PELICAN BOOKS

COMPARATIVE GOVERNMENT

Advisory Editor: Jean Blondel

Professor Samuel Edward Finer, Professor of Government at Manchester University since 1966, was born in 1915. He was educated at Holloway School in London and Trinity College, Oxford, where in 1937 he received his B.A. In 1946 he received his M.A. (Oxon.). He spent the years from 1946 to 1950 at Oxford, first as Lecturer in Politics at Balliol, and then as a Junior Research Fellow at the same college. After twelve years at Keele University he was made Deputy Vice-Chancellor in 1962, until 1964. Professor Finer is Chairman of the Political Studies Association of Great Britain.

S. E. Finer

COMPARATIVE GOVERNMENT

PENGUIN BOOKS

Penguin Books Ltd, Harmondsworth, Middlesex, England
Penguin Books Inc., 7110 Ambassador Road, Baltimore, Maryland 21207, U.S.A.
Penguin Books Australia Ltd, Ringwood, Victoria, Australia
Penguin Books Canada Ltd, 41 Steelcase Road West, Markham, Ontario, Canada
Penguin Books (N.Z.) Ltd, 182–190 Wairau Road, Auckland 10, New Zealand

—

First published by Allen Lane The Penguin Press 1970
Published in Pelican Books 1974
Reprinted 1975

—

Copyright © S. E. Finer, 1970

—

Made and printed in Great Britain by
Hazell Watson & Viney Ltd,
Aylesbury, Bucks
Set in Monotype Times

FOR ANN, JEREMY,
JESSICA AND JOS

CONTENTS

PREFACE

It takes a long time to acquire the art, but life is short, the crisis rapid, experimentation dangerous, the cure uncertain.

Hippocrates: *the first Aphorism*

THIS book is meant as my introduction to the study of politics. I have written it for my students and for the general public. In it I have tried to present a vision of the ubiquity of political behaviour, and the paradoxical omnipotence and frailty of the effort to channel and domesticate it – which is what we call 'government'. Deliberately, I have set out to systematize, simplify and codify our ever-widening, ever-flowing range of data and circumstances, so as to provide a first – and I really mean a first – step on a long journey which I hope will absorb and enchant.

Why I should attempt this is best explained in terms of personal history. I have been teaching in this field for over twenty years, I still hold the perhaps old-fashioned view that undergraduates need more attention than graduates and beginning students more attention than the senior ones; and so over this period, I have considered it a matter of honour and duty and indeed of love to give the first year introductory course in comparative government. The first rudimentary approach to this book was initiated in lectures I gave at Cornell University in 1962. Then, at Keele University I modified it substantially, in the years 1963–6. But the book as it now stands follows and elaborates the First Year undergraduate course in government which I have been giving at the University of Manchester. Indeed, it is the written version of this course: somewhat less picturesque and mediterranean than my lectures, but fuller, more *nuancé*, and, I hope, rather more elegant.

It is not surprising, therefore, that much in the book records the conventional knowledge of the profession, nor that some of my views are idiosyncratic. But part of it, I hope, makes an original contribution to the discipline and this is true, I consider, of the way I have expounded my theme. To the best of my knowledge it is a novel one. It is not the now rightly discredited juxtaposition of this that or another country's form of government which only ended, as one wag had it, when one ran out of countries – or of time. It is a *systematic* exposition. In the first chapter I explain why I begin the study of government with governmental institutions, and from there I classify the governments of the modern world into five major types. The subsequent chapters elaborate on this, explaining the characteristics of each type in greater detail. The rest of the book consists of chapters which illustrate these various forms as in the cases of Britain, the U.S.A., France and the U.S.S.R., and analyse further the sub-varieties of the main forms. In one sense there is an illogicality in devoting a separate chapter to each of the major states mentioned above while treating the governmental forms met with in the Third World in a largely analytical fashion, but my reason is this: rightly or wrongly most students of the subject are today required to have a somewhat detailed knowledge of at least these four great states. Hence it seemed to me that, illogical or not, the book would be the more useful if it were laid out in the way it is.

Currently there is a vogue for teaching 'politics' by what is known as 'the functional approach'. Briefly, a checklist of functions is established, which functions are held to be performed by any 'political system' (whatever that may be) in every society, from the Eskimos to the U.S.S.R.; and the governmental institutions of societies are then compared with each other in terms of this list of functions. I do not dispute the fruitfulness of this approach – in its good time. But my experience as a teacher has convinced me that the first step must be the study of whole systems at work, since it is only in this way, for instance, that what in the army we used to call 'the naming of parts' becomes meaningful; the beginner grasps what is meant by pressure group, party, parliament when he sees institutions called by these names at work in very different systems. Once this has been done, the way does indeed lie open to functional or other kinds of analysis as I indicate in my final chapter; but, in my view, *only* after this.

For all that, I recognize the incompleteness of this book. It is incomplete in the first place even in terms of its own ground plan. Britain and France and the U.S.A. do not exhaust the varieties of the liberal democratic state; ideally I should have liked to insert a chapter on Israel whose polity is a remarkable example of what is sometimes called the 'party state' wherein political parties mediate the main functions elsewhere performed by autonomous pressure groups; and also a chapter on the curious and fascinating mixture of adaptation and transformation that occurs in the ground-rules of the liberal democratic polity when these operate in a non-industrialized society like Gambia, or the Lebanon. Likewise the U.S.S.R. does not exhaust the concept of the 'totalitarian' state and I should have wished to deal with somewhat more pluralistic societies in Eastern Europe, such as Poland and Hungary and certainly with Yugoslavia. But with the book already nearing one fifth of a million words I felt that to add still more detail would be counter-productive. If I am wrong – then *mea culpa*; and after all this is a fault that is remediable at a later date.

But the book is incomplete in a profounder sense, and irremediably so. The range of fact is so great and the changes are so rapid that, as one draft succeeded another, not merely have some of the facts taken surprising new twists, but one's own self has altered in the interim. *Tempora mutantur nos et mutamur in illis.* This book has gone through some five drafts. If I put it aside to write it again in four years' time, I know that I should still be feeling this same sense of incompleteness that I do now. Tennyson put it exactly:

> 'For all experience is an arch wherethrough
> Gleams that untravelled world whose margin fades
> For ever and for ever as I move . . .'

Yet it is in this very experience that lies the endless beckoning adventure of research and teaching; ever new facts and ever new perspectives. This book reflects how I see things now. I hope that at the very least it will draw many, many people who were unfamiliar with this field into that same endless and marvellous quest along with me.

University of Manchester

1 December 1969

ACKNOWLEDGEMENTS

I OWE a great debt of thanks to friends who have helped me in so many various ways to complete this book. First, I want to thank Mrs Maureen Ball (*née* Bryan) who audiotyped the first version for me over four years ago; and Mrs Agnes Cox of the University of Manchester for the indispensable help she has given me in its last stages.

Dr J. Lees and Dr J. Hayward, of Keele University, both read and criticized individual chapters and I am under a great obligation to them for the numerous helpful corrections and suggestions they made. Those who have read the entire draft and made their important comments thereon include Professors Brian Chapman, Dennis Austin and Ghita Ionescu, my colleagues, partners and friends in the Department of Government in the University of Manchester; and those other two tried and esteemed friends, Professor Leonard Schapiro of the London School of Economics and Professor Jean Blondel of the University of Essex. Mr Clement Dodd, another of my friends and colleagues in the Department at Manchester, was also good enough to go through the entire manuscript, and his comments have much assisted me.

The blemishes that remain in this book are clearly my own; I admit them; I apologize in advance for them; and I trust they will by now be venial ones. But I am glad to say this in conclusion: that they are very considerably less in number and importance than they would have been, is due to the exceptionally able and painstaking copy-editing of Mrs Margaret Phillips of the Penguin Press. I would like to pay this special tribute to her skill, her knowledge and her care.

1 December 1969   *S. E. Finer*

Part One

THE MAIN FORMS OF
MODERN GOVERNMENT

Chapter 1

GOVERNMENT: A PRELIMINARY SURVEY

I. 'GOVERNMENT' AND 'POLITICS'

'WILL the study of politics ever become a science?'
'Not until it has acquired a vocabulary totally unintelligible to the normal well-educated layman.'

So Lawrence Lowell, one of the greatest students of comparative government is alleged to have replied. This was fifty years ago. But today, the coinage of neologisms has become almost frantic. Whether this has put the study on the road to becoming a science is questionable. What is certain is that it still wallows in semantic confusions. Some of the most commonly used terms are homonyms – one identical word with several meanings. Others are stipulatory: whether he consciously knows this or not, the writer is using the term in a special and often highly personal way. Some terms are both.

It is a nuisance to start reading a book only to be told that the first matter to be attended to is the definition or clarification of the terms that are to be used in it. Nevertheless this is how we shall have to proceed.

This book is about different forms of government: yet the word *government* is a homonym capable of bearing at least four meanings.

In its first sense, *government* denotes the activity or the process of governing, i.e. of exercising a measure of control over others. We use it in this sense when, for example, we say: 'the government of small states is usually easier than the government of large ones.' But *government* may also be used in a second sense denoting the state of affairs in which this activity or process is to be found – in short a *condition of ordered rule*. This is a rather special sense of the term, common in the eighteenth century. A good instance of this usage is to be found in Jeremy Bentham's

Book of Fallacies (1824). There, commenting on the sentence 'Attack us (the rulers) and you attack Government', Bentham explains that the fallacy consists precisely in confusing two senses of the word government – that meaning a group of people, and that meaning ordered rule. Thirdly and obviously, we use the word *government* to denote those people charged with the duty of governing. This is a very common usage and I shall have to employ it very often in the course of these pages, so that whenever it appears to be ambiguous I shall replace it with the expressions 'the rulers' or 'the governors' or even 'the public authorities'. Fourthly and finally, *government* may denote the manner, method or system by which a particular society is governed. When we say that we are about to compare French and British government it is in this sense of the word that we are using it, and the very expression 'comparative government' itself embodies this particular meaning. Since I shall have to use it very frequently in this sense also, whenever an ambiguity seems likely to occur I shall substitute such terms as 'system of government' or 'form of government' or 'régime', all of which I intend to be taken as synonymous.

This is all fairly straightforward because each of these meanings is well accepted and the only problem is to sort out the different usages and keep them separate. But when we turn to the term *politics* the problem is of quite a different order. Here the differences of usage are not just semantic but substantive – they reflect the fact that each individual's usage of the term embodies his personal conception of how human conduct in society is motivated and ordered. Consequently, what follows is my own individual concept.

Politics, then, is neither the same thing as government, nor is it necessarily connected only with those great territorial associations which possess a body of governors, i.e., *a* government, and which go under the name of 'the state' – another debatable term which will have to be explained in due course. For, if we may take *government* in its first sense, that of 'governance' or 'the activity of governing', we may conceive such government of society as existing at three levels.

(a) By far the vastest area of human conduct and activity in society proceeds quite unregulated or controlled by the public authorities. This is not to suggest that it is chaotic or turbulent, but rather the reverse. It forms a coherent set of patterns and regulates itself. It does this by two chief means. In the first place many of our activities fairly evidently entail fairly evident consequences. It really is unnecessary for a body of persons in a community to forbid others to sell in the cheapest markets and buy in the dearest. Anybody who did so would go bankrupt. Actions which obviously entail pleasant or disastrous consequences may be left to the individuals themselves. This class of actions is what Bentham called *sponte acta*. In principle the entire economic aspect of society could be left to the operation of such *sponte acta*, though in practice this policy has had to be severely qualified. Yet even in this qualified form a vast tract of human affairs does regulate itself after its own fashion, free of intervention by public authorities.

(b) The second chief mode by which society forms its own patterns and regulates itself is the process of so-called 'socialization' of the individual, with which is associated the concept of 'social control'. 'Socialization' describes the way by which, as we grow up in our society, we are led to absorb the ideas, the beliefs, the tastes and aversions and standards of the groups in which we find ourselves: the families, friendships, schools, clubs, churches, professions and the like. To some extent we absorb these in such a way that they become a part of our being, so that we regard the world through the frame of reference which they provide. In that case, these standards etc. are said to have become 'internalized'. Even to the extent that they are not internalized, however, the various groups and associations of which we form a part exercise over us a mixture of incentives and constraints which put a premium on conformity to these socially standardized and approved modes of social behaviour, and this mechanism is what is known as 'social control' in its more specific and restricted sense. By virtue of *sponte acta*, socialization and social control, a great area of human conduct in society regulates itself; and some societies, those called 'simple', such as the Manus society described by Margaret Mead in her *Growing Up in New Guinea*, got along perfectly well in their rather static and restricted way without ever experiencing the need for establishing a formally constituted body of persons charged with the duty of taking decisions in their name. Such societies have 'government' in the sense that there is a recognizable manner or system by which their affairs are regulated: but this is not such as to require a functionally differentiated group of 'governors'. They are not, to use a common expression, 'societies without government'; they are societies without government*s*.

(c) Most societies in the modern world, however, *are* equipped with governments. The point is, however, that even in those where the activity of such governments is at its maximum – in the so-called totalitarian states – there is still a vast tract of human affairs which continues to regulate itself by the mechanisms described. Now at this self-regulatory level, we have 'government' but no politics. Even if we presuppose that a formally constituted set of rulers does exist in a society, but has as its role only the purely mechanical task of executing decisions arrived at elsewhere; this routine execution of agreed social policies is certainly governmental, but it is not political. For government, in its sense of *the process of governing*, consists of two elements – choosing a course of action and carrying it out. Politics is related to the first of these; and it is the choosing of a course of action that constitutes the point of contact between the two concepts, 'government' and 'politics'.

So in a given society not all policy activity is governmental; some may be societal. And, again, not all governmental activity is political: some may be routine administration. Government and politics come into contact at the point where a course of action has to be selected for the whole of the society – under certain conditions. This qualification requires an extended definition of 'politics'.

II. THE NATURE OF POLITICS

In our everyday lives we sometimes fall into situations where, willy-nilly, we are forced into making a decision – in the sense that in these situations even not to decide is a kind of decision.

When Squire Allworthy opened his door to find a baby lying on his doorstep, he could not avoid a decision. To have 'taken no action', i.e., to have left it there, would have been tantamount to deciding to let it die of starvation and exposure. Life is full of such situations (aptly described, by a happy image, as 'to be left holding the baby'!). For want of any technical term, I shall call such situations 'predicaments'. Politics flows from a special kind of predicament (as does economics, albeit from a different one).

Politics connotes a kind of activity, a form of human behaviour. More specifically it is a social form of behaviour in that it presupposes the interaction of at least two persons. Still more specifically, what distinguishes it from other types of social behaviour, like economic behaviour, is not the range of issues with which it is concerned, nor necessarily the methods by which it proceeds, but the characteristics of the predicament which gives rise to it.

It is not distinguished from other types of social behaviour simply by reason of its dealing with a specific and restricted subject matter. Political behaviour has been generated by religion, by morals, by questions arising from the production and distribution of wealth. As Swift perceived, it could in principle be generated by a difference as to whether to crack one's egg at the big end or at the little one. Nor is it necessarily distinguished by the methods it employs. For instance, it is common to hear economics described as 'the science of the allocation of scarce resources between alternative uses', while politics is often described as 'the exercise of power'. Yet it must be clear that the detergent war between Unilever and Procter & Gamble, fought out as it has been by mass persuasion on the television screens, is an exercise of power; while an exercise of power may well take the form of a rationing system to determine the allocation of scarce resources among alternative uses.

No: what distinguishes political from economic and other types of social activity is the originating predicament. Of course, in real life, this one kind of social predicament is often superposed on or commingled with another type of social predicament: in this way a situation may give rise to behaviour which is economic from one point of view, political from another. There is nothing startling or disconcerting about such a conclusion, either. In talking of *political* predicaments we abstract certain specific features from the context of the whole social situation. Economists have been doing this for a century and a half, with considerably misleading consequences for their conclusions, to be sure, but without being accused of methodological error. Human beings are a mixture of motives, and human society is a seamless web of activities which we distinguish one from another by a deliberate act of abstraction and classification in the hope of understanding each one of them better.

Two features must coexist to create a political predicament – one that will give rise specifically to *political* activity. They are: (1) that a given set of persons of some type or other require a *common* policy; and (2) that its members advocate, for this common status, policies which are *mutually exclusive*.

I use the word 'policy' where, previously, I used the expression 'course of action'. I do not intend 'policy' to mean a sophisticated and premeditated programme of action, although of course this is precisely what it sometimes may be. I use it to cover what may be simply a common rule on, for example, a matter of defence or a tax. Such a decision may be a specific and limited one. In the old days, before modern forms of government, few governments had a coherent policy in the sense of programme: the organs of the government issued a succession of often unconnected detailed decisions on the matters arising for their consideration. But in so far as any one of these became the subject of dispute in the way formulated above – i.e., was contested either on the grounds that no decision was required at all or that another and preclusive one should be the one adopted – in that sense it is 'policy', as used in the text.

The first condition makes the situation a predicament, in my sense of imposing an inescapable necessity for a decision. The second condition gives this predicament its *political* character; i.e., makes it one that generates specifically political activity. Take any kind of continuing group or community – bridge club, trade union or state – and the moment any member demands that a common rule be adopted on any matter whatsoever, a predicament is created; for even if all other members unanimously decry the need for any common policy, they are also in the circumstances of the case propounding a common policy – namely, that there shall not be one. And furthermore this particular predicament will be a *political* predicament too, since not only *must* the members now decide on whether to establish a common policy or not, but two mutually exclusive views about this are being propounded.

If this seems highly paradoxical or even trivial, consider Abraham Lincoln's epigram about the genesis of the terrible American Civil War: 'We will say to the Southern disunionists: we won't go out of the Union and you *shan't*.' The Southern States, inflamed over the failure to have the slavery issue settled on their own terms, decided that they no longer wanted common policies for the entire United States – and hence decided to secede. Lincoln and the Northern States took the view that, irrespective of any particular solution of the slavery question, common policies for all the United States there must be. Hence the issue of the 'preservation of the Union', and Lincoln's summary: '*We* won't go out of the Union and *you* shan't.'

Thus the moment a voice is raised in a group or community for a common rule on any issue whatsoever, a predicament is created, in the sense that even to decide against this demand is to take a decision. The first of our two conditions therefore is inescapable: given the demand from within the community, a common policy *must* be established, if only to have no policy. Suppose, however, that there was full agreement on the need to establish a common policy, and also that everybody was in full agreement as to what this policy should be: then no further problem would arise. The further problem arises only if members of the community advocate mutually exclusive policies. Where that happens, the first condition (the establishment of the common policy) can only be achieved if and when, by one means or another, one policy and only one policy is acted upon, i.e. put into effect. In this sense it could be said that the choice as to which of the mutually exclusive policy suggestions is to be acted upon is reduced to one and one only. And one other point should also be noticed here. When we talk of 'mutually exclusive policies' what matters in generating political activity, i.e., the effort to reduce the choice to one, is not whether *in fact* they are mutually exclusive but whether their respective advocates *think* they are.

Politics connotes activity. By contrast there are certain situations describable as political *rest*. Suppose all agree that a common policy is necessary and then suppose that all members of the community 'spontaneously' agree on what that policy should be. In that case, the only activity required is the execution of the policy. This is a matter of simple administration in its most mechanical and narrow sense. This may be governmental activity; it is not political activity.

One difficulty here lies in defining the adjective 'spontaneous'. In this context, we cannot rule out the possibility that this 'spontaneous unanimity' may well have been effectuated by past pressure – by socialization, or by deliberate governmental conditioning or brain-washing in the past, as a result of which members of a given community have come to think alike on a large number of matters. These past pressures must be taken at any given moment to have become part of the current character of individuals: they have become internalized; and where unanimity on a policy issue can be traced only to such past pressures, it seems right to regard this as genuinely spontaneous. On the other hand, there are few surer ways of bringing people to support or tolerate one policy rather than another than the application of external pressures: on the one hand rewards and punishments, on the other propaganda and persuasion. Where these are currently applied, it would be quite inappropriate to consider the unanimity as spontaneously achieved; on the contrary it would be artificially contrived. By 'spontaneous unanimity', then, is meant that type of unanimity that has arisen without *current* external pressures or persuasion of any kind.

Now a situation where all are freely agreed in this way on an object or policy clearly generates no activity at all except the physical procuring of that object or policy, i.e., simple administration. It will be a situation of *political rest* in that it will not start up any cycle of *political activity* since this is defined as the ways and means of reducing mutually exclusive policy viewpoints to one – unnecessary in this case as only one policy is being advocated.

By the same token it may be that, even where mutually exclusive viewpoints are *initially* advocated and a cycle of political activity thereupon starts up, rational discussion, or the effects of indoctrination over a long period of time, or long habituation to and experience of the policy adopted, will ultimately bring all the population to acquiesce in it; i.e., the standards it embodies will become internalized. In Britain the various sects once took the line that only their own church discipline was right and that it should therefore be adopted and enforced as a common policy. Later 'toleration' was adopted as a common policy, though legal and social discrimination against Dissenters, Catholics and Jews persisted. But, over the course of generations, the public at large has come to adopt both the policy and the practice of toleration; and this policy – for it is a policy – may today be said to rest on spontaneous unanimity. So, just as a situation of political rest does not start up any political activity, it also closes down a cycle of political activity.

If even one member demands a common policy, then a predicament exists. That predicament is solved, however, if either everybody spontaneously agrees on what that policy should be, or, in the event of more than one policy being advocated, those policies are mutually compatible. In neither case is any cycle of activity generated other than the administrative one, the physical execution of the policies. On the other hand, where what appear to be mutually exclusive policies are advocated, the predicament can only be solved if the choice is somehow 'reduced to one' for the purpose of action.

This can be achieved in one of two main ways. By processes of persuasion, reasoning, diplomacy and a consequent series of adjustments, the competing agents may come piecemeal to abandon first one part and then another of each of their original policy schemes until in the end they arrive at one which is mutually acceptable. This is the method of compromise. If carried out thoroughly enough it would imply that in the end the society had reached a state of spontaneous consensus, and thereby of political rest. Alternatively, there is a second method:

by processes ranging from reason and persuasion at one end, but in this case extending to threat and coercion at the other, one of the policies may wholly or largely prevail over the other.

There is an important distinction between the two cases. In the first, the competitors begin with mutually exclusive policies and it is only after a period during which each has tried to make his views prevail over the other that the condition of spontaneous consensus is reached. That period constitutes a train of political activity. The predicament has generated *politics* and this is practised; but the cycle ends once the spontaneous consensus is reached.

In the second case, however, the cycle is *not* ended. As in the former case, the various competitors begin with mutually exclusive policies and this initiates a period during which each tries to make his policy prevail over the others; but here the predicament, although resolved when one such policy does prevail, still leaves the competitors preferring their original policies, albeit acquiescing for the moment in the victorious one. They do not acquiesce because they agree with it, but as a consequence of the application of continuing external pressure and persuasion. Where the battle between the competitors is fought out within the framework of rules which are mutually accepted – where, that is to say, the competition is 'institutionalized', i.e., conducted in the light of some socially standardized and accepted code – that pressure may appear to be fairly mild. In other situations, where the struggle is not institutionalized but fought out by any means to hand, those who continue to oppose the victorious policy may suffer extreme penalties. But in either case, the policy which has been adopted remains in being through the continued application of some kind of pressure on its opponents – whether propaganda and attempts to win them over, or the penalties of the law. The issue is – in a current phrase – 'still in politics'; political activity still continues, i.e., the effort to alter the policy adopted, and this cycle will not be ended until by some means or other a spontaneous consensus is reached on the matter.

The capacity to make one's own view prevail over that of others is a special case of the more general category, 'the capacity to achieve desired results', and this is what is meant by the word *power*. An engine's capacity to achieve desired results – say, fifty m.p.h. – would be a measure of its power. Politics, being an exercise in the attempt to change the conduct of others in one's own desired direction, is thus an exercise of power. This use of the word 'power' in the context of politics has been under considerable attack, on three main grounds: one is that politics is a word whose use should be reserved for a special *kind* of power struggle, one that is highly institutionalized, where the rewards and punishments used in the struggle are not barbarous nor even harsh. There seems little justification for this restricted use of the word which leaves us, in many cases, with the need to find a word for the more coercive modes of decision-making. Another reason for not using the word 'power' in connexion with politics flows from a belief that power is equivalent to violence or coercion. If this were so, then the statement that politics is an exercise of power would indeed be quite false in most cases. But, as used here at any rate, power is taken to denote the whole spectrum of those external influences that, by being brought to bear upon an individual can make him move in a required direction. It is commonplace to talk of the 'power of love' and equally so to talk of 'the power of reason'. The spectrum of Power ranges widely. At one extreme we find the modalities which carry no sanction: the power of love and affection in getting others to do as one wills, the power of pure personality (charisma), the power of reason and above all of pseudo-reasonings, especially when these are tricked out with emotion-stirring imagery. All these are used, e.g., by mothers to induce desired behaviour in their recalcitrant children, or by cabinet ministers to secure support for themselves or their policies. At this point in the spectrum begin those modalities of power which depend on sanctions, i.e., rewards and punishments; these range in severity along the spectrum until, at its very end, they terminate in coercion and ultimately in death itself. Power implies the use of any or every modality in the whole spectrum not just the 'sanctions' end of the scale. It ranges from the love that an individual evokes in others to the fear of death he may induce in them.

A third objection is that the word 'power' alone is not adequate to describe the activity of politics; the notion of 'authority' is also necessary. This is true, and logically this is the right place to expound the notion of authority and the vast qualification it makes to my treatment so far. Unhappily there is also much more to be said regarding power in politics. For this reason, and for no other, the central notion of authority is treated later at some length and can be understood as qualifying what is being said here. This is a literary problem, a question of the order in which matters are to be explained. This much can be said at this point, however. Firstly, even where the spectrum of power is invoked to reduce the choice of mutually exclusive policies to one, it is usual for some modes of persuasion or coercion to be socially sanctioned and approved and others to be disapproved. In short, it is usual for the power struggle to be pursued according to certain socially approved standards – that is, for it to be *institutionalized*. Thus, in Britain, it is regarded as right and proper to decide on a change of government by a general election, and wrong to do so by means of violence. So the electoral system is a political institution; and revolution is not. Next, the power struggle is not usually pursued in terms of who is the most popular or violent, but in terms of the rightness or wrongness of the policies being advocated. But thirdly, and most important of all, the various modalities we have mentioned – love and persuasion, rewards and punishments – are not the only modalities for 'inducing desired results in others', i.e., for exercising power. Desired results in others can also be induced by the *authority* of the actor. *Authority also is a source of power*. It is a fact, not a piece of sermonizing, that one of the most influential means of getting others to behave in the way required is to invest the policy with authority: i.e., to put it crudely (for the moment), with a degree of moral acceptability. The policy may appear morally acceptable by reason of its sources or by reason of its anticipated results. In the first case, it may appear so because its advocates are generally regarded as the wisest, or the best, or the most representative in the community, or because they are agents of a higher power, such as God or Reason or Progress, which is held in universal esteem. In the second case, it may be regarded as morally acceptable because it appears conducive to Happiness or Welfare or Greatness, or whatever other value has an overriding importance. The greater the authority of the policy-makers – or of the policy itself – the less will be the need to employ the other modalities of power. But, for the moment, let us pursue the analysis of politics in terms of the exercise of these modalities of power, so that this can be completed before the qualifying note of 'authority' can be introduced.

'Politics' therefore connotes a special case in the exercise of power. The case is special because the context that gives rise to action – the predicament – is special. Its essence lies – we repeat – in the necessity for a number of actors to agree on a common policy, although initially each or some of them advance policies which preclude other policies which are also being put forward. Now this situation is not confined to a state and to those who govern it. On the contrary, it is ubiquitous throughout modern society. The mother and her child, at odds over the hour of bedtime, provide just such a situation: and the train of political activity this generates might proceed from appeals to the child's common sense ('you will be tired in the morning') or to its affection ('mummy must cook'), to bribes (a sweet, a bedtime story); then, if these all fail, it might progress to threats of punishment and finally, it may well be, to some minor application of coercion or violence. A domestic dispute where the husband wants blue curtains and the wife green may likewise constitute a political predicament, generating a train of political activity until a decision is reached. Such situations are not different in kind from the disputes over public policy which nobody would fail to classify as 'political'. Even more strikingly, the domestic affairs of what (in the context of a state) we call 'private' associations, like trade unions, board meetings, churches and universities, frequently throw up situations which in our terminology are political predicaments, and generate a train of internal politics. In modern society, politics is ubiquitous.

There is a vital qualitative difference, however, between modalities of power applied to solve predicaments inside private associations, and those originating with the state. This difference turns upon the respective *cohesiveness* of the two types of association in question. Most private associations are voluntaristic – they are easy to join and easy to quit; compared with them most states are compulsive – certainly to the extent that they are difficult to quit for practical if not for legal reasons. Now the degree of voluntarism, i.e., the looseness of the links uniting members of a group or community, profoundly affects the nature of a predicament. Such a predicament is created when, whatever the reason, the members have to adopt a common policy; and we call it a predicament precisely because, as soon as even one solitary member of a group demands a common policy on some matter or other, a decision *must* be taken by all the other members. In short, we have called it a predicament because it imposes an inescapable necessity for decision. But suppose a group that is entirely voluntaristic, both in theory and in practice, i.e., which each of its members may at any time leave to go his separate way. In such a group there is *never* a political predicament because the necessity to adopt a common policy is completely escapable – dissatisfied members simply quit. As it becomes more inconvenient or difficult to quit a group, however, so the necessity for common policies becomes less and less escapable, until at the extreme limit, where it is both practically and legally impossible to quit, the predicament is completely inescapable.

In a highly voluntaristic association, then, it is more or less open to members to escape from what would otherwise be a predicament by leaving the group. Hence, in such groups, each contending faction is aware that if it presses its demands too far it will drive its antagonists out of the group altogether. To the extent that it does not desire this it will modify its demands. And so in such cases the modalities of power will be confined to the persuasion/diplomacy end of the spectrum. But one of the chief distinguishing marks of the state is its high degree of compulsiveness. And this is why, historically, the politics of *public* policy, i.e., that concerning a territorial community which is organized as a state, has generated such arduous, protracted and bloody struggles, and why the modalities of power have so often shifted down to the rewards, punishments and coercion end of the power spectrum.

This relationship between private associations and the great and paramount association called 'the state' must therefore be explored; and in the course of doing this it becomes possible to give a first, highly simplified illustration of what constitutes the 'political process'.

III. THE POLITICAL PROCESS

Historically all human beings have been found in association with others, even if this association is of the extended-family type. The 'solitary individual' of Hobbes or Locke is only a methodological fiction designed to point up some necessary characteristics of social life. Furthermore, by far the greater part of our life in a modern society is mediated through the groups and associations of which we are members. In so far as societies may be regarded as 'more developed' or 'less developed', too, they may be said to form a spectrum, ranging from those composed of a single group or of a limited number of simply structured and homogeneous groups and associations, to those composed of numerous groups and associations each of which is of a complex and heterogeneous kind.[1] In the so-called simpler societies, the typical groupings are based on kinship and lineage, expressible in terms of tribe, clan and sept. Superposed on this may be groupings based on neighbourhood, and to this broadly corresponds that type of political organization described as feudal – or, by analogy, as 'neo-feudal' where it is met with in certain areas today. At a more developed level, kinship groupings and neighbourhood ones decline in importance when compared with functional associations, which have been roughly classified as those concerned with economic, religious, cultural and political matters. Industrialized societies are composed of a myriad groups of all kinds, but with the functional ones attaining a prime importance. Furthermore, in such industrialized societies, not only is society divided into these so-called 'vertical' compartments, but it is also stratified: it is divided horizontally into classes representing layers of subordination and superordination.

1. cf. A. H. Spencer, *First Principles*, Williams & Norgate, London, 1863.

In modern society few groups are 'politics-free'. In most of them political predicaments will arise from time to time albeit in weak form. But wherever, for one reason or another, cohesion is deemed necessary by the group's members, while competition and rivalry over common policy exists – there will predicaments arise and politics be generated.

In modern society, again, few groups have no 'governments' in the sense that they lack a body of individuals charged with specific duties of policy formation or execution on behalf of the group as a whole. The elucidation of why this should be so is a huge field of sociological inquiry in its own right. Briefly, it would appear to be due partly to the nature of individuals and partly to the nature of organization. As to the first, it so happens that some individuals show a marked desire for and capability for directing others, while some show the reverse characteristics. If this were not so, and if all individuals competed equally strenuously for posts of leadership, we should have the situation which Hobbes envisaged, 'the war of all against each'. At the same time, organization itself tends to create a functional requirement for posts of leadership, which can be filled because of the existence of would-be leaders in the group. Organization tends to create this functional requirement for three reasons. The first is the effect of increasing complexity, i.e., specialization within a given group or association. This multiplies the number of alternative courses of common action and so makes for more frequent clashes of will and personality. Some leadership role would be required if only to regulate the discussion. The second reason is the effect of increasing size. Size limits the possibilities of intercommunication. As this becomes less easy to arrange on an informal face-to-face basis, so formal channels and fixed procedures become more necessary: and this implies that some functions and roles must reside in a predictable manner in known persons. Furthermore, coupled with this increasing complexity, size increases the difficulties of co-ordinating the specialized activities within the group, for the number of possible inter-relationships rises exponentially as the number of members increases. Finally, the group may become increasingly busy, i.e., the flow of intercommunication may increase sharply, irrespective of either complexity or numbers. When a group simultaneously becomes more complex, larger and also busier, the functional necessity of certain leadership roles is overwhelming.

In this way some groups, and it may be the majority of groups and associations in a society, create specialized roles of 'leadership' – a word left deliberately vague here, because the duties of the leader would vary with the requirements of the group, as would the number of the leadership roles created. The effect is that most private associations tend to develop their own 'governments'.

In each group there exists a reservoir of folk who are just as able and willing to lead as those that currently occupy the 'governmental' positions. The entire reservoir of the able-and-willing may be described for these purposes as the *political élite*. Those who actually fill the leadership roles at any one time may be called the *governing élite* and those who are willing and able to take their place the *counter-élite*.

Now human groups are *purposive*. Human beings do not congregate together like a herd of cows just because they feel a need for propinquity: they gather for purposes, even if the purpose is only to carry on an idle conversation, and most durable human associations have more important purposes than that. Out of this fact arises the politics of the private association. The members have certain objectives or values which they have come together to forward, or alternatively have certain common objectives or values which they stay together to preserve – as in the case of a crescive and 'natural' association, like the family. These purposes are forwarded by organizational structure, i.e., by the creation of procedures, structures, and leadership-roles. Those who fill the roles of leadership, i.e., the 'government' of the association, exist, implicitly at any rate, to enable the purposes of the association to be forwarded more effectively. The members grant their allegiance to this 'government' in so far as they believe and continue to believe that this is indeed forwarding their purposes and values as they conceive them. In this sense, therefore, the incumbency of the leaders is conditional. It is most true that in certain associations the leadership would have to stretch the patience of its followers very, very far indeed before the latter sought to depose them, but, in the last resort, these may certainly be expected to express their dissatisfaction in whatever ways lie open to them. This tenure of office by the leaders becomes more precarious as the counter-*élite* becomes more able and more aggressively willing to replace them.

Now in the context of a larger society, where the group is not alone in a given area of territory but shares that territory with other groups, or where it is functionally interconnected with these other groups – as it may be by trade relationships or (as in the modern state) by virtue of a functional specialization which impinges on the purposes and interests of a host of other groups – in such contexts it sometimes occurs that the purposes and values of any one group can only be realized at the expense of the purposes and values of another or many other groups. Group competition then arises. And inside each group the tenure of the office-bearers is now doubly precarious: to maintain the allegiance of the group's members against the competition of the counter-*élite*, they may well have to impose their own way upon the leadership of those other groups whose values and purposes run counter to theirs.

The larger the number of groups within the territory, the higher is the degree of their functional specialization and hence their mutual impingement; and the busier the tempo of inter-action, the greater is the possibility that they will pursue mutually exclusive policies. In the absence of a common government which all obey, the political struggle that ensues between them is necessarily both intermittent and inconclusive. Sometimes, as where a number of ethnic or tribal groups compete within a given territory, it takes the form of intermittent wars. Elsewhere, where regional groupings have evolved to the point where each establishes its own government, it may take the form of frontier raids. Where the arena is a more evolved, single and functionally interdependent society, the conflicts may take the form of religious or economic disputes. In all such cases the conflict either ends in a stalemate or in the temporary victory of one group over the other; no group has a ready means at hand of *guaranteeing* its victory over its opponents, or – if it is victorious – of making sure that that opponent will not be able to reverse the situation on some future occasion, when it has grown relatively stronger.

It is out of such historic situations that the peculiar association we know as 'the state' has slowly and intermittently evolved. Some societies, fairly simple in structure, and with little or no sources of inter-group conflict latent within them, like Manus society, have never evolved into states. Others have evolved the state only in what, compared to the state as it exists in the industrialized society of today, is a weak and incomplete form. The feudal state (if indeed it can be properly called a state) was less comprehensive, less powerfully endowed with a central organ of decision-making and enforcement than the state of the European Renaissance, and this again was incomplete compared with the state as we know it, e.g., in contemporary Britain or France or the U.S.S.R. Our current and generally accepted criteria of what constitutes 'the state' is very much a normative definition rather than a description based on the facts of the case. If that definition and its entailed criteria of recognition are accepted, then it must also be accepted that some historic 'states' fulfil the definition much less completely than others. And furthermore, just as some simple societies have never evolved into states, and just as some that have evolved do not match up to the generally accepted definition of the state so well as others, so, on the world scale, despite the conflicts of value and interest inherent in the coexistence of a multitude of discrete and independent territorial entities occupying the planet, no world-state has yet emerged. This underlines the fact that the conflicts latent in inter-tribal, inter-territorial, inter-functional or class conflict create a functional *need* for some organ of conciliation regulating them; but this does not entail that such an organ comes into existence. And when it has done so, historically, it has not always come about in the same way. In some cases such an organ followed the conquest of one territorially-based society by enemies. In other cases it came about by the domination of some elements in a society by another element. In yet other cases it evolved by a process of grudging and intermittent concessions on the part of all or the most significant of the groupings, whether ethnic, territorial or functional, in a given territory. And in most cases it has involved a blend of all three.

In its most primitive form, and hence most primitive definition, a state is a territorially delimited population who have accepted a common 'organ of government'. This leaves two vitally important questions unanswered for the moment: first, whether such an organ of government is accepted with respect to all the political conflicts arising within the population, or only to some of them: in the medieval English state, for instance, the king was accepted as this 'organ of government' in the 'Pleas of the Crown', but not with respect to church matters, or to much of the daily discipline arising in the feudal manor or municipal corporation. The second and even more important matter is what manner of 'acceptance' this is: whether it is simply the recognition of overwhelming force or similar sanctions on the part of the ruler, or whether it is some kind of moral acceptance as well. As I have said, this moral acceptance involves a concept that has yet to be discussed, namely, the concept of 'authority', which is of overwhelming importance in any consideration of politics and political organization. I have omitted it so far and conducted the discussion in terms of power alone simply for the sake of exposition; the next section will show that the 'model' we are expounding at this stage is radically incomplete and false to the facts until the concept of authority is built into it.

Let us put these two unanswered questions aside and return to them later, in order to pursue the corollaries of the definition of the state as 'a territorially delimited population who accept a common organ of government'.

The first corollary is that, even if this population were a mere aggregate of individuals with no other point of contact between them than their common acceptance of an organ of government for some or all of the issues they dispute, the single fact of their accepting this common organ of government *interrelates* them. All are connected to one another via each one's acceptance of this common government. In much the same way, a body of individuals who have never met before but congregate in a hall to hear a lecture thereby acquire the most rudimentary of all social structures: they constitute the type of association called 'an audience'. This is indeed a most rudimentary form of corporate existence; but it *is* corporate. In practice we need make no such supposition about existing or historic states. In all of these the government emerged from, or was superposed from the outside upon, an already structured society – which sometimes consisted of a single, fairly simple structured association, but more often consisted of an interconnected system of social structures, i.e., one with defined sub- and sub-substructures within it.

The second corollary is that this organ of government, in the sense of a set of offices occupied by certain individuals, is the *final* arbiter in matters disputed between the individuals comprising the state, or the various associations of which they are members. In order to fulfil this condition of finality it must be more powerful than the associations whose affairs it is trying to regulate, or it would be ineffective. This power may derive from a spectrum ranging from its popularity at one end of the scale to its coercive capacity at the other. But, as will be seen below, its power may *also* depend on its moral authority. Whichever it relies upon, and in most cases it must rely on both, to act as the final arbiter the organ of government will have to be able to deploy a power and/or authority superior to that of any one sub-association or group of these within its sphere.

The third corollary is precisely that this sphere is defined in terms of a stretch of territory. It is this that determines where an association called State A ends and another called State B begins.

The fourth corollary is that, with qualifications, all of those living within the territorial area are subject to the rules drawn up by the government for the population, *whether they like this or not*. This phrase 'with qualifications' has to be inserted because, as already mentioned, in some states in the past certain categories of inhabitants could, by virtue of certain characteristics, secure immunity from some of the common rules drawn up: 'benefit of clergy', by which a priest could secure immunity from some of the territory's rules, is a case in point. As time has passed, the area of these immunities has shrunk until, in the modern state, the proposition that the state is a compulsory organization in the sense that its rules are mandatory on *all* those living inside the territory has become almost entirely true. In its modern form, at any rate, the state is very markedly a compulsory association.

Those within its territory are inside its field of competence and command whether they like this or not; they are not asked whether they wish to obey it or not, and by the same token whether they leave it or not is not always a simple matter of individual choice. The rulers may decide, and have the power to enforce this decision, that they may not leave it.

The defining characteristics of a state then are: (1) It is a territorially defined association. (2) It embraces, compulsorily, all the persons in that territory. (3) It possesses the monopoly of violence throughout this area, by virtue of which it has the capacity, even if not the moral authority, to guarantee the finality of its decision in political disputes arising from the con- flict of individuals or groups within its territory. (4) As a necessary accompaniment of all this, it has a body of persons who exercise this monopoly of violence in its name, namely, the common government.

The individual differences between the state and the sub- associations inside it are matters of degree rather than of kind, but, taken together they are sufficient to make the state a very different kind of association, and to bring about a radical change in the manner in which one association conducts its conflicts with others. First, while it is true that some associa- tions, like the Roman Catholic or Greek Orthodox churches, are communities of faith and discipline and transcend geographical frontiers, many private associations are, like the state, based on territory. The British Legion, for instance, is geographically cir- cumscribed. Secondly, the compulsory nature of state member- ship is certainly approached, though it may not be equalled, by some private associations. In India, for instance, a man or woman is born into a certain caste. This is automatic and ineffaceable and, as long as they remain in Indian society, it may govern their private as well as their social relationships, for as long as they live. This is an extreme example. Many other cases occur, on a more domestic plane, e.g., a particular social environ- ment may dictate that an individual must enter a given church or political party; and there are others where, although an individual is in principle free to quit such a 'voluntary' associa- tion, this is in practice very difficult – either because he would suffer financial hardship or because he would suffer in his friendships or in social esteem. Thirdly, the compulsive capability of the state may well be matched by that of certain private associations. Despite the state's claim to a monopoly of violence, in practice private associations may also wield so great a coercive power that they can execute summary justice on their dissidents without fear of the public authorities: the Mafia provides one ready example, and the horrible private war that went by the name of *la violencia*, in Colombia, provides another. Nor is that all. Death is sometimes held cheaper than certain other deprivations, and private associations can coerce their members by holding out the fear of some tragic after-life: for instance, religious belief may induce a Buddhist monk to burn himself to death rather than acquiesce in the state's policies, or may cause Hindu sadhus to court death by gunfire rather than have their holy cows put down in violation of their religious scruples.

Yet, when all the qualifications have been made, it is rare, if indeed possible, to find associations that *combine* all of the state's distinguishing criteria in that pre-eminent degree that is characteristic of it. By and large, the state is an altogether more compulsory and more comprehensive association, and more formidable, than any other in its territory. And it is this that brings about a qualitative change in the mode in which these private associations conduct their conflicts with other groups once they are working inside the context of a state.

For, in the absence of a common government, the victory of one of these associations over its opponents is, as we have seen, neither certain, nor durable. On the other hand, what the government decides in the name of the state as a whole, is both: it offers the most certain guarantee of victory because the government has a monopoly of violence in the territory; and it offers the most durable settlement, because its decision can apply to all associations throughout the whole of the territory. So, in the normal way, its decision is both universal and binding. Clearly, a private association's hope of success in its competition with other groups is maximized if the full power of the state, as mediated through the government, is put behind it. And so it is that, once such competition takes place within the framework of

the state, what would otherwise have to be a private and intermittent struggle of one group against another now becomes a
public competition with other groups, either to get the government to espouse its policy and enforce it, or else to go forward
and become the government. And the set of procedures whereby
the private associations within a state seek to influence the
government, or to participate in policy formation by the government or to become the government, is 'the political process'.

Crudely we can express it in the form of a simile (see Figure 1).
Each of the associations and sub-associations in the society has,
as we have seen, its *élite*; some members of this are in office and
form the government of the private association; others, the
counter-*élite*, are waiting the opportunity to displace them. The
aggregate of all these *élites* forms the total *élite* in the society as
a whole. This may be thought of as the skin of an orange –
except, of course, that in life this 'skin' merges with the pulp
through a number of minute gradations. Again, each section of
the orange may be taken to represent some politically important

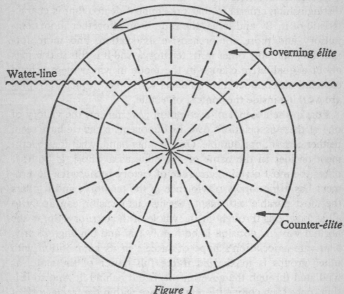

Figure 1

association – except that, in life, a considerable cross-membership may exist between some associations and others, whereas this simile gives the impression that society is compartmentalized. Furthermore, there is no way, in this simile, of portraying the divisive effects of class. The simile is indeed most defective; yet it may serve to make the main point without committing us to anything but a general concept of the relationship of associations *and* classes to the state as a whole, and the relationship of *élite* and non-*élite*.

This orange, with its skin representing the *élite* of society, floats in water; that portion of the skin that is above the water-line represents the governing *élite*, and the segments which it covers represent those associations in society which have succeeded in the competition to have their leadership participate or hold office in the government. All those segments under the water-line, however, represent those associations which have lost this competition, and whose policies are temporarily being subordinated to those of the victorious ones, and the portions of peel that cover them represent, for society as a whole, the counter-*élite* that seeks to displace the governing *élite* at any point of time. This counter-*élite*, impelled by its need to maintain the allegiance of its associations' memberships, strives to make the orange roll from right to left, or left to right, in order to push the governing *élite* and the membership it represents out of office and below the water-line, and to take its place. And the mere fact that such a push could have precisely this result tends to make the *élites* of the 'governing' segments anxious to minimize the purely sectional aspects of their own policies so as to discourage the counter-*élites* from the concerted effort to overthrow them.

IV. AUTHORITY

Quite apart from the defects already pointed out in this illustration, however, there is one other so cardinal as to make the entire simile misleading save for one special case – revolution. As it stands, the illustration assumes a naked scramble to attain the offices of government by any means that come to hand. It represents a catch-as-catch-can, which ends with the installation of a group of persons whose power is greater than that of its competitors – whether this power be based on popularity, rewards, or coercion and elimination of its opponents. It would serve, perhaps, as a preliminary (and little more than a preliminary) sketch of the way in which, in the course of the French Revolution, the Royalists were displaced by Feuillants, Feuillants by Girondins, Girondins by Jacobins and so forth, all the way to the Empire of Napoleon. Or it might serve to portray how, during the Russian Revolution, Royalists and Constitutional Democrats were swept away by Socialist Revolutionaries and Bolsheviks, and then how the Socialist Revolutionaries were dispensed with by the Bolsheviks, and so on through the civil wars, until the final triumph of the Bolshevik fraction.

But these are highly exceptional situations. In practice, the struggle for governmental office is usually conducted through some socially standardized and approved procedures; and even if these are violated, as they are more often than not, the government of the day does not in fact, save for brief periods, base its possession of office solely or even wholly upon emotions, economic rewards and penalties, or coercion and violence. For one thing, all of these are satiable. Power based on love, affection and respect is not in its nature durable. To secure office simply by handing out rewards and donations to those who have smoothed the path is not durable either – those who receive clamour for more and more, as did Geoffrey de Mandeville in his alternating support for the claims of Stephen and Matilda to the throne of England. And even a reliance on force is not durable: there comes a point where a population has endured so much coercion and bloodshed at the hands of its government that it feels it has little to lose by chancing its arm and attempting to overthrow it. Nor are governments founded on these exercises of power necessarily stable. For a government which claims to govern simply on the grounds that it is more popular than another is laying itself open to a popularity contest with other aspiring *élites*; one that bases its claim solely on the rewards it has given to its supporters invites others to offer still greater rewards as a price of office; and above all, those that claim to govern solely on the grounds that they are stronger than others openly invite overthrow by any group that can prove itself stronger still.

> The same Arts that did gain
> A power, must it maintain,

wrote Marvell; and, more succinctly, Rousseau pointed out:

If force creates right, the effect changes with the cause. Every force that is greater than the first succeeds to its right. As soon as it is possible to disobey with impunity, disobedience is legitimate; and the strongest being always in the right, the only thing that matters is to act so as to become most strong.

Nor is this all. Physical compulsion, applied as the ultimate means of securing the obedience of recalcitrants, is an uneconomical way of going about the matter. It diverts a high proportion of resources, time and effort from the tasks of policy-making and execution. Take a fairly simple example – the compulsory lecture – and suppose, in this case, that the students obliged to attend are still determined to resist as far as they are able. There is little doubt that the lecturer and his minions can get most of them to the lecture. They can be roused from their beds at dawn, rounded up, piled into trucks and driven to the lecture room, decanted and frog-marched into the auditorium. They can be prevented from whistling and heckling by further attentions from the strong-arm men. But what the lecturer will achieve in delivering his lecture in these circumstances is very doubtful – for even at this point he has no guarantee that they will listen to what he is telling them. Nor would other forms of coercion necessarily prove more effective. The university might threaten to expel the absentees, but if it did this it would certainly not be able to fulfil its function – which is, to teach them. Yet this whole system of sanctions, culminating in physical compulsion, is avoidable once the students recognize the *authority* of the university and of the lecturer in particular, to have them attend at a particular time. Thereupon the simple announcement that the lecture will take place at a given time and is obligatory will secure a mass attendance. Admittedly not all will attend – there are usually marginal recalcitrants in any organized society. But the bulk of the students will attend – not because of any coercion or violence but simply through the magic of authority, that is to say, their *recognition of a duty to obey*.

Certainly, most of the régimes in the contemporary world make a show of violence against their recalcitrants, and the spectacles of the Nazi régime in pre-war Germany, or of the Stalinist régime in the U.S.S.R., suggest at first sight that machine guns and concentration camps alone secured the allegiance of the populations of these countries to their respective governments. Unquestionably far, far more coercion was used against these populations than is common in, say, the U.S.A. or Britain or the Netherlands. But to assume that Hitler and Stalin retained the allegiance of their subjects solely by their use of violence is mistaken. Hitler undoubtedly had his enemies, and these would have multiplied if they had been empowered to conduct propaganda and organize political parties in opposition to him; and the same is true of Stalin. But it is also true that both had vast multitudes of officers and supporters, as well as beneficiaries, and that both could and did rely on a widespread belief – artificially inculcated by their monopoly of the mass media – that they were the rightful government, that it was wrong to disobey them. They commanded not only by virtue of their physical might but by virtue of their *authority*.

The stable and effective exercise of a government's power is that which derives from its authority. By this I mean that the commands to do or to abstain proceed from persons who – no matter whether this is logical or reasonable or justifiable by any objective criterion – are *believed* to be persons who have the moral right to issue them: so that, correlatively, those to whom the commands are addressed feel a moral *duty* to *obey* them. Authority represents a two-way process: a claim to be obeyed, and a recognition that this claim is morally right. No public recognition of a claim means no authority.

Where a population recognizes a moral duty to obey, there is no need for the government to reason with it, persuade it, bribe it or threaten it, though all these exercises of power may be necessary for the marginal recalcitrants. The mere recognition of a duty to obey achieves for the government what an overwhelming application of violence would not satisfactorily achieve. As Rousseau said: 'The strongest is never strong enough unless he succeeds in turning might into right and obedience into duty.' As human nature goes, fear is certainly the father of power, but authority is its mother. To inculcate the population with the belief that their rulers have the right to demand obedience and they the corresponding duty to give it is the principal art of government.

How then do governments acquire or enjoy this authority? Basically by making use of some belief, or even a sub-intellectualized attitude ('mentality'),[2] or 'sentiment' which is to be found amongst their subjects – or which they, the government, have themselves successfully planted there. Authority depends upon what one political scientist has called the *miranda* and the *credenda* of power: the things that arouse favourable emotional responses (the *miranda*, or things to be admired) and the 'rationalizations that contain the reasons which oblige the intellect to give assent . . .' (the *credenda*, or things to be believed).[3]

Sometimes the *credendum* is a belief in the actual, alleged or presumed extraordinary quality of a person. This is what Weber called *charismatic* authority. It rests on a wide public belief – what he describes as the belief in magical powers, revelations, and hero worship. Hitler claimed, and a very large number of persons unquestionably believed him, to be just such an extraordinary superhuman person. (See below, Chapter 3.) Sometimes the belief is in the everyday routine as an inviolable norm of conduct. Rule that rests on such 'piety for what actually, allegedly or presumably has always existed' is what Weber called 'traditionalistic authority'. Examples are the authority of the father or the senior of the house over the household; of the lord over his serfs or peons, or of the Renaissance prince over his subjects. Such a basis of authority is the foundation of the so-called 'traditional régimes' (but also for those which we shall later

2. See p. 43 below for 'mentality'.
3. The expression is Charles Merriam's. cf. his *Political Power*, Free Press, Illinois, 1934, Chapter 4 *passim*.

classify as 'façade-democracies'). In both the foregoing cases the authority is vested in specified *persons*.[4] In a third type, it is vested in impersonal rules and the offices created under them. This is called 'legal' authority, though 'procedural authority' would be a better term, for this kind of authority extends to other human associations than the state, to which alone the terms 'law' and 'legal' are applicable.[5] But of course the compelling nature of these rules itself depends on a set of prior beliefs – beliefs which, according to Weber (though we do not need to follow him here in all respects), hinge upon the recognition of expediency, or on rational values, or both. In fact, the recognition of these rules as duty-worthy usually turns not so much on a rational attitude as on an impulsion which is given the appearance of logical and/or scientific reasoning.[6]

The assent to the authority of the government, based on this 'platform of rationalization'[3] may, as Merriam pointed out, be given to (1) *government* in its most general sense (as the condition of being governed), or to (2) '*the government*' in the sense of the special system of rules in force at the moment, or to (3) *the individual holders of office* at the time. The most common reason for obedience is, as he says, 'no reason at all' – it is just assumed. But, in the rationalized stage, it may be alleged and believed that the power of the government in any of its three aforementioned senses is ordained from God, or that it is the highest expression of wisdom or expertness, or that it is the will of the majority or of some specially important section of the population; and so forth. The moral viewpoint which is widely accepted by the masses, and in the name of which a group of persons can successfully claim authority to govern them, is what[7] Pareto called the 'derivation' or what G. Mosca called the 'political formula'. The last-named succinctly expressed the notion thus:

3. Merriam, loc. cit.

4. For the three 'ideal types' of authority see M. Weber, *Theory of Social and Economic Organization*, Hodge, Edinburgh, 1947, pp. 300 ff.

5. H. H. Gerth and C. W. Mills. From *Max Weber*, Routledge & Kegan Paul, 1964, pp. 295–9.

6. V. Pareto, *Sociological Writings*, ed. S. E. Finer, Pall Mall, 1966, pp. 33–50.

7. idem.

By this expression, *political formula*, is to be understood the fact that in all countries which have reached an extremely modest level of civilization the governing class justifies its power by basing it upon a sentiment or belief which, at a given moment and among a particular people, is generally accepted. Such sentiments could be – according to the individual circumstances – the presumed will of the people or the presumed will of God, traditional fidelity to a dynasty or confidence in some individual actually or apparently endowed with extraordinary qualities.

Naturally, each political formula must correspond to the degree of intellectual and moral maturity of the population adopting it at that particular time. It therefore follows that it must correspond to a conception of the world which is held by the particular people in question at a given point of time and it must constitute the moral link between all the individuals who share it.

Consequently, when, for one reason or another, a political formula becomes outmoded, when belief in its basic principles grows cool, this presages that grave transformations are imminent in the governing class. The Great French Revolution broke out when the vast mass of Frenchmen stopped believing in the divine right of kings; the Russian Revolution took place when virtually every intellectual and possibly the majority of workers and peasants ceased to believe that the Tsar had received a God-given mission to govern Russia as an autocrat. By the same token when a political formula corresponds with the mentality of the age and with the most widely shared sentiments of a people, its utility is unquestionable. For it often serves to *limit* the activity of governments while, at the same time, in some measure it ennobles obedience because this is no longer simply the result of material constraints.[8]

The 'divine right of kings' is one example of just such a political formula that was highly effective in its time. In the late Middle Ages, when this belief was widespread, a king or prince could secure the obedience of a population on the grounds that, in his capacity of prince, he had been entrusted by God with the authority to rule them. This was the major premiss in the argument and was itself founded on a widespread belief that the Bible, from which this axiom was derived, was a holy book, the word of God, and so to be trusted without question as an article

8. G. Mosca, *Histoire des doctrines politiques*, Payot, Paris, 1936, pp. 321–2.

of faith. But the prince had also to establish the minor premiss in the argument, namely, that he really was a prince; and to this end he had to prove his claim to be the lineal descendant of the ruling line according to the rules of lineage and succession currently accepted. Then the syllogism of authority ran: 'Princes are appointed by God to rule their subjects, I am the prince, therefore I am divinely appointed to rule ..' The establishment of that intermediate, minor premiss, however, was not always easy. This is precisely why, during the Middle Ages, there were such arguments about whether a particular nobleman of royal blood was descended from the male or the female line, whether he was born in wedlock or whether he was a bastard – and indeed, in the last resort, whether (as in the cases of Lambert Simnel or Perkin Warbeck, in the reign of Henry VII of England) he was a nobleman at all, and not some common impostor. Shakespeare's history plays are stiff with arguments of precisely this kind. This is why, in *Henry V*, which in all other respects is a play of action, the unfortunate groundling is treated to that interminable scene[9] where Henry V, seeking to invade France, demands from the archbishop of Canterbury a verdict on his moral claim to the French throne. The archbishop, playing with the 'Salic law', argues that because of its operation the current incumbent of the French throne is not the true prince but a usurper, while Henry V of England, on the other hand, is the lawful king of France. Henry presses him: 'May I with right and conscience make this claim?'; and to this the cleric gravely replies, 'The sin upon my head, dread sovereign.'

The history of political thought is a cemetery of political formulas. A political formula can be attacked by denying the major premiss (the axiom on which it is founded), or the minor intermediate premiss, or both. The example from *Henry V* illustrates an attack by way of rejection of the minor intermediate premiss. Another way to attack the divine right of kings, however, would have been to argue that what the Bible said was not true, or, alternatively, that it was true but had been misinterpreted in this particular respect. In England, the divine right formula was attacked in the latter way and had lost its hold by

9. *Henry V*, I, 2.

the end of the seventeenth century, only to be replaced by a new formula. This started from the axiom that the relationship between ruler and ruled was a tacit and mutual understanding of a contractual nature by which the ruler ruled the population provided that he fulfilled certain conditions for them; from which it followed that breach of the conditions by him would void the contract, and thus justify rebellion. It was along precisely these lines that the English Whigs rationalized the ejection of James II from the throne and his replacement by William of Orange.

Today the contract formula is also dead. It has given way to the notion that the will of the population as a whole or, in default of unanimity, a majority of the population is the sole moral basis for exercising power. In some quarters, however, even this has become outmoded; it is argued that the will of only a special part of the population can provide the moral basis for this exercise of power – for instance the 'proletariat' or the 'Volk'.

Where a particular political formula is challenged and replaced by another, the moral authority of the government which rests on it is, by the same process, also challenged. In such cases, the government has three choices. It can adapt itself to the new formula – or at least try to do so, because sometimes the new formula is such as to make adaptation impossible. (For instance, for decades past, the masses of Asia and Africa accepted without question a belief in the supremacy of the white man, and consequently his derivative right to rule over them. This formula of white supremacy has been successfully challenged by other formulas, namely, those of popular sovereignty and the right of nations to self-determination. It is impossible for the white rulers to adapt to these new formulas because, by their nature, they imply the replacement of the white by the indigenous inhabitant.) Where adaptation is not possible, the rulers have only two other alternatives: to rely increasingly upon coercion, or to abdicate.

In societies in which there is wide consensus that the office holders or the system of government have a rightful claim on the obedience of the population, i.e., where government in either of these senses reposes firmly on a current political formula, government will be stable. If, on the other hand, the tenure of the office holders or the system of government are out of line with or contradict the current political formula, then there will be political instability, with government relying much more upon coercion. Instability will likewise ensue if, in a given society, there is no widely shared political formula but a number of competing formulas. This question of consensus, and the support which a political formula brings to the system of government and the office holders at any time, is one of the central considerations in the comparison and contrast of various families of governments. Where consensus is weak, coercion tends to be strong, and vice versa.

So far we have talked of the *credenda* of power, the rationalizations 'that contain the reasons which oblige the intellect to give assent to the continuance of authority'. But *'the heart has its reasons which reason knows not of'*.[10] Systems of government, as well as the persons who form governments, have from time immemorial contrived to identify themselves with the emotions of men and not just their reason. They appeal by and to *symbols*. The political group, wrote Merriam,

has appropriated more days of the calendar than any other except the ecclesiastical. It has taken over perhaps the largest proportion of territorial space for public use and has endowed streets, ways, places with power group names, and has generously equipped them with monumental advertisements of power. Public buildings are more impressive than those of any other group with the exception, again, of the church and in modern days the factory and skyscraper. Music and song have contributed to the glorification of the power association in some of the most striking rhythms ever devised, rivalled again, however, by those of the church and by other types of music. What should we do without the Marseillaise, Deutschland über Alles, the Internationale, America, God Save the Queen. . . .[11]

Public holidays, statuary and monument, music and song, flags and uniforms, legend and history, ceremonials and processions, mass demonstrations, have all been pressed into service to identify the system of government, and the office bearers under

10. Pascal, *Pensées*, 4, 277.   11. Merriam, op. cit., p. 105.

it, with the inarticulate and perhaps inarticulable values, attitudes, prejudices and velleities of the population.[12] And, at the same time, they have been used to make the system of government and its office bearers appear more than life-size in the eyes of those they command: in short, to 'glorify, magnify, praise and extol'.[13] As Pascal, that most perceptive of philosophers, remarked: 'A very refined reason is required to regard as any ordinary man the Grand Turk, in his superb seraglio, surrounded by forty thousand janissaries. . .'[14]

V. COMPARATIVE GOVERNMENT

What is government? From the foregoing, it is seen to be a standardized arrangement for taking decisions affecting the group and for giving effect to them. Most organized human groups have such arrangements, whether they are small primary face-to-face groups like the family, or the territorial state itself. The government of units like the family, the Church, the trade union or the firm may properly be called 'private' government. It is, however, to what might by contrast be called 'public' government, that is to say, the government of the territorial state, that the term 'government' is commonly applied; and it is with this type of government that this book is concerned.

This is not to say, however, that we shall not be concerned with such 'private government' in any given state that we examine. And the reason for this is to be found in the answer to a second question, namely, *why have government?* The answer that has been given to this is that government is a response to political predicaments, i.e., to situations where the group in question (in this case the territorial association called the state) *has* to adopt a common policy, but where rival bodies of members advocate policies which are mutually exclusive. To secure a common policy, the condition of self-division must be replaced

12. loc. cit.

13. The phrase used in the Hebrew *Kaddish* prayer, a kind of 'Magnificat'.

14. Pascal, *Pensées*, II, 82.

by one of unanimity. The creation of this admittedly artificial and it may be fragile unanimity is effectuated by the exercise of political power, ranging from affection and persuasion at one end of the spectrum to coercion at the other. Government, as an arrangement for taking the common decision, defines and channels these exercises of power. In the territorial association of the state, various groupings, as we saw, provide the members of that state with rival focuses of authority and with alternative sets of sanctions; the mutually exclusive policies of these groupings are, precisely, what generate the demand for a common public policy and formulate its alternatives – in a word, then, make 'public' government necessary or at least desirable; finally, those who govern these groupings seek to further their exclusive aims either by becoming the governors of the state or at least by getting those governors to espouse their own aims and objectives as opposed to those of their rivals, so as to ensure that their own policies will be translated into general rules that bind the whole of the community with the full moral authority and the penal sanctions of the state behind them. Government, as a set of standardized arrangements for taking and effectuating group decisions, cannot be considered in isolation from these 'private governments' because it is a response to the problem which their conflicting interests and attitudes have created. These interests and attitudes of the groups and associations, the relationships existing between such groups and associations, condition the form of the arrangements, who shall handle them, what support or resistance these persons or the arrangements themselves shall receive, and the issues that are to be decided under or by them. Government is a regulator of society so that its form, its scope and its procedures are all to greater or lesser extent outcomes of that society.

Hence arises the study of 'comparative government'. For the form, the procedures, the scope of government differ from one society to another, often very widely. It is the task of comparative government to establish, first how – and then, as far as possible, *why*.

The 1966 *Statesman's Year Book* listed 122 different independent states and, even as these words were written, no less than four new states were in the process of being formed. Clearly the task of comparing and contrasting all of these in every respect would be difficult – and would be so confusing as not to be rewarding. Fortunately no such extended comparison is necessary. Although each and every one of these states differs from the others, there are family resemblances; and the most direct practical way of going about our business is to group these states into their respective 'families' and compare and contrast these.

Unhappily, though this disposes of some difficulties, it also creates new ones. In one sense all these 122 states are unique – hence there ought to be 122 'families'. In another sense all are identical: all are ruled by a group of influential individuals who are less numerous than those they govern. In this sense all are oligarchies. The problem is to establish categories that are neither so numerous as to make comparisons impossible nor so few as to make contrasts impossible. And how many categories there should be, and of what type, depends upon the initial criteria we select. But what one observer thinks an important or significant criterion of comparison and contrast may appear trivial to another. At one time, for instance, it was common to distinguish states according to whether they were monarchies or republics. Today this appears to be of far less importance than other criteria. In the fourth century B.C., Aristotle classified forms of government into three main types, using as criteria the numbers and the wealth of those who held formal authority in the state; then he sub-divided each of these three categories into two, according to whether those who held authority were concerned for their own private wellbeing or for that of the community as a whole. So he derived his three pairs, monarchy–tyranny, aristocracy–oligarchy, *politeia*–democracy. And then, when he came to treat each one, he sub-divided it further – monarchy ('the rule of one man'), for instance, was sub-divided into five distinct types.

What Aristotle did, political scientists are still continuing to do; and it would seem that the best one can hope for is to produce a typology that (a) covers all the known varieties of governmental forms with (b) the most economical set of distinctions, so as to (c) provide the receiver with what he, at any rate, regards as a satisfactory basis for explaining what forms arise in what given circumstances and, (d) hence, has some power of predicting what vicissitudes or alterations any given form may undergo should circumstances change in named respects. And even this may be too much to expect. The study of comparative government is as old as Plato and Aristotle but, as its history has shown, is so enormously complicated that its findings and even its basic typology are still fluid. The best one can do, then, is to try. And this necessitates, at the very outset, that the basic criteria of comparison and contrast must be made explicit. This in itself depends on a vision of politics and government; and so the basic families or types to be established here depend on these basic criteria of comparison and these in turn upon one's own perceptions. In the first place: if 'to rule' or 'to govern' signifies the exercise of a preponderant influence in initiating, deciding and executing policy, then everywhere the few rule the many. What differentiate one system of government from another are: (a) how far the mass of the public are involved in or excluded from this governing process – this is the *participation–exclusion* dimension; (b) how far the mass of the public obey their rulers out of commitment or how far out of fear – what may be called the *coercion–persuasion* dimension; and (c) how far the arrangements are designed to cause the rulers to reflect the actual and current values of the mass of the public or how far they may disregard these for the sake of continuity and future values – what may be called the *order–representativeness* dimension.

(1) *Participation–exclusion*

In all modern states the extent to which the mass of the population share in the process of governing is marginal compared with the extent to which the *élite* do, but, due allowance having been made for this, states exist in which the public are sufficiently involved in that process to be styled participants.

This may occur through formal methods, or informal ones, or by a combination of both. Informal groupings and associations of sectors of the public may secure a hearing from the authorities, because tradition or because their social, political or economic importance warrants it. Of the formal methods, one is the direct consultation of the public on a particular issue on which they are called to vote – the 'plebiscite', or 'referendum'. But the principal formal mode of securing popular participation in, or, at least, control of, the activities of the government is by the institution of 'representation'. This will be dealt with more fully later, at page 63, but for the moment let me merely say what I mean by this term – namely, that legal provision is made for a larger or smaller proportion of the adult population to elect persons to 'represent' their views, values and interests in an assembly, which has greater or lesser authority as between one state and another. Now many qualifications must be placed on this generalization. A few states still make no such provision – Saudi Arabia is one. Others – not a few – have 'temporarily' suspended its operation – Malaya, for example. In still more cases the elections are falsified. And even where they are not, and the elected assembly is genuinely representative, this may enjoy only limited powers.

These things having been said, then, the public may play some part in initiating policies by making demands through the associations of which they are members; in some states, such as Switzerland, they may even enjoy the legal right to make the rulers take cognizance of such demands through the device of the 'popular initiative'. Furthermore the public may also participate in deciding the issue, either mediately, because their voting power gives them the possibility of turning out an unpopular government, or directly, as in Switzerland or France, by accepting or rejecting the policy in a popular referendum. The public may also participate to some extent in executing the decision – either by their right to elect judges and officials, or else by serving in such offices in a voluntary capacity.

In many states, however, participation would be too strong a word to describe the relationship: there the principal role of the public is to *control* the activities of the rulers, to exercise a sort of veto power, rather than to participate. This broad veto power may be exercised by means of the ability to select or reject a particular set of rulers, as in a British or an American general election, or by the passive and in extreme cases active resistance of affected groups to the proposed policy – and so forth. In the great majority of the 'liberal-democracies' – i.e., states such as Britain, France, the U.S.A. or the German Federal Republic – the relationship of the public to its rulers is one of control rather than one of participation. But in by far the largest number of modern states the public neither participate in nor control the activities of their rulers, but more or less passively *acquiesce* in them. And in some this acquiescence is *submission* to coercion by their rulers. We can thus recognize a spectrum in which the ruler–ruled relationship ranges from popular participation, to popular control, then to popular acquiescence and finally to popular submission to the coercive capability of the authorities.

(2) *Coercion–persuasion*

All rulers secure the obedience of their subjects by a mixture of persuasion and coercion: but the mix differs significantly from one state to another. Compared with Haiti, probably the worst-governed state in the entire world, the British government employs very little coercion indeed, and compared with the British government Dr Duvalier of Haiti uses very little persuasion. We can analyse this coercion–persuasion spectrum by distinguishing various government operations designed to elicit obedience together with the corresponding pyschological attitude which they invoke. There are four main varieties: all governments at all times make use of all four – but some lay predominant stress upon one, some lay predominant stress upon another; and they can be arranged accordingly.

First of all, some governments – Haiti is a case already mentioned – rely much more exclusively upon *coercion* than upon the others: the psychological attitude they invoke is *fear*.

Next, there are a number of so-called 'traditional' societies in which the public is accustomed to regard certain persons or strata of persons – such as tribal chiefs, sheikhs, religious leaders or noblemen – as being their social and political superiors. These persons *manipulate* the public, relying on their sentiment of *deference*.

Thirdly in an increasing number of states the rulers *regiment* (or *organize*) the population – by which is meant that they 'form persons . . . into a definitely organized body or group', that they 'bring or put [them] into some definite order or system.[15] The practice of many African governments of creating single monopolistic political parties, along with ancillary organizations like trade unions, co-operatives and women's and youth sections, illustrates what is meant. In some of these states the psychological attitude which this regimentation invokes might be described as 'ideological' but it is pretty clear that in most of them the appeal lies with sentiments and beliefs which are too inarticulate, inchoate and diffuse to justify the use of this term. Indeed, even in the so-called 'ideological' states like the U.S.S.R. or China, it is none too clear that the non-party masses (who form the overwhelming bulk of the populations) do not respond by virtue of such inchoate and diffuse beliefs rather than by anything so intellectualized as 'ideology' connotes. This distinction has been noticed by the German sociologist, Theodore Geiger, who accordingly talks not only of ideology but also of what he styles *mentality*. While an ideology is a system of thought which has been intellectually worked out and organized usually in written form by scholars and intellectuals or with their help, mentality denotes a way of thinking and feeling which is more emotional than rationalized – something like a 'cast of mind'. In just such a way we might speak of 'the military mentality' or the 'boy-scout mentality'. Mentality has an oddish sound in English. I shall use the term 'sentiments'. Consequently, we have forms of government – régimes – in which the rulers *regiment* their population by invoking their *sentiments*.

Finally, in a large number of states the primary mode of securing public allegiance is by *persuasion*. This method implies a politically sophisticated public which can view the claims of its government (and those of its detractors) with some critical awareness of the values invoked, the sacrifices demanded and the rewards promised. Such an attitude might be styled *cognition*. This state of sophistication may indeed be attained in advanced industrial and highly literate societies – and yet, even in these, as general election studies have shown, it is neither universal nor

15. Definitions derived from *The Shorter Oxford English Dictionary*.

unalloyed. Not only do the electors of these states think and vote in terms of stereotypes and 'images', but even these, and the politicians' appeals (that is to say, the advocacy or persuasion to which voters are subjected), are often based on or at least conditioned by the supposed *interests* of the various sectors of the public. To the extent that this is so, then, the persuasion is admixed with *bargaining*. Now in a large number of less industrialized societies, especially those where primary allegiances (e.g., to family, clan, ethnos) are still very strong, bargaining based on purported interests predominates over the persuasion/cognition/component: examples are the Philippines, Lebanon and (at the grass roots, certainly) India. But in all these states the two components are intermingled, and so I shall style the last of my categories *persuasion/bargaining*, and the popular attitude which these invoke, *cognition/interest*. These four main types of the *coercion–persuasion* dimension may be arranged as in Table 1.

TABLE I

Coercion (Fear)	Manipulation (Deference)	Regimentation (Sentiments)	Persuasion/Bargaining (Cognition/Interests)

Furthermore these types can also be related to our first dimension – that of participation–exclusion. The régimes which have to rely primarily upon coercion are also, by their nature, régimes which exclude the public from the governmental process – though slight steps may be taken towards limited participation in selected issues, as, for instance, the elections to the workers' syndicates in Franco's Spain (the Cortes, part elected, is virtually functionless however). These coercion/exclusion régimes are, pre-eminently, of the military junta type, exemplified by Iraq, Greece or Argentina. The manipulation régime, based principally upon the traditionalistic deference of the population, is also, to a very large degree, exclusive: the population defers to its superiors and leaves government to them. But some of these régimes admit some elements of genuinely independent popular feeling, to the extent that some popular groups manage (despite the régime) or are permitted (by licence of the régime) to secure representation in consultative or parliamentary assemblies; though in all cases these, consistent with the definition of this class of régime, are dominated by the traditionalistic ruling oligarchy. The regimentation régime also tends to exclude its public from participation in initiating policy and in determining it, nor does the public control the activities of its ruler; on the other hand, many of these states attempt to draw the masses into participation in the execution of the policies that have been decided for them, and try also to give them a vicarious sense of involvement in these. In these various ways the U.S.S.R., China, Tanzania and the Ivory Coast exemplify this type of regimentation/exclusion régime. Finally come the persuasion/bargaining régimes; only in these do the mass of the public have a measure of participation in or control over the governmental process.

We could easily visualize therefore a combination of our participation–exclusion dimension with the dimension of coercion–persuasion, to produce a table like Table 2. But on the whole

TABLE 2

	Coercion (Fear)	Manipulation (Deference)	Regimentation (Sentiments)	Persuasion/ Bargaining (Cognition/ Interests)
Participation	Indonesia	Afghanistan Iran	Mexico Tanzania	U.S.A. U.K. France
Exclusion	Iraq Burma Argentina	Saudi Arabia	Albania U.S.S.R.	

this is not worth while, and the reason is that régimes using coercion, manipulation and regimentation are, by definition, ones that largely or wholly exclude their populations from decision-making or controlling (save with the minor qualifications already noted). Consequently we can proceed on the understanding that the dimension of participation–exclusion is largely subsumed under the dimension of coercion–persuasion.

(3) *Order–representativeness, Present goals–future goals*

The qualities expected of government are by no means simple. On the contrary, they form a complex of requirements which are mutually inconsistent, and so the composition of this complex tends to differ from one society to another. The organs of government do not simply represent or reproduce the consciously expressed values of the public – even assuming that it has these: and it is arguable whether they should indeed do so. A government does not simply 'represent', for the public will also expect it to provide continuity, and they will also expect it to show foresight. These statements are so bald, however, that they demand not a little explanation.

If an American or Englishman were asked what the first indispensable requirement of his government should be, it is ten to one that he would reply that his government was the servant of the people and its principle duty was to give the public what they told it they wanted. Even if this is taken as the starting point, it is no more than that: for it raises another trickier set of questions. Who are 'the people'? Are not some more knowledgeable than others, or more valuable and so forth – and, if so, should not their demands or views be given more weight? If the answer is 'No: every person must count as one and no person as more than one' – a fine democratic sentiment – this still does not fully answer the question, for now suppose that not one single policy is put forward from among the people but two mutually exclusive ones. In such a situation – and it is the normal one – who now are 'the people'? The Western tradition has been to decide this by counting heads and to adopt the policy supported by most people. Thus 'the people' turns into 'a majority of the people'. At this stage two new problems present themselves. The first relates to the size of the minority. After all there is not much to choose between forty-nine and a half and fifty and a half per cent. In such circumstances the minority may well be inclined to feel that, with better organization or more time to develop its case, it could have been the majority. The greater the importance that it attaches to the issues under discussion the stronger it is likely to feel about this. In such instances it may well be inclined to resist the application of the policy until or unless a much clearer verdict has been delivered – a majority of two-thirds or of three-quarters, for instance. Many constitutions – i.e., the written documents that contain among other things the ground rules of a governmental system – contain provisions which 'entrench' certain highly controversial matters by demanding that they be changed only by something larger than a simple majority.

The generalization may be hazarded that the more importance is attached to a particular rule the more those favoured by it will be prepared to resist its alteration. Logically one ought, therefore, to expect that there are certain particular states of affairs which are of such paramount importance to some people that they would resist any majority verdict, no matter what its size, that sought to alter it. And this is precisely what occurs. This forms the first of the practical limitations to the principle of majority rule, i.e., the assumption that the voice of the majority is also the voice of 'the people'.

The second arises where those who constitute the minority are always the same group of persons: this creates the problem known as the 'permanent minority'. The recent break up of the Nigerian Federation illustrates the point. Until 1966 this great state was dominated by its Northern Region, principally inhabited by the Hausa-Fulani peoples, by virtue of the fact that its population was larger than that of all the others combined. In this way the other ethnic groups, notably the Yoruba of the West and the Ibo of the East, found themselves permanent minorities. It was this that led to the first of the military revolts – an Ibo-inspired coup to break the Hausa-Fulani monopoly of power – and it is this that has led the Ibo-populated Eastern Region to secede from the Federation. From the Ibo point of view, the principle of majority rule, as it had hitherto operated, condemned them to permanent subjection.

The conclusion to be drawn is that the principle that the first duty of a government is to 'represent the people' raises difficulties which are not just philosophical, but practical as well. Many devices have accordingly been invented to protect minorities against the full implications of the 'majority' doctrine. Federalism, upper houses of legislatures, the system of 'checks and balances' (to be explained below) are such devices. Those states that have adopted such devices form a family of *qualified* democracies, to which the name '*liberal*-democratic' has been given.

This consideration gives rise to a most important distinction between régimes, and constitutes another dimension by which they can be judged. This dimension is the degree of *autonomy* enjoyed by minority groups. In some societies, groups may constitute themselves freely, may express their particular interests and view points and may intervene in the political process up to the point of criticizing, embarrassing or even hindering the activities of the government. In others, groups may only constitute themselves with governmental permission, may express views and interests only to the extent that government allows and, far from criticizing, let alone frustrating, the activities of the government, are expected to conform to and actually further its policies in every way. No existing state permits absolute freedom to its sub-groups and few, if any, reduce these to total subservience: but a broad spectrum certainly exists between states where the autonomy of the sub-groups is relatively uncontrolled, such as the U.S.A., Britain, France or Israel, and those where their status is relatively dependent, such as the U.S.S.R., Mali or the U.A.R. The dimension of sub-group autonomy–dependence can be combined with the dimension of coercion–persuasion, as shown in Table 3.

While it is easy to supply illustrations for six out of the eight cells in the matrix below (Table 3), problems arise in respect to two. Where does one find a régime which combines sub-group dependence with deferential respect to a traditional ruling group? I know of no modern state that exhibits this combination but I suspect that the reason for this is simple: in modern states, society is always pluralistic, but only in modern states is it also technically possible for the government to suppress the political expression of this social pluralism. In short, sub-group dependency in a modern state is factitious not natural. On the other hand, in simpler societies and states the degree of sub-group autonomy was sometimes very limited: the society was relatively homogeneous and undifferentiated. It is in certain primitive

TABLE 3

	Coercion (Fear)	Manipulation (Deference)	Regimentation (Sentiment)	Persuasion/ Bargaining (Cognition/ Interests)
Sub-group autonomy	Spain Indonesia Brazil	Ethiopia Afghanistan Iran	Ivory Coast Senegal Yugoslavia	U.S.A. France U.K. Israel
Sub-group dependence	U.A.R.		U.S.S.R.	

states, in Africa, for example, that one would find examples of this particular type of régime.[16]

The other problem concerns the régime that combines sub-group dependency with a persuasion/bargaining basis of political allegiance. Again, I know of no extant state that exhibits this particular combination. But this is not because the combination is self-contradictory. The concept is not merely thinkable but has been thought, and thought very fiercely. For this is the amalgam that produces the concept of 'totalitarian democracy' as explained by Talmon,[17] and the concept put forward by Saint-Just and Robespierre, and indeed by J.-J. Rousseau. In the state thus conceived, there would be no sectional associations, nothing but atomized individuals; but since each of these would be guided by Reason, the result would be a 'General Will' (Rousseau), or '*Une Volonté une*' (Saint-Just). The Jacobin régime failed to realize this, and it is permissible to believe that no other régime

16. Possibly, for instance, the Barotse. See M. Gluckman, *Politics, Law and Ritual in Tribal Society*, Blackwell, 1963.

17. J. L. Talmon, *The Origins of Totalitarian Democracy*, Heinemann, 1952, Chapters 1, 3 and 2, II, 3 *passim*.

ever will either. The concept is Utopian: but like Utopia it is *thinkable*.

But an entirely new difficulty arises from the axiom that 'governments must represent the people' when we ask next: with what frequency is the public to be consulted? In Britain the law prescribes that it is to be consulted by way of a general election every five years or after a shorter period if the prime minister so decides. But why five years? Why not four? Three? Two? Or even annually? Again, in certain states the voters have the right to 'recall' their representative at any time and hold a new election, so that in principle the population is able to alter the composition of its government as its own views and values alter. But now that public opinion polls have become so sophisticated, why not consult the public through them on every occasion when a division of opinion becomes apparent? Technically this would be quite possible and so would nation-wide campaigns carried out through the medium of television. In this way we could go back to the direct democracy of the Greek city state. The two considerations that arise from this prospect, however, are these. First, suppose that the public were to demand something that in the opinion of objective experts would be positively harmful to themselves? Secondly, what would be the likely consequence if it turned out, as there is every reason to suppose it would, that, on a number of critical economic or foreign policy issues, the opinion as registered in the polls were to reverse itself from year to year – or even from month to month? These two considerations bring into the open two requirements of government which are largely *latent*. That average American or Englishman mentioned earlier does not carry them in the forefront of his mind as he does the requirement that his government is there 'to give him what he wants'. The first of these latent requirements is that government policy should be in some large measure *predictable*, which implies certain dimensions of public order and continuity in its operation. The second of them is that the government ought to show some degree of skill and foresight in its conduct.

As to the first: men do not want individual objects as soon as they think about them, like children or cats. Men – and increasingly so as they grow up and assume responsibilities for others – want a framework inside which they can plan ahead for themselves and their dependants. They require a measure of predictability. Nobody has better explained this than Jeremy Bentham who called this 'security' and regarded it as the 'principal object of the law':

> Man is not like the brutes limited to the present time either in enjoyment or suffering but . . . is susceptible of pleasure and pain by anticipation and . . . it is not enough to guard him against an actual loss but also to guarantee him as much as possible his possessions against future losses.
> This disposition to look forward . . . may be called expectation – expectation of the future. It is by means of this that we are enabled to form a general plan of conduct: it is by means of this that the successive moments which compose the duration of life are not like insulated and independent points but become parts of a continuous whole. . . .[18]

But this need for predictability, and hence for order and continuity, clashes with the principle of representativeness. The second demands that as soon as public opinion alters, the government alters with it; the first demands that it remain the same. The second demands that rulers trim their policies and programmes to the changing likes and dislikes of their subjects; the first demands that they are independent of these likes and dislikes. Representativeness demands a turnover of rulers; order and stability demand their permanence. In the old days this order and stability could be supplied by some natural aristocracy like the Whig cousinhood, contemptuously dubbed 'the Venetian oligarchy' by Disraeli, which effectively controlled British society from 1688 to 1760. In default of hereditary rulers, the want is often supplied in the modern state by self-perpetuating military or civil juntas and also by the increasing responsibilities everywhere assumed by the corps of permanent qualified officials – the civil service or bureaucracy.

But in addition to predictability, men also expect their governments to show a degree of prudence and care for the future. It is a commonplace that individuals prefer immediate to future

18. J. Bentham, *Principles of the Civil Code*, Chapter 7.

pleasures even if the former are less satisfying than the latter promise to be, and equally that they prefer exertions that procure them a direct personal return to those that advantage them only by way of bettering the whole society. Despite this, they recognize, albeit only intellectually, that their government ought to have a regard for the community as a whole and for future generations. But this also clashes with the representative principle. The latter, dependent upon public opinion, is impassioned by and interested in what this demands: care for the community and for the future has to be dispassionate and disinterested about current clamour. Again, representative government is government that responds to overt expressed preferences; regard for the community and for the future requires government to see beyond these immediate preferences to the damage that they may do to the community as a whole and to its future prospects. Thus the futurity/community principle, like the predictability principle, requires a government skilled enough to see the future implications of current demands, and to make projections for the future, independent of current popular pressures and imbued with a sense of community and posterity. In the contemporary world many rulers trample upon the representative principle and erect personal or collective despotisms precisely in order to give effect to these corporate and proleptic values. Elsewhere, in those régimes where the representative principle still remains the cardinal one, as in the 'liberal-democracies', it is everywhere eroded and attenuated by the increasing influence of the permanent bureaucracy and its chiefs, which have become indispensable to the modern state. Hence the universal trend towards a decline in the influence of the elected legislatures and a corresponding strengthening of the 'executive branch' of government, i.e., the bureaucracy and the heads of state.

Thus we acquire two more dimensions by which systems of government may be differentiated: the dimension of *order–representativeness*, and the dimension of *present goals–future goals*. They may be represented as in Table 4.

The U.K. and the U.S.A. combine representativeness with an emphasis on present goals; Tanzania might conceivably be regarded as a state that combines it with future goals. A military despotism like Argentina's illustrates a régime which combines emphasis on stability or, as I have called it, 'order' with the pursuit of present goals, while the U.S.S.R., for example, combines it with an emphasis on future goals.

TABLE 4

	Present goals	Future goals
Representativeness	U.K. U.S.A.	Tanzania
Order	Argentina	U.S.S.R.

Now this particular matrix can be superimposed upon my earlier matrix (Table 3) which relates the coercion/persuasion dimension to the dimension of sub-group autonomy/dependency. And this will yield the shape shown in Table 5.

TABLE 5

By combining the two matrices, we can envisage no less than sixteen separate combinations of characteristics: sixteen possible syndromes. In fact, our possibilities are even wider, for it permits us also to conceive of régimes which lie across the borders of the four perpendicular columns, i.e., that in some measure combine coercion and manipulation, or manipulation and regimentation, or regimentation and persuasion; moreover, if we replicated 'manipulation' on the right-hand side of the 'persuasion' column, we would have the characteristics of such régimes as Lebanon, the Philippines or India, which combine persuasion and manipulation.

Even so, a schema of this kind will only be a crude approximation to the living realities of 122 different independent states. But as one has to begin somewhere, I choose to begin here. And the entire point of what follows in this book is to elaborate, to refine – and this will mean to qualify – the distinctions based upon the foregoing table. The mind is sharp, but life is hazy.

To begin with column I, the régimes relying peculiarly upon coercion (fear): the most obvious examples are military régimes whose principal, albeit not sole, operation for securing obedience is coercion. In their strict military form, as in Greece or Peru, these are usually short-lived, imposing a temporary truce of order on a confused situation. Most of them – as in Argentina or Greece, for instance, are concerned with immediate goals; but some, like the Nasser régime in Egypt, are concerned with future goals. Again, many of them permit a degree, sometimes a high one, of sub-group autonomy – Indonesia is a case in point; but others, like the Nasser régime, permit little or none. Thus the coercion régimes can be characterized as being divided into those permitting or not permitting sub-group autonomy: and those concerned with order and present goals, or those concerned with order and future goals. These can all be placed in appropriate cells as shown in Table 6.

But that table also makes provision for a coercive régime which is representative and concerned with present goals. How can a coercive régime be also representative – or at least partly so? Further analysis of such régimes at Chapter 11 does identify two kinds of military régime of just this type – there styled

TABLE 6

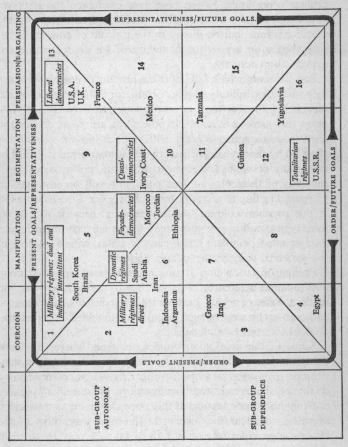

'dual' régimes, and 'indirect-intermittent' régimes, both of which in different ways combine reliance on the military as a source of power and policy-making with reliance on organized civilian forces. South Korea serves as an example of the first type, and Brazil of the second. These additional sub-types of the coercive régime can be placed in the top cell of column I: but they should lie across the boundary of the coercion and the manipulation columns.

Some régimes which fall under the heading of coercion are not in fact based on military coercion. Haiti, for instance, is a coercion régime but the coercion is supplied by Dr Duvalier's private army, the '*tonton macoutes*'. In others, the army has disengaged itself from an active concern with politics but the coercion is supplied by the police, particularly the secret police. It would be technically possible, therefore, to establish 'police states' as a sub-class of this column. This possibility will be envisaged in Chapter 11; but to simplify terms I propose to call *all* states in this coercion column 'military régimes' because this is the most typical and the most common form that such régimes take. As a result, I postulate a *first* class of states, with a number of sub-varieties, namely, the *military régime*.

Passing on to column II (the régimes based primarily upon manipulation/deference), I have already pointed out that no modern states of which I am aware combine this characteristic with sub-group dependence, though a number of simpler traditional societies have done so.

States of the manipulation/deference type, where they exist today, are ones which are governed – whatever a paper constitution may say – by a historic oligarchy whose power is based on the social esteem it traditionally enjoys. Most military régimes can rely on a fair measure of this same deference as a support, as well as the fear they evoke; in the same way, most of the historic oligarchies rely on a dash of salutary coercion to help along the habitual deference which perpetuates their power. Now some of these historic oligarchies, for reasons which will be explained in Chapter 9, have to work through liberal-democratic forms. Some, however, do not. Saudi Arabia is an example. This state is simply a *dynastic* state – which forms a *second* class of régime after the military kind. But the remainder of these historic oligarchies work in the trappings of liberal-democracy: constitutions, civil liberties, elections, parliaments, etc. In practice, however, these are neglected or perverted to ensure the retention of power by the historic oligarchy. For this reason they can be called *façade-democracies*. They form a *third* type of régime in the contemporary world. Some of them are more representative than others for reasons already explained at page 44 above. Their nominally elected assemblies or consultative councils do to some extent reflect opinion from outside the oligarchy. This is true of Morocco, for instance, but much less true of Ethiopia. Thus this class of régime can be placed on the matrix according to whether it exhibits a degree of representativeness or not. In like manner, a number of these régimes rely heavily on military support. To this extent they can be shown to do so by being placed athwart the coercion–manipulation boundary line. Iran provides an example. In all these cases it is part of the nature of the régime that it does not tamper much with the social structure: so that sub-groups, like landlords or the clergy, enjoy a wide autonomy.

Fourthly come those governments that qualify popular participation or control of their activities by *regimenting* the population in officially sponsored, favoured, or controlled associations so as to lead, *de facto* or *de jure*, to the monopoly or the hegemony of a single party. This in itself implies some measure of sub-group dependence, but some governments go much further than others in this respect. Some, like Guinea, go almost to the limit in denying sub-group autonomy; although, for a number of reasons, of which the most important is the lack of an adequate material sub-structure, they cannot enforce this dependence in anything like the completeness they claim. Such states can be placed low down the column, on the borderline between the representativeness–future goals cell and the order–future goals cells. On the other hand, some, like Tanzania and Mexico, provide more representativeness than Guinea, though equally committed to future goals. But Mexico differs from Tanzania in that it permits a high degree of sub-group autonomy, while Tanzania markedly does not. Hence its place in the column. Finally, there are a number of states wherein the single or dominant party, partly representative as it is, is devoted more to the immediate present than to the future: the Ivory Coast or Mauritania may serve as illustrations.

Interestingly, many of these dominant parties, which all began their careers as agitational mass parties and were heavily 'regimentary', have begun to abandon regimentation as their chief method of securing mass support: instead they are increasingly beginning to rely on manipulation of the population to retain power. This can be shown by placing them across the manipulation–regimentation boundary line. The Ivory Coast serves as an illustration.

The members of the three top cells in this column have a characteristic in common: one party monopolizes effective control, while unable or unwilling to bring the entire range of social groups within its scope. They constitute a *fourth* main class of state which I shall style a *quasi-democracy*.

They differ from a *fifth* class of state, which also relies on regimentation and on single or hegemonic party control, but which goes further in the scope of the authority it claims, the degree to which the present is subordinated to the future, and the effectiveness of its control over sub-groups. In these states, regimentation is extended to its limits, the representative quality of government is all but extruded and sub-groups are all but entirely dependent. These are the *totalitarian régimes* and they occupy the lowest cell in the 'regimentation' column. But some of the states that belong to this class have permitted free discussion inside the ruling party. Yugoslavia provides an example. Yugoslavia therefore can be placed across the boundary line of regimentation and persuasion. There may soon be a time when it ought to be moved out of the cell altogether and put into the one immediately above it, namely, the representativeness/future goals cell.

A *sixth* and, for my present purposes, final class of régime consists of those which rely upon the critical awareness of the population, and seek to convince them by a process of persuasion. This is not to say that this persuasion is rational: not only is it likely to utilize stereotypes and images, but as has been seen, it often takes the form of deals and bargains struck with various interests among different sectors of the public. But these rulers are sensitive to the immediate and overtly expressed demands made on them by the population and indeed parade their deference to the representative principle. In this class the extent of the sub-group autonomy is very high; which implies, among other things, competitive party politics. Because the rulers are thus so highly dependent upon public mood for their tenure or capture of office, the public participates in, or at least controls, the governmental process. The elements of continuity and care for the future and for collective goals reside, if anywhere, in heads of state and the bureaucracy: i.e., in the *executive* rather than the legislative branch of government. Thus they can be differentiated by the extent to which this is so. France, for example, has a system which currently permits the executive much more discretion than in Britain. Thus, if this is a distinction we care to stress, these régimes can be placed in either of the two top cells of column IV, the persuasion (cognition) column. Obvious examples in this class are Britain, the U.S., Sweden and the Netherlands. They are the *liberal-democracies*. But here a serious difficulty arises. To put it concretely: the general pattern of political powers, authority and processes in Lebanon outwardly resembles that of Britain; certainly it resembles British forms far more closely than it does any other type of régime so far mentioned. Lebanon indeed should be 'typed' as a liberal-democracy; and yet liberal-democracy clearly does not function in Lebanon in the same ways as it does in Britain, any more than it functions in the same ways in Ceylon or in Chile. The functioning of the régime as met with in Britain certainly provides a basis for comparison. Yet if this comparison is carried out, it must be in terms supplementary to the criteria used in Table 6.

The fact is that the liberal-democracy is, of all the various types of régime mentioned, by far the most complex and demanding. For in this type of régime much more depends on the internal structure and functioning of the parts of the government apparatus than in any other class of régime. In order to distinguish the operation of one liberal-democracy from another, new and ancillary criteria, not present in the table, are required.

These will be supplied in Chapter 2, and will be further commented upon in the final words of this book; but for the moment I certainly intend to classify Lebanon with Britain and Ceylon as falling into the liberal-democratic class of régime. One important distinction can be made here and now, however, since it does involve criteria already employed. In many countries of the Third World which are just embarking on their experiment with liberal-democracy it would be foolish to assume that the working of the régime depends on the degree of political sophistication present in Britain or the Netherlands. In countries like India, Ceylon, the Lebanon or the Philippines, the operation of the liberal-democratic system is largely and in some cases predominantly based upon bargaining with local, sectional, communal or other indigenous interests. To this extent their style differs markedly from the style in literate industrialized liberal-democracies. The issues which generate politics are exotic; the collection of votes at local level is often in the hands of some notable; the aggregation of the constituencies into a working national party, and hence the structure of that party, tends to be cellular and indirect rather than direct and hierarchical – and so forth. Furthermore in such countries a great deal still depends upon manipulation of the voters either through their social deference or through more material inducements. It would be possible to show this in Table 6 if one chose to duplicate the manipulation column on the right of the persuasion (cognition) column and place a number of régimes – of which the named ones are good examples – athwart the border line. This point, and other criteria of distinction, will be taken up in the concluding pages of the book.

I embark on my comparisons, then, on the basis of five major and one minor type of régime. The minor type, which is not worth examining in any detail since only Kuwait and Arabia belong to it, is the *dynastic*. The five major types are: (1) coercion/fear régimes of various kinds, the most common form of which is the *military régime* in its manifold aspects, henceforth styled the class of military régimes; (2) the manipulation/deference class, of which the most common and characteristic form is the régime called *façade-democracy*; the regimentation/sentiments class, which comprises two distinct types, namely, (3) the *quasi-democracy* and (4) the *totalitarian régime*; and finally, (5) the persuasion/bargaining types, associated with political pluralism: these, for all their variety, I call the *liberal-democracies*. And each one of these types contains a number of sub-varieties.

The remainder of this book elaborates the criteria for each main class, explores the nature of at least some of their sub-varieties, and describes some of them in closer detail.

Chapter 2

THE LIBERAL-DEMOCRATIC STATE

LIBERAL-DEMOCRACY is an English export. Some states have maintained this form of government for well over a century: for instance, the United Kingdom, Canada, Australia, New Zealand, Belgium, Holland, Switzerland, the Scandinavian countries and the United States of America. In others with shorter histories, e.g. Iceland, Israel and the Irish Republic, this form of government appears to be equally firmly founded. The list also includes many states which today are certainly liberal-democracies but whose past has been chequered, like France, Germany, Italy and Japan. Others are experimental, like India, Gambia and Ceylon. Many, like the Lebanon, Chile and Uruguay, are rickety.

This form of government is fragile, as is seen by the fewness of the countries which fall into the 'proven' category. It ought also to be noticed that many of these 'proven' countries were populated wholly or largely from Britain – for instance, the North American liberal-democracies, Australia and New Zealand.

Added together, the populations of all the countries with a liberal-democratic form of government, whether 'proven', or experimental or feeble, amount to some one thousand million people – about one-third of the world's population.[1]

I. ASSUMPTIONS OF LIBERAL-DEMOCRACY

Certain presuppositions or basic assumptions underly this form of government. Obviously the first of these is that it is 'democratic'. Now, no political terms have been so subjected to contradictory definitions as 'democracy' and 'democratic', since it has become fashionable and profitable for every and any state to style itself in this way. The Soviet Union and communist states

1. See Chapter 12 for a list.

of Eastern Europe, the Chinese People's Republic, North Korea and North Vietnam all call themselves democracies. So does Nasser's Egypt; so does General Stroessner's Paraguay; so did Sukarno's Indonesia. Yet, if anything is clear, it is that these states do not all meet the same definition of democracy.

Where so many diverse definitions of democracy exist – and new ones are continually spawned – it is rash to give another; yet it is necessary. We must start somewhere. I therefore *stipulate* this definition: (1) The primary meaning of democracy is government which is derived from public opinion and is accountable to it. As to *accountability*; this implies that it is not sufficient for a government to justify its existence because at some time in the past it was representative of popular opinion; for the two may have diverged since then. 'Accountability' entails that a government must continuously test its representativeness, that is to say whether its claim that it is 'derived from public opinion' is still valid. (2) This public opinion, it must therefore be presumed, is overtly and freely expressed. For if it is not, how can anybody *know* that the government is still 'derived from public opinion', i.e. is still representative? But 'overtly and freely to express opinion' implies some opportunity and machinery for making that opinion known, and therefore implies some kind of a suffrage, some kind of a voice or vote. A distinction is drawn between the direct democracy, in which the people are gathered together and consulted, or alternatively where the people are polled by a referendum or plebiscite, and the representative democracy, where the people periodically elect persons who are supposed to represent their opinion in a central law-making body. But in either case the condition is 'that the public opinion from which government is derived and to which it is accountable is to be expressed overtly and freely' does imply suffrage, and this brings us to the third part of the definition, which is that (3) in matters of contention between sections of public opinion it is the majority opinion that prevails. It is precisely because democracy, both historically and logically, implies and involves majority rule, at least in the last restort, that since the great French Revolution of 1789 pressure has been inexorably exercised to extend the suffrage to a wider and wider body of the people. This in turn explains why until quite recent years, certainly seventy years ago, 'democracy' was a term of abuse.

These three characteristics must, it seems, form part of any definition of democracy, whether this is to be taken historically back to the Greek world from which the term derives or to the struggle for the extension of the suffrage in the name of democracy which occurred in the nineteenth and twentieth centuries.

Thus the first assumption of liberal-democracy is that it is a democracy in the sense expressed above. But liberal-democracy is a *qualified* democracy. In this type of government there are other presuppositions or assumptions beyond the one which we have already stated.

The first of these is that government is *limited*. This implies that the government is operating in a world of autonomous, spontaneously self-creating, voluntary associations. In such conditions the government operates only at the margin of social activity. That it ought to interfere and regulate or even suppress these autonomous, self-creating, voluntary associations is a matter for it to prove: it is not assumed. There is no doubt, of course, in anybody's mind that it has a large and wide duty to interfere, if only to provide the minimum conditions of order and civil peace and defence from invasion without which this world of autonomous voluntary associations could not exist at all. But government only comes in, as it were, after the free play of these autonomous voluntary associations has failed to produce desired results or where its results are civil strife, unrest or breakdown, or other evils with which the public is dissatisfied. The authority of government therefore is limited; and this can be expressed by saying that certain rights of the individual and of the private association are safeguarded. A kind of ring fence is drawn around them and the onus lies on the government to show whether, why and to what extent this ought to be breached.

The second qualification to democracy in this particular 'liberal' form is that society is recognized as being *pluralistic*. To say this is not just to state that it is made up of a host of autonomous sections and associations, but to believe that each enshrines values or interests dear to its members. To recognize society as being pluralistic, therefore, carries the additional assumption that the government sets out to rule, not in the interest of any one group or alliance of groups, but in the common interest of all. This itself implies that such a government is rather tender-minded towards the minorities and gives them a long run for their money. It also carries the implications, however, that judgement is fallible, and that there are many points of view and all of these have to be considered and, if possible, reconciled by the government.

This highlights the third qualification: the liberal-democratic type of government is one in which *it is denied that there is any objective science of society or of morals.* On the contrary, it is assumed that in the last resort truth is a matter of individual consciences where all consciences are held, by an act of faith, to be equal either in the sight of God or in the sight of man. Two working conclusions follow from this, namely, toleration and the qualification of majority rule.

Why toleration? Because if there is no objective science of society and morals, then clearly no group, not even the government, has any moral justification for imposing any creed, philosophy, religion or ideology upon the rest of society. Again, since it is assumed by this act of faith that all individuals are equal in the sight of God, man or both, then dissent must be tolerated and each has the right to put his own point of view. Again, since truth is held to be individual and also fallible, rulership will be both conditional and also temporary; because clearly the views as to what is true and therefore proper for government to act upon will change from time to time as opinion fluctuates amongst the body of the people. So, this qualified form of democracy entails that the government is representative of and responsive to public opinion; and that where this opinion is not unanimous it is representative of and responsive to the majority. But these majorities will usually be constantly changing. As we shall see later, where there are permanent minorities and permanent majorities in a liberal-democratic state, serious problems arise for the maintenance of the system.

But even majority rule is seriously qualified in the liberal-democracy. It is certainly true, as we have already said, that government must in the last resort express the wishes of the majority (assuming that they have any), otherwise it could not be a democracy. But being a liberal-democracy also implies that the minorities must be given a chance to become a majority; and that means, therefore, that they must be given a chance status and a means to convert the majority. In order to make this possible, certain guarantees and machinery would have to be established.

II. CHARACTERISTIC FEATURES OF LIBERAL-DEMOCRACY

So much, then, for the preconditions or assumptions of the liberal-democracy. How, then, are these given practical effect? This brings us to the 'type' and the composite picture of this form of government. The form has four characteristic features. First, all governments of this type contain a representative organ in an elected legislature – and in some cases, too, an elected head of state or president. Secondly, and accountable to these representative organs, there goes a stabilizing and expert organ, both advising it and executing its instructions; this is the 'executive'. Thirdly, there exists a system of social and economic checks and balances, a network of centres of private power which acts as a brake upon the activity of the government. And fourthly, this system of social and economic checks and balances is paralleled and assisted by a system of political checks and balances.

(1) *Representative organs*

It is a part of the democratic assumption that government must represent and be accountable to the overt and actual wishes of society in so far as these are expressible and expressed. And this in turn either involves polling of the people's opinion by plebiscite or referendum, or alternatively, as we have said, the election by the people of representatives to a central legislature. Leaving the first of these aside, let us examine the system of electing the legislature.

This has two implications. Firstly, if it is really to represent the opinions of the public, then the election of the representatives must be secret, uncoerced and uncorrupt. Otherwise they do not represent these opinions; they either misrepresent them or represent pseudo-opinions. If the object of the legislature is truly to represent public opinion, there is no point in falsifying the elections: it would be like cheating at chess! Secondly, in preparing to elect representatives, and also in order to influence the government between one election and another, members of the public must have the right to petition government freely and to express themselves freely both in print and speech. For without freedom of speech and of the press, members of the public cannot make their views known at all; without a second freedom, the freedom of assembly, it is difficult, if not impossible, for them to exchange these views among each other; and without a third freedom, the freedom of association, it is impossible to see how they can get together in order to put up the candidates who represent their opinions. Free elections, freedoms of speech, press, assembly and association are necessary conditions for a legislature to 'represent' public opinion in any meaningful sense at all. Any legislature which has been brought together without these freedoms operating could only represent the opinions of the public by sheer chance; and of course nobody would know that it did accurately represent these opinions.

There is, however, a further condition. How are such freedoms guaranteed? Every one of these rights could be nullified if the judiciary or its equivalents were not independent of the government of the day. For, in the modern state, if the elections were not free, or if bribery were attempted, if the freedoms of speech or of the press or of association were abrogated, it would be necessary to prove this in a court of law or some specially constituted tribunal. If such a court of law took instructions from the very government or political party which had, in fact, abrogated these freedoms, the public would secure no redress. It is necessary, therefore, not only to have these rights but to have an independent judiciary or set of tribunals to see that they are duly enjoyed.

(2) *The executive*

The executive fulfils two tasks. In the first place, it executes the decisions reached by the government – and in this sense all modern governments require an executive (a body of agents with professional and technical qualifications) to carry out the tasks assigned to them by those authorized to make policy for the state. But, in modern states, the higher ranks of the executive fulfil another task: out of their professional and technical experience they advise the policy-makers on policy, help to shape it and may indeed be entrusted with a wide discretion in actually formulating it.

This is the forward-looking function of government, although in a liberal-democracy policy is supposedly a matter only for those who are representative of and responsive to the opinions of the public, namely, the elected legislature or head of state. Yet this advisory role of a policy-forming executive is necessary in the liberal-democratic state: this is evident the moment we examine the characteristics of elected legislatures. Though an elected legislature is not necessarily composed of amateurs, it is very likely to be so, because it is part of the nature of a liberal-democracy that anybody who has a mind to do so can stand for election, and that anybody with a persuasive tongue may very well be elected. It is therefore more likely that an elected legislature will consist of amateurs than that it will consist of specialized and trained technicians. Secondly, in the nature of things, it is likely to be partisan and highly politicized. Thirdly, by the same token, it is likely to be composed of passionate men, men who have got themselves elected in order to carry out policies which they think are for the public advantage, and who would not, indeed, ever have stood for election had they not had something of the nature of a *prima donna*; they are men who feel their opinions to be so important that they must be put forward and if possible implemented in law. And finally, a legislature is bound to be transitory, for the elections will be for a limited period and there is nothing to make us assume that the candidate selected last time will be returned at the forthcoming election.

Thus legislatures tend to be amateur, partisan, impassioned and transient. But, as we saw in an earlier chapter, one of the qualities which men require of government, whether they express this consciously or not, is a degree of predictability and stability. This is the dimension of 'order and future goals'. To provide this, the elected legislature (which embodies 'representativeness and present goals') must be advised by persons who are removed from the hurly-burly of political controversy and electioneering and trained in the matters which come to governments' attention, and who, moreover, will be there permanently and not change with every whim of public opinion. It would, however, be contrary to the very notion of democracy as we have already defined it if this group of people – skilled, neutral, dispassionate and permanent – were themselves to govern the people, because by their very nature they would not be representative of the opinions of the public. Indeed, they might have views which were diametrically opposed to such opinions at any point of time, or all of the time. And so it follows that, although it is desirable to have such a body of skilled, neutral, dispassionate and permanent officers, they would have to be only advisers to the legislature: not required to make policy, but to help in making it.

This is the rationale for a permanent, trained and politically neutral 'higher civil service'. The legislature in the liberal-democracy is directly accountable to public opinion, from which it derives its authority to govern. But at the same time it is advised on practicability by this permanent, dispassionate body of neutral experts. The typical device is the one shown in Figure 2, of two pyramids linked together in some way by the political head or heads. In the United States model, the president, who is the head of the executive branch – elected by the whole people and directly responsible to the whole people – is also in some senses responsible to Congress. In the British model, the Cabinet acts (to quote Bagehot) as a 'hyphen or buckle' between the legislature on the one side and the permanent body of trained experts on the other, being the head of the latter and at the same time a member of the former.

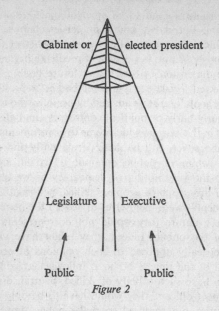

Cabinet or / elected president

Legislature   Executive

Public   Public

Figure 2

(3) *Social and economic checks and balances*

The third characteristic of liberal-democracy is the existence of social and economic counter-pressures on its activities. We have seen that, typically, this form of government is associated with a relatively untrammelled and spontaneous formation of private associations and the high degree of independence or autonomy which they are permitted to enjoy. Certain quite vital areas of decision-making are 'effectively' devolved upon these private bodies and not undertaken directly by government. For instance, the bulk of the economic decisions in liberal-democratic societies is not taken by the government, but by a multitude of private firms and their associations through the play of the market mechanism. Likewise, many professional decisions are taken by assocations of professional men. In Britain, for instance, the General Medical Council, the Law Society and the Inns of Court, police, discipline and arrange for the training of their own members. Again, in all similar liberal-democratic states, religious and moral decisions or points of view are developed and expounded in complete independence of the government through churches and various promotional groups. And finally, even the political decisions are formulated, expressed and pressed into effect through private associations – the political parties. The duty of the government in such societies as these is viewed as being to harmonize and co-ordinate and only in the last resort to impose and coerce. The extent of its interference may vary greatly indeed. Some such states have traditionally regulated commerce and industry far more than others. Some give a privileged position to one particular church. Some, again, maintain much stricter control over professional activities than do others; but generally speaking, the existence of social and economic counter-pressures, expressed through private firms and associations and private bodies of all kinds which act as a check and balance upon the free activity of government, is a fundamental characteristic of liberal-democratic governments.

(4) *Political checks and balances*

Not only is the government trammelled by outside centres of power which seek to bend it to their views and to hinder its activities where these are felt to be injurious, but the existence of political checks and balances practically enhances the status and magnifies the importance of minorities. 'Liberty is power cut into pieces,' said Hobbes. If minorities are to be protected and given a chance to challenge the views of the majority and time to mobilize and organize their own forces in order to convert that majority to their own way of thinking, the notion of political checks and balances follows. This has taken three main forms, although there are often others. The first of these is 'the separation of powers'. The notion here is that the government should be organized into three branches, the judiciary, the executive and the legislature, all held by different hands and never united under control of the same man or body of men; and, furthermore, that none of these three branches should have the power to coerce or override either of the other two. Therefore, the theory goes, if an act of government is to be carried through at all, it can be carried through only if all three branches concur. The failure of even one of the three branches to concur would abort the policy. Now, it must be obvious that, if all three branches were united under a single head, the opportunity for an act of government to go through rapidly would be very much greater than if three individuals or sets of individuals had to concur before that act went through: and so the separation of powers imparts a friction and a brake to the activity of government. When all three powers act in concert the matters go forward; let one of them refrain and nothing can go forward at all. This means delay. The principle is similar to that of a three-legged race: running on his own, a child can moderate or accelerate his pace as he wishes; if he is tied to another, then he must adjust his pace to that of his fellow. If he stops and the other child does not, one or the other will fall down flat. Not unnaturally this slows down the speed of the race to that of the slower runner. In the United States, as we shall find, this system is seen in a fairly complete form. In Britain it is found in a much weaker form, for (unlike the American Congress) Parliament can override the judiciary and itself combines the executive and the legislature. Nevertheless, the judiciary once appointed is independent of Parliament, and if it should produce a legal decision contrary to the desire of Parliament, that decision must stand, at least until such time as Parliament takes the necessary powers to override it. Furthermore, the fact that inside the British Parliament the opposition has a special status does act as a delaying power, albeit in a weaker form than the full-blooded separation of powers as it is seen in the Constitution of the U.S.A.

Another form of political brake is the division of the legislature into Upper and Lower Houses. In the United States, the Upper House (the Senate) has virtually coequal status with the Lower (the House of Representatives). If it disagrees with the Lower House, therefore, a delay ensues, until by some means or another both of the houses can be got to agree. In Britain, the Upper House (the House of Lords) can delay the measures of the Lower House (the House of Commons), if it so dares, for up to one year. On the continent of Europe the delaying power of the Upper House is generally much weaker even than this.

Nevertheless the general principle remains true: that by sub-dividing the legislature and by giving each branch of it certain delaying powers, frictions are imported into government enabling minorities to win the time in which to publicize their dissent and possibly to convert a majority to their point of view.

A third method of providing political checks and balances is to divide the powers of government between two sets of authorities: on the one hand, a national (or 'federal') authority whose writ runs over the whole national territory but only in respect of one particular set of matters, and, on the other, a number of other governments each with a restricted area to govern but responsible within this area for another range of powers. This arrangement is the basis of the territorial device, to be described later, known as federalism. The division of powers between two sets of authorities, Federal and State, can, in matters of disputed or concurrent jurisdiction, lead to friction between the two authorities and delay. In these circumstances, minorities which might have been defeated at the national level are able to rally within the security of the individual States of the federation. Britain is not federal but unitary, but even there the local authorities, although they could be abolished by Parliament at any time and although for the most part they owe their powers and responsibility to Parliament, have historically played a very prominent role in the government of the country. Furthermore, they have banded themselves into powerful protective associations, like the County Councils' Association and the Association of Municipal Corporations. As a result of this they, too, are very often able to resist suggestions by the central government; here again, therefore, delay and friction is brought into government. The essential point of all of these devices – the separation of powers, the creation of Upper and Lower Houses, the territorial division or devolution of powers – is to bring friction, delay and the necessity for consultation and compromise into the operation of government. All of them demand that, if government is to go forward, consultation must take place and some form of consensus between the contending bodies must be arrived at.

So much, then, for the main characteristics of a liberal-democratic type of state. It presupposes the existence of a host of autonomous private associations. The personnel and the policy of government emanate from these groups and the potential or actual situations of conflict which exist between them. Its duty is seen as being to mitigate and control the conflict and friction between them, but without destroying them in the process.

Chapter 3

THE TOTALITARIAN STATE

THE TOTALITARIAN TYPE

I CONSIDER a state to be *totalitarian* when two conditions are fulfilled. First, that the entire society is politicized; if private areas of life do still survive, they do so conditionally, on sufferance, as it were, from the government which at any time and for any reason may control, invade or take them over. Secondly, that not only is the entire society politicized but that the viewpoints which so politicize it are reduced to one alone, from which no dissidence is tolerated. It is therefore the veritable contradictory of the liberal-democratic type of government. The scope and authority of government is not limited but, just the reverse, is total. And the plurality of viewpoints, the hallmark of the liberal-democratic state, is here suppressed in favour of one single viewpoint.

In principle there could be a totalitarian state in which a personal despot was supreme provided that he had devised suitable instruments for exercising his control. In Stalin's Russia, it was nominally the Communist Party which expressed the single and total viewpoint: in practice the state bureaucracy and secret police, which were nominally subordinate to it, exercised a parallel or even a superior power under the personal guidance of Joseph Stalin, the general secretary of the party.

In practice, the characteristics which in greater or lesser measure have been or are exhibited by régimes of this kind are these: the authority claimed by the government is, in principle at least, unlimited in its scope; a single political party enjoys a *de facto* or even *de jure* monopoly of power; inside it, authority is transmitted from the top to the bottom so that it is hierarchical; and this authority is then transmitted outwards from the party to the society as a whole. This monopolistic and hierarchical organization controls and directs the organs of administration, no matter what their formal powers of decision-making may be; it formulates and also interprets an ideology which is binding upon its members and makes this the official creed of the state; it transmits and enjoins this upon the rest of the population, partly through its control over the formation and functioning of all associations, partly through its monopoly of the mass media, partly through coercion or even terror.

Spain and Portugal are sometimes described as totalitarian, but this is a misnomer. There might have been a time, between 1939 and 1942, when Spain was moving in a totalitarian direction but this is no longer true. Nowadays both these countries are varieties of the military régime to be described in Chapter 11. In practice, ever since the defeat of Nazi Germany in 1945, there have been no totalitarian states of Fascist, Nazi or other right-wing-radical tendency. The totalitarian type is nowadays exemplified only in communist states.

Of the numerous states of this political tendency, the oldest established is the U.S.S.R. and it is still the one that comes closest to the 'type' formulated above; that is to say, the one that most nearly approximates to the characteristics described. There follow the east European 'socialist' states: Poland, East Germany, Czechoslovakia, Hungary, Romania, Bulgaria and Albania, and then the People's Republic of China and three other Asian examples, namely, Mongolia, North Vietnam and North Korea. Yugoslavia has moved away from many of the totalitarian characteristics mentioned above and Cuba also is a remote variant on the totalitarian type. Indeed Yugoslavia today resembles increasingly the quasi-democratic type of state, rather than the totalitarian. But taking all these states as closer or more distant variants of the totalitarian pattern, their combined population adds up to about one thousand million. This is roughly the same number as those living in the liberal-democratic states and, like them, comprises about one-third of the world's population.

I. PRESUPPOSITIONS OF TOTALITARIANISM

(1) *Presupposition of the communist variant*

Unlike the Fascist and Nazi varieties, the communist variant of the totalitarian form derives from two currents of political thought, one stemming from Lenin and the other (though no communist would ever admit to this) from an older source which had been absorbed into the views of Marx and Engels imperceptibly.

(a) Marxism-Leninism

From this source there derive three assumptions: firstly that society is *monistic* and therefore that minority or sectional rights must be eliminated. It is denied that the government ought to recognize and accept the existence of various sections of society and undertake to conciliate the claims of one as against another; on the contrary, only one section of society – the proletariat and its allies – is worthy, and government has the duty of suppressing all other sections and governing in the interests of this worthy section alone. Secondly, a government so acting is supposed to be doing so in the name of some transcendent end – of something which has been described as a 'consummatory value': one to which all individuals and groups in society, and present generations as against future generations, must be subordinated. In the communist case, this consummatory value is the realization of an ideal social system, called communism, on an international scale. And, in pursuing this ideal, Marxist philosophy suggests that the government of the state is simply 'giving History a push', since the laws of society, as discovered by Marx and Lenin, indicate that the transition to communism is an ineluctable trend in society. Thirdly, these 'laws' of society are held to be scientifically demonstrable; and so, instead of judgements on society and morals being regarded as matters of individual choice or conscience, they are held to be matters of scientific certainty. It follows, therefore, that there neither are nor ought to be minority or sectional rights. For, clearly, if there is an objective science of society and morals, then those who disagree with its findings – once taught them – are not merely in error, but in sin. If a child continues to assert that two and two equal five,[1] then beyond a certain point of correction it must be assumed that he is not stupid, but deliberately refractory.

Thus the rulers claim that there is an objective science of society and morals, which points out a transcendent end to which society must move or be made to move. In the communist variant of totalitarianism, this science is Marxism-Leninism. It is then further maintained that there are expert exponents of this scientific system, a sort of high priesthood. In practice, this turns out to be the communist party. Consequently, those outsiders who disagree with the party on such matters are either ignorant or heretical; and those insiders who disagree with the party's triumphant faction are heretical pure and simple.

This is precisely why, whenever a split occurs in the ruling party of, let us say, the U.S.S.R., those who are defeated are described much as the early Christian Church used to describe heretics like Marcion. They are not described as being simply mistaken but are stigmatized as wicked. When Molotov quarrelled with Krushchev and was defeated, he and his supporters were described as 'factional', as 'anti-party bankrupt splitters', as 'intriguing careerists'. They had not merely stumbled in error: that 'such a position was not accidental', was the charge constantly levelled against them.

It clearly follows that there can be no toleration of dissent from the party line. If dissenting minorities do exist, they must be captured in some way or another, and, if that is impossible, they must be extinguished. (The euphemism coined in the U.S.S.R. is 'liquidated'.) Every sectional group must be subordinated to a general conception which, in its turn, derives from the objective science of society, Marxism-Leninism. Furthermore, even if a majority overtly and freely expresses a view contrary to what the 'objective science' says – it must *still* be subordinated to this 'objective science' and, in the Soviet Union and states modelled upon it, this science is infallibly expounded by the communist party at any and all points of time. Thus,

1. On a denary base, of course.

paradoxically, the majority must give way to the minority if the latter is the communist party expounding the 'objective science'.

The formulae by which this peculiar view is justified are 'democracy equals majority rule', and 'majority rule equals rule in the interests of the majority'. It is held that democracy means the subordination of the minority; but it is further held that the responsibility of the government is not to give way to the overtly expressed wishes of the majority, but only to its *real* interests, and what its real interests are in these cases is not defined by what the majority actually says or thinks it wants, but by what science (Marxism-Leninism) indicates are objective and scientifically ascertainable wants – not subjective ones. This is quite clearly and openly expressed by Vyshinsky. In his *Law of the Soviet State*, a large and still standard text book in the Soviet Union, he wrote: '[The Soviet government] is democratic in social essence because it is directed to the *defence of the interests of the majority* of the toilers against the exploiter minority';[2] and continues that, in the liberal-democracies, whenever the opinion of the majority runs counter to those 'interests', then 'the so-called "general will", which was so advanced as the basic motive power of the democratic state, remains, and cannot but remain, *a fiction, a false ideological pendant* to the bourgeois state-apparatus of class oppression'.[3] The party, therefore, basing itself upon the scientific principles of Marxism-Leninism, always expresses what the majority 'want' even when popular opinion as actually and freely expressed is flatly opposed to what the party proposes to do.

(b) Rousseau

The second component to be found in the assumptions of the communist variant of the totalitarian state derives from Rousseau; not directly, to be sure (Marxists affect to despise the '*bourgeois*' Rousseau), but via the theory and practice of the Constituent Assembly and particularly of the Jacobins at the time of the French Revolution, which Marxists venerate. This is

2. A. Y. Vyshinsky, *The Law of the Soviet State*, Macmillan, New York, 1948, p. 162.
3. ibid., p. 169.

the view that 'the people' (defined in the communist state as 'the proletariat and its allies') 'is the source of all legitimate authority'. Sovereignty, the ultimate authority and power to decide in a state, resides only in the 'people': but this sovereignty is indivisible and so cannot be split between different agencies which have to collaborate as in the United States of America. It is also 'inalienable'. 'The people' in whom this power is collectively vested can no more get rid of it or transfer it to other hands than the individual can give away the pigment of his skin or the colour of his eyes to any other person. Hence, the people must be directly consulted: no individuals can 'represent' it. The only form of democracy properly so called is direct democracy, by which every individual speaks and votes directly for himself without the intermediation of any elected representative. Alternatively, Rousseau goes on to argue, if this is impracticable because of geographical or other conditions and if people *have* to be chosen to come together and carry out 'the will of the people', these people must be mandated and pledged to follow their electors' instructions. They must be what we call today *delegates*, and they ought to be subject to recall by their constituents if these so desire it. In this way, the barriers of communication and geography are overcome. We could thus have a system of direct democracy in which the government simply replicates the public will at any point of time. There would thus be a *direct transmission* of what is assumed to be 'the will of the people', (more accurately, the opinions of the public) to the government. And the government itself would have no responsibility at all other than being simply *un commis* – one might say, an agent, or even an errand boy – of the opinions of the public. No check or balance would be – nor ought to be – interposed between the viewpoints of the public and what the government did. It is precisely because Rousseau argued that there should be no check and balance between what the people wanted and what the government actually did on their behalf, that Vyshinsky argued so strongly[4] against the separation of powers – the principle discussed in the previous chapter, which in strong or weak form is a characteristic of liberal-democracy.

4. In *The Law of the Soviet State*, op. cit.

His argument is very interesting indeed in this respect. Historically, the liberal-democratic notion that the executive, the legislature and the judiciary should all be in separate hands, which could check or balance one another, was derived from a desire to check the autocratic tendencies of the French monarchs who, at one time, did indeed combine under their hand all three powers in their own persons. This was certainly the intention of the propounder of the theory, Montesquieu, in his *Esprit des lois* in 1748. But Vyshinsky, arguing from a tacitly Rousseauist standpoint, stands the whole of this argument on its head. 'Not "separation of powers" but predominance of executive power characterizes the organization of the state government of capitalist countries.'[5] The reason for this apparently astonishing statement is to be found two pages earlier where, talking of Montesquieu and his theory, Vyshinsky comments: 'According to him the essence of the matter is not whose hands held the authority, whether those of the monarch or those of the people, but that the three powers constituting the supreme power be concentrated in different hands.'[6] According to Vyshinsky, and, indeed, the whole Marxist-Leninist argument, what alone is important is who holds the power, not whether there should be any checks of balances. And it is maintained that 'the people' (or, in practice, the custodians of the popular interest) ought to hold the power, and that, the more unfettered that power, the easier it is for them to act in the (purported) interests of the public.

The assumptions of the communist-type totalitarian model, an amalgamation of viewpoints derived from Lenin on the one side and Rousseau on the other, result in the following features:

(1) There is a direct transmission between government and the governed, without any interposition: no checks or balances, no artificial frictions of any kind. But, in practice,

(2) The line of command does not run from periphery to centre, but exactly the other way. The line of command runs first of all from the centre (the communist party) to the periphery (the various associations in this totalitarian society). The co-operatives, the trade unions, the state enterprises, schools and universities and the like are all the creations, or the emanations, or the

5. ibid., p. 314.   6. ibid., p. 312.

extensions of this power centre, the communist party. Without a will of their own, without any autonomy, they resemble zombies – the walking dead.

(2) *The Fascist and National-Socialist variants*

A similar type of state was achieved in Fascist Italy (1922–43) and National-Socialist Germany (1933–45) but by quite different intellectual routes.

Like the communists, both the Fascists and the Nazis were monistic – but in a totally different way. They regarded society as an organic whole, an entity that had evolved and whose various parts were functionally specialized and interconnected like those of a living organism. For Mussolini, this whole was the nation-state – 'not a race, nor a geographically distinguished region, but . . . a community historically perpetuating itself, a multitude unified by one idea which is the will to existence and power, self-consciousness, personality. . . .'[7] 'The Italian nation is an organism endowed with purposes, a life and means of action transcending in power and duration those of individuals, singly or grouped, which compose it. It is a moral, political and economic unity which realizes itself in the Fascist State. . . .'[8] For Hitler, it was the German *Volk*, a community of human beings who are physically as well as spiritually kindred, a 'national being based on a unity of blood'.[9]

Inside such communities, whether nation-state or *Volk*, there is no place for individuals or groupings except in so far as they serve the purposes of that community as a whole. 'Anti-individualistic,' wrote Mussolini, 'the Fascist conception is for the State, and it is for the individual in so far as he coincides with the State, the universal conscience and will of man in his historical existence.'[10] For Hitler, 'the individual is transitory, the *Volk* is

7. Quoted, H. Finer, *Mussolini's Italy*, Grosset & Dunlap, New York, 1965, p. 215.

8. ibid., p. 219.

9. A. Hitler, *Mein Kampf*, Hurst & Blackett, London, 1939, pp. 330, 333.

10. Quoted in Finer, op. cit., p. 198.

permanent. The position of this single ego is exclusively determined by the interests of the *Volk* as a whole.'[11]

Both, too, envisage a 'consummatory value', a transcendental goal or end to which the whole society must move, indifferent to the fate of individuals or generations. This is not the communist goal of the international victory of the world proletariat and the establishment of the millennial communist system over all the earth; it is the particularistic, indeed, tribal vindication of the power and grandeur of nation or *Volk* in which the individual realizes himself. According to Mussolini, 'Our mythos is the Nation'; 'the past century was the century of our independence, the present century must be the century of our power.'[12] 'For us,' said Hitler, 'the permanent element is that substance of flesh and blood we call the German People. Party, state, army, economic organization – these are but institutions and functions which have only the value of a means to an end.'[13] 'The State [is] only the living organism of a *Volk*, an organism which does not merely maintain the existence of a *Volk*, but functions in such a way as to lead its people to a position of supreme liberty by the progressive development of the intellectual and cultural faculties.'[14] 'Its task is not only to gather in and foster the most valuable sections of our people but to lead them slowly and surely to a dominating position in the world.'[15]

In the communist state, the end or goal of the community and the means by which this is to be realized derive from a written corpus, the works of Marxism-Leninism, and are expounded by the skilled interpreters of this – the communist party. In theory this reaches collegiate decisions, after full discussion by the rank and file. In practice, as has been noted and as will be demonstrated later, the decisions are made by the top group of leaders or even – in Stalin's day – by one man. In the Fascist and National Socialist variants, however, this personal autocracy is openly advocated. As in the communist systems, an official and authori-

---

11. N. Baynes, *Hitler's Speeches*, Oxford, 1942, Volume I, p. 872.
12. Quoted in Finer, op. cit., p. 182.
13. Quoted in Baynes, op. cit., Volume I, p. 428.
14. Hitler, op. cit., p. 381.
15. ibid., p. 334.

tative exposition of the supreme values and judgements is required: but as these relate to the mystic non-rational quality of 'nation' or '*Volk*' so they are intuited, not intellectually excogitated. There is an official *creed*, in its original sense of something that is believed, rather than an official *science*. Pareto, who rightly held that all political formulae were ideologies, distinguished between pseudo-scientific ones (into which class Marxism-Leninism falls) and anti-scientific ones: the Fascist and National-Socialist ideologies are of this latter kind. Furthermore, in the Fascist and National-Socialist systems, there was never any pretence that the end and the means thereto were discovered and interpreted by the official party as a collective body; nor was there ever a pretence that the rank and file of that party had any right to determine its policy. Instead of the party as a caste of priests, Fascism and National Socialism substituted *the* high priest (the leader) and a party which served him merely in the capacity of acolyte. In the Fascist Party, the leader was called *Duce* – the Italian word for 'leader'; in the Nazi Party, he was called *Führer* – the German word for 'leader'. Both these movements openly espoused authoritarianism under the concept of the *Führerprinzip*, the 'leadership principle'. There was not even the nominal bow to democracy which the Communist Party of the U.S.S.R. felt obliged to make.

In Mussolini's words:

Three conditions are necessary for the full, complete, integral and revolutionary fulfilment of the Corporate State: a single party by means of which there shall be effectuated political control as well as an economic control and which shall be above the competing interests a bond which unites all in a common faith. Nor is that enough. We must have, as well as the single party, the totalitarian state, i.e., the state which absorbs in itself, to transform and make them effective, all the energy, all the interests and all the hope of a people. The third . . . is to live a period of the highest ideal tension. . . .[16]

Now, each member of this single party took as his oath 'I swear to execute the orders of the *Duce*', while the *Duce* himself proclaimed: 'My words . . . come after the facts, which do not

16. Quoted in Finer, op. cit., p. 231.

draw their origin from assemblies, nor from previous councils or inspiration of individuals, groups or circles; they are decisions which I alone mature.'[17] Among the Commandments of the so-called Fascist Decalogue, one ran: 'Mussolini is always right', while the slogan proclaimed for the people as a whole ran: 'Believe; obey; fight!'

In Nazi Germany, the supreme value was the spirit of the people, the *Volksgeist*. This mystic entity could only be intuited, and only some more-than-normal person could at once evoke it, feel with it and for it, and embody it. In so far as he did this, he was the *Führer*. As to the National-Socialist Party of which he was the leader, its members served the *Volksgeist* only through obedience to him. When a fellow Nazi, Otto Strasser, suggested to Hitler that leader and subordinates were alike servants of 'the Idea', Hitler impatiently broke in with:

This is all bombastic nonsense. . . . It boils down to this, that you would give to every member of the Party the right to decide on the Idea – even to decide whether the Leader is true to the so-called Idea or not. That is democracy at its worst and every member of the Party has to do what the Leader orders. The Leader incorporates the Idea and alone knows its ultimate goal. . . .[18]

The communist and the Fascist-Nazi systems of totalitarianism resemble each other, then, in that, in their different ways:

(1) Both are monistic.

(2) Both recognize a transcendent value or goal.

(3) Both endow a leader or group of leaders with unique responsibility for discerning this and for constraining all members of the society to accept this goal and the means laid down for pursuing it.

But the *justifications* advanced for these positions differ radically. The communist justification was derived, as has been shown, from an amalgam of Rousseauism and Marxism. The Italian Fascist position was supported by a well-established European philosophical tradition, namely, 'idealism', which goes back as far as Plato but which, in its more immediate form,

17. ibid., p. 287.
18. Quoted in Baynes, op. cit., Volume I, p. 460.

drew its inspiration from Hegel and – to some extent – from a strand in the self-contradictory works of J.-J. Rousseau. But it is difficult to find any intellectual antecedent of Nazism, which was distinguished above all by its ruthless nihilism, its rejection of reason, its open advocacy of mystic belief.

In examining the Marxist-Leninist ancestry of communist totalitarianism, it has been shown that, while the original position was 'democracy equals the rule of the majority', at the close this was re-interpreted as 'democracy equals rule in the *interests* of the majority'. A distinction was drawn between what people overtly want or say they want, and what some other people – in this case the communist party – think that they *ought* to want according to the canons of the Marxist laws of society. Italian Fascism, in espousing idealism, drew on a theory which *overtly* proclaims this same distinction between what people actually desire and what they ought to desire – the distinction between 'actual will' and the so-called *Real* Will.

Owing to his isolation, his ignorance, his frailty and so forth, what the individual desires is narrow, arbitrary and inconsistent. Contrasted with this stands an ideal – a will which 'would be completely or more completely what ours attempts to be and fails'.[19] By the same token, the individual's freedom is not a mere absence of external restraint but 'being oneself in the fullest sense of the word' – i.e., behaving completely as we attempt, but in practice fail, to do. It is in this sense that Hegel had said: 'The Real Will is the Will that wills Itself', which is not the piece of gobbledygook which at first it appears to be. It means, roughly, that the individual who lays down a code for himself, such as teetotalism, and sticks to it is freer than that man who either lays down no such code or fails to adhere to one and is, in consequence, a 'slave to alcohol'. Individuals as such *cannot* will their Real Will. They are too isolated and too ignorant to know where their true interests lie. They are too frail to stick to a personal code. But in so far as individuals find themselves in a wider society, this, which harmonizes and rationalizes the desires and motivations of a large number of individuals, presents the

19. G. Bosanquet, *The Philosophical Theory of the State*, Macmillan, 1899, p. 108.

solitary individual with wider horizons and with wiser counsels, and also imposes external restraints, and so forth in ever widening circles until the limits of such an organized society are reached. At the present moment, these limits are those of that state in which the individual finds himself. Embodying all individual wills, past as well as present, and looking to the future, this territorial association embodies a wider, a more tested, and a more coherent set of standards than any individual could reach by himself. Thus, the state becomes 'the flywheel of our life. Its system is constantly reminding us of duties which we have not the least desire to neglect but which we are either too ignorant or too indolent to carry out apart from instruction and authoritative correction.'[20] The state, therefore, is the individual mind writ very large, and straightened out in the process. What the state commands through the laws which its government lays down is our Real Will. If a policeman locks us up for stealing, or for a traffic offence, this is what we ourselves *really* want – had we been less selfish, foolish or frail, we should never have stolen, or parked our car in heavy traffic, in the first place. The state, in locking us up, is, therefore, making us *free*! For freedom is – after all – 'being ourselves in the fullest sense.'

Enunciated in a massive form by Hegel, 'received' in Britain in the later nineteenth century by lesser philosophers like Bradley and Bosanquet, this line of thought can also be discerned in Rousseau. For in his *Social Contract* there are two lines of thought which he himself and all his subsequent commentators tried in vain to reconcile. One is the simple majority principle and it is this on which the Marxists seized. But there is a 'yardstick' or 'standard' principle, which is not necessarily a majority principle at all and may, indeed, be an anti-majority principle. For, in Rousseau's thought, the sole basis of all legitimate authority reposes in what he calls the General Will. Now, this is not the summation of the individual wills of all the persons composing the state. On the contrary this is merely a 'sum of selfish desires' and he calls it 'the will of all'. The General Will is that which arises when all are consulted, which is general in its application and which, above all, responds to the question

20. op. cit., p. 152.

'What is the general, and not my own particular, interest in this matter?' Now, in some places Rousseau wrote as though a simple majority would automatically represent this General Will. Elsewhere, however, he seems to think that only an extraordinary and highly-perceptive Individual, somebody whom he calls the Legislator, would be able to elicit such a response from the population he consults. This implies that the General Will is distinguishable from what the population overtly desire and, furthermore, that it may be perceived by a single Individual, even though the majority continue to be intent on their own particular and selfish interests. Thus, the General Will, in this latter sense, comes near the Real Will of the later writers, such as Hegel, Bradley and Bosanquet. And the conclusion Rousseau drew is identical with that which they also drew, to such a degree indeed that Rousseau is approvingly quoted by Bosanquet as a forerunner. For Rousseau wrote: 'The social pact tacitly includes the covenant . . . that whosoever shall refuse to obey the General Will shall be constrained to do so by the whole body, which means nothing else than that he *will be forced to be free*.'[21] Nor is that all, for he went on: 'We might add to the gains of the civil state the moral freedom which alone makes man master of himself: for the impulsion of appetite alone is slavery and obedience to the law which we have prescribed to ourselves is liberty.'

It is easy to discern in these and similar writings such typical Fascist doctrine as:

Anti-individualistic, the Fascist conception is for the State, and it is for the individual in so far as he coincides with the State, the universal conscience and will of man in his historical existence . . . Fascism re-affirms the State as the true reality of the individual.[22]

and:

All is in the State and nothing human or spiritual exists, much less has any value, outside the State. In this sense Fascism is totalitarian and the Fascist state, the synthesis and unity of all values, interprets, develops and gives power to every aspect of the life of the people. . . .[23]

21. J.-J. Rousseau, *The Social Contract*, Book I, Chapter 7.
22. Quoted Finer, op. cit., p. 198.   23. ibid., p. 201.

No such eminent intellectual pedigree could be claimed for Nazism, for which Hegel was too intellectualist, too much a devotee of reason. Hegel glorified and extolled the state as the 'march of God on earth', but Hitler glorified, not the state, but the *Volksgeist* of which the National-Socialist Party was an emanation and he himself the single and unique interpreter. This *Volksgeist* is no mere momentary opinion, for this may be falsified and misled, and so 'public opinion' is no guide to it. It is a subconscious sentiment until there arises a *Führer* who evokes it and by that token is known *as* the *Führer*. This title is not conferred upon him. He is not mandated. He incarnates the *Volksgeist* and the *Volk* recognizes itself and its destiny in him. Nor did the Nazi Party owe anything to the state. Through its obedience to the leader it, too, incarnates the *Volksgeist*.

> The National-Socialist State is the pure political State . . . controlled by the Party, the incarnation of what is political: the embodiment of a *volkisch* community-will-for-self-preservation regardless of all other controversial issues within that community. . . . The Führer State according to the words of A. Hitler (Party Convention at Nuremberg, 1934) – 'It is not the State that commands us – it is we that command the State. It is not the State that has created us; it is we who make the State for ourselves. . . .'[24]

This notion of Leadership or *Führertum* gave rise to a host of competing explanations. Marr wrote of the relationship between *Führer* and *Gefolgschaft* (his following) as 'unconditional affinity . . . mystical holiness of the blood . . . a permanent connexion . . . certainly proof against intellectual doubt. . .'[25] Schott lyricized: 'In this man's mortal frame the original Germanic stature is incarnate. . .'[26] 'The representation and the popular will', wrote another, 'is discharged by the Führer who feels with the Volk and thus is enabled as its representative to make its will effective. . .'[27] 'The Führer is legitimate,' wrote a fourth, 'because he has sought the Volk and called upon it and

24. W. Roessle, quoted, Aurel Kolnai, *The War Against the West*, Gollancz, 1938, p. 159.
25. Quoted, Kolnai, op. cit., p. 149.
26. ibid., p. 151.
27. ibid., p. 153.

the Volk has followed him. . . . The Volk is personified by the Führer.'[28]

The appeal, in short, is to *un*-reason. 'National Socialism,' wrote Schnabel, 'does not demand from its adherents that they should be convinced of the rightness of its doctrines but that they should believe in it. A refutation of the mythos of National Socialism there cannot be for National Socialism is a faith.'[29] The adherents, the 'following', were adjured to 'think with their blood'.

Yet, despite these very different justifications, the Fascist-Nazi type of totalitarianism results in institutional features similar to those of the communist variant:

(1) There is a direct link, with neither interposition, check or intermediary, between the *Duce* or the *Führer* and the spirit of nationality or *Volk* which he incarnates.

(2) The leader, assisted by his party, is supreme, and the line of command runs from top to bottom, down to the lowest ranks. At the same time, the organic and monistic principle, whether this is expressed as the supreme moral authority of the state or by the *Volksgeist*, demands the absorption into the party of all private associations – schools, universities, trade unions and so forth – inside the state territory.

(3) Just as the party does not tolerate dissent from associations outside it, so the leader demands total obedience from those inside it. In short, *mutatis mutandis* with the communist variant, absolute power is assumed by the party, and there is an unlimited politicization by it of all outside elements and associations.

II. CHARACTERISTIC FEATURES OF THE TOTALITARIAN STATE

(1) *The government and its powers*

In the totalitarian state, the government propagates the official myth, the official ideology. It seeks to persuade and has powerful means of doing so. In all totalitarian states, the ruling party and

28. ibid., p. 158.   29. Baynes, op. cit., Volume I, p. 415 (footnote).

the rulers supported by it control and operate all the mass media. In addition, the party itself wields an army of what, in the U.S.S.R., are called 'agitators' – political propagandists who spread the word throughout the fields, the factories, the workshops, the schools and, indeed, all organized sectors of society.

But where persuasion falls short, coercion, even terror, is called upon. As compared with the liberal-democratic states, the totalitarian ones rely very heavily upon secret and security police forces. Furthermore, in political matters, the judges are not independent but are regarded as another state instrument by which the ruling doctrine of the party and its leaders or leader may be realized. And, because of this, the criminal codes of all such states carry the notion of the 'counter-revolutionary crime'. Such political crimes may be hunted down with all the apparatus of terror, as in Stalin's Russia or Hitler's Germany, or else may be pursued under orderly processes of law, as in the trial of Daniel and Sinyavsky in the U.S.S.R. in 1966. The significant point is that, whatever the means employed, what is punished is 'counter-revolutionary crime'.

While the government uses persuasion and deterrence to inculcate the official myth, it simultaneously uses its powers to nullify and to suppress minority opinion. For one thing, the right to associate is severely limited. By laws of the U.S.S.R., for instance, no persons may form an association without first disclosing its constitution to the public authorities and receiving their permission to go ahead; and that permission can always be revoked if the security police (who are entitled to sit in upon the meetings of such associations) decide that the association is conducting operations which are contrary to the constitution as deposited with them. Again, the right to express opinions is subject to state-censorship. It is subject also to material restriction, in that access to newsprint, to films, to jobs on newspapers, magazines, television and the like, is controlled by the dominant party and the government agencies which it has established. Both Nazi Germany and Fascist Italy exercised a similar total control of stated opinion.

Thus, the government both limits and channels the opinions expressible in society. And, finally, elections, however free they may appear to be according to the constitution, are in practice falsified or nullified, as we shall see later.

(2) *The government is the party*

In the totalitarian state, the unique or hegemonic party controls the administrative apparatus at all levels from top to bottom. It permits the members of this apparatus no latitude or discretion. The government is to the party what the glove is to the hand. The central institution of such totalitarian states is the party. It is the party which wields all of these powers: the powers of persuasion, of deterrence, of the licensing and control of expressed opinion, of the control of elections. But the party itself – which is quite numerous – is itself controlled. It would be practicable to have a party-controlled society, where, inside the party, members were quite free to form and state their opinions and to carry the party their way. This would be a limited form of democracy, but it would, at least, be a nearer approach to democracy than what, in practice, occurs. For the principal features of parties in the totalitarian states where 'party' is king are: that there is only one party permitted (with a qualification to be noted below); that this party is disciplined as an army is disciplined – no factionalism or splitting is permitted and, once a line is laid down, it has to be obeyed by all members on pain of expulsion; and that it permeates the whole of society.

That the Communist Party of the Soviet Union is the sole party is implied by the Soviet Constitution at Article 126, supplemented by administrative action. In Germany, the National-Socialist Cabinet, in its decree of 14 July 1933, declared the National-Socialist Party to be the sole political party and laid down harsh penalities for whomsoever undertook to maintain previously existing parties or establish new ones. In Italy, the Law on Association of 1925 and the Defence of the State Act of 1926 achieved an identical effect; in 1928, the Fascist Party, now the sole legal one, was entrusted with the legal right of making the final list of parliamentary candidates to be submitted, as one list, to the electorate, while a further act of that year declared the party to be the supreme organ for co-ordinating and integrating the entire activity of the régime. As such, it was vested with the right to give advice on all constitutional questions and the further right of nomination to all government posts. In some of the communist totalitarian states of the present day – in the German Democratic Republic, for instance – other parties are indeed permitted to exist; but they do so on sufferance and by licence of the communist party and as its subordinate allies. They are mere ancillaries to the communist party which maintains its leading role.

Inside such ruling parties there is no 'inner party democracy'. In Germany and Italy, this was ruled out overtly from the start, by the leadership principle. The parties in these two countries were 'followings', subordinate to the leader. In communist countries, the communist party is, in theory, a democratic organization, whose decisions are made by a conference elected by and representative of the membership at large, but, in practice, the higher echelons direct the lower ones. This is the principle described as 'democratic centralism' and, in the U.S.S.R. for example, by its means the Politbureau of the party effectively controls the Party Congress which is the body which is supposed to debate and decide the party line. That Congress, in fact, merely endorses what the leaders put before it and, once they have dispersed, vests in those leaders the formal right to run the party until the next Congress – in four years' time. So, for practical purposes, party policy is that of the Politbureau and by the centralist principle all lower echelons must comply with it on pain of expulsion. Thus, when the Congress is reassembled, the Politbureau, having been in the position of autocratic authority for the last four years, finds no difficulty in 'arranging' the election of delegates to the conference. When this assembles, therefore, it does little but endorse all the decisions taken in the past and enthusiastically applaud all the proposals the Presidium puts forward for the future.

In practice, then, in all these states, it is the *Führer* or the *duce*, or the top committee of the ruling party which effectively controls and lays down the line for the whole membership. The party, then, is the sole party, or else the hegemonic party, with others existing only under its licence and by its sufferance: it is monolithic and its members obey the orders of its leading group of officials. These members permeate the rest of society. The party membership fills all the important posts in all walks of life. The party organization keeps a check upon them; from the information fed into it by its party members, organized as primary units in every government and social organization, it is able to manipulate them as it wills. In this way, the party cements and binds all the organs of all the associations in the society together.

A RESTATEMENT AND A SUMMARY

Thus, decision-taking in the totalitarian state is concentrated, not dispersed. All sections and associations in society are emanations of and colonies of the party. Nothing throughout society escapes the party except through accident or administrative incapacity. The great Russian Revolution ground to powder and dispersed to the winds all the great associations of Tsarist society except the Church. The army, the bureaucracy, the industrial corporations, the central and local organs of the state – all were smashed to pieces and replaced with new, Bolshevik ones. As to the Church, its revenues were cut off, it was subjected to a harsh and rigid control, and its doctrines were held up to public ridicule and contempt. Thus, totalitarianism reached very far and very deep into the minds and hearts of men. In Italy and Germany, however, the totalitarian-minded ruling parties took over an existing social structure complete with its institutions. In Germany, the army was not Nazi, and, although the party made strenuous efforts to infiltrate and indoctrinate it, it never entirely succeeded. The Churches too, continued their independent existence, although they were careful not to fall too foul of prevalent doctrine. In Italy, the army was never Fascist, nor did the Fascists exert much control over it. It owed its allegiance to the monarchy – an additional and distracting pole of loyalty that did not exist in Germany. The Catholic Church was tougher and embarked in a fierce battle with Mussolini over its youth movement and over teaching in the schools – a battle which, in the end, was settled by a concordat. Private enterprise too, was less state-regimented than in Nazi Germany. In these ways, totalitarianism was less complete in the Fascist–Nazi régimes than in the contemporary U.S.S.R.

But, apart from such qualifications as these, the single party in a totalitarian state becomes the leading and directing institution, and, inside that party, policy is not decided by the rank and file but by the leading oligarchs. Inside that leading oligarchy, it is determined by secret collisions – collisions of the kind that have led, for instance, to those continuous changes, promotions, demotions and expulsions of leading members which have continued without cease in the Communist Party of the Soviet Union from Stalin's death in 1953 to the present day.

Thus, the two prime conditions for totalitarianism are: the total or all but total politicization of society, and the reduction of that politicization to one single standpoint. 'All conscious and arbitrary movement or organization is *totally* controlled by the State; the State is *totally* expressed in the actual governing authorities and coincides *totally* with the ruling body.'[30]

30. Kolnai, op. cit., pp. 160–61.

Chapter 4

THE THIRD-WORLD STATES

I. 'THE THIRD WORLD'

'THE THIRD WORLD' is an expression that is much used nowadays, without any precise generally accepted definition. There are however two 'strong' senses in which it is understood. In the first of these it means those states that are neither unambiguously communist-totalitarian, nor unambiguously liberal-democratic. In the other sense it refers to the succession states resulting from the dismemberment of the European and Ottoman empires, excluding the territories of European settlement (like the United States and Canada) but also including a number of independent states, like Iran, that were subjected to colonialist infiltration and pressure. It so happens – and this is by no means accidental – that the two conceptions, albeit not identical, do very largely overlap. For instance: taking the latter, geographical definition, then only China, North Korea, Mongolia, North Vietnam, and the former Balkan states (excluding Greece) are unambiguously communist-totalitarian, and taking the former, only the following liberal-democracies have functioned stably since 1948: Costa Rica, Chile, India, Israel, the Philippines and Uruguay; a number of others, like Ceylon or Lebanon, are shaky; and a rather larger tally, which includes countries like Jamaica and Trinidad, are of such recency that they are relatively untested.[1]

In what follows I shall use the political definition: the Third World means the world of states that are not unambiguously liberal-democratic nor unambiguously communist-totalitarian.

Though the 'hard core' of the Third World is ex-colonial, it also includes a handful of states which never formally lost their independence: Liberia and Ethiopia in the African continent, Turkey, Afghanistan, Nepal, Iran and Thailand in Asia. However, although nominally independent, all these states were sub-

1. See Chapter 12 for a list.

jected to persistent colonialist pressure, both diplomatic and economic, and have reacted against this in a fashion similar to that of the ex-dependencies.

This Third World of seventy states seems at first sight a mere residual category, since its component members are disparate in size, in population and in resources, as well as in political, social and cultural characteristics. It will be noticed also that these states became independent in different eras. Iran, Afghanistan, Turkey, Thailand, Ethiopia, Egypt, to name but a few, are all of considerable antiquity. The Latin American republics which seized their independence between 1810 and 1828 are almost coeval with the United States. Greece became independent in 1832. Such states are the elder of two groups in the Third World. The second, and younger, group comprises those that became independent between the two world wars, and – by far the larger part – those that have attained independence since 1945. Egypt and Iraq fall into the former category: into the latter fall the sixty-odd states created since 1945 out of the collapse of the British, French, Belgian and Dutch overseas empires, mostly in Asia and in Africa.

Furthermore, some Third-World states have continuous traditions of statehood, while others have none. Egypt, India–Pakistan, Annam and Tonkin (i.e., the Vietnams), Burma, Cambodia, Laos, to name a few, were states for centuries before their colonial interlude. Other states in the Third World, notably the Latin American republics, became states because of their colonial experience; for instance, the frontiers of the Latin-American states are largely adaptations of the viceroyalties and captaincies established by the Spaniards and the Portuguese. On the other hand, very many Third-World states are quite new. They are areas which were traced out on the maps of Africa or the Middle East by the various European powers, partly for administrative convenience, partly through diplomatic rivalry. Most of the sub-Saharan African states are of this kind, despite an effort on the part of some to assert their continuity with such medieval African kingdoms as Mali or Ghana. Those kingdoms did not endure and left nothing behind them but a vague historical memory.

Yet, despite superficial appearances, the Third World is not a rag-bag, a miscellany, a mere residual category of the states that are neither stable liberal-democracies nor totalitarian. It is significant that it lies *outside* Europe; that most of it lies south of the Fortieth Parallel; that nearly all its component states are agrarian, possibly with some extractive industry, but with little heavy industry; that most of them are much poorer *per capita* than their neighbours to the north; that all were either dependencies or subjected to deep diplomatic and economic penetration by the Western powers.

Moreover, the governments of most of these countries also share – or purport to share – a common set of political presuppositions. They wish, or claim to wish, to '*modernize*', whatever that may mean. But the very term implies that they regard their societies as in some sense *non*-modern. It is precisely from this confrontation, the attempt to 'modernize' what is not 'modern', that their political experiences and institutional experiments flow. More specifically: the ambitions and imperatives of the rulers of these states derive expressly from Europe and North America, and so, initially, did their political institutions. Yet, being 'non-modern', their political and economic and social structures at independence did not (in the case of a few older states) or do not (in the case of the great majority) readily support these novel political institutions and practices. On the contrary, these modernizing ambitions actually further fragment such meagre public support as these institutions initially received.

This is the argument to be expounded. First these political presuppositions, expressed by the term 'modernizing', must be examined; then the social, political and economic structures of the receiving societies; and finally the consequences of the interpenetration of the two for the political institutions of these various states.

II. PRESUPPOSITIONS

The presuppositions of the modernizers, with no exceptions at all, derive from Europe. *None* are indigenous.

Their inspiration was the French Revolution of 1789. For the most part it still is; recently, however, it has been supplemented by the received image of the Russian Revolution. And Europe provided more than the inspiration: together with North America, it also provided the example – the powerful, healthy and wealthy secular state. Thus European and North American principles are at once an object of admiration and of envy: of admiration because there is a sufficiency of persons who value them for themselves; of envy because they appear to the modernizers to be the means of becoming as healthy, wealthy and powerful as the Northern and Western states.

To be more specific, these presuppositions derive from three European events or trains of events – the French Revolution, the industrial revolution and the Russian Revolution.

(1) *The French Revolution*

From this derive two of the constitutive principles of the succession states – constitutive in the sense that it was on the strength of them that these states demanded and finally received their independence. They became the new political formula which revolutionary minorities opposed to that of the colonial ruler; through which they captured the allegiance of the population; and by which they secured territorial independence. The first is the principle of nationality: the claim that each group feeling itself to be a nation has the right to *independent existence* governed by its nationals and its own laws in its own territory. This notion was never propounded in this uncompromising and universalized form until the French Revolution. Since then it has become one of the great revolutionary inspirations of the world, the grave-digger of empires. It stimulated and justified the revolt of Latin America against Spain and Portugal, of the Balkans against the Turk, of Asia and Africa against Britain, France, Belgium and Holland.

The second principle is that of *popular sovereignty*: the dogma that no government is legitimate unless it can demonstrate to its subjects that its powers are derived from them. This dogma, it should be noted, does not predicate any particular form of régime. It will permit of any form – liberal-democracy, autocracy, oligarchy, even totalitarianism – providing only that the office-bearers are able to convince the public that they have received office by popular mandate – however this may be interpreted. Until Napoleon's accession the crowned heads of continental Europe had claimed to rule by divine right. Once Napoleon acceded, this hoary old political formula was on the defensive. For it now appeared that any Tom, Dick or Harry might come forward and seize control of the state, provided he took sufficient pains to make it appear that he had attained his high office as the result of a call from the people.

These two principles have important negative implications also. Whatever 'popular government' may turn out to be in practice – and Hitler's tyranny was a version of 'popular government' – there are certain things it quite certainly is *not*. It is not compatible with theocracy – the principle that for so long held the disparate nationalities of the Ottoman Empire together, and provided likewise a justification and method for governing the non-Moslems. It is not compatible with hereditary despotism such as justified the monarchs of Spain and Portugal in their hold over their Latin American subjects. It is not compatible with traditional allegiance such as justified the rule of a sheikh in the Middle East or of a chief in Africa. All of these forms are 'traditional', and it is precisely because the principle of popular sovereignty is antithetical to every one of them that it is a part – the first – of the syndrome of modernization. Nor is this all. The implication – indeed the intention – of popular sovereignty, is that the people shall be consulted on and determine their political future. In short, it implies that public policies shall be a matter of *conscious purpose*. This sharply contrasts with the unreflecting loyalty to existing authorities which is implied in all the traditional formulae. Conscious social purpose, then, is another part – the second – of the syndrome of modernization.

The principle of nationality, also, has its negative aspects, dissolvent of traditional formulae. For the idea of the *nation-state* – the notion that the boundaries of the state should coincide with the national community and vice versa – is also an extremely recent idea, not older than the French Revolution. Till that time and for long afterwards, even persisting today, the territorial unity of a community was held to inhere in common loyalty to a certain dynasty (as in, say, Austria-Hungary or Tsarist Russia), or in common ties of kinship or lineage (as in an African tribe), or in community of religious observance (as in the Arab empires), but not in the concept of a common nationality. 'Nationality' in this sense was meaningless until the French Revolution. This concept also, therefore, was and is antithetical to those formulae and their institutional embodiments which are nowadays classed as traditional, and is thus another – the third – of the component parts of the syndrome of modernity. It must also be noted that, in so far as it rejects theocratic authority, it is a *secular* notion, and as will be seen, secularization is yet another of the components of the modernization syndrome.

Finally, it must be emphasized that the two principles of nationality and popular sovereignty are difficult to keep apart, and indeed they are to be found in fusion as early as 1789 in Sieyès's *What is the Third Estate?* And this fusion is quite simply achieved: for the Nation is identified as the People, and the People are identified as the Nation – the entire community within the national territory. Each principle reinforces the other. A perfect example is to be found in the current conflict in Rhodesia. There the African nationalists, governed as they are by a white minority, demand 'one man one vote'. In one and the same slogan they assert the principle of popular sovereignty and justify an African nation state with Africans ruling a small white *minority*.

(2) *The industrial revolution*

It was neither Europe's manpower nor her wealth that created her vast overseas empires, but arrogance, courage, fire-arms and fleets. The disparity in national wealth between Europe and, say, Latin America or India was by no means so marked in the eighteenth century. In the nineteenth century, however, Britain, America and France became noticeably wealthier and technologically superior. The principles on which these states were erected – nationality, popular sovereignty and secularization – and the embodiment of these in the liberal-democratic system, suggested to the peoples of Latin America and, later, the Balkan peninsula, that these were the preconditions for national wealth and power, and not simply desirable in themselves. By the last quarter of the nineteenth century this conclusion appeared inescapable in the light of the upsurge of Germany and Japan alongside the former industrial powers. For these too were erected on the modernizing principles and had adapted liberal-democratic institutions. So, as the French Revolutionary principles began to penetrate India from the 1880s, even revolutionizing Iran in 1905 and Turkey and China in 1908, those principles, along with the parliamentary system, were regarded as a *means* to affluence and power. The desire to industrialize and grow rich went alongside the strictly 'political' aspects of modernization and, as the nineteenth century ended, often began to supersede them. But it became increasingly observable in the already independent states, like the Latin American republics, or Iran, or Egypt (under the khedive Ismail), that their efforts to industrialize had given them communications, mines and public utilities, but not a heavy industry; that even those enterprises they had were largely owned by Americans and Europeans; that far from becoming wealthier they were head over heels in debt to foreign creditors; and that far from becoming more powerful they had become economic – and often political – satellites. Thus the principle of economic modernization had apparently ended in a contradiction of two of the main principles of political modernization – those of national independence and popular sovereignty. From henceforth, *economic independence* figured as yet another of the components of the syndrome of modernization.

(3) *The Russian Revolution*

The Russian Revolution and the 'reception' of Marxism in the Third World had two, contradictory, effects. It reinforced the principles of the French Revolution and it cancelled the admiration for liberal-democratic institutions.

Marxism is not inimical to the Western rationalist tradition: on the contrary. And to the Third World, the Soviet Union presented its 'Western face'. It was received, not so much for what it was as for the principles it announced. To begin with: the Marxist concept of the nineteenth-century state as a coercive organ wielded by a minority of wealthy exploiters, irrespective of liberal-democratic institutions, happens to be far truer to most post-colonial reality than any other put forward. It has become fashionable to 'disprove' the Marxist concept by reference to the operative liberal-democracies of the U.S.A. or France or Sweden. It is just as easy to prove it by reference to the historic oligarchies of Latin America (many of which still persist) up to 1930. For the notion of rule by an oligarchy drawn from the economically most powerful class and governing from behind a façade of parliamentarism, which is Marx's picture of the nineteenth-century state, was *true* of Latin America or Iran or the Balkan states; and the notion of such an oligarchy being in league with the colonial power was not far from the truth in a large number of the colonies. And it was there that the modernizing minorities pondered their situation, not in Britain or America. Secondly the October Revolution had proclaimed the principle of nationality, abolished the 'unequal treaties', conceded the right of national minorities to form their own independent states and, in the 1924 Constitution, recognized their right to secede from the Union. The hollowness of these gestures will be demonstrated later: but they reinforced the *principle* of nationality. The Revolution likewise justified itself in the name of popular sovereignty and has never ceased to do so. Moreover it was not only rationalist and secular but militantly scientistic and anti-religious. Finally, its system of a planned economy and Stalin's slogan of 'socialism in one country' represented the principle of economic independence to its ultimate degree. For here (so Soviet propaganda claimed) was a primitive, illiterate and disease-ridden agrarian economy that had succeeded in pulling itself up by its own boot-straps and transforming itself, in a mere generation, into the second most powerful state in the world. If health, wealth and power were prime desiderata, then here was an obvious short cut.

In all these ways, then, the Russian Revolution reinforced even more heavily the principles behind the various components of the modernization syndrome. But it also cast doubt on the appropriateness of Western liberal-democratic institutions.

(4) *'Modernization'*

Most of those who use the term 'modernization' seem to conceive of it as something objective, fixed and precise, and then proceed to define it. This seems to be the wrong way to go about the matter. 'Modernization' is not an objective datum, fixed or precise: it is an *image* of Europe and America as received by their emulators in the Third World. To be a modern state is to be like any of the states that they regard at that particular moment as clearly outstanding in terms of health, wealth and international power. In the early nineteenth century Britain filled the bill. For the modernizers of Japan, later in the century, it was the German *Kaiserreich*. No nineteenth-century state attempting modernization tried, as far as we are aware, to emulate Russia or Austria-Hungary! In the nineteen thirties modernizers in the Middle East turned from the Western exemplars to Nazi Germany and Fascist Italy for inspiration. Today America and the Western powers still provide one model; but the U.S.S.R., China and the so-called popular democracies provide an alternative. So, what 'modernization' is depends on the age, and on the eye of the beholder. Nowadays it consists of a syndrome of principles deduced from Western or totalitarian models. This syndrome, if reproduced at home, is expected to produce a 'modern' state instead of a 'traditional' one.

We have discussed these principles. They are five. First comes the nationality principle, as the basis of territorial organization, contrasted with the 'traditional' bases of dynasty, kinship and lineage, or religious community. The second is the principle of popular sovereignty as the legitimizing principle, contrasted with the 'traditional' bases in theocracy, divine right, noble birth, or caste. The third is the secular principle, the separation of the political processes from religious sanctions and activities and values. The fourth is social purposiveness – even wilfulness – as against the traditional unreflecting reverence for pre-existing authority, whether this be cultural or religious or political. The fifth is economic independence – the construction of an independent and nationally sovereign basis for health, wealth and power; this implies extensive industrialization, as contrasted with the 'traditional' rural economy.

It is implicit in these principles that the rule of the *imam* or the sheikh, of the chief or the monarch, are alike obsolete and must disappear. But, as a replacement, the time has gone when the liberal democratic system was universally regarded as the *dernier cri*. It is a historical fact, however, that nearly every state attaining its independence in the Third World has started out with liberal-democratic institutions, and that in this way, until the most recent present, modernization *has* meant 'Westernization'. It is from this point that the analysis must start.

III. THE RECEIVING CULTURES

The first signal difference between the receiving cultures and the transmitting ones – till very recently the Western powers – is this: in not a single one of the states of the Third World are the five basic presuppositions of modernization shared by any but a minority. In the Western states, by contrast, the principles of nationality, popular sovereignty, secularization, social purposiveness and industrial independence are taken for granted: indeed they form the very texture of these societies. Historically each one developed parallel with all the others. Not so in the Third World. Whether it was the Latin American struggle for independence a century and a half ago, or the Asiatic or African struggles in the recent past, always these were spearheaded by a very small group who had – mostly through Western-type education – come into contact with the West, absorbed its principles and envied its example. This group, divided on many a domestic issue, were united on at least one thing – the desire to get rid of the foreigner. And they were able to achieve national independence not because the masses accepted their modernizing principles but simply because they too shared in this desire to get rid of colonial rule.

Algeria, Mali and Guinea are very exceptional in starting their independent existences with institutions modelled on those of eastern rather than western Europe. By and large, the nationalist and modernizing *élites* demanded and received institutions of the liberal-democratic type. This experiment with liberal-democratic forms – dismissed in pretty short order in a large number of the states after independence was won – is easily explained. The older group of Third-World states won their independence at a time when the West was the only transmitter of the constitutive principles and when its prestige was at its highest, while the newer group were all ex-colonial, i.e., dependent on the Western metropolitan countries. In these, contact with Moscow was suspect and 'communist' activity repressed. By contrast, Western notions were openly transmitted through the school systems, through education in Western universities, by contact with or employment in the colonial administrative services and by participation in the various advisory or consultative councils which the colonial powers usually established. Furthermore, once the independence movement had gathered such force that the colonial power was ready to quit, the latter preferred to hand over to the 'moderate', i.e., the liberal-democratic, faction rather than to any Soviet-orientated rivals: partly because it genuinely believed in the greater humanity and tolerance of liberal-democracy, partly for clear and obvious reasons of international diplomacy.

Now the societies which these modernizing minorities sought to transform through the principles of modernization were and are, with few exceptions, quite differently structured from the Western societies which had evolved these principles. First, nearly all are agrarian. Where industry exists on a large scale, it tends to be extractive – oil, minerals and the like. Any other industry is usually light industry to supply the home market and much of it has been established as part of a policy of import substitution. In any event most large aggregations of capital investment tend to be foreign. Next, a large majority are rural, not urban. Here one must beware. Some of these states – Chile, Uruguay, Mexico and Argentina in Latin America, Egypt in Africa, Thailand in South East Asia – contain vast cities. But these are 'pre-industrial'. Their swollen populations are made up of ever-increasing numbers of migrants from the poverty-stricken countryside, who drift in to live in shanty towns and pick up work in the service trades of the metropolis. Such societies are sharply divided between a parasitic urban sector and a peasant one. Thirdly, nearly all of these societies are, by Northern-world standards, miserably poor; and the extent of their poverty is concealed by the statistics which give *average* national *per capita* income, disregarding the extreme inequality of income which is general to most of these lands. (For instance, Chile is regarded as fairly prosperous by world standards: her average *per capita* income in 1960 was $320. But a mere one-eighth of the population there enjoyed *two-thirds* of the total national income! In Peru, with an average *per capita* income of only $140 in 1960, one-fifth of the total national income was enjoyed by a mere *thousandth* part of the population, while four-fifths of the population had to subsist on one-quarter of the total national income!)[2]

Fourthly, nearly all these societies lack adequate means of communication, in the intellectual as well as in the physical sense. In terms of distances, roads and railways are inadequate: hence regionalism is pronounced. It is reinforced wherever, as is most usual, the rural and isolated population is illiterate. In such cases, outside the great cities, ruralism, localism and political unawareness go hand in hand, and by consequence 'traditionalism' reigns. For again, in all these societies except the most advanced, like Argentina, great sectors of everyday life are still powerfully influenced or even governed by traditional observances. Sometimes the traditional influence is cultural, like Buddhism in South East Asia, Hinduism in India, Islam in Indonesia, Pakistan and the Middle East as well as in the Maghreb and parts of sub-Saharan Africa, or the influence of the Roman Catholic Church in Latin America. All these cultural and religious influences have a political bearing; but sometimes a direct traditional politics still operates, where old traditional *élites*, such as sheikhs or clan heads in parts of the Middle East, or chiefs in certain of the African ex-dependencies (notably those governed formerly by so-called 'indirect' rule as in British West Africa), still retain a measure of power.

2. C. Veliz (ed.), *Obstacles to Change in Latin America*, Oxford University Press, 1966, p. 86.

Finally, these societies are deeply riven: in Latin America mostly by class lines, in Africa mostly by tribal and ethnic ones (which, as in Kenya, may also be economic), in Asia by either or both. The Latin American societies are markedly stratified. At the peak stand the tiny minority of the conspicuously rich, often ancient aristocratic families. The middle sectors, in so far as they have developed (as in Argentina, Chile and Brazil), have aspired to join this aristocratic *élite* by copying its way of life and its pattern of education, and above all, so they hope, by intermarriage. At the bottom of the pyramid lies the vast mass of down-at-heel clerks, urban slum dwellers, and *campesinos* or Indians in the countryside. The figures just quoted above give some idea of the polarity between the two extremes. Only Mexico, which underwent a genuine social revolution between 1911 and 1922, Uruguay, which began to develop a measure of social democracy even before the First World War, and contemporary Cuba form qualified exceptions. In Latin America the aristocracies have shown astonishing powers of endurance. 'For many generations the same handful of families have always been near the sources of political power, have obviously enjoyed great wealth, and have had a clear monopoly of social prestige.' The urban interests, according to the same observer, by dint of zealous application in social climbing, 'have finally succeeded in becoming very much like them, thinking like them, and defending their traditional interests with the zeal of the newly converted'.[3]

In some of the Latin American republics the horizontal stratification is complicated by vertical division. This is notably true of the 'Indian' republics – Mexico, Guatemala, Ecuador, Peru and Bolivia. There the indigenous Indians retain their identity. They do not speak Spanish. They cannot read a newspaper. They cannot comprehend a political broadcast. They do not leave their districts. They remain aloof, unincorporated in the nation.

On the other hand, the societies of sub-Saharan Africa are not yet markedly stratified. There, on the whole, peasant or tribal landholding prevails. The middle sector, save in some instances for the professions, is very often occupied by expatriates, often

3. Veliz, op. cit., p. 7.

Asians, brought in for such purposes by the colonial power, while the management of industry was until recently a preserve of the Europeans – though in some states (Kenya again) this is altering rapidly. On the other hand these societies are deeply riven by tribal, regional and ethnic lines, accentuated by the way in which their frontiers were drawn up. These usually correspond to no ethnic or tribal or historic tradition. They are mere lines of convenience, established by the former colonial power either for ease of administration or as a consequence of diplomatic bargaining. These societies are 'plural'. Any identity their peoples can feel is one that has still to be created by the modernizing *élites*.

Asia presents a mixed picture. Indonesia, for instance, is not markedly stratified by socio-economic class, though it is by status grouping. Its deep divisions arise from its diverse religious communities, and from the historic antagonism between Java and the outer islands. On the other hand, Pakistan is both stratified *and* plural: there is a world of difference, in language, cultural heritage, land tenure, between West Pakistan and East Pakistan, while in West Pakistan itself, society is divided horizontally between a handful of great landowners and the peasant mass. India is likewise divided by socio-economic class, albeit the middle class is large, intelligent and able; and she is also divided in countless ways by ethnic and linguistic and religious community. And so one could go on. Few, if any, of the Asiatic ex-dependencies are homogeneous societies. Nearly all are plural, by virtue of one consideration or another; and many, in addition, are cleft into the rich–poor and urban–rural dichotomies.

In earlier chapters, when discussing a liberal-democratic or a totalitarian 'type' of governmental system, we had occasion to give this warning: that the 'type' was a mix, compounded of the features of many disparate members of a family, and that in the real world individual states only approached this type to some degree or other, but never fully coincided with it. This warning must be repeated here with respect to the social characteristics of the Third World. What has been presented here is a *composite*. Some societies approach it very nearly, others resemble it in a number of its features and one or two (Argentina springs to mind) are exceptions. The table (Table 7) gives some idea of the range of deviation. It is true to say, however, that in the Third World *most* of the societies exhibit *most* of the features here described.

**TABLE 7. SOME SOCIAL CHARACTERISTICS
OF COUNTRIES IN THE THIRD WORLD**

	G.N.P. per capita	Percentage urban	Percentage adult literacy	Percentage higher education per 100,000	Inhabitants per physician
Argentina	490	48·3	86·4	827	660
Turkey	220	18·2	39·0	255	2,800
U.A.R.	142	29·1	19·9	399	2,600
Iran	108	21·0	15·0	90	3,800
India	73	12·0	19·3	220	5,200
Laos	50	4·0	17·5	4	100,000

Source: B. M. Russett and Associates, *World Handbook of Political Indicators*, Yale, 1964.

To the extent that most of them do in fact approach this composite type, two conclusions follow. The first is that there does not exist in them *an organized public opinion* of sufficient strength to support liberal-democratic institutions. The second is that the principles of the modernization syndrome not only do nothing to help create such an organized opinion in the short and medium terms, but actually enfeeble whatever of that nature already exists.

IV. THE ABSENCE OF 'ORGANIZED PUBLIC OPINION'

It has already been stated that if governments are to rule stably and give way to alternative governments peaceably, they must not rely on naked coercion, except in an emergency and at the margin, but upon their legitimacy, i.e., their moral authority, which they derive from the political formula current in their society. We can expand this a little and say that the stability of a government depends upon *organized public opinion*. Public opinion is necessary in so far as it upholds, sustains, the political myth; in so far, that is to say, as it believes that government has a moral claim to its allegiance. This public opinion must be *organized*, however, because the government is always likely, even in the best conducted country, to be challenged by dissidence either at home or abroad, and a small minority of resolute men could overturn quite a well-established and popular government by force unless some counter-forces among the public could rally to its defence. Stability demands dependency upon a political formula, but the notion of the political formula itself must be elaborated to imply the existence of an organized public opinion. Now the stability of many totalitarian governments (for example, the U.S.S.R.) is readily explicable in these terms because, as we have seen, in these states the government organizes supporters for its own 'official' formula and puts them in positions of authority throughout the rest of society while at the same time it pulverizes the supporters of opposing opinions. Thus a political formula is fabricated by the government and organizations are created to disseminate it. This forms the basis on which the government rests and, so long as its measures in giving effect to its myth are effective, that government is likely to be tolerably stable. But what happens, we may ask, in the open societies of the West, the so-called liberal-democratic societies? For here, by definition, no official support is given to any particular formula at all and the clash of organized opinion and counter-opinion is freely permitted. Yet many of these societies – the United States of America, the United Kingdom, the Irish Republic, the Scandinavian countries, Switzerland – are extremely stable in their form of government. Why is this?

The answer can only lie, surely, in that somehow or other, despite the opportunity for dissent, there is a freely achieved *consensus* on important – and potentially divisive – issues. And this, in turn, brings us back to our hypothesis that the governments, to be stable, must rely upon the support of organized public opinion. Where this exists, liberal-democratic government can function stably; where it is feeble, such a government functions erratically; where non-existent, such a government will not function at all. This may seem a bold claim to make, but it will become less bold if we recognize that the expression 'organized public opinion', consisting as it does of three words, is susceptible to analysis under the three headings of 'opinion', 'public' and 'organized'. Let us then examine these three parts of the term and see their implications.

(1) *'Opinion'*

First of all 'opinion'. As traditional loyalties are challenged and eroded by the new principles of nationality, popular sovereignty, secularization and social purposiveness, so they have to be replaced by a new nexus of loyalty and allegiance. The old traditional loyalty is to a man or body of men – to individuals: the new one is to an abstraction, to a set of rules which apply to any person, provided he is put into office by an agreed procedure. Unreflecting loyalty, by the same token, must be replaced by critical awareness.

Now these new principles, and the type of allegiance they imply, require certain material preconditions to become widespread in a society. They demand, to begin with, some measure of industrialization. The reason is that the traditional societies, as we have seen, are largely agrarian and often subsistence economies, with relatively little internal trade and interchange of products. In this they resemble, more or less, the manorial economy of the European Middle Ages. In such an economy, economic processes are based on geographically isolated areas, each largely self-contained. The state boundaries enclose communities – but not 'a community'. Industrialization brings about the growth of *communal* economic activities because it stimulates a division of labour and the interdependence of one occupation upon other occupations and of one local area upon other areas.

The second material precondition – necessary for the effectiveness of the first – is the growth of physical communications. The breaking down of the hermetic economic areas which we have already mentioned can only come about if, in fact, communications can be easily established between them by water, road or rail. Only when these communications are established can a wider community be established instead of a number of largely insulated local cells. Then, not only will trade and commerce flow between one area and another, but the communications will also make possible an interchange of views such as is not practicable where distance and geography impede travel.

Thirdly, to follow this up, it is important, if public opinion is to become widespread and effective, that there shall be media of mass communication. At one time it was held that this required widespread literacy. This is probably no longer true, owing to the fact that broadcasting and television are even more effective methods of communication with the masses than books and newspapers. But some such media as the press, television and radio are required in order that increasingly homogenized masses, who move so much more freely about the whole national territory and are increasingly interdependent upon one another in their economic life, should also be able to communicate their political views to one another. It has been shown by Lerner and his associates, in his book *The Passing of Traditional Society*,[4] that in the Middle East, the countries that are advanced in one of these three respects tend to be advanced in the other respects also. Interestingly enough, this same interdependency of industrialization, communication and the growth of mass media can be discerned in British society between 1760 and, say, 1860, in the century of the industrial revolution. Now it so happens that there are still very many countries in the world, notably in the Middle East, in South East Asia, in Latin America and in Africa, where these conditions simply do not obtain at all. In such countries, 'opinion', in the sense of a reflecting and self-conscious set of ideas about allegiance and civic duty, either exists only in a slight degree or not at all. Where this is so, where there is very little in the way of a self-conscious opinion about what constitutes a rightful claim to government on the part of those who are ruling the country, public office tends to be the prey of a narrow set of *élites* and counter-*élites* contending for

4. D. Lerner, *The Passing of Traditional Society*, Free Press, Illinois, 1958.

power by the means best adapted, in that country, for their achieving it. For example, in Haiti, where an 'opinion' on politics can hardly be said to exist at all, there has been almost continual despotism throughout its history. In Thailand, there has been continuous military rule from 1932 to the present day. The French-speaking states of West Africa, such as Upper Volta, the Central African Republic and Dahomey, in which tiny military forces have taken the government over without any difficulty, provide further examples.

(2) *'Public'*

So much, then, for the importance of there being an 'opinion' – in any shape or form – if government is to be stable. The second term in our expression, however, is the word 'public'. I have postulated that stable government demands not just opinion but an organized *public* opinion. 'Public' in this sense means just what it says – namely, *widely disseminated* throughout the community. It implies that there are no permanent minorities, or that if there are, they are, on the whole, insignificant. It implies, in short, some *homogeneity* of view throughout society; for unless certain basic values are widely shared, the society will be cleft by irreconcilables, each struggling, not to convince the others (for, by definition, this would be impossible), but to *suppress* the others. Some issues are so passionately or fanatically contentious in some societies that the minority is not prepared to accept majority rule. Where the minority sees no opportunity of ever becoming the majority, its resistance is likely to be still more uncompromising, for it can foresee no possibility of ever being able to reverse the policies on which it feels so deeply. In such societies it is very difficult to see how a government can remain in power except by relying upon coercion.

Extremely sharp economic cleavages, and the cleavages caused by ethnic, religious or tribal division – these, common in the Third World, are precisely the kind that make for the existence of irreconcilable factions each struggling to suppress the other; for they are unwilling to compromise and fearful of 'taking turns'. In societies so divided, while there may well be 'opinion', it is not 'public', because there is no one public but a number of them.

The political effects vary with circumstances. Some societies are split into a number of identifiable and permanent minorities which differ from each other in so many ways that even if they resemble another group in one respect they differ from it in all others. This situation produces so fragmented an opinion that coalition is impossible. Although Spain is not a part of the Third World, it is a striking illustration of this principle. For it is precisely to this circumstance that Ortega y Gasset, in his *España invertebrada*, ascribed that country's inability to operate liberal-democratic institutions. Here the persons who were separatists were sometimes clericals, sometimes anti-clericals; the clericals might have been separatists or, equally, centralists; the socialists were sometimes centralists, sometimes separatists; equally, the *bourgeoisie*, though anti-socialist, were sometimes separatists and sometimes centralists – and so forth. The entire society was split into a large number of small but entirely uncompromising groups. Something of this kind of situation is to be found in Argentina where the three great sectors of society, the old *estanciero* aristocracy, the trade unions and the urban middle class, so differ that no one of these is prepared to coalesce with the other two. All three are pitted against each other and no one of the three sectors is strong enough to overcome the opposition of the two others.

But in other circumstances different social divisions may be congruent; this situation leads not merely to mutually hostile factions incapable of coalitions and hence to intense instability – it may lead to civil tension or even civil war. This was the situation in Mexico before the 1911 revolution. On the one side were the *criollos* who were at once wealthy, powerful and white; on the other, the *mestizos* and the Indians who were dark-skinned, poor and had no part in the governing of their country. One finds similar situations in Peru or Bolivia today; two-thirds of their populations are Indian, and these are the poor, the dispossessed, the individuals who are governed but have no say in the governing of their country. In Guatemala the situation is even more extreme. There the franchise used to lie in the hands of the *ladino* minority and was confined to one tenth of the national total. The remainder of the population, mostly the Indian descendants of the Incas, were, effectively, both economically and politically subject.

There is a similar congruence in, say, Rhodesia with its society divided between the white minority and the African majority. The whites are the wealthy and they are also the powerful; the Africans are the poor and the subject. The same situation was observable in Algeria during the struggle for independence. Here it was the *colons* who had wealth and political power and the native Algerian who was kept in subjection and in poverty.

In societies of one or the other of these types, i.e., where the self-divisions are either congruent or multiplex, the live-and-let-live assumptions of liberal-democracy are not maintained, and, indeed, cannot be maintained, because it would be far too dangerous for any of the minorities concerned. For liberal-democracy requires for its maintenance and operation the absence of any permanent minorities hostile to the government of the day, since it assumes that minorities will, at some time or another, be able to turn themselves into majorities. Clearly this cannot occur in certain of the conditions given above. It was impossible to imagine the white *colons* in Algeria being able to turn themselves into a majority of inhabitants in a situation where the majority of the inhabitants were poor and politically subject to the white minority. That white minority was always going to remain a minority. This is why it fought so desperately to prevent the democratic franchise coming to Algeria. It knew that, the moment all Algerians had a vote, it would be outnumbered and, because it was rich and because it had previously held the majority in subjection, it would in turn be despoiled as well as oppressed. The same fear is clearly behind the thinking of the white minority in Rhodesia.

The truth of the matter is that permanent minorities see no virtue at all in rule by the majority, and a moment's reflection will show that they are perfectly right. Why should they see any virtue in subjection to the majority? Subjection is still subjection, whether it is subjection to a mass of people or subjection to a single despot.

(3) *'Organized'*

So much then for the importance of the second element, the word 'public', in our formula 'organized public opinion'. This leaves us with the third element: that this widely diffused opinion must be *organized*. For even if a widely shared opinion does exist, it will be incapable of supporting the government unless it is so organized as to be able to sustain it against any violent, dissident group in society. For we must always assume such to exist, even if they are groups of criminals without any political objective.

Now in traditional societies, such associations and groupings as exist tend to be of the first two types on the list mentioned at page 17. That is to say, they tend to be based either upon the blood tie and kinship, clans or tribes; or upon neighbourhood and territory, that is to say, upon some regional allegiance; or upon religious community. They are 'primary' groups. And as we have pointed out, associations of this kind are, by their nature, mutually exclusive. It is impossible to conceive overlapping membership between tribes, between territories and between religions. (This is an additional reason why the traditional society, or the society which is modernizing but which has still large traditional elements in its rural areas, tends to be unstable, because of the disintegrative effect of sub-organization in that society.) Now industrialization tends not only to help public opinion to come into being, but to create organizations strong enough to sustain a government. These are the so-called 'secondary' associations.

As we have pointed out before, firms, industries, trade unions, political parties, are not necessarily mutually exclusive associations; on the contrary, they often admit of a very wide overlapping membership. Hence they do not necessarily tend to disintegrate opinion into naturally hostile assemblies, but often help to integrate it into a 'public' opinion. At the same time, they *mobilize* it.[5] Perhaps the most important of the mobilizing

5. 'Mobilize: (Mil.) To prepare (an army or fleet) for active service' (*Shorter Oxford English Dictionary*). Hence, by analogy, to prepare opinion-holders for active service. This commonplace expression is being given a lot of fancy meanings nowadays. All except the one here given seem impermissible.

organizations which can sustain a government is the political party. In any society in which a genuine 'opinion' really does exist, the party is the vital link between the government and the governed.

Of course, in many societies, particularly non-Western societies, similar and supporting roles are played by industrial and religious organizations. It is significant that it is where these do not exist or where they are feeble, as, for example, in Ghana, Turkey, Guinea and Algeria, that such ultimate reliance is placed upon the political party as such: in Western societies, as we pointed out earlier, firms, industries, labour unions and the like can and do also play an important part in sustaining the government of the day. The effects of the creation of powerful and permeative political parties are twofold. Where parties are strong – for instance, the Partido Revolucionario Institucional (P.R.I.) in Mexico or the Néo-Destour Party in Tunisia – a degree of integration has been attained, and stability imparted to the government. Where, on the other hand, parties are fractionalized and are merely personalized cliques, as in Syria and Iraq and in many Latin American countries, there ensues a perpetual instability of government.

(4) *'Organized public opinion' and the Third World*

Briefly, then, some of the societies of the Third World – Ruanda and Burundi, for instance – contain no 'opinion' in the sense of self-conscious and critical awareness of, and involvement in, government activity. In others, where such opinion does exist, it is fragmented into bitterly hostile uncompromising groups. And, even if this is not so and it is relatively homogeneous, it may be weakly organized. In any such state the mass of the people have, or had, little attachment to, or even comprehension of their political institutions. There are no clear and well-established political formulae. In such countries politics will not usually run in well-defined channels; there is no widespread consensus as to what channels it should run in and, even if there were, that opinion would be too amorphous to make it do so.

Unfortunately this is not all. For in many of these states the principles of modernization not only run counter to the contours of society, but they accentuate the divisions, making an organized and public opinion even more difficult to obtain.

V. THE DISRUPTION OF SOCIETY

Independence is won through and by the 'modern' principles of national self-determination, of popular sovereignty and of economic independence: yet, after it has been obtained, these principles work on, and in certain circumstances may disrupt society.

(1) *The principle of nationality*

The principle of nationality may well disrupt a polyethnic society. The experience of the Latin American republics is instructive in this respect. They have the great advantage of being much older than many of the other states of the Third World, and consequently the first half century of their existence was occupied with problems that are still threatening many of the newly constituted states, namely, the problems of territorial organization and national frontiers. Argentina, Colombia and Mexico were fought over for decades by rival armies of federalists (decentralizers, representing the agrarian hinterland) and unitarists (centralizers, usually representing the capital). Nor were national frontiers easily established: Bolívar's Gran Colombia split into its component Venezuela, Colombia and Ecuador; the Central American Federation broke into Guatemala, Honduras, San Salvador and Nicaragua; and Paraguay split off from La Plata Province. Similar tension between Chinese and Malay has led Singapore, which is largely Chinese, to quit the Federation of Malaya. In Pakistan there is ever-present danger that the two halves, Western and Eastern, which differ culturally, economically and linguistically, will fly apart and stay apart. Who ordained that Kurds should be subject to Arabs? Or black 'Sudanese' to the northern Arabs?

The problem is most acute in those states which had no antecedent identity – those of sub-Saharan Africa. Ghana is reckoned as particularly homogeneous by comparison with her neighbours: yet even there the hostility of the proud Ashanti to the coast tribes, and the difference between both these and the Moslem peoples of the Northern Territories, have threatened to disrupt the state. In Nigeria, a vast country of some fifty millions, in which no less than fifty-two different languages are spoken, the deep divisions of tribalism led to the adoption of a federal constitution: a Yoruba Western Region, an Ibo Eastern Region and a vast Moslem Hausa-Fulani Northern Region, which almost immediately dominated the other two. Even federalism was not flexible enough to contain the fierce pressures of tribal nationalism: the army itself fell prey to it; and at the time of writing the country is in the throes of civil war.

(2) *Popular sovereignty*

Where the society lacks functional associations and is divided by tribe, region or religious community, 'one man one vote' can and often does mean that political parties are merely tribe or region or religious community in liberal-democratic trappings. It by no means follows that the representatives elected by such groupings will work together any more than the groupings themselves have done. Again, where – as in most instances – there is just enough industry to exacerbate division between employers and workers but not enough to create state-wide functional associations, and where also there is widespread illiteracy and a want of communications – then universal suffrage, endowing the members of these mutually antagonistic groupings with a vote, produces a confused and pulverized party structure. Indonesia, Pakistan, Ceylon and the Congo (Kinshasa) may serve as illustrations. There would be many more if elections had not been suppressed throughout one half of the Third World and controlled or falsified in most of the other half.

(3) *Economic independence and industrialization*

No country in the world has as yet industrialized itself without disrupting traditional patterns of behaviour and inflicting great hardships, indeed cruelties, upon its population in the process. In order to extract the social surplus needed to supply the capital investment, in order to attract, train, mobilize and discipline the labour force, 'all human ties' (we quote Karl Marx) 'were set aside and the cash nexus became the only link between man and man'. Britain had its poor-law bastilles and its Tolpuddle martyrs; on a vast and crueller scale, the U.S.S.R. had its liquidation of the kulaks and its slave camps. The Third-World countries are exceptional only in that their effort to industrialize is even more strainful. For none of them have the technicians, the trained labour force, the supervisors – all must be created. None of them have much surplus capital, and what there is tends to remain in private hands or be invested in landholding: if any is to come the government must provide it – and since foreign aid usually has 'strings' attached, and since neo-colonialism is feared, it can in the last resort only come from forced public savings or labour. At the same time, this same public has usually been assured by the modernizers that it was colonialism that retarded their industrialization and caused their poverty, and that, conversely, independence will make them wealthier. The governments are committed to a 'modern' policy of social welfare (something, it should be noted, that the Western societies dispensed with for three-quarters of a century), as well as industrialization. Their exiguous resources would be strained to provide either, let alone both. The resentments caused by their apparent failure to honour their promises; the hostility of traditional sectors of the economy, whose political power or social prestige rests on land or trade; the demands of the labour force which their policies have created: all these impinge upon the modernizers. Where the liberal-democratic institutions operate, even if only at half-cock, these resentments are translated into electoral demands and give rise to radical populist parties. Where, on the other hand, the institutions have been suppressed, resentment simmers until it breaks out in revolt. In all cases, however, the effort to industrialize impels government to strengthen its powers and to curtail the liberal-democratic order. It is precisely this that has made so many modernizers look with sympathy on Soviet rather than on Western institutions. For the Soviet Union is the success story of how a small group of wilful men, without much mass support but with stupendous ruthlessness, could transform a traditional agrarian and poverty-stricken society into a leading industrial power in the space of half a human lifetime.

VI. POLITICAL SYSTEMS OF THE THIRD WORLD

In some societies public opinion is an artifact: it is consciously formed and organized by the government in order to maintain itself in power and deviation is either prevented or suppressed. This is the totalitarian system. In other societies public opinion forms and organizes freely and with sufficient basis of agreement between the varying viewpoints to maintain the system of government, though from time to time one set of rulers is, peaceably and by pre-established rules, displaced in favour of another. This is the liberal-democratic system.

In the Third World, with a few exceptions (Algeria, Mali, Guinea), a large number of states have experimented with liberal-democratic institutions in societies which, for reasons described, provide only a feeble and faltering public support for them. In some, opinion is organized but not public: it is fractionalized into powerful but mutually hostile and irreconcilable groups. In others, opinion is neither public nor oganized. Here opinion is broken into mutually hostile but feebly organized groups, all of which are largely alienated from the ruling minority: as in the Middle Eastern countries and in most of the Latin American ones, excepting, perhaps, Mexico, Costa Rica, Chile and Uruguay. In still others, an opinion can hardly be said to exist: the masses are rooted in invincible ignorance, prejudice and illiteracy as in Haiti, Paraguay, or Rwanda and Burundi.

A small number of ex-colonial states have managed to work liberal-democracy with some success: Israel, where it is firmly rooted and stable, India, whose great success must be qualified until a longer period has elapsed, and the Philippines, Gambia and Ceylon, whose success must also be qualified, since all these states are so young. On the other hand one state, Cuba, has adopted a system akin to the totalitarian. Outside the states that are firmly liberal-democratic or firmly totalitarian lies a penumbra of weak, unstable or experimental liberal-democracies.

But the greatest number of the ex-colonial states have either qualified away the liberal-democratic institutions or abandoned them. The régimes they have established in their stead are pragmatic ones, fed by the apparent exigencies of the moment. These favour two main styles of government: some form of autocracy or some form of oligarchy.

I use these terms here for want of better ones. If in a loose sense autocracy means a régime where one person alone wields overwhelming power without any effective accountability to the public, then this would equally apply to the régimes of Mussolini or Hitler or Stalin; and again, if in its loose sense an oligarchic régime is one where a small group of individuals wield overwhelming power without any effective accountability to the public, then this is applicable to the U.S.S.R. and the other communist states today.

But, for reasons already explained, I have preferred to characterize all the above-named régimes as totalitarian. The term totalitarian subsumes the characteristics of autocracy or oligarchy, but is more than just autocracy and oligarchy: how much more has already been explained. Hence, for purposes of analysis, I am going to use the terms (unqualified) *autocracy* and (unqualified) *oligarchy* to mean these in their non-totalitarian form. In this sense these characterize a very high proportion of the countries of the Third World in the geographical sense of this term.

Autocracies, then, form one sub-variety of rule in the Third World: indeed, strictly speaking, they form two because there still survive two or three dynastic states, like Saudi Arabia, as well as the commoner form, namely, the *military* autocracy. In addition, moreover, the oligarchies are of two types, a new and an old. The consequence is four sub-varieties of rule, the dynastic, the military or military-supportive autocracy, the historic oligarchy and the neo-oligarchy.

Up to the end of the eighteenth century, the vast majority of states were dynastic autocracies or historic oligarchies: that is as much as to say that they were governed by autocrats or oligarchs of lineage or wealth or – more usually – both together. But, with the French Revolution and the reception of its notion of popular sovereignty throughout the world, the autocrats and the oligarchs felt compelled bit by bit to bargain with this new political formula. Hence the piecemeal introduction of liberal-democratic constitutions.

But this by no means meant that the dynasts and the oligarchs had abdicated power. Far from it. In most states, though not all, they continued to govern in despite of the new constitutional and popular order. So arose the *façade-democracy*. In this type of régime, historic oligarchies of lineage and wealth govern from behind a façade of liberal-democratic forms which serve as a cloak or screen to their rule. But in this kind of régime also, the exercise sometimes proves too exacting or the oligarchs quarrel among themselves: in which case, for a space, they yield to an autocrat, often a social upstart, and nearly always a military man.

The façade-democracies are on the wane. Few continue to exist and even those are being eroded. In their place, often, *neo*-oligarchies have arisen. These are composed of professionals of modernizing and nationalist bent. They are what sociologists call men of 'achieved' as against 'ascriptive' status – much the same distinction that historians have been wont to draw between the *novi homines* and the aristocracy of blood and lineage. And the form through which these 'new men' govern is, currently, the *quasi-democracy*. I give this name to a largely improvised and pragmatic system of single or hegemonic party rule. But these neo-oligarchs, also, find the going too hard sometimes; or, like the old oligarchs, they fall to quarrelling among themselves. And when this happens, and it is happening frequently, the quasi-democracy itself gives way to *military rule*. Military rule forms a fourth type of government. But sometimes the military govern openly in their own name and sometimes from behind the scenes, through a civilian façade; and this gives rise to various sub-varieties of the military régime.

I do not propose to examine the vestigial dynastic form of régime, but only the three main types: façade-democracy, quasi-democracy and military régimes. But I should not like it to be thought that the distinctions between these three types and other types of régime are always clear and easy to apply.

All three *resemble* the liberal-democracies and the totalitarian states in that they all pay lip service to popular sovereignty. Their governments sometimes go to absurd lengths to make it seem that they owe their being to the expressed wishes of the people. But all three *differ* from the liberal-democracies in that their governments manipulate the electoral procedures of liberal-democracy in order to achieve a pre-ordained result, namely, their continuance in office. And all three *differ*, too, from the totalitarian state in that their governments do not – or perhaps cannot – direct or control all areas of public life.

Now even these preliminary distinctions serve to show that the system of classification is not clear-cut. Is Colombia a façade-democracy or a liberal-democracy? For there, since 1957, only two parties are permitted to exist; they share seats equally in the Congress irrespective of the votes cast for them, and the presidency alternates between them. Is not this the manipulation of liberal-democratic electoral procedures to achieve a pre-ordained result? And similarly, at the other end of the scale, the government party of Guinea certainly tries (but vainly) to impose its control over all areas of society in a manner which is hard to distinguish from that of the Communist Party of the Soviet Union.

The distinctions between the façade-democracy, the quasi-democracy and the military régime can also become blurred. Though the façade-democracy is so called because it operates from behind the façade of liberal-democratic forms, this may be true to a greater or lesser degree of both the other types. All in fact may indulge in electoral malpractice to falsify a popular verdict. In this respect, a military régime can use almost identical tactics to those of a façade-democracy (as in Thailand), and so can a quasi-democracy (as in the constitutional referendum of 1964 in Ghana).

It is therefore not just electoral malpractice that distinguishes one of these three types from the others. The distinctions lie elsewhere – in the social character of the ruling *élite*, in the nature of its relationship to the ruled and in the structure of the régime;

and each one of these is interconnected with the others. For instance, a façade-democracy is so called partly because of the electoral malpractices of its rulers, but partly, also, because the latter are the traditional rulers – the historic oligarchy – and consequently their manipulation of the vote is made more practicable as a result of the traditional deference paid to them, as social superiors, by the electors. And the structure of their régime tends to be cellular and collegiate because this corresponds to the social structure of the oligarchy itself.

The distinctions can be set out in tabular form (see Table 8).

TABLE 8. REGIMES ALL MANIPULATING LIBERAL-DEMOCRATIC FORMS

Type	Social character of ruling élite	Nature of élite-ruled relationship	Structure	Typical Party Structure
Façade-democracy	Historic oligarchy	Traditional social deference	Cellular, Collegiate Clientelist	1 No-party 2 Plural personalist cliques
Quasi-democracy	Modernizing élite	Single- or dominant-party regimentation	Hierarchical, Centralist (theoretically) Collegiate	Single or hegemonic hierarchical party
Military régime	Armed forces	Coercion	Hierarchical, Centralist, Personalist	1 No-party 2 Single or hegemonic 3 Personalist

These distinctions will be elaborated as I examine each type in the chapters that follow, but even here it is easy to see that they are not clear cut, either. Take first the distinction between a façade-democracy and a military régime. In the former it often happens that, as traditional deference fades, so the historic oligarchy has to rely increasingly upon its army in order to employ coercion.

At a certain point, the military, now the main prop of the régime, begins to dictate policy. In such an event, is the form of rule an indirect military régime or a façade-democracy? In a sense it is either or both. Similarly, with the distinction between façade-democracy and quasi-democracy: into which category does Liberia fall? For if Liberia resembles other quasi-democracies in that the government exerts its control via a dominant and officially-favoured political party, yet that government and party are the political expression of the historic Americo-Liberian oligarchy! Specialists themselves recognize the difficulty in classifying Liberia because of these peculiarities.[6] And again, the distinction between quasi-democracy and military régime may blur where, as in Algeria, a one-party state, the chief of the armed forces deposes the president and head of the party and assumes the presidency himself. Provided they are recognized openly and at the outset, these difficulties need not worry us unduly. They are inherent in any scheme of classification, from library indexing to a decision as to whether algae are vegetable or animal; for instance, witness the two historic legal cases to decide whether a tomato was a fruit or a vegetable. Life is more complex and fluid than classification systems; the smaller the number of classes the larger the number of overlaps – and the larger the number of classes the smaller they are until one is back with an aggregate of individuals.

6. J. G. Liebnow, 'Liberia', in J. S. Coleman and C. G. Rosberg, eds., *Political Parties and National Integration in Tropical Africa*, Berkeley, California, 1966.

Part Two

LIBERAL-DEMOCRACY

Chapter 5

THE GOVERNMENT OF BRITAIN

I. THE COUNTRY AND THE PEOPLE

BRITAIN provides an outstanding example of the liberal-democratic type of government. The régime is stable and has been so for generations, and so are the individual governments generated and sustained by it. The executive enjoys wide authority and extensive administrative capabilities, and yet, as a whole, government is both representative of public opinion, and liberal in its concern for minorities.

These characteristics stem as much from the nature of British society as from the specifically governmental arrangements and norms. The long-enduring stability of the régime is due to the characteristics of the party system – but also to the relatively homogeneous and politically consensual nature of British society. The extensive authority and administrative discretion of the executive is immediately due to constitutional norms such as the 'sovereignty of Parliament' and the status of the Cabinet and to the solidarity of the parties on which Cabinets depend – but all these are tolerable and tolerated only because society is consensual. The representative nature and liberal attitude of the régime is in the first instance due to constitutional factors such as the nature of the electoral system and to the procedures in Cabinet, Parliament and civil service which put a premium upon consultation – but is also due to the powerful and pervasive role of interest groups. This in turn is related to the wide proliferation of autonomous private associations, which in turn is related to attitudes of the British and to their common law rights of free expression, free assembly and free association. The 'constitution', taken in its very widest sense as 'the general set of arrangements that regulate the conditions of political struggle in the country', is a facet, a particular aspect of the wider life of the British community. It is an emanation not an epiphenomenon: it springs out of British social structure and values, it is not something that some group has superimposed upon these.

The political consensus

In 1963 two American political scientists (Professors Almond and Verba) made a survey of what they called 'the civic culture' in five countries.[1] These were the U.S.A., Britain, the Federal Republic of Germany, Italy and Mexico. In the course of this they conducted opinion polls on certain relevant topics across these five countries. Answering the query as to 'which aspects of national life they took most pride in', only two-and-a-half per cent of the Italians named their governmental arrangements and only four per cent of the Germans. In Britain, however, thirty-three per cent of the respondents named their governmental arrangements. Furthermore, more than one-half believed that civil servants would give their individual problems 'serious consideration' and three-quarters believed that the police would. Two-thirds of those questioned believed, further, that it was in their power to affect a national policy and four-fifths thought they could affect a local policy. Finally, four-fifths of the respondents believed that the civil servants would treat them fairly and no less than nine-tenths believed that the police would. By international standards these proportions are very high indeed, and they express what has long been asserted: that on the whole the British esteem their political arrangements and have confidence in them.

This establishes what may be called a *procedural* consensus – agreement on how to go about managing differences of view on substantive issues. But there is also a large *substantive* consensus. Differing from many a distempered polity today, Britain is untroubled by profound and embittered ideological disputes. World ideologies like Marxism or Fascism never had, and do not have, any great place in political life. The great national parties are parties of programmes, not of ideology or 'tendency'; the rival programmes they put to the nation at the periodical general elections resemble each other more than they differ; and when

1. G. Almond and S. Verba, *The Civic Culture*, Princeton, 1963.

one of the parties is in office and comes to honour such election pledges it tends to modify this programme still more in the direction of its defeated rivals – so that the Conservative policies from 1951 to 1955 resembled in marked degree those of the Labour governments of 1945 to 1951, while Labour's handling of the economy from 1964 to 1969 soon came to differ in no major respect from the policies of the Conservatives from 1959 to 1964 except that (as the event turned out) it was far less effective.

For one thing, the competitive dynamics of the two-party system impels the two main parties to try to consolidate a majority by reaching out for the middle ground; consequently, a large part of the rival programmes runs in parallel, not on a collision course. Secondly, the legacy of the past and the structure and values of British society in the present have made these programmes not of 'all or nothing' but of 'less and more'. Few individuals want to abolish the 'capitalist class': but a very large number want to tax it, control it and limit it. Few persons want to uproot the trade unions: but a very large number are tired of their pretensions and want to check their power over their members and limit their capacity to disrupt basic industries. And so forth. Furthermore, with rare exceptions – the Suez crisis is the only outstanding recent example – most conflicts arise over domestic issues, not foreign ones. And these domestic issues have increasingly reduced themselves to two: on the one side, the government's handling of the economy, on the other, the issue of social and economic equality. These are interconnected. Essentially British politics are about national productivity, and social and economic inequality – or, if one wills, about increasing the gross national product and dividing it up. Unlike struggles over national, religious or ideological claims, such issues are instrumental and/or negotiable; they permit of compromises.

And yet national, religious, even at times ideological, conflicts are the very stuff of British *history*. Officially, the state, loosely called 'Britain', is 'The United Kingdom of Great Britain and Northern Ireland'; 'Great Britain' is the official designation, not adopted till 1706, for the larger of the two main British islands, which comprises the two units of England-and-Wales on the one hand and Scotland on the other. This points up the fact that the

British community comprises *four* peoples. Four-fifths of the total population are English, and the remaining fifth is made up of the Scots, the Welsh and the Northern Irish. The relationships between the four ethnic regions are different. Northern Ireland, which is represented in the Westminster Parliament also possesses its own local parliament for local matters. Wales, though its population is double that of Northern Ireland, is an integral part of England-and-Wales and has been so since the Act of Union in 1536. Scotland, which until the Treaty of Union in 1706 was an independent state (albeit one that shared the same monarch with England and Wales from 1603 to 1706), is today represented only in the Westminster Parliament; but, by virtue of the 1706 Treaty, Scotland enjoys her own national Church and legal, educational and local governmental systems. But for all this, the 'Constitution' – the overarching rules within whose compass dispute is regulated – is not British at all. It is *English*; it is the Constitution of the quondam Kingdom of England which was forced upon or adopted by the other three nationalities in the past.

Certainly, today, the four different nationalities have different political preferences. England is a predominantly Conservative country. Except in 1945 and 1966, a majority of its people have always voted Conservative since the Second World War. Wales, however, is overwhelmingly Labour; Northern Ireland is equally overwhelmingly 'Unionist' (i.e., the peculiar local brand of Conservative): and Scotland has swung about between the two parties. But the important feature of this voting behaviour is that it is expressed in terms of and through *national* parties, and at general elections it is expressed on *national* issues. Certainly, strident nationalist parties exist: the Irish Republicans in Northern Ireland, Plaid Cymru in Wales, the Scottish Nationalist Party in Scotland; but hitherto – except in by-elections (especially of late where Plaid Cymru and Scottish Nationalists have scored spectacular gains at the expense of the Labour Party) – their political support has been meagre. One of the best attested facts in British political life is precisely the *relative* insignificance of specifically regional loyalties in voting. It has been shown that the political preferences of the various regions is not due to local national or religious factors but to local *class* structures.[2] The British political consensus transcends the religious and national conflicts that took place in the past. There is only one rift in the lute: a class cleavage. This is a national, not a regional factor; and it is prominent in British politics not because it is wide, deep and clear cut, for it isn't, but simply because other cleavages hardly exist.

The making of the consensus

(a) The importance of being an island

At least three important consequences have followed from the fact that Britain is a set of offshore islands. The first is the insulation of British political development. Briefly, at no time for more than nine hundred years were the institutions of England, the most powerful of the political units of the British islands, ever subjected to the radical torsion or reconstruction to which the states of continental Europe were subjected during that long period: notably during the wars of the French Revolution and Empire and during the period of the Third Reich. English institutions followed their own, separate, sequence of adaptation and evolution, at their own self-imposed pace.

Another consequence was the early political unification of the country – though it is easy to ante-date this. The island of 'Great Britain' is not subdivided by high mountains, impassable deserts, or wide rivers; but it is all of it girdled about by the sea. The sea is the natural frontier and this sea once circled no less than three distinct political units – Wales, Scotland and England. Of these, England was the most populated, prosperous and powerful and it became the first ambition of its kings to expand their territories up to the natural frontier. Wales, still tribal and miserably poor when England was already a well-established kingdom, was subjugated and annexed as early as the fourteenth century. Scotland, which was not in much better shape politically, was, however, able to thrust the English back at Bannockburn in 1314; as a result she was able to gain enough

2. R. Alford, *Party and Society*, John Murray, London, 1964, pp. 289–90.

time to attain statehood and conduct incessant wars with her powerful southern neighbour down to the time of the unification of the two kingdoms under a sole monarch in 1603, and the subsequent Treaty of Union in 1706 which for the first time created a united state of the two – 'Great Britain'. The kings of England also strove to subdue the neighbour island of Ireland – still tribal even at the time of Elizabeth I. That unhappy country was invaded, conquered, colonized, re-invaded, re-conquered and re-colonized from the twelfth century onwards until, in 1801, it too was absorbed into Great Britain in what became – until 1922 – the 'United Kingdom of Great Britain and Ireland'. But here, significantly, the sea intervened. Ireland never became an integrated part of the British political community as Wales and Scotland did; English policy vacillated between treating it as the farthest region or the nearest colony. Irish nationalism, powerfully reinforced by the fact that its southern counties were Catholic and hence religiously different from the rest of the now United Kingdom, and nourished on economic exploitation, reawakened in the late eighteenth and nineteenth centuries. In 1922 all but the largely protestant six northern counties seceded from the United Kingdom as the Irish Free State, later the Republic of Ireland. This secession mightily strengthened the religious, social and political homogeneity of the territorially diminished 'United Kingdom of Great Britain and Northern Ireland', and greatly simplified the main issues – and strategies – of its politics.

Finally, insularity has had a bearing upon 'the liberties of Englishmen'. Since the kings of England had nothing to fear from land invasion, they did not have the same incentive as their continental cousins to develop a standing army; whereas their need for a navy was imperative. Now because navies are at sea for long periods, because their personnel is not numerous, and because they are made up of a large number of small units, maritime forces present little threat to civil institutions. To ensure effective control of the localities in their kingdom, therefore, the kings of England relied on the co-operation of the local lords and gentry, rather than over-awed them by royal officials backed by the royal army. From the earliest times English governmental arrangements had a markedly legalistic and civilian character, and, compared with the 'new monarchies' of Spain or France, they were extensively decentralized. Far more was left to local initiative than on the other side of the North Sea and the Channel.

(b) The flux of time

Like many of the new states of today, Britain too has had its 'nationalities' problem, its 'language' problem, its 'religious' problem, not to speak of its 'constitutional' problem. These are problems no more; not because 'time has resolved them', for this is meaningless, but because, in the course of time, either the problems have been eroded by the unintended side-effects of legislation designed for quite other purposes, or else because the conditions which gave rise to the original problem have altered, doing away with that original problem and not necessarily creating another in its place.

The nationalities problem provides one illustration. With the glaring exception of Catholic Ireland, which wrenched itself loose in 1922, national separatism has long been muted, as already noted. Demography provides one reason. As recently as the beginning of the nineteenth century, the non-English peoples of the United Kingdom equalled the English in number. Today, even if one includes the population of the Republic of Ireland, they amount to only about one-fifth of the entire population. Meanwhile intermarriage has gone on uninterruptedly and few can boast a purely Welsh or Scots or English lineage. Moreover, industrialization – of which more later – has not only made the various economies interdependent but has caused vast internal migrations. The resulting homogenization is partly the cause and partly the consequence of the extinction of yet another problem – the language problem – which is common among the new, post-1945 states of the world and which also taxes 'old' states like Belgium or Canada or Spain. English is the common language of the United Kingdom – although this situation is barely a century old. In the middle of the last century most Welshmen and Irishmen were still speaking their native Celtic tongues, and together they accounted for about one-third of the total British population. It was not till the decade 1840–50 that Welsh and Erse went into rapid decline. In Wales today, despite frantic efforts to keep Welsh alive, English is not only spoken by virtually the entire population but is the sole tongue of over two-thirds of it. As to Erse, despite official efforts in the Republic of Ireland to establish it as a national tongue, English remains the common language of everyday life.

The religious cleavages, once the mainspring of national history and a prime determinant of party attitudes and allegiances until well into the beginning of the twentieth century, are another of the problems bypassed in the course of time. The struggle between Scottish Presbyterianism and English Episcopalianism which played so large a part in perpetuating the feud between Scotland and England, was finally put aside when the Treaty of Union guaranteed Presbyterianism the status of the national Church in Scotland. The strife between English and Welsh nonconformity and episcopalianism continued to inspire English and Welsh party politics up to the end of the First World War; but since then, the general decline of religious faith has robbed Dissent, Catholicism and Anglicanism of all political importance. British politics have become secularized.

As for the political institutions of the country: at one level British history is the usual record of assassinations, depositions, rebellions, abdications and proscriptions. At another, and more significant level, the basic institutions have grown piecemeal out of or alongside their predecessors. The continuity of these institutions constitutes at once the supreme fact about the historical evolution of the United Kingdom and, at the same time, its supreme enigma. Certainly it is not possible here to volunteer reasons why this should have occurred. But it is a fact that, in the past as now, large areas of the Constitution were enshrined only in custom and tradition. Even the one radical violent break in the continuity – the interregnum of 1649–60 – ended with the cancellation of all the laws passed in this brief span, and the restoration (in form) of the previous political arrangements.

So it is that the Constitution has developed *ad hoc*, by adaptation first to one immediate problem, then to another. Today, it is a democratic one – but poured into an antique medieval mould. It is still stuffed with officials, terminology and procedures that originated in the Middle Ages. The government is the Queen's government; ministers are Ministers of the Crown; the armed forces are the armed forces of the Crown; officers hold their rank by virtue of the Royal Commission. The courts and the judges are Her Majesty's courts and Her Majesty's judges. High officials still bear titles like Lord Chancellor, Lord Privy Seal, Chancellor of the Exchequer, which all go back five or six hundred years. The place where Parliament meets is the *royal* Palace of Westminster.

The importance of this tradition is that it has preserved not only medieval forms but the medieval essence: this was that the king governed – but conditionally, not absolutely. At the heart of the English political system – now embracing the entire United Kingdom – there was always a core of officials, who initiated, formulated and executed policy. Only at one time – during the extraordinary period of the Long Parliament (1640–49) – was this tradition suspended, and even then this was because the king 'went missing' (so to speak) and with him this key-nucleus of the working constitution. For the rest, political opposition has never sought to abolish this group, but only to control it. British constitutional history is in sum the story of a continuous struggle for the control of this executive machinery. In the beginning, it was the king and his hand-picked officials versus the barons in the Great Council. Today it is the prime minister and his hand-picked ministers in his Cabinet, versus the Commons, or – more realistically – the opposition party. The form taken by an Act of Parliament links the present to the past and attests the underlying continuity of the medieval conception of government. An Act begins with these words: 'Be it enacted by the Queen's most Excellent Majesty, by and with the advice and consent of the Lords Spiritual and Temporal, and Commons, in this present Parliament assembled, and by the authority of the same . . .'

Today, in practice, it is the prime minister and his colleagues in the Cabinet that enact, but 'by and with the advice and consent of the . . . Commons . . . and by the authority of the same . . .'

(c) Industrialization

Britain is the most industrialized and urbanized country in the entire world. Only a bare four per cent of the working population work the soil, over seventy per cent of the population lives in cities of over 20,000 inhabitants, and half of these are concentrated in a mere six conurbations.

With industrialization has gone a high standard of living, an elaborate division of labour and an extensive network of communications and mass media. This industrialization-cum-urbanization (the two are not necessarily connected) has had two effects on British society and they pull in different directions. On the one hand, the phenomenon has homogenized British culture – enhancing the political consensus by a socio-cultural one. On the other hand it has divided society into new social classes. The former mitigates political conflict; the latter generates or exacerbates it.

The homogenization of culture

Such local, regional or religious differences as still remain are being eroded – or perhaps overlaid is the better expression – by the effects of the mass media. As far as the Press is concerned, not only had Britain in 1968 a higher *per capita* circulation than any other country (506 per thousand) but this circulation is dominated by the *London* newspapers. In this Britain differs sharply from the countries of the European continent and also from the U.S.A., where regional newspapers are the rule and not the exception. Again, in broadcasting – the sound radio is all but universal in Britain – the British Broadcasting Corporation, which enjoys a monopoly in sound radio, standardizes information and news on a national plane. Most noteworthy of all – so does television. The B.B.C. transmits television as well as sound broadcasts and, despite regional programming, the overwhelming impression is one of national programmes. 'Independent' (i.e. commercial) Television is, in its constitutional arrangements, more geared to the local or regional programme than is the B.B.C. but in practice, again, nationwide transmissions predominate. Thus most people watch identical programmes for most of the time. In addition Independent Television transmits sales advertisements. These go beyond the informational aspects of B.B.C. and Independent Television telecasting, and shape *tastes*. And the fact that Britain is so highly urbanized provides a fertile field for such national messages: townsfolk, wherever they are, have similar environments and similar problems.

Meanwhile, industrialization has made Britain, by world standards, a wealthy society, and so helped to close the gap between rich and poor. The standard of living improved sharply between 1951 and 1964, when consumer expenditure rose by forty per cent – more than for the entire previous half century. This began to equalize the distribution of goods and services, putting what were once luxury goods within the reach of common folk. Compared with 1951, by 1964 more than twice as many persons were taking their holidays abroad and the proportion of house owners had risen from twenty-nine per cent to forty-four per cent. And by 1964 over two-fifths of the population owned a car, rented a telephone, owned a refrigerator.

As this standard of living spread more widely, so, at the same time, the labour force was changing. Heavy manual labour was declining; by 1966 only forty-one per cent of the total labour force was employed in mining and manufacturing, and of that percentage one-quarter was engaged in administrative and clerical work. Calculations made by various organizations show that non-manual occupations now account for one-third of the entire labour force, and it is reckoned that by the late 1980s the proportion will exceed fifty per cent. A trend of this kind increasingly blurs the traditional distinction between 'capitalist' and 'proletarian'.

And yet, that distinction still exists and supplies the main motive force of British politics. In the fifties someone coined the expression: 'Socialism is about equality'. However that may be, equality is what British politics is about. For one thing, a trend towards the equalization of incomes, which was marked in the 1938–56 period, came to an end after that date – even when the effects of progressive taxation are taken into account. In 1963 one-tenth of the population took one-quarter of the national income, while another thirty per cent of the population took only twelve per cent of the national income. And income is much more equally distributed than wealth, for, roughly speaking, four-fifths of the total wealth of the country is held by less than one-tenth of the population. Furthermore, educational opportunities are still highly unequal, and this is important since the life chances of an individual, including his income, occupation and social class, are closely correlated to his education which is in turn correlated to his home background – which includes his parents' wealth or income. About four per cent of the school-age population go to private schools and yet this minute sector of the population supplied one-fifth of the entire university population (1961–2), half the officer cadet intake at Sandhurst Military Academy (1960), thirty-seven per cent of the entrants to the top grade (i.e. the Administrative Grade) of the Home Civil Service (and far, far more of the entrants to the Foreign Service). Even in 1966, with a Labour majority of nearly one hundred in the House of Commons, this private school sector supplied forty-seven per cent of M.P.s. But the state school sector also produces inequalities. The higher the occupational status of the parent, the more likely is his child to go to a grammar school at the age of eleven, and not to a secondary modern school. Next, of those going to a grammar school, the children with parents of higher occupational status are more likely than their fellows to stay on after the age of fifteen and take the school leaving exam-inations which are the principal passport to professional careers and the university. Indeed, though the number of university places has doubled over the last twenty years, the proportion of manual-working-class children attending university was only twenty-five per cent in 1960 as compared with twenty-three per cent from 1928 to 1947.

It is over such inequalities that British society is divided and the main parties – Labour, Liberal and Conservative – are in dispute. There is a correlation between social class (as measured in this case by income) and the way individuals cast their votes, as can be seen from Table 9.

And yet, for all this, it will not do to put too much emphasis on this class analysis. Class is important – indeed central – in British politics only because nothing else is; and there are two fairly simple ways of demonstrating this. One is to compare the indices of inequality with other liberal-democracies. To hear some publicists go on, one would think that class distinction and social

TABLE 9. PARLIAMENTARY VOTING BY SOCIAL CLASS (I)
(Range of percentages voting for Conservative, Labour and Liberal Parties in general elections, 1945–66)

Class	Conservative	Labour	Liberal
Upper-middle (6%)[1]	72–90	6–14	2–14
Middle (22%)[1]	56–77	16–30	2–15
Working (61%)[1]	32–44	52–57	2–14
Very poor (11%)[1]	24–44	54–68	2–12

1. Percentage of total vote.

Source: British Institute of Public Opinion, 1945–66.

inequality were either exclusive to Britain or, at any rate, far worse than in other liberal-democracies. But educational inequality is far more pronounced in say France or West Germany than it is in Britain. In Britain a quarter of the university intake comes from working class families; in the other countries mentioned only between five and seven per cent. The middle- and upper-middle-class origins of civil servants in those two countries is ever higher than it is in Britain. The 'worker' percentage in parliament, which is some seventeen per cent in Britain, is a mere six and a half per cent in France (1967) and fifteen per cent in the German *Bundestag* (1961).[3] Few observers have, seemingly, tried to apply to the U.S.A. those same indicators of social inequality which are so unsparingly applied – and notably by American

3. An overstatement: the figure comprises both employers *and* officials of the trade unions and of the social administration. G. Braünthal, *The Federation of German Industry in Politics*, Cornell Press, 1965, p. 157.

observers – to class-ridden Britain. Nobody would ever pretend that income differentials or the inequalities in the distribution of wealth were less in the U.S.A. than in Britain, and, as far as the U.S. Congress is concerned, the manual 'worker' is almost totally absent. And although, to be sure, educational opportunity is more widespread in the U.S.A. than it is in Britain this seems to have singularly little effect upon the class composition of the 180 top executive posts in the government. These comprise the Cabinet, the military secretaries and under-secretaries, the under-secretaries and assistant secretaries and general counsel of the departments, the administrators and deputy administrators of the largest federal agencies and the members of seven of the extremely influential regulatory commissions. Between 1933 and 1965, 1,029 men and twelve women held these posts. There is a popular legend that this corps is predominantly W.A.S.P. (White Anglo-Saxon Protestant) from the eastern seaboard, and this popular legend has been proved right. During this period, over half came from the large cities of the eastern sea-board; three-quarters were protestant and one in four was Episcopalian – a sect that comprises only three per cent of the total population. Jews had their proportion of these posts – but Roman Catholics, who make up thirty-six per cent of the population, only held nineteen per cent of the posts. Nor is that all. Of the entire set, no less than four out of ten went to private schools and twenty per cent to very exclusive ones; and over twenty-five per cent had proceeded thence to Ivy League universities. In the most import-ant of the departments the ratios were much higher than these average figures for the entire set. Though only six per cent of the U.S. school population go to private schools, sixty per cent of the Treasury men, and roughly the same proportion in the State Department, were privately educated.[4]

The other method of demonstrating the relative, rather than the intrinsic or absolute, nature of class polarization in Britain is to examine voting statistics in a different way. Table 10 shows that British parties are by no means based exclusively on class differences, and, above all, that a high proportion of 'working-class' and 'very poor' electors vote Conservative.

4. *Men who Govern*, The Brookings Institute, New York, 1968.

Nearly two-thirds of the Conservative vote in 1966, a disastrous
year for that party, came from the working and very poor classes!
This fact alone blurs the facile assumptions of a class-orientated
politics. Which brings us back to our earlier point: that whereas

TABLE 10. PARLIAMENTARY VOTING BY SOCIAL CLASS (II)
(Percentage share of each class in voting for Conservative, Labour and
Liberal Parties, in 1959, 1964, 1966)

Class	Conservative			Labour			Liberal		
	1959	1964	1966	1959	1964	1966	1959	1964	1966
Upper-middle	9	10	10	–	2	2	5	5	6
Middle	34	34	31	8	11	14	28	27	20
Working	52	50	52	76	75	70	56	61	65
Very poor	5	6	7	16	12	14	11	7	9
Total vote:	100	100	100	100	100	100	100	100	100

Source: British Institute of Public Opinion, 'quota' samples.

religion and notably the position of the Catholic Church are
important in French and German and Italian politics, whereas
ethnic differences play a vital role in Belgian or Canadian politics
and whereas the region is important in U.S. politics – none of
these is very significant in British politics. Social inequality and
class cleavage are likewise, in their various ways, factors in the
politics of all these countries. In Britain however, where they are
also factors, there are no other cleavages to compete with them.
It is in this qualified sense that British politics are about equality.

II. THE CONSTITUTIONAL FRAMEWORK

(1) *Basic characteristics*

For my purposes, *constitutions* are codes of rules which govern
the allocation of functions, powers and duties among the various
governmental agencies and their officers, and define the relationships between them and the public. They are, however, often
much more than this. Some contain lengthy preambles setting

forth moral prescriptions and political, social and economic aspirations. Some go farther and prescribe details regulating secondary issues like social security or labour law provisions. At the same time, they are seldom as complete as my own definition suggests. Political parties, for instance, are a major political factor today; yet many constitutions omit even a mention of them. The electoral law is another major political factor; again, it is rare to find this prescribed in the constitution.

But whether the rules be prolix like India's or economical like those of the U.S.A., they are, overwhelmingly, *codified* in a single document – and a document, moreover that usually has a special status in law. In the entire range of the 122 sovereign independent states existing at the time of writing, there are only two exceptions. One is Israel. The other is Britain.

So, the first feature of the British Constitution is that it is *uncodified*. To find the constitutional position on any one point, any (or all) of five different sources must be consulted. This source may be a statute, i.e., an Act of Parliament: for example, the responsibility of a minister for acts of the National Coal Board is defined, in the first instance at any rate, in the Coal Mines Nationalization Act, 1946. Or else the source may be a judicial pronouncement on the meaning of the relevant words in such a statute. Or, again, the source may not be a statute, but a principle of the Common Law – from which certain basic principles, notably those relating to freedom of expression, of assembly and of association are, in the first instance, derived. Then there is a very special and narrow body of law that relates to the status and operation of Parliament and its members, the *lex et consuetudo parliamenti*, which, in so far as it protects members from 'molestation' (e.g., intimidation and other kinds of outside pressure), sometimes plays a significant role in the political process. Now all of these sources are, in one way or another, *written down*. This is why I have not used the old fashioned distinction between written and unwritten constitutions. The true distinction is between codified and uncodified ones; the more particularly since, in the British case, there is a fifth element which is not written down nor codified at all, and is a set of usages, not juridical rules. This element, the most significant, is referred to as *the conventions* of the Constitution. The conventions are rules of practice and interpretation which by their antiquity and utility have acquired a normative, a binding quality. It is often asked: 'What makes the convention (which is not a law) binding?', and one of the (albeit undeservedly) famous works on the Constitution, Dicey's *Introduction to the Study of the Law of the Constitution* (1885), was a (typically perverse) attempt to solve this conundrum. But the answer is simple: the conventions are held to be binding by the political actors because, if they were not, they would not be 'conventions'. Because a convention is, precisely, 'a general agreement or consent as embodied in any accepted usage, standard' (O.E.D.). It is fruitless to ask why a 'general agreement' is 'binding', because that is the natural entailment of 'general agreement'. (More meaningfully, one might ask why the British rely on general agreements of such a nature to so much greater an extent than other nations. But that is a different question.) Among these conventions, then, are some of the key points of the working constitution: that Parliament must convene at least once in a year, that the sovereign does not attend Cabinet meetings, that ministers who lose the support of the Commons on a major policy issue must resign, or try to reverse the situation by requesting the sovereign to grant a dissolution of Parliament so that they can try their luck at a general election. And so forth. Nearly all codified constitutions have to be supplemented by conventions. The British Constitution is unusual in that its conventions are so numerous and so important relative to the written elements.

In the second place, the Constitution is *flexible*. With a very few exceptions (notably the Parliament Acts of 1911 and 1949, where Parliament has provided a more complicated procedure for amending a statute than the common one) no greater legislative sanctity attaches to a law of constitutional significance than to any other. The number of M.P.s could be altered by a procedure identical to that used to change the law relating to gaming and lotteries.

Thirdly, the United Kingdom, despite the terms of the Treaty of Union with Scotland and the existence of the Northern Ireland Parliament, is a *unitary* not a federal state. No territorial assembly inside its frontiers enjoys a coequal legal status to that of the Parliament of Westminster. This contrasts signally with the situation in the U.S.A., as will be seen later.

Fourthly, by the same token, Parliament is supreme. The courts of law recognize a statute, passed in due form by Parliament, as being binding upon them, and that they must therefore apply it. Neither they nor any other authority in the U.K. is competent to set statutes aside or override them. This holds true irrespective of the content of the laws – even of laws that act retrospectively. Here again the position contrasts sharply with that in the U.S.A.

Fifthly, in the 'type' of the liberal-democratic régime as expounded in Chapter 2, the 'separation of powers' was mentioned as one of its characteristic features. In the U.S.A., as will be seen, this principle operates in a strict form; but not so in Britain. There, Parliament comprises both the supreme executive branch (the Cabinet) and the supreme legislative branch. In law, too, Parliament is regarded as the highest court in the land – this is how lawyers explain why the law courts cannot query or set aside its duly enacted statutes; they argue that they are inferior courts to the 'High Court of Parliament'. Yet on a more mundane plane, the principle of the separation of powers does operate in a 'weak' sense. Parliament – whether considered as a legislature or as the executive – does not interfere in the day-to-day workings of the courts of law; the tenure of the judges is protected from day-to-day political pressure. Again, the inferior ranks of the executive – i.e. the civil servants – are, likewise, neither appointed by nor dismissed by Parliament. They are appointed by an independent commission under strict rules of public competition. Once appointed they are immediately answerable to their minister, and it is through him that their views are conveyed to Parliament and vice versa.

Sixthly and finally, the system of government is most conveniently described as *cabinet* government – unlike other possible liberal-democratic forms such as the 'parliamentary' system of the French Third and Fourth Republics, the clear-cut presidential system of the U.S.A. or the muzzy presidential form of the French Fifth Republic.

(2) *A cabinet system*

At the moment of writing, a learned debate is proceeding as to whether the term 'cabinet government' is not a misnomer and whether 'prime ministerial government' is not a more accurate description of the British system. This is a question that I shall pick up later, since it is not intelligible at all except within the framework of the conventional 'cabinet government' concept.

In law the government of the United Kingdom is vested in a composite body styled the Crown-in-Parliament. This consists of the Sovereign, nominally the supreme executive, in whose name ministers carry out the duties with which they have been charged – either by custom and precedent (the 'prerogative powers') or by statute; of the House of Lords; and of the House of Commons. In practice, the effective political authority of the sovereign is all but negligible, that of the Lords marginal and of the Commons itself becoming ever more formal and nominal as the power of the ministers and particularly of the prime minister has waxed.

As to the Sovereign: it is debatable whether or not she still retains the right to refuse a request by her prime minister to dissolve Parliament – and thus precipitate a general election. Formally this right exists but it has never been exercised in the present century. The Sovereign also possesses the rights to 'be consulted, to encourage and to warn' and in this capacity has access to all governmental information; but these so-called prerogatives only give access to influence, they do not confer an authority to intervene. Finally, however, the Sovereign may in certain circumstances have some discretion as to the choice of a prime minister: briefly, when the majority party in the House of Commons has no recognized leader or deputy leader, or, even if it has, is bitterly divided over his merits; or when there is no single majority party in the House. The former situation occurred in 1957, when the question arose of appointing a successor to the then Sir Anthony Eden who had resigned the premiership; the second arose in 1923, and again, in a sense, in 1931.

As to the Lords: this strange and antique body, from which the Commons is historically sprung, and which is currently composed of over one thousand hereditary peers, some prelates and about one hundred and sixty life peers of singularly recent creation, has no power to reject a finance bill of the Commons and has no veto power over other types of bills – merely the power to delay them for the maximum of a year. Moreover, under the Labour governments (1964 to the present day) it has never dared to use even this limited power (though it has sometimes put the Commons in the dilemma of accepting 'wrecking' amendments or dropping its bill).

So it is that what the old lawyer Blackstone termed 'the omnipotence of Parliament' has come to reside in the Lower House: the elected House of Commons. And inside this, it has come to reside in that inner council of ministers called the Cabinet – and inside this, increasingly, in the prime minister.

The Commons consists of 630 members, elected in single-member constituencies by universal suffrage at intervals of at most five years. It is organized along party lines, the government party on one side and the opposition party or parties facing it on the other. The bulk of its business, and certainly all the most important business, revolves around the proposals of the *Cabinet*. This does not comprise all ministers by any means. It consists of some twenty (in 1969, twenty-one) ministers, who form the policy-making inner circle. The Cabinet – and hence the government in general – is headed by the prime minister. The leader of the majority party, he is the personal choice of the sovereign; and the members of the Cabinet are *his* personal choice. The whole ministry, including the Cabinet, is a corporate body, all ministers being jointly responsible for policy, and this is called, collo-quially, 'the government'. But, inside the government, the Cabinet is the policy-making body and prime mover.

Certain working conventions regulate Cabinet rule. Parliament is legally supreme throughout the United Kingdom; at least one session of Parliament takes place each year; the majority party are entitled to have their leader entrusted by the Crown with the formation of the ministry; and this ministry is collectively responsible to Parliament for all acts of policy, though for any mishandling or omissions that may occur in the administration of his department the individual minister is responsible, and not his colleagues as a whole. Fifthly, the opposition has a special status inside the House of Commons, a status which is implicitly recognized in the standing orders of the House, as well as in parliamentary usage. (For instance, it is part of parliamentary usage that, if the opposition puts down a motion of censure, the Cabinet must find time to have that debated and cannot morally refuse to have it debated.) Sixthly, a government out-voted in the Commons on a matter of confidence must resign, while a government that cannot carry the House with it on a vital issue may resign if it so wishes. Another convention is that if the prime minister resigns, the whole of his government must resign. Finally, if a general election returns a majority against it, then it must resign.

Inside the Commons the Cabinet conducts a dialogue with the opposition, which is led by its own 'shadow Cabinet'. The Cabinet controls the time-table of the House within certain limits laid down by standing orders, it initiates most laws and all financial measures and it carries on the day-to-day administration. It must at all times convince its back-benchers – although these are likely to be three-quarters convinced already by the exhilaration of being on the governing side of the House. On the other hand it faces the opposition and it is primarily with this, the minority in the House, that the dialogue is nowadays conducted.

The opposition, however, is doubly circumscribed. To begin with, it is excluded from any share in formulating the policy to be presented to the Commons; and secondly, when the government presents this policy to the House, it is in a minority there. Certainly, it shares some of the offices of the House with the government party, it is guaranteed large blocks of time for airing issues or censuring the government and it is consulted on the business of each week. But floor votes are rigidly disciplined and in this century governments have made even trivial issues 'matters of confidence' on which they stake their life; so that the likelihood of the opposition turning out the government on a straight motion of censure is *nil*.

So, to outward seeming, the Cabinet is powerful, durable and stable. In practice it is circumscribed and vulnerable to pressure.

One reason lies in the pluralistic character of British political activity – i.e. in the existence of social and economic associations which counter-check the power of the government. Another lies in the electoral system and the natures of the parties, as a consequence of which only a tiny margin of votes is necessary to turn out a government and install the opposition in power. A third lies in the way the House serves as an arena wherein the leverage of these two factors is brought to bear upon the government's policies. That this is so, and how it is so, is the burden of what follows.

III. PRESSURE GROUPS

As I have already pointed out, in Chapter 2, the freedoms of expression, of assembly, and of association are *constitutive* elements of a liberal-democracy. Unless these exist in a fairly unqualified form, the system of government is either falsified (it becomes a façade-democracy) or else it is frustrated, since the government cannot (except by chance) represent public opinion, and cannot be made accountable to it. But, by the same token, these freedoms are an open licence to any individuals or groups to set up in opposition to the government. In so far as they are able to defy the government by virtue of their numbers, wealth or other forms of social influence, and deny it the collaboration of which it stands in need, they circumscribe its freedom of action.

Thus it is that in all liberal-democracies there exist, not one, but two channels of popular representation. Political parties and the electoral process are one; pressure groups provide the other.

There are some liberal-democracies, of which Israel is the striking example, where the pressure groups are controlled by the various political parties or by a number of these, or else put up their own candidates and run for election themselves and thus turn into fragmentary and highly sectional parties. This characteristic is present to some extent in France also, though less so today than a decade ago. But in other liberal-democracies, of which the U.S.A. is the outstanding example, the pressure groups are, by and large, autonomous and politically neutral bodies, which bargain with the political parties and the bureaucracy irrespective of the political complexion of the government in power.

With the massive exception of the Labour Party/trade-union relationship, Britain resembles the U.S.A. Here, then, party and electoral system provide for a (maximal) term of five years' general programme of policy; the pressure group system, however, qualifies this. Without the disciplined party majority the Cabinet policy would be incoherent; without the pressure groups to modify this policy it would be ill-conceived or unrepresentative and probably both. Party and pressure group are distinguishable, but they are not isolated. On the contrary they interconnect, and even interpenetrate, at bureaucratic, party and ministerial levels. In brief, pressure groups are an auxiliary circuit of representation. And the British system of government depends on them just as much as it does on the party system.

They fall into two main groups, together with a hybrid. Those having a function or economic good at stake are 'interest groups', like trade unions, churches and universities. Others, whose purpose is propagandist, like the societies for the protection of wild birds or children or animals, are 'promotional' groups. In the first the association (or firm) exists for the benefit of its members (the Automobile Association is an outstanding example), though universally each interest group believes that its interest is also the nation's and to this extent all are 'promotional'. In the second, the members belong to the association for the good of the cause it is promoting. The hybrid group includes such associations as the Roads Campaign Council, which is avowedly propagandist but overtly financed and indeed established by interest groups which have a material stake in road use or construction.

British society is extremely rich in groups like these. The number of those serving the needs of commerce and industry is not known but is in excess of 2,500. Among them the National Farmers' Union (200,000 members, some seventy-five per cent of the total number of farmers (1967)), the Confederation of British Industry (180 trade associations, nearly 13,000 individual firms and a bureaucracy of 300 (1966)) and the Association of

British Chambers of Commerce (representing 60,000 firms (1966))
are the most influential. Of the civilian labour force, which
numbers some twenty-four million, nine and a half million
belong to trade unions, and nearly nine million of these to unions
affiliated to the Trades Union Congress. Likewise the co-operative
movement comprises (1966) 801 retail trading societies with a
combined membership of over thirteen million. The professions
are increasingly well organized and becoming more militant:
among these the British Medical Association, the National Union
of Teachers and the National Association of Local and Government Officers are highly influential.

To achieve their aim – i.e., to influence policy – pressure
groups aim at any or all of three targets: the executive (ministers
and the civil service), Parliament, and the general public. The
choice of target is governed by expediency. In general, the more
material the interest, the greater the tendency to aim at the civil
service, and, failing that, the House of Commons. The more
propagandist the association, the greater the tendency to aim at
the general public and then the legislature.

Civil servants need the knowledge, the judgement and often
the collaboration of the affected interests when they come to
formulate a policy. Indeed in some cases the policy is not
applicable at all unless the interest groups acquiesce – for instance, to decree a wage freeze without first ensuring that trade
union leaders will co-operate with it would simply cause a rash
of strikes. In fact, the contact between interest groups and civil
servants is continuous. Groups are invited to express their views
to official inquiries such as royal commissions or departmental
committees of inquiry; representatives of appropriate groups are
invited to serve on the 500 or so advisory committees attached to
the various departments in order to assist them; and in certain
cases a tradition has grown up of ministries consulting the
relevant interest group before formulating a policy. And side by
side with those formal contacts the informal ones – telephone
and personal conversations – are close and continuous.

Members of Parliament (and indeed, Peers also) frequently
'represent' an outside interest group. Some are members, officers
or spokesmen of such a group when still parliamentary candidates;

others become so, on the invitation of a group, when they enter the House; other M.P.s may be approached *ad hoc* to speak up for a group on a particular occasion. Equally important, the great parties incorporate powerful outside interests. Seventy-nine trade unions are affiliated to the Labour Party; they provide most of its campaign funds, almost all the running expenses of its national H.Q. offices and command an overwhelming number of votes at its annual conference. In 1969, trade-union-sponsored M.P.s held 127 of the 348 Labour seats in the Commons. No business or finance groups are affiliated to the Conservative Party in this formal way but the personal linkage between them and the Conservative Party, in the House and in the constituencies, makes the Conservative Party their spokesman. Currently, (1969) at least seventy of the Conservative Party's 263 M.P.s are company directors and another thirty-eight are farmers and land-owners, and this much under-represents the true situation, since many listed as lawyers, for instance, direct companies also.

Interest groups turn to the House of Commons either to reinforce the representations they are making to ministers and civil servants or to modify the decisions of these where representations have failed. Their pressure is usually checked by the disciplined voting of the parties in the House but this does not prevent marginal amendments being adopted in large numbers. Substantial concessions are rarer. Nevertheless, whenever the opposition does appear to extract a substantial concession from the government it will usually be discovered that this is because they are expressing the representations of powerful outside groups which the government decides it must placate. Thus the very material concessions made by the Labour government in its Finance Bill of 1965 were almost entirely in matters where outside interests had already made their position known to the Chancellor in private meetings. This could be known as the 'Esau phenomenon': 'The voice is Jacob's voice, but the hands are the hands of Esau.'

The groups that cultivate the general public tend to be the promotional ones rather than the interest groups. By their nature these groups do not perform functions which are indispensable to society and which the administrators, as a consequence, have a vicarious responsibility to keep going. Hence the bargaining power of such groups *vis-à-vis* administrative departments is limited or non-existent. Usually, any influence they can wield over the administrators comes from a public outcry, taken up by M.P.s or entire parties. This is how the Campaign for Nuclear Disarmament tried to influence the government. In contrast to this, although some interest groups do – or have in the past – conducted public relations campaigns to keep their names sweet in the public nostrils, few openly cultivate the public support of specific objectives. For one thing, they are reluctant to intervene in favour of one party rather than another in election campaigns – which in any case would do them no good because parliamentary candidates adhere to the programmes laid down by their parties and are warned by their respective H.Q.s not to go beyond them. For all this, some groups have launched public campaigns. The National Union of Teachers, for instance, has on several occasions mounted a 'selective' campaign aimed at local opinion leaders; and some industries, notably the steel industry, have mounted 'saturation' campaigns at enormous cost to ward off the threat of nationalization by a triumphant Labour Party. (The evidence shows that these steel campaigns were a waste of time and money.)

Returning to the interest groups: it should be clear that these groups work pre-eminently at the executive level. And the ambition of an interest group is to acquire a close working relationship with the appropriate government department. The crown of this ambition is what may be dubbed 'consultative status'. This means that the ministry recognizes a group as so widely representative of its membership and so influential among it that the organization has, like the British sovereign, 'the right to be consulted, the right to encourage and the right to warn'. It is because they have so largely acquired this consultative status that the most influential of the pressure groups are the most silent. The Confederation of British Industry, the Trades Union Council, the County Councils Association and the like usually achieve their results closeted in secret within the ministry. Nearly always the noise a pressure group makes is inversely proportional to the influence it wields.

Such groups perform an essential function in the liberal-democracy. They provide the government with information it cannot in the ordinary way possess; they challenge government policy or conversely suggest new initiatives, so permitting their membership access to government independent of the only other two channels open, namely, the local M.P. or the local party organization; they often perform indispensable administrative services for the government departments; and in so far as they dispose of a social and economic leverage they act as so many checks and balances upon the executive.

But at the same time the arrangements present dangers. For one thing, not all pressure groups enjoy the same access or influence. Interest groups, because they can withdraw their needed collaboration, enjoy much greater access and influence than promotional groups. Among the interest groups, the ones that represent producers – whether employers or the labour force – are more influential than groups representing, say, the universities or the consumers. True, they can only rarely make a government do what they want; but they can and do hinder or even veto what a government would like them to do. This imbalance among the various groups gives society a permanent bias in favour of the socially powerful.

A second danger lies in the effects of 'consultative status'. I have stressed how closely civil service and interest groups work together. In a number of instances the relationship has become so close that it is *closed*. The narrow specialized public has, rightly, been brought into policy-making; by the same exercise, the broader generalized public has been shut out of it. Increasingly, what the minister presents to the Commons is a package arrangement agreed between the civil servants and the representatives of the outside groups. In the House, party discipline inhibits back-benchers from challenging their government; even if it did not, the information and evidence on which the package depends are confidential and have not been disclosed; and even if they had been, the nature of the package is so well balanced a set of compromises that if any one part were overturned in the House the entire deal would have to be re-negotiated. The closed relationship between interest groups and civil servants has left the Commons without a role – except the one which David Wood of *The Times* has so well described as the role of a pianola, 'mechanically rendering tunes composed jointly by departments of state and whatever organized interests happen to be affected'.[5]

IV. THE PARTY SYSTEM

For many years Britain has been alternately governed by Cabinets drawn from either the Labour or the Conservative Parties. The Liberal Party is a mere remnant, for all that it improved its situation in 1964 and 1966 and has (1969) twelve seats in the Commons. The two-party system is the key to understanding how the Constitution really works; it is responsible for six of its characteristics: the near certainty that one party or the other will have a clear majority in the House; the consequent formation of a Cabinet drawn from this majority party; the stability of this Cabinet, since its majority is guaranteed; the durability of this Cabinet for the full term of the Parliament's life; the unambiguous responsibility of the Cabinet for what happens during its term of office; and the presentation to the electorate of a clear choice between the government party and the opposition.

The Labour, Liberal and Conservative Parties have deep roots. Membership of a political party implies some commitment at least, much more than 'registration' of membership in a political party as understood in the United States. In Britain nobody will carry a party card and pay the party subscription, unless he is, to put it at its very lowest, what the public opinion polls describe as 'a Labour or a Conservative *incliner*'. The total electorate is some 37,000,000 people. Of this, Conservative Party members number some two and a half million and Liberal Party members about one and a third million; the Labour Party claims six and a half million members. The total, well over nine million, is one in four of the total electorate. This degree of penetration is very high indeed. The British parties also differ from the French parties or American (national) parties, in their high degree of organization. Each possesses paid local agents and paid

5. *The Times*, 29 January 1963.

regional and headquarters staff. All publish party literature and carry out extensive programmes of party activities. A further characteristic is their high discipline. In both the Labour and the Conservative Parties the parliamentary candidate has to satisfy certain minimal requirements laid down by national headquarters: no candidate is likely to secure the party leader's endorsement and the support of his local association headquarters organization unless he is a member of the party and pledges allegiance to its programme; and, if elected to the House, he is expected to vote with his party on the summons of a 'three-line whip' unless some matter of conscience arises. In practice, voting discipline is not only high, but is fairly regularly maintained. Floor revolts are rare, and, when they do occur, usually involve abstaining rather than crossing the floor of the House and voting with the other side.

A further characteristic of these parties is that they are *programmatic*. They spend a good deal of the time before an election in preparing a programme of action which they expect to carry out if returned with a majority. From these party programmes are extracted the parties' election manifestos. These consist of a list of fairly specific promises; the party that wins will claim a 'mandate' to carry them out and will, indeed, be expected to do so, unless it can produce convincing reasons to the contrary.

The British parties are not exclusively class parties, but they are undoubtedly orientated towards class issues and supported along broadly class lines. It is here that social cleavage between capital and labour makes itself felt. On the whole the Labour Party is the party of organized labour and the very poor, while the Conservative Party is a very much more heterogeneous party which draws support from all sections of the population. Briefly speaking, nine-tenths of Labour support comes from the working class and the very poor, but, in the Conservative Party, the proportion is only fifty-five per cent. For the Labour Party only ten per cent of support comes from the upper-middle and middle classes; for the Conservative Party the proportion of support drawn from these two classes is forty-five per cent. The manual working class is split roughly in the proportion of two Labour voters to one Conservative; for all that, there is a wide overlap of manual-working-class votes between both parties.

The two-party nature of the system is undoubtedly assisted by the mode of election. The country is divided into 630 constituencies, each returning one member, and it is the candidate with most votes who is declared elected. In a three-cornered contest a candidate can be elected with only thirty-four per cent of the total vote. If one party has for some reason or another lost electoral support and tends habitually to come third in such a race, it soon begins to lose its votes to one or other of the two parties which tend to top the poll. In this way, once a party has consistently dropped to third place it tends to be pushed out of the race altogether. Its supporters feel that a vote for it is wasted and they tend to 'polarize' between one or other of the two commanding parties. Furthermore, it is very difficult to reverse this situation: the third party would have to make a very large leap in public esteem before coming near enough to the two top contenders to convince voters it had a real chance of winning, and so take votes from them.

There is a second point to be noted in connexion with the effect of the electoral system upon the parties: the *extreme* sensitivity of the electoral mechanism. This can be shown first of all by what is known as the 'cube law'. This is a law, not in the sense that it is 'necessary', but in the sense that empirically it seems to fit past elections which have been contested primarily by the two main parties. In such situations it has been shown that the distribution of seats in the House of Commons is not directly correlated with the distribution of votes in the country but varies according to the following formula: the seats of Party A stand in respect to the seats of Party B as the cube of the votes cast for Party A stands to the cube of the votes cast for Party B. The effect of this is that a very slight edge in votes in the country will give the leading party a very much greater margin of seats over its rivals in the House of Commons. In short, the electoral system gives a bonus of seats to the party which is ahead, even though it may be ahead by only a small fraction of the popular vote. And the further it is ahead in popular votes the greater does this bonus tend to become.

The other way of looking at this is to consider the nature of 'swing'. Swing is a notional concept: to put it at its crudest, it is a measure of the change in either party's share of the vote. Consider the case of an election in which candidate A secures forty-nine per cent of the vote and candidate B secures fifty-one per cent. Now consider a second election in which these proportions are reversed. Candidate B receives forty-nine per cent of the vote and candidate A now receives fifty-one per cent. This is as if two people out of each hundred had deserted one candidate in favour of the other. It therefore represents a swing of two out of one hundred or two per cent. Such is the closeness of the division of the British electorate between the two major parties that a very large number of constituencies are held by majorities which are so small that a very tiny swing of opinion from one party to another would be sufficient to turn the existing candidate out and put his rival in. It was because of this that in the 1964 election a Conservative majority of nearly one hundred was not only wiped out, but converted into a minority of fourteen seats by a swing of opinion away from the Conservatives of only 3·5 per cent. This is as much as to say that little more than *three votes in every hundred* were able to turn one government out and install another.

The party structures

Conservatives become party members by joining a local association and paying a weekly subscription; in this way, all the party members are individual members. The structure of the party comprises three elements, which nowadays intertwine with one another. One is the 'representative organ' – the National Union of Conservative and Unionist Associations. This holds an annual conference (as well as an annual sort of half conference which goes by the name of the 'council' of the association). The conference gives equal representation to each of the constituency associations. On the whole it is a tame affair, partly due to its very large size (over 4,000 delegates), partly due to its constitutional status: it has no power to make policy but can only make recommendations to the party leader. It is primarily a sounding-board although in the past, notably in the nineteen thirties, it became a decisive influence when the leadership was split on major policy. The second party element, the leader, is formally entrusted with the task of defining policy. Elected by the parliamentary party on a system of run-off ballots, he holds office indefinitely, which is not to say that he cannot be induced to resign – as for instance Sir Alec Douglas-Home was, in 1965. At his disposal the leader has the party's third component, the Central Office. This is a powerful organization of full-time party officials, at headquarters and also in the regions. And it takes under its wing the professional party agents in the constituencies although these are chosen and paid by the membership of those constituencies. But training, pay and conditions are laid down by the Central Office organization, and the local agents form part of its operational network.

By contrast with the Conservatives, the Labour Party has a dual membership; and indeed it also features another and unfortunate duality in its organization, namely that of the annual conference and the parliamentary party.

There are two ways of becoming a Labour Party member, namely, either membership of an affiliated organization, or direct membership of and subscription to a local constituency organization. Some members enjoy both types of membership at once, a fact that complicates the true reckoning of total membership.

Most of the affiliated organizations are in fact trade unions (but *not* the Trades Union Congress itself). While the total party membership stands at some six and a half million (including the dual members), only about 800,000 of these are individual members. With few exceptions the remainder are members of trade unions who become members through paying a subscription called the 'political levy' each week to their trade union which, itself, is an affiliate of the party. At present seventy-nine trade unions are so affiliated. But whereas the trade unionist who wants to become a member of the party simply pays his weekly subscription – or rather does nothing to prevent this being deducted every week from his pay packet – the trade unionist who does not want to belong has to sign a form to that effect.

The trade unions provide most of the party funds and the vast bulk of the running costs of the central headquarters (Transport House). Of its 1965 revenue (£380,000) about £280,000 came from the trade unions. In 1966 the trade-union contribution was £270,000. Their contribution to election fighting funds is much greater – since 1945 they have never contributed less than eighty per cent of these. If one considers the entire expenditure of the party in a normal year, i.e., including both headquarters' and constituencies' expenditure, then the trade unions contribute fifty-five per cent of it.

Quite apart from the leverage which such massive contributions afford them, the trade unions are highly influential because they preponderate in the annual conference. There, they are represented in proportion to their declared Labour Party membership, so that in total they exceed the constituency party votes in the ratio of six to one. Now, unlike the Conservative Conference, the Labour Party Conference has two very important privileges, namely, that of electing its National Executive, which is the highest organ of the party while the conference is not sitting, and that of formulating policies: on a two-thirds vote, a conference policy resolution becomes part of the party programme. To attenuate the vast preponderance of the trade-unionist-member vote in the elections to the National Executive, seven special places are reserved for the constituency parties, and one for the co-operative movement. Twelve more are reserved for the trade unionists, and seven seats, which are reserved for women, are voted on by the entire membership, trade union and other. The leader of the Parliamentary Labour Party and the deputy leader are *ex officio* members; finally there is the party treasurer, who is elected by the entire conference.

The relationship of the annual conference to the parliamentary party has always been a bone of contention, since in theory the latter is autonomous. The issue was tested in 1960 when the conference rejected the resolution on nuclear weapons which the parliamentary party approved and substituted one which it did not approve. A period of high tension between the two followed until, in the succeeding year, the conference suffered a change of mind and the two bodies found they could agree.

The party ideologies

The Conservative Party is the 'national' and to that extent the 'nationalistic' party. It claims to stand for the entire nation not for any one section. The desirability of national unity is the centre piece of its ideology, such as it is. It is by reference to this dogma that it resists the notion of class struggle, and in contrast proclaims the necessity for capital–labour co-operation and a 'property-owning democracy'. It proclaims the need for freer competition in industry and the end of restrictive practices both between employers and among employees. It is the party of social mobility. 'Quality and not equality' and 'opportunity rather than security' are two of its slogans. In its eyes, private enterprise and the profit motive fulfil vital social and economic roles. It proclaims the desirability of promoting private initiatives and on these grounds stands for decentralization of administrative functions, private enterprise rather than public ownership of industry, the 'little man' as against the monopoly, and the right of minorities against the majority – though, as might be expected, it is very selective about *which* minorities are to be so favoured (e.g., note its attitudes towards coloured immigrants). In foreign affairs it still is the party of national self-assertion, though it has slowly and reluctantly come to realize that the country is not nowadays capable of asserting itself overmuch. It is the *ex-imperial* party. But since the Empire was liquidated and succeeded by the Commonwealth, and since the latter has ceased to be a small number of 'white' Dominions and become an association of ex-imperial dependencies which is overwhelmingly inhabited by coloured peoples, the mass of the Conservatives have become highly disenchanted with it.

Yet the party eschews ideology. It has always claimed to be realistic and empirical, and indeed between 1959 and 1964, as will be seen, its 'realism' became so marked as entirely to discount its claim to consistency. From the party of the Commonwealth it has become the party of accession to the Common Market. After its defeat in 1945 it was able to accommodate itself very rapidly to the Labour concept of the Welfare State, and likewise, though the champion of private enterprise, it is not always opposed to public ownership or control; indeed the earliest experiments in these forms, e.g., the B.B.C., the Central Electricity Board and the agricultural marketing boards set up in the thirties, were all introduced by the Conservatives.

More than half its total vote is working class, and therefore this vote is vital for its survival. Hence, whatever else it may do for other classes of the community, it must retain a firm anchorage among the manual workers who make up seventy per cent of the employed population. And until 1964 it was remarkably successful. Yet despite this working-class basis, its leadership and notably its M.P.s are overwhelmingly from the richer sectors of society. In the 1966 Parliament, forty-six per cent were from the professions and thirty per cent were businessmen. But this grossly underestimates the proportion of the latter since many professional men (lawyers, in particular) have business interests. In addition the party draws its M.P.s very largely from the public schools. In 1966 no less than seventy-seven of the 253 M.P.s came from three schools – Winchester, Eton and Harrow – while 204 came from some kind of public school, and well over half the party had been to Oxford or Cambridge.

The Labour Party, on the other hand, is more overtly ideological. In home affairs it lays its stress on the need for equality: as between classes and as between races. It demands equality of opportunity and, also, equality – or near equality – of rewards. It gives a very high priority to social provision, and advocates an indefinite extension of public ownership and control. In foreign affairs the party outlook (not its leaders' in the cabinet) is pacifist and parochial and fervently anti-colonial and has a touching faith in the United Nations. It is far less hesitant about cutting defence expenditure and closing overseas bases than any Conservative government is ever likely to be. It was – until recently – stridently anti-European and pro-Commonwealth – the latter embodying its ideal of a multiracial association. It used, also, to have strong reservations about the possession of a nuclear capability in defence affairs. Economically, it stood for expansionist policies, in contrast to the alleged Conservative emphasis on deflation, the money mechanism and low growth rates. But in all these respects it has changed since it reached office in 1964.

Conservative and Labour policies 1959–64

With the Conservative Party's third successive electoral post-war victory in 1959 a change came over both the main parties. Conservative successes, 1951–9, had been achieved through a number of reasons. First, they had adopted as part of their policy the encouragement of self-advancement among what one might call the 'rising working class'. Secondly, there was a much greater will to win on the part of Conservative supporters than on the part of Labour supporters. (This becomes quite clear if one compares the answers given by respondents to Gallup polls.) Thirdly, they showed much greater adaptability than their rivals. They adapted themselves to full employment, to the Welfare State, to the break-up of the Empire. A fourth reason was that, long before the Labour Party did so, they adopted professional standards of organization. In all this they were assisted by manifest confusion and, indeed, obsolescence on the part of the Labour Party, especially from 1958 to 1963, when it was divided over nuclear defence and confused about the Common Market, argued over the necessity and scope for further nationalization, held obsolete notions about public ownership and appeared to surrender too much to trade-union vested interests. Furthermore, all this time it was unwilling to raise money and spend money on public relations.

From 1963 this entirely changed. Indeed the situation of the two parties reversed itself. The Conservatives had pressed their empiricism too far. By deciding to seek accession to the European Common Market in 1961 they had, except for a minority, turned their back upon the special position of the Commonwealth which hitherto had played a central role in their attitudes. In trumpeting 'modernization' they now confessed belief in the concept of 'planning', a doctrine buried for ten years and which they had hitherto abhorred. In 1964 their M.P.s entered upon a self-destructive orgy when many of their back-benchers rebelled against the Resale Price Maintenance Bill. The party seemed to be governed by no intelligible principle. In addition when Mr Macmillan, the prime minister, resigned in 1963, leaving the party no obvious successor, the party tore itself to pieces in discreditable manoeuvring while selecting a leader. In the event the choice went to an elder statesman, brought down from the House of Lords, Sir Alec Douglas-Home. Sir Alec, who had many virtues and was able to rally the party very ably between its nadir in 1963 and the general election of 1964, nevertheless appeared to the country to lack the dynamic of a prime minister and compared unfavourably with his Labour counterpart, Mr Wilson. Moreover, the mode by which his election had been determined left whirlpools of intrigue and dissidence in his party and a profound feeling of *malaise*. And finally, for all its thirteen years in office, the party had failed to dominate the 'stop-go' economic cycle.

The Labour Party had, on the other hand, staged a remarkable recovery, not the least part of which was the shedding of its cloth-cap image. After the dramatic Scarborough conference of 1960, when the issue of unilateral nuclear disarmament so bitterly divided the party, it had begun to come together. The unilateralist policy was reversed in 1961. Next (still under the leadership of Mr Gaitskell, a man regarded as somewhat to the right of centre), the party came whole-heartedly out against accession to the Common Market on the terms which the Conservative Party was then approving. This united both right and left of the party (except for a highly respected but small minority). It was united, too, over its policies for social welfare, on which it had always been strong in popular esteem, and it also benefited from the evident failure of its opponents to regulate the stop-go cycle. In these circumstances the Labour Party's own proclivity for planning and controls once more enjoyed a vogue and it was able to put plans forward with a degree of plausibility which hitherto had been lacking. Thirdly, it had in Mr Wilson (the successor to Mr Gaitskell) a man somewhat left of centre in the party, who had the calibre of a prime minister and who made an immediate hit with the electorate. Fourthly, and lastly, the Labour Party after 1961 decided to shed its old-fashioned image and follow its Conservative rivals in taking the skilled advice of public relations consultants in order to project its policy in a form palatable to the electorate. At the same time it devoted a great deal of time, and money, to the reorganization of its electoral machinery.

The result of all this was a general election which was as near a dead heat as any that had taken place in Britain since the elections of 1950 and 1951 – the Labour Party being returned with a majority of only four over the Conservative and the Liberal Parties. It was with this slender lead that it undertook the task of governing the country, in October 1964. Eighteen months later, after vicissitudes in which it alternately topped the heights or plumbed the depths of popular favour, it swept back to power with a huge majority of one hundred. From that moment fortune ceased to smile on it. Its colonial policy (the Rhodesian independence issue), its foreign policy (the bid to enter the Common Market) and its economic policy, all proved unsuccessful. Dogged by a balance of payments problem like all its Conservative predecessors, it was forced to pursue an 'orthodox' economic line of deflation, stagnant production, unemployment and wage slow-downs. For all that, it failed to hold sterling to its parity and, in November 1967, was forced to devalue the pound and follow up this defeat by a package of cuts in public expenditure which with majestic impartiality simultaneously ended Britain's role as a world power and put the welfare provisions of the Labour Party's manifesto into cold storage. By February 1969, after more than six years of office, the Labour Party was in a state of self-division and doubt worse than that of the Conservative Party in 1963–4; its outlook, too, had become empirical, cynical and devoid of any single intelligible principle. From this it slowly began to emerge in 1970 as the door to Europe was opened and the balance of payments improved.

V. THE GOVERNMENT

It is imperative to understand that in Britain, quite unlike the U.S.A., the 'executive', by which I mean the governing body, is not a separate structure set apart from the legislature. On the contrary. The senior level of the executive – called loosely 'the government' and containing an inner council called 'the Cabinet' as its top echelon – itself consists of members of the legislature, mostly members of the House of Commons. This body commands a majority of votes in that House; and, as we have seen, it is a central feature of the British system that this parliamentary majority is permanent and solidary. A general election today is a plebiscitary affair to decide which of two rival teams shall command a majority of votes in the House – on the implied condition that the winning team will sustain a government chosen by its leader from among its members for the duration of the Parliament. And this is just what in practice these majorities do. British governments, if they have a majority of seats, *do not lose floor votes*. Moreover, floor votes of the Commons ratify policy, they do not create it. Policy is made elsewhere and earlier: in the ministries where civil servants strike bargains with pressure groups, and 'upstairs' in committee rooms where ministers strike bargains with their parliamentary supporters.

(1) *The Cabinet*

Once a party has won a parliamentary majority, the sovereign appoints its leader as prime minister and in turn he selects for formal approval the remainder of the ministers. This is a sizeable group – in 1966 it numbered no less than ninety-nine in the Commons and eighteen in the Lords. A smaller group of indeterminate size, which, since the end of the war, has been as low as sixteen and as high as twenty-three, is appointed by the prime minister to form a policy-directing body to whose decisions the entire 'government' is expected to adhere. This is the Cabinet. Its members attend all Cabinet meetings, which are ordinarily held once a week, and receive memorandums and minutes in full. Non-Cabinet members of the government attend only when specially summoned.

For matters of personal conduct, and for the purely departmental aspect of their duties, each minister is individually responsible to the Commons. If he commits a personal fault, like Mr Profumo in 1963, or if he makes a hash of departmental management, like Sir Thomas Dugdale in 1954, and the House feels he should resign and the Cabinet is unwilling to protect him, then a minister may have to resign, though the convention is more honoured in the breach than the observance.

For policy, however, the entire Cabinet assumes a collective responsibility: 'one out, all out'. A minister who disagrees with the policy must either grin and bear it, or resign. The secrecy of Cabinet proceedings serves to make this doctrine of collective responsibility practicable.

Formally, the Cabinet is the supreme body for determining the policy to be put to Parliament and for controlling the civil service. In practice most of this formal authority is exercised outside the plenary meetings of the Cabinet, either by Cabinet committees, or by the prime minister and the ministers who are specially involved in any given issue, or – as is often the case – by both. This arrangement is ensured by three devices – the agenda, the committees and the Cabinet secretariat. Almost all Cabinet business proceeds on the prior circulation of papers: before a minister can have an item placed on the agenda he must first have circulated his proposals to all other interested departments – this will always include the Treasury – and it is the prime minister, with the assistance of the head of the Cabinet secretariat, who decides whether to place the item, and at what place in the agenda. By the time they reach this agenda, most of the items are formal, being the products or recommendations of numerous Cabinet committees, most of them *ad hoc* but a few of them permanent, established and nominated by the prime minister. All of them are serviced by the Cabinet secretariat. Between 1945 and 1950 there were some thirty Cabinet committees at any one time, most of them consisting of three or four ministers. But if the Cabinet committees are defined more broadly as being all ministerial committees serviced by the Cabinet secretariat, then they ramify all the way down into the individual departments and number as many as one hundred. The secretariat takes minutes for all these committees, as well as minutes of the plenary sessions of the Cabinet, and circulates these to all members of the government. Thus, in principle, every member is aware of the proceedings of the entire team and is notified for what he is individually responsible. The secretariat scrupulously cross-indexes these minutes. In this way the secretariat serves as the memory-bank of the Cabinet.

Inside the Cabinet the prime minister overshadows his colleagues. Hence the current thesis that 'Cabinet government' has given way to 'prime ministerial' government. But if this is intended to mean that on any issue on which he feels strongly the prime minister can and does always get his own way, then the thesis is false. For instance, in 1967 Mr Wilson and Mr Brown wished to take a strong line against Egypt's closure of the straits of Tiran, but were overruled by the opinion of the rest of the Cabinet. Again, Mr Wilson, though he did in the end get his way over sustaining the arms embargo to South Africa in 1967, did so at a very heavy cost to his authority, and this was reflected in the collective, rather than autocratic, way in which the post-devaluation package-deal of economies was handled in the Cabinet. On the other hand, in the sense that the prime minister is by far the most important individual in the Cabinet, the statement is true; and there are good reasons for this.

To begin with, whereas other ministers are important because they control a ministry, the prime minister is important for other reasons too; and he can and does use strength in one arena to repair weaknesses sustained in another. To begin with, he is the spokesman for and representative of the nation, he can speak directly to it through the mass media, and public opinion polls provide a monthly indication of his popularity. Next, he is the leader of a national party; he therefore disposes of a national network of professional spokesmen and party loyalists who are available to repeat and disseminate his views throughout the constituencies. Furthermore he is this party's master tactician and strategist, playing the greatest individual role in setting its course and devising the run-up for the next election. Thirdly, he is the leader of the parliamentary party. This is his power base. If it is dissatisfied with him, it can bring him down, and indeed, short of a general election in which his party loses its majority, there is no other force in the British system which can do so. However, he wields over it the impressive patronage of one hundred-odd ministerial appointments and of other honours and rewards, and is also the supreme conciliator of its diverse factions in moments of internal strife. And finally, he is the leader of the Cabinet; it is *his* Cabinet. If he resigns, it must resign also. He selects its members, he dismisses them. He convenes it, decides its agenda, arranges its order of business, determines who shall sit on which of its subcommittees, who shall be heard and not be heard in plenary session – and it is he who sums up the sense of the meeting. In practice, with the possible exception of the Bevin period (1945–50), it is the prime minister who effectively controls foreign affairs.

Nor is this all. For the Cabinet secretariat, which prepares and circulates the Cabinet and Cabinet committee agendas and minutes, is also the prime minister's own secretariat. 'The Cabinet Secretariat,' Prime Minister Wilson has said, 'is the private department of the Prime Minister. Each member of the Cabinet Office staff services and serves the whole Cabinet, but they are also my own staff. . . . But the Permanent Secretary of the Cabinet is also my Permanent Secretary in the same sense that any other minister has a permanent-secretary/chief adviser. He advises me, briefs me, not only for Cabinet meetings over which I preside, but on the general running of the government so far as policy is concerned.' And yet, he added, 'The power lies . . . in the Cabinet. To the extent that a Prime Minister appoints the Cabinet, obviously he has a considerable amount of power but he is not a completely free agent. The power really lies in the Cabinet to the extent that the Cabinet keeps the confidence of the House.'[6]

With this important proviso concerning the role of the prime minister, then, the Cabinet is the powerhouse of the entire governmental system. And it enjoys this unique status because its members combine three roles. Firstly, they are 'Ministers of the Crown': they are the directing heads of government departments, i.e., the 'executive' in its strictest definition. But the Cabinet is also the steering committee of the legislature, and its members initiate all financial measures as well as all major legislation and decide on the order and time-table of business; for, with the exception of the three or four peers from the House of Lords, all its members are also M.P.s. And finally, the Cabinet

6. The *Listener*, London, 9 February 1967, 6 April 1967.

is the majority party's policy committee, composed for the most part of tried party chieftains. In short, in Britain it is as true to say that the executive is an appendage of the legislature as that the legislature is an extension of the executive. The executive acts by and with the consent of the legislature and the latter gives that consent because the executive is a committee formed from its majority party. The majority party is the power base of government and as long as party and government hang together they will never hang separately.

But how does the Cabinet maintain this support? Why does the majority party sustain it through thick and thin? Not principally because the Cabinet has the power to expel rebels or have them expelled from that party, for this tactic would work only if the rebels were few in number – and if they were, they could do little damage anyway. Nor again is it principally because of the prime minister's power to secure the dissolution of Parliament and so to plunge any recalcitrant members into a general election. For a prime minister to do this when his party was seriously split would be suicidal for himself as well as for the dissidents. The main operative reasons are, in fact, four. In the first place, the 'government' in its most extended sense includes almost the entire leadership and potential leadership; prime ministers, especially Prime Minister Wilson, have become acutely aware of the truth that a dog cannot bark with a bone between its teeth; for instance, in 1966 the new 'government', including its unpaid hacks (the parliamentary private secretaries), formed more than one third of the total number of Labour M.P.s. Secondly, there is the factor of ambition. Most of the two M.P.s out of every three who are not 'in the government' desperately want to be; moreover, of those who are already in the government, members in a junior capacity want to be senior ministers, and those who are senior want to be Cabinet ministers. And this leads the less influential to defer to the more influential and these, in turn, defer to the prime minister. Thirdly, there is a constant communion between the ministers and the back-benchers – hence the importance of the British executive being simultaneously part and parcel of the legislature. And finally, on most issues the non-ministerialists are willing to let the minister make the running;

for all were elected on the same platform and all have an equal stake in remaining in power and keeping their opponents out.

(2) *The House of Commons*

Nominally, the power of the Commons is vast. Its effective powers are limited. To begin with, it is not a law-initiating assembly, like the U.S. Congress. Though individual members may introduce bills, their opportunities are limited, the bills may not impose a public charge, and, unless the government is at least neutral, have no chance of success. In practice it is the Cabinet that initiates all major legislation and a great deal of minor legislation too, and which controls the time-table and gets exactly what it requests in the way of finance. Secondly, members vote in a predetermined way, along party lines; abstention is uncommon, cross-voting almost unheard of. Thirdly, Cabinets make even trivial issues into matters of confidence, on which their existence is staked. Hence Cabinets are never overturned. This does not mean that they are absolute. As a matter of fact it is doubtful if any ruler ever was or could be absolute. British Cabinets have to work to a 'law of anticipated reaction': the reaction of their own supporters and that of the opposition.

Parliament – which in effect means the Commons – is, as we have seen, the supreme authority in the United Kingdom. The opposition is a built-in check and balance to the government. It has five distinctive characteristics and five distinctive functions. It is organized; permanent; representative (of something like half the nation who look to it to fight their battles); a participant in selecting issues for debate; and the alternative to the group in power. If the government falls the opposition takes office. This is the logic of the two-party system. It is a zero sum game: what the government side loses the opposition side gains: 'the more there is of mine the less there is of yours'. Theoretically, a dissatisfied electorate could withdraw support from both the parties and plump for a third. It has not happened that way for over a generation and it is unlikely to do so.

The functions of the opposition are: to participate in parliamentary deliberation; to oppose objectionable policies; to try to make the government modify them; to create a public revulsion against the government; and, above all, to pose an *alternative*. Of all its functions the last is the most important. If the government fails to deal with some problem, the opposition will rush in with its own suggestions: then the government, not to be outdone, has to follow suit.

No opposition seriously expects to overthrow the government on a floor vote. This has not happened since 1895. At the very most, it might shame enough of government supporters into abstaining, thus cutting the government's majority to so small a fraction that it felt a moral obligation to resign; this is what happened in the famed Narvik debate of 1940 (although in that debate the government had the mortification also of seeing nearly thirty of its supporters actually voting against it). But the Narvik situation was altogether exceptional. In normal conditions, the opposition can hope for only three things. Firstly, it can wring amendments out of the government, the more so where these amendments are being supported by powerful outside interests which the government wishes to conciliate. Next, it can expose weaknesses and inconsistencies in government policy and, as a result, have them cancelled. Thirdly, and most important, it can cumulatively create a mood among the electorate. It need today capture only four votes in every hundred to convert the government side into a minority and bring itself to power.

Obviously a government is much more responsive to its own supporters than to the opposition. This is where the power and authority of a U.S. president and that of a British prime minister significantly diverge. The former derives his power from the authority vested in him as the president, and this authority is independent of the Congress. The latter derives his authority from being prime minister but is prime minister by virtue of the power he exerts over his majority in the Commons. The South African arms embargo affair of December 1967 illustrates this. Prime Minister Wilson in effect overruled the Defence and Foreign Affairs Committee in this matter: they wanted to abandon the embargo, he to continue it. Mr Wilson then resorted to the extraordinary expedient of getting the party whips to solicit signatures to a motion supporting the continuance of the embargo. In short he appealed (successfully) to the rank and file of the party against his Cabinet colleagues.

Ministers and back-benchers are linked by a nervous system. The parliamentary parties establish a large number (twenty to thirty) of specialist committees, as well as meeting in general caucus. The whips attend all these committees and serve – often with the honorary officers of the committees – as a two-way communication channel. Ministers themselves often attend the committees to explain their activities and can gain a first-hand impression of back-bench feeling. This two-way communication usually suffices to modify the views of both sides and keep them on the same course and there have been a number of well-attested occasions where back-bench disquiet has made the government reconsider its attitude.

This disquiet is most evident but also most effective where things are going badly – indeed, it is necessary to say *very* badly – for ministers. Given even a mediocre success the Government can usually carry off a situation by its general prestige together with the normal party feeling that however badly they are doing the opposition would be twenty times worse. For in the normal way back-bench influence is severely qualified. The proportion of ministerialists is high. Most back-benchers have a ravenous appetite for recognition and esteem by the prime minister, and this usually quells rebel ardour. Moreover, too serious a rebellion, even if not sufficient to overthrow the government (than which, of course, nothing could be worse in the eyes of nearly all back-benchers) may so discredit it publicly as to jeopardize success at the next election. And finally, so many government proposals are package deals negotiated with outside interests that even if the back-benchers had access to the information on which the bargain was based – and they have not – they could not unpick the package without making it unacceptable to the outside interests.

(3) *The Commons as a legislature*

The Commons is not a true legislature but an extension of the executive. Nine-tenths of the bills that are enacted are government bills. The Commons debates on these bills are only the last, not the most important, and never the most creative part of the legislative cycle. Bills emanate from the departments. As a result of discussion between the minister and his senior civil servants a memorandum is prepared stating the object and scope of the proposed legislation. It is then circulated to all interested ministries, always including the Treasury. Only at this stage does the memorandum go to the Future Legislation Committee of the Cabinet, which considers it alongside other proposals from other departments, and only if this committee assigns it a given priority on a provisional list of bills may the department request Treasury Counsel to sit down with its own staff to draft the proposals into legal language. The draft of the bill will then be considered by the Cabinet – almost always by a Cabinet committee, not the plenary session – and it may go through several drafts before being approved. The bill will then be mentioned in the Queen's Speech (the speech put into her mouth by ministers, which outlines the session's legislative programme). Once the session opens, the bill passes from the care of the Future Legislation Committee to that of the Legislation Committee, which is responsible for piloting it through the two Houses during the current session.

The predominance of the executive asserts itself once more, even when this stage has been reached. Firstly, the bill is debated by the whole House and its general principle approved; it is not routed to a committee of the House for scrutiny and a recommendation as to whether the House should consider it at all, or in modified form, as it is in the U.S. Congress and in the legislatures of continental Europe. Furthermore, in this debate (the Second Reading, since the First Reading is formal) party discipline is invoked in its full rigour. Sometimes the reception is so hostile, or so tepid, that the government thinks better of the matter and withdraws the bill. This is most unusual. But a bill is never defeated on Second Reading. This would be tantamount to a vote of no confidence.

Secondly, if the bill has financial implications, the proposals to meet these may be made only by the ministers. They move a Financial Resolution which the House debates after resolving itself into committee.

Thirdly, only when the bill has received its Second Reading

and its Financial Resolution does it go to committee for discussion in detail. Sometimes – where the bill is of great or constitutional importance – this may be a Committee of the Whole House. But, most usually, a bill is considered by one of the eight standing committees which consist of about thirty M.P.s. apiece, drawn proportionately to the party strength of the parties in the House. Here again executive predominance is assured. These committees are unspecialized, they have no power to summon witnesses or call for papers; they may not challenge the general policy of the bill but merely consider it line by line and clause by clause within the general policy framework. Admittedly, it is possible to re-argue some of the basic provisions of the bill even within these restrictive rules of order, and there is large scope for amendments and new clauses. Sometimes significant details are substantially amended or even dropped. In general, however, the main lines of the bill remain intact.

The bill, as amended, must now be considered by the House as a whole and this initiates the Report stage – a prolongation, in sort, of the committee stage – where new clauses may be added, and substantially new amendments may be moved. The bill as amended in Report is then presented to the entire House for a short debate on its Third Reading, a stage whose consequence is foregone; and thence it proceeds to the Upper House, the House of Lords, for its three readings there. (It should be noted though that for non-controversial legislation it is the practice to initiate the measure in the Lords, and then bring it down to the Commons for the procedures that have been outlined. This is done to save time.)

Finally, during this entire process, the time-table is the one laid down by the government. It will try to reach an understanding with the opposition; but, if it cannot, it has the power to closure debate, not only on the floor of the House but if necessary in the standing committees as well.

(4) *The Commons and money matters*

There is a fiction that the House 'controls' taxation and expenditure. In fact it does neither.

Taxation proposals are put by the government in a series of resolutions, later incorporated in a Finance Bill. This the House debates intently and intensively – but to little avail. Chancellors of the Exchequer keep a few million pounds in hand to make marginal concessions to opponents of minor taxes which happen to arouse antagonism; for the rest they insist – successfully – on approval of their Budget. True, the government had to make serious concessions to the opposition over the 1965 Finance Bill – but the circumstances were hardly ordinary, since not only was the bill complicated, long and poorly drafted, but the government's majority at that time was only three. Against this, if the following facts are considered – that no resolutions concerning the raising or spending of money can be put forward except by members of the government, that proposals for taxation are the work of the Chancellor and his department (the Treasury) and the tax-gathering departments (the Board of Inland Revenue and the Board of Customs and Excise), and that government defeat on a major tax proposal would be tantamount to a vote of no confidence – the supremacy of the government is manifest.

It is still more complete in the matter of 'supply' i.e., the authority to spend. The decisions on how much to spend, and what to spend it on, are taken by the Chancellor and the spending departments, and if necessary argued out in the Cabinet. All these decisions are embodied in the 'Estimates' which are presented to the House and show exactly how much is to be spent, on what, in meticulously itemized detail. The opposition is entitled to select at its own discretion the 'votes' it wants to challenge and no less than twenty-six days, known as the 'Supply Days', are set aside for this purpose. But these debates are simply general ones, on policy, not on detail; and, even if pressed to a vote, the government is certain to win it since defeat on an Estimate is treated as a confidence matter; and the opposition cannot even obstruct the flow of funds to the government since standing orders say that, at the end of the twenty-six Supply Days, all outstanding Estimates must be put to the vote without further debate. In practice then a government decides the level of its expenditures and presents them to the House in the certain knowledge that at the end of the session it will receive everything it has asked for, to the last penny on every item it has specified.

(5) *The House and the challenge to policy and administration*

What the Commons can do – and does do – is *criticize*. It can force the government to disclose its policies and where necessary to defend these. As long as its administration is even modestly competent, a government can take an enormous amount of this criticism without seriously impairing its hold on its own supporters or public opinion. Governments, at least of late, have been undone by their own mistakes: when these occur on a serious scale as they did for the Conservatives after 1961 and for the Labour Party after 1966, something of a vicious spiral seems to develop. The rank and file's complacent confidence in their government is shattered, the solidarity of the majority party gives way to mutual recrimination, and in these circumstances enforced debates on critical areas of policy can prove disastrous to the government's hold upon public opinion. The opinion polls and by-elections point this up; this causes further uneasiness among the majority – and so on.

The Commons has two instrumentalities for its challenge: the first via specialized organs, the second by the general procedures of the House.

The first affects the details of administration and this includes that very large area of sub-policy which passes under the name of administration. It is effected through a number of select committees. Of these the oldest and most influential is the Public Accounts Committee. An officer of the House, the Comptroller and Auditor General (with his staff), annually audits the accounts of every department. If his inquiries throw up instances of irregularities or of wasteful or even unwise spending, he reports these to the committee, and this in its turn interrogates the civil-service heads of the named departments and both makes recommendations to them and reports to the House. Its activities are taken with great seriousness; but of course, they are *ex post facto*. Nevertheless, the departments' natural dislike of interrogation and rebuke acts as a powerful proleptic deterrent. Another committee, the Select Committee on Estimates, was originally intended to examine the annual Estimates presented to the House and advise it before it came to debate and vote on the proposed expenditures; but it never has time to do so and its reports, too, are *ex post facto*; the money has been voted and spent long before the committee has reported. But here again, the knowledge that they may be the subject of an inquiry provides a proleptic check on the activities of departments. The Select Committee on the Nationalized Industries is a comparative newcomer. The government does not have to heed its criticisms – but, as it has performed well, its reports do enjoy some esteem and hence have some controlling effect. Latterly other select committees, on agriculture, on science and technology and on education, have been set up with power to interrogate civil servants. But none of these committees – with the possible exception of the Public Accounts Committee – has a tithe of the power and responsibility of a legislative committee of the U.S. Congress or the corresponding committees of most of the European continental legislatures. In Britain, on the whole, the details of administration and administrative sub-policy are *arcana imperii* and as little as possible is disclosed. This provides yet another example of the pervasive hegemony of the executive.

It is rather the second instrumentality – the general procedure of the House – that can rise to punishing heights (though it does not usually do so). And one of the principal reasons is that, unlike the French parliamentary opposition, the British opposition is afforded opportunities to oppose on a lavish scale. No less than one in every four parliamentary days is 'opposition time' ('government time' is only one in two days).

The most important probing device – open to all individual M.P.s and not just the opposition – is the 'parliamentary question'. On the first four days of the week, three-quarters of an hour is set aside for ministers to reply to oral questions; and since the original question may be followed by supplementary ones, a weak or controversial answer by a minister results in cross-examination at the hands of the entire House. Exposed in Question Time, an issue can be taken further by adjournment debates – either the half-hour debate that takes place at the close of each day's business in the House, or the 'urgency' debates, arranged at short notice, which go on for some three hours when a member, supported by one hundred of his colleagues, succeeds in adjourning the House on a matter of 'urgent, immediate and public importance'. Until very recently, it was difficult for a member to succeed in such a motion, since it had been interpreted very narrowly by successive Speakers of the House. Today the restrictions on its use have been eased.

There are also great blocks of time set aside for debates on government policy and administration, so that any or all of the issues which still retain their controversiality despite the foregoing procedures can be taken further, virtually for as long as the opposition likes. To begin with, there are the six days of debate on the government's legislative programme – the Debate on the Queen's Speech – which takes place at the beginning of each parliamentary session. Then there are the twenty-six Supply Days, ostensibly on the government Estimates, already described. In addition usage permits the opposition to challenge the government from time to time by putting down 'votes of censure'; and, *noblesse oblige*, the government has to afford time to debate such motions.

To sum up:

Although Parliament is commonly called 'the Legislature' it has to be recognized that legislative initiative lies mainly with the Executive and that in such cases the function of Parliament is limited to examining and criticizing these proposals, requiring the Government to justify them and accepting them with or without modification, or rejecting them.

Parliamentary scrutiny of the Executive is fundamental to the whole business of parliamentary reform. For though it is the business of Government to govern, it is also their business to give a running account of their stewardship to the House of Commons which was elected to support them and to submit their action or inaction in any particular instance to the judgement of that House.[7]

7. Fourth Report, the Select Committee on Procedure, 1964–5, HC303, H.M.S.O., pp. 132, 135.

VI. AN APPRAISAL

It looks at first as if Britain is governed, for all practical purposes, by a prime minister standing above his Cabinet, a Cabinet standing above the Commons, and a Commons standing above the electorate: a power pyramid. In short, government by the executive branch tempered by periodical elections. Nothing could be more misleading. In practice the government is under almost intolerable popular constraints and its freedom of action is severely limited.

(1) *Democratic constraints*

Like all other governments, the British government is constrained, to begin with, by what the administrative machine – the civil service – can manage. The Labour government, entering office in 1964 with a mandate for 'planning' found it had no organization to hand with which to act, and tried to create one in the Department of Economic Affairs. Next, and again like other governments, it is constrained by unexpected emergencies. The entire domestic programme of the Labour government of 1966 was wrenched askew by the sterling crisis of 1966, and had to be altogether jettisoned because of the more severe crisis of 1967 which forced the government to devalue the pound. And, of course, in foreign and commonwealth affairs, what it can do is limited by what foreign states wish to do.

But, in addition to constraints like these, a British government is subjected to particular ones arising out of the influence of public opinion.

To begin with, it must reckon with its parliamentary majority. It goes without saying that it will always have a majority in the House on matters it considers to be vital. But the majority party is not an isolated body: it shares national values, which is to say that its members think and act on certain issues just like the most uninstructed of their constituents. Furthermore they are in constant communion with these constituents and are expected to intercede for them – for instance, on local issues like unemployment – and so forth. So that the majority party back-benchers become much more highly disturbed about wage freezes and rising prices and the like than ministers who try to take a long and detached view. Ministers have to defer to them; otherwise they find a revolt on their hands, as the Conservative leaders did over the Resale Price Maintenance Act of 1964, or the Labour leaders over the public expenditure cuts in 1966 and 1967 and, above all, on the issue of the 'penal clauses' against wild-cat strikers in 1969.

Secondly, the Cabinet is highly sensitive to public unpopularity. This is why the opposition is significant. A loss of one party's popularity registers also as a rise in the other's popularity. Hence if a government has sinned by omission it acts to prevent the opposition outbidding it. If it has sinned by commission then it tends to drop the offending act or policy or modify it.

Certainly, a government is more sensitive to unpopularity at the end of the parliament's five-year term than at the beginning; but throughout the entire period it is under pressure from organized interests. Their pressures sometimes reinforce the pressures engineered by the parliamentary opposition. At other times, what the government presents to the House is simply a package of arrangements already made with these outside interests: this is true of the annual Farm Prices Review, for instance, or even of the ill-fated 'National Plan' of 1965. Thirdly, these same outside interests often act as veto groups, blocking off an area of policy from a government. It has proved impossible (whether desirable or not) to arrange a national incomes policy without the active assistance and concurrence of the major trade unions and the T.U.C. This has been the perennial lesson of events since the notion of a national incomes policy was first mooted, in 1962, up to the time of writing. The 'pressure groups' form a sub-system in British political life and it is remarkably stable. In 1966 I revised a book which I had written in 1958 about these pressure groups. The most striking feature of the enterprise was that, with minor exceptions, the same groups were still playing the same roles and pursuing the same policies, by the same techniques, on much the same sorts of occasion.

(2) *Stability – or immobilism?*

For all this, the constant burden of commentary on the British Constitution is the massive strength and authority that it gives to the executive, that is to say, the Cabinet. In my view nothing could be more delusive. How does this misconception arise? Firstly, because the passage of legislation through Parliament is mistakenly equated with effective power over national affairs. In 1965 Mr Wilson told the Labour party Conference that his government – and hence theirs – had passed more bills during its term of office than its Conservative predecessors despite its slender majority of four in the House of Commons. But the object of these bills, if the 1964 manifesto is a guide, was to increase the gross national product and improve the welfare services, little of which aims was in fact achieved during the following four years: in this respect, perhaps the worst record of *any* post-war British government. In brief: legislation *per se* is pointless if the powers conferred by it are irrelevant or ineffectual to attaining the aims sought.

The second reason for the misconception springs from the fact that a great deal of legislation or administration is of little concern to the general public and interests only specialized and limited publics. In all such cases the government undoubtedly has great latitude as far as the general public is concerned; for it is in these circumstances that it arranges those package deals with outside interests, like the Farm Prices Review, which the Commons passes, *en bloc*, because it can do little else. But when these two aspects of governmental power – the secure passage of legislation and the secure managing of bargains with outside interests – are put aside, it is very questionable indeed as to whether a British Cabinet has any of the massive strength and authority claimed for it. On the contrary it is very arguable that, where opinion is genuinely *public* and chooses to express itself, British governments do not command it but surrender to it. The Labour government's surrender to popular prejudice in 1968 on the question of restricting immigration from the Commonwealth provides one example. Another is provided by the Labour government's persistent reluctance to introduce the deflationary measures and curtailment of public expenditures demanded by the country's economic situation after 1964 – a reluctance which resulted in the forced devaluation of 1967. A third is its surrender to the trade unions over its trade union legislation in 1969. The Labour government, like its Conservative predecessors, was not prepared to face the unpopularity that comes to any government from taking such measures.

One of Mr Wilson's ministers at one time nourished the hope that government could stand above group pressures, saying: 'if the State machine, including Parliament and the Civil Service, can really acquire an impetus of its own, . . . then there is hope.'[8] In fact British governments, reflecting, as they do so closely, the values, prejudices, aspirations and interests of British society, are too involved with the electorate and the pressure groups to acquire any such impetus of their own. This is what makes régimes so stable and durable. By the same token, where large interests are affected, it makes governments immobile. Vilfredo Pareto postulated a situation where no individual in society could increase his own satisfactions without thereby causing someone else to diminish his: this is known as 'Pareto optimality'.[9] Britain appears to be in a similar condition, with her pressure groups so disposed – or at any rate thinking they are so disposed – that each one fears that any increased satisfaction on the part of other groups is bound to be obtained at its own expense, and consequently resists the policies of these other groups, striving desperately to preserve the *status quo*. Some of these groups – notably the producers' organizations and the professional bodies – are important enough to society to impose a veto on government intentions. So it comes about that for several years past, the British Cabinets, despite all the power and authority attributed to them by constitutional observers, have not governed so much as reigned – even presided – over a system of power points which they could at best affect only marginally.

8. *Public Administration*, Volume 36, 1958, p. 403, R.I.P.A., London.

9. V. Pareto, *A Treatise on General Sociology*, Dover Publications, New York, 1963, p. 1461 et seq.

Chapter 6

THE GOVERNMENT OF THE U.S.A.

I. THE COUNTRY AND THE PEOPLE

(1) *The American paradox*

UNITED STATES society is highly pluralistic: as in Britain, a myriad freely-formed associations coexist, of all types and traditions. But U.S. society contains a larger number of sub-cultures than British society and some of these constitute groups or loose associations which are of the 'disintegrative' type. Of such are the sub-divisions based upon ethnic origin, upon religion or upon territory. Yet the institutions of the United States resemble the liberal-democratic 'type' far more closely than do those of Britain. As in Britain, these associations and these sub-cultures are autonomous, freely-forming and possess the basic freedoms to speak, to assemble, to organize and to vote; and elections are held at regular intervals. So, while government is founded upon, dependent upon and accountable to the organized public opinion in society, this society is, comparatively, fragmented and incoherent. One would therefore expect the government to reflect this fragmentation and incoherence, and hence one might well expect it to be unstable. In fact, it is the reverse. This is the initial paradox of U.S. government; the existence of a stable, well-ordered, already traditional form of government despite the apparent fragmentation of the public opinion upon which this is founded.

The short answer to this paradox is that U.S. society is 'consensual'. The meaning of this term was proleptically expressed in a famous number – Number 10 – of the *Federalist*, written by Madison in 1787. 'A greater number of citizens and extent of territory ... within the compass of ... government' would, he said, render 'factious combinations less to be dreaded'. The reason?

Extend the sphere and you take in a greater variety of parties and interests; you make it less probable that a majority of the whole will have a common motive to invade the rights of other citizens; or, if such a common motive exists, it will be more difficult for all who feel it to discover their own strength and to act in unison with each other.

This *a priori* argument has been borne out in practice.

America is a land of minorities. No solid majority possessing the common motive that Madison speaks of exists there; in the United States a majority is necessarily a coalition of a number of minority groups.

There is yet another sense in which U.S. society is 'consensual' – the sense described by Calhoun in his *Disquisition on Government*. Calhoun was a sectionalist who upheld the rights of the slave-holding Southerners against the pretensions of the Northern States in the middle of the nineteenth century. If majorities were to be reckoned by numbers alone, the numerical majority would prove just as tyrannical to the Southern minority as a single person. Instead of the 'numerical majority', Calhoun propounded the doctrine of *concurrent* majority. Accepting the existence of diverse sections and interests, he argued that no act of government should ever be promulgated unless all the interests affected by it concurred in it. Curiously, in practice this represents something very much like the operational formula of U.S. government today. It is necessary to bring a large number of interests and minorities into a fairly durable coalition with a high degree of pertinacity as regards its temporary objective in order that a controversial measure of government shall, in fact, be acceptable at all. The way this type of coalition comes about is the result of the peculiar way in which the governmental institutions of the United States have been arranged.

Briefly speaking, the territorial organization of the United States is very loose indeed compared with that of Britain or France or the Federal Republic of Germany; moreover, the way in which the organs of government are arranged in relation to one another – what we might call the functional structure of the federal government and of each of the individual governments within the fifty States that comprise the U.S.A. – is both incoherent and self-stultifying. Both of these arrangements, the territorial *division of powers* and the functional *separation of powers*, enable and encourage recalcitrant minorities to fight long rear-guard actions. It requires the coalition of a large number of different interests before a measure of government can be put through. This self-stultifying, divisive system of government indeed sometimes produces no movement or action at all; but, in the United States, this situation, where government can grind to a halt and produce no action for a very long time, is not only tolerable but often even agreeable, and in any case is usually irrelevant because the United States is, by world standards, an empty country and a most wealthy one, so that the slowness with which new measures may be introduced there does not bother the average U.S. citizen anything like as much as it would bother his counterpart in the more crowded and considerably poorer states of Europe.

The main factors which ought to be considered in discussing the social basis of U.S. institutions are: first of all, the enormous influence of sheer size and space on the functioning of U.S. institutions; secondly, the open and mobile nature of its society; thirdly, the comparatively high proportion of ethnic, religious and regional sub-cultures to be found in it; fourthly, the dynamic nature of its motivations; and fifthly, the peculiar nature of the unifying forces which, despite all these self-divisive aspects of U.S. society, give it coherence and self-consciousness – in short make the U.S.A. a *nation* and thus enable its government to function stably and effectively.

(2) *The influence of area and space on United States society*

The U.S.A. is a vast country, the fourth largest state in the world: its area is 3,615,211 square miles, thirty-six times larger than the United Kingdom. On the other hand, by British standards, this vast sub-continent is virtually empty. Whereas Britain's population density per square mile is 575, that of the U.S.A. is only fifty-three; so that for every ten persons per square mile in Britain there is only one in the U.S.A.

One effect of this has been to promote regional cleavages. The

South (the area of the old Confederacy that fought and was defeated in the Civil War) and its rivalry with the North Eastern States is the most dramatic instance of this, but it is not the only one. The Middle Western States have an atmosphere of their own; they have their own economic interests and they, too, were for a long time in uneasy opposition to the bankers and the merchants, the importers and manufacturers of the North Eastern States. Again, the sparsely populated Plains States, Nebraska and the Dakotas, which were settled largely by German immigrants, have atavistically retained something of a pre-1914 German outlook on foreign affairs, and this fact has been used to explain U.S. isolationism during both the First and the Second World Wars. The 'Silver States' which lie adjacent to the isolationist Plains States, the States of Nevada and Idaho, for instance, also have their own peculiar problems and their own peculiar outlook deriving from their sparse populations and their dependence upon extractive industries.

Nor is regionalism the only factor which area has introduced into U.S. society. Another is the distinction between small town and megalopolis. If one compares the percentages of the population living in towns with over 20,000 inhabitants, there is not very much to choose between Britain and the U.S.A. In the former, seventy per cent of the population live in such places, in the latter, the proportion is fifty-two per cent. However, if one compares the percentages of the population living in towns of over 100,000 people, there is a sharper distinction. In Britain the proportion living in such towns is fifty-five per cent, in the U.S.A. it is not much more than twenty-five per cent. Now a town of 20,000 is not a 'town' at all. It is little more than a village by British standards. It is a 'hick' town. And the great majority of Americans live in such towns or have only recently migrated from them to the metropolitan areas of Chicago or Los Angeles or New York City. The predominance of this small-town culture in American folk-ways, *mores* and attitudes is one of the most pronounced features of its society. Furthermore there are striking contrasts between a megalopolis and the people living up-state, in villages or small hick towns. There is considerable conflict, for instance, both political and in attitude, between Chicago (that is to say, Cook County) and the people living in up-state Illinois, just as there is between the people of New York City and the people living in up-state New York, or again, between the people of Louisiana and the citizens of New Orleans. To some extent this conflict represents the age-old contradistinction in attitudes between the 'hicks' and the 'city slickers' – between the farmers on the one side and the bankers, the money-lenders, the manu-facturers, the merchants on the other. In the United States, however, it is also tied up with the facts of immigration. Over the last hundred years, immigrants, who came largely from Europe and contained a much higher proportion of Roman Catholics than the original settlers in the U.S.A., have tended to congregate in the large towns; and so, whereas the countryside is largely protestant and 'Anglo-Saxon', there is a high proportion of foreign-born Catholic and Jewish immigrants in the large cities. These have become not merely metropolitan but cosmopolitan.

A final social factor born of the huge areas and distances of the United States is the parochialism of most of its areas. The distances have to be thought about to be imagined. If one spreads a map of the United States over a map of Europe and Asia with the State of Oregon where Britain is, one finds that New York lies somewhere in the Urals and Miami lies somewhere in the area of the Mosul oil wells. The U.S.A. is a very, very large country. Now the mass media of communication do not do anything like as much to span this country and to unify local attitudes as they do in Britain which is so very much smaller. British newpapers, for instance, have a national circulation, some of them of over five or six million apiece; people can read the *Daily Mirror* or *The Times* simultaneously all over the country, with news headlines and front pages made up in London. This is simply not so in the United States. The quality newspapers which are best known to Europeans – for example, the *New York Times,* the *New York Herald Tribune,* the *Washington Post* – have not much of a circulation beyond the cities in which they are produced, and, in so far as they do have, it is a belated one. If one lives in up-state New York, it may take the *New York Times* half the morning to arrive; one would certainly not be reading it at breakfast. In Chicago one would have to wait till late in the day for one's copy, and in San Francisco or in Portland, Oregon, it would be later still. And, just as there is a lack of national newspapers, so there is a vast proliferation of local ones. These will certainly carry national news, but they carry precious little international news, and may even ignore what is going on in neighbouring States.

This failure of the press to cover the whole of the Union has, if anything, actually accentuated the parochialism of the various cities and regions of the United States. Such 'nationalization' of attitudes as is brought about through the newspapers is the result of the syndicated columns. These are glosses on the news, by commentators mostly living on the East Coast, which are reproduced simultaneously throughout the country; but these, it must be stressed, are commentary, not hard news. What is true of the newspapers is also true of broadcasting and television. Certainly there are coast-to-coast hook-ups for popular programmes, and also for some documentary and news programmes; but this must be qualified by two other considerations. In the first place, television newscasts contain, not merely international and national news, but a proportion of local news which would consternate the British visitor, particularly since in the United States the local news tends somehow or other to subdue and soften the impact of national and international news. The other qualification is that there is a very large number of local television broadcasting stations, as parochial and district-minded as the provincial newspapers. Thus, even the mass media of television and of sound broadcasting do not create national attitudes to the high degree that their counterparts do in Britain. On the contrary, like the newspapers, they tend to pander to, and consequently perpetuate – possibly even extend – localism and parochialism.

One ought not to look at the government of the United States in the light of European models. Europeans are accustomed to a strong central government whose authority over all other institutions in the country is paramount and to which regionalism is not of overriding importance; they tend to think of government as reaching outwards from the centre to the periphery and downwards from the top to the base. In the U.S.A., however, the institutions of government should be looked at from precisely the other way round – as leading upwards from their base, the county court-houses (that is, the local government offices), to confederations of these, working up to State level; and finally, to a confederation of States, working up to federal level. In the U.S.A. the governmental system starts at the bottom and works up to the top and the top merely caps an already existing edifice. It does not create that edifice, as it often seems to do in the states of Europe.

(3) *Class, status and section in United States society*

It would be an exaggeration to say that U.S. society is open-ended both at the top and at the bottom. And yet there is more truth in looking at U.S. society from this point of view than in considering it from the usual European angle, which thinks of a sort of ruling group, a cultivated *élite*, tending to dominate the high positions of State at one end of the scale, and of a working class somehow in opposition to them trying to dominate the state machine at the other end.

In the U.S.A. one could say, exaggerating slightly, that there is neither a traditional ruling *élite*, nor a working class in the European sense. To begin with, a traditional landed aristocracy, such as has persisted in Britain till the twentieth century, does not exist in the United States. It did, at one time, but it has been destroyed in the course of the Republic's history. There was indeed a landlord class before the War of Independence in 1776. Many of these great landlords took the Loyalist side during the war, the side of King George III (for it must be remembered that the War of Independence was not a united national effort against the British Crown; it was as much a civil war in thirteen colonies as a war of independence against Britain). But, in the event, the Loyalist side lost in 1781, and the estates of the defeated were confiscated. This was the first great blow at the landed aristocracy. The second occurred when the plantocracy of the old Southern Confederacy was destroyed in the reconstruction of the South after it had lost the Civil War in 1865. That Civil War had simultaneously brought about the opening up of the West; the passing of the Homestead Acts encouraged individuals to migrate westwards with their families and take up yeoman farming in the middle of the continent and on its west coast. These three events together effectively destroyed any landed class that had persisted from pre-revolutionary times and no such class any longer exists.

In much the same way any tendencies towards the establishment of a hereditary ruling class have been destroyed in the course of the Republic's history. The first stroke came with the failure of the Loyalist cause in 1781 and the expulsion of these Loyalists, after their estates had been confiscated, into Canada. But there still remained the aristocracy of intellectual gentlemen which produced, immediately after the success of the Revolution, that remarkable line of presidents who are known as 'the Virginia dynasty'. These and their colleagues were the folk who wrote the *Federalist*, who drafted the new Constitution of 1787, who pushed it through and who operated it. If they had remained dominant, there might well have been in existence today a class of people who, through historic service to the state, the possession of wealth and the transmission of rare intellectual and educational standards, formed an intellectual and political *élite* in the United States. But the Virginia dynasty and those who supported it were early overwhelmed by the votes of the newcomers who had settled west of the Alleghenies with Andrew Jackson, president in 1828, at their head. And with the destruction of the Southern plantocracy in 1865, the renewed tendency towards the formation of a ruling class was thwarted. From that point on, the differentiating criterion between Americans has become the possession of wealth: for, in the absence both of a landed aristocracy and of a hereditary ruling class, there has never arisen instead, as there might have (and as there has in France, for instance), a sentiment of deference towards an aristocracy of intellect. Despite the vast contributions of American men of science, men of letters and men of learning, there is throughout the U.S.A. even to this day a widespread antipathy to the intellectual.

Thus there is no basis – unless it be wealth, perhaps – for any kind of permanent ruling *élite*. At the same time, at the foot of the scale, the manual worker is not imbued with the attitudes so common in Europe. Unionization, even today, is neither as extensive nor as politically effective as it is in, say, the United Kingdom. The attitudes of the U.S. manual working class have been shaped by two factors which are, paradoxically, opposite ones – namely, the shortage of labour on the one hand and the dilution of labour on the other – and which have alternated throughout the Republic's history.

For a very long period of time, from the colonial days up to, perhaps, 1890, American society was marked by a very great shortage of labour. North America was an empty continent and those workers who were dissatisfied with their lot on the east coast could and did migrate westwards in order to set up their own establishments or to take up farming. The advice of Horace Greeley, 'Go West, young man, and grow up with the country', was indeed followed. In this way individual enterprise rather than collective self-help became the way of life of the American migrant worker, and the need to combine in trade unions was not felt anything like as early or as strongly as it was in Britain and on the continent of Europe. But after 1890, even where gross economic exploitation inspired a desire to form unions – and this was mostly on the industrialized East Coast – the great tide of immigration which bore people into the U.S.A. from Ireland, from Italy, from the Balkans, from Germany, made unionization very difficult. For the new immigrants were willing to take any jobs at any prices, and this undercut the effort to unionize. Not till shortly before the First World War were any widespread efforts to form a working-class movement and trade unions attempted, and these were not very successful. It was not until the 1920s that unionization took firm root, and not until the Wagner Act of 1935 that trade unions were publicly recognized as a necessary adjunct of the U.S. capitalistic society and a necessary component in its working. And, significantly, this recognition did not occur until after the Great Crash of 1929 and the depression that followed it showed that labour was a potentially revolutionary force and that it was necessary to bring it, as it were, inside that system of shared favours which has characterized U.S. government from the very beginning of the Republic, and forms the material sub-structure of its consensus.

Thus, unionization began late in the U.S.A.; it has still not progressed as far in terms of the proportion of the labour force as it has in Britain; except in the period just before the First

World War, it did not form a revolutionary force; and it was and is still pragmatic. Whereas it is characteristic of European manual workers to accept socialist leadership, this is not so in the United States. There the tradition of self-help which originated with the first migrants has persisted, and the principal characteristic of U.S. organized labour is that it forms a section rather than a class. Certainly it attempts to exploit its organized position in U.S. society to better its own situation, but it does not oppose the capitalist system as such. On the contrary, it is prepared to work with it, through it and for it, providing only that it gets its fair share of the enterprise – or indeed, a little more.

It is in this sense, then, that U.S. society may be conceived of as open-ended, with neither a ruling *élite* at its top nor a working class at its base. This brings us to the third salient feature of U.S. society – its pluralism.

(4) *Pluralism in United States society*

Whereas the one great cleavage that still persists in Britain is the horizontal one between capital and labour, this is not only greatly attenuated in the United States, but is simply one amongst a great number of other cleavages, which are very different in kind. In the U.S.A. the farmer plays a far more important role in the economy and certainly in politics than he does in Britain. Whereas in Britain somewhat less than five per cent of the working population work in agriculture, in the U.S.A. the proportion is closer to ten per cent. Like industrial workers, these farmers seek to drive the best bargain they can with the economy and in many instances, therefore, the interests of the farmer and the industrial worker clash. This is nowhere seen to better advantage than in the disputes which have racked the United States for decades over high and low tariffs. The farming communities are traditionally for low tariffs because they would like cheap manu-factured goods from the rest of the world to reach them. The industrial communities, on the other hand, with their high costs, high prices and high wages, seek to protect their own market and to sell their expensive products to the farming communities behind the protection of a tariff wall.

Side by side with such economic sectional cleavages there go other cleavages of a kind no longer politically important in Britain. Some of these are ethnic. The statistics of ethnic origins of Americans can be and often have been juggled, and anyway a vast amount of intermarriage has taken place in the course of the last 150 years. But in 1954, when the population of the United States was 160 million, it was reckoned that one-third (or fifty-two million) originated from British stock; that fourteen million, or roughly one-eleventh, were of German origin; that seven million, about one twenty-second, were of Italian origin, with Scandinavians (six million) and Poles (five million) following hard upon the Italians' heels. In addition, of course, about one-ninth of the population is Negro.

The descendants of European immigrants into the U.S.A. still retain some atavistic attitudes towards their land of origin. This can have important political repercussions. We have already mentioned how the isolationism of the German-populated States results from the fact that they are largely composed of people who emigrated from Germany in the 1890s and 1900s. It is not that such ethnic communities are anti-American or non-American. Just the contrary. They are often more American than the descendants of the British, who have been there longest. It is that they are American with certain traditional outlooks and preferences. Many places in the United States are densely populated still by people of the same ethnic origin, such as Milwaukee by Germans or New York City by Jews, Italians and Negroes in very high proportions. Such communities wear their Americanism with engaging differences which are politically significant. To woo the German vote, or the Italian vote, or the Polish vote can become an important political exercise at certain times. And, of recent times, the Negro vote has become a critical factor in the election of a president.

Another cleavage is religious. The earliest settlers in the thirteen colonies were British protestants. It was only later, in the second half of the nineteenth century, when the Irish started to come in, followed by Italians, Poles and others, that the proportion of Catholics began to rise. Today one in every five Americans is a Catholic. Jews, too, are an important and influential com-

munity numbering five and a half million – some two and a half
per cent of the total population. Catholics and Jews – and
Mormons – are no less American than any other religious
denominations but they do tend to have political attitudes which
are to an extent shaped by the kind of religious faith they hold.
Thus stratification of the horizontal class type, such as we know
in Europe, exists very much more tenuously in the United States
than in Europe, but at the same time the society is divided by
what we might call vertical cleavages: the industrial section of the
community and the agricultural section, one religious section
juxtaposed with another, and all of these placed side by side with
certain ethnic cleavages. And to these must be added the regional
sectionalism already mentioned in the discussion of the importance of space and area in U.S. life.

Since it is impossible to belong to both the Protestant and the
Jewish communities at the same time, or to be a Texan and at the
same time a New Yorker, or to be both part of the Italian-
descended community of New York and part of the German-
descended community of Milwaukee, overlapping membership
between sections of this kind is clearly limited. In short, U.S.
society comprises a large number of somewhat divisive vertical
sub-cultures, living side by side with each other and mingling
largely by intermarriage and migration.

This, then, is the anatomy, the crudest anatomy, of U.S.
society. But what 'makes it tick'? What are its motivations? This
is the fourth salient feature that has to be discussed.

(5) *Motivations in United States society*

The U.S.A. is a country of immigrants. All its people, then, save
the North American Indians, are the descendants of pioneers.
And the story of the United States is a great success story. These
pioneers, coming to what was originally wilderness, have moved
throughout it, have exploited its natural resources and have built
the most powerful industrial society in the world today, all in a
period of some 170 years.

A prime characteristic of U.S. society as it strikes a European
is its ferocious degree of competitive individualism, of enterprise

and of acquisitiveness. A second, which links up with the first, is the extent of voluntarism and the absence of any 'sense of the state' such as we find in Europe. The American tradition, from the very earliest times of the immigrants and the frontier, has necessarily had to be one of self-help, of individualism and of voluntary co-operation with one's neighbours. This was reinforced from the very beginning by the existence of a powerful tradition of religious sectarianism. Early America was peopled by strange sects from Europe; not merely Calvinist or various other protestant sects which were persecuted at home like the puritan Pilgrim Fathers, but also quasi-religious sects like the utopian society of Robert Owen. And, furthermore, established settlers frequently developed sects of their own, such as Mormonism. The Constitution of the United States decrees a separation of church and state. This itself reflects the existence of numerous sects in American society at the time of Independence; but it also looked forward beyond the existence of these sects to what was to be an ideal of American society, that the independent United States should, in fact, become the home of those who wished to worship freely without interference from the government or from their neighbours.

But competitiveness also was linked with the self-help and co-operative tradition of the immigrants and the frontier. For America did not merely attract people from Europe because they were religious sectaries who were persecuted at home and wished to worship in freedom abroad. It also attracted people because they were poor at home and wished to get on in life in a country where there was land in plenty to be had. And so a strong streak of competitiveness ran in those who emigrated to America. Linked with all these tendencies, there has always been, throughout the U.S.A., the ideal and tradition that government should be limited. From the very beginning the role of the government was less to regulate than to give: to give in the shape of free land, of subsidies, of tariffs. Regulation came very much later and, in so far as regulation now exists side by side with help to individual sections and localities, the tradition stops short of actual direction and management by the state. On the whole, government is mostly regarded as a dispenser of gifts and favours to various sections of the population, at the worst as a regulator of the autonomous groups which enjoy such favours, but rarely, if ever, as a *directing* force in the economy or in social life.

But this excess of individualism, this confidence in self-help, this dislike of governmental interference, have their dark sides. Their concomitants are lawlessness sometimes bordering on anarchy and the habit of violence. The homicide rate in the U.S.A. is 64·4 per 10,000 as compared with Britain's 2·7 per 10,000 (1966). The sociological and psychological determinants of this anomie are beyond the purview of this book, and – to judge by the literature – largely escape the understanding of those in whose disciplines the answers could be found. What can fairly be remarked, however, is that both the dislike of government interference and the habit of violence are part of a historical tradition. Resentment of governmental regulation is not merely part of frontier individualism; indeed, it was because the British government decided to tighten its administrative controls over such matters as smuggling and the protection of the Red Indians that the thirteen colonies erupted in revolt in 1776, and it was the fear that the government would intervene in the slavery issue that sparked off the rebellion of the Southern States in 1861. As for violence: the War of Independence, frontier troubles, the Indian wars, the Civil War, the industrial warfare of scabs and 'yellow' (company) trade unions (assisted by paid thugs) against the unions in the last years of the nineteenth and the opening decades of the twentieth century, the old exhortation to the Middle Western farmers to 'raise less corn and more hell' – all these are also part of the American historical tradition. So too is that 'freedom to bear arms' which is to be found in the Constitution and which has become so hallowed that today arms and even sub-machine guns can be freely bought by mail order. Individualism verges on contempt for the law and the forces of public order: the sense of self-assertiveness finds its expression in armed private associations, like the Ku-Klux-Klan, which are in direct line of descent from frontier vigilantes and lynching.

The Supreme Court itself has a powerful tradition of defending the common law rights of the individual as enshrined in the first Ten Amendments and guaranteeing *inter alia* the freedoms of speech and writing. But these rights can be and have been negatived by the procedures of legislatures, by the passage of laws against 'anarchism' or 'syndicalism', as well as by the activity of so-called 'un-American activities committees' in the federal Congress and in some of the State legislatures. True, these laws and these legislative committees may and usually do lie dormant for long periods at a time; but when, as occurred after the First World War or during the period of McCarthyism from 1949 to 1952, a panic takes hold of the country, these laws are reactivated and the legislative committees hold what are in effect trials without any of the guarantees that the courts afford the accused. The civil liberties of Americans are hailed by the population as the feature which most distinguishes the U.S.A. from 'inferior' régimes such as the communist ones – and to a large extent they are right. But not always; as sociological inquiries have shown, while obeisance is made to these liberties, prejudice lurks not far behind.

When habits of excessive individualism, distrust of the law, recourse to private violence and surrender of principles to private prejudice coincide with the social and economic hardships of a protesting minority – then the consensual framework is rudely shaken by waves of public violence. The violent protest of the minority is countered by the violent 'backlash' of the majority. At one time the trade unions were the harassed minority. Today it is the Negro minority whose awakened self-consciousness has begun to cause riots and looting in the great city centres during the long hot summers.

A third motivating force in U.S. society is the high degree of social mobility. Individual opportunity, which beckoned on the original immigrants and those of the 1890s, still exists today. It is by no means uncommon, for instance, to find some poor Greek leaving his native shores, settling in some small town in, say, northern New York State, opening up a grocery store, working very long hours, and finally realizing his first ambition – to have made enough money not only to own his own store, but to send money home to his family, bring his fiancée back to the United States, marry her and found his family there. Another aspect of the search for opportunity is reflected in the steady

Negro migration from the Deep South to the great cities of the North and the West where they can better their condition. Whereas in 1910 nine out of ten Negroes lived within the confines of the old Confederacy, today barely more than fifty per cent do so. Such geographical restlessness is not confined to the Negro. It is a marked feature of American history. From the very beginning the population has shifted westward, westward, westward. It is still shifting westward, so that in 1964 the State of California overtook New York to become the most densely populated State in the Union, and Chicago or San Francisco or Los Angeles, which were mere shanty-towns a century ago, are now vast metropolitan areas.

But if fluidity, incoherence and self-division were all there was to U.S. society, how could any government based upon it fail to topple? The opinion upon which it was based would be so fragmented and mercurial that the government which reflected it would itself be unstable and insecure. But in fact there are powerful forces which serve to unify U.S. society – even if they do not unify it to the degree that British society has attained. These unifying forces form the last of those features of U.S. society which we have at this stage to consider.

(6) *Unifying forces in United States society*

I once met a Somali who maintained that the Somalis were a nation but the Americans were not. His definition of a nation appeared to be 'people of the same ethnic stock' and he could not see how the Americans, of so many different ethnic stocks, could form a nation. But in fact the Americans do form a nation, and their nationalism is a powerful unifying force. The U.S.A. was the land of the immigrants' choice, and it still is: the immigrant who goes to the U.S.A. is selecting his own culture because he deliberately prefers its values to those of his native land. And it is a most characteristic feature of the newly-arrived immigrant that he becomes very rapidly more American than the Americans. (It is, after all, a society composed of immigrants which has imposed restrictions upon further immigration into the United States.) The system of instruction in the primary grade schools of the United States was designed from the beginning, and still continues, to inculcate this sense of U.S. patriotism and nationalism. For one thing, the grade school (what in Britain would be called a comprehensive school) is far more notable for its social qualities than its educational ones. It inculcates the sense of equality amongst citizens and also the sense of nationalism: school text books with legends and heroes of the great War of Independence are a central feature of its curriculum. So, too, are the cults both of the presidency and of the flag. It is unheard of in Britain to have a flag-raising ceremony at a state school just as it is unheard of in the United States to have a religious ceremony in a state school. But in the U.S.A., saluting the flag is part and parcel of the school tradition. The songs and anthems which children sing throughout the United States carry the same message. 'The land of the free, and the home of the brave' is the concluding line of the U.S. National Anthem, 'The Star-Spangled Banner'; and this anthem, it may be remembered, commemorates American reaction to the British invasion of 1812. The U.S.A. certainly has a sense of nationhood, all the more marked because the more recent the immigrant the more he wishes to identify himself with the nation he finds; and this sentiment is transmitted through educational channels, of which the grade school is the most important.

A second important unifying factor is the economy. It is a commonplace that the U.S.A. is the greatest industrial complex in the world today. The U.S.A. is the home of the giant trust and combine, and these nationwide enterprises, which span the continent from coast to coast and from Canada to the Rio Grande, make the whole economy interdependent.

A third unifying force comprises the shared beliefs of Americans, the myths of American democracy. The first and most important of these is the widely-shared attachment to the common law freedoms. The Americans took over the British Common Law at the time of the Revolution. Their common law freedoms ante-date the Declaration of Independence in 1776. The Declaration of Independence actually restates those common law freedoms for Americans: for, as the rebels saw it, it was precisely because their common law freedoms as British citizens were being menaced by the British government that they sought independence. When, therefore, their Revolution triumphed in 1781 and in 1789 they ratified their constitution – which is the one which exists today – one of the first matters to which they bent their minds was the place of these common law freedoms; and they incorporated them in the document by a set of ten amendments (the 'Bill of Rights'). These guarantee in specific terms freedoms which in Britain are held neither by statute nor by a codified constitution, but at common law – the freedom of speech, the freedom of association, the freedom of the press, and so forth. Not only are these enshrined in the Constitution, but the courts and notably the Supreme Court of the United States, are responsible for interpreting them. Sixty years after the formulation of the Bill of Rights the need to uphold one of these freedoms – the right of Negroes to participate in elections – became a major issue in the Civil War. But, as I have already pointed out in what many Americans themselves might well regard as exaggerated language, these beliefs and principles are sometimes (and, to some marginal extent, always) more honoured in the breach than the observance. Public prejudice, police arbitrariness, the extraordinary laws often to be found on the statute books of some of the less enlightened States – all contrive to mitigate these liberties. For all that, these derogations are deviations from the norm. The norm itself is powerful, widely approved and equally widely implemented.

Another generally shared belief is in the importance of consent on the part of the governed. The Declaration of Independence of 1776 states in its first paragraph in quite unequivocal terms: 'governments derive their just powers of government from the consent of the governed.' The Gettysburg Address, defining democracy as 'government of the people, by the people and for the people', repeats this in Lincoln's own words. The thesis that government must depend upon the consent of the governed was in a sense inevitable, for government by consent anteceded the existence of State government in a wide area of America. Not only was the Constitution itself formed by consent of the various colonies which had succeeded in breaking their ties with the British Crown; in addition, as American society pushed the frontier of population ever westward, the pioneers moved out of the settled States and came into frontier areas in which they very largely had to frame their own laws and maintain their own protection. The Western frontier communities, therefore, were profoundly dependent upon the consent of the inhabitants and, without any military force at their disposal with which to repress the citizenry, were naturally led to some form of representative government. This is precisely why the suffrage was extended first of all in the new Western States and only later, and by imitation, in the Eastern States which were the oldest and had the most traditional forms of government. The Jacksonian revolution of 1824–8 by which the trappers and settlers of the Western frontier were able to use their voting power to bring Jackson, their hero, to the presidency, was another stage in the development of the doctrine of government by consent. It meant the dilution of the more traditional and hidebound attitudes of the Eastern States by the new sentiment of general consent which had been engendered in the pioneering communities of the West.

Thirdly, Americans share a belief in the 'destiny' of the United States. In American political thought there has always been a strain of political utopianism representing America as a kind of 'anti-Europe': whatever Europe was, that America must not be. Europe was corrupt; so America would be uncorrupt. Europe was class-ridden; so America must be egalitarian. European society was bigoted; so the people of America must be free. This notion has continued to affect American thought, and an ideal society has been framed from generation to generation as the goal for Americans to aspire to. From this it is a short step to the idea that it was their 'manifest destiny', to use the grandiloquent phrase of the early Americans, not to confine themselves to the coastal strip of the original thirteen colonies, but to extend ever westward until they covered the whole continent from coast to coast. Where other peoples sailed the seas in order to take land for themselves to settle their inhabitants, this was and is looked upon by Americans as 'colonialism'. Where the original American settlers took 'prairie schooners' and moved westwards to take the land of Red Indians and southwards to annex part of Mexico, this was not described as colonialism; it was just 'manifest destiny'. Furthermore, this belief in the destiny of anti-Europe seemed to prove itself. The early inhabitants of northern America were able to work their country and construct a society which before their very eyes was clearly rising to a fabulous wealth and power unlike, for instance, the Portuguese-settled Brazil; and this enormous and tangible success, ascribed by the settlers to their own merit and not to fortune, provided a continuing incentive for further generations to move ever westward until they had seized all of the continent that they thought worthwhile.

All of these beliefs have combined to reinforce American patriotism and they run through and infuse all of the sectional sub-cultures which we have already mentioned. The newcomer to U.S. shores is struck not only by the wealth, the business, the dynamic, the power of U.S. society, but also by its self-confidence, founded upon these beliefs; and, if he is an immigrant to the U.S.A. by choice, he becomes one of the most forward to embrace these beliefs and to become as American or even more American than his fellows.

(7) *The American consensus*

So much then for the salient characteristics of U.S. society – its divisive factors on the one side, and those powerful shared beliefs which tend to unify it on the other. This brings us to consider what is the nature of the American consensus of which we have already spoken briefly.

There have been two great traumatic experiences in U.S. history. The one was the revolutionary struggle of 1776 to 1783. In this the defeated united empire Loyalists – chased out of their homes, stripped of their possessions and driven into the Canadian wilderness to the north – were despised and forgotten and have remained so even in the school history text books. The dead past has buried its dead. But this has not been so with the second traumatic experience, the great Civil War of 1861–5. There, the defeated Southern States were a reproach and have remained a reproach; and from that has been drawn a conclusion to be found in practically every U.S. text book about the U.S. political system and parties – a conclusion which, whether true or false, has become one of the great political myths of the U.S.A. And it must be remembered it is upon such myths that governmental practice is founded. That myth is that the Civil War demonstrated the danger of pressing minorities too far; that if they are pressed too far, this confederacy of minorities which is U.S. society might, in fact, fragment, as it did indeed at the time of the Civil War. This very fear has been vividly illustrated by the effects of the Vietnam War and, simultaneously, by the Negro riots since 1964. From tiny and obscure beginnings both grew like the biblical mustard-seed until, in the year of the 1968 presidential elections, opposition to the war (though always in a minority) had become so passionate, so dedicated, so irreconcilable that it threatened to split the nation into two conflicting factions. At that same time the Negro riots pointed up the existence of a horizontal class-cum-ethnic cleavage in the nation – a phenomenon mention of which is conspicuously absent from the usual run of junior college and school text books. 'Consensual politics' appeared to be breaking down and the unity of the nation seemed threatened as it had not been since the Civil War. It is this above all that explains the constant preoccupation of the 1968 presidential contenders with policies which would lead to conciliation – promises to bring the war in Vietnam to some honourable conclusion, to pay more attention to the needy, to remove the Negro ghettos, and so on.

So, willy-nilly, perhaps because of fear of such a trauma, perhaps by sheer force of circumstances and the rise of economic groups of such power that they could bring the whole economy and society of the U.S.A. to a grinding halt, Calhoun's notion of the concurrent majority has become, in fact, the tacit assumption upon which current U.S. government is founded: government has to be loose, it has to be limited, it has to be slow, in order to handle the U.S.A.'s wide variety of geographical, ethnic, religious, sectional and economic cleavages. And so the peculiar governmental institutions of the U.S.A. have been adapted to try to extract the highest common factor from this very variegated collection of minorities and sub-cultures. The point is, however, that they do not in fact abstract the highest common factor but only the lowest common denominator. Nevertheless, in this they are successful and it is to this rather low level of governmental activity, this low level of centralization, that U.S. government has been geared to function.

What then are these governmental features? They are four. First, the very loose geographical bond is formulated in *federalism* and also in the recognition given to localism. By federalism we have a division of the functions of government between the centre, represented by the 'national' government in Washington, and the localities, represented by the governments of no less than fifty separate States. The functions which in Britain are exercised by the sovereign Parliament of the United Kingdom are here chopped in two: one half is handed to the governments of the individual States, the other remains in the hands of the federal or national government. With this goes localism; the effective pyramid of power runs from below upwards, from the county to the State, and from the State to Washington itself.

The second feature is the self-contradictory governmental bond. There are fifty-one governments in the United States – the federal government and fifty individual State governments – and each one of these is based upon the 'separation of powers' principle (described earlier in discussing the liberal-democratic model and the nature of checks and balances). This arrangement, as already described, is designed to stultify government – to enable one bit of the government to say something different from the other bit and, whenever this occurs, to prevent government *as a whole* from saying anything at all. Nor is this all. There are areas, too, laid down by the written Constitution in the 'Bill of Rights', which permit of no government meddling whatsoever; these are areas in which neither the federal government nor the State government can intervene unless that Constitution itself is changed. And it is difficult to amend the Constitution – so far, only twenty-five amendments have been made to it, ten of them in its first few years of existence.

The third governmental feature is the remarkably loose structure of the two main political parties and their lack of coherent programmes or ideologies. In so far as we can talk of national parties at all in the United States, they have so adapted themselves to the localism and regionalism and the federal nature of U.S. government that each is also a cross-section of the entire population. Neither is founded on a particular geographical section nor on the support of one particular class. Both represent, and strive to be completely representative of, all the regions, all the sectional divisions and all the class-stratifications. Both parties therefore do unite the nation, but unite it so loosely that each one tends to be little more than a temporary coalition of bits and pieces. It is in this way that the prophecy of Madison has been fulfilled: in other words, by creating a society of such diversity as U.S. society is today, the majority has been deprived of any 'single motive force' – to use Madison's own expression.

The fourth and final feature is its sole focal centralizing point: the presidency. In all the welter created by the loose territorial bond as reflected in federalism, by the self-contradictory governmental bond as reflected in the separation of power in the federal and the State governments, by the incoherent parties, without fixed structure, ideology or programme – in all this there is one focus of policy-making. This resides in the office which is filled by the choice of the whole of the people, whose constituency is therefore the whole people and which is therefore responsible to the whole people by a process of universal suffrage. That office is the presidency. This and this alone is the great centre of power and coherence in what is otherwise a self-stultifying system.

II. CHECKS AND BALANCES

As has been said in Chapter 2, one of the characteristics of the liberal-democracy is the existence of a set of political checks and balances which import friction and delays into the decision-making and policy-executing processes of the government. The U.S.A. is particularly rich in such devices. One of these, not to be found in Britain or France, for example, is the federal 'division of powers' between the national government in Washington and the governments of the fifty individual States that comprise the Union. Something must therefore be said about this term '*federalism*' – the more so because, in the U.S.S.R., which is also a federal union of States, the device as there practised does not serve as a check or balance to the activities of the central government at all. Unfortunately 'federalism' seems to be just as much an artificial term as most of the terms used in political science.

A 'federal' arrangement always envisages two sets of authorities, one making decisions for the entire territory, the other only for their local sub-divisions of that territory: so that the full range of governmental duties is divided between the two sets. But an indefinite number of variations is possible on this simple theme and there is no consensus among political scientists as to which arrangement is 'truly' federal and which is not. If one brought together all the states that call themselves federal and sought to extract from them their common characteristics in this respect, one would be brought back to our starting point: one would find only that in all of them there was some kind of local/national division of governmental powers. But this of itself is not a sufficient criterion of differentiation because many states which call themselves 'unitary' (i.e., which claim that all governmental powers emanate from one single national centre) also divide governmental powers between a central authority and a number of local ones: and some give these local authorities a very free hand. Moreover, what is claimed by the 'federal' states, by reference to their constitutions, is often a poor guide to what happens in practice, as the later example of the U.S.S.R. will amply demonstrate: and so we have the spectacle of some nominally federal states confining all or most of the government's power to the national government, while other, nominally unitary, states give their local authorities a great deal of latitude.

In an effort to break out of this difficulty, political scientists have mostly been forced simply to stipulate a definition of federalism and then use this as a yardstick to measure how far a particular state can be said to be federal. Unhappily there is no consensus as to the yardstick to be used.

One school, however, has for a long time chosen to regard the juridical characteristics of American federalism as the paradigm for federalism in general, and to measure off other self-styled federalisms by comparison. Provided that one realizes how arbitrary this procedure is, there is no harm in starting off this way. If that be done, the characteristics of a federal state would be as follows: the duties appertaining to government are divided between two sets of governing authorities, one of which exercises its functions over the whole of the national territory, while each of the authorities of the other set exercises another range of functions inside its own local borders; the legal status of the former (the 'national' government) and of the latter (the individual 'State' governments) is co-equal – neither may legally invade the jurisdiction of the other, nor override nor veto the operations of the other in the conducting of its own peculiar set of duties; the operations of each governing authority (i.e., the national and the State authorities) are usually executed by their own sets of officers, neither of whom may invade or veto the work of the other set in the execution of their due powers. These features – and local modifications of them – are set out in a written document, the constitution. Usually, though not always, the national (sometimes called the 'federal') legislature consists of two chambers, one representing each of the constituent states of the union as such; and again, usually, but not always, the division of powers between the two sets of authorities as set out in the constitution is interpreted by a supreme court.

The United States, consisting of fifty individual States, is such a federation as this. And its system of government is marked by four salient characteristics: the elective principle; the principle of the supremacy of the Constitution; the federal principle – as already outlined; and the principle of the 'separation of powers'.

The elective principle

The elective principle goes much further in the United States than in Britain or France. In Britain, for instance, even including the parishes as effective governmental units, there are not more than 15,000 jurisdictions governed by meetings of the population or persons elected by them. If the parishes are excluded, the number sinks to approximately 1,500. But in the United States the number of area councils and special authorities is enormous, and, with some rare exceptions mostly at the national level, all are elected. First of all, the whole population itself forms a single constituency for the purpose of electing the president. Next come the fifty individual States, the vast majority with two-chamber legislatures, and all possessing a governor and various chief officers (such as state treasurer and state attorney), their own supreme court, and in most instances a large number of elective boards and commissions. Then, inside each State, the cities and self-governing municipalities each possess their councils and elective executive officers. Still lower down come the counties containing townships, and though counties are usually administrative units without their own councils, all the townships and villages within them do elect their own officers and councils. And finally there are any number of special authorities, such as school boards and water boards, each with its own jurisdiction. All in all, it is reckoned that there are some 155,000 units and some 875,000 representatives and officials – as against the British totals of (at most) 15,000 units and only 80,000 elective posts.

The supremacy of the Constitution

Drawn up in 1787 and put into effect in 1789 and since then subjected to only twenty-five amendments, the Constitution is the supreme law of the land. And all governmental acts which contradict the Constitution as interpreted by the courts – in the last instance the Supreme Court of the U.S.A. – are null and void, since no legal authority for them had ever existed.

The Constitution allocates the powers and the duties of the main governmental organs of the United States. In the first place it divides the federal government into three branches: the legislative branch, i.e., the Congress, which is divided into two chambers, the Senate and the House of Representatives; the executive branch, of which the (elected) president of the U.S.A. is the head; and the judicial branch, of which the highest organ is the Supreme Court of the United States. And, furthermore, it lays down the specific powers and duties appertaining to each of these three branches. In the second place the Constitution allocates powers and duties between the federal government (established as described) on the one hand and the fifty individual

State governments on the other. And finally, it allocates powers and duties between these fifty-one State-cum-federal governmental bodies on the one side and the people, collectively, on the other. By this we mean that the Constitution specifies certain powers which are *denied* both to the federal and the individual State governments: most of these appear in the first Ten Amendments (the 'Bill of Rights') and in the Fourteenth and Fifteenth Amendments. Unless a constitutional amendment is made, these powers lie outside the range of any governmental agency whatsoever.

So complicated an allocation of powers and responsibilities raises more questions than it resolves. Who is to decide? In the U.S.A., it is the courts of law and, in the last resort, the Supreme Court of the U.S.A. which are the final agency for saying what the words of the Constitution mean. So wide ranging and yet so broadly drawn are the clauses of the Constitution that it is hardly exaggerating to say that any citizen can challenge pretty well any act of the public authorities by alleging that it has acted unconstitutionally – although it is for the Supreme Court in the last instance to decide whether or not it regards the matter as justiciable; on the whole it entertains such cases. For instance, we have already mentioned the flag-raising ceremony that opens the school day in the U.S.A. Suppose one is a member of the Jehovah's Witnesses and regards this as contrary to one's religion? Can one claim that one's constitutional right has been invaded? In the Gobitis case in 1940 the Court refused to accept this view, but in 1943, in the case of West Virginia *v.* Barnette when the same claim was made, the Supreme Court upheld it. Again, suppose a Negro child living in the South is refused permission to attend the local school or State university because this is all-white? Is this not an invasion of its constitutional right to equal protection under the laws? In 1938 in the Gaines case the Supreme Court held that it was: the school authority had the duty either to admit the student to the State university or provide an alternative college for it to go to. Since then the Court has gone further, arguing that the 'alternative but equal' facility is itself not enough to fulfil the constitutional provision: all children and all undergraduate students have the right to admission to public educational institutions – hence the clash in the South between the local proponents of the segregated school and college and the Supreme Court's 'integrationist' interpretation. Again, if one employs child labour, is one's constitutional right invaded by the federal government if it passes a statute to regulate the employment of such labour? In 1918, in Hammer *v.* Dagenhart, the Court ruled that it was – the Constitution did not allocate such power to the federal government.

It is important, indeed vital, to note that in the course of its history the Court has enormously *enlarged* the powers of the federal government, both absolutely and relatively to the States. Indeed, this is the chief way in which the Constitution, drawn up when 'commerce with the Indian tribes' was still important enough to merit a specific mention, has been able to cope with the multifarious complexity of the twentieth-century industrialized U.S.A. And of late the Court has pushed the federal jurisdiction further; in the days of the New Deal, in the thirties, it opened the way to federal regulation or management of social security, of the trade unions, of labour relations and of practically all matters affecting the conditions of employment throughout the U.S.A., as well as permitting a hitherto unheard-of degree of intervention in the economic life of the nation. In the last two decades it has pressed federal intervention in the field of civil rights, long regarded by the Southern States as being of purely domestic concern; and its very recent judgements have asserted the right of the federal government to intervene, where necessary, to guarantee 'one man one vote, one vote one value' where it thinks individual State practices seriously limit or deny this. But the Court may often *deny* a power to the State or the federal government. For instance, in 1895 the federal government sought, for the first time, to introduce income tax, only to have the Court state that this was unconstitutional, i.e., irreconcilable with the tax provisions as laid down in the Constitution. In the event of such a denial there are only two courses open. One is to wait until vacancies occur in the Supreme Court and then appoint successors who are known to be favourably disposed to legislation of the kind that has been declared unconstitutional (for it is the president, with the concurrence of the Senate, who appoints justices of the Supreme Court). The other is to take steps to alter the Constitution – as was done, for instance, after the 1895 Income Tax Law had been declared unconstitutional.

Now, altering the Constitution of the U.S.A. is no simple matter, as witness the fact that only twenty-five such amendments have actually been passed although thousands of resolutions to amend the Constitution have at one time or another been introduced into Congress. For the most usual procedure for altering the Constitution requires, first, that a resolution containing the proposed amendment be passed by a two-thirds majority of both houses of Congress; and practically all the proposed amendments have fallen at this hurdle. (The Constitution also permits an amendment to be initiated thus: on the application of two-thirds of the several States, the Congress shall call a convention for proposing amendments; and any such amendment proposed thus becomes valid if ratified by the legislatures of three-fourths of the State legislatures, or by three-fourths of the States at special conventions.) But even if the resolution receives its necessary vote in the Congress, it must then be submitted to the legislatures (or to special conventions) of the individual States. In practice (with the exception of the Twenty-first Amendment) the resolutions have all gone before the State legislature; but, since it requires the assent of three-quarters of these legislatures to be carried, a mere thirteen State legislatures (or indeed only the senates of these thirteen legislatures) need oppose, and the amendment fails. The difficulty of altering the Constitution is indeed the principal reason why the Supreme Court has become the main channel through which the Constitution has been adapted to modern conditions.

The division of powers

The division of powers between the federal and the State governments respectively as laid down by the Constitution is also determined, effectively, by decisions of the Supreme Court. In recent years, the Court has tended to enlarge the federal jurisdiction at the expense of what was formerly regarded as that of the individual States, while the federal government has come vastly to outspend the individual States, and has even come to give them financial grants in aid for specific projects within their jurisdiction, such as highways. Hence there is talk of 'the obsolescence of federalism' in the United States. Obsolescent it may be, but it still has a vast deal of life in it, and its continued effects on the working of American federal government can, even today, hardly be overstated.

For, partly by the constitutional barring-off of certain matters from the competence of any governmental agency at all, whether State or federal, and partly by the powers that the Constitution gives to the States, and partly because of the political role of the States in the working of federal government, federal politics is, by European standards, denatured. Consider first the effects of the Bill of Rights. This separates Church and state; compare the struggle between Church and state which has been or is a foremost feature of the politics of France, of Italy, of Germany, of Israel. Consider the civil liberties secured in the Bill of Rights: guarantees against preventive detention, imprisonment without trial, restrictions on the freedom of Press and assembly, and the like. These are still political issues in Latin America, in Africa, in Asia. Yet, in the U.S.A., they are taken out of the sphere of federal politics altogether. At the very most, they are matters for a Supreme Court ruling.

Next, consider the powers allocated to the States – and hence denied to the federal government – and try to imagine what the British Parliament would be without them: powers over civil and a good deal of criminal law (including the issue of capital punishment); school education and higher education; health, sanitation and housing. These are the very stuff of British parliamentary politics; in the U.S.A. they are the stuff of State politics but only marginally the concern of the central government.

Moreover, the States as States enter into the make-up of the federal government and influence its outlook and the way it works at every turn. Here is a supreme illustration of the truth that, in the U.S.A., government begins at the bottom and each successive layer is built on the foundation below it until the federal government itself is reached. It is one thing to see the federal government as doing more things than it did, often at the expense of what the States used to do; it is another when it is realized that the composition and day-to-day workings of that federal government are affected by the internal processes of those States themselves. Until the last few years the States determined who were to vote, not simply in their own elections but in federal elections also; and, in a rich variety of ways, many used their powers in order to discriminate against certain classes of their citizens. For instance, in the South, elections for the offices of congressman (member of the House of Representatives) and senator are almost always won by the Democratic Party, which is locally supreme. This being so, securing the Democratic candidacy for such offices is obviously tantament to election. In the U.S.A., as will be seen later, candidacy is secured by a special pre-election election called the 'primary'. Now, until the Supreme Court ruled differently in Smith *v.* Allwright (1944), Southern States used to prohibit Negroes from voting in these primaries, by claiming that they were 'private party meetings'. Also many States used to refuse the vote to citizens who could not pay a poll tax; again, most of these were Southern States and most of those who were so disfranchised were Negroes. This practice is now forbidden in respect of all federal elections by the Twenty-fourth Amendment adopted in 1964.

Nor is this all. It is for the individual States to divide their territory into electoral districts (constituencies), whether for the elections to federal offices or for elections to their own State legislatures. As far as the former were concerned, the States were supposed, by law, to redistrict their territories every ten years after the census, in order to keep the number of voters in each district roughly equal; but many did not and even those that complied did not always equalize the districts. Instead, the sparsely populated rural areas were favoured at the expense of the town areas. The consequence was a vast over-representation of rural areas in the U.S. House of Representatives. Not until the Supreme Court's judgement in Wesberry *v.* Sanders in 1964 was such mal-apportionment declared a violation of 'the equal protection of the laws' and the States required to mend their ways. Many States had permitted even more flagrant over-representation of their rural areas in districting their territory for the purposes of electing their own legislatures; the over-representation of the countryside in the upper houses of such legislatures usually reached proportions only describable as grotesque. Now the effects of this went well beyond the politics of the individual State – since, for instance, a constitutional amendment requires the assent of three-quarters of the State legislatures. In Baker *v.* Carr (1962), and in a number of subsequent cases, the Supreme Court had ruled such mal-apportionment unconstitutional and required 'equal electoral districts'.

But while such pronouncements have severely curtailed the power of the individual States to modify their local electorates, they have by no means abolished it. For one thing, States can and do require citizens to register before they are entitled to vote; this can be and has been perverted so as to render it difficult for all but the most pertinacious – or the most favoured – to secure the vote. States are still entitled to deny the franchise to any citizen who has failed to pass a literacy test and some States have used this means to disfranchise Negroes, Red Indians, Mexicans and 'Orientals'. And finally, even though the States must give equal electoral value to the electoral districts, it is still open to the State – or rather to its ruling party – to draw the boundaries of these districts in such a way as to improve the electoral chances of one party and reduce those of the other. This juggling of boundaries to favour or disfavour a particular party or even a particular section of the population is known as 'gerrymandering' and, although practised elsewhere than in the U.S.A., it ought not to be forgotten that it was in that country that the term originated. In all these ways the States still influence the composition and character of the United States Congress.

The States as States also affect the policies of the Congress. The Constitution lays down that candidates for the federal Senate must be residents of the State for which they stand. By convention this same 'locality rule' is applied to candidates for the House of Representatives. Here its effects are more pronounced than in the Senate, for the congressional district is a very small area compared with that of most of the States, and the congressman is elected for only two years at a time. If defeated in his district he cannot stand again in some other district as can a defeated British parliamentary candidate. Thus the locality rule has two effects. It narrows the range of talent available for the House of Representatives; and it ensures that the congressman is a prisoner of his local pressure groups and interests. The House is both more mediocre than it need be and exceedingly parochial in its outlook.

The Constitution also lays down that in the Senate each State is represented as such by two senators from each State regardless of population. Since there are more sparsely populated States, more rural States and more poor States than there are densely populated, urbanized and industrialized wealthy States, this immediately distorts the representative character of the very powerful Upper House of the U.S. Congress. It is such an unrepresentative House as this that must concur with the Lower House, by a two-thirds majority, before a resolution to alter the Constitution is allowed to take its chance before the State legislatures.

Even the presidency itself is affected by the independent existence of the States. In the first place this affects the nomination of the presidential candidates. Each party nominates its candidate in a party convention which consists of delegations from each of the fifty States, whose voting power varies according to the rules agreed on by the party. The contenders for the nomination (with the exception of an incumbent president seeking re-election) aim to win over those State delegations with high voting power; this can usually be done only by transactions between him and the leaders or controllers of each State delegation, i.e., the State party potentates. Furthermore, in the election of the president, the States act as so many electoral constituencies. Each State is credited with a number of votes in an electoral college and, formally, it is this college which elects the president. To be elected outright he must have an absolute majority of the votes in the electoral college. The votes of each State vary, being an aggregate of the number of their senators (always two) *plus* the number of their representatives in the House of Representatives (proportional to population). In this way the more populous States have more votes – though by no means proportionately more votes – than the sparsely populated. If a candidate captures the majority of votes in a State, he receives *all* the State's electoral college votes. Thus both candidates exert themselves to capture, above all, the States that have most votes in the electoral college. To do this they must rely heavily on the party workers and above all the party leaders in those States. Once more, such support must often be cemented by transactions and deals. This will be described more fully when we discuss the electoral system.

Finally, the States affect the personnel of the federal administration. Certainly the federal government administers its vastly increased powers inside any given State through its own personnel; but, for most key positions, the State itself has a hand in selecting who these shall be. This is because the president's appointment of a wide band of high-ranking officials is dependent on the 'advice and consent' of the Senate. Now the Senate has long operated a convention of 'senatorial courtesy'. This means that the senators of a given State, when of the president's own party, may exercise the right to veto presidential nominations that displease them; in exercising such a right, their fellow senators will back them up, on the 'you scratch my back and I'll scratch yours' principle. This usually results in discussions between the president and the State senators as to who shall be appointed.

Thus the influence of the individual States on the composition and practical workings of the federal government must never be ignored. Legally, indeed, federal government and State governments are equal and independent. For practical politics, however, they are interdependent. And as will be seen later, the organization of the U.S.A. into its fifty States has had the most profound effect on the structure, the ideology and the operation of the two great American political parties.

The separation of powers

Of the three branches into which the Constitution divides the federal government, one, the judicial branch, is dependent upon the other two. The Constitution prescribes that there shall be a federal judiciary with the Supreme Court at its head; it does not prescribe the number of justices who shall comprise the Supreme Court. That is done by an Act of Congress. Originally there were five judges and today there are nine. Like other high-ranking federal officials these justices are appointed by the president with the advice and consent of the Senate. Thus, in principle, there is no reason why a president, with a compliant Senate, should not appoint justices of his own political persuasion; and there is nothing to prevent Congress, with presidential assent, from passing an Act enlarging the Supreme Court and thus creating vacancies. In practice, the respect in which the Court is held has defeated the more obvious attempts to 'pack' it. President Roosevelt tried but failed in 1937. At that time the Court was in its most obstructionist mood and repeatedly declared unconstitutional important Acts of Congress which formed part of Roosevelt's radical New Deal policy. After his prodigious victory at the polls in 1936, President Roosevelt in 1937 introduced a Judicature Bill into the Senate, which among other things, provided for the addition of a new justice for each member of the Court over seventy. This bill was rightly seen as a deliberate attempt to create additional vacancies on the Court or encourage the retirement of certain justices and allow the president to appoint more congenial successors. The Senate Judiciary Committee reported adversely on the bill and it was defeated. But shortly afterwards, first one and then more vacancies appeared as justices retired or died, and Roosevelt had no difficulty in replacing them with others who viewed his New Deal legislation as constitutional. This practice of a triumphant president and his congressional majority appointing justices whose construction of the Constitution is attuned to their own has in fact been a feature of the history of the United States since its very earliest days. Indeed, it is thanks to this alone that the Supreme Court has been able, albeit at a distance, to keep the interpretation of the Constitution in tune with the broad current of political thought and presumptions.

Thus the Supreme Court follows the prevalent political trend. On the other hand, once a Justice is appointed he can only be removed through the dramatic and cumbersome procedure of impeachment. However, the quality of the Justices appointed is guaranteed, as it is in Britain, by the public opinion of the legal profession, backed, in the U.S.A., by the severe cross-examination a candidate usually has to face from the Senate's Judiciary Committee.

The other two branches of the federal government – the presidency and the Congress – are, for practical purposes, politically independent of one another; but their functions are dependent upon one another.

The two are appointed by different bodies at different times. The president is elected by the nation at large every four years. The Congress may impeach him, but otherwise cannot remove him. The one and only attempt to impeach a president was made in 1865 when President Andrew Johnson, who had succeeded the murdered Abraham Lincoln, was impeached by the House and tried – as the Constitution lays down – by the Senate. The impeachment failed. Except in some dire emergency, therefore, the president is irremovable. The House of Representatives comprises 435 members, each representing a congressional district, and is elected every two years. The Senate (100 senators, two from each State) is elected one-third at a time, elections taking place every two years. Neither the House nor the Senate can be dissolved by the president. The elections take place regularly according to the calendar. Thus, effectively, neither the president nor the Congress can appoint one another or remove one another. They run their respective courses independently.

On the other hand, they function *inter*dependently. The president's principal powers derive first from his designation in the Constitution as head of the executive branch: thus the federal civil service, including his own Cabinet members, are responsible to him alone. Next, he represents the United States abroad, appointing and receiving ambassadors and conducting foreign relations. Thirdly, he is the commander-in-chief of the armed forces and in times of war or threatened war his 'war powers' become almost dictatorial. Fourthly, he uses the annual State of the Union message to Congress to announce his own legislative programme and seeks to have the measures it announces introduced and carried there, through his supporters in the Congress. Finally, he can veto congressional measures of which he disapproves and his veto is only surmountable by a two-thirds majority in both houses of Congress – a stipulation that is not easy to comply with.

But these powers depend for their effectiveness on the concurrence of the Congress. The powers of president and Congress resemble the two halves of a bank-note – each useless without the other. For, in the first place, only Congress may legislate. This means, to begin with, that it may refuse to pass the measures the president puts before it; it may amend them, possibly out of all recognition; or it may pass measures which the president dislikes and force them through despite his veto. It means, secondly, that the Congress and Congress alone has the power to grant the president the finance to carry out the laws, or any law in particular, and by the same token it can refuse to grant such money, or grant it only for some measures and not for others, or vary the amounts from the recommendations the president has put before it, or attach 'riders' to the bills appropriating the money.

In addition, the Senate has special powers of its own and these also act as checks upon the president. Federal appointments – in principle all such, but in practice only a broad band of upper echelon posts – are made by the president (to whom the holders are responsible) but only, as we have seen, by the 'advice and consent of the Senate', and the convention of senatorial courtesy considerably restricts the president's appointing power. Secondly, all treaties negotiated by the president have to secure a two-thirds majority of the Senate to become operative. This made the Senate's Foreign Relations Committee a powerful check upon the presidency. For this very reason, presidents have latterly sought to avoid this problem – on the whole successfully – by making 'executive agreements' which do not need the Senate's approval.

It will be seen, then, that neither the executive nor the legislature can act to much effect without the concurrence of the other. And of course, as we have already seen, even if they have concurred to enact a statute or vote moneys, their action might be declared unconstitutional by the Supreme Court, which once appointed is, in practice, independent of them both.

But this does not exhaust the list of checks and balances in the federal government. A further check on what opponents or recalcitrant minorities would most likely call 'hasty, rash and ill-considered legislation' exists in the internal organization of the Congress itself. For this is not a monolithic body with one single corporate will at all. Indeed, one might almost go so far as to say it has as many wills as there are senators and congressmen. For, to begin with, it consists of *two* houses – the Senate and the House of Representatives – which enjoy virtually identical powers in respect of legislation and finance and neither of which can in any way at all override the other! Should the Senate dislike a House bill, it can reject it or amend it; the House can do nothing about this except appoint a conference committee with the Senate to try to reach a compromise. Furthermore, the loose rules of debate in the Senate permit of the 'filibuster' – a manoeuvre by which a small number of speakers, taking advantage of the procedural rules, can talk continuously and so bring the business of the Senate to a halt. If well timed so as to hold up important legislation, this filibuster can compel the Senate to drop the disputed business before it in order to get on to the urgent business that awaits it. Thus a small minority of senators can force the abandonment of a measure even if this has the goodwill of the president and has been passed by the House of Representatives. Thirdly, the structure of the House of Representatives itself puts power into the hands of specialized committees and, inside these committees, concentrates much of it in the hands of the chairman – who, unlike his British counterpart, is a partisan advocate and not in any sense neutral. Bills are allocated to these legislative committees according to their subject matter. The committee studying a bill can and usually will call witnesses to testify on its proposals. The choice of such witnesses, which effectively lies within the chairman's discretion, can largely discredit a bill, or, conversely, lend it powerful support. After the hearings, the committee can report the bill out substantially unchanged; or report it with amendments; or report against it; or – and this happens quite often – simply fail to report it out at all. The House has long alternated its procedure, at times giving a majority of the House the power to force such bills out of the committee on to the floor, at times condoning this tacit suppression of bills.

But even if a bill is favourably reported out of a committee, there is no guarantee that it will get any further. The Calendar of the House is so full that, for a bill to receive discussion out of its due order – and if it is not taken out of due order it will not be taken at all – a special resolution or 'rule' must be passed by the House. The functions of making recommendations as to which bills shall have a rule passed for them to receive an early hearing, and of specifying the time to be taken in the various stages on the floor of the House, are vested in the Rules Committee. This committee, together with the Speaker (who again, unlike the British Speaker, is a partisan), therefore controls the time-table – a role which the executive in the form of the Cabinet performs in Britain. And if the Rules Committee refuses time, the bill will lapse just as surely as though a committee had sat upon it and failed to report it out. Once again, the procedure of the House has alternated between giving the majority power to override the Rules Committee and compel it to give bills time, or leaving this to its discretion.

Thus the federal government does not consist simply of three bodies which must concur for an act of government to be sanctioned; it consists of many more; and each one of these, by its refusal to concur, can veto the operations of all the others.

Now, this system of checks and balances is not confined to the federal government alone. On the contrary. Each one of the fifty States of the Union possesses, in its governor, its legislature (in all but one case bicameral) and its own supreme court, a replica of the threefold separation of powers that obtains at the federal level: and in their State boards and commissions for special purposes they have additional time-wasting devices.

Thus, the imperfect consensus of American society, the self-divided and sometimes inchoate condition of its organized public opinion, is matched by governmental institutions that are loosely articulated and self-frustrating. The proliferation of bodies, throughout the Union and its component States, which have power to obstruct or veto the will of other governmental bodies and so abort legislation, provides protection to minorities.

Defeated in one governmental organ, they can yet succeed in another. Thus legislation is often imperfect, or slow, or both; and it cannot be enacted in any shape unless a 'concurrent majority' has been secured.

III. PARTIES AND PRESSURE GROUPS

The parties of the U.S.A. are a unique phenomenon. They are what parties in Europe might perhaps become if there were a United States of Europe and the parties had to organize themselves, not only for the national parliaments of the constituent States, but also for a European Parliament. Would not they, too, then tend to be wide coalitions of individual State parties, denatured of doctrine and even of all but the broadest programme, without continental cohesion or leadership and with a membership of obscure or ambiguous significance? For this is what the two major American parties, the Republicans and the Democrats, are like: based on their States and the localities within them, lacking national coherence and focus, and ideologically denatured.

The most essential characteristics of the American party system are these. First of all, like the British, it is a two-party system. 'Third' parties do exist – the American Socialist and Liberal Parties, for instance – but they are at present of no major significance. And in the past, when a third party arose as a potentially serious contender, as did the Populists in 1892, it was swiftly absorbed by one or other of the two traditional parties – as the Democrats absorbed the Populists in 1896 when they nominated Bryan for the presidency, thus driving their whole party to the left. The reason for the endurance of a two-party pattern is primarily the result of two factors, one sociological, the other relating to electoral machinery. As to the first: some three-quarters of Americans vote according to local historical tradition. For local, State and congressional elections (but not latterly for the presidency) this tendency is most marked in the eleven States of the South that made up the former Confederacy. Here the tradition is 'Vote as you shot' – that is, Democratic. Other areas, notably in the North East, are rock-ribbed Republican for similar historical reasons. Such traditional voting areas coupled with traditional voting habits create the basis for voting 'machines': bailiwicks of Democracy or Republicanism scattered over the country; and these factors give the two major parties the momentum of a vast 'going concern' which is difficult, to put it at its lowest, for any third party to resist.

The other part of the explanation lies in the electoral machinery. Candidates for all major offices except the presidency are elected on the 'first past the post' system, the one used in Britain: to be more technical, by a plurality (not an absolute majority) of votes cast for the candidates in single-member constituencies. As in Britain, this puts a premium on the chances of the two leading-party candidates: the party that tends always to trail third loses its supporters, who 'polarize' between either of the two leading parties. And, for the presidency, the fact that the president is elected by the votes of the electoral college (as described earlier) leads to the same result, though by a different path. For, to win the presidency, the candidate needs an absolute majority of votes in the electoral college; if there are more than two candidates and the leading one receives only a plurality of the votes, the choice of president falls to the House of Representatives, in which each State counts as *one* and not more – despite the number of congressmen it returns to that House. Winning the presidency is the prime ambition of the American political party and electing his candidate president that of every American elector. Hence the polarization of electors' choices for the presidency between the two major contenders and the shunning of the others who might split the vote and so cast the election into the hands of the House of Representatives.

But although, for congressional and presidential elections, the system rates as a two-party one, the parties are based upon locality and State. This is due to the 'elective principle' to which attention has already been drawn: i.e., to the wealth of local and State offices for which candidates have to be elected. It is not uncommon for the electors to face a 'long ballot' containing the names of from fifty to one hundred candidates – to elect half a dozen state officers apart from the governor, to elect state commissioners and judges, state treasurer and state attorney, as well as their mayor, their councillors, the members of their local school board, their city court judges, their tax collectors and many more

Except only for the presidential, vice-presidential and congressional candidates, all this voting refers to the State or local officials. And this has two consequences: it empties the party of doctrine and it robs it of discipline at the same time. For the vast number of offices to fill has stultified the electoral process by sheer surfeit. To almost all the voters most names are so many unknowns. Early in the life of the Republic this led to the 'party slate'; the party caucus put up its candidates and urged the electors, bewildered by such choice, simply to 'vote the straight ticket' – i.e., to vote for all the Republican or for all the Democratic candidates on the ballot, without questioning individual choices. The abuses so engendered led in turn to the demand that the party members should themselves choose the candidates to be put forward, and hence to the primary election.

The primary is (or was, originally) an *intra*-party contest to nominate candidates for the *inter*-party contest. These party primary elections, which precede the real or 'run-off' election, have now become the general rule. Consequently, the decision as to who is – and hence what is – a Republican (or Democrat) has been taken from the hands of the party bosses, whether at local or at State or at federal level, and vested in local populations. This means that anybody, no matter what he professes or promises, may secure Republican or Democratic status: and this means that Democratic or Republican mean just what this or that locality, in this or that year or set of circumstances, has decided they shall mean. And that varies all over the country from election to election. Compare this with, say, the British system, where the Labour or Conservative candidate, to secure official endorsement (and thus the help of his national headquarters, let alone the local party militants), must be a member of the party and agree to support its policy and its programme, and it is clear why the candidates of the American parties lack any common basis of ideology, or programme. By the same token, they are also free of discipline. In Britain, the failure of the candidate to secure official party endorsement will usually lose him his election. In America, where it is the local electorate that 'endorses' a candidate by virtue of the primary election, the local electorate is the only force the candidate has to reckon with: national endorsement, even if it were proffered – which it is not – would be otiose. The primaries have yet another effect. They have *doubled* the number of elections – as though the original number were not itself too much!

Thus, a second characteristic of the American party system is that American parties are, primarily, local parties and State parties, and only once in every four years, and then for only seven months, are they national ones. For whom the Republicans are choosing as candidate for governor in California is of no concern to the Republican Party of Iowa. The multifarious elections which go on, some each year, some every two years, some every three, and all the massive organization of campaigning and 'turning out the vote' that they necessitate, occur *inside* – not across – a State's boundaries, they have no bearing on or connexion with the doings of the State next door, engaged in similar practices, though they may be bearing an identical name. Come every four years, each individual State party, with its tally of voting support, its network of organization and organizers and its potentates – be they governor or senator or State party committee chairman – has to come together with the other forty-nine State parties which bear the same name, first to nominate a candidate for the presidency and then to try to get him elected. But every party comes to that nominating convention with its local coloration, its local commitments, its local organization – and, as the sanction that these will be respected by the others, its own kernel of voting support to be brought into the national presidential pool. The presidential nominating convention is a congress of ambassadors of the fifty State parties: and, as Clinton Rossiter has justly observed, they are conscious that they are more important to the party than the party to them. 'When the Convention is over they return to their principalities secure in the knowledge that their own position of power depends only peripherally, or not at all, on the results of the presidential canvass.'[1]

1. Clinton Rossiter, *Parties and Politics in America*, New American Library, New York, 1960, p. 25.

The third characteristic of the two parties is that, although their appeal is rooted in post-Civil-War history and in the traditional family voting patterns that help perpetuate this appeal, neither history nor geography nor habit form a sufficiently permanent base for either to guarantee a national majority for their presidential candidate. To achieve this they have to extend their appeal – to the different strata of American society, to the economic sectionalism of its regions, to its ethnic and its religious groupings, to mention only the most important of the 'voting publics' in the sub-continent. And here both sociology and electoral machinery step in to push them both to appeal to identical groupings. For in the first place, although more American voters 'register' as Democrats than as Republicans, the Democrats, comprising as they do more of the low status groups than the Republicans, tend to abstain more at the polls; in addition, a high proportion (twenty to twenty-five per cent) of the electorate register with neither party, but are independent – i.e., uncommitted voters. For both of these reasons the result of a presidential race is not predetermined by rooted attitudes. And in the second place, the 'unit rule', by which the winner of the presidential election in a given State receives that State's entire electoral college vote although he may have won the State by the barest margin of votes (as Kennedy won Illinois in 1960), forces the candidate to neglect no grouping whose votes have any weight at all: the Jewish vote, the Polish vote, the Negro vote – indeed nearly all *blocs* of votes – may prove to be the decisive *bloc* in winning a State's electoral college vote and with it the presidency. Thus, as we shall see in a moment, both parties edge towards the centre – both comprise, albeit in varying degrees, voters from every class, section, region and interest of any significance inside the nation.

The parties: doctrine and support

Just as the Liberal and Conservative Parties like to trace their pedigree back to the seventeenth century – even perhaps to the latter years of Queen Elizabeth I(!) – so the apologists or ideologists of the two great American parties like to trace their origins back to Independence. They may well be right. But, for practical purposes, the two parties are the product of the period since the Civil War (1861–5), with the Roosevelt election (1932) constituting the great watershed in their history. In 1860, when it nominated Abraham Lincoln for president, the Republican Party was a new party formed from the detritus of former parties (Whigs and National Republicans) and from new forces. The Democratic Party, tracing its origin further back to President Andrew Jackson (1828–36), split at that same election into two fractions, the northern and the southern. The Republican Party became the party of the embattled North; the southern wing of the Democratic Party became the party of the Confederacy.

The Republicans, then, are the party of the victors of the Civil War. The industrial and moneyed interests of the North Eastern States leapt on their bandwagon; thus they also became the party of high tariffs and, since the war had been fought over the right of the (Democratic) Southern States to secede from the Union, the party of federal centralization. In an uneasy alliance, sporadically broken by Middle Western farmer–labour alliances and by populism and by progressivism, they linked together the industrial North East and the agricultural Middle West against the defeated third section of what was then the U.S.A., namely, the States of the Southern Confederacy.

The Democrats, by contrast, were the party of the vanquished South; and yet, very soon indeed after the Civil War, they were able to rally sections of the North's population to their ranks. For as the Republicans became the party of triumphant industrial enterprise, so the Democrats appealed to the various victims of that enterprise – to the minority groups, like the Irish, who were beginning to pour into America in vast numbers. Thus they became the party, not only of the Southern rural protestants, who were still voting as they shot, but of the immigrant minorities of the mushrooming cities of the North and Middle West, many of whom were, like the Irish and the Poles and the Italians, not Protestant, but Catholic. Hence the Republican jibe that the Democrats were the party of 'Rum, Romanism and Rebellion'. Just as the Republicans, representing industry, were protectionist, so the Democrats, because the southerners were agriculturalists, supported a low tariff; and as the Republicans were the party of federal centralization, so the Democrats continued to uphold the doctrine of States' rights that had sparked off the war.

These characteristics became ever more shadowy, and, at the great turning point of 1933, the 'Roosevelt Revolution' imposed new features on both the great parties. The pre-1933 historical features, indeed, still appear, but rather like a palimpsest. For Roosevelt was elected after a twelve-year period of Republican rule and came to office when the Great Depression had shattered faith in the leadership of big business and the unfettered free enterprise system, and his great strategic feat was to create an alliance between the hard core 'solid South' and the great cities of the North East and Middle West, leaving the Republicans isolated in their rural and hick-town strongholds. Roosevelt turned the Democratic coalition towards federal regulation of and intervention in the economy, towards social welfare legislation and towards federal encroachment on States' rights. So it is that from Roosevelt's time the Democratic Party has become the popular party and the 'party of movement'. As its character changed, so the alliance between the great city populations of the North East and Middle West on the one side, and the Southern 'Bourbons' on the other, became more and more strained. Traditionally the champion of the ethnic minorities, the party found it more and more difficult to keep in line the anti-Negro racists of the South and its own Negro supporters in the Northern cities. With Presidents Kennedy (1960) and Johnson (1964) this strain reached breaking point. The 'solid South' had already begun to crack in 1948. When Harry Truman wrote civil rights for Negroes into his campaign, four Southern States cast their electoral college vote for a third candidate, failing by only a narrow margin to abort the election in the electoral college and thrust it, for decision, to the House of Representatives: and, from that period on, the South has never solidly supported the Democratic presidential candidate in an election, though certain individual States have of course done so.

The Roosevelt revolution left the Republican Party in the dilemma of either opposing the basic reforms of the Roosevelt era, which were widely popular, or of becoming the 'me-too' party with the refrain 'anything you can do, I can do better'. Until 1964 they chose the latter course as the wiser. But the hard core of the Republicans is still the supporter of *laissez faire* and individualism; the party of the businessmen, suburbanites, and farmers; the foe of the federal government and the champion of States' rights. It is an alliance of the agrarian Middle West and Plains, the Pacific Coast, and the up-state areas of the North Eastern States. Under Eisenhower (1952–60), a benevolent father figure, the alliance succeeded. With Nixon as candidate in 1960 it just failed. The Democratic Party launched its new wave of forward movement, separating itself from the 'me-tooism' of the Republicans once more, with the concept of Kennedy's 'New Frontier'. Fatally, the Republican Party Convention now chose the other of its two alternatives: to become an ideological vehicle of the right-wing radicals, opposed to welfare legislation as 'creeping socialism', opposed to the cities and their pop culture, ambiguous if not hostile towards civil rights for the Negro. This was the ideology of Barry Goldwater: and under its impact the Republican popular vote withered away. Lyndon Johnson, a shrewder, earthier candidate than Kennedy, won easily, benefiting by his opponent's mistakes, and promptly set about translating Kennedy's new-look Democracy into action.

The hard-core regions of the Democratic Party are the South (except, as we have seen, where the presidency is concerned): those of the Republican Party are the northern part of the North East, the Western Reserve and the upper Mississippi. The Democrats are strong in the great cities: outside the South there are fifteen cities of more than half a million inhabitants apiece and, in 1960, of their sixty-five congressmen, fifty-five were Democrats and only ten were Republicans. The Republicans are strong in the rural belt (outside the South) and – a new important phenomenon – in the suburbs. The Democrats are the party of the ethnic minority groups with the exception nowadays of the Irish and the Italians who have become evenly divided between the two parties; but the Jews (forming one-quarter of the electorate in four of the great cities) vote three to one for the Democrats, and the Negroes (half in the South, half in Northern cities) vote four out of every five for the Democratic Party, even in

the South where traditionally they used to vote Republican.
Table 11 shows the way in which various groups distributed

TABLE 11. THE 1960 PRESIDENTIAL ELECTION

	Republican	Democrat	Other	Non-voting
Designation of head of family				
Professional/Managerial	46	39	3	12
Other white collar	46	37	1	16
Skilled/Semi-skilled	31	44	3	22
Unskilled	27	41	–	32
Farm operators	50	25	2	23
Trade unionist	27	48	2	23
Non trade unionist	44	35	1	20
Metropolitan areas	34	46	2	18
Towns/Cities	41	36	1	22
Rural	40	35	2	23
Protestant	47	28	1	24
Catholic	16	68	1	15
White	42	38	1	19
Negro	15	36	3	46

their votes in the 1960 election. Some of these patterns change
from election to election, but the groups that consistently favour
the Republicans over the Democrats comprise the professional/
managerial class, the college-educated, the voters of the towns
and smaller cities, the Protestants and the non-unionized. By
contrast, those that consistently favour the Democrats over the
Republicans comprise the unskilled worker class, the Negroes
and unionized labour. The shifts, however, continue. Three are
particularly significant at the moment. The first is the Negro
vote. Nearly all that vote was corralled up in the old South some
fifty years ago; today half of it resides in the great cities of the
North where it is of decisive importance in governorships and the

presidential election. The second is the vote of suburbia; as in Britain, the centres of the great cities are emptying and their populations moving into the suburbs. And this suburban vote is predominantly Republican. Not that a voter changes his allegiance with his address: what lies at the root of both the ecological and the political movement is the rising status of minority groups – the Irish, the Italians, the Jews are successively moving outwards from the centres, stepping into one another's home places and, as they do so, reflecting their elevation by turning Republican. The third shift is the change of voting pattern in the South. In the first place, as already remarked, the eleven Southern States are no longer solidly Democratic in the presidential elections. Next, the Negroes – who, after all, were the minority supported and emancipated by the Republican Party – have switched their voting support to the Democrats. And finally, as they have done so, the white suburbanites have begun to desert the traditional Southern party, the Democrats and lay the foundations of a Republican revival.

Congressional elections

The result of the plethora of elections, with the other factors we have considered, is twofold. First, as far as the congressional elections are concerned, they drain the parties in the Congress of all coherent ideology, programme and discipline and so convert the legislature into a tissue of unrelated localisms. These parties are not parties in any European sense, but undisciplined cohorts of local interests. Secondly, however, this very lack of cohesion and common purpose faithfully reflects the multivariate nature of American society with its manifold sub-cultures. And hence it permits and even encourages the self-stultification of the electorate's purpose: for it permits them to vote for one thing in choosing a congressman or a governor of their State – and for an entirely different thing in choosing their next president. The States may all go one way, say the Democratic way, by choosing predominantly Democratic governors, while the presidency goes to a Republican, thus creating a tension between the federal government and the States collectively.

Two other features, both familiar, exaggerate this tendency. The locality rule makes sense for the election of senators; after all, New York State or California have populations of about one-third the size of Britain's. New York's area is about half of Britain's; California's is twice its size. Texas, indeed, is three and a half times larger. It is not unreasonable that the senators, to qualify as candidates, should be residents of their States – particularly since their task, in the Senate, is to represent the State *qua* State. But, as we have already remarked, these arguments do not hold for the congressman, whom the locality rule – plus biennial elections – ties to the strings of his electorate, turning him into its office boy in Washington.

Secondly, the party primaries, already mentioned, denature the ideology and programme and discipline of the parties even more than has been stated so far. In theory the party primary is the party membership's choice of candidates; in theory it is a *party* election, not an election *between* parties. This is not exactly how it works out in practice. For how is the election officer to know whether a voter is a bona fide member of the party whose primary election is being held? Does he insist that the voter shall have registered his name with the State authorities as a Democrat or a Republican? Some States do this. Or does he demand proof how the voter actually voted in the last election? Or a promise that he will vote a particular way in the next? Some States do it the first way, others the second. But obviously there is no guarantee of how the voter did vote last time or will vote next time, since the ballot is secret. So that in principle it is possible, even under all of these systems, for a voter who is secretly going to vote Democrat to cast a vote in the Republican primary: i.e., to help decide who the Republican contenders shall be!

Now, in the States which exact some test or pledge, these primary elections are known as *closed*. On giving the requested proof or pledge, the voter is handed his party ballot form, containing the names of rivals who want to stand as the party candidate for various elective posts to be decided at the election. And the primary voter 'checks' the names he approves.

But, precisely because such proofs and pledges are both meaningless and invidious, many States have resorted to the *open* primary. Here the voter gives no proof whatever of his party affiliation. He simply picks up a single sheet on which *both* the parties have put down their slates of rivals for the candidacies; and he can select either list he pleases. He may well be a life-long Republican, but, because the Republicans have no hope in that particular area (in the South, perhaps), decide to mark the Democratic primary ballot, thus helping decide which Democrat shall be nominated as candidate for, let us say, congressman or State governor. Thus the decision as to who or what is a Democrat is not even decided by Democrats; it can be decided by anybody else who cares to vote on the Democratic ballot – by a Republican, a Socialist, a communist.

The open primary, therefore, takes the decision as to the nature of 'Democracy' or 'Republicanism' away even from the members of the respective parties and gives it to the public at large. And with this disappears any hope at all of distinctive doctrine or programme as between one party and another. What is a Democrat? Anybody who can win a Democratic primary, anywhere in the U.S.A. And the same is true for Republicans *mutatis mutandis*.

But this is not all. The plethora of elections, all coming together, with the rival candidates for as many as fifty or a hundred national, State and local offices all printed on the same ballot paper, makes the entire electoral process self-contradictory. The ballot paper contains two (Republican and Democrat) or more (Progressive, Socialist, etc.) lists of party candidates, ranged in columns against the appropriate office for which they are standing. At the top of each column there is a symbol – usually a circle standing beside the name of the party whose column it is. The parties urge the voter to vote the 'straight ticket', e.g. vote for the Republican candidate for every post from president to the local dog-catcher; and he can do this by just putting a cross into the circle standing by the word 'Republican' at the head of the Republican column. And many voters do. But, equally, large numbers of voters do not. They discriminate. They may, and sometimes do, vote for, say, a Democratic president and vice-president, a Republican senator, a Republican congressman, a Democratic governor, a Democratic mayor, a Republican this and a Democratic that, all the way down the 'ticket'. And they do not vote by hand. With all those names to put crosses against, they might get writer's cramp. So they mark their ballots in a voting *machine*: they press the appropriate buttons, and the ballot sheet is marked. It is not only possible, but often happens, that the electorate returns one party choice for the presidency, another for the Congress, one for the State governorship or legislature, and another for the local mayoralty or council. There is little guarantee that the Congress will be of the same party as the president. Of the fifty Congresses that sat between 1868 and 1968, in no less than sixteen at least one branch of the Congress was controlled by the anti-presidential party. Again, the president may have most of the State governments controlled by his party: equally, he may not. Thus the system of checks and balances in the U.S.A. is not exhausted by the division of powers between the federal government and the States, or between the three branches of government in the federal and the State governments. These checks and balances are compounded by the political cleavages between the presidential, congressional, State and local levels of government. America is the only country in the whole world where an elector can vote for two opposed things at the same time – and get them!

The presidential election

State parties – fifty of them; but a *national* election! How is it done? The United States, when it elects a president, is the largest single-member constituency in the world. For no other country of such a size votes directly for its president.

The process takes place in two stages: 'first catch your hare', said Mrs Beeton, before telling the housewife how to cook it. 'First pick your candidates', says the electoral system; 'then choose between them.'

The choice of the candidate is not a public matter but a matter for the delegations of the fifty States' parties assembled together, every four years, in a Convention. Who makes up the delegations? There is no common rule. It depends on the procedure established by each State party. Sometimes the State Committee goes, or else people whom it appoints. Sometimes the State holds its own convention to decide who shall go; sometimes it decides this by an election (another!). And behind all these processes looms the power of the local potentates or bigwigs who are influential on the State Committee, or so powerful in their own right as to dominate it, or even make it otiose, and these shadowy people are the ones who either comprise the delegation, or select it, or tell it what to do. Sometimes it is the State governor; sometimes it is the State senator; sometimes it is the chairman of the State Committee; sometimes it is none of these. There is no telling. Theodore White has put it superbly when he writes:

There are fifty states in the Union, each endowed with a separate sovereignty by the Constitution. These sovereignties are genuine; they create in each state two major parties; and within each party from two to four separate groups contend for capture, first of the state party's leadership, then of the state's sovereignty. Where true power lies in these hundreds of revolving, dissolving, nascent and fading political groups is known only by local folklore, below the threshold of public report. . . . The laws of libel, the decencies of political reportage, the conventions of friendship and custom, the obstacles of distance, and parochialism all effectively conceal the ever-changing topography of American politics. It is impossible to report publicly which world-famous Governor of what state was commonly called 'The Boob' by his political boss; which apparently sinister boss is only a paper tiger in the hands of other men; which labour leader can really deliver votes and money and which can not; which great industrialist is a political eunuch while his neighbour is master of the state; which nationally eminent Negro is considered an 'Uncle Tom' by his people, while some unknown kinsman really controls its county leaders. . . .[2]

Nor is there any common rule as to how the delegation should cast its votes: whether it should only vote as a *bloc*, or whether it may split its vote and, if so, under what conditions; whether it shall have discretion as to whom to support, or whether it is mandated to vote for only one candidate – and, if so, under what conditions it may switch this vote if that candidate has no hope of winning.

But, of course, all this is known to the contenders: and well in advance, for it governs their electoral strategy. And so too is the

2. Theodore White, *The Making of the President*, Cape, 1960, pp. 135–6.

voting strength of the delegations, for these have unequal votes in the choice of the candidate. How these votes are apportioned is a matter for the party's national committee; and this is the one factor in the matter which is public and routine knowledge.

Long before the Convention the candidates throw their hats into the ring. Their strategy is twofold. Firstly, they try to convince the masters of the most influential States that, given the nomination, they could win the presidency: for the chief object of the party bosses is not to pick a candidate who is wise and good – though he may well be – but one who can win. And, secondly, they try to lobby or nobble a sufficient number of State delegations to win the necessary majority in the balloting. (In the Republican Convention of 1960 this was 666, and, in that of 1964, it was 655; in the Democratic Convention of 1960 it was 761, and, in that of 1964, it was no less than 1,159). As to the former, the presidential primaries have a part to play. Sixteen States hold such primaries – they have not caught on, unlike the congressional primaries, and in most cases they are nothing better than straw votes without political significance. But a few of them are more. For instance, it was John Kennedy's smashing win over his rivals in the West Virginia primary that convinced the doubters among the State bosses that he could, if nominated, carry the country. Likewise it was Rockefeller's defeat by Goldwater in the California presidential primary that demolished his hope of becoming the Republican presidential candidate in 1964. As to the latter part of the strategy, long months of negotiation with the leading personalities of the influential States precede the Convention.

Once there, and once the delegations have been recognized by the platform, the imposing roll call of the fifty States begins. Each in turn, in alphabetical order, rises to declare its choice; and those among the As and Bs who have no 'favourite son' of their own whose name they want to place before the Convention, yield their place to some State with a lower letter – like New York, away down among the second half of the States – to allow it to put its candidate before the Convention early in the proceedings. The cheers and caperings that are part of the folksy build-up of the

Convention – half meeting, half jamboree – mount as the great, the leading names, are put forward. And so, by the end of the call, the votes are tallied. If one candidate has the necessary majority, he is the presidential candidate. If not, further ballots are held until one candidate does secure that majority. And then the whole Convention votes to make the endorsement unanimous. For the fortune, the leadership, the programme, the machinery, the *mana* of the party is now irrevocably in the hands of that man. The first thing he will do is to nominate his choice of running mate – the vice-presidential candidate. (This, too, is often negotiated beforehand.) Then, he makes his keynote speech. Now in its earlier sessions, the national committee, presiding from the platform, has established a committee to present the programme – the 'platform', as it is called. It makes promises to all. It is as diffuse, as comprehensive, as the span of American society itself. This document becomes meaningless after the presidential nominee has spoken; for he selects, enlarges, attenuates and adds to that platform speech in such a way as to make it specific as well as personal, and henceforth his speech becomes the electoral programme of the party. From this point, the whole party unites behind him, however faction-ridden and bitter the divisions in the Convention have been. The aim is clear and specific; whatever he is, they must secure his election.

The tactics of candidates vary. The strategy is and must be the same. The winner will be the one with an absolute majority of votes in the electoral college (in 1964 this college had 538 votes; the winner had to have at least 270). He can get this majority by winning the eleven most heavily-weighted States, plus any one of the others – by carrying, that is, twelve States out of fifty, provided only that they are the right ones. But, to be 'right', they not only have to have a large number of votes in the college, but also they must be balanced evenly enough to make it worth while campaigning there. For years – certainly until the Eisenhower electoral campaign of 1952 – there was little point in a Republican campaigning for the States of the former Confederacy. For one thing, they do not carry many votes between them in the electoral college, but for another, he would never have won them anyway – they always voted Democrat. Nor did a Democratic candidate spend much time on them: they did not amount to many votes, and he was going to win them anyway.

So, attention concentrates on the densely populated, evenly divided States: States both influential and winnable. These include States like New York, which in 1964 had forty-three votes, California (forty votes), Pennsylvania (twenty-nine votes), Illinois and Ohio (twenty-six votes each), and Texas (since 1952, when Eisenhower carried it for the Republicans, though it is traditionally Democrat), with twenty-five votes. By and large, the areas that are criss-crossed by the campaigners are the industrialized North East, California and Illinois. All of these contain huge urban centres. And in the neck and neck race with Nixon in 1960, Kennedy owed his victory to winning – by hair-breadth margins – seven out of nine of such bigger urbanized States.

This is one reason why it can happen, particularly since 1946, that the president is of one party and his Congress of the other. For the House of Representatives and Senate over-represent the rural areas: the Senate because each State sends two senators to Washington, and there are more rural States than industrial-urban ones; the House because the districting carried out by the States has, as stated, favoured the rural areas over the urban ones, and because, in any case, the population of the U.S.A. is concentrated in towns of between 20,000 and 500,000 rather than in towns of over 500,000. But winning the presidency turns on the pivotal strength of the urbanized States. The 'unit rule' ensures that these States can be swung by a very narrow majority. That majority can be ensured in those States when the voting is on a state-wide basis because then the urban masses and the rural and small-town areas form one great pool. The presidential candidate can win if he captures the metropolitan areas, with their polyglot populations and their appetite for social welfare, while the up-state vote may bring victory to his opponents in the Congress.

And even if it does not quite do this – even if the president's party also wins the Congress – that difference in their respective constituencies still persists. Whether Republican or Democratic, the candidate for the presidency must court the urban masses. Not so the Congress.

IV. THE PRESIDENCY

The agency which suggests things; the agency which gets approval for them; the agency which sees they are carried out; the agency, in short, which leads, devises and executes, and which symbolizes the country – this is what the common man regards as his government. And, in this sense, the government of the U.S.A. is the president. He is, constitutionally, the head of the whole civil service. He commands the armed forces. He appoints and receives ambassadors, negotiates agreements, signs treaties. He proposes legislation to the Congress. He suggests to it how much the authorities should spend and on what. He symbolizes the nation.

The enormous upsurge of the U.S.A.'s industrial power and its central role in world politics have enhanced all these roles. The U.S.A. is the world's diplomatic centre. In present-day conditions, foreign policy is negotiated, if not made, by face-to-face meetings of heads of states. As the head of the most important of all states, the presidency has grown with America's world role. Again, as the sub-continent has filled up and become the world's workshop, so the national government has been expected, increasingly, to regulate industrial relations, social conditions and the economy. What President Roosevelt took as almost an emergency power to right the economy in the Great Depression has now been written into statute after statute, so that this has become the duty of the presidency, not simply its right. And with this, the federal civil service has grown from a mere 131,000 in 1884 to the vast figure of 2·4 million in 1963. The president is the chief executive – he appoints and he dismisses from this vast corps. And finally, with the growth of mass communications, Press, broadcasting and television, he has stepped ever more prominently into the father-figure role created by the first and most revered of all America's presidents, George Washington: the Abraham of the Chosen People.

The president is the one focus, the one centre of coherence in the bewildering variety, profusion, confusion which mark

American society and its governmental expression. Or, more justly, one must say: the one *possible* focus, the one *possible* centre of coherence. For some presidents have not filled the role, and others have barely done so. Only a few have filled it completely.

For consider what confronts the presidency: first of all, the legislature – Congress. Its orientation is different, for its constituency is different, as has been said already. No president can lean *away* from the great metropolitan demands: he can only lean towards them in a lesser degree than other presidents. The presidential candidate who tries to win an election by relying on the rural, suburban and hick-town belts will lose hands down, as Barry Goldwater did in 1964. Then again, Congress is incoherent. It is composed of a congeries of individuals, self-divided into two bands of nominal partisans, bisected into an Upper and a Lower House; and each house is sub-divided into a number of committees who have the first – and usually the final – bite at legislation, and some of which are further split into sub-committees; like the House Appropriations Committee which divides itself into twelve. Next, Congress is intensely parochial: the Lower House because its members are tied hand and foot to their districts which they have to meet for re-election every two years, so that they have barely got to Washington before they must think of their next campaign, and the Senate, parochial on a larger scale (there are fifty parishes and not 435), because the senators from Arizona or Idaho have as much legislative weight as those from New York and California.

Party allegiance *might* weld all these bits and pieces into coherence, but it does not. The right wing of one party has much the same outlook as the right wing of the other. That is its natural affinity, even when it comes to the vote. And the same for the liberal wings, and for the respective centres. The La Follette–Monroney Committee of 1945–6 suggested that each party should establish a 'policy committee' in either house, to give coherence to its outlook and legislative programme. But this advice has borne little fruit. In 1949 the House Republican Policy Committee was set up, but did not become fully active until 1959. Since then, it has become useful as a means of providing internal recognition

within the ranks of the younger Republicans. The House Democrats do have a committee also, but it rarely meets. Neither of
these policy committees do or can draft programmes, and even if
they did there is not the slightest guarantee that the party members would support them. The party whips, led by the majority
(or minority) leaders, can cajole and persuade: they cannot do
more. They wield few sanctions. All votes for bills, whether these
have emanated from members themselves or from the president,
are bipartisan in some degree. One American scholar has palely
pleaded that party allegiance is the best single predictor of the
vote of a member.[3] Certainly; 'So shines a good deed in a
naughty world.' But the hard facts of the situation are to be
seen in Table 12, which shows samples of voting figures for some
recent legislation.

TABLE 12

Farm Act, September 1962			Democrats	Republicans
House of	for		200	2
Representatives	against		37	100
Senate	for		52	7
	against		–	34

Revenue Act, 1964				
House of	for		218	108
Representatives	against		20	63
Senate	for		53	21
	against		10	9

Civil Rights Acts, 1964				
House of	for		152	138
Representatives	against		96	34
Senate	for		46	27
	against		21	6

3. N. W. Polsby, *Congress and the Presidency*, Prentice-Hall, 1964, p. 113.

In the 1961 Senate, only fifteen Democratic senators supported the president, a Democrat, in eighty to ninety per cent of his measures; only another twenty-two supported him in seventy to seventy-nine per cent of his measures.

In any case, there is no guarantee that the president's party will have control of the Congress – for instance, Democrats controlled it for six out of the eight years of Eisenhower's presidency. In such circumstances, the usual indiscipline is weighted against the presidency.

For leadership, for initiatives and for public intelligibility the Congress is useless. As Bagehot put it, 'it is a body hanging on the verge of government.' Never mind if it reflects public opinion more faithfully than does the president, as its apologists contend, for that is precisely its drawback. American society is too variegated for its reflection to be anything but diffuse and unfocused. Perhaps the trouble with Congress is precisely that it is too honest a reflection. Or, to change the simile, it is like a window-pane which lets the sun's rays pass through it, where what is needed is a burning glass.

In 1946 the Congress tried to reform itself, to become an effective alternative to the presidency. It reduced the number of its committees and defined their terms of reference more precisely. It gave them better and more numerous staffs and improved the congressional intelligence service – the Legislative Reference Service. It recommended that each party in each of the two houses should establish policy committees. But all the reforms achieved was to make the Congress better at its traditional role of interfering with the presidency. They did not make the Congress into a substitute focus of leadership. When Congress is at its best, when it functions most effectively, it is not because of its own spontaneous efforts. Left to its own devices, it would reduce itself to a number of legislative vortexes. It functions well only when and because the initiative in major policy, and the inducement to enact it, come from the outside – from the president.

What else confronts the presidency? The pressure groups. So far we have not mentioned them. But, given a society as multifarious and populous as that in America, in which, too, the freedoms to speak and print what one likes, to assemble, to associate and to vote are fundamental, of course there are pressure groups. Indeed, for a long time America was regarded as the unique home of pressure groups. Not until 1957 and 1958 did British scholars discover pressure groups in their own country and not till a few years later did the French and the Germans discover them in theirs. It has been reckoned that there were (1947–8) some 1,800 organizations with lobbying offices in Washington; and (1950) 150 national labour groups, 40,000 to 50,000 local labour groups, 3,000 national business groups and some 2,000 local ones. According to the U.S. Department of Commerce (1949) some 4,000 national, professional, civic and trade associations existed, divisible thus: associations of manufacturers, of distributors and of businessmen in the fields of transportation, finance and insurance; professional and semi-professional groups; labour unions; women's organizations; ex-servicemen; farmers; Negroes; public officials; fraternal associations; sport and recreational associations; and, finally, an 'all other fields' category, which would include a multitude of ethnic associations. Some American pressure groups are internationally famous: the National Association of Manufacturers, the American Federation of Labor and Congress of Industrial Organisations (A.F.L.–C.I.O.) (the equivalent of the British T.U.C.), the American Medical Association, the National Grange (farmers), the American Legion (ex-servicemen), the National Association for the Advancement of Colored People.

Now, the open-ended nature of the American parties, and the functioning of the party system and of the congressional system, all invite the attention of pressure groups. To begin with, in the United States, pressure groups can, and therefore try hard to, influence elections – an almost useless preoccupation in Britain, where the national endorsement by party headquarters means much more to a candidate than the vagaries of any section of his electorate. In the U.S.A. it is, precisely, the vagaries of the local electorate that 'endorse' the candidate in the primary and serve to elect him as Democrat or Republican to the Congress. So some American pressure groups often make a point of 'endorsing' a candidate – the A.F.L.–C.I.O., for instance, makes a feature of this. Next, the organization of the Congress positively invites, nay demands, the presence of pressure groups. For instance, a bill goes to its appropriate committee; there it is usually subjected to a hearing – i.e., outside witnesses, for and against, are called before the committee. These outside witnesses are nothing else and can be nothing else than the pressure groups. Furthermore, unlike the British Parliament, the Congress itself initiates legislation. The British pressure group can hardly hope for much from the legislature unless the Cabinet of the day will endorse a private member's bill and give it facilities. This is not so in the U.S. Congress, where a private member's bill may be brought in and carried with some ease, if it commends itself. Again unlike the British Parliament, the Congress is independent of the executive and can amend or reject legislation sponsored by it. Thus Congress attracts pressure group activity for this reason, too. And having attracted it, it finds it impossible to be rid of it, because there is neither party tradition nor party discipline to ensure that it is disregarded or defeated. The only authority that can defeat it is outside the Congress: it is the president, using his veto.

Finally, the whole separated-powers structure of the government invites the attentions of the pressure group and this for two reasons. The first is that, since any one branch of government can veto a proposal, it is useless for a group to concentrate on the House alone or the Senate alone or the executive alone. It must not only try to ensure that all three are favourable but that they are favourable simultaneously. This is why American pressure groups have turned more and more to 'grass-roots lobbying' – orchestrated attempts, via the electoral process, via letters to, and personal lobbying of, congressmen and senators and even the president, via mass advertising in the newspapers and over the television networks, to create a favourable public opinion. Secure that, and all the interlocking branches of the government become receptive simultaneously. The principal reason for the common belief that pressure groups are more prominent and successful in the United States than in any other country is because they are forced to campaign on this lavish scale, and in the open, in a way that is either otiose or vain in Britain. As a consequence, the groups are certainly more prominent in American public life than in British; but not necessarily more successful.

The second reason why the separated-powers structure attracts pressure group activity is that concentration upon the executive branch offers no guarantee of success; whereas in Britain it affords a very high possibility of success, since there, espousal of a proposal by the executive will have the support of the party's majority in the Commons and in more than nine cases out of ten, therefore, to win over the minister or civil servant is to win the campaign. This is not so in the U.S.A. Certainly the pressure groups besiege the bureaux and agencies that make up the federal executive; and even more than in Britain there exist closed relationships of client–patron nature between the pressure groups and their sponsoring agency. But this difference exists: in the United States the support of the executive agency does not dispose of the matter in the Congress, for it may well run into a hostile committee; conversely, the disapproval of an agency does not dispose of the matter, for the group can – as it cannot in Britain – go behind the back of the agency and secure appoval in the favourable committee. In short, the United States lobby can, as the British ones cannot, play both sides against the middle. And very often it does.

Consequently, the whole of the American legislative and administrative processes are shot through with the pressure of the various groups. They enter into the electoral processes, and so help shape the very composition of the two houses; they dispose the two parties in Congress towards the claims of various sections; they inspire bills in the Congress and in the White House; they influence the executive of the laws. Only the strategy is different. In Britain, the interest group starts by trying to persuade the ministry; only failing that does it move to try to influence the Commons; only to assist in this, or when this approach has failed, does it try to manipulate public opinion on a mass scale. In the United States the order is inverted. First and most important is the public-cum-electoral campaign; then the influencing of the Congress; only if this is a failure, is an attempt made to win over the president or his departmental heads.

Thus the president has to face a Congress that is not only amorphous, but convulsed by the efforts of group pressure. And at this point he is assailed on another flank also. For, as we have seen, in the modern state, the representative, partisan and 'interested' legislature, the representative of today's wishes and pressures, is offset by the neutral, dispassionate, forward-looking bureaucracy. But the American executive 'branch' is not a solidary hierarchical body which can interpose a collective veto upon the legislature or the pressure group. No bureaucracy is, of course; but some, like the French and the British, possess a cohesion, a chain of command and a common outlook in far higher measure than the United States. To call it the executive 'branch' is a misnomer. It is a congeries of thrones, principalities and powers. For one thing, a number of extremely powerful bodies stand outside it altogether: the so-called 'independent commissions', like the Federal Trade Commission, the Interstate Commerce Commission and the Federal Power Commission. The jealousy of Congress, eager to curb the growth of the presidential power, has established these in such ways that they do not come directly under the president's control. These are the agencies collectively described in a bizarre but nevertheless effective image as a 'headless fourth branch of government'. Next, each of the main secretaryships – the main departments of state, whose members sit in the presidential Cabinet, like the Department of State and the Treasury – is subjected to a two-way stretch. In theory it owes allegiance only to its head – the president. In practice, if it wants to see its budget through, if it wishes to retain its powers and its private way of doing things, it had best be friends with the congressional committees which exercise the power, not only of scrutinizing proposed legislation and of withholding funds, but of generally supervising groups of executive agencies. The department, or a bureau in the department, faces two ways.

Nor are the departments solidary units. The American practice of staffing their top ranks with politicians, the friends of the administration in power, rather than with career-bureaucrats (the permanent secretaries, etc., of the British system) has permitted the departments to crumble into their primary units, the bureaux. Unlike the departments themselves, these are headed by career officials and are cohesive units, although few, if any, of these bureau chiefs care a fig for the bureau next to them. And so the number of individuals whom the president has to supervise is immediately multiplied to a prodigious degree. To complicate the pattern still more, most bureaux will have some specific clientele with whom they work and whom they try to satisfy: for instance, farmers, small businesses, the army or navy. Neustadt has painted an admirable picture of the executive:

Like our governmental structure as a whole, the executive establish¬ ment consists of separated institutions sharing powers. The President heads one of these: Cabinet officers, agency administrators, and military commanders head others. Below the departmental level, virtually independent bureau chiefs head many more. Under mid-century conditions, Federal operations spill across dividing lines on organiza- tion charts; almost every program calls for interagency collaboration. Everything somehow involves the President. But operating agencies owe their existence least of all to one another – and only in some part to him. Each has a separate statutory base; each has its statutes to administer; each deals with a separate set of sub-committees at the Capitol. Each has its own peculiar set of clients, friends, and enemies outside the formal government. Each has a different set of specialized careerists inside its own bailiwick. Our Constitution gives the President the 'take-care' clause and the appointive power. Our statutes give him central budgeting and a degree of personnel control. All agency administrators are responsible to him. But they are *also* responsible to Congress, to their clients, to their staffs, and to themselves. In short they have five masters. Only after all of those do they owe any loyalty to each other.[4]

Thus the amorphousness of the Congress, the polymorphous- ness of group pressures, the fragmentation of the executive branch itself – all thrust the presidency into the centre.

The amorphous Congress reflects, the multifarious lobbies refract, the labyrinthine bureaucracy services, the needs and aspiration of polymorphous U.S. society. The presidency focuses them. If it did not exist it would have to be invented. It is the one point of contact between the three. The entire burden is thrust upon the shoulders of one man.

'*The President needs help.*' So reported a famous American Commission on Administrative Management in 1936; and since

4. R. E. Neustadt, *Presidential Power*, Wiley, New York, 1962, p. 39.

that date the unparalleled and ever-increasing burden on the president has been matched by offices, agencies and boards designed to help him in the task of co-ordinating and focusing the pressures from Congress, from the claim groups and from the executive branch itself.

The traditional instrument, the presidential Cabinet, which comprises the secretaries of the departments, has never been effective. It is unknown to the Constitution. It was the invention of America's first president, George Washington, after the Senate (then only twenty-six in number) had declined to act as his privy council, and after the Supreme Court (then five justices) had similarly declined that role. The Constitution says quite clearly that the president is the head of the executive branch and lays the duties of this office unequivocally on him and him alone. So, the Cabinet is advisory only. It is not a collective body, like the British Cabinet. The American equivalent of the British Cabinet is the president, and the British equivalent of the president is the collective presidency of the Cabinet. From the earliest times presidents used advisers other than their Cabinet members. From Andrew Jackson's term (1828–36) dates the expression 'kitchen cabinet' – meaning informal advisers as opposed to formal ones. Whether a president is swayed by his Cabinet or overrides it; whether he works through it – as President Eisenhower liked to do – or whether he works with small groups of selected advisers, is a personal matter. Certainly, the Cabinet is not the place where all pending legislation is 'cleared', where all interested ministers advise and recommend on the problems raised by the proposals of one of their group, as in Britain. It is an adjunct to the government, i.e., the president; it is not, as in Britain, the government itself.

The newest instrument is the National Security Council, a direct response to the Cold War. Established by statute, it consists of the president, the vice-president, the secretaries of state and defence and the director of the Office of Emergency Planning. The chairman of the Joint Chiefs of Staff and the director of the Central Intelligence Agency are *ex officio* advisers. Its scope is defence and foreign affairs. But, once again, the president does not have to work through it, and although he may delegate problems to it, they still remain his personal responsibility. Like the Cabinet, it is an adjunct. And, like the Cabinet, it is relied on by some presidents, such as Eisenhower, and by-passed for smaller working groups by presidents such as Kennedy and Johnson.

The two instruments which do act as ears, eyes and arms for the president are more modest. Both are creations of the Roosevelt era. They are the Bureau of the Budget (created in 1921 but moved directly under the presidency in 1939) and the White House Office. The first of these is of great importance. It does three things: it acts as a clearing house for all bills introduced in Congress, expressing an opinion on each, and making sure that they are in accord with presidential policy; it annually scrutinizes the budget estimates of each bureau, thus exercising a control over administrative policy, again in accordance with the policies of the president; and it carries out administrative surveys in the executive branch, again at the president's request. It is the effective focus for all minor policy and administrative sub-policy making. But, by its nature, it cannot resolve matters which bring it up against a powerful secretary or senator. The only person who can reconcile major policy differences is the president, personally.

To help him in this he has the White House Office – a group of aides and assistants, the so-called 'trouble shooters'. Some of these are assigned to expedite presidential legislation before Congress, some to look into specific problems as they arise. They are, in fact, a secretarial staff; and again, their effectiveness derives entirely from the man behind them. If, like President Johnson, he is a former senator and skilful political operator, they really can succeed in their task of expediting legislation before Congress. If, as in Kennedy's day, they are regarded by the senators and older congressmen as the 'jet set' or the 'whizz kids', they will do more harm than good: between the elder statesmen at the Capitol and the administrative aides from the White House there existed in Kennedy's time what has been described as only a 'mutuality of contempt'.

It will be noticed that every one of these agencies, Cabinet, National Security Council, Bureau of the Budget, White House

Office, is an adjunct of the president: not one of them divests him of a shred of his constitutional responsibilities. In the last resort, to fulfil his duties as chief executive, initiator of legislation, commander-in-chief, chief diplomat and head of state, he must rely on the bargaining weapons with which the Constitution has equipped him, and on his own personality and shrewdness. Given the latter, he can make the weapons effective. Without them, they are too feeble and too few.

His task is to secure the concurrence of Congress. Congress is congenitally hostile, and we have seen why. And Congress has very sharp weapons at its disposal. A glance at these and it is easy to see how good a *tactician* the president must be if he is to be effective.

V. PRESIDENT AND CONGRESS

It is not often that a Constitution does just what is expected of it. But the rivalry between Congress and president was planned by the Founding Fathers; and it has duly occurred just as it was planned.

The great security against a gradual concentration of the several powers (of government) in the same department [wrote Madison in Number 51 of the *Federalist*] consists in giving to those who administer each department the necessary constitutional means and personal motives to resist encroachments of the others. The provision for defence must in this, as in all other cases, be made commensurate to the danger of attack. Ambition must be made to counteract ambition. The interest of the man must be connected with the constitutional rights of the place.

The ambition of the senator or the congressman is opposed to that of the president. This is because, firstly, his future is bound up with deferring to his locality, not with representing the Nation. Secondly, his time scale is different: most senators and congressmen want to stay in Congress indefinitely, and this means surviving several presidents whose personal terms are limited to a maximum of two full terms (eight years), in the normal way, ten years as an abnormal vacuum. (The Twenty-second Amendment, adopted 1951.) While the president wants to pack everything possible into his four or eight years of office, the senator or congressman wants to stay longer; hence both the latter will often be disposed to vote down the president's policy if this means perpetuating their own tenure of office. Thirdly, the highest pinnacle which the congressman – and the bulk of senators – can attain is not, as in most European countries, to become a minister and part of the government, but to become a chairman of an important committee and this, again, under the conventions governing the selection of chairmen, demands that he hang on to his seat as long as possible, owing to the operation of the 'seniority rule'. The Chairman of each Committee, in either branch of the Congress, is by convention always the member of the majority party having the longest unbroken length of service on that Committee.

In the Senate, power lies with the chairmen of committees, but it also lies with individual senators or groups of them in so far as these can utilize the rules of debate to delay or filibuster. The longest and greatest of these filibusters may serve as an example: that over the Civil Rights Bill, 1964. Here eighteen senators, all from the Southern States, and all of the president's own party, held up all Senate business for eighteen days on end, by dividing into three platoons of six senators apiece, each working one day on and two days off, and by this means chain-talking continuously. (To break it, the Senate used its one defence, so difficult a one that it has only been successfully applied three times since 1945. It carried the closure of debate: for this a two-thirds majority of those present and voting is necessary. It was carried by seventy-one to twenty-nine.) In the House of Representatives, however, the problem is to find time, not to waste it. The House is inundated with bills: between 1961 and 1962, a fairly average session, there were no less than 13,420 of them. The alleyways to debate and vote are the nineteen standing committees, and then the Rules Committee. Blocked in any of these alleys, a bill fails. The 1961–2 figures tell their own story. Of the 13,420 bills introduced only 1,812 were reported on by the committees, the rest suffering silent euthanasia at their hands. Of these reported out, 1,017 were passed. The committee is enormously more lethal than the floor of the House.

These alleyways to floor consideration – the committees – are guarded by the committee chairmen. By their patronage over the committee staffs, their power to allocate tasks to sub-committees, to arrange the committee agenda and to pre-select the witnesses, they have a major place in determining the attitude the committee will take. But these, as we have seen, are appointed on the principle of seniority. And this means that the most likely chairmen are those from 'safe' areas – rock-ribbed Republican or Democratic areas that rarely if ever change their voting allegiance – in short, from the most bigoted sectors of each party: from the Southern States in the Democratic Party; from the rural or hicktown up-state areas of the North East or the Plains in the Republican Party. Thus the divergence between the president and the Congress is widened. Whether he is a Democrat or a Republican, the president must always be more liberal than the chairmen; for he is responsive to the metropolitan pressures and they to their rural ones.

And they have the sharpest of weapons at hand, with which to check, thwart or entrammel the president. They can and do delay or refuse to act upon the bills he recommends; between one-third and two-thirds only of presidential proposals are enacted in some recognizable form – and the median, as against the arithmetical average, is well below fifty per cent. They can and they do cut and change the appropriations from the estimates put before them by the Bureau of the Budget. They can give instructions or pass statutes to enforce the most stringent and detailed requirements upon the executive agencies; and every new agency, every alteration and re-allocation of functions within the executive branch, must receive statutory authority – at their hands, therefore. They have the duty of general surveillance over the executive performance of the agencies within their field of subject matter, and they press this often to extreme lengths. Furthermore, the Congress can, at will, establish special inquiries into certain aspects of the executive's activities, the transcripts of evidence often running to mountainous heights. And, through the General Accounting Office, they can and do carry out post-audit examinations of the work of the agencies and bureaux.

All these powers thwart: they are no substitute for government or for leadership. These are for the president. He cannot brow-beat the congressional committees. He cannot override them. His strategy is twofold: to push them to a parley – and then parley to good effect. The Constitution provides him with weapons for the first. He himself is responsible for the second.

For he, in his turn, can thwart congressmen and senators in the things that they want. First of all, he can veto bills treasured by knots of senators and congressmen: the two-thirds majority needful to overturn that veto is not easy to obtain. This is one bargaining counter, then. Next, he can hold up the spending of money appropriated to some purpose – and to do so may mean the loss of a factory, a road or a port to some congressman's district. Then, he has inducements to hold out. There once was a time when the president held thousands of petty official appoint-ments at his own discretion. Most of these have now been 'classified under civil service rules' and are no longer discre-tionary political appointments, but enough still remain to make these *douceurs* effective in certain instances. Postmasterships, for instance, are at his disposal; these are usually delegated to the congressmen of the president's own party to hand out in their districts, but, of course, only if they are pliable. The same is true of federal judgeships and collectors at ports. In addition, appoint-ments to the Supreme Court, to the 'independent commissions', to the top management posts in the bureaux and agencies, are all within his nominating power: he appoints to these – subject to the advice and consent of the Senate, it is true, but they are the subjects of bargains between himself and the senators concerned. Another inducement is the traditional 'pork barrel'. The Small Business and Area Redevelopment Corporation grants loans to various areas: the president can steer such a loan, for a considera-tion; he can also steer defence contracts, research contracts and the location of various administrative headquarters – and these projects touch the local-minded congressman in his sorest spot.

These are the president's weapons. Used well, they will give the Congress pause. There are others too, but these are more personal. Party loyalty is thin, but it does have some power; especially where the president is politically prominent and popular, his support or endorsement will carry weight in the next round of elections. While it is not at all impossible to resist a personal appeal from the president, it is embarrassing to say 'no' and it may even be unwise. And, where the president has appealed successfully to the nation over the television channels, it may even favour a congressman's political chances to associate himself with the presidential policy. It is in these fields that the personality of the president is paramount. He must be popular with the public, an electoral advantage to the congressmen of his own party, but also a shrewd and easy-mannered diplomat in his dealings with the two houses. He must be a lion, but he must also be the fox. If he can handle Congress, his power and authority is indeed immense; if he cannot, it is blighted; if he will not, policy marks time and government declines into administrative routine. But, always, he must reckon with the Congress. This division of the legislature from the executive branch weakens each, and also both; that is it weakens the entire aggregate power of the national government as a whole. But that, as we have seen, was precisely what the Founding Fathers wanted to do; and that too is precisely what – for most of the time, in the long periods of fatness and 'normalcy' which America has enjoyed – this immensely pluralistic society has licensed it to do.

Chapter 7

THE GOVERNMENT OF FRANCE

I. DISSENSUS

ONE good reason for taking France as the third example of the liberal-democratic state is that she has a longer continuous development as such than any other European country of her population, resources and world-involvement, excepting Britain. Italy and Germany are not good alternatives since they did not exist as unified states until 1860 and 1870 respectively. Furthermore, in both cases, constitutional development was arrested by a long spell of totalitarian rule followed by foreign occupation, so that their current liberal-democratic régimes must be regarded still as to some extent under trial.

But there are other excellent and more positive reasons for selecting France. No other European state so epitomizes the civilization of continental Europe. No other European state has so perennially excelled in so many fields of human endeavour simultaneously: in the visual, the plastic and the architectural arts, in music and poetry and literature, in philosophy and in natural science, in the art of war as well as in the science of administration and the law. Well might Joachim du Bellay sing: '*France, mère des arts, des armes et des lois.*'

Nor is that all. Few states, even European ones whose power of resurgence so puzzles and surprises the citizens of the U.S.A., have so frequently suffered disaster and so unfailingly recovered, stronger and more self-confident than before. The tough resilience of the French people, their national aptitude for '*se débrouiller*', has led to one glorious renaissance after another, occurring just when least expected, at the point where foreign observers expected France to be at her last gasp: her recovery after the foreign occupation and humiliation of the Hundred Years War, after the Wars of Religion, after the Revolution, after Napoleon's humiliating defeat, after Sedan – and recently under de Gaulle, after she had been written off as the sick man of Europe. France might well take unto herself the motto of her capital city: '*Fluctuat nec mergitur*' – 'it rocks but it does not founder'.

More important still, France is the world's ideological factory. It seems to be her peculiar faculty to absorb influences from elsewhere – the experience of Britain, or the experience of Germany, or wherever you will – and transmute these into abstract terms. In the realms of ideas and particularly political ideas, French influence has been paramount throughout the world, excepting, peculiarly enough, in the United States.

But the most important reason for taking France as the third example of the liberal-democratic state lies in the contrast she affords to Britain and the U.S.A. Britain is, comparatively speaking, a highly united community, and so she can tolerate a form of government that is unitary, concentrated and strong willed. The U.S.A. is not so highly united a community: her government, decentralized, self-frustrating, uses a looser rein. But France is self-divided. Political opinion exists there in highly ideological form – unlike Britain and the United States where differences arise over minor programmes not major principles; it is organized, as in Britain and the U.S.A., in parties and pressure groups; but it is not 'public', in our sense of being widely dispersed throughout the various sections and strata of society as it is in Britain and the U.S.A. On the contrary it is fragmented into mutually exclusive compartments.

The result has been extreme political instability as government has alternated between two types. The first of these has emphasized representation of and accountability to this fragmented public opinion at the expense of 'order and future goals'. The other type has stressed 'order and future goals' at the expense of representation and accountability. The first has found expression in a peculiarly French type of parliamentarism, '*gouvernement d'assemblée*' (government by the Assembly), and the second in varieties of personal rule, whether that of Napoleon I and Napoleon III in the First and the Second Empires, or in the Vichy régime, or – 1958/1969 de Gaulle's presidential Republic.

French society

French society is very rapidly altering. Her population, almost stagnant in the nineteenth century, has leapt from thirty-nine million in 1900 to fifty million today. Agriculture, which in 1870 accounted for as much as forty per cent of the French labour force, now accounts only for some twenty per cent. Since 1930 production has nearly trebled: aluminium production has increased threefold, pig-iron doubled, electricity quadrupled. There are over six times as many motor cars, and over thirty times as many tractors in use. Industrial productivity, in 1960, was more than double that of the year 1939, and the national income has risen over that period from an index figure of 107 to 175. France has entered the twentieth century along with the U.S.A., Britain and Germany, and her rate of growth is prodigious.

For all that the structure of society is 'old-fashioned' compared with Britain and the United States. It is less industrialized, less urbanized, less concentrated and more parochial, and the 'small man' still predominates. France is double the size of Britain, but far less densely populated: Britain has 217 inhabitants per square mile, France only eighty-three. Furthermore a far higher proportion live in tiny towns than in either the United States or Britain: in Britain seventy per cent of the population lives in towns of over 20,000, in the United States fifty-two per cent, but in France only thirty per cent. Nor is that all. Apart from Paris, only six cities in France have populations of over a quarter of a million; and one-third of her population lives in villages with under 2,000 inhabitants apiece.

Of the working population, a far higher proportion is engaged in agriculture than in either of the two other countries: nearly one-fifth, as against less than one-tenth in the U.S.A. and less than one-twentieth in Britain. Furthermore industry, although rapidly modernizing and concentrating itself into giant enterprises, is still preponderantly small scale; ninety-six per cent of industrial firms employ less than fifty workers apiece – indeed, eighty-three per cent of them employ less than *five* workers apiece! Moreover, the 'small man' is ubiquitous. There are one and a quarter million self-employed 'bosses' in industry and commerce, and of the four and a half million or so 'farmers' only about 800,000 are labourers: the rest own or lease their own farms and work them. Thus French society is not just polarized between 'capital' and 'labour'; side by side with these two sectors it also contains a large number of economically independent small producers, in industry, commerce and agriculture alike; and this has profound effects on French political life, creating a clientele for parties which have no counterpart in either the United States or Britain.

In one sense, French society is more homogeneous than either the United States or Britain. The people are *ethnically* the same: with the exception of Alsace and Lorraine, they have been French speaking – and part of the French *nation* (as opposed to *patrie* – a different concept) for centuries: and the great majority of the population is nominally Catholic. In another sense it is somewhat less markedly homogeneous: localism and regionalism are more pronounced than in Britain (though less so than in the United States) but this is of only marginal political significance today. But, whereas Britain has newspaper circulations of 506 per 1,000 inhabitants, France has only 252 per 1,000; moreover, these newspapers are provincial not national, and few have circulations of over 500,000 – unlike some British ones with ten times that figure.

But, i n a third sense, French society is not homogeneous at all. On the contrary it is cruelly self-divided, to a degree and in a manner unknown in the United States or Britain. And this is a product of history.

Like Britain, France is a very old state. Like Britain, her origin lies in the feudal society that followed the break-up of the Roman Empire. Like Britain, the making of the state – and the national community – was the work of feudal monarchs, imposing their will on unruly subordinates. Here geography, which came to the aid of the English by giving them a natural rampart in the sea, was less kind to the French. The distances – for the Middle Ages – were too great for the easy imposition of central rule; and the frontiers were too long, too numerous and too open. The sea coast is only a rampart if the navy can defend it, and the French sovereigns had to watch not only the sea but also the exposed land frontiers of the east and north east. So, in disposing of their feudal vassals, they were doubly handicapped: their rebellious feudatories were not only out of easy reach, but had access to foreign support. Nevertheless, partly by the persistent cunning of the royal lawyers, partly by force of arms, they were bit by bit subdued, or else their estates fell in by convenient deaths to the royal demesne. The lawyers, the officials and the standing armies of what was then the central power overmatched them. There was a final civil convulsion, brought about by the struggle between Catholic and Protestant in the sixteenth century when the centralizing process was nearing its goal, and this was not resolved until 1635. But when it was, there was a state, called France. Governed by an absolute monarch, and supported by the hierarchy of the Catholic Church whose faith was the official state-religion, it was, by contemporary standards, centralized and bureaucratized. It was a very different evolution from that of Britain, where Parliament had triumphed over the king, where a central civil service could hardly be said to exist, where localism luxuriated, and where nonconformity persisted; and it ushered in two centuries of European glory, wherein France was at once the wealthiest, most populous and most powerful of the European comity of states, and where 'France' and 'culture' became synonymous. Then occurred the great trauma: this evolution was terminated by a convulsion which has, to this very day, split Frenchmen into two camps. French politics is entirely incomprehensible except in the light of the Great Revolution of 1789. This, rather more even than socio-economic structure, is the key to French politics from that date to the present.

The Great Revolution, 1789

The point about the French Revolution is that it was not simply a great political or economic convulsion. While it lasted it was a break with the entire daily pattern of former existence. Nothing at all of this magnitude and completeness was ever experienced in the U.S.A. or Britain; only the experience of the Soviet state is comparable. Imagine a situation where, in a few short days or months, the old seven-day week is abolished and 'decades' substituted; where the familiar names of the months are changed; where the customary units of weight, height, distance are all altered to a completely novel system; where all the ancient provincial boundaries and their proverbial names are abolished and the whole country is re-districted into new units bearing the names of some geographical feature – rivers, mountains, etc.; where the state religion is not merely disestablished, but actively persecuted, and where its temples are turned over to a variety of novel and often bizarre cults. Very few revolutions seek to reach down into the humdrum routines of everyday existence. The Great Revolution did. It was not remote from the popular folk; it reached into the most trivial details of their lives. The Revolution convulsed the entire society.

The facts are familiar. In 1789 a desperate court convenes the Estates General, last brought together in 1914, its very protocol half forgotten. The Third Estate – the commonalty – promptly declares the meeting a 'National' Assembly. It invites the other two estates, the clergy and the nobility, to join it. Most of their members refuse to do so, but the so-called 'National' Assembly acts up to its name and, in a great burst of activity, abolishes or reforms away most of the old feudal prescriptions of the state – the privileged position of the Church and the clergy, the guilds, the nobility. Then, within two years, the mobs of Paris, under the auspices of their local government, the Commune of Paris, march on a newly elected Assembly and make it to the *claque* of the extremist factions, the Girondins and the Jacobins. The king is deposed, France is declared a Republic. The king, later followed by his queen, is put on trial, condemned and guillotined. Now the extremist factions dispute supremacy. The Girondins are declared traitorous; they are guillotined at the orders of the Jacobin faction. Faced with revolt in the south, in Brittany and the Vendée, and beleaguered by enemies without, the Jacobins establish the Committee of Public Safety: a ferocious collective despot that shows itself as merciless to its internal opponents as to the foreign armies on its frontiers. It beats off both; and then, amid the excesses of the Terror, itself falls victim to a coalition of factions emboldened by utter fear at falling victims to the tyranny they had themselves established. They seize Robespierre, Saint-Just and the other leaders of the Jacobin faction and guillotine them in their turn. The Terror comes to an end and the Constitution is changed (once more). This time the state is entrusted to the Directory: a committee of five men. Seeking public endorsement of its rule, the Directory prescribes elections, but, since it fears the return of the Jacobins, it arranges that two-thirds of the Convention's current membership shall retain their seats. In protest against this 'Law of the Two-Thirds', the Jacobin sections of Paris rise in a new insurrection. But no acquiescence in popular rule this time! Instead the Directory calls on the new revolutionary armed forces, an unknown Corsican lieutenant of artillery places his guns on the steps of Saint-Roch, and from there he mows down the advancing pikemen. This is the famous 'whiff of grapeshot', and thanks to it the Directory continues in office. Now, in the country generally, but particularly in Paris where the Jacobins have been hunted down, opinion actually demands the return of the *monarchy*! In Paris royalist *sections* march against the Directory. Once again the Directory brings out its troops and the insurrection of *Fructidor*, 1797, is crushed. But by now the country is riven by the rebellion in the Vendée and by yet other insurrections elsewhere; it is in a state of economic collapse and everywhere its once victorious armies are on the retreat. The Republic needs a sword. Since General Moreau has died in battle the Directory's choice falls on the victor of Saint-Roch: on Napoleon Bonaparte. A plot is woven between Sieyès, one of the Directors, and Napoleon, back from triumphs in Egypt. This *coup d'état* is sadly bungled; but it goes through. This is the *coup d'état* of 18 *Brumaire*. The Directory is swept away and replaced by a three man Consulate, Napoleon is named the first consul and the year is 1799, and, in Hugo's words, '. . . *Rome remplaçait Sparte. Déjà Napoléon perçait sous Bonaparte*'. Once in the saddle, Napoleon rides. The other two consuls are reduced to ciphers, to rubber stamps. Napoleon goes out to battle in Italy once more. His political future hangs upon his fortunes there. In 1800 he smashes Austria at Marengo and, when he returns to France, it is a Roman triumph. In 1804 he completes the cycle: in Notre-Dame, in the presence of the Pope but with his own hands, he crowns himself Emperor of the French.

The Revolution began as a rebellion against an effete autocracy. It ends with public support, by popular plebiscite, of an autocracy more ruthless, more centralized, more efficient than any France had ever known.

Now this account is just a string of dates, and in Britain and the U.S.A. no emotional significance attaches to it. It is otherwise for a Frenchman. He is personally involved in the events – even today, as we shall shortly see. Outside France, especially at this distance of time, the Revolution is seen simply as a great historical event, a most momentous one which, like all such, was 'inevitable', and on the whole 'a good thing'. But inside France, what is plain to all is that there is a dark side to the moon. If there was grandeur in the epic of the Revolution – and there was – there was also vileness. What the Revolution said is one thing. What it did is usually quite another. Consider the matter of *political authority*. The Revolution proclaimed the great levelling gospel of the contemporary world: 'Sovereignty resides in the people'; but what did it do? It established the Jacobin dictatorship. When the fate of the king was in play after he had been condemned to death, the government refused to hold a popular plebiscite – because the sovereign people would have pardoned him. When the Jacobins rose in 1795, they were mown down by grapeshot. When the royalists rose in 1797 they were treated in the same way. When the Chamber protested against Napoleon's decision to abolish the Directory, its members were marched off by the soldiery. By what criterion then does one judge the Revolution's attitude to political authority? By its proclamations? Or by its performance?

Again, consider its opposition to censorship and the intellectual and moral domination of the Church and its dedication, instead, to free thought and freedom of conscience. How does this square with the persecution of the non-juring clergy? The desecration of the churches? The abolition of the Christian Sunday? The support of novel cults like the Religion of Humanity? Or the altars raised and services read to the 'decadal cult' or *la patrie*, inside the walls of the proscribed churches?

Such instances could be multiplied. Consider 'social equality'. The Revolution abolished the last vestiges of feudal privileges in matters of law, status and taxation; but the Revolution also fostered and protected speculators, army contractors and bankers. Or consider the attack on dynastic loyalty. In its place the Revolution inculcated a furious nationalism, the cult of *la patrie*, one and indivisible. National unity was to replace loyalty to a person. But what kind of national unity was it which required civil war in the Vendée, the suppression of the *Chouans*, the '*noyades*', the razing of rebellious cities, the cry '*Lyon n'est plus*'? It is not generally realized that some part or other of the country was up in arms against the central government during the whole period from the Vendée revolt of 1793 until after Marengo in 1800. Napoleon, not the Revolution, was the peacemaker.

Finally, consider its attitude to religion. This was dubbed 'superstition'; it was to give way to what has been called the 'heavenly city of the eighteenth-century philosophers', to the Republic of Virtue, to the cult of 'progress'. These are noble and humanitarian phrases, but what was *done* was ignoble and vile. What other words are suitable for public authorities who mock the mourner by inscribing on cemetery doors 'Death is an eternal sleep'. Or for those in power who indiscriminately massacre the inmates of their prisons? For those who disposed of their enemies, male and female, by tying them together and sinking them in the river – a form of execution known as the *noyade*? For the procedures of the revolutionary tribunals? For inducing the dauphin, a child of ten, to give public testimony accusing his mother, Marie Antoinette, of committing incest with him? For the abominable treatment meted out to this pathetic imprisoned little boy at the hands of a brutalized sadist of a warder?

It is possible to support the revolutionaries *despite* all these things, even to justify all these things; but the fact remains that, since these things happened, it is equally possible to condemn them. The reason for mentioning these things is not to make a case either way but to show that there *is* a case against, if one feels that way inclined, and that, for one hundred and sixty years, many Frenchmen have felt that way. This issue, for or against the Revolution, became a kind of mould, into which each successive generation of Frenchmen poured its political emotions and interests; a pair of lenses, through which every generation interpreted the events of its own day. The entire subsequent political and economic history of France has been expounded and explained in terms of categories derived from the course of the Great Revolution.

The French dissensus

The Revolution has become all things to all men. There is no generally accepted interpretation. For Taine i t was the canker in the French state, directly responsible for the defeat at Sedan; for his rival Aulard it was the precursor of the Third Republic; for the socialist Jaurès, it was a class struggle; for the royalist Gaxotte, it was a sinister conspiracy; for the Marxists it is the red dawn of the proletarian struggle against the capitalists; and so one could go on. The important point is that as the two sides, the side of 'movement' and the side of 'order', competed for power, so they both invoked the Revolution. It has not been enough that French conservatism accepted the republican form of government in the end, and prepared to work through its institutions; as Bourgeois told a man of the right who said '*J'accepte la République*': '*Vous acceptez la République . . . ? Monsieur, c'est entendu. Mais, acceptez-vous la Révolution?*' Clemenceau, too, refused to admit the permissibility of distinguishing between the 'good' and the 'bad' sides of the Revolution. '*La Révolution*', he maintained, '*est un bloc.*'

The Revolution has thrown a spell over all the actors who have succeeded on the political stage. To all it has provided a great example – or a terrible warning. Each cast himself in his favourite role from the revolutionary repertoire; and it is this, not any objective regularity in the historical process, that accounts for the recurring situations in French nineteenth-century history that prompted Marx to the remark; 'Hegel says somewhere that all great events and persons in the world history appear, as it were, twice. He forgot to add that the first time they appear as tragedy, and the second as farce.'[1] After all, if all the main actors on the

1. The famous opening words of Karl Marx in his *The Eighteenth Brumaire of Louis Bonaparte.*

political stage are going about the business of mimicking their predecessors' lines, one ought not to be surprised if the drama they enact bears some resemblance to the original! In 1848, France had enjoyed eighteen years of static conservative parliamentary monarchy in the interest of that mixed crowd of speculators, contractors, professional middle-class people and sprigs of the ancient and the Napoleonic nobility who make up the cast of Balzac's *Comédie humaine*. In 1848 the king, Louis-Philippe, was overthrown by a rising in Paris (and nowhere else). France had sneezed and all Europe caught a cold. The great Revolution had come again! And forthwith everybody began to behave as though this was really true. At the head of the republican forces stood the poet and man of letters, Lamartine. Now Lamartine was also the author of the long and famous *Histoire des Girondins*. These were his heroes. For him the Revolution was about to be re-enacted; and so, under him, it should be a Girondin, not a Jacobin, Revolution. But, within six months, the Paris workers, infuriated by the decision to close the National Workshop, came out on the streets: was the Revolution, then, moving into its Jacobin phase? Was the Paris Commune on the march again? General Cavaignac bethought himself of Napoleon and of the 'whiff of grapeshot' and in the 'June days' his troops mowed down the incipient Commune on the streets. *Thermidor* had been successfully negotiated then; would this not be followed by another 18 *Brumaire*? At least one person was determined on this course: the furtive Louis-Napoleon, nephew of the great Napoleon, author of *Les Idées napoléoniennes*, perpetrator of two unsuccessful attempts upon the French throne. Elected by universal suffrage as president of the Second Republic, he schemed for the chance to quarrel with the National Assembly, and manipulate this excuse to suppress it; and so, on 2 December 1851 he carried out his own '18 *Brumaire*' – not very much better managed than his uncle's but just as successful. Then, submitting himself to a plebiscite, he inaugurated the Second Empire, taking the title of Napoleon III.

In parenthesis: the *bourgeoisie* is much blamed for its support of the repression of the Paris workers during the June days and for rallying to Napoleon III. Without attempting any excuses, it must be said that their behaviour is entirely understandable – in terms of the Great Revolution. These *bourgeois* remembered fathers and mothers who had been stripped of their possessions, exiled and even murdered, at the hands of the Parisian mobs and their self-appointed leaders. To them the seamy side of the Revolution was vivid and terrifying. If they had learned one lesson – and indeed it was the lesson of Lamartine, the historian of the Girondins – it was that the Paris mob was Jacobin and lethal. It must be stopped in its tracks. Their reaction was natural. It would have been surprising had they acted otherwise.

The apparent parallel between the courses of the first and the second revolutions, the First and the Second Republics, 18 *Brumaire* and 2 December, struck all observers. The Great Revolution was unfinished business: it was for each new generation to finish it. And so, when Napoleon III was forced to abdicate by the reaction of the Paris politicians and masses after the defeat at Sedan, in 1870, the Revolution was 'on' again. To most, the situation seemed to resemble the defeat of Napoleon in 1814 and the restoration of the monarchy. When, however, the Paris artisans barricaded themselves in Montmartre, then seized the city and actually proclaimed 'the Commune' the atavistic memories turned to a different chapter: the Paris Commune of 1791 – coupled with the Parisian workers and their barricades of June 1848! How could one expect the head of state, the venerable Thiers, who was the historian of a multi-volumed history of the French Revolution, Consulate and Empire, enemy of the Jacobins, protagonist of constitutional monarchy, to have failed to give the orders to suppress the Commune even with the help of the German besiegers!

And so further still, through the subsequent years of the Third Republic: every time the Church or the army or the right wing – or all together – took a political initiative, as in the days of General Boulanger (1887–91) or the Dreyfus affair (1894–8), the situation was interpreted in terms of the past: of the Communards and their enemies, of the 1848–51 period, of the Great Revolution.

Throughout all these evolutions, the questions posed were: for the Revolution, or against it? And next: whose revolution?

That of the constitutional monarchists or that of the Girondin republicans or that of the Jacobins? Or whose counter-revolution? That of the Orleanists? Or of the legitimate Bourbon line? Or of the Bonapartists? It was in answers to these questions that the French dissensus expressed itself.

The first great cleavage was over political issues; the next was over social and class issues; and the third was the result of the temperamental differences between Frenchmen. And the lines of division did not necessarily coincide: they crossed, ending in six divisions of French opinion.

The first issue arose over where authority should reside. The 'revolutionaries', or, as they were soon called from the place they took up in the hemispherical chamber of the national legislature, the 'men of the left', were the proponents of popular sovereignty. Authority resided in 'the People'. It derived from below. It was expressed through elections to a legislature. This legislature was sovereign, since it represented the Will of the People. Hence the government – the executive – was its creature and must do its bidding. The Will of the People must not be impeded: hence the necessity for freedom of speech, assembly, association and elections. It must not be distorted either, hence no censorship, and above all, no brainwashing. And brainwashing in nineteenth-century France meant the influence of Catholic priests, particularly in the schools. So *laïcité* in the schoolrooms, and the disestablishment of the Catholic Church, was another cardinal feature of left-wing opinion. It amounted, in its most dilute form, to civil liberties and anti-clericalism, a powerful elected legislature, and a weak and pliable executive. And the left's opposition to a strong executive, as to the Catholic Church, was reinforced by the example of history: for strong executives, whether a Napoleon I, a Charles X or a Napoleon III, had, consistently, been the assassins of free and representative institutions. And the Catholic Church had consistently supported them, and used them to restore its pre-revolutionary position.

But many others desired the exact opposite. Some hankered after the glories of the Bourbon line, some were content with a Bonapartist substitute. But all these men of the right wanted a strong executive: they believed that authority should be acknowledged wherever it lay, and that it should transmit its mandates downwards from on high. They distrusted the masses. They expressed their view of society in the threefold slogan: 'family, religion and nation'. The Altar must buttress the Throne. In practice this was expressed in a programme promoting a strong executive, limitations upon thought and expression, and the re-establishment of the place of the Church in schools and society generally.

The chasm between these two groups of Frenchmen continued and persists to this day. It divided them into two main groups, which may be called the *political* left and the *political* right.

But this is not the only division in France. Industrialization has created a second one; and it cuts across the first. Industrialization came to France comparatively late in the nineteenth century. Furthermore, it was concentrated in a few scattered centres: there was the textile industry in towns like Lyons, there was commerce in ports like Marseilles, there were the service and luxury goods industries in Paris; and only in the north east, in the Pas-de-Calais area, were there coal and iron industries. It was overshadowed by the peasant mass, and by a particularly avaricious and ruthless type of *bourgeoisie*. Hence unionization came late in the century and was, generally, ineffectual. But it was natural for the industrial workers also, like other classes, to interpret their experience in terms of the Great Revolution. Hence arose the hitherto unfashionable Jacobin interpretation of the Revolution. The Jacobins had made various social efforts, particularly in the field of price and commodity control. They were now interpreted as proto-socialists. Jean Jaurès's *Socialist History of the French Revolution* constitutes a landmark in this development. The industrial workers took the side of the left; but they added to it an ingredient that was not at all shared throughout the left, namely, their socialist aspirations. Far from sharing these, the bulk of the left, the 'small men' of whom France is so full, as well as some of the merchant and industrial republicans, detested and feared socialism just as much as they feared the men of the right. Many of them deserted left for right which seemed to afford a more secure protection against these thrustful and unwanted would-be allies. But the ranks of the right were not entirely united against the social aspirations of the workers. There were some, particularly certain Catholics, who looked back nostalgically to a paternal state in which authority protected and nourished the masses. This was the sort of programme that was, in 1891, outlined in the papal encyclical, *Rerum novarum*.

Thus the cleavage between capital and labour produced two new divisions in French opinion: the socializing, *étatiste* wing, and the free-enterprise wing. And so four great families of opinion were formed in France by the time of the Third Republic (1870–75), and the new divisions scored themselves deeper and deeper as the century wore on and industrialization advanced. And so we get the pattern of French political opinion, at about 1914, as shown in Table 13.

TABLE 13

	Anti-capitalist	Capitalist
Left	Socialists	Radical-socialists
Right	Small groups of 'Christian Reformers	'Moderates' Republicans

But this is to omit a third factor: that of temperament. And here again, the Revolution was a great example and inspiration. In Britain, and in the U.S.A., opinion tends not to be fiery and impatient, at any rate, not in its political expression. In both countries the vast bulk of the population, whether through apathy or unimaginativeness or long habituation to constitutional forms or psychological make-up or all of these, operates and only seeks to operate within the forms of the constitution. But French history, to begin with, hardly encourages so placid an outlook. From 1789 to this day, France has had no less than sixteen new constitutions, most of them overthrown by violence. Violence, the achieving of aims by direct action – the rigged-up coup on the right, the popular insurrection on the left – have become a recurrent pattern in French political tactics.

And so, at the extremes of opinion, whether on the left or the right, there have been, from the revolutionaries of 1789 to the terrorist groups of the Organisation de l'Armée Secrète (O.A.S.) of 1962 and the massed university students and left-wing trade unions of 1968, groups of people who reject constitutionalism and preach and practice direct action: the so-called 'activists'. The French labour movement has been divided into activists and constitutionalists since its beginnings. In the late nineteenth century this expressed itself, first of all, in the enmity between the followers of Jules Guesde (activist) and those of Jean Jaurès (the constitutionalist). In the decade preceding the First World War, it projected itself in the mutual hostility of the syndicalists and the parliamentary socialists. The former would have no truck with Parliament. Instead, they advocated the political strike, culminating in the 'general strike', which would bring *bourgeois* society to its knees, and leave the way clear for the trade unions (*syndicats*) to take over society themselves. And, since 1918, the rivalry has expressed itself in the shape of the two major working-class parties: the Communists and the Socialists.

The same kind of cleavage has occurred on the right. In the early days of the Third Republic, royalist and clerical groups were prepared to conspire against the Republic. Then, in 1891, they – and also some working-class elements, it should be noticed – were prepared to put themselves behind Boulanger in an assault on the Republic. After Boulanger came the threat from the army and the Church, during the Dreyfus years. Between the two wars, there flourished petty activist groups: royalists, Camelots du Roi, Francistes, the Croix de Feu. During the occupation years, 1941–4, supporters of such groups backed Marshal Pétain and served in his police force and torture chambers. Finally, the Gaullist following, in de Gaulle's original Rassemblement du Peuple Français (R.P.F.) contained many of this political hue until Gaullism became constitutional, when they were succeeded by even more violent right-wing activists, such as the ex-Poujadists or the O.A.S. terrorists.

And so, the fourfold division of opinion has become sixfold (see Table 14). Thus one comes to know the so-called *éventail des parties*, the 'fan-tail' of the parties. The dividing line comes between the Radical Socialists and the Christian Democrats

TABLE 14

	Anti-Capitalist		Capitalist
Left	Communists	Socialists	Radical Socialists
Right	Christian Democrats (M.R.P.)		Independent Republicans Gaullists Extreme Right e.g. Republican Alliance

(the Mouvement Républicain Populaire or M.R.P.). To the left of the former, all is 'left'; to the right of them, all is 'right'. Starting from this centre point, and working out thus,

PSU	REPUBLICAN ALLIANCE
COMMUNISTS	GAULLISTS
SOCIALISTS	INDEPENDENT REPUBLICANS
RADICAL SOCIALISTS	CHRISTIAN DEMOCRATS

we have, first, the Radical Socialists. They are of the political left: they are on the economic right – free enterprisers; and temperamentally, they are constitutionalists. They make a great appeal to the 'small' – the independent producers and clerks. As the saying goes, their hearts are on the left, their wallets on the right. To the left of them is the 'double left': those who are politically and also economically left; they are anti-clerical, parliamentarian, but in favour of socialism. These are the Socialists. Today their clientele comes from the trade unions in the state sector – e.g., those of posts and telegraphs and the railwaymen. To the left of them stands the 'treble-left'; anti-clerical, anti-capitalist and also anti-parliamentarian. These are the Communists. Today they are being outflanked by a 'new Left' group – the P.S.U.

On the right, starting from the centre point, come first the remains of the M.R.P.; they are parliamentarian and favour a measure of state control of the economy and welfare legislation, but they are clerical, drawing inspiration from the social encyclicals of the popes. On their right stand the Independent Republicans, the traditional conservatives: willing to work the parliamentary system, pro-clerical, but, unlike the M.R.P., die-hard defenders of private enterprise. On their right there stand today the Gaullists; they themselves contain left-wing and state interventionist elements as well as right-wing private enterprise elements. They were bitter opponents, however, of the Fourth Republic and the kind of parliamentarianism it embodied. When they disappeared from the electoral contest in the 1955 election, a large part of their former vote went to an even more unrestrained and extreme group, the followers of the shopkeeper Poujade – frenetically *laissez faire*, activist, anti-parliamentarian and authoritarian.

The names of the French political parties are more confusing than the reality. The fact is that these names form a kind of code, and understanding this code greatly helps one to understand the system. The clue to this code lies in the fact that, historically, the general trend of French politics has been to the left, as it has in Britain – so that the substance of party policies has become more interventionist and socialistic as time has gone by: but at the same time the names of the parties have moved to the left very much further than the substance of their party programmes. What has happened is expressed in the French phrases, *le glissement à gauche* (the slide to the left), and *le verbe vengeur* (the avenging word). The hold of the French Revolution on the French political imagination is so strong that one certain way of picking up votes from a rival is to adopt a name that is more evocative of the Revolution, i.e., that is more 'left', more 'progressive' or 'advanced'. And this outstrips the slower leftward trend of the programme itself. It is not nearly as confusing as it looks, if one bears three things in mind. The first is the historic evolution of the party labels (very greatly simplified, however). Look at the family tree in Table 15.

Today, a 'Left Republican' is a very very right-wing animal

TABLE 15

Approximate date	LEFT	CENTRE	RIGHT		
1884	Radical Republicans	Moderate Republicans	'Orleanist' Monarchists	Imperialists	'Legitimate' Monarchists
1902	Socialists / Radical Socialists	Radicals Republicans	Nationalists Conservatives		
1914	Socialists / Radical Socialists	Radical Left / Federation of Left	Republican Federation	Nationalists	Conservatives
1928	Communists Socialists	Radical Socialists / Radical Left / Democratic and Socialist Left	Popular Democrats	Democratic Alliance	Federation of Republican Democrats
1945	Communists Socialists	Radical Socialists / Popular Republican Movement	Republican Liberal Party	Gaullists	Independent Republicans
1956	Communists Socialists	Radical Socialists / Popular Republican Movement	Independent Gaullists: Republicans Rally of the French People	Poujadists	
1967	Communists United Socialists	Radical Socialists / Popular Republican Movement	Gaullists (Union for the New Republic) and Independent Republicans.	Republican Alliance	

Federation of the Left

Democratic Centre

indeed, and his devotion to republican institutions might well be suspect. The extreme left-wing position these former heretics once took up in the political spectrum has now been occupied by the Communists – birds of a very different colour, since, to their original attitudes of anti-clericalism and popular sovereignty, have been super-added, first a 'left' opinion on the place of the workers in French society, and next, anti-constitutionalism. But, as these words are printed there is reason to suppose they are moving into the constitutionalist – or at least, the non-revolutionary orbit; and their place as revolutionaries is being taken by Maoists and Trotskyists. As to the groups on the right of the original Left Republicans, because of the *glissement à gauche* they would not dare to express themselves today as Bonapartists or royalists even if – as is really the case – time itself had not rendered such aspirations quite idle. The authoritarian anticonstitutionalists today look on the monarchy or the Bonapartist line as decaying political albatrosses. They have had to invent new names to conceal their aspirations. And this brings us to our second point: the inverted logic of the vocabulary used in French party labels. In interpreting the names, it is necessary to remember three things: first, in a party label, 'left' really means 'right'. The logic is simple. Every party is assumed, in post-revolutionary France, to be on the left. So why mention the fact in its name? It is taken for granted in all left-wing parties. Any party that features the word 'left' must therefore be adopting it for propaganda purposes – it is really on the right. Secondly, in a party label, a qualifying adjective *means* a prefix of the word 'not'. So to call one's party 'Radical-Socialist' really means 'non-socialist'. Again the logic is simple. *Of course* a socialist party is radical. How can it be otherwise? To make a feature of the word 'radical', in conjunction with expressed socialist opinion is, necessarily, to qualify those socialist opinions. Socialists are socialists – *any* prefix is a qualification of their socialism.

The third point is this: a number of terms serve as indicators that a party is on the right. 'Republican' in the party title is one. Everybody is republican. To state that the party is republican is simply to conceal whatever else it is, for, if its only concession to progressive opinion is to label itself republican, then it must be pretty far to the right. Otherwise it would call itself radical or socialist or communist. Likewise with the word *populaire*. *Populaire* – 'of the people'! What else in the land of popular sovereignty and universal suffrage! Likewise with the words *union* and *sociale*, but for different reasons. These expressions evoke the notion of the state as a family, a great organism, together with the allied concepts of paternalism, corporate identity, authority, social integration: the opposite of the atomistic mechanical model of the state held by the individualists of the left parties.

Now consider some of the party names in the light of this. Currently, the extreme right party as represented in the Chamber of Deputies is the Gaullist party. Its name was, originally, the Union pour la Nouvelle République (U.N.R.). Here, then, are two of these horrid question-begging words – *union*, and *république*, sure indicators of the right. Today (it changes its name frequently) it calls itself the U.D.R., i.e. Union of Democrats for the Republic. Again, M.R.P. stands for Mouvement Républicain Populaire: another two question-begging words, *populaire* and *républicain*, again indicating that the party is on the right. Or the Radical Socialists: 'radical' qualifies away the name 'socialist'.

Substantially, therefore, the division of French public opinion is the sixfold one indicated in Table 15. The parties mask this by their names, and by the constant *glissement à gauche*.

These six divisions are not new ones. They are very old. The French parties represent these divisions. But, first, they give themselves fancy names. More important, in taking up these ancient positions they clothe themselves in *selective myths* culled from the French past. They reproduce too, the clash of temperament of the past. And they interpret these selective myths, they act out their temperamental make-up, to fit the new conditions and demands thrown up in French society.

II. THE THIRD AND FOURTH REPUBLICS

There has already been much more history in this chapter than in the preceding ones, which dealt with Britain and with the

U.S.A., and there is now going to be more: for in this section I shall be describing the Third Republic (1870–1940) and the Fourth (1944–58). In much current work in the field of comparative government, every state discussed is considered under the same fixed number of characteristics, to each of which equal consideration is supposed to be given, in a fixed order. Certainly, as we have already shown in the first four chapters of this book, there are certain 'dimensions' in terms of which we ought to carry out our comparison of the various states; but each state is also to a greater or lesser degree idiosyncratic; and if an idiosyncratic feature is of great importance, it ought to be given due prominence and treated at far greater length than in the case of the other states. So it is with the constitutional history of France. The Third and Fourth Republics embodied the aspiration to 'representativeness and pursuit of present goals'; the present régime, the Fifth Republic, embodies the contrary emphasis, towards 'order and future goals'. There are therefore two excellent reasons why this chapter should deal with the French political past in a measure so much greater than that required for Britain and the U.S.A. The first is specific to an understanding of the French political scene; it is that this past is not forgotten and the Fifth Republic, as it crumbles, will increasingly have to come to terms with it. The second is of general significance to the method of study in comparative government. Our usual procedure in this field is to compare and contrast a number of contemporaneous régimes (this is the procedure which by and large is adopted in this book). But it is also permissible to compare and contrast the governmental arrangements of one state at different points of time.[2] This is less rewarding in the British and American cases than in the French because in the two former countries the present political arrangements have persisted, slowly evolving, over a long period of time. In France,

2. In France the adjectives used for these two procedures are respectively 'synchronic' and 'diachronic' and the usage is spreading to the U.S.A. I regret this, not because the words themselves are not useful – they are: but because words form families, and we must take in their relatives as well. So, we shall expect such terms, no doubt, as 'anachronic' and 'catachronic' – and, perhaps, just 'chronic'?

on the other hand, the pendulum has swung from *gouvernement d'assemblée* to a highly personalist régime in a comparatively short span. Consequently, a comparison and contrast of the two serves two distinct purposes, both of them highly relevant to the study of comparative government. Firstly, it permits the study of two distinct variants of the liberal-democratic type of régime. Secondly, neither of these types has quite 'fitted' French society: both types did (or do) encounter opposition. To explore why this is so should throw light on French political attitudes and on the general problem of the congruence of régime and society.

French parliamentarism

The characteristic of the French variant of parliamentarism whose institutions outwardly resembled those of Britain was precisely that Parliament, rather than the Cabinet, had the last word. The French calls this *gouvernement d'assemblée*. The reference is, inevitably, to the Great Revolution: it recalls the way an early representative legislature operated – the Legislative Assembly of 1791. Its distinguishing traits are the feebleness of the Cabinets and the predominance of the legislature. From 1870 to 1958, punctuated only by the Vichy years (1941–4), France was governed in this way.

During this time governmental policy was made by an amalgam of the legislature, in which rural, local and sectional interests and pressures were over-represented, and the *haute administration* – the higher civil service. Socially, the régime was profoundly conservative. This is the peculiar combination of political and social attitudes characteristic of the Radical and Radical-Socialist Parties, and it is no accident that throughout the whole of the period that culminated in the débâcle of 1940 the Radicals and Radical Socialists should have held the balance of power. They were the anchor-men of the Third Republic, its hinge-party, or *parti-charnière*.

The Third Republic: 1870–1940

Il n'y a que le provisoire qui dure. The Third Republic lasted longer than any other régime from 1789 to the present day; yet it was the only one *not* endowed with a 'codified' constitution. Instead it was founded on a set of 'Organic Laws' passed by a Provisional Assembly between 1873 and 1875. The period 1870–75 was a kind of interregnum, with a provisional government established after Napoleon III's defeat by the Prussians in 1870. The Provisional Assembly, convened under foreign occupation, was strongly royalist in sympathy, and indeed at that time the restoration of the 'legitimate' Bourbon line appeared imminent. Consequently the Organic Laws of 1873 and 1875 were passed in a form that envisaged the re-establishment of a constitutional monarchy. For one reason and another – the arrogance and stupidity of the pretender (the Comte de Chambord) and the resurgent strength of republicanism – this restoration never occurred. Instead the Organic Laws served, ironically, as the basis of yet another republic – the Third. This proved a watershed in French constitutional history for two reasons. It signified, though nobody knew it at that time, the definitive triumph, since 1789, of republicanism over monarchism; and it gave republicanism a very broad and diluted meaning which became the possession of the political *left*. For up to this time the Bonapartists also had claimed to be heirs to the republican tradition. Henceforth they were relegated to the right-wing of the political spectrum.

The organs of government may be simply described: they consisted of a president, and two legislative chambers. The president, elected by both chambers jointly for a seven-year term, was commander-in-chief, head of the executive branch and president of the Council of Ministers; he received and appointed ambassadors; he symbolized the state. And he was politically irresponsible, for all his acts required the counter-signature of a minister. He was, in fact, cast in the mould of a British sovereign. The establishment of such a presidency was a seat-warming operation for the expected royal restoration.

The Lower House, the Chamber of Deputies, was elected for a fixed four-year term by universal manhood suffrage. The Upper House, the Senate, was indirectly elected, the ninety[3] depart-

3. Since 1964, there have been ninety-five departments.

ments of France serving as the constituencies, and the electors consisting of electoral colleges in these areas, made up, in the greatest part, of the municipal and departmental councillors. The Senate, like its American counterpart, was never dissolved, for the senatorial term was nine years, and one-third retired in rotation.

Superficially, the resemblance to British institutions is very close. Even the powers of the Senate were not too dissimilar from those of the then House of Lords except for finance (but even this was put out of the reach of the House of Lords in a definitive way only as late as 1911). Yet, despite the similarities, the mode of operation was radically different. The deputies – and senators – held the power – not the executive.

For this there were a number of reasons of which the first is the difference between the British and the French party systems. The French dissensus pulverized the French parties. At the turn of the twentieth century France possessed only one reasonably coherent and nationally organized party: the newly founded Socialist Party. The remainder, all on its right, were coalitions of local personages highly dependent on their constituency organizations, which in turn consisted of the local notables of the town or district: the *comités*. The Radical Socialists pretended to some form of departmental organization but had a feeble national one. To the right of them, to use the word national 'parties' is a misnomer. They were electoral coalitions formed every four years. Nor was this all. For once inside the Chamber, the deputies could and did form their own parliamentary 'groups'. The standing orders of the Chamber recognized 'groups' not national parties: each group was entitled to representation upon the various specialist committees into which the Chamber was divided and which, like the American committees, did the spadework on bills. Thus the parties were numerous; excepting for the Socialists, incoherent; and apt to split into further groups once their members had reached the Chamber. The British Cabinet stood firm because it had a firm majority to rely on. The French Cabinet was based on a coalition of groups all of which were unreliable, and all of which were likely, themselves, to fly apart.

Next, a most important weapon against such unreliability was missing. There was no dissolution power. Or rather, the Constitution contained such a power, but convention denied its use. This was because of the circumstances surrounding the one time that a president did dare to use it: in 1877. From that time on no prime minister ever dared to ask for a dissolution or no president ever dared to grant one. Every Chamber lived out its full term. There was, therefore, no incentive for the opposition groups to temper their attacks on the ministry with the knowledge that they too might have to honour the promises they made. There was no reason – for nearly four years at any rate – for the various groups to reckon on a public accounting for the ministries they overthrew, the alliances they made and the ones they quitted. The parliamentary manoeuvres went on in a 'house without windows', in a 'closed arena'. A parliamentary profession grew up, playing its own private game by private rules. The *mot* went round that deputies, of even the most divergent views, had more in common with one another than with their own constituents.

Thirdly, these deputies were strongly favoured by the standing orders of the Chamber, especially as compared with their British counterparts. For one thing, no bill or amendment to a bill could be debated by the Chamber until or unless it had been reported out by one of the nineteen specialized legislative commissions into which the Chamber was divided and on which all groups were proportionately represented. Furthermore these commissions commented on a bill or amendment in the form of a report; and it was this report which the Chamber debated, not the original governmental text of the bill. The chairman of the commission was certain to have sat in his place longer than had the minister whose bill was being considered; and the Committee's '*rapporteur*' (reporting the deliberations to the Assembly), usually a bright young man on the make, could frequently impress the Chamber and more often than not acted as a sort of counsel for the prosecution with the minister on the defensive; furthermore the shifting government coalitions of the day were not always reflected by a similar alignment of members in the commission. So each bill tended to be a duel between the minister and his colleagues on the one side and the *rapporteur*, the chairman and the commission on the other. This was not the only procedural advantage of the deputy. For instance, the weekly agenda (*ordre du jour*) (simply announced by the Leader of the House in the British House of Commons) was settled by a committee of the leaders of the various groups; their views did not necessarily coincide with those of the ministry and many a debate had to take place – and many a ministry fell – simply on the question of what the agenda should be – the debate on '*l'ordre du jour*'. Deputies were permitted (unlike British M.P.s) to suggest increased public expenditures during the Budget debate: another opportunity for log-rolling or demagoguery which the ministry had to risk its fate to withstand. Then there was a procedure allowed called the *interpellation*: a type of debate on a question of topical importance, ending in a vote. The standing orders allowed several of these issues to be voted on together, i.e., the *interpellations* were 'joined'; thus could be concocted a temporary coalition of malcontents, who were often at opposite ends of the political spectrum, but whose combined vote could vote down the ministry. Add to all these hazards a final one: the power of the Senate to hold up bills indefinitely or to send them back with amendments so unacceptable to the ministry that it could do nothing but drop its bill.

The consequence was extreme Cabinet instability. It was entirely dependent on the goodwill of the legislature, which was precisely what good republicans thought it should be; to their mind the legislature, elected by universal suffrage, represented the 'Will of the People'. It was sovereign. This was the triumph of representativeness over 'order and future goals'. Between 1872 and 1928, there were no less than sixty-eight distinct Cabinets: an average life of not much more than nine months. And, on the manoeuvres that led to these changes, the electorate were never – and, because of the lack of the dissolution power, never could be – consulted.

Two other points must be remembered about the Third Republic. It was socially very conservative. This was due to a number of factors. The most usual mode of voting – the laws were changed many times – was the second-ballot system. In this, voting takes place in single-member constituencies as in Britain or the U.S.A.; but to be elected on the first ballot the candidate requires an absolute majority of all votes cast. Should nobody succeed in this, a second ballot is held one week later. In this interval the less favoured candidates withdraw after making various deals with the two or three leading candidates who remain in the race. At the second ballot, the leading candidate is elected. Now this sytem favoured the middle-of-the-road parties and, in the Third Republic, this position was pre-empted very soon by the Radicals and Radical Socialists. The right-wingers, particularly those on the 'economic right' – the capitalist groupings – would obviously vote for a Radical Socialist rather than a Socialist: and on the left, a Socialist would clearly vote for a Radical Socialist, who was at least a democrat and anti-clerical, rather than for a man of the right – some *Républicain de la Gauche*, for instance. Thus the 'heart on left, wallet on right' group held the balance of power. The Radical Socialists typify the Third Republic. But another reason for the social conservatism of the régime was the Senate. The make-up of the departmental electoral colleges which elected the senators was heavily weighted in favour of the villages and small towns as against the few metropolitan areas. The political attitude there was like the Radical Socialist attitude, republican but 'free-enterprising', and definitely anti-proletarian. Therefore, when-ever the Chamber did become somewhat 'demagogic', and passed 'progressive' social legislation, the Senate could be trusted to reject or amend it in the name of financial orthodoxy. Thus the legislature as a whole represented the small man, the small towns and the provinces as against Paris; the countryside as against the large cities: the peasant and the *bourgeois* as against the industrial worker.

The second point to be borne in mind is that, once it was established, there was no practical constitutional means of altering the Republic! The leading politicians of the régime were Republicans. (The irony of the régime, indeed, is precisely that it was intended for a monarchy but was captured by Republicans.) And once they had got their hands on it, they quite deliberately excluded the right – even after the *Ralliement* of 1892, when the

Catholics formally abandoned their monarchism and stated their intention of working through the republican Constitution. Those of right-wing opinions – and this usually meant practising Catholics – were purged from the civil service; and at elections, given the possibilities of the second-ballot system, the left-wing parties formed electoral alliances against them, leaving them entirely isolated and hence in a minority at the second ballot. Thus they could never form a Cabinet, nor even participate in the administration. It was in these circumstances that so many of the younger sons of the Catholic nobility and gentry began to enter the officer corps of the army for a career.

The right therefore became bitterly resentful. Excluded from influence by way of the legislature, it placed its hopes in capturing the executive. All the proposals to strengthen the hands of the executive came from the right: the Boulangists, the anti-Dreyfusards, later (in 1934) the Doumergue proposals; but all such attempts to strengthen the Cabinet or presidency against the legislature were defeated by the electoral coalitions of the Republicans – the so-called 'Republican defence'. On every occasion they interpreted the constitutional issue in terms of the Directory defying the coup of the new Bonaparte, as the Assembly of 1851 defying the threats of Louis Napoleon or as the Chamber of 1877 defying President MacMahon! Thus any attempt to strengthen the executive power was identified with anti-republicanism, with counter-revolution; and by the same token, parliamentarism in its weak form was identified with republicanism: a strange fate indeed for an ideology which among other things had supported the Jacobin Committee of Public Safety!

The Fourth Republic: 1944–58

The Third Republic collapsed in the aftermath of the Nazi conquest of France in 1940. While northern France was occupied by the Germans, the south received a new Constitution at the hands of a rump parliament called together at Vichy. This Constitution provided for an authoritarian head of state: the senile Marshal Pétain. This régime in its turn was brought down by the collapse of the Germans under the allied offensives of 1944, and the subsequent triumph of the Free French forces under General de Gaulle. A provisional régime was established with the General as President of the Council; a Constituent Assembly was convened: and a new Constitution was drafted. The first draft, submitted to the electors in a referendum, was rejected. The second draft was accepted.

The three dominant parties in the immediate post-war era were the Communists, the Socialists and the Christian Democrats (the M.R.P.). The latter was a new party but it captured those who wanted to vote for the old-fashioned right but either dared not do so or had no candidates to vote for.

These three major parties diagnosed the ills of the Third Republic as due to the lack of party discipline, the weakness of the Cabinet and the inordinate powers of the Senate.

To cure the first, all prescribed the abandonment of the old second-ballot system and the adoption of a system of proportional representation.[4] Now this may seem odd in view of the widely held belief that proportional representation multiplies the number of parties and increases their propensity to split. In fact there are many different systems of proportional representation, and factors other than the electoral machinery also have a bearing on the number of parties. The system adopted in France divided the country into a number of multi-membered constituencies (the departments were in fact used) and the voter had the choice of voting for the lists of candidates put up by any party contesting the election. This favoured the larger parties capable of forming such lists of candidates to stand in all or a great many of the constituencies. It also greatly strengthened their central committees, for it was they who decided on the order in which the candidates appeared on the party list: and, self-evidently, the candidate at the head of the list stood a much better chance of being returned than the one at the bottom. For the latter to be elected would imply that the party had made a clean sweep of all the seats in a constituency: a most unlikely event in France where a large number of parties were contesting the election. Thus the

4. The electoral law embodying this, however, was not a part of the new Constitution.

adoption of the 'list system' was a very rational way of encouraging the internal discipline of the parties.

In addition, however, the votes were counted according to the method known as 'highest average'. The arithmetic need not concern us here. The fact is that this method did not give *exactly* proportional representation: it tended to favour the leading parties in the constituencies. A third consequence of the electoral system was indirect. Under the second-ballot system, in the pre-war years, the Socialists had secured parliamentary seats that were in fairly just proportion to the number of votes cast for them in the country; but not so the Communists. These had been under-represented in the Chamber of Deputies. Under the new proportional representation system, they secured seats in proportion to the votes cast for them and this meant an enormous jump in their parliamentary representation. Thus the two parties of the economic and the political left collared almost the whole of the 'left' vote. The men of the right, of all shades of opinion, could not at first vote for the traditional '*Modérés*' and '*Indépendents*', partly because these were discredited and partly because they had never had a national organization and found it impossible for the moment to put up national lists like the Socialist and Communist Parties which had always been disciplined and nationally organized. The men of the right therefore voted for the candidates of the only right-wing party that did have a national headquarters organization: the newly founded M.R.P.

Thus, in the elections, first to the Constituent Assembly (a trial run for the P.R. system before the Constitution was adopted) and then to the first National Assembly of the duly constituted Fourth Republic (1946), the Communists, the Socialists and the M.R.P. secured roughly one-quarter of the seats apiece. So, for the first time in French parliamentary history, three-quarters of the legislature was in the hands of three coherent parties. This system lasted for the whole of the first term (now fixed at five years) of the new National Assembly. Then as we shall see it was modified.

The old Senate was abrogated. Instead a much enfeebled Upper House, re-styled the Council of the Republic, was instituted. This was indirectly elected, in much the same way and by much the same persons as before; but it was shorn of the powers the Senate had formerly possessed. It could not veto, only delay; and, if the Cabinet of the day chose to invoke the so-called 'urgency procedure', the maximum delay was only one hundred days. Furthermore, the Council of the Republic could not (until 1954) amend. It could either accept or reject.

Finally, the status of the Cabinet and the prime minister was reviewed. This was the centre-piece of the new Constitution. The intention was to emulate the British example and make the prime minister the leader of the Assembly by giving him the powers commensurate with this role. First, his administrative powers were increased: certain duties hitherto carried out by the president were transferred to him, and the power of the president was correspondingly diminished. The two most important of these powers were his chairmanship of the Office of *la fonction publique* (the Civil Service), and his chairmanship of the Armed Services Committee. The first gave him the patronage and control of the entire civil service. The second put him at the centre of defence policy and foreign affairs.

Next, the Constitution took steps to enhance his political authority in the Assembly. The idea was that he should be personally invested with his office, and then pick his team. So it was laid down that the prime minister designate, selected by the president in the old style after 'soundings', should prepare a statement of the policy he proposed to follow and present himself to the Assembly. To be invested with the prime minister-ship he must then receive an *absolute* majority of the Assembly's vote. With this authority behind him he would then go forward and select his team of Cabinet colleagues.

Once this was done, how ensure that the Cabinet would be longer-lived than its predecessors of the Third Republic? First the Assembly's power to overthrow Cabinets by means of the conjoined interpellation was substantially reduced. More import-ant, so it was thought, the Cabinet could only be forced to resign on formal votes of censure, or by the loss of a formal vote of confidence, by an *absolute* majority of the Assembly. Short of this it could remain in office: it was not 'overthrown' according to the meaning of the Constitution. And, to give deputies time to reflect on what they were doing, the vote on such formal motions entailing the possible resignation of the Cabinet were to be taken forty-eight hours after the debate.

Finally the prime minister was given the power to secure the dissolution of the Assembly and the holding of new elections. But such was the fear of the executive and so vivid the memory of the affair of the MacMahon dissolution of 1877 that this was qualified. No dissolution could take place until eighteen months of a new Assembly's five-year period had elapsed. The prime minister could then dissolve if there had been two cabinet crises ('*crises*') within at most six months of one another. These provisions were drafted so as to avoid a snap election immediately after the election of a new Assembly, but, thereafter, to ensure that an Assembly which overthrew Cabinets at the average rate of one every six months should be dissolved to face the verdict of the electorate.

From the Fourth back to the Third Republic?

For a variety of reasons these provisions never worked. Within a few years the Fourth Republic was behaving just like the Third! For one thing, this was partly due to the evolution of the political parties after the post-Liberation euphoria had evaporated. This narrowed the majority on which a Cabinet could rely to impossibly fine limits. For another, the provisions themselves were defective. Finally, deputies remained deputies, and more and more boldly worked the institutions of the new Republic by the conventions that had governed the old.

The turning point came in 1947. In that year the Communists were ejected from the three-party coalition and went into opposition. Simultaneously, in the country at large, the Gaullists, newly formed into the opposition R.P.F., scored up huge victories in the local elections. Thus the defenders of the Fourth Republic, pathetically calling themselves the 'Third Force', were attacked from extreme right and extreme left.

The first effect was the retreat from the electoral law of 1946. The Third Force parties – the Socialists, the M.R.P. the Radical

Socialist remnant and a section of *Modérés* (C.N.I.P.)[5] were justly terrified that, under the 1946 law, the Communists and the Gaullists would together command an absolute majority of the new Assembly to be elected in 1951. So they changed the law by permitting *apparentement* – the combining of party lists. The new rules were as follows. If a single party list in a constituency secured an absolute majority of all votes cast there, it carried all the seats. If an affiliated set of lists secured an absolute majority of the votes cast, then it carried all the seats and these were divided among the affiliated parties by proportional representation. If, finally, no list secured an absolute majority, then the old law stood: the seats were divided among the party lists by proportional representation. This was an absurd and unjust system. The intention was clear enough however. No parties at all would affiliate their lists to the Communist lists: so the only seats these would win would be where they took an absolute majority of all the votes in a constituency (a rare occurrence) or in the confused situations where no lists, affiliated or otherwise, secured an absolute majority of the votes. By the same token, the Third Force parties were unlikely to affiliate their lists to those of the Gaullists, and in any case these were loudly proclaiming their intention of having nothing to do with the political parties. (This is why their organization called itself a *rassemblement*. De Gaulle loathed parties, and aspired to a 'rally' that would transcend them.) Thus the centre parties, champions of the Fourth Republic, would hold the interior lines and cut down the representation of both the extremist, anti-constitutionalist wings. They only narrowly succeeded in this expectation.

A second retreat from the 1946 settlement came in 1954, when the powers of the Council of the Republic were somewhat increased. Characteristically the councillors had taken to styling themselves Senators. One of the drawbacks of the revised Council of the Republic was its lack of amending power. Even the lower

5. The Centre National des Indépendants et des paysans: this grew out of the C.N.I. or Centre National des Indépendants, which was a committee set up in 1948 to co-ordinate the activities of the P.R.L. (Parti Républicain de la Liberté) and other Independent Deputies who rejected de Gaulle. This C.N.I. was extended early in 1951 to embrace the Peasants.

house had felt the inconvenience of this. In 1954 the amending power was restored: but the limitations on the delaying power of the Council remained.

The most important retreats, however, came over the provisions respecting the Cabinet. The effort to improve its stability and authority *vis-à-vis* the Assembly proved a complete failure. To begin with, the rule relating to the personal investiture of the prime minister transformed itself, in many cases, into a *double* investiture. First the prime minister designate came to receive endorsement by an absolute majority of the Assembly. Having received it, and picked his team, he often found himself compelled to come back and receive another absolute majority to ratify the composition of the Cabinet he had selected. Within a short time, therefore, prime ministers designate reverted to the Third Republic practice of picking their team and letting their names be known before meeting the Assembly for endorsement.

Nor was this all. The simple fact of the matter is that, from 1951, the enemies of the Constitution in the country not the Assembly all but out-numbered its supporters, and these supporters were themselves riven into four groups, pro-clerical and anti-clerical, socialists and anti-socialists; so that in these circumstances the issue before the Fourth Republic was not so much what it should do but whether it could survive at all.

In 1947, once the Communists had gone into opposition, there were 183 opposition deputies out of 635. In 1951 there were 221, made up of the Communists on the left and the Gaullist R.P.F. on the right. In 1956 there were still 201 although most of the Gaullists had quitted the parliamentary scene: their place was partly taken by the followers of the shopkeeper, Poujade. Thus the constitutionalist fraction was at most 452 (in 1947) and at worst 414 (in 1951). Up to this time, under the original terms of the Constitution, it will be remembered, the prime minister designate had to be endorsed by an absolute majority of the Assembly. Thus in the normal way he needed 318 votes out of a possible 635. But after 1947 he had to draw these 318 votes from the constitutionalist fraction of only 452; in 1951 he had to draw them from the constitutionalist fraction of only 414! So that, of those deputies prepared to play the constitutional game at all, he needed about three-quarters of the votes. No wonder it became so difficult to fulfil the requirement that, in 1954, the Constitution was amended so that the endorsement became valid by only a *relative* majority of the Assembly.

This was not the worst. Not by any means. Once endorsed, the prime minister had to find majorities for his measures not from the full complement of the 635 members but from the 452/414 constitutionalists; that is as much as to say that he always had some 200 votes against him from the start. The desertion of a mere one hundred constitutionalists to the extremes was enough to overthrow him. This represented only one in four of the constitutionalist *bloc* – but it was not a *bloc*: it was an aggregation sundered by France's historic cleavages. The Socialists and the M.R.P. were united perhaps over governmental planning but at loggerheads over church schools. The Radical Socialists and the Socialists were united over church schools but not over economic planning. The Radical Socialists and the Independents or 'Moderates' were united over free enterprise but at loggerheads over the church schools issue. Other issues plagued them also. One of these was the question of European unification. The Socialists and the M.R.P. favoured this; the Independents did not. The other issue was the future of the Empire. It was this in the end that proved too daunting for the flimsy coalition and brought it and the Fourth Republic crashing into ruin together.

Finally, this constriction of the constitutionalist fraction in the National Assembly frustrated the provisions that were supposed to guarantee the stability of the Cabinet. The assumption had been that the Cabinet need only resign if defeated by an absolute majority of the Assembly. The authors never laid it down, however, that the Cabinet must remain in office unless defeated by an absolute majority, merely that it might do so. Nor did it lay down (as the Fifth Republic was to do) that *unless* the government were to be defeated by an absolute majority of the Assembly its bill would pass automatically. In practice, then, Cabinets saw their bills thrown over by only relative majorities – but defeated nevertheless. Why then remain in office? And what purpose would this serve? Throughout the entire life of the Fourth Republic the number of Cabinets that fell after a defeat by an absolute majority, on a vote of confidence, was only *five*!

And because of this the automatic dissolution procedure became (except in one instance) a dead letter, and the Assembly remained a 'house without windows'. For the Constitution, when it said that after the first eighteen months of its life an Assembly might be dissolved if two Cabinets were successively overthrown within a six-month period, made an important stipulation: that to be 'overthrown' meant overthrown in a vote of no confidence by an absolute majority of the Assembly. And since nearly all Cabinets chose to fall rather than be pushed, or to resign after defeats by relative majorities, these 'overthrows' did not count, as far as the dissolution was concerned. Only once was this procedure invoked: in late 1955.

For all these reasons, therefore, Cabinets were no more stable than under the Third Republic. In fact they were less so. The Fourth Republic saw twenty-five Cabinets between 1946 and 1958. The average life of a Cabinet, therefore, was less than seven months. But under the Third Republic it had been nine!

Social and political characteristics

The 'dance of the portfolios' is to some extent misleading. In Britain, the replacement of one Cabinet by another usually suggests that there has been the replacement of one party policy by another, one set of ministers by another. Not so in France. There the same leading politicians tended to reappear over and over again in subsequent Cabinets, and some parties managed to maintain a more or less continuous hold on some important ministry. For instance, the M.R.P. held the Foreign Office continuously except for one very short break from 1945 to 1954. In fact, the change of Cabinet in France, as compared with Britain, resembles the change of scene in a French play as compared with an English one. In the latter, a change of scene means just what it says: the *venue* has altered. In a French play, every time a new character comes on, or goes off, this is labelled as a change of scene, though the place may be exactly the same.

Nevertheless, the fragility of the Cabinet in the face of the obstinacy or opposition of the Assembly prevented it from ever constraining political pressures. It had to give way to them or abdicate: and Cabinets did both. While they changed, the pressures in the Assembly were continuous. Hence, not very long after the adoption of the 1946 Constitution, a position of deadlock between these pressures resulted. This deadlock is what in France is called *immobilisme*. Meanwhile, by the same token, bold planning or orientation of the society and its economy was beyond the reach of ministers. Instead they lived out their short lives by trimming to every sectional interest in turn. France, like any liberal-democratic state and for the same reasons, had its pressure groups and, as in any complex industrial society, these groups were extremely numerous. Indeed, the ones that catered for the largest sectors of society – labour, the employers, the teachers, the farmers and the like – were more numerous than in Britain and the U.S.A. (though by the same token, less powerful) precisely because they, too, like French society in the large, were riven by ideological differences. There were three peak organizations for labour, for example: the Confédération Générale du Travail (the C.G.T.) mostly representing heavy industry, which was Communist-controlled; the C.G.T.–F.O. (Force Ouvrière), catering for the state enterprises and white collar workers, which was broadly socialist in sympathy; and the Confédération Française des Travailleurs Chrétiens (C.F.T.C.), a Catholic organization, which in the immediate post-war period looked towards the M.R.P. Among the farmers' organizations, the Confédération Générale de l'Agriculture was a loose, umbrella organization and the Fédération Nationale des Syndicats D'Exploitants Agricoles was broadly conservative or M.R.P. in its political sympathies. The '*jeunesses agricoles*' (Centre National des Jeunes Agriculteurs) were attracted by left-wing Gaullism; while the M.O.D.E.F. was communist in outlook. Among the ranks of the employers, the Conseil National du Patronat Français is a powerful peak organization; the young business-men's organization (French Centre for Young Businessmen) is to some extent attracted to the left-wing Gaullists, as is the Con-fédération Générale des Petites et Moyennes Entreprises. Now these, and a host of other interest groups, were most powerfully entrenched in the machinery of the Fourth Republic. Given the localism of much French politics, they were able to intervene in the electoral process in a manner similar to that of the American groups. In the Assembly they were particularly well positioned, since they flocked into the membership of the nineteen legislative *commissions* which each specialized in a particular field; so that the agriculture committee, for instance, simply turned into a focus for the farmers' lobby, and so forth. Given the immense power of these *commissions* over the bills introduced, the interest groups were able to maintain a firm hold over 'dangerous' legislation. The drink lobby, for instance, was able to defy all governmental attempts to limit alcoholism in France. Again, given the loose rules of order in the Assembly, the groups found it easy to introduce bills in their own interest and even easier to introduce amendments into government legislation. But these groups were also very influential in the ministries themselves. Each powerful group tried to 'colonize' the bureaucracy, either by planting spokesmen in the appropriate ministries or conversely by employing ex-civil servants (a practice known as *pantouflage*). These exercises were, on the whole, very successful. But the weakness of ministers worked against the pressure groups as well as for them. For though all pressure groups were successful up to a point – that point was where they were met by the determined resistance of another pressure group. A sort of balance of power established itself: in short, the *immobilisme* of which we have been speaking.

During this period, therefore, France was not ruled; she was administered. The government of the day carried on through the efforts of the most highly trained and intelligent of any group of civil servants in continental Europe. Neither the Monnet Plan nor the Second, Third and Fourth Economic Plans were ever effectively debated by the Assembly. They were largely the work of anonymous bureaucrats. Nor did the Assembly debate or otherwise control the negotiations that led to the formation of the European Economic Council: all it was allowed to do was to ratify the Treaty of Rome after the negotiations were complete. Yet the Plans, and the E.E.C., were the two most important domestic initiatives taken under the Fourth Republic, and it is no exaggeration to say that it was they which prepared the domestic prosperity which the Fifth Republic inherited.

The end of the Fourth Republic

The Assembly of 1956 contained few Gaullists. Under instructions from the General, the R.P.F. had dissolved itself. But, if he had renounced the hope of political power, his friends in the Assembly and the Senate, in the army and the bureaucracy, never halted their efforts to 'draft' him – should the opportunity offer. And many were willing to create this opportunity.

It came in 1958 over the war in Algeria. This polarized French opinion. The Communists were out and out for Algerian independence, the far right – the so-called 'Moderates' and the followers of Poujade – were for out and out repression. The constitutional parties all split down the middle.

Meanwhile the Algerian right had spawned a host of those clandestine 'activists' who perennially gather at the sick-bed of the parliamentary régime in France – as they had in the time of Boulanger, or Dreyfus, or in the middle thirties – only to be beaten off by 'Republican defence'. Some of these secret societies moved in France. Others were local to Algeria. What exactly all these groups looked for it is hard to say. Some wanted a military dictatorship, others to come to power with military support and subsequently form some right-wing dictatorship. But all relied on insurrection or murder to end the parliamentary régime.

This might not have mattered but for one thing. For decades the army had been styled *la grande muette* – 'the great deaf-mute'. But in 1958 the army ceased to be reliable. On the contrary; it assumed a political role. A variety of causes contributed to this: longer tours of duty which took soldiers from their homes and made them feel unwanted when they returned; the adoption by some of the general staff of a doctrine of counter-revolutionary warfare, a kind of mirror-image of Maoism, which provided them with an ideology – and, in so far as they assumed certain civil functions in Algeria, the opportunity to put this into practice; but above all a feeling of humiliation. Since 1940 nothing had gone right. Beaten in 1940; beaten in 1954 at Dien Bien Phu;

victorious in the Suez zone only to be withdrawn by *les frocs* (the civilians); and now they had staked their reputation on one simple promise to their allies in Algeria: that Algeria would remain French. The moment the politicians in Paris appeared to cast doubt on this, their mood darkened and, like so many armies before them, they began to blame the politicians and the régime for their train of humiliations.

The defection of the army proved the final straw. After the Socialist-centred government of Mollet was brought down in May 1957 by the desertion of the 'Moderates' (not on the Algerian issue but on a question of social legislation!) two short-lived Cabinets, each led by Radical Socialists, succeeded one another without moving any nearer to a solution of the Algerian affair. The second of them fell in April 1958, in a blaze of nationalistic rage at what the right was disposed to see as an Anglo-American effort to squeeze France out of Algeria in the wake of the Sakiet bombing. (Sakiet, a border town in Tunisia, had been strafed by French aircraft on suspicion that it was a refuge for the Algerian liberation army.) A Cabinet crisis followed, until on 8 May an M.R.P. leader, Pflimlin, was designated prime minister and prepared to meet the Assembly on 13 May.

On hearing this the activists in Algiers decided to bring down the régime by striking on that very date. They planned an insurrection in Algiers. They were successful. There followed the vortex of events which sucked the army into the insurrection, stiffened the resolve of the parliamentarians in Paris by that same token, and then – as France feared civil war – led to the call for de Gaulle to return to office as the one man who could lead France out of the impasse. De Gaulle himself assisted this evolution of opinion when, on the afternoon of 15 May, he stated: 'Let it be known that I hold myself ready to assume the powers of the Republic.'

From this point the Republic was finished. The officers of the armed forces publicly demanded de Gaulle. In the hope of averting civil war, more and more of the parliamentarians also did so. Faced by an army threat to invade the mainland of France, the Minister of the Interior found that he had no armed support to counter it. The Communists did indeed beseech the Socialists to join them and defend the Republic but, once the Socialists had refused to do this, by a wafer-thin majority, the jig was up. All that remained was to negotiate the most decent possible rites of interment for the expiring Republic. It took time but finally it was achieved – without bloodshed, and with due respect for constitutional forms. On 1 June 1958, de Gaulle appeared in the Assembly as prime minister designate and was accorded confidence by 329 to 224, with full powers for the next six months, authority to revise the Constitution, and an immediate recess of Parliament until its next session. The General was back in the saddle again. This time he would ride.

III. THE FIFTH REPUBLIC: DE GAULLE, 1958–69

Two tentative conclusions can be drawn from the collapse of the Fourth Republic. The first is that where sharp dissensus exists, particularly of the murderous nature we have described, popular loyalty to abstract procedures gives way to trust in some outstanding individual, the heroic leader. Secondly, the existence of this murderous self-division means that society calls, if government is to be carried on at all, for a stronger and less representative state authority to repress, coerce, perhaps ultimately persuade this dissensus into some larger unanimity. This, as we have seen earlier, is a tendency which has been often repeated in France. The year 1958 was not the first time that France had swung from institutions which laid their emphasis upon representing public opinion to institutions which tend to diminish this in favour of those other two essential ingredients of a government form, namely stability and foresight. In France this swing has historically taken the form of a change from government by a representative assembly to government by some individual or small knot of individuals, backed up by the bureaucracy – in short by a swing from parliamentary institutions to some kind of Bonapartism. This is what occurred now. The key to the current institutions of France lies in a simple sentence of one of the Constitution's main architects, Michel Debré: 'Since in France government stability cannot result primarily from the electoral law, it must result from making governmental rules. [6] Expanded, what Debré was saying was this. Because of the dissensus in French opinion, elections were bound to throw up numerous parties, none of which would have a working majority; hence coalition governments; hence fragile governments. Hence a government that is not fragile must be created *factitiously*, as an autonomous or largely autonomous authority.

As will be seen, the same problem faces many of the less favoured new states in the Third World, and in some of them this same line of reasoning has led to the establishment of a single official party whose leader, endowed with governmental authority, is strengthened by virtue of being the only personage permitted to have an organized body of followers. This device being ruled out in France, the aim has been realized by a more sophisticated arrangement in which the personality of de Gaulle and the prescriptions of the new Constitution were intermingled. In the U.S.A., an irremovable president confronts but is checked by an equally irremovable Congress. In Britain, a removable prime minister, who is the emanation of the majority party, faces a removable Parliament. But, in France, an irremovable and constitutionally irresponsible president appoints a prime minister in a Parliament which he can dissolve at will and whose opportunities for striking back have been whittled down far below the most supine level of the British Parliament let alone the American Congress.

The new Constitution – general

The new draft Constitution was drawn up rapidly and on 28 September 1958 it was submitted to the people of France in a referendum. The response was overwhelming: four out of five of the voters approved. The next step was to elect a president: for under the new Constitution the president was to be elected by a system different from that of the Fourth and, indeed, of the Third Republic. He was to be chosen by an electoral college, consisting for the largest part of the local municipal and depart-

6. M. Debré, 'La Nouvelle Constitution', p. 2 (*Revue française de science politique,* January 1959, p. 7).

mental councillors throughout France. There was no effective opposition to General de Gaulle's candidature, and he was elected by a majority of 78·5 per cent of the votes. Thus the institutions of the new Republic were established.

Superficially the Constitution looks much the same as before. There is a president, and a prime minister and Cabinet responsible (in this case specifically) to the Lower House, and there are two houses, the National Assembly and the Senate. But there are four vital differences. The parliamentary respresentation of the public has been deliberately distorted. The legislature has been muzzled. The executive has been given a much greater weight in decision-making; and, notably, the presidency has been exalted at the expense of the prime minister and the Cabinet.

But this exaltation owes more to practice than to the letter of the Constitution. On paper the prevalent notion is of a 'two headed executive' with a division and balance between the president, elected by universal suffrage for a seven-year term, and the prime minister whom he appoints and who is (nominally) responsible to the Parliament and particularly the National Assembly which is elected for five-year periods (although it can be dissolved before the period expires). It is important to glance at the formal distribution of the presidential and prime ministerial powers immediately so as to be able to see them in the context of the other constitutional innovations. For in this way the presidential usurpation of power is clearly displayed.

The new presidency retains all the former powers of that office; for instance the incumbent presides over the Conseil des Ministres (i.e. the cabinet), exercises the power of pardon, countersigns government bills and so forth. But, in addition, he resumes control over the administration since Article 13 makes it clear that he appoints to the great military and civil posts of the state. He accredits and receives ambassadors and negotiates treaties. He presides over the Supreme Council of National Defence. He appoints one-third of the Constitutional Council (the other six being appointed, three apiece, by the speakers – *presidents* – of the two houses of the legislature respectively.)

On the other hand, the Constitution says that it is the 'government' which, chosen by the prime minister, 'decides and directs the policy of the nation'; also that it 'has at its disposal the administration of the armed forces' (Article 20). Again, while the president is responsible only to the High Court of Justice and then only for the crime of high treason (Article 67), it is the government that is 'responsible to Parliament'.

What then are the interrelationships between the constitutionally irresponsible, unaccounting, unaccountable president and the responsible prime minister?

To begin with, the prime minister is *appointed* by the president (Article 8). This is utterly different from the provisions of the 1946 Constitution which laid down in detail how the president had to hold consultations with the parliamentary parties (called 'groups' in France), and then 'designate' the prime minister, who could not be appointed (*nommé*) by the president until or unless he had received a confidence vote from the Assembly. There is no doubt that the president can now appoint whomsoever he pleases to this vital office without consulting anybody. On the other hand, this power is checked by virtue of his constitutional incapacity to *dismiss* the prime minister, unless the latter chooses to present his government's resignation. Furthermore – in constitutional theory – it is not the president who appoints the other ministers but the prime minister who does so.

Next, the president has the right to dissolve the Assembly whenever he thinks fit (exceptions to be noted below), whereupon a general election must take place. Nominally the provision is qualified by the requirement that he must first 'consult' the prime minister and the presidents of the two houses of the legislature, but 'consultation' gives them no power to obstruct the president in his chosen course. In fact there are only two substantial limitations upon the president's power to dissolve; he cannot do so twice in the same year, and, if he is governing through the emergency powers of Article 16, he cannot dissolve Parliament at all.

Thirdly, the president has a qualified right to break out of the 'house without windows', by virtue of a *referendum*. But the subjects on which he can consult the electorate are limited to three: 'the organization of the public authorities', the approval of French Community agreements and the authorization of ratification of a treaty which affects domestic institutions; and furthermore, the initiative to hold the referendum does not reside in him but in the government or in the two houses of the legislature. They, not he, must put the proposal forward.

Fourthly, the president possesses an emergency power of great dimension – indeed, the power of exercising a constitutional dictatorship. Under Article 16, 'When there exists a serious and immediate threat to the institutions of the Republic, the independence of the Nation, the integrity of its territory, or the fulfilment of its international obligations, *and* the regular functioning of the constitutional public authorities has been interrupted, the president of the republic takes . . .' Takes what? He '*takes the measures required* by the *circumstances*'. Yet even this is qualified. He must tell the nation of his measures in a message. And Parliament reconvenes automatically as of right and sits throughout the emergency.

And finally he is the 'umpire' – or, in Gallic style, he is the 'arbitrator'. Article 5 states: 'The president of the Republic shall see that the Constitution is respected. By his arbitral power he shall ensure the regular functioning of the governmental authorities as well as the continuance of the State.' On the surface this is a transcendent power of conciliation, fully compatible with the political irresponsibility of the presidency, similar, one at first supposes, to the concept of the British sovereign who stands over and above the day-to-day political battle. In practice this clause has thrown the cloak of constitutionality around flagrant breaches of the Constitution and enabled Charles de Gaulle to make it mean what it suited him to mean.

In practice, as will shortly be seen, this two-headed executive became a single-headed one in every major respect mentioned above. It was the president, General de Gaulle, who decided and the prime minister and his Cabinet simply managed and executed his decisions. Prime ministers (there were only three during the first decade of the Fifth Republic) regarded themselves as the personal appointments of the president and at his disposal. Through this, their ministers were effectively hired and fired by de Gaulle. He used his dissolution power – in 1962 – when it suited himself – not his ministers or, for that matter, the opposition. He invoked the emergency power under Clause 16 when it was manifest that the 'regular functioning of the constitutional authorities' was continuing. Though constrained by the Constitution to permit Parliament to reconvene during his exercise of these emergency powers, he took it on himself to decide what it might and might not discuss. Through the complicity of his prime ministers he used the referendum power both as a personal plebiscite and, in one flagrant case, in 1962, to amend the Constitution in flat contradiction of Article 89. At all times, in all matters in which he chose to take a personal interest, it was he who communicated to his prime minister the decision to be taken by him and his ministers.

If a minister had proved recalcitrant, the prime minister removed him on behalf of the president. If the prime minister had proved recalcitrant (like Debré over de Gaulle's Algerian policy) the president induced him to resign and appointed his successor. If the opposition had proved difficult, the Constitution and its rules of procedure allowed the government, acting for the president, to override it. If parliamentary opposition had been so widespread as to overthrow the government, as it did in 1962, the president was able to appeal, and did so, to the electorate. And up to 1969 this backed him. And, if ever a constitutional nicety stood in the way of the president, he did not scruple to brush it aside by invoking his arbitral power under Article 5.

How did this come about? By three main processes. First, a new electoral law favoured the united Gaullists over an opposition which is still riven by the historical dissensus, and particularly the division of the left into Communists and Socialists. Secondly, the Constitution abrogated most of the opportunities which a parliamentary opposition used to enjoy. And, finally, de Gaulle interpreted his role in accordance with his own imperious character.

(1) *The electoral law, and elections 1958-67*

The Fifth Republic abolished proportional representation and reverted to the single-member constituency second-ballot system which had been the most customary mode under the Third

Republic. As we have seen, this system favours the middle-of-the-road party, the one that can form alliances with both sides of the political spectrum, or, alternatively, can draw voters from both sides. In the 1958 election, the Gaullists unexpectedly found themselves cast in this role. In a country which dreaded the spectre of civil war, the Gaullists took the anti-communist vote in constituencies which were left wing, and took the left-wing vote in constituencies normally held by the rightist 'Moderates'. Furthermore, at that stage no other parties were prepared to negotiate agreements even at local level with the Communists, this being regarded at that time as a veritable kiss of death. Consequently the Communists were able to win seats only in those areas where they scored over fifty per cent of the votes on the first ballot – a rare occurrence. And on top of all this there was a pronounced right-wing swing in public opinion.

The Gaullist party – by now called the U.N.R.–U.D.T. (Union Démocratique du Travail) – secured no less than 188 seats. It had not been represented, *qua* party, in the 1956 Assembly: now it was the largest party. To its right stood a massive contingent of the traditional conservative 'Moderates' (C.N.I.P. and others), though these were by now the most extremist, as far as Algerian policy was concerned, in the Assembly: they numbered 132. This Gaullist and right-wing coalition easily dominated the Assembly, for on the left the Communists were virtually extinguished. They held only ten seats. Even the Socialists had only forty-two and the Radical Socialists only thirty-five. In the centre, the M.R.P., once the party of fidelity to de Gaulle, came back with fifty-seven seats. The British system of parliamentary representation does unquestionably distort the result in terms of parliamentary seats, as has been seen. But not to this wild extent. 'Moderates' and Gaullists together took some forty-nine per cent of the popular vote: they had 320 seats between them. The opposition parties secured fifty-one per cent of the popular vote: they received only 144 seats. Again, the Communists, though their vote had greatly declined, did still receive nearly twenty-one per cent of the popular vote: the Gaullists received some twenty-eight per cent. But whereas the Gaullists came back with 188 seats, the Communists secured only ten!

Though his party was in a minority, de Gaulle selected from it his first prime minister, Michel Debré. Paradoxically, however, the minority status of the Gaullist party enabled de Gaulle to expand the role of the presidency. For, as he began to move in the direction of conciliating the Algerian rebels, he came into conflict with the inflamed nationalists among the 'Moderates' on his right – but, by the same token, he could rely upon the tacit support of the forces of the left. These acquiesced in his increasingly high-handed actions against the spirit of the Constitution – feeling, no doubt, that once an Algerian settlement was reached, and the menace of a civil war was lifted, they could manoeuvre him from power.

Their opportunity seemed to come when de Gaulle climaxed his usurpations of authority, in September 1962, by putting his constitutional amendment (to alter the mode of electing the president) directly to the electors in a referendum, instead of going through the procedures clearly laid down in Article 89. For on this the entire non-Gaullist membership of the Assembly was in opposition and had no difficulty in carrying a vote of no confidence by the absolute majority which the Constitution requires. The president accordingly dissolved that Assembly and called a general election. The result staggered all the opposition parties, both left and right. On the right the 'Moderates' found their thunder stolen by the Gaullists, and they almost vanished. On the left the parties still had not learned that under the second-ballot system they had to form a *bloc* of 'republican defence' as in the old days, if they were to beat the right. Instead they continued as separate entities, except that a limited number of local alliances began to be forged between Communists and Socialists. These Marxist parties made but a meagre gain in the popular vote: but the local arrangements proved highly effective – mostly to the advantage of the Socialists. Whereas the Communists raised the number of their seats to forty-one, and the Socialists raised theirs to sixty-five, the Radicals, left in the cold, gained only one extra seat. But for the Gaullists the election was a landslide. They won no less than forty-six seats outright on the first ballot; on the second ballot there was a wholesale transfer to them of votes from the centrist M.R.P. (which lost twenty

seats) and from the 'Moderates', the Centre National des
Indépendants (C.N.I.), which lost seventy-eight seats, and from
even more right-wing independent conservatives who lost all
their seats. In vain did the General's opponents claim that the
moral victory was theirs since the parties which had opposed de
Gaulle's unconstitutional referendum had won sixty per cent of
the total popular vote. For the hard political fact was that, with
his minority vote of forty per cent, de Gaulle had picked up 229
metropolitan seats – only thirteen short of an absolute majority
in the Assembly; and since in this election the Independent
Republicans of M. Giscard d'Estaing had fought as allies of the
Gaullist party, and had won twenty seats, this ensured the General
and his prime minister something no government had possessed
since the beginning of the Third Republic, and something that
Debré, who was the chief architect of the 1958 Constitution, had
never envisaged when he pioneered its drafting: namely, an
absolute governmental majority in the Assembly.

On strict proportionality the Gaullist U.N.R.–U.D.T. would
have held only 150 seats and the Communists would have held
100 – not unlike the Assembly of 1951! As it was, the election
proved to the opposition parties that, unless they ceased their
makeshift arrangements, they could never expect to win an
election. The ancient dissensus worked against each of the
opposition parties to the advantage of a united body like the
U.N.R.–Independent Republican *bloc*. The future pointed to the
necessity for an electoral coalition and electoral programme
common to the opposition, but the past beckoned with the
traditional lines of cleavage between the components of such a
coalition. Meanwhile, until the next elections, the presidency,
supported by a majority party in the Assembly, could expand
itself without concern, and without forcing matters. And in this
time the Constitution, hitherto widely regarded as a makeshift,
began to institutionalize itself.

The opposition parties of centre and left – the parties, one
might say, of the Fourth Republic – began to take the lesson to
heart. This thinking, initiated by the imperatives of the second-
ballot system, was rudely reinforced by the electoral logic implicit
in the new mode of electing the president, adopted in 1962. For

now the president was to be elected by an absolute majority of the electorate: if this was not obtained at first ballot, all the contenders had to withdraw except the two leading candidates, who then contested for the prize in the second ballot. This thrust upon the French people, for the first time in republican history, the necessity of choosing one thing or another thing. There is a comedy by Musset entitled, reasonably enough, *Il faut qu'une porte soit ouverte ou fermée*: a door is either open or it is shut. The intellectual and ideological tradition of France does everything it possibly can to avoid such brutality, more reminiscent of England's Dr Johnson than of the *lycée* and the *école normale*. It seeks and expresses itself in a host of elaborate intermediate positions. Not so now. For the presidency, two rival coalitions must be formed. On the one side there would be no difficulty; the Gaullist party formed the nucleus of one of the two opposing *blocs* of voters. But how to construct a coalition out of the mutually competitive Socialists, Communists, Radicals, Christian Democrats and traditional conservatives – the parties of the old Fourth Republic?

It is increasingly argued that Gaullism, and even more the economic and social changes that are occurring in France, have rendered obsolete the old ideological differences between the parties. Maybe: but not, apparently, in the minds of the party leaders and their central committees. The analysis of the French dissensus given at pages 271 ff. above is still valid, as far as electoral manoeuvres go, at any rate. Certainly this was illustrated by the run-up to the presidential election of 1965.

The first attempt to create an anti-Gaullist coalition was made by M. Gaston Deferre, a Socialist of right-wing and anti-communist *tendance*. Reasoning that the Communists would have to support him in any case rather than vote for de Gaulle, he set his heart on a coalition with the centrist Christian Democrats (the M.R.P.). But, while these two parties could agree on some things, they failed to agree on church schools, long-term policy towards the Communists, and on 'socialism'. The attempt foundered. The next attempt was made by M. Mitterrand, a member of a small left-wing group called the Union Démocratique et Socialiste de la Résistance (U.D.S.R.) and an obdurate opponent of the Fifth Republic. Supported by the Socialists, Mitterrand formed the '*petite fédération*': Socialists, the small U.D.S.R. group, and the Radical Socialists – the 'Fédération de la Gauche'. Mitterrand made no bargain with the Communists but knew he could rely on their support against the General. On the other hand he had effectively renounced alliance with the M.R.P. and this party, having attracted to itself a number of radical and conservative politicians, adopted M. Lecanuet as its presidential candidate. Thus there were three candidates: Mitterrand, Lecanuet and de Gaulle. In addition, three minor, independent, candidates presented themselves.

The split in the anti-de Gaulle ranks proved fatal. True, at the first ballot they did unexpectedly well. For this, the new role of television is responsible. Under the Fifth Republic the Press is free; broadcasting, however, has hardly been politically neutral, while television was heavily biased in favour of de Gaulle and the government. Under the rules, however, the opposition parties were entitled to a fair share of television time and the result was startling. For the first time – Parliament having been put into decline by the General – the population of France was able to see and hear the Fifth Republic on the defensive. Instead of grandly carrying all before him, the General was thrust into the humiliating position of scoring less than fifty per cent of the votes cast, and was forced to enter into a second, run-off ballot. He took 44·6 per cent of the vote: but Mitterrand took 31·7 per cent and Lecanuet, of the Comité des Démocrates,[7] took 15·6 per cent. On the second ballot, Lecanuet and the lesser candidates withdrew; and at this stage, with the contest resting between Mitterrand and de Gaulle, the latter carried the election (see Table 16).

There now loomed up the legislative elections of 1967. Could the opposition parties learn from their experience of the presidential elections and form a common platform? No, they could not. They remained divided into their three parts, although they still faced the cartel of the U.N.R. and the Independent Republicans. Lecanuet, the M.R.P. leader, expanded his base somewhat by forming the Centre Démocratique: he had attracted to

7. Mostly M.R.P. but supported by the C.N.I.P. also.

himself some of the former 'Moderates' (those that had belonged to the C.N.I.P.) and a few ex-Radicals. But the bulk of the Radical Socialists now formally entered the Federation of the Left which now styled itself the Fédération de la Gauche Démo-

TABLE 16. PRESIDENTIAL ELECTION, 1965:
PERCENTAGES OF VOTES CAST

	First ballot	Second ballot
De Gaulle	44·6	55·2
Mitterrand	31·7	44·8
Lecanuet	15·6	
Tixier-Vignancourt	5·2	
Marcelhacy	1·7	
Barbu	1·1	

cratique et Socialiste (F.G.D.S.). And this, in its turn, made a formal electoral pact with the Communists. Both groupings agreed to withdraw on the second ballot in order to assist the 'best placed candidates of the left'. The second-ballot system was certainly producing a simplification of the party structure; unfortunately, however, instead of there being two *blocs*, there were still three: left, centre, and the Gaullists. For all that, the left-wing electoral pact did a great deal to mitigate, though not abrogate, the distortion of the representational system. With 42·6 per cent of the vote, the Gaullists and their allies got 244 seats. With 45·4 per cent of the vote, the two left-wing parties secured 189 seats. With seven per cent of the votes, the Democratic Centre secured twenty-seven seats, and together with the fifteen odd 'Moderates' it held the balance of power. For the most striking feature of this election, after the second ballot, was that the Gaullists and their Independent Republican allies had lost their absolute majority. But, save for some strikingly horrific act of the president, the Centre was obviously going to maintain the Gaullists in power, unless and until it felt that a dissolution of Parliament and new elections would favour its chances. Until then, the Gaullists and the government were safe.[8]

8. For the 1968 election, see below, pp. 325–31.

Thus, in the first of the Assemblies (1958–62), the Gaullists, because the president was of their party and also because they were the largest single parliamentary party, formed the Cabinet, and – owing to the Algerian issue – were able to depend on tacit support from the opposition when they turned away from their own 'Moderate' allies. In the second Assembly (1962–7), the Gaullists and their allies had an absolute majority. In the 1967–8 one, they and their allies were just short of this majority but could rely upon the support of the Centre. There was therefore a congruence between the political complexion of the Assembly, of the Cabinet and of the presidency, and in these circumstances the personalist interpretation of the Constitution and the exaltation of the presidency have flourished.

It must be noted, however, that there was no such congruence between the presidency-cum-government's political complexion and that of the Upper House – the Senate. For this is still elected in much the same way as it was before: indirectly, by an electoral college, which is primarily composed of the local and departmental councillors in each department of France. As always this over-represents the rural and small town areas: and it is a striking testimony to the traditional nature of the vote in these areas that the elections to the Senate produce results similar to those of the Fourth Republic. The Gaullists are in a small minority, and the overwhelming majority represent the centre-of-the-road parties, characteristic of the Fourth Republic. Thus, while the Assembly backs the Cabinet and president, the Senate has become the chief focus of party opposition to them. But the significance of this is greatly diminished by the manner in which the Constitution has reduced the importance of Parliament as a whole, and exalted the executive at its expense.

(2) *The debilitation of Parliament*

When they were drafting the Constitution, in 1958, the Gaullists thought they would have to rule against Parliament or without it. They envisaged the old fragmented Assembly. In practice they found themselves with majorities or near-majorities. In 1958 they laid down the constitutional conditions for a semi-autonomous

TABLE 17. PERCENTAGE OF VOTES CAST FOR THE MAIN PARTIES, 1956-67

Party		election dates		Party		election dates	
	1956	1958 (second ballot)	1962 (second ballot)		1967 (first ballot)	1967 (second ballot)	
Communist	25·7	20·5	21·3	Communist	23·1	21·4
Other left	2·1	0·8	1·2	Other left	2·4	0·9
Socialists	14·8	13·8	15·2	Federation of the Left	19·9	24·0
Radicals	13·4	3·3	4·2			
Centre left		2·4	2·8			
M.R.P.	11·0	9·1	5·3	Democratic Centre	12·8	7·0
U.N.R. (Gaullists)	4·4	28·1	40·5	U.N.R.-U.D.T.	35·3	42·6
Republican Centre	–	2·4	0·4			
C.N.I.	14·4	19·9	7·6	Various moderates	5·6	3·7
Independants			1·6			
Extreme right	13·3	3·0	–			

executive power, and enormously strengthened it at the expense of the legislature: but thereafter their majorities or near-majorities in the Assembly made it stronger still.

In drawing up the new Constitution they did three things: transferred a number of formerly legislative powers to the executive; diminished the powers of the Assembly relative to the Senate; and subjected the powers of the opposition and of the individual deputy to crippling restrictions.

(a) The legislature is no longer omni-competent. The Constitution lays down, in so many words, the matters on which it may legislate, and the remainder are reserved to the executive to decree, by means of ordinances. It may legislate within the field of civil liberties, nationality questions, crimes and penalties, taxation, electoral arrangements and the issues involving the nationalization of private property. In addition it may lay down the principles but not the details of laws on education, local government, defence, party relationships and social and labour matters. 'Matters other than those regulated by laws fall within the field of rule-making' (Article 37).

Furthermore, the time at Parliament's disposal has been curtailed. Under the Fourth Republic it had to sit for at least seven months in the year and usually sat for longer. Now it is confined to two sessions totalling some five and a half months, and even these tend to be curtailed by sundry holidays and other interruptions. The time has proved too short even for the government's own legislative programme.

It may also be mentioned in this connexion that a rule of incompatibility (Article 23) forbids a deputy to hold a ministerial appointment. If a deputy is made minister he has to resign his seat. The idea was that the overthrow of Cabinets under the Fourth Republic had been spearheaded by ambitious deputies eager for ministerial appointment. Recent research has in fact disproved this hypothesis.[9] But in any event the incompatibility rule is neither as radical nor novel as is commonly supposed. A similar rule has long prevailed in Holland, but in that country it has become common form for ministers to sit in the chambers

9. cf. D. Macrae, *Parliament, Parties and Society in France, 1948-1958,* Macmillan, New York, 1968.

and behave in all respects like their British counterparts. It is most doubtful whether this particular provision has had any significant effect on the behaviour of either the deputies or the government.

(b) Inside the legislature, the Senate has been strengthened as compared with the old Conseil de la République under the previous Constitution; but this accrued strength is all geared to the advantage of the government. The Senate's powers are equal to those of the Assembly save in two respects: it is for the Assembly to examine the Budget first, and only the Assembly can censure a government and so force it to resign. The Senate can, however, veto the legislation of the Assembly. This apparent limitation on the power of the government is turned into an important weapon in its defence. For, supposing that the Senate has exercised its veto, the Constitution nowadays gives the government *three* choices. It can convene a joint conference of the two houses and persuade them to a compromise. Or, if it wants the bill which the Senate has just vetoed, it can ask the Assembly to rule 'definitively' – i.e., to override the Senate. Or, if it does not like the bill which the Assembly has passed, it can do nothing at all and thus implicitly uphold the veto of the Senate!

(c) Finally the opportunities of the opposition and of individual deputies have been minimized. The Gaullists seek to defend the changes they have introduced by arguing that they make the Assembly approximate to the position of the Commons *vis-à-vis* the Cabinet. Superficially many of the changes may appear to do so. Taken together, however, they form a grotesque caricature of the British situation.

Three individual changes do indeed escape this censure. Firstly, the power of the legislative commissions has been reduced. Previously nineteen in number, highly specialized, the nests and strongholds of pressure groups, they now number only six and are so large that the pressure groups are submerged by the numbers of independent deputies. Not only this but the Assembly no longer debates on the commission's text and report, but must debate on the original government draft together with any amendments the government has chosen to introduce. This has seriously weakened the influence of the commissions as such, in the Assembly. Next, the procedural rules on the Budget and financial matters resemble British practice in that motions to increase taxation or reduce expenditure can be moved only by the government. Lastly, as in Britain, it is the government which nowadays fixes the agenda – the famous *ordre du jour* over which so many battles used to be fought in the past.

Beyond these innovations, the changes increasingly penalize the opposition. In Britain the standing orders of the House guarantee 'opposition time' equivalent to some twenty-six per cent of the entire session, while question time and the other rules of procedure permit the government's critics to raise the most embarrassing questions at the most politically opportune moment. Not so in France. Apart from the Friday which has been set aside for questions, the opposition have *no* guaranteed time at their disposal. All time is the government's. Questions themselves have been treated perfunctorily by the government, and – to be fair – grossly mishandled (*qua* engine of criticism) by the opposition. Again, in Britain, where the government makes an important policy statement, this is not only the subject of question and answer but can be and usually is followed by debate. In the Fifth Republic, the government can and usually has refused a vote on its policy statements and in most cases has succeeded in preventing debate. The Debré government (1958–62) made twenty-seven policy statements: ten to the Senate, the remainder to the Assembly. On eight, the government refused any debate at all. On one, the debate did take place but the government did not bother to make any reply. On the remainder, where debate did take place, it was pointless since the government had let it be known that there would be no vote – so that no deputy felt he had any need to convince the Assembly.

The opposition may, however, table a motion of censure. The rule is that this must be signed by one-tenth of the deputies and that they can do so only once in each session. This means that, if (as in 1967–8) one-half of the Assembly was composed of opposition deputies, it is theoretically possible for these to table (between them) a total of five motions of censure per session: roughly one per month. This is not a large number but in any case the procedure is vitiated by the provision that to succeed the motion must collect an absolute majority of the entire membership of the Assembly. This means that those who abstain are considered as having voted for the government! And this same convention is used for the voting on government issues of confidence: which brings one to the procedure for voting government bills.

Quite simply; if the government is prepared to stake its life upon a bill, it declares this a matter of confidence and it is then for the opposition to put down a censure motion against the government within twenty-four hours (such censure motions are not rationed like those already mentioned: they can be put down every time the government challenges the opposition to do). If the opposition fails to put down the motion of censure, then the bill not only passes – it passes undebated! If, on the other hand, the motion of censure is duly tabled, then to defeat the bill the opposition must muster an *absolute* majority of the *entire* Assembly (Article 49). In addition the government may require the Assembly to either accept or reject the bill (or any part of it) *as an entirety* – the so-called *bloc* voting – staking its life on the result. In that case, unless the government is defeated by the motion of censure, the entire bill passes. It may be argued that where the government's party is in a minority, as under the Fourth Republic, this collection of rules was sensible in that it guaranteed that the government would get its legislation as long as it was not opposed by an absolute majority of the Assembly. The government party was in a minority in the first of the Fifth Republic parliaments, and it could also be argued that the procedure was necessary then. During that Parliament the *bloc* vote was utilized forty times, about six times in each session. But in the second Parliament the Gaullists had an absolute majority: yet the *bloc* vote was used no less than 118 times, or fifteen times per session. And clearly, the procedure is useless against out-and-out opponents who will vote against the government in any case. Those whom it penalizes are the moderate critics who wish to amend the bill in particular rather than in principle, and this includes the government's own back-bench supporters.

The changes have guaranteed the Cabinet's stability and continuity but only by robbing the legislature of its role as a forum of grievances, as a check on administrative abuses, as a defender of civil liberties and not least as the place where the reputation of government and opposition is made or unmade as the months tick by to the next election. In every single one of these respects the new National Assembly falls far short of the Commons which it is supposed to resemble. And it falls short of the Commons even in that matter wherein it is supposed to bear the strongest resemblance: in sustaining a strong and continuous executive. For a British Cabinet is no stronger than the party which supports it. If this party cracks open, so does the Cabinet. And the Cabinet is part and parcel of the majority that supports it; it reflects its political tendencies. It is, so to speak, a 'sample' of the majority party; and when this is troubled, so is the Cabinet.

Not so in France. The Cabinet is not in any sense 'selected', even vicariously, by the majority *bloc*, but appointed by the constitutionally irresponsible, seven-year-tenure president. It does not generate the policies it pursues but pursues the policies dictated to it by this same president. Its job is to act as his parliamentary agent. In this exaltation of the presidency, lies the final magnification of executive over legislature, and of 'order and future goals' over 'representativeness and present goals'.

(3) *The presidency*

That the Constitution indubitably endows the presidency with powers in excess of those possessed by that office under the Third and Fourth Republics has already been made plain. But most of these are, in some measure, qualified powers: and three provisions – the constitutional irresponsibility of the president (Article 67), the arbitration power (Article 5) and the attribution to the government and not to the president of the power to 'decide and direct the policy of the nation' – all suggest that the president is over and above the political battle: more mundanely, that he does not pursue political policies of his own.

This was not de Gaulle's conception of his office. In his view:

The keystone of our régime is the new institution of a president of the Republic, designated by the reason and feelings of the French people to be the head of state and the guide of France. Far from requiring that the president must, as was once the case, remain confined to the role of advisory and representative functions, the Constitution confers on him the outstanding responsibility for the destiny of France and of the Republic. In accordance with the Constitution the president is, in effect, the guarantor of the country's independence and integrity. In short, he is responsible for France. At the same time it falls to him to ensure the continuity of the state, and the working of the public powers. To bear these supreme responsibilities, the head of state must have adequate powers. The Constitution gives them to him. It is he who designates the ministers and chooses the premiers, it is he who takes all important state decisions by means of decrees or ordinances. It is he who appoints officials, officers, judges. In the essential fields of foreign policy and national security he is required to act directly, since by virtue of the Constitution he negotiates and concludes treaties, is head of the armed forces and presides over national defence. Above all, if it should happen that the country and the Republic are directly in danger, the president is personally invested with all the duties and all the rights which public safety involves.[10]

De Gaulle established this conception of the presidency through four avenues. The first was the subservience of his Cabinet. It was not simply that de Gaulle looked on them as his agents and subordinates: the real point is that this was how they saw themselves. Whenever he thought fit he communicated his decisions to them; these by no means always had their prior knowledge or consent. In foreign affairs, the first they heard of many items was often through the Press conferences which the president made a habit of giving. On Algeria, he outlined the phases in his policy as this developed, with scant or no mention of the government. On numerous occasions, statements by the government were contradicted by statements issuing from the presidential palace. The Cabinets loyally abided by it all and translated it into parliamentary effect. Their parliamentary support, and the new rules of procedure, facilitated this task. So it was that the president ruled his Cabinet and the Cabinet ruled the Assembly.

10. Broadcast, 20 September 1962.

A second avenue was the use of the government's decree powers. Whereas the Constitution firmly prevents the legislature from taking over functions assigned to the executive, Articles 38 and 16, in their different ways, do permit the executive to take over functions assigned to the legislature. Article 38 permits the government to request Parliament to grant it powers, for a limited period, to act by decree in fields that are normally 'in the field of legislation' – i.e., the matters specified by the Constitution as being within the scope of Parliament. To 1968, Parliament had given the government its decree powers on eight occasions. Mostly there was a good argument for doing so: for instance, the three cases that arose during the 1962–7 Parliament were all concerned with translating provisions of the Treaty of Rome into practical effect. No such excuse can be made for the example in 1967, after the Gaullists had lost their absolute majority in the general election. No sooner had the new Assembly met than the government, relying (with reason) on the reluctance of the Democratic Centre to overthrow it, insisted on taking a six-month grant of special powers to handle economic and social legislation by decree: and, without the Democratic Centre, the other opposition parties could not muster an absolute majority of the Assembly to deny these powers to the government. The way in which explosive economic and social welfare matters have been withdrawn from parliamentary check and criticism in France has to be contrasted with the long Calvary the British Labour Party has had to endure as every stage in its unpopular prices and incomes policy has come before the House of Commons.

In contrast to Article 38, the emergency powers of the president, under Article 16, have been invoked but once – when the Four Generals' Revolt occurred in Algeria in April 1961. That an extreme emergency existed is indubitable and de Gaulle's invocation of his special powers was welcomed. But whether it was constitutional remains in doubt. For the article only allows the invocation of the powers if the emergency has 'interrupted the regular functioning of the constitutional organs of government', and this it certainly had not done, at least in metropolitan France. Furthermore, though Parliament automatically reconvened according to the letter of the article, de Gaulle then decided on what matters it could or – according to him – could not discuss. This high-handed personal interpretation of the clause, which led the opposition parties to put down a motion of censure, will be mentioned later. In the event, the exercise of Article 16 proved so embarrassing to the government that it was abandoned after five months.

The third avenue was de Gaulle's usurpation of the right to interpret the Constitution. He usually, but not always, did this under cover of Article 5 – the 'arbitration' clause. The Constitution has indeed established a Constitutional Council which must be consulted in a range of situations; but, in all cases, it is able to express an opinion only when asked to do so, the citizen cannot appeal to it and its decisions are simply statements without binding juridical force or any other machinery of execution. Furthermore its political complexion is biased. Its nine members are appointed, three apiece, by the president of the Republic, the president of the Senate and the president of the Assembly respectively. The first and the third of these personages have naturally appointed Gaullists. In addition to this Constitutional Council, there is the venerable and esteemed – and truly independent – Conseil d'État, which is the supreme court of jurisdiction on administrative matters including the legality of decrees and ordinances. It has been easy for de Gaulle to skirt round the authority of both these bodies when so minded and to take refuge in Article 5 – or even in no particular constitutional provision at all. Some examples will make clear the contemptuous interference of de Gaulle with the text of the Constitution.

(i) In the spring of 1960 serious trouble erupted among the agricultural communities of France at a time when Parliament was in recess. A majority of deputies signed a petition for an extraordinary session of Parliament, as Article 29 entitles them to do. The article says that, in such a case, 'Parliament meets in special session . . .', which (Article 30) is opened and closed by a decree of the president. De Gaulle, surprisingly, refused to sign the decree and so prevented Article 29 from being followed. According to him, the deputies' request was unconstitutional under an earlier article (27), which states that an 'imperative mandate' (i.e., special instructions to a deputy by which he is bound to vote a certain way in Parliament) is 'null and void'. According to him, the deputies had requested the special session because of pressure from the farmers. This particular ruling begged three vital questions: firstly the factual one as to whether pressure had been applied; secondly, whether such pressure was the same thing as an 'imperative mandate'; and thirdly, whether declaration that such imperative mandates were 'null and void' does not merely mean that they had no contractual validity in a court of law. He also rejected the deputies' request on the grounds that the bills they proposed to introduce were unconstitutional since they proposed to incur expenditure, a right conferred on the government and not on the deputies. While this contention may well have been correct, one fails to see how or why it should be the president who decides such a matter in advance of the meeting of Parliament! And finally, he refused to sign the decree opening such a special session on the grounds that this violated his 'duty of securing the regular functioning of the public authorities' – i.e., that it violated Article 5! *Quelle blague!*

(ii) A somewhat similar case arose in August 1961, once again provoked by agricultural unrest. This time the General could not forbid Parliament to meet, because he was at the time governing under Article 16 under which Parliament reconvened automatically. It so happened that it had just gone into recess and now desired – by the required absolute majority – to recommence its labours. This time, unable to prevent its meeting, de Gaulle simply refused to let it debate its agricultural bills. Under Article 16, he said, the Parliament, meeting in automatic session, was limited to debating *only* those issues arising out of the emergency. This unexpected interpretation provoked widespread anger; so, even more, did the president's self-assumed right to make this interpretation. The opposition promptly tabled a motion of censure on the government (the president, as we have seen, is not accountable to Parliament). To their amazement, the Gaullist president of the Assembly ruled the censure motion out of order on the quaint grounds that in *his* view the president did have the right to interpret the Constitution under Article 5; and that, since he had ruled that the deputies' agricultural bills would be out of order when Parliament met under emergency powers, the right of the deputies to table a motion of censure was *a fortiori* even more out of order! This bizarre logic defies analysis. But it did have the effect of permitting the president to shuffle off all responsibility by telling the Socialists, when they complained to him: 'But it was not I that said this! It was the president of your National Assembly who said it!'

(iii) A more trivial example, and for that matter all the more revealing, shows a similar contempt for constitutional forms. It arose in the wake of the 1967 elections when the Gaullists, having lost their absolute majority, were no longer sure of being able to elect their candidate to the speakership of the Assembly. They were in a minority of one. To make matters worse, however, no less than twenty-two of the deputies were ministers and would therefore have to vacate their parliamentary seats on assuming their ministries, so that these votes would be lost too. So, if they went to their ministries, the Gaullist vote would be twenty-three down, but if they remained deputies they could not administer their ministries. Characteristically, de Gaulle accepted the resignation of the Cabinet (thus freeing the twenty-two votes for the election) while asking the outgoing ministers to carry on the current business of their departments.

(iv) However, the classic and unquestionably most important utilization of the 'arbitration power' to violate the Constitution was the use of the referendum to amend the Constitution, in 1962.

Originally the president was indirectly elected: by an electoral college which for the greater part consisted of local councillors. This was neither wide nor representative enough to satisfy de Gaulle's wish that the president should have as good a democratic title to govern as the directly elected National Assembly. The Algerian extremists' efforts to assassinate him in 1961 and 1962 raised the question of presidential succession and so provided him with the chance to bring about what he had always desired: a presidency elected by the entire electorate. It is certainly arguable that such a change was desirable and it is equally arguable that it could not be attained unless Parliament was by-passed. It is certain, however, that the amendment clause of the Constitution (89) requires the assent of Parliament. It lays down two methods of proceeding. The president can put an amendment to the two houses and, if they pass it by a three-fifths majority, it becomes law. Alternatively, the president (on the proposal of his prime minister) or the deputies themselves can introduce the amendment: if the two houses then pass it, it goes to the electorate by way of a referendum. In either case, Parliament *must* approve.

Instead, in September 1962, de Gaulle stated his intention to submit his proposed amendment directly to the people in a referendum. His minister of education promptly resigned on the grounds that this was a breach of the constitution, the president of the Senate likewise declared it unconstitutional, and so did the Conseil d'État, while the (Gaullist) Consultative Council declined jurisdiction. The president pressed on, and invoked Article 5. It was for him, he stated, to interpret how the Constitution should be applied, and in his judgement the appropriate article was not the amendment clause (Article 89) but another clause, Article 11. This gives him the power, on the proposal of his prime minister, to submit to a referendum any bill dealing with the 'organization of the public authorities'! In that case argued his opponents, why was Article 89 in the Constitution at all? And we may well echo them. In the event, Parliament passed an overwhelming vote of censure of the government, so provoking a dissolution of the Assembly and new elections. But, disregarding this, the president put his referendum to the vote. If the political maturity of a people is indicated by its ability to distinguish between procedure and substance – and I maintain that it is – then the French electorate again displayed its immaturity. A majority ratified the constitutional amendment. At the ensuing elections it returned the president's party in an absolute majority.

The final avenue to presidential supremacy has been the abuse of the referendum. Not merely has Parliament been shackled and diminished. Nowadays, in certain cases, it can be dispensed with altogether by way of a direct appeal to the people. In January 1961 the General – conformably to Article 11 – launched a referendum to justify his decision to establish a provisional executive for Algeria. What was not envisaged was that he would treat this as a personal vote of confidence. 'I am the country's guide,' he told the voters in his broadcasts. 'To succeed I must have the support of the nation. That is why I appeal to you over the heads of intermediaries' ('intermediaries', of course, means the Parliament). In April 1962, when in another referendum he sought power to ratify the Évian agreements with the Algerian nationalists, he not only treated the vote as one of confidence in himself and in his régime: in addition, acting on some unspecified constitutional authority, he demanded – and received – a grant of special powers to conclude all agreements necessary to execute the Évian agreements by way of decrees and ordinances. And then, some six months later, came the unconstitutional referendum to amend the Constitution. This time the meaning of the Constitution itself was turned into a personal matter between the president and the electorate. Later utterances of the General, not speak of his henchmen, made it clear that the referendum was in fact the preferred style of conducting business – notwithstanding the qualifications which the paper Constitution imposes on that method.

The events of May 1968

And so this régime approached the tenth anniversary of its accession – the famous (or notorious) 15 May – with pride and excessive self-confidence. It could and did congratulate itself on having given France stability, public order, a booming economy, a vast gold hoard and a popular if idiosyncratic foreign policy of anti-Americanism.

At this very moment, like thunder from a blue sky, the entire fabric toppled and seemed about to disintegrate.

Political scientists will long analyse those extraordinary days of May and June 1968 which none of them foresaw, and many will be the contradictory explanations. Here, at a short distance from those events, let one man's opinion stand. Briefly, a badly managed confrontation between the authorities and a handful of ultra-left-wing students got out of hand and sparked off a sympathetic general strike of workers; this in turn got out of hand and provoked a mass standstill until no less than ten million were on strike (including the girls at the Folies Bergères); the government was paralysed and on the point of disappearing and the way was clear for a *coup d'état*. It did not happen, because of a covert (it may indeed turn out to be an overt) complicity between the so-called revolutionary party, the Communists, and the Gaullist government. Brought to the jump, the Communist race-horse 'refused'; the government regained the initiative and in new general elections scored a momentous victory over all its opponents of the centre and the left.

The immediate conclusions that I draw are these: firstly, the tradition, nay the cult, of insurrection, of Michelet's concept of the Revolution as the Goddess, is still alive and numbers many worshippers. Secondly, the Communist Party has quitted this cult. Since May 1968 it should no longer be placed where it is in the table at page 275 above. It should be moved into the 'constitutional' box alongside the Socialists, and its place, as an extraconstitutional and insurrectionary force should be taken by the diminutive Parti Socialiste Unifié (P.S.U.) and the various ultra-Marxist 'groupuscules', which include anarchists, Maoists and Trotskyites as well as others. Thirdly, the concept of a unified 'opposition of all the lefts', symbolized in the 1968 common programme of the parties of the Fédération de la Gauche and the Communist Party, is only credible as long as there is no likelihood of its being returned to office: given the alternatives of Gaullism and a government containing the Communists the French electorate unhesitatingly support the first. Fourthly, the Communist Party became – to use its own Marxist jargon – an 'objective' accomplice of the General; i.e., even if it thought and felt that it opposed him, in practice it acted in such a way as to support him. And the reason is clear. Provided it could satisfy the demands of the Communist-led trade unions and so retain its grip upon them – and in the end it was able to do this – the party was only too glad to have the General at the helm: for the simple and sole reason that he, far better than they in a coalition with Socialists whose foreign policy they did not share, could carry out the anti-American policy which, for the previous four years had ranged France at the side of the Soviet Union, largely disrupted the North Atlantic Treaty Organization and was at that very moment trying to force the devaluation of the American dollar.

The French Communist Party was at this period one of the few large European communist parties that faithfully followed the Moscow line; and that line is, as it always has been, that the interests of the homeland of communism, i.e. Soviet foreign policy interests, must take precedence over any domestic concerns.

The events took place in a drama of five acts. In the first (2–13 May), the activities of the ultra-left student agitators at Nanterre provoked the authorities into closing the faculty, the students demonstrated, clashes took place with the police, the remainder of the student community joined the few 'enragés' and a series of pitched street battles took place in which the police used indiscriminate, revolting and useless barbarity. The students, true to their romantic brands of Marxism appealed to 'workers' solidarity'. The Communist-dominated C.G.T. union, always alert to being outflanked on its left (it cordially detested these youngsters), met this threat to its leadership by calling, jointly with the C.F.T.C., a general strike in Paris for 13 May, the tenth anniversary of the Fifth Republic. The strike was obeyed, and ended Act I. Now began the 'rising action': Act II.

A spontaneous movement spread through the country, with strikes and in many cases the physical occupation of the factories by the strikers. The strikes spread with astonishing rapidity and by 22 May no less than eight million workers were 'out'. Meanwhile the opposition political parties decided to climb on the back of the movement. While de Gaulle was returning hastily from his state visit to Romania, a vote of censure was tabled in the Assembly. As was to be expected, it was lost – but less than half a dozen centrist deputies supported the government so that the motion was lost by eleven votes. Meanwhile, the prime minister, M. Pompidou (who was gallantly holding the fort while the president was expatiating in Bucharest), got the unions to agree to sit down with him to reach a settlement of the economic issues. It seemed the entire episode was about to close. The Communists were now ostentatiously turning their backs on the students; they had apparently retained their leadership of their unions, and the government – and its precious foreign policy – would not fall.

Wrong! This proved just the curtain on Act II. The climax, Act III, was just at hand. The president, very like a caricature of himself, gave another of his television performances, in which he promised that, while order would be sternly maintained, he would shortly hold a popular referendum on some vague concept, then very voguish, called 'participation'. The effort failed. In the capital the riots broke out worse than before, while in the provinces the speech was treated with indifference if not disdain. Though the Communist-dominated C.G.T. pursued its talks with the prime minister and reached a provisional settlement, this was to be repudiated by its followers, who were not satisfied and who remained on strike. Indeed the strikes spread further; by 29 May the strikers numbered *ten million*. This was the revolutionary climax. The government clearly had no control over the situation and widespread demands were voiced for the resignation of the prime minister, and for the retirement of de Gaulle. The political parties staked their claims to the succession: Mitterrand, leader of the Federation of the Left, declared he would be a presidential candidate in the event of an election, the Communists stated that they would naturally expect to share in any new government, and Mendès-France, the leader of the doctrinaire P.S.U., himself announced his willingness to head a new government of 'all the lefts'. But nobody *did* anything to bring all this about. They sat, apparently expecting the government would quit. It was at this moment, above all, that the verbalism, the domestication, the 'objective' complicity with the régime, of the famed French Communist Party, which attracted one in four of all the voters in France, now became obvious. That 'complicity' is well enough attested by the Russian Press. It suppressed the anti-Communist references of politicians like Pompidou; it censored out references to the sloth of the French Communist Party; it guarded total silence about de Gaulle.

The high point in the drama came on 29 May. The president, it was broadcast, had left Paris – in order to take a 'grave decision'. Would he then resign? He returned next day, and 30 May saw the opening of Act IV: the 'falling action'.

He told the nation, in a broadcast, three things: he was staying in office; he had cancelled the referendum; he was dissolving

Parliament and new elections would be held immediately.

The moment for the revolutionary parties to take revolutionary action had passed. If they interfered with the elections they were insurrectionists, fearful of a popular vote, and could be treated as such. They had to play along. Their immediate reaction was quite typically *verbal*. They denounced the broadcast as 'an act of civil war', as 'an act of dictatorship'. This arrant nonsense merely showed their ineptness. They had not condemned the rioting, but had tried to ride to power on its shoulders – hence they had discredited themselves with moderate opinion. They had not led the rioting and seized power – hence they had – or at least the Communists had – forfeited their *raison d'être*. And now, in this invidious position, they were condemned to a fortnight's debating match with a prime minister who made his chief electoral appeal the communist/totalitarian threat to the Republic! Meanwhile, at the signs of a revivified de Gaulle, a vast pro-governmental demonstration had taken place in Paris. Elsewhere, the negotiations with the unions began to bear fruits. The strikers fell away. France slowly returned to work and when, in the middle of June, the police moved to eject the students from the premises which they had been occupying, they met with no resistance. Order had returned. And so came Act V – the dénouement.

The electoral line-up was the same as in the previous year, with the Gaullists and their allies, the Independent Republicans, facing the centrist 'Progress and democracy' grouping (the new name for the Democratic Centre), and the joint Federation of the Left–Communist alliance. But the situation was vastly different from the previous year. To begin with, the Gaullists and their allies benefited from an invisible party: '*le parti de la peur*' ('the party of fear'). They were assisted, too, by deserters from the Socialist Party, shamed and shocked by Mitterrand's apparent readiness to pick the presidential sash out of the debris of the barricades. They were assisted, finally, by the widespread fear and dislike of the Communist Party: this meant that the collaboration of that party with Socialists in the local contests, on second ballot, was a veritable kiss of death.

The result of the election was a Gaullist landslide. The Gaullists and their allies won no less than 142 of the 487 seats outright at the first ballot. In the second ballot, the local arrangements between Socialists and Communists held less well than in the previous year and, in any case, the mere association of the two parties led a number of voters to vote against a Communist-supported Socialist at the second ballot. So was initiated a number of marginal shifts to the right which led to a final result unprecedented in French electoral history: *one* party, the Gaullists, alone had an absolute majority of all seats. They could afford even to dispense with the Independent Republicans. As for the Democratic Centre Party, the Socialists and the Communists – their parliamentary force was shattered. Table 18 tells its own tale. It will be seen that the aggregate votes of the opposition

TABLE 18. THE 1968 ELECTIONS IN FRANCE

Party	Percentage of votes first ballot	Percentage of votes second ballot	Seats in Assembly	Percentage of Seats in Assembly
Communist	22	20 ⎫	34 ⎫	
Other Left	5	1 ⎬ 42%	– ⎬	· 18
Federation	18	21 ⎭	57 ⎭	
Democratic Centre	11	8	33	8
Gaullists (U.D.R.)	38	46 ⎫ 49%	292 ⎫	72
Various Right	5	3 ⎭	61 ⎭	
Extreme Right	–			
		(Not grouped)	10	2

parties form fifty per cent of the total; the Gaullist tally of seats is totally out of proportion to its popular vote. France is still a very evenly divided country, even after a shock like the events of May and June. The elections did not prove there was a consensus. What they proved instead was the total incredibility, the non-viability of the cartel of the lefts.

This sweeping victory was followed by an extraordinary *coup de théâtre*. By every account, the man who had held the fort during the paralysis of France was the prime minister, M.

Pompidou, and his public credit and popularity had risen accordingly. Now, on the very morrow of his stupendous electoral success, the president removed him from office and appointed as his successor the former foreign minister, M. Couve de Murville: the third prime minister of the Fifth Republic.

IV. THE FIFTH REPUBLIC LEGITIMIZED
JUNE 1968–JUNE 1969

'Nothing will ever be the same again,' was the verdict of some observers after 'the Events'. 'Everything is the same as before, only more so,' was the verdict of others as they surveyed a left-and-centre shattered to fragments: an enormous Gaullist majority in the Assembly; and a President who celebrated his triumph by the political execution of the man who had engineered it.

At that stage, however, one might also have suggested these five hypotheses:

(i) The most important element in the development of the Fifth Republic during its first decade had been the personal. It is very doubtful whether any President other than de Gaulle would have dared to take such liberties with the law and much more doubtful still whether the masses, consulted in his referendums, would have said 'Yes' so often to anybody else. But – would they always do so?

(ii) As it stood, and leaving out the personality of de Gaulle, the Constitution provided no solution for that situation where a President of less imperious temper faced an Assembly in which his party was in a minority, and was forced to work with a Prime Minister of different complexion than his own. Indeed the text seemed bound in such cases to generate a constitutional crisis of the first magnitude. The President would not be able to dissolve the Assembly for twelve months after the election, so that for that period he and his Prime Minister would be at loggerheads. If, after twelve months, new elections still returned an antagonistic majority, then he would, like the President Marshal MacMahon, in 1877, have to give in or get out – '*se soumettre ou se démettre*'. By the same token, as long as a President had a solid majority in the Assembly, so long would the régime remain, not a 'semi-presidential régime', as Professor Duverger, the French pundit is complaisant enough to style it,[11] but, in fact a *hyper-presidential* one. Unlike the presidential régime of the U.S.A., the President lacks the check of an independent Congress and the constraint of the Supreme Court's judicial review, to say nothing of the limitations imposed by federalism. Unlike the British 'parliamentary' régime, its supreme policy-making organ, which is the presidency, is constitutionally irresponsible and neither accountable to nor removable by the legislature. The French presidential régime is *hyper-presidential* because it compounds the strengths of the executives of the U.S.A. and Britain while being subject to the limitations and constraints of neither.

(iii) The French dissensus persisted: but worse than before the elections. The Communists and the Socialist-Radical-Centrist grouping did not see eye to eye on foreign policy. Likewise the mere prospect of a Popular Front acceding to power with the Communists as one of its components was enough to frighten the Catholic 'Democratic Centre' into the arms of the Gaullists despite their disagreements on foreign and defence policy, and to drive a significant number of Socialist Federations there also. There was also dissensus on industrial and financial policy between the U.D.R. and their electoral allies, *viz.* Giscard d'Estaing's 'Independent Republicans'. After the General's electoral victory of June this pulverization became worse: the components of the left and the centre quarrelled the more fiercely among themselves in the shock of their defeat, the Socialists began to try to re-found their party while at the same time permitting its organization to sink into further deliquescence, and the Soviet invasion of Czechoslovakia (August 1968) drove a wedge between them and the Communists. At the same time the U.D.R.'s absolute majority in the Assembly permitted them the new luxury of being able to dispense with the Independent Republicans' support, and when the General and his new Prime

11. *Le Monde*, M. Duverger, 'Les Institutions après de Gaulle: Un régime Semi-presidential', 26 November 1969.

Minister used this opportunity to lean to their so-called 'left-wing Gaullists' and invoke all kinds of 'participation', the gap between the two groups began to open. Meanwhile, secure in its majority, the U.D.R. was the master of all its master surveyed.

(iv) There was a vital potential difference between the possibilities open to the opposition in an electoral contest and in a referendum. So far the results of the two had turned out to be similar; but would this always be the case? In an election the anti-Gaullist elements had to form a 'coalition of the yesses' if they were to win: and the historic dissensus inhibited this. The second ballot system then gave a premium to the Gaullists, who did form such a bloc of yesses. But the referendum only called for a coalition of noes – and not even a formal coalition, either. So far the electors had always said 'Yes' in the referendum; but if there were one way in which they could defeat the government it was, precisely, in such a referendum, not in an election. Up to date the President had turned the referendums into a personal plebiscite, invoking in the last resort the challenge 'after me the deluge'. By doing so he had unquestionably carried a decisive number of electors who would otherwise have voted No, or abstained. But by the same token, this was a dangerous game, for the time might come when the voters would say 'No' despite the General; in that case, they would not only throw out the referendum-bill, but the General with it. In short, the General played a 'double-or-quits' game with his referendums: he chose to increase the likelihood of a favourable vote by putting himself at risk. Not so the prudent Swiss. In their country the government never feels its survival bound up with the way the voting goes in one of their referendums.

The General's personality and the fear of disorders in the event of his resignation had so far carried the day. But from July 1968 a significant new element entered into the calculation: for the first time there was an alternative Gaullist, another strong man: none other than the disgraced ex-Prime Minister, Georges Pompidou, the man of May.

(v) The Constitution was far less likely to be modified in the direction of the Fourth Republic; it had begun to win wide acceptance. In 1962 it had still appeared to be provisional. Now, apart from the Communists the elements of the opposition seemed reconciled to it. They recognized that even if the French electorate disliked the style or substance of General de Gaulle's rule (and so far they had supported both) they certainly approved the new stability it had given the government of the country. So, apart from the Communists, the opposition parties were increasingly speaking in terms of minor modifications: e.g. limiting the presidential term to five years so that it coincided with the elections and so minimized the possibility of the clash outlined in (ii) above; similarly, they urged the end of the practice of bloc-voting on bills.

But one other element of the historic dissensus still remained, and as long as it was manifested the Constitution was still not fully legitimate. That element is the one I have described as impatience of constitutional restraints. Latent from 1958, it had burst out in May 1968. The Gaullists had not played fair with the opposition. This was in the common tradition of French politics. It could only rebound on the Gaullist clans when they themselves, at some future date, were put into a minority. For, to a great many of the opposition, the régime suffered from a vice of origin. The rulers were usurpers. M. Mitterand, who received nearly eleven million votes as presidential candidate in 1965, left no doubts on this score. In a television appearance (9 May 1968) he said,

We still remember 1958. We know that the group who are in power today got there first of all by force and then by trickery and have not hesitated to break the law. And it is said – and I personally am tempted to believe that it is true – that the ruling group would not hesitate to retain power by illegal means.

For him, and many, many like him, the régime was still provisional.

What happened after de Gaulle's electoral triumph in 1968 provides a commentary on each one of these propositions. The events fell into three phases – the Gaullist restoration; the referendum of 27 April 1969, and the struggle for the succession.

A. *De Gaulle's restoration, July 1968–April 1969*

With his dismissal of Pompidou and the appointment of the *verkrampte*, Couve de Murville, the General seemed to want to show that Gaullist policies would be pursued even more rigorously than before. Certainly foreign policy lost nothing of its anti-American, anti-Canadian, anti-British, anti-Israel and pro-Soviet bias; except that the Events had rendered the franc so weak that the President could no longer continue his vendetta against the U.S. dollar. Instead, faced with the necessity of devaluing his own currency, he made the characteristic gesture of ostentatiously refusing to do so. But then foreign affairs and defence had long been accepted as part of the President's so-called 'reserved powers'. It was what was to happen on the domestic scene that illustrated, to an exaggerated degree, all his long-standing contempt for the letter of the Constitution, the seemingly unappeasable appetite for erasing all constitutional constraints to his personalism, and his extraordinary egotism.

He set the avalanche in motion in September 1968, when he announced that he proposed to make two drastic changes in the administrative and constitutional structure: to establish twenty-one regional councils, each with its own regional prefect, and also to alter the powers and composition of the Senate. Furthermore, he made it clear that these two reforms were linked (as institutionally, in some ways, they were) and would therefore be considered as a single major reform on which the nation would have to pronounce. The regional reforms do not concern us in any detail since they raised no acute constitutional issues. There seems to be no doubt that these plans could have been handled as an ordinary piece of parliamentary legislation or, alternatively, could have been put to the electorate by referendum under Article 11, the one concerning the 'organization of the public authorities'. There was considerable dispute as to whether they did, as suggested, amount to decentralization or, as others contended, a degree of even more effective centralization. The reforms would have disturbed the grass-roots political influence of many anti-Gaullist notables, but would not have led to any significant shift in the constitutional balance of institutions. Not so with the second part of the reform – that which concerned the Senate. The details of what de Gaulle proposed were vague at first and indeed the final text was not to be produced before the March of the following year (1969); but already, by the end of 1968, the main lines became apparent.

The composition of the Senate was to be altered. It was to be merged with the existing consultative body, the Economic and Social Council, a body representative of the major interest groups. This had long been a wish of the General. One could point to hints of it in his Bayeux speech of 1946, to his intentions, temporarily shelved, in 1958; and to further moves also abandoned in 1963-4.

Some half of the Senate was, as of wont, to be indirectly elected by the local councillors of the communes, départements and the (proposed) regions, by the deputies for the constituencies in such regions, and –a new element – by the organized interests. The remainder were to consist of elected representatives of these organized interests as in the existing Economic and Social Council. But the *powers* of this new Senate were also to be changed. It was to lose both the legislative powers and powers of conditional veto it had been permitted to gain under the 1958 Constitution. Instead it was to become a purely consultative body. In the normal way it would receive bills before the National Assembly and would tender its views to that body before debate.

This reform has to be seen in the context of the cold war that had developed between the Senate and the General ever since the referendum of 1962, and which was personalized in the feud between the General and the Senate's president, Gaston de Monnerville. The latter retired in October 1968, and, after two ballots, the Senate elected a compromise candidate, Alain Poher, an old Christian Democrat Senator, in the hope that he could effect some reconciliation. It must be remembered, when considering this 'cold war' and the new project of the General, that the Senate, unlike the Assembly, had never been Gaullist; that, on the contrary, it tended to reflect the middle-of-the-road centrism that was typical of the small-town mentality in France.

So the proposed reform must be seen in this context, as an effort to sweep away an impediment, an annoying obstacle, which still retained the mentality of the old Fourth Republic.

The difficulty about sweeping it away, however, was this: that under the Constitution, the amending clause was Clause 89 (see page 324 above); and that under this clause a constitutional amendment required the consent of the two houses of parliament. In short, before the amendment could go forward, either for three-fifth majority by Parliament (which was one way of proceeding) or by way of referendum (the alternative way), the Senate would have to approve the very bill which provided for its own destruction. Of course it would never do this, and the debates in that Chamber on the proposed reforms, which took place in December 1968, made this perfectly clear.

So, instead, the General decided to invoke once again the illegal procedure of 1962: instead of Clause 89, he would proceed by Clause 11. Hereby, on the proposal of the government (i.e. the President's government), the President could simply by-pass the legislature and put the proposal directly to the electorate in a referendum.

This was not all. The President seemed to have no notion of where it was prudent to stop. For one thing all the discussions, up to within a few weeks of the referendum itself, took place on somewhat vague and fluctuating government statements – not on the actual text of a bill. This was not produced, even in draft form, until February 1969, when the text was sent to the Conseil d'État. Despite the government's attempts to keep the findings secret, it soon leaked out that the Conseil had pronounced the decision to put the Senate reform part of the text forward to the electorate by referendum under Article 11 as unconstitutional; and it rejected the government's view that, since that method had been used in 1962, a 'convention' for its use had thereby been established. Secondly, the President decided to be hung for a sheep rather than for a lamb: if the referendum were to go forward additional clauses could be stuck in. One of these had the extremely important effect of permitting the President to choose his own immediate successor. Under the existing constitution it was the president of the Senate who automatically became acting President in the event of a vacancy; now it was proposed that it should be the Prime Minister who automatically became the acting President. Since the President is the one who selects his Prime Minister, this was tantamount to decreeing that he could nominate his own acting successor; and it was well known that even the temporary occupation of the Elysée Palace would confer important advantages for its incumbent in the Presidential contest that would follow.

As if this were not enough, the text also contained the proposal that the amending clause should itself be changed: that Clause 89, heavily modified, should remain but that, in addition, the controversial procedure of Clause 11, permitting the President to submit governmental reorganization to simple referendum, should henceforth be recognized as valid for amendments to the Constitution itself. Having, by the illegal use of Article 11, whipped the French electorate on its bare arse, the General was now inviting it to kiss the rod as well.

Despite the Conseil d'État's ruling that the use of Article 11 was illegal as far as the Senate reform was concerned, the government ignored it and went on to prepare the text. This ran to a booklet of fourteen pages, containing 68 Articles, which would alter, delete or replace no less than twenty-three of the eighty-nine articles of the current Constitution. Despite the pleas of even the most moderate critics, the government decided that to this gallimaufry, the elector was to return a single Yes or No.

The arguments by which the arrogant procedure was defended were curious in the extreme. One was that since the method, though pronounced unconstitutional, had been used in 1962 and received an affirmative answer, this made it constitutional to use it in 1969. The General himself, in speeches and radio broadcasts, also argued that the referendum had now become the usage by which constitutions were made and unmade: he instanced the referendum on the draft constitutions in 1945 and 1946, and on the 1958 Constitution, and claimed that the 1968 parliamentary elections had themselves been in the nature of a referendum. These arguments were irrelevant. Nobody disputed the fact that under Clause 89 a constitutional amendment could be put by referendum: the point was that the two houses of the legislature had to pass the proposal first. This was the law as it stood; and to by-pass the legislature by the use of Article 11 was, according to the Conseil d'État, illegal. But to this the General made a singular (but entirely typical) reply, tantamount to saying, 'Never you mind what the Conseil thinks Article 11 means. I know better because I put it there.'

I . . . being myself the principal author of the constitution . . . drew up and proposed the text because Article 11 means what it means . . . otherwise I should obviously have neither drawn it up nor proposed it . . . (Broadcast, 10 April).

The preceding narrative illuminates two aspects of Proposition (i): the General's desire to expand the domain of *pouvoir personnel* by doing away with the obstructionist anti-Gaullist Senate, select his own immediate successor, and eliminate Parliament's role in the matter of constitutional amendment; and secondly, his contempt for constitutionality. The third aspect of Proposition (i) is his exorbitant egotism, and this became more and more pronounced as the day of the referendum approached. In January 1969 the ex-Prime Minister Pompidou had told journalists that he could envisage a situation where he would enter a Presidential election; in frigid retort the General declared a few days later that he intended to go on to the full length of his presidential term, i.e. until 1972.

The 10 April broadcast, in which he claimed unique personal authority to interpret the arcane mystery of Clause 11, added yet another paroxysm of egotism. Up to this point his entourage had spoken as though the General did not see his presidential office as engaged in the outcome of the referendum. The campaign was not due to open, officially, till 14 April, but in fact the battle was in full swing. Senators and local notables, led by the Senate president, Alain Poher, were campaigning against it; as many groups and, notably, sections of the U.D.R. party were campaigning in favour. At this point the opinion polls suggested a clear, if somewhat narrow majority for the government's text. But on 10 April, to the consternation of his Cabinet, the General threw his personal fate into the balance; if the country voted

No, he would resign! And this threat was henceforth accompanied with the familiar menace – the choice between stability or chaos. It reached its climax in this remarkable statement, in the final broadcast before the referendum, delivered on 25 April:

> Your reply is going to decide the destiny of France because if I am disavowed by a majority of you, solemnly, on this capital subject . . . my present task as Chief of State would obviously become impossible and I would immediately cease to exercise my functions.
>
> How then would be mastered the situation resulting from the negative victory of all these diverse, disparate and discordant oppositions, with the inevitable return to the play of ambitions, illusions, machinations and treason in the national upheaval that such a rupture would provoke? . . .

B. *The Referendum, 27 April*

The moment the General staked his personal future on the outcome of the referendum, it changed its nature. Is it significant that from that point – 10 April – the opinion polls showed a steady rise in the negative vote? Not if Proposition (iv) is valid. In elections, the electorate had always polled a majority of anti-Gaullist votes, but had always come off with a disproportionately lower number of seats: this was because the anti-gaullists were not combined, as the gaullists were. But it did not need to combine in order to vote No. And in the new circumstances, it was not only the left that were going to vote No. For the centrists and even for the Independent Republicans the threat of chaos had become far less credible now that there was a Georges Pompidou in the offing. The sentiment was active even among some of the gaullists themselves. So the referendum became a personal plebiscite. And at this the various parties began to react ominously. One or two hardy gaullist notables even declared they would vote No. Giscard d'Estaing himself said he would vote No, although his Independent Republicans split on this issue. In the centre, the P.D.M. group split, but the rest of the centrist groupings declared for No. And, as was to be expected, the Radical Socialists, Socialists, Communists, and even the Unified Socialist party all decided they were going to vote No.

On the extreme right Tixier Vignancourt's Republican Alliance, which hated the General, pronounced it would vote No, and so did the Algerian refugees. By 20 April the polls suggested that the referendum was no longer a foregone conclusion. By the 24th, even defeat seemed possible.

All de Gaulle's usurpations, his personalist incursions into the fields marked out for the legislature and the Cabinet, had been rooted in and upheld by the confidence the people vested in him. Consulted in referendums, they had upheld him. His personalist policies were, as suggested in propositions (i) and (iv), an outcome of the direct popular support which he evoked to override the constraints the Constitution laid on him. Now, it was like that scene in *Anthony and Cleopatra* before the fatal battle, where the guards hear strange music. One asks whether this foretokens good, and the answer comes that it does not: that it signifies

> ... the god Hercules whom Anthony loved
> Now leaves him.

For, by midnight on 27 April 1969 the country had spoken; spoken thus:

Yes	47·58 per cent
No	52·41 per cent

The country had said 'No', and no single explanation seems adequate. However one looks at the figures, they show that all classes were affected, both sexes, most areas, in a roughly equal degree. Some occupational groups did indeed react somewhat more strongly than others: but not, it would seem, in sufficient numbers to affect the total result, nor to offer a clue as to what psychological processes were at work. Perhaps, for once, the result may be taken at its face value: that is (to quote a remark once said to have been made by Britain's former Prime Minister, Harold Macmillan) the French had finally said, 'Enough is enough'.

C. *The Succession*

From Colombey-les-Deux-Églises, at a few minutes past midnight on 28 April 1969, came the following curt message:

I am ceasing to exercise my functions as President of the Republic. This decision takes effect today at noon.

Allons enfants de la patrie   Le jour de chaos est arrivé?

Nothing of the kind! Curiously, the sun rose as usual on the 28th, the earth continued to turn, people went to work whistling. And M. Alain Poher peacefully acceded to his functions as acting President.

This was to have the greatest effect upon the struggle for succession that now opened. Under the (reprieved) constitution, elections had to be held for a new President at least twenty and not more than thirty-five days after the formal declaration of the vacancy.

These elections illustrate two of the propositions advanced above: Proposition (iii), which stresses the continuance of the historic dissensus of France, Proposition (iv), which shows that while it is possible for a conglomeration of Noes to reject a referendum, this is quite another story from expecting an alliance of Yesses to appear against the gaullists to win a parliamentary or a presidential election. Georges Pompidou was the obvious candidate for the gaullist U.D.R. No so for their quondam allies, the Independent Republicans of d'Estaing; and this notable tried to queer Pompidou's pitch by bringing in an elder statesman, René Pléven. The ploy did not work, however, and on Tuesday the 29th Pompidou announced his candidature and the U.D.R. rallied behind him.

He was a powerful candidate: able, prestigious, of strong personality, well known to the electorate, and a good television performer with a strong organization behind him. He could count on a large part of the gaullist vote – say some 40 per cent of the electorate – as a start. Hence to beat him there would have to be some kind of coalition on the left. Since some 60 per cent of votes were needed, it might have seemed logical to look where the public was already looking – at the acting President, who radiated serenity, was clearly in charge of the situation, and had not, as predicted by his predecessor, produced disorder and chaos. But such a candidature required the centre, the Socialists and the Communists all to line up behind him. This was asking a lot. The game was spoiled from the outset by the ambitions of the leftward-leaning socialist leader, the Mayor of Marseilles, Gaston Deferre, who jumped in immediately with his own nomination, much to the vexation of the Socialists. These were trying to refound their party. Half their federations were prepared to support Deferre and lean towards the Communists on their left, though without a formal agreement; the other half leaned to an alliance with the Centrists, even under Poher. In the end the Socialist congress most reluctantly endorsed him. He would never get into second place: but he had destroyed the chance of a moderate left–centre coalition. Instead he had given the Communists their opportunity for putting up their own candidate: they had no use for Poher, and indeed a coalition led by him would have been a disaster for them as it would have revived a Third (Centrist) Force, pushing them out into isolation on the left, whereas what they wanted to demonstrate was that no anti-gaullist candidate could succeed without first coming to terms with them. So they put up their old secretary-general, Jacques Duclos, who was to turn out to be a first-rate candidate. In addition the Unified Socialist Party, to the left of the Communists, also put up their candidate, Michel Rocard; and the Trotskysists, not to be outflanked on the left, put up theirs, Alain Krivine.

Thus the old dissensus had wrecked from the start the chances of a first-ballot win against Pompidou. It is doubtful if in these circumstances Alain Poher would have decided to run; but, very unexpectedly, the opinion polls showed him not only as a close contestant for second place to Pompidou in the first ballot, but actually as leading him in a second run-off ballot. This caused great excitement; and so, at a very late date in the nominating process, Poher also announced his decision to stand.

From that time onwards the polls showed a steady erosion of Poher's support, a fixed ceiling of about 43 per cent for Pompidou, and an increase in the Communist vote for Duclos. In this, two points are noteworthy. First, the appeal of the Communists. For their part the front runners were Poher and Pompidou; they made it clear that their choice was, lightly, for

Pompidou – the two candidates, they said, were like a choice between 'cancer and scarlet fever'. Few failed to catch the innuendo that a gaullist victory was curable – not the first; and the reasons are pretty obvious. Gaullism has always been a lesser evil to the French Communists than a centre/left coalition which left them isolated on the left; and, under de Gaulle, gaullism had been a much better bet; for nobody, not even in their own party, could have done a better job of underwriting the U.S.S.R.'s foreign policy, opposing and denigrating the U.S.A., wrecking the prospects of an enlarged European Economic Community and keeping France out of N.A.T.O. Pompidou might not be able to follow all these objectives, or achieve as much success as de Gaulle; but at least he was unlike Poher in all these matters, who was pro-Nato, pro-American and pro-Israel. The second point of note is that with the Poher candidature the skeleton in the Constitution's closet was suddenly exposed: that nightmarish prospect of a President who faced a huge and hostile gaullist majority in the Assembly. In these circumstances Poher would have to battle against a hostile Prime Minister and then dissolve the Assembly as soon as constitutionally possible. If and when he did so, the further prospect opened of a gaullist recession, and the absence of a clear majority. For all the safeguards in the Constitution, would not this greatly resemble the Fourth Republic? And would not the Communists play a great part in any parliamentary manoeuvres? To some the prospect was titillating, and for these reasons they favoured the Poher candidature. But to most the prospects of a return to instability was unwelcome. Thus was evoked the point made in Proposition (ii) – the inability of even the 1958 Constitution to cope with a return to minority government.

The object of the anti-Pompidou contenders was, for the minor leftist parties, to chalk up a respectable vote; for the Poher coalition and the Communists to beat each other to second place. Because in that event the candidate placed second to Pompidou would be the one to face him in the second ballot.

When the results were announced it was clear that the Poher effort was doomed. His position had slipped badly; that of Jacques Duclos had correspondingly advanced.

Presidential election: 1st ballot, 1 June 1969

	per cent
Pompidou	44
Poher	23
Duclos	21
Deferre	5
Rocard	3·6
Others	3·4

Some three and a half per cent more of the electorate had voted anti-gaullist in this election than had voted No in the Referendum; but with what an outcome – split six ways! This is a further vindication of Proposition (iv). And furthermore the outlook for these divided anti-gaullists was dismal. Whereas Pompidou needed only some 6 per cent more votes to win, Poher needed some 27 per cent. This meant he had somehow or other to attract most if not all of the Communist vote; and the moment this was twigged, and it was twigged immediately, his chances became even more remote, as, in accordance with Proposition (iii), the mere prospect of a President acceding on Communist votes was enough to frighten off the centre-leftists. But this was to assume that the Communists would ever have contemplated support of a Centrist, a pro-European, a pro-Israeli and a pro-American – in short would ever have contemplated supporting an anti-gaullist. Their tactics were sublime. Gravely they restated that there was no difference between the two leading candidates (though to their mind there was a whole world of difference) and that therefore the proper course for Communist voters was to abstain. The rationalization was perfect; the effect perfectly predictable. If even half of the Communist voters abstained, Poher's chances of success were minimal. So it turned out to be. Poher gamely refused to concede or to retire and leave the field to a contest between the Communists and Pompidou, as he was urged to do; he struggled on. His tally was really quite respectable. Honour had been saved. But Pompidou had been elected.

Presidential election: 2nd ballot, 15 June 1969

Pompidou   57·6 per cent
Poher   42·4 per cent

The election closed the de Gaulle chapter. It opened another. This had been a free, fair and open election. All fractions had taken part in it – even the Trotskyists and the Unified Socialist party. And the gaullist candidate had won. Henceforth it was unplausible for anyone to argue as Mitterand had argued the previous year that the gaullist clique had come to power by force and then resorted to trickery. For the first time the credentials of the head of state were above suspicion. The Fifth Republic had become legitimate.

The questions are, how suitable are France's political institutions likely to be; and what lines of evolution – or, for that matter, revolution – suggest themselves to the observer?

In the first place, it looks as if for the moment the main provisions of the constitution of the Fifth Republic are likely to remain in place. This constitution is by no means ideal, as we have pointed out; because it only works smoothly if the head of state – the President – has behind him a solid majority in the National Assembly (as at present). The constitution will be sorely tested if the President faces an opposition majority in the legislature. Since there appears to be little risk of this in the next few years it may well be that there will be no further modification of the constitution: but if risk there is, a way out is suggested by reducing the presidential term from seven years to five and making it coincide with the parliamentary elections. This would cut down the chances of the President and the parliamentary majority being of opposing parties, though it would not altogether eliminate them. However, as long as there appears no great likelihood of this, it seems unlikely that President Pompidou would consent to have his term reduced in this way.

As long as the present situation obtains, i.e. the head of the gaullist majority party resides in the Elysée Palace, so long there will be a high degree of personalism in the conduct of French politics, both domestic and foreign. This is due to the fact that the gaullist party adheres to General de Gaulle's view of the Presidency as the head and fount of office honours and policy, and continues to uphold his view that the Prime Minister is his personal choice and politically responsible to him, and the Cabinet likewise. Nevertheless, it is going to be personalism with a difference. Pompidou is not de Gaulle. There is little evidence that he is as exigent and avid of power as his predecessor, and, in any case, neither his history nor his personality give him anything like the same hold over his party or the electorate as the General possessed. It is hardly likely that Georges Pompidou would seek to emulate his predecessor in the abuse of the referendum, in overflowing constitutional restraints, and in setting at naught the influence of the Conseil d'État. And even if he tried to do so he is unlikely except in some grave and threatening national emergency to do so with anything like the success of General de Gaulle. In this sense the Fifth Republic under its second President is likely to be gaullism in a low key.

All this is predicted on the continuance of a gaullist majority commanding both the legislature and the presidency. Dissensus at the centre and left is going to continue for some time to come. While the Communist vote may be expected to hold reasonably steady, the old Christian Democrat party, the Radical Socialists, and the Socialists are all obsolescent organizations, in search of a role and a character. The likelihood that any serious political initiatives will come from them in the next five or ten years seems at the moment remote; it is to the two wings of the Assembly, the gaullists on the one side, and the new revolutionary forces of the Unified Socialist party and the Trotskyites to which one would have to look. As to the first: it has often been predicted that, after de Gaulle's departure the gaullist party would disintegrate, since it was the party of a man and a personality rather than a party of doctrine. This is not quite exact; but in any case this view overlooks what has been called, in America, 'the cohesive force of public plunder'. If one is talking about the parliamentary group of the U.D.R., then it would take some very great vicissitude indeed to induce a sizeable group to splinter away from the main body of the gaullists and to go into opposition – simply because the opposition in the French legislature has such a limited range of action under the rules of the Fifth Republic. More considerable is the threat that on some great public issue the group would split under two rival leaders in a presidential contest. But here the rules of the presidential election themselves exert a tendency towards party unity. By putting up two presidential candidates the rival factions of the gaullists could run the risk of losing the election. It is true that under the rules of the second ballot they could always close ranks after one or other of their candidates had attained either the leading or the second place in the presidential election; but the risk could never be quite discounted that by putting up two rival candidates they might lose the first round outright. There might indeed be circumstances which would split the party to such an extent that its factions would take this risk; but, for the reasons advanced, it is as well not to make too much of this. The likelihood is much more that the gaullist party would remain a solidary organization intent on winning the Presidency and thus securing the most important office in the state. At the same time, as long as it remains solidary, the rules of the parliamentary election, as we have seen, favour it as against its disunited opponents of the centre and the left. In the foreseeable future the most that is likely to happen to this party, therefore, is some degree of fraying at the edges.

The other source of political initiative, however, lies in the small groups on the left of the Communist party. These are more radical than the Communist party, more irresponsible, and, above all, they have become the present-day vehicle of the insurrectionary and activist tradition which blew up in 1968 and which has been such a perennial feature of French politics from 1789. A time may come when these again put themselves at the head of protest movements, but more successfully than they did in May 1968; that is to say, when they, rather than the Communist party, appear to striking farmers or workers and the like as the more credible leaders. In this sense, the more stable the institutions of the Fifth Republic, the more likely it is that these extreme left-wing elements will grow in significance and stature. The denaturing of the legislature, the limitation of the powers of parliamentary opposition, and the corresponding strengthening of the central government institutions of Presidency and Cabinet have given the Fifth Republic more motive power, but at the expense of depriving it of that set of safety valves which the National Assembly provided for dissident groups under the Fourth Republic. If another great social collision arrives, or an acute sense of social frustration and impatience occurs, these stable institutions may prove – as in May 1968 – too insensitive to respond quickly. These are the circumstances in which the extreme left could increase its political power.

For the moment, however, all is still; but one is bound to say that the political vicissitudes of France, as catalogued and commented upon in the pages above, caution against too facile an assumption that the weather is all set fair for the Fifth Republic.

Part Three

TOTALITARIANISM

Chapter 8

THE GOVERNMENT OF THE U.S.S.R.

I. MARXISM–LENINISM

IN a material perspective, the U.S.S.R. is in many ways comparable with the U.S.A. Like the U.S.A. it is a huge country; its area, eight and a half million square miles, one-sixth of the land surface of the globe, makes it the largest state in the world, double the size of the U.S.A. Its population is 230,000,000, compared with the U.S.A.'s 187,000,000, and so it is even more sparsely populated than the U.S.A., whose population density per square mile is 53 while the U.S.S.R.'s is only 27: it is still an empty land. Its ethnic variety, however, is quite different from that of the U.S.A. There, immigrants from different cultures have assimilated themselves rapidly to the American national values and become more national and nationalistic than the people whom they have joined. The U.S.S.R., on the other hand, comprises over one hundred nationalities, of whom the Russian people form only just over fifty per cent. In addition to them there are the Ukrainians, the White Russians (Byelorussians) and many others, including a whole train of Asiatic peoples – for example, Tartars, Tadzhiks and Uzbeks. In this respect, Soviet society is far less homogeneous than that of the U.S.A.

The two states are also comparable in the perspective of their economic and social life. The U.S.S.R. ranks second only to the U.S.A. in world industrial production. It produces more coal than the U.S.A. (534,000,000 metric tons, as against 428,000,000). It produces 201,000,000 metric tons of petrol, as against the U.S.A.'s 372,000,000; 80,000,000 tons of steel as against the U.S.A.'s 100,000,000; and 400,000,000 kilowatts of electricity, as against the U.S.A.'s 1,007,000,000. The U.S.S.R., therefore, is an industrial state. Admittedly, its national income per head is considerably lower. Figures here are very problematical, owing to the doubts which cloud Soviet statistics. Figures for 1969, culled from various handbooks published by the United Nations Organization, suggest that, in terms of dollars, the *per capita* income of the U.S. in 1960 was $3,520, as compared with that of the United Kingdom ($1,620) and that of France ($1,730); whereas that of the U.S.S.R. was only $890, i.e. a quarter of the U.S.A.'s. Nevertheless, this is sufficient to include her in the ranks of the industrialized states.

In terms of their urban/rural profiles, the U.S.S.R. and the U.S.A. are even more comparable. In the U.S.S.R., 35·5 per cent of the population lives in towns of over 20,000 inhabitants, while in the U.S.A. the figure is not very much larger – only 52 per cent. If we take the population of the two countries living in big cities over 100,000, then nearly a quarter, 23·5 per cent, of the population of the U.S.S.R. lives in such towns, as against 28·4 per cent of the population of the U.S.A. In short, the U.S.S.R. is not only industrialized, but urbanized. This is reflected in the figures of the population working in industry and ancillary activities as against agriculture. Forty-eight per cent of its population is still engaged in agriculture (whereas in the U.S.A. the proportion is only ten per cent and in the United Kingdom only five per cent). Nevertheless, the fact that over half of its population is engaged either in industrial or white-collar work again puts the U.S.S.R. into a position comparable to, rather than in contrast to, that of the U.S.A.

Now, if we followed the approach of the previous chapters, we should go on and deduce from the profile of U.S.S.R. society the interests, beliefs and ideologies of the various sections of its peoples. But in this case, that approach would be quite wrong. For the U.S.S.R., it is necessary to reverse the order entirely and the reason is to be found in the following quotation from the Third (and most recent) Programme of the Communist Party of the Soviet Union (C.P.S.U.), adopted in 1961:

Unlike all the preceding socio-economic formations, Communist society does not develop spontaneously, but as the result of the conscious and purposeful efforts of the masses, led by the Marxist-Leninist Party. The Communist Party which unites the foremost representatives of the working class of all the working people, and is closely connected with the masses, which enjoys unbounded prestige among the people and understands the laws of social development, provides proper leadership in Communist instruction as a whole, giving it an organized plan and a scientifically based character.[1]

The operative words here are the first ones: 'unlike all the preceding socio-economic formations, Communist society *does not develop spontaneously, but as the result of the conscious and purposeful efforts* of the masses, led by the Marxist-Leninist Party, [the] Communist Party'. In the liberal-democratic states, the only ones which we have explored so far, society, which *is* spontaneously and freely formed, gives rise to opinions and to ideologies which are reflected in parties and numerous other groups, each representing specialized sections of the population. These in their turn generate the leadership and its viewpoints which organize the machinery and assume the control of the state. In the U.S.S.R. precisely the reverse has happened. In the U.S.S.R. it is inappropriate to start with the history or the geography and work up to the state of opinion. On the contrary, we must start with the state of 'opinion', which is a datum in the U.S.S.R., and work down to the mechanism of government which is its product.

Firstly, we must explain the doctrine in whose image and according to whose objectives the society has been formed. This is the doctrine described in the foregoing quotation as 'the laws of social development'. Then we must examine the vehicle by which this is conveyed to Soviet society as a whole, and this is the Communist Party of the Soviet Union, described above as 'the Marxist-Leninist Party'. Only at that stage will it become appropriate to discuss the organs of government and how they function. The purpose, then, of this preliminary section is to give a short account of that *official* doctrine of society which forms the mould into which for the last fifty-two years, ever since the Bolsheviks took power in 1917, Soviet society has been self-consciously poured.

The doctrine is known as Marxism-Leninism, and derives from three great sources: Marx (1818–83); Engels, his collabora-

1. *Third Programme of the C.P.S.U.*, 1961, Part VII.

tor, somewhat younger, (1820–95); and Lenin, who died in 1924, and who developed from the work of Marx and Engels the theories of imperialism, of the dictatorship of the proletariat and of the nature of the state. Leninism, it must be stressed, is only one strand of Marxist exegesis, but, until it was recently challenged by the interpretations of the Chinese political leader, Mao Tse-tung, it became the world *orthodox* interpretation of Marxism; for it was Lenin's own Bolshevik faction of the Russian Social-Democratic Party (now styled the Communist Party of the Soviet Union) that made the October Revolution of 1917, seized the state power of the former Russian Empire and was able thereafter to give assistance, leadership, support and an example to all other communist parties throughout the world.

What we have in the U.S.S.R. today, therefore, is not simply Marxism. 'Leninism' is Lenin's peculiar but by no means necessarily correct or even definitive interpretation of what Marx and Engels meant. Furthermore, the present-day doctrine of the C.P.S.U. is not necessarily even what Lenin meant. There has been a continuous elaboration, discussion, re-discussion and re-elaboration of the original Marxist-Leninist canon, and this has led to various schisms and factional struggles inside the leading strata of the party. The role of the various dissidents inside the party from 1917 to the present day – the role of such men as Trotsky, Zinoviev and Bukharin or, more recently, Molotov or Malenkov – has always been to be branded by those who defeated them as heterodox or heretical. There have been charges of 'revisionism' or 'dogmatism' according to the fashion of the moment. The interpretation which has triumphed has done so simply because it was the interpretation favoured by the winning side. There is no one objectively true or correct or final interpretation of the work of Marx and Engels; merely the interpretation which the leaders of this vastly powerful state have adopted. This becomes orthodox only because they have won – won in a very earthly and highly pragmatic struggle for power.

In order of generality we can conceive Marxism-Leninism as consisting of three concentric circles. The widest circle, the most general expression of the philosophy, is the theory of dialectical materialism; a more particular application of this, applied to world history, is known as historical materialism. In the centre of this is the critique of capitalism; this in turn has been re-interpreted to produce the more specific theories of imperialism and of the state. And finally, an even more applied form of it is to be found in the inner core, the bull's-eye of the whole of this great coherent interconnected doctrine: the theory of the revolutionary party. In what follows we shall not concern ourselves with the general theory of dialectical materialism, but begin with historical materialism.

Historical materialism is the Marxist view of the way in which society changes. Man, it is said, makes himself; his consciousness drives him on. But it drives him on, he makes himself, only under certain material conditions, which provide both the stimulus, but also the restraint, to his own creativity. These material conditions are basic in the evolution of human society. The remainder, the laws which man throws up, the religion he adopts, the morality he cherishes – these are mere superstructure, and they change with the change in the conditions on which they rest. But, under these conditions, man makes himself. The social agencies through which he does so are not his personal efforts, nor even sectional efforts such as we have mentioned earlier. The great mobilization of human endeavour takes place through the social and economic *classes*, and the socio-economic class is, according to Marx, a stratum of people which he defines according to the relationship in which it stands to the means of production, distribution and exchange on the one side, and to its consciousness of common interest on the other.

The objective and the subjective factors are both necessary in order that a class should not only *be* a class (that is to say observable by the outside observer as a class) but also act like one. Thus one could distinguish right away between those who own the fields, the factories and the workshops in a society, and those who own merely their two hands, their labour power. And one can distinguish between these two sharply opposed groups on the one side and the farmer who owns his own land on the other. This would make at least three classes. And one can think of certain other classes which stand in still different relationships to the means of production than the ones already enumerated.

But, in so far as people who stand in the same objective relationship to the means of production *realize* that they do so, they become conscious of their common interests, they develop a common ideology and they begin to work as a unity. This forms the active class; and, according to Marxism, it is such classes which have driven society on, and have been the agents of change in society.

Now, as the material basis of society alters, so do relationships between the classes alter. In a primitive agricultural society, those who are wealthiest and who because they are wealthiest are able to hire armies to defend themselves, are those who own the land and who can keep others off it except under conditions which they themselves impose. And so society would consist, broadly, of those who own the land and those who work it (who might be in a condition of slavery or serfdom, or who might even be agricultural labourers, but who nevertheless own nothing except their bare labour power). But suppose now that a new form of production arises – that techniques alter. Suppose, for instance, that industry makes it appearance. In that case a new class of individuals will arise, who will own, not land, but factories, workshops and machines; furthermore, these persons will be faced by another kind of property-less class – those who have to work in their factories and subject themselves to their discipline, and who will have to submit to the conditions imposed upon them by the industrialist proprietor because they have no resources to fall back upon but their own labour power. In that case, as well as the existing dichotomy between the landowner and the day-labourer on the one side, there will now be another dichotomy – that between the industrialist and the industrial proletariat – i.e., the rightless and property-less people who work in the industrialists' factories and workshops.

Now it is axiomatic to Marxism that those who are wealthiest in society are those who rule, since they are able to secure the high positions of state by virtue of their wealth and their command over the economy. In so far as they achieve domination of the state in this way, they use their power to promulgate laws to universalize their own peculiar interests – which are not necessarily those of the rest of society. The laws of an agricultural society will be such as to favour the economic interest of the predominant class, the landowning oligarchy, who rule. But, with the coming of a new class of industrialists, a clash will arise between the old dominant class and the class which has risen in standing and which, in so far as the new methods produce wealth more rapidly and under more favourable conditions than the old, is likely to become a dominant class in its turn. The laws which suited the old governing class, the landowning aristocracy, will not necessarily, and in fact will almost certainly not, favour the new and challenging class of industrialists. Thus, opposed to the old morality, social structure, laws, customs, superstitions and the like which have been adopted in the period of landed domination, there will arise a new standard of political belief, a new morality, a new outlook, which the industrialists will seek to embody in law. In short there will be a 'contradiction', to use a Marxist term, between the interest of the rising class and the legal-economic structure which has been shaped in the interests of the class dominant up to that particular time. There will therefore arise a struggle between the two classes, and there will be an attempt to alter this superstructure of law, custom and the like so as to fit the aspirations and the economic interests of the rising class. This will be resisted by the older class, which still retains the leadership of the state and the control of all its activities although its economic power is now waning compared with that of the rising class. This struggle will ultimately produce a revolutionary crisis, a confrontation which (according to Marx and Engels) must, in most societies (but not necessarily in Britain or the U.S.A.), be solved in the way that it had been solved in 1789 in France: by the violent overturn of the older but still ruling class by one which is now economically dominant and which seeks to replace the former as the ruling group. Thus the class struggle would culminate in an armed encounter between the old order and the new. With the destruction of the political control of the former ruling class, the latter will be repressed and ultimately extinguished by the new class, which will rule in its place.

'All history', according to the *Communist Manifesto* (1848), 'is a history of class struggles'; and the evolution of all past society has taken place, *mutatis mutandis*, in the way just described. Now this is the most general formulation of the theory of historical materialism, and Marx went on to make a particular application of it to the circumstances of his own day. According to him and his collaborator, Engels, Western history had moved through a series of cycles. Originally there had been no states but merely societies in which property was held in common. Once private ownership was introduced, then classes arose, formed of those who owned and those who did not; and, with this cleavage, the state came into existence as a machine of repression, a mechanism by which the economically dominant class could repress by force the efforts of the vast and property-less majority to dispossess it. So, departing from primitive communes, Western history had moved through various stages of slavery to serfdom and from serfdom to capitalism (the era of 'wage-slavery'). Up to this last era, many classes had co-existed inside a single society. But capitalism had simplified this class struggle. It had polarized these many classes into just two. On the one side were the *bourgeoisie*, those who owned the means of production; on the other were the proletarians, the rightless and the property-less wage-slaves. Classes of yeomen farmers, of peasants, of office workers and of artisans who owned their own tools might indeed stand between them. But, according to Marx, these would rapidly be ground out between the two great classes of capitalist society and would either become part of the tiny minority of the possessors, or sink among the vast ranks of the underdogs. In short, capitalism had simplified class conflict into a basic struggle between two opposing sides.

This polarization constituted one of the inherent and fatal weaknesses of capitalism. Another was its tendency to move in economic cycles of boom and slump. Massive crises, throwing millions out of work, generated revolutionary situations in which the rightless and the property-less could not find any employment even at a subsistence wage. This itself would suffice to drive them into realizing that the small knot of property-owners was their enemy. Nor was this all. War also was inherent in the capitalist system. This too would depress the condition of the proletariat. These two inevitable tendencies in capitalism – slump and war –

concluded in the so-called 'immiseration' of the proletariat, whose condition could become only more and more wretched. As capitalism progressed, so, therefore, the revolutionary tensions which always existed between the rightless and property-less on the one side and the propertied on the other would become increasingly sharpened. And, given the conditions of capitalism, the class war could eventually only end in one way. For where there were only two classes, constantly set at one another's throat by the immanent operation of the system, only one of two alternatives was conceivable. If the capitalists won, the situation would recur again: for they needed the proletariat to carry the system on and so they could not exterminate it; they could win a battle, but would still find themselves faced with the war. Sooner or later, therefore, the alternative situation would occur: the proletariat would win. And here there would be a difference. It is impossible to consider the capitalist mode of production without capitalists on the one side and workmen to work their factories on the other. But, according to Marx, it was perfectly possible (as well as desirable) for the proletariat to take over these factories and workshops, and work them themselves for their own benefit, and there was not the least need to retain a class of proprietors to own them. This expropriation of the private property of the possessing classes was the true goal of the proletariat. At one stage or another in its class struggle, it would seize control of the machinery of the state. The moment it had done so, it would strip the possessing classes of their possessions, which would pass into public ownership and be operated for the benefit of the whole of society, minus only their former owners.

The foregoing critique of capitalism is to be found in its most detailed and elaborate form in the three volumes of Karl Marx's *Capital*, the first of which was published as early as 1867. Now by 1917 it was quite obvious to every objective observer that Marx's predictions about the increasing wretchedness of the proletariat were false. The middle classes – the white-collar and service groups in society – had not sunk into the ranks of the proletariat; nor had their numbers diminished, either absolutely or relatively but, on the contrary, they had grown. In the second place, far from the condition of the proletariat becoming worse either relatively or absolutely, their condition had vastly improved and showed every sign of improving further; despite booms and slumps, there had been a rapidly rising standard of living for the whole of the community in the industrialized countries. In Germany, then the great home of Marxism, these observations provoked a split between the orthodox and dogmatic Marxists and those led by Bernstein, who drew the conclusion that the revolutionary role of the proletariat was finished, and that henceforth it should adopt a reformist stand, to soften, attenuate and control the operations of capitalism. It was at this point that Lenin, a young Russian who had taken part in revolutionary activities since his university days and had had to flee and live in exile, intervened in the controversy. Lenin re-vindicated the revolutionary tradition in the thought of Marx and Engels by giving an entirely new explanation of the apparently increased prosperity of the proletariat. And this explanation is most elegantly set out in his book *Imperialism*, which he wrote in 1916, shortly before he was able to engineer the Bolshevik revolution in October 1917 in Russia. Its full title is *Imperialism: the Last Stage of Capitalism*. It is a re-interpretation of what Marx had said in the light of the new conditions.

Briefly, his argument ran thus. Once capitalism was fully grown, it developed an inherent tendency to turn into a *new* kind of capitalism, namely 'monopoly' capitalism. He argued (and there was some justification for this in the works of Marx) that, starting with a large number of tiny competitive enterprises competing savagely for the home market, the industrialist's propensity to maximize his profit would impel him to try to absorb his competitors. This would not result in increased competition, and the consequential depression of the working classes, but in the integration of company with company, and the formation of more and more massive units – i.e., of monopolies or near-monopolies. Ultimately the entire home market would be more or less quartered up between a small number of giant monopolies. At this stage, to invade their competitors' markets would bring them a falling rate of profit. The leaders of industry, therefore, always looking for higher rates of profit, can only find these overseas. Consequently they begin to funnel their surplus capital (piled up by the monopoly conditions at home) into investment abroad: in Malayan rubber plantations, African coco-nut oil plants or South American oil wells, for example. And, as they begin exporting their capital to these countries, so they find, not unnaturally, that their exploitation rouses the animosity of the local inhabitants and makes this capital insecure. They therefore turn to their governments (who, according to Marx and Engels, are of the same socio-economic class) and press them to protect these overseas investments. From the mere protection of capital abroad these home governments soon find it necessary to station permanent garrisons there. In this way monopoly capitalism first leads to the export of capital abroad; the export of capital abroad leads in its turn to the military occupation of the country into which it has been exported. Thus monopoly capitalism turns into *imperialism*; it generates great empires which are held by the metropolitan countries.

Now this is why, according to Lenin, the proletariat in the Western countries was so much better off. Had the capitalists been unable to invest their capital abroad at enormously high rates of profit, then the inherent tendencies of capitalism, as described by Marx, would have been confirmed. But, by exporting their capital abroad, they were able to secure a very handsome return on it and, when this was repatriated to the metropolitan country and added to its national income, some of it filtered downwards, and in this way actually increased the *per capita* income of the proletariat. The prosperity of the English or French or Belgian worker was drawn from the sweat of the exploited African, the peon, the coolie. But this, according to Lenin, would all pass. It was a mere phase – the last dying phase of capitalism. For at this juncture Lenin injected into the Marxist system a new axiom – the axiom of the *uneven development of capitalism.*

According to him, the way in which capitalism took root in various countries such as Germany or Japan, and the rapidity with which those countries were industrialized, was unpredictable and uneven. Britain and France had industrialized first, and because of that had reached the stage of monopoly capitalism first, had felt the need to export capital first and consequently had been the first to seize colonies. And as a result most of the under-developed countries of the world had been partitioned between France and Britain. But then, somewhat belatedly – and unpredictably – the countries like Germany, Italy and Japan had also begun to industrialize. They too had gone through the same phases that had earlier occurred in France and Britain until they too found that it was necessary for them to export capital abroad. But they could not do so; could not, because all the best areas for such investment had already been pre-empted by the British and the French. For this reason, said Lenin, a struggle would occur between the *bourgeoisie* of the countries who had reached the stage of monopoly capitalism late, and the *bourgeoisie* of those countries which had already seized all the outlets. In this way imperialism, which divided up the world like a melon between the possessing countries, would be challenged by the counter-imperialism of the countries which sought to re-divide that melon in their own favour. Thus the relief which monopoly capitalism gave to the *bourgeoisie* of an industrial country, by enabling it to buy off its home proletariat, would be short-lived because it would inevitably thrust them into war with their neighbours and, in the miseries which that war caused, the class struggle would once again become acute. And this would be not merely a struggle of the proletariat to prevent their 'immiseration': it would also be a struggle to prevent their own butchery in the class-interests of their own *bourgeoisie*.

Nor was that all. Even if this state of war could be postponed, the imperial occupation of foreign countries must sooner or later bring about a revolt of the native peoples against the exploitation of the metropolitan country. So, for two reasons, imperialism was merely the last straw at which monopoly capitalism could grasp: on the one hand, because it provoked colonial revolt against the metropolitan country; on the other, because the metropolitan country would itself be involved in wars to defend those colonies or, alternatively, to win them from others. So, monopoly capitalism led to imperialism and imperialism led to war. But monopoly capitalism and imperialism were both doomed. In the world chain of capitalism, as Lenin observed it in 1916, the colonies, he maintained, were the weakest links. Snap them and you break capitalism. And this became a cardinal doctrine, not only of Lenin, but of his successors in the U.S.S.R. after they had seized power in 1917: 'Imperialism is the weakest link in the chain of capitalism.' This is why the Soviet leaders devoted so much time after 1917 to stirring up revolts in the French and British colonies and spheres of influence. Once these states were shorn of their colonies, their standard of living must necessarily suffer and the immanent contradictions of capitalism as described by Marx must ensue. The workers would be increasingly 'immiserated' through boom and slump, would turn against their own domestic *bourgeoisie* and would finally bring about its fall and the liquidation of the capitalist system.

The eventuality brings us to an even more narrow application of Marxism-Leninism – the theory of the state. What were the proletariat to do once they had achieved the victory in a civil war or revolution against their own proper ruling class? Were they to take the state machine over and simply work it in their own interest? Were they to destroy it, as the anarchists wished to do, and have no state machine at all? Were they to break up the old capitalist state machine and create one which was more suited to their own interests? One can see the problem is of more than mere academic interest.

Marx had discussed this question in the course of his struggles with his anarchist opponents who conceived the goal of the proletariat as the smashing and abolition of the state machine altogether and immediately. Basing himself upon such indications as Marx gave and upon references in his correspondence, and also upon Engels's *The Origin of Private Property, the Family, and the State*, Lenin developed his own theory. First outlined in *State and Revolution* (1917) it became official doctrine in the U.S.S.R. until 1961. Lenin defines 'the state' differently from the way in which most political scientists define it today. It is defined, not as a form of association, but as an *instrument of* an association. It is the apparatus of coercion – the system of police, prisons, armies – which is used by one group in society to repress the other. Thus some societies do not 'possess' states; they are simply societies, communities. Others, however, do 'possess' states: they possess an apparatus of coercion. For instance, the primitive communist society, of which Engels had written in the book cited above, did not 'possess' a state. It did not need one. Where property was held in common there were no cleavages sufficiently serious to warrant the repression of one group by another. An apparatus of repression only became necessary the moment land fell into private ownership. This created two antagonistic classes, those who owned land, and those who did not but wanted to. And the state was invented in order to give the possessing classes a machine by which to repress the aspirations of the have-nots.

Thus the state is a historical manifestation which arose at a specific historical point of time. There is nothing inevitable about its arrival, and there is nothing eternal about its existence. The state is simply the inevitable outcome of a particular and peculiar social situation, namely, class cleavage and the exploitation of one of these classes by the other. Wherever one group own and the other group do not, there must be a cleavage; there must, by definition, be exploitation, because that is the object of such a cleavage; and there must, therefore, be an apparatus of coercion. So the existence of two or more classes in a society is *ipso facto* a proof that it is a state. By the same reasoning, where there are no classes there is no apparatus of coercion and therefore no state.

The state did not always exist [wrote Engels]. There are societies which got along without it, and without any conception of state or state authority. At a certain stage of economic development, necessarily connected with the split of society into classes and by reason thereof, the state became a necessity. We are now fast approaching the stage in the development of production where the existence of these classes has not merely ceased to be a necessity, but has become a direct impediment to production. The future disappearance of classes is just as inevitable as was their rise. With their disappearance the state will inevitably disappear as well.

According to Lenin, the state is a machine to sustain the domination of one class over another, but the *form* of state domination may vary. Private capital exercises its power in different ways: but it does always exercise it, whether political rights are based on some property qualification or otherwise, and whether or not the state is a democratic republic. Indeed, the more 'democratic' it is, the more 'crude' and cynical is this domination by capitalism, and Lenin pointed to the United States of America as an illustration. Nowhere else, he wrote, was the power of capital among a handful of millionaires manifested so crudely and with such open venality as in America. Once capital exists it dominates the whole of society, nor does any democratic republic, nor any right to vote, change the essence of the matter. Even in a democratic republic, e.g., a Western liberal-democracy, the state exists; and equality before the law, the right to vote, the freedom of speech and of association are purely formal. They simply advantage the propertied as against the non-propertied, and indeed buttress them by giving the masses a false view of what their situation really is.

From this Lenin deduced the task of the proletarian revolution. Once the proletariat has seized power, its task is to break up altogether the apparatus used by the former possessors of capital and land, and to establish its own machinery. Through this it must carry out a programme of repression of the former possessing classes. The proletariat, or those who act for it, must establish an *in*equality of rights, and deprive the former possessing class of its right to vote and to participate in government. This régime of inequality and destruction of the former possessing classes is 'the dictatorship of the proletariat'. Ultimately the former possessing classes will be eradicated. When this time comes, only one class, the proletariat, will remain. But if there is only one class in society, this is tantamount to saying that there are no classes in society: if everything is owned by this one class, then there is nobody who seeks to take its property away from it: in short there is nobody whom it must repress. There is no object, therefore, in it maintaining an apparatus of coercion because there will no longer be any class to coerce. There will be no need for the state apparatus, and in that case the 'state', as defined by Lenin, will simply 'wither away'. As Engels put it: 'The political direction of man gives way to the administration of things and material processes.' This will take a long time. The proletariat must first repress the previously propertied classes, and change the traditions of those who have hitherto supported them; it will also have to raise the standard of living to such a height as to make possible the norm of socialist distribution, namely, 'from each according to his ability, to each according to his needs'. Thus society will move through two phases before the state withers away. The first will be the stage of socialism, in which all property is owned by the public, that is to say, by the proletariat, and used solely to their advantage; and the second stage will be that of communism, where there is such an abundance of goods and services that it will no longer be necessary to exert any kind of control over the processes of production or distribution or exchange. It is during this latter period, and not before, that the state will finally wither away.

II. THE COMMUNIST PARTY OF THE SOVIET UNION

'The Communist Party of the Soviet Union', says Article 126 of the Constitution of the U.S.S.R., 'is the leading core of all organizations of the working people, both public and state.' The theories just described form the ideology of this party. It is in the terms of these theories that it views the world, the Soviet Union and its own role in both. These theories are a guide to action.

There must be no mistake about either point. They are not the invention of 'hostile bourgeois sources'. They are the open boast of any Soviet publication itself.

A good helmsman steers his ship on a set course in any weather, through storm and gale. Likewise, the Communist Party steers the Soviet State ship.

A helmsman must have a compass in order not to deviate from his course. The revolutionary theory of Marxism–Leninism serves as the Party's compass. The theory is omnipotent because it correctly sets out society's requirements in the development of its material and spiritual life.[2]

As to the governing role of the party, any textbook of Soviet law makes a feature of expounding this. *Soviet State Law*, a current textbook by Professors Denisov and Kirichenko, may serve as an example:

2. *U.S.S.R. Today and Tomorrow*, Moscow, 1959, p. 63.

The Soviets [it states baldly] are *guided* by the Communist Party of the Soviet Union. It is the *leadership* of the Party which ensures the successful work of the Soviets. *The Party takes an active part in the formation of state organs.* Its organization, like all other public organizations and societies of the working people has been granted the right to nominate candidates for the Soviets. *The Communist Party directs the selection, distribution and training of the personnel of the Soviet State apparatus. It checks* [upon] *the activity of the organs of power and state administration. Not a single important decision is taken by the Soviet state organs without preliminary guiding directions and advice from the Party.* . . . The Party is the leading core of the power of the working people . . . [3]

The theory of the party

Marxism began to be studied in the Russian Empire in the last three decades of the nineteenth century, but, by its close, had been subjected to various interpretations. As a consequence, there were rival theories as to what type of party a working-class party ought to be. Here Lenin struck out a distinctive line. To begin with, he disagreed with those Marxists in Russia who interpreted Marx as saying that the movement towards an ultimate clash of the working people with the owners of the means of production was an inevitable historical process, and therefore concluded that the working people could sit back and wait for these developments to happen. Lenin re-emphasized, quite rightly, the role of consciousness in bringing about this consummation. The Marxists, he argued, must form a party to 'give history a push'. Furthermore, Lenin also opposed those revisionists like Bernstein who wished to make social democracy a movement for reforming capitalism rather than overthrowing it. Against these, Lenin re-emphasized the revolutionary content of Marxism: that the role of a truly Marxist party was to make the socialist revolution, and, in this sense, to be 'the vanguard of the proletariat'. But this was not all. Lenin also had to face those who, while willing to go all this way with him, wished to create a party along the lines of the German Social-Democratic Party, that is to

3. A. Denisov and M. Kirichenko, *Soviet State Law*, Moscow, 1960, p. 143 (my italics).

say, a very large mass party which would work by constitutional means. To Lenin this seemed an impossibility in Russian conditions. The Russian Empire was an autocracy. Its representative institutions were limited. The labour movement was weak, and its leaders were watched by the secret police and punished by exile or death. And from this he elaborated that theory of the party which is to be found in his famous pamphlet of 1902, *What is to be done?*

I assert [wrote Lenin] (1) that no revolutionary movement can endure without a stable organisation of leaders that maintains continuity. [. . .] (2) that the wider the masses spontaneously drawn into the struggle, forming the bases of the movement and participating in it, the more urgent the need of such an organisation and the more solid this organisation must be . . . (3) that such an organisation must consist chiefly of people professionally engaged in revolutionary activities. [. . .] (4) that in an autocratic state the more we *confine* the membership of such an organisation to people who are professionally engaged in revolutionary activity, and who have been professionally trained in the art of *combating* the political police, the more difficult it will be to wipe out such an organisation and (5) that *greater* will be the number of people of the working class, and of the other classes of society, who will be able to join the movement and perform active work in it.[4]

The party must be a party of professional revolutionaries; it must be conspiratorial; and it must be hierarchical and centralized.

In 1903 a group of forty-three delegates from the various Marxist organizations of the Tsarist Empire met in London to found a social-democratic party and to decide upon its rules. It must be remembered that the organizations they represented were feeble and had an almost nominal membership. They were, in fact, a scattered group of intellectuals from the vast areas of the Russian Empire. At the meeting (officially it was the *second* meeting of the Russian Social-Democratic Party, nominally founded in 1898) Lenin put forward his own theses and managed to carry the majority with him, despite strenuous opposition from the minority; and since the Russian word for 'majorities' is *bolsheviki*, Lenin's victorious faction was dubbed 'the Bolsheviks', and retained that name thereafter.

4. *What is to be done?*, Moscow State Publishing House, no date, p. 206.

The subsequent theory of the party has gone hand in hand with the work it has performed, but through it there run two unvarying themes: that it is indispensable and that it must be united. The arguments by which these twin conclusions have been reached have altered: the conclusions have ever remained the same.

The years before 1917 were those of 'preparation for the socialist revolution'. Since the party's self-appointed task was precisely to act as the vanguard of the proletariat in bringing this revolution about, it was *ex hypothesi* indispensable; and since it had to do so in the repressive conditions of Tsardom, it had to be, as Lenin's pamphlet had argued, conspiratorial, disciplined and united. Once the party succeeded in seizing power in 1917 the argument changed. The subsequent years were regarded as those of the 'dictatorship of the proletariat'. As the vanguard of the proletariat the party was the agent of the dictatorship: it was, therefore, once again indispensable. And since the concept of the proletarian dictatorship implied the repression of the former ruling classes, any self-division in its ranks could only strengthen the class enemy. Hence, once more, the party had to be disciplined and united.

In 1938, Stalin, the general secretary of the party – by now the undisputed ruler of the Union – declared that the class enemy had finally been crushed. The next period was therefore described officially as the stage of 'socialism in one country'. In this the role of the party was formulated as that of guiding the working people of Russia towards the accomplishment of this socialism. It was therefore, again, indispensable. But it was socialism in *one* country only; this implied that the U.S.S.R. was beseiged by ravening imperialist powers anxious to destroy it. Though the internal class enemy had been destroyed, enemy agents continued their fell work. Once again, then, the party must be disciplined and united so as to prevent them from taking advantage of its self-divisions.

But, possibly from 1953, and certainly from the Twenty-second Congress of the Party in 1961, the official doctrine has been that the Soviet Union has reached a new stage. First, socialism has been attained and the country is on the road to full communism when, according to the Marxist theory of the state, the state will 'wither away'. Secondly, it is officially admitted – indeed, pro-claimed – that the capitalist encirclement is over; the 'socialist camp' is now superior. Yet the party is still proclaimed as indispensable – in order to guide the working people towards full communism. And it must continue to be as tightly disciplined as before. For, the argument runs, as the coercive apparatus of the state is dismantled and control turned over increasingly to organizations like the trade unions, co-operatives, factories and collective farms – so the only way of unifying society, of prevent-ing it from dissipating its gains in mutually destructive conflicts, will be through the guidance and control of all of these by a disciplined and wholly united Communist Party!

In short from 1903 onwards, and for an indeterminate future, the uniform conclusions have been that the party must (1) have a monopoly of power, and (2) never weaken this by internal dispute. In this respect it is enlightening to compare and contrast the conclusions drawn in the first (and Stalinist) *History of the Communist Party of the Soviet Union*, published in 1938, with those in the revised (Krushchev) edition, published in 1960.

The 1938 version draws the following two conclusions:

(1) This history of the Party further teaches us that unless the petty-bourgeois parties which are active within the ranks of the working class and which push the backward sections of the working class into the arms of the bourgeoisie, thus splitting the unity of the working class, are smashed, the victory of the proletarian revolution is impos-sible.

(2) The history of the Party further teaches us that unless the Party of the working class wages an uncompromising struggle against the opportunists within its own ranks, unless it smashes the capitulators in its own midst, it cannot preserve unity and discipline within its ranks, it cannot perform its role as organiser and leader of the proletarian revolution, nor its role as the builder of the new Socialist society.[5]

In the 1960 version, a quite different and much longer book than the original 1938 version, we find the following statement:

(1) The history of the C.P.S.U. teaches that unity of the working class is an essential condition for victory in the Socialist revolution, and

5. *History of the Communist Party of the Soviet Union*, Moscow, 1943 edn.

that such unity cannot be achieved unless the petty bourgeois parties are exposed and isolated from the masses, unless they are routed ideologically.

(2) The history of the C.P.S.U. teaches us that the Party would not have been able to preserve its militant unity and to perform its role as leader of the Socialist revolution, as the directing and leading force of the dictatorship of the proletariat, its role as the builder of the Communist Society, had it not waged an uncompromising struggle against the opportunists, conciliators and sceptics within its own ranks, had it not defeated and overcome them.

(3) The historical path travelled by the C.P.S.U. shows that the party can effectively lead the struggle of the working class for power, for the establishment of socialism and communism, only if the internal life of the party is highly organised, if all its organisations and all its members have one will, if they act as a solid force, if there is iron discipline in its ranks. The methods of party work and the forms of party organisation depend on concrete historical conditions. *But the basic principles of organisation which were worked out and substantiated by Lenin, and are now an integral part of Bolshevism are immutable.*[6]

The monolithism of the party

If, as we have been told, the party is 'the leading core of the power of the working people', then the party secretaries and their associates are the 'leading core' of the party. This corps of professional partisans services every unit of the party from lowest to highest in an ascending ladder of power and responsibility until they reach the highest level of all, in the person of the general secretary of the Communist Party of the entire Soviet Union. It forms a spinal column, a brace, to the twelve million rank-and-file members and the twenty-three million Komsomol members (the Young Communists).

Again, if it is true as the authorities state, that 'not a single important decision is taken by the Soviet state organs without preliminary guiding directions and advice from the Party', it is also true that the party itself takes no important decisions without the preliminary guidance and advice of its secretaries and that no

6. *History of the Communist Party of the Soviet Union*, Moscow, 1960, pp. 752–4.

secretary takes any important decision without preliminary guidance and advice from the secretary of the higher echelon – and so on all the way up to the general secretary of the party, in the Kremlin.

In short: at each governmental level, the people of the Soviet Union are regimented and directed by the party organization at that level; but the party at that level is regimented and directed by its secretarial 'apparatus' and the apparatus at each level is directed by the apparatus at the next highest level, and so on until the highest level of all – the level of the Politbureau and Secretariat of the all-Union Communist Party.

Numbers and formal structure

In March 1966 the party contained 11,673,676 full members and 798,403 probationary ones. The Komsomol organization – which works to the direction of the party functionaries – comprised twenty-three million members at that same date.

The party is organized pyramid-wise. The base consists of some 300,000 party primary units, and the apex of the Politbureau and Secretariat. Party primary units (P.P.U.s) must be formed in every work-place where there are at least three party members. Their structure depends on their size. Those with fifteen members or less select a secretary or deputy-secretary and hold a general meeting once every month. Those whose numbers are larger than fifteen but less than 300 elect a bureau which includes the secretary and the deputy-secretary. The large ones, with over 300 members, elect a committee and it is this committee which elects the bureau. In these very large organizations the sub-units in each of the various plants or departments of the enterprise are themselves accredited with the status of an ordinary P.P.U.

The secretaries are part-time officials in the smaller P.P.U.s – those defined, for this purpose, as containing less than 150 members. Once a unit has more members than this, the secretary is a salaried full-time official. The 'apparatus' begins at that point. The current trend is towards larger P.P.U.s. In 1962 there were 296,444 P.P.U.s of which 13,220 were over 300 strong; the corresponding figures in March 1966 were 326,000 P.P.U.s and the number of them with more than 300 members had increased (since 1962) by fifty per cent.[7]

The '*P.P.U. is organised and confirmed in its work by the next highest party organisation*' (Rule 50 of the C.P.S.U.): namely, by the city, borough or *rayon* (regional) party organization. Such an organization is nothing but a biennial *conference* of delegates from each of its constituent P.P.U.s; but this then elects a committee which in turn elects a bureau (including a secretary or secretaries). Thus, *in practice*, the city, borough or *rayon* 'organization' is just a committee – and, to speak still more practically, just the bureau appointed by that committee. Hence the importance of Rule 49 stating that the secretary must be of at least three years' standing and that his appointment must be confirmed by the next highest echelon, and of Rule 47 which, equally bluntly, states that that the next highest echelon both 'directs its work' and 'inspects' it. These higher echelons are the party organizations in the administrative units called the *krai* (or the appropriate ethnic unit) or, most commonly, in the administrative units known as *oblasts*. Just as before, the *oblast* party organization (or its equivalent) is a biennial conference of delegates from the lower organizations, in this case those of the city, borough or *rayon*: and again, in practice, this means simply that the 'organization' is just the committee it elects (the *obkom*) and, in still more practical terms, its bureau and secretariat. But at this level the secretariat is considerably differentiated. There will be second and third secretaries, and specialized departments for indoctrination (*agit-prop*), for the press, for the selection and placement of personnel in party posts and in industry and agriculture generally, as well as departments supervising the operations of these economic sectors. The heads of these specialized departments will be subjected to a dual control – to the first secretary of the *obkom*, but also to the heads of the corresponding departments in the bureau of the next highest party organization.

Except for the largest of the Republics, the Russian Soviet Federated Socialist Republic (R.S.F.S.R.), whose superior

7. Report of the Credentials Commission of the C.P.S.U., April 1966, edition 14, *Current Digest of the Soviet Press*, Columbia, 1966, Volume XVIII, No. 13, p. 14.

echelon is the all-Union party itself, this 'next highest organization' is the Union-Republic party organization – e.g., the Communist Party of White Russia, or of the Ukraine, or of Tadzhikstan, as the case may be. Excluding the R.S.F.S.R. (the Great Russian Republic), there are fourteen of these. Each consists of a party congress meeting biennially, and composed of the delegates of its constituent *obkoms* and their equivalents. The congress elects its central committee and this in turn its bureau-cum-secretariat. The functions of such congresses are to receive reports from their lower units and from their own central committee, to discuss other party matters at their discretion and to choose delegates for the all-Union quadrennial Congress of the whole party. And this, the highest of all levels is described (in Rule 31) as the 'supreme organ' of the C.P.S.U. It meets every four years. It elects a Central Committee which must meet at least twice a year and this in turn elects a Politbureau and Secretariat. And, since Stalin's day, the first secretary of the all-Union party organization has been recognized as the *de facto* ruler of the Soviet Union.

Three features of this party organization are particularly noteworthy. The first is the remoteness of the highest party organizations from the rank and file. In the largest of the Republics (the R.S.F.S.R.) the rank and file members only elect to the city or *rayon* conference; it is this conference which in its turn elects to the *oblast* conference; and it is this that then elects to the all-Union Congress. In the other Republics there are *three* intermediate steps from lowest to highest: first to the city or *rayon*, then from this to the *oblast*, then again from this to the Republic congress, and only then, from the Republic congress to the all-Union Congress. Secondly, at each ascent in the pyramid, party officialdom – secretary or bureau – becomes more numerous, more differentiated and more professional. And finally, the activities of every level are subjected to the direction and control of the superior ones. This is stated in so many words in Rule 19, which says that 'democratic centralism' implies:

(b) *Periodical reports* of party bodies to their party organisations *and to higher bodies.*

(c) Strict party discipline and the subordination of the minority to the majority.

(d) *The decisions of the higher bodies are obligatory on lower bodies.* An organisation serving a given area is higher than any Party Organisation serving part of that area. All Party Organisations are autonomous in their decisions on local questions *unless their decisions conflict with Party Policy.*

Apparatus and apparatchiki

In the rule just quoted, the first line (omitted above) runs: '(a) *election of all leading Party bodies from the lowest to the highest.*' This phrase constitutes the supposed democratic guarantee in the doctrine of democratic centralism which the rule expounds. In practice these leading party bodies are self-recruiting. It is certainly true that at the very lowest levels, in the smaller P.P.U.s, the party meeting does, very rarely, adopt its own candidate for secretary despite the disapproval of the superior echelon. But these are glaring exceptions. It is not to secure such a result that every party bureau, from *oblast* level upwards to the Kremlin itself, contains a 'party organs department' whose task is, precisely, to deploy officials throughout the party. Nor is it to secure such a result that the Party Rules specify that the Secretariat of the all-Union party 'directs current work, *chiefly the selection of cadres* and verifications of fulfilment of party decisions', nor that the Central Committee of the all-Union party has the function of 'selecting and appointing leading functionaries', nor that Republic, *oblast*, city and *rayon* organizations 'select and appoint leading personnel'. The blunt phrasing of these rules makes it clear that these bodies have the power to carry out these appointing functions – electivity nothwithstanding. The semantic contradiction is solved in practice or – as the Russian comrades would phrase it – 'by life'. Suppose a party meeting is about to vote by secret ballot (as prescribed) for its committee and secretary: then a representative, usually the secretary, of the next highest organization is always present at such a meeting. He is not permitted by a party custom *to impose* his list; but he is charged with *directing* the election – a nice distinction. For, as Professor Schapiro aptly quotes from a Soviet source – which describes such elections – 'Democracy has nothing to do with spontaneity, when any chance result may emerge.'[8] The representative of the higher organization in fact helps to prepare the list of candidates and speaks as often and as pressingly as necessary in the open discussion which precedes the ballot; except for trivial exceptions this suffices. Effectively the lower officials are appointed only with the approval of the higher. The apparatus recruits itself by what in practice is a system of co-option.

A bizarre interlude in the history of the Party Rules aptly illustrates this point. At the Twenty-second Party Congress of 1961, Nikita Krushchev, then first secretary of the party, took steps to 'preclude the concentration of excessive power in the hands of individual functionaries and to prevent them placing themselves above the control of the collectivity'.[9] To this end a new rule, Number 25 was introduced. P.P.U.s and city, borough and *rayon* organizations were to retire half of their functionaries and committee men at each regular election; *oblast* and Republic organizations were to retire one-third of them; and at the very top, in the Central Committee and the Politbureau itself, one-quarter were to retire at each regular election. Exceptionally talented individuals might, however, be retained, but only provided they received a seventy-five per cent vote to that effect. Nevertheless the effect was dramatic. Up to that time, about one-third of the secretaries of the P.P.U.s had been changed every year; now the proportion doubled – each year, sixty per cent of them were replaced. It was then found that there were not enough 'mature and experienced workers' to man the party committees[10] and the *apparatchiki* complained bitterly. And so, four years later, when Krushchev was gone and Brezhnev had supplanted him as the general secretary, the rule was abolished.

8. L. Schapiro, *The Communist Party of the Soviet Union*, Methuen, 1960, p. 575.

9. *The Road to Communism: Documents of the 22nd Congress of the C.P.S.U.*, Foreign Languages Publishing House, Moscow, 1961, p. 379.

10. Twenty-third Congress of the C.P.S.U., *Current Digest of the Soviet Press*, Committee on Slavic Studies, Columbia University, New York, 1966.

The intertia of the machine, the vested interests of quarter of a million *apparatchiki* had, not unexpectedly, proved stronger than any individual.

Only among Western intellectuals, apologists and '*marxisants*' are efforts made to deny or to extenuate the power of the *apparatchiki* over the party rank and file and of the higher *apparatchiki* over the lower. In the Soviet Union these are simple facts of life. Solzhenitsyn's novel, *For the Good of the Cause*, was much attacked in the Soviet Union when it appeared in 1963 – but because he had misrepresented the motives of his *apparatchiki* not because he had misdescribed their relationships. This latter aspect of the book attracted no attention at all, for it described a state of affairs that everyone knew and took for granted.

The novel is indeed enlightening. It concerns a technical college in a small provincial town, where the staff and students are making their final preparations to move to new buildings which are almost ready and which they themselves have helped to construct, their existing quarters being cramped and inadequate. At this moment a delegation of officials arrives. One member is an official of the 'Ministry in Moscow', another is the head of the local Building Trust, a third is an electronics expert and the fourth is the supervisor of the industrial department of the *oblast* committee. They offhandedly inform the college principal that the new buildings are to be taken away from his college and turned over to a government research institute.

Aghast, the teaching staff want to convene a special meeting of their college party primary unit, but its secretary simply refuses; he forbids the Komsomol committee to convene a meeting also. This refusal is quite good enough – the meetings do not take place. (So much then for the influence of the '*aktiv*', i.e. of the rank and file, on the course of events!)

The secretary of the borough party, however, is sympathetic to the college principal; but even he immediately adds: 'If Knorozov' (the *obkom* secretary and hence his superior) 'has already given his okay, then, my friend, you are in trouble.' The principal, in despair, suggests sending a telegram to the Council of Ministers in Moscow. A revealing passage follows:

Grachikov [the town secretary] studied him closely for a minute. Suddenly all the sternness vanished from his face giving way to a friendly smile.

'My dear Fyodor, how do you picture this being arrived at, this decision by the Government? Do you imagine the whole Council sitting at a long table, discussing what to do about your building? Do you think they've got nothing better to do? And then I suppose you think your telegram will be brought in at just the right moment. Is that what you believe? No! A Government decision means that one of these days a Deputy Prime Minister will see one of the Ministers. The Minister will have some papers with him to make his report and at some point he will say: "This research institute has, as you know, top priority. It has been decided to locate it in this town, in which there happens to be a building it can use." The Deputy Prime Minister will then ask: "Whom was it built for?" And the Minister will reply: " For a school. But the school has got rather decent premises for the time being. We sent a commission of experts down and the Comrades studied the matter on the spot." Then before giving his final okay, the Deputy Prime Minister will ask one more question: "Does the Oblast Committee have any objections?" Do you get this – the Oblast Committee! Your telegram will be returned right to this place with a notation on it saying: "Check facts".' Grachikov pursed his lips. 'You've got to know how these things work. In this case it's the Oblast Committee that holds the power.'[11]

One final point emerges in the novel. For all his misgivings, Grachikov, the borough secretary, does interview Knorozov, the *oblast* secretary, and tries to get him to change his mind. He does not succeed. In fact there is a furious row. And then, after a silence, Knorozov quietly sneers: 'You're not the man for the job. We made a mistake.' Notice the phrase – '*We* made a mistake.' So much for the elective principle in the borough party!

The supreme organs of the C.P.S.U.

The chain of command from the lowest P.P.U. to the highest party organ terminates – in official theory – in the quadrennial Congress of the C.P.S.U., and the bodies it elects: the Central Committee which in its turn elects the Politbureau and the

11. A. Solzhenitsyn, *For the Good of the Cause*, Pall Mall, 1964.

Secretariat. In practice, the order of importance is reversed. The supreme party organs are the Politbureau and the Secretariat. The Central Committee's role is intermittent and limited and the Congress is a rubber stamp. And the elective order, also, is the reverse of the official theory: in practice, the Politbureau and Secretariat pre-select the Central Committee and the members of the Congress.

The Congress is simply an organ of ratification, It neither originates policy nor represents the opinions of the rank and file. For this there are four reasons. In the first place it is not the master of its agenda. Rule 27, which ostensibly permits the raising of issues, in practice restricts them by imposing the following conditions: 'Party-wide discussion is necessary on three conditions, (a) if the necessity is recognized by several Party organizations at Oblast or Republic levels. . . . (b) if there is not a sufficiently solid majority in the Central Committee on major questions of party policy and (c) if the Central Committee considers it necessary to consult the Party as a whole.' The last two conditions mean in effect that party-wide discussion takes place only if the leadership desires it, or cannot prevent it. As to the first of the three conditions, it states an impossibility; Republic and *oblast* organizations are continuously subject to the direction and control of the higher echelon, i.e., of the Central Committee, the Politbureau and the Secretariat of the all-Union party; at the slightest signs of dissidence in any of these inferior organizations, the supreme organs would (and do) purge them of malcontents and replace them with more pliable persons.

In the second place, the Congress does not reflect the opinion of the P.P.U.s but of the delegates of the Union Republics together with those from the *oblast* conferences of the R.S.F.S.R.

In the third place, at each level in the electoral pyramid that culminates in the Party Congress, the election of the delegates for the conference or congress of the next highest body takes place in the presence and under the guidance of the party's officials. In short, pressure is applied by the apparatus at each level in the long ascending ladder of indirect election. This can readily be seen from such a calculation as this: the total number of party members is approximately twelve million; the total number of *apparatchiki* is approximately 250,000, or 2 per cent of total membership; but the proportion of *apparatchiki* to the total number of delegates to the Congress was, in 1961, no less than twenty-six per cent!

Finally, the Congress meets too infrequently and is too unwieldy to play any positive part. Under Stalin, Congresses met less and less frequently, until at last a gap of thirteen years elapsed between the Eighteenth Congress and the Nineteenth. Since then, the Congresses have met every four years: but this is far too infrequent to ensure any continuity, particularly since the Congress consists of some 5,000 delegates.

So, the Party Congress approves and ratifies: not only the actions that have been carried out in its name by the supreme organs of the party, but also the lists of candidates submitted to them for election to the Central Committee which is, in official theory, to carry on the party's affairs on its behalf for the next four years.

It is in this Central Committee that the dominance of the *apparatchik* becomes striking. The Central Committee is an omnium gatherum of the Soviet *élite*. It contains the admirals and the marshals, the trade union and the Komsomol leaders, the leading ministers, and all the members of the Politbureau and many from the Secretariat; but the largest single component consists of the first secretaries of the more important party organizations, chiefly those at Republic and *oblast* level. In the Twenty-second Congress of 1961, no less than forty-nine per cent of the entire Central Committee consisted of party officials. If Party Rules were, in this case, a true guide to practice, the Central Committee would be the most influential organ of the party. Indeed, in the early days of the Soviet régime this is precisely what it was. It was Stalin who, after 1924, undermined its influence and concentrated power in the organs which, in theory, it elects: Politbureau and Secretariat. As they stand, the Rules – like the word 'Soviet' in constitutional theory – are a mere historic testimony of the heroic past. The powers which officially are wielded by the Central Committee serve to show, not that it is the effective organ of power in the party, but just that the Congress is a mere cipher. For the Rules say that 'in the intervals between Congresses, the Central Committee of the Party *directs the enitre work of the party and the local party organizations*'. It 'selects and places executive cadres' – i.e., it manages the entire (and enormous) Soviet bureaucracy. It 'directs, via the Party inside them, the work of the central organizations and public organizations of the working people' – i.e., it manages the entire society. It 'establishes various Party agencies, institutions, and enterprises and directs their work'. It 'appoints the editorial boards of central newspapers and magazines that function under its control'. It 'distributes the funds of the party budget and supervises its execution'.

In fact it does none of these things. The Politbureau and Secretariat do them for it. For one thing it is too large to do them – the 1966 Central Committee comprised 195 members with voting rights plus another 165 without. It meets too infrequently – four times in 1957, six times in 1958, but on the average not more than twice or three times a year. Thirdly, it is a body of yes-men. Once a fraction has triumphed inside the Politbureau, its first care is to purge and reconstruct the membership of the Central Committee. For instance, once Krushchev had ousted Malenkov as first secretary of the party in 1953, he manipulated the Central Committee membership to such effect that the body elected by the Twentieth Congress (1956) contained 215 of his hangers-on out of a total membership of 309.

The Central Committee, a mere shadow under Stalin, has only once played a significant political role. This was in 1957. In that year Krushchev was outvoted in the Politbureau, but he successfully appealed to take his case to the Central Committee. The fact that his supporters were in a majority there, together with the ostentatious support which the army accorded him, was sufficient to enable him to turn the tables on his opponents. Ignominiously they were condemned by the Central Committee and Krushchev was confirmed in his post.

All the functions which, according to the Rules, are the province of the Central Committee are in practice exercised by the supreme organs, Politbureau and Secretariat. Rule 39 says, laconically: 'The Central Committee of the C.P.S.U. elects a Politbureau *to direct the work* of the Central Committee between plenary sessions' (i.e., all the time save for two or three occasions in the year!). And it continues: 'it elects a Secretariat *to direct current* work chiefly in the selection of cadres' (i.e., key personnel) 'and in the organisation of the check-up on fulfilment.' The rule of politics in the Soviet Union is thus: the higher the fewer and the fewer the stronger.

Between Politbureau and Secretariat there is an overlap. For instance, in 1966, of the eleven full members of the Politbureau, four were also members of the Secretariat. It is clear that the two bodies work hand in hand. The Secretariat is the advisory and executive body, the Politbureau the policy-making one. And how effectively the Secretariat oversees and controls every aspect of Soviet society – not just the party – can be seen from its organization chart. The Party Organs Department is responsible for placing, promoting and removing the officials throughout the entire party, the Komsomol and the trade union organization, together with the supervision and direction of these bodies. The Ideological Department is responsible for indoctrination throughout the Union: by means of personal persuasion (called 'agitation' in the U.S.S.R.), the press and the other mass media. Then comes a series of departments which direct the personnel policies and the activities of the various sectors of society: Transport and Communication, Agriculture, Heavy Industry, Light Industry, Machine Tools, Construction, Higher Education, Science and Culture. And finally, it has departments responsible for the direction of what goes on in foreign affairs, and inside the Soviet armed forces. Most important of all is the Administrative Organs Department: it is this that appoints and controls the police, judges, procurators and armed forces.

Employing perhaps five or six hundred officials, the Secretariat is the peak of an extensive network of patronage and power the like of which the world has never seen before. From it depend, directly, the careers of about 2,000 officials of the Republic parties, some 9,000 officials of the *oblast* committees, and about 200,000 officials at the city, *rayon* and party primary unit levels; those of the leading ranks in police, courts and armed forces; as well as those of the quarter of a million members who work as specialists in the national economy, and those of another one and a quarter million who work as administrators and managers. Through them the twelve-million-strong party is controlled; and through the party the whole of Soviet society.

The party's monopoly of power

In 1917, when the Bolshevik faction of the Russian Social-Democratic Party seized power by a *coup d'état*, there were many parties in existence; and indeed, the first government to be formed by the Bolsheviks after the insurrection was in coalition with the Left Social Revolutionaries. But the '*bourgeois*' parties, such as the Constitutional Democrats, were harried from the start and soon proscribed. In the exigencies of the civil war, pressure was brought upon the 'socialist' parties – Social Revolutionaries and Mensheviks – and by 1922, whatever the legal position, the Bolshevik faction, who after 1917 described themselves as the Communist Party, was *de facto* the ruling party. Its monopoly position is implied but not formally guaranteed by the 1936 Constitution (Article 126), and is arrived at administratively.

Admitted this party is only a minority in the state. With some twelve million members, it comprises only five per cent of the population. But this is somewhat misleading, for it contains no less than nine per cent of the over-eighteens, i.e., those eligible to join; while the Komsomol members, twenty-three million strong, make up about two-thirds of the eligible age group, aged between fifteen and twenty-six.

However, though the Communist Party comprises only five per cent of the population, it is so distributed, and assigned such duties, that it permeates the whole of public life. For, in the first place, the P.P.U.s are based on the *work-place*: in every office, factory, workshop, collective farm, university and school, regiment and battleship where there are more than the minimum number of party members. Next, these units are required to propagandize in these work-places in favour of the policy of the government, to admit and enlist new members, to give these members political education and – in so doing – 'to oppose all attempts at revisionist distortion of Marxism-Leninism and its dogmatic interpretation'; which is as much as to say that it is required to pursue orthodoxy. And what is or is not orthodoxy is ensured by Rule 58 (h) which reiterates that the unit is accountable for its work to the next highest echelon – the area, city and *rayon* committees of the party.

But Rule 59 gives the party membership an even more important role. It distinguishes two sets of establishments: state organs; and others such as industrial and agricultural enterprises, drafting and design offices, industrial and agricultural research institutes. In the latter the P.P.U. has 'the right to control the work of the administration', i.e., call to account before it the managers who run the office or works. This is not permissible in the state organs: it might be very awkward if a pip-squeak of a party secretary of some tiny P.P.U. tried to call a state official to account. Hence the chief task of the P.P.U. in such offices is 'to inform the appropriate party bodies in good time of shortcomings in the work of the respective offices and individuals regardless of what post the latter may occupy'. To put it bluntly: the chief task of the P.P.U.s throughout all the work-places, the universities and schools, the military units and the public establishments, is to act as a body of gad-flies, critics and licensed sneaks. There are some 300,000 of these P.P.U.s: thus in every working establishment throughout the whole vast country there are knots of dedicated Communists, responsible exclusively to their party superiors, to control, check upon and inform against their official superiors and managers. The party is not simply a body of persons devoted to securing office for its leaders and maintaining them in power: it is a set of command posts distributed throughout every important institution in the Union.

This control is guaranteed and completed by two other devices: the party's hold over key personnel; and its apparatus of policy-direction and its grip on the electoral process.

As to the first, it has already been stated that the all-union Secretariat has a number of departments (the organization has shifted back and forth since its establishment) which nominate, distribute and promote key personnel throughout the Soviet Union, not only in the party hierarchy but in industry, agriculture, the mass media, the military units and the government departments. The result is a significant overlap between managerial position, educational attainment and party membership. In 1961, of the approximately 3·8 million persons who had completed their higher education, 1·3 million were party members. Of the 8,784,000 specialists working in the national economy, 2,495,000 were party members. Of the administrative-management personnel, numbering 4,403,000 persons in 1956, 1,230,000 were party members. And for years virtually all officers in the armed forces have been party members.[12]

Secondly, at all levels, the appropriate party committee and its bureau is keyed into the formal machinery of government. The party committees are, indeed, founded to parallel the state organization: hence the hierarchy, from the city, *rayon* and borough levels, up to the *krai* or *oblast*, then to the Republic, and finally to the all-Union (or federal) level: for this is the hierarchy of governmental units in the U.S.S.R. At each ascending level, the party apparatus – the bureau – becomes increasingly differentiated and complex, with divisions elaborated to work parallel to and to control the appropriate government departments; until the apex is reached, with the all-Union Secretariat and its elaborate compartmentalization which parallels in all significant particulars the great departments of state and economy.

Its control is achieved in three ways: by the personal overlap between the leading party members and the key posts in the government of that level; by the influence of the party groups in the elective organs of the state and other important public organizations; and by the party's control over the elections.

As to the first, all that need be said is that it is a general and cardinal rule in the Soviet Union that the higher (and therefore the more important) the ranking of an official body, the higher will be the party proportion of its membership. In other words: though a village soviet may have relatively few Communist members, the committee it elects will have a far higher proportion, and so forth; and by the same token, though a village soviet will have relatively few Communist members, the *oblast* soviet is sure to have many more, the Republic soviet still more, and so forth.

12. Quoted, Z. Brzezinski and S. P. Huntington, *Political Power, U.S.A./U.S.S.R.*, Viking Press, New York, 1964, p. 168.

As to the second, Rule 67 is specific:

at congresses, conferences and meetings and in the elective bodies of Soviets, trade unions, co-operatives and other mass organizations of the working people, having at least three Party members, Party groups are formed for the purpose of strengthening the influence of the Party in every way and carrying out Party policy among non-party people. . . . The Party groups are subordinate to the appropriate Party bodies: the Central Committee of the C.P.S.U., the Central Committees of the Communist Parties of the Union Republics, territorial, regional, area, city or rayon Party committees. . . . In all matters the groups must strictly and unswervingly abide by decisions of the leading Party bodies.

Finally, the party controls the elections. Direct election to the Supreme Soviet of the U.S.S.R. was not introduced till after the 1936 Constitution. The first elections were scheduled for 1937, and the C.P.S.U. found itself in something of a quandary. If it insisted that only party members could stand, it would open a cleavage between itself and the rest of the population. If it allowed non-party candidates to stand, there was the risk that they might oppose the party. The solution was the so-called '*bloc*', described in the official *History of the Communist Party of the Soviet Union* thus: 'The Party entered the elections in a bloc, an alliance, with the non-party masses by deciding to put up joint candidates with the non-party masses in the electoral areas.[13] The phrase 'joint candidates' was a masterpeice. For by insisting that only one candidate should stand for any vacancy, and by insisting too that this candidate should be nominated after joint consultation of the party and the non-party other organization, the party was able to ensure with the greatest ease that the candidates elected should either be party members or, at least, sympathizers. And so it has worked out. No candidate may stand without the grace and favour of the party. In addition to this, the electoral mechanism, as will be seen later, guarantees that almost nobody will abstain, still less register a formal protest vote. The result is that the various elective bodies contain proportions of Communists which vary directly with their importance – and the decision of the party. In the local bodies, on

13. op. cit., 1943 edn., p. 350.

average, forty-three per cent of the elected candidates were party members in the 1965 elections. In the Union Republics, 68 per cent of the elected candidates were party members in the 1963 elections. In the Supreme Soviet elections in 1962, seventy-six per cent of the elected candidates were party members.

The Communist Party: a summary

Thus, the party is a pyramidal, hierarchical organization in which, at any one point of time, the top group of leaders in the Politbureau and the chief secretaries of the Secretariat make the decisions, which are then transmitted downwards, according to the principles of democratic centralism, through the 'apparatus' – the spinal column of the party – and thence outwards through the rank and file; then, adopted by these and duly executed, they are carried forward by the 300,000 party primary units into all the working organizations of the Soviet Union. Though the Party Rules stress again and again that it is the right and privilege of each party member to discuss party issues, the sealing off of the rank and file from its adjacent committees (save through the intermediation of the next highest authority) gives little or no opportunity for concentrated action at the grass roots; and such action would in any case be regarded as factionalism, and prohibited. Furthermore, the operation of Rule 27, prescribing – or rather proscribing – the opportunities for rank and file discussion, effectively excludes inner-party democracy. Instead a self-perpetuating oligarchy, located in the Politbureau and Secretariat, directs the work of the party and lays down its policies.

Under Stalin, between 1928 and 1953, the party was turned into a Byzantine bureaucracy. Among the defects noted by Malenkov in 1952 at the Nineteenth Party Congress were: 'self satisfaction and smug complacency', 'fear of reporting defects to superiors', 'concealment of the truth about local affairs', 'laxness in securing action, over-indulgence in giving orders', 'gross nepotism in making appointments', 'individual actions instead of consultation', 'delations, the removal of opponents, the promotion of yes-men'. This was a fine result after thirty-five years of the Bolshevik Revolution! And it was this that Krushchev sought to remedy after 1953, by insisting on strict application of the Party Rules and above all by laying down in 1961 a new rule, Number 25, for the 'systematic renewal' of the committees of the party from bottom to top. But this rule, making for more frequent changes of party officials and committeemen, clearly did not commend itself to the *apparatchiki*. With the removal of Krushchev – and perhaps the rule was a cause of his removal – in 1966, this rule has been abrogated; and it remains to be seen whether the party, still intent on shouldering its crushing burden, will not rigidify once more.

III. STALIN'S RUSSIA

(1) *Chronology*

In the thirty-six years between the Bolshevik seizure of power in 1917 and the death of Stalin in 1953, the former Russian Empire, known from 1924 as the Union of Soviet Socialist Republics, became industrialized, urbanized, socialist – and totalitarian.

The Bolshevik seizure of power did not long go uncontested. By 1918 the forces of opposition had rallied and taken up arms, assisted by British and French forces. Thus the Wars of Intervention began and lasted till 1920, dragging on in the East until 1922. The Bolsheviks, their enemies defeated and their former friends proscribed, were now supreme.

Decrees of the years 1917 and 1918 had nationalized the land, private industry, the entire credit system and the means of transportation. The wars, however, had inflicted such destruction on the country's by no means advanced economy, that by 1921 industry was almost at a standstill, consumer goods had largely disappeared and grain was made available only by forced requisitions from the peasantry. In these circumstances the party, at the instance of Lenin, permitted a certain recrudescence of private enterprise. This was the N.E.P. – the New Economic Policy – and the entrepreneurs and speculators who rapidly emerged were known as the N.E.P.-men: under their efforts the economy made some small progress towards recovery. But N.E.P.

was only a temporary solution. When Lenin died, in 1924, the economic options were all open. But so too was the problem of the succession. In such reverence did the party hold Lenin that his survivors – the most advanced revolutionaries in the world – took the decision to embalm his corpse and display it to the multitude in a mausoleum in the Red Square of Moscow! The problem of who should or could replace this demigod, and the problem of economic policy, became inextricably intermingled.

As it posed itself to these Marxists, the problem was something like this. According to Marx, the proletarian revolution would erupt first in the advanced industrial societies of the West, those with a large proletarian base. But Lenin had decided otherwise: the revolution was here, in a primitive and unsanitary peasant economy, with a proletariat that was fractionally small. The 'dictatorship of the proletariat' meant the uneasy exercise of power by a handful of industrial workers atop a mass of primitive and superstitious peasants anxious only for one thing – their free and undisturbed possession of the land. And they held the whip hand, for without them the revolution would starve to death. The fear and distrust of the 'dark masses' was nowhere better expressed than in the provisions of the Constitutions of 1918 and 1924 which weighted the franchise heavily in favour of the towns as against the rural areas.

In principle, once the revolution had broken out in Russia it should have been taken up by the industrial proletarians of the West: their triumph would guarantee the survival of the revolution in Russia. But the Red Army had been halted before Warsaw in 1920, and each succeeding year saw the red waves in Central and Eastern Europe grow feebler until, by 1924, they had subsided and left the national *bourgeoisies* in control as before. Only in China, where a nationalist revolution was in progress in alliance with communism, was there hope of further spread of the revolution.

The principle that the revolution could only succeed through the support of Bolshevized Western states was elegantly expressed by one of the obvious contenders to the succession, Trotsky, in his doctrine of 'permanent revolution', with the corollary that the Soviet state must promote and assist revolution abroad.

Trotsky was a brilliant orator and polemicist, and a superb organizer withal. It was he who had raised and organized the Red Army, now triumphant. In the public eye he stood inferior only to Lenin. But Trotsky had always neglected political manoeuvre, relying on his personal ascendancy. And he had made a host of enemies – not least in the Southern Army group, the one that had defended Tsaritsyn under the leadership of Stalin and Voroshilov and Budyenny. Furthermore his notion of the permanent revolution offended not only Stalin but others even more cautious – for instance, Zinoviev and Kamenev, both 'old Bolsheviks'. And, for that matter, Trotsky was *not* an 'old Bolshevik'. Before 1917 he had been neither Menshevik nor Bolshevik, but in between; he had joined Lenin only in 1917.

In 1924 his chief rival appeared to be either Kamenev or Zinoviev. In fact it was a third person, Joseph Stalin. The history of Russia from 1924 to 1936 is the story of Stalin's rise to personal dictatorship.

Stalin was the very antipodes of Trotsky. He was no intellectual: his maunderings in the field of Marxist doctrine are clumsy, mechanical and banal. He was no orator: his speech was laconic and curt. He was not middle class, like both Trotsky and Lenin: proletarian in origin he had joined the Bolsheviks early and, while its pundits were in exile in the West, had carried out revolutionary work in the oil-fields of his native Caucasus along with a fellow Georgian, Lavrenti Beria, later to become the dreaded head of his secret police. Stalin was a crafty, devious, suspicious and utterly ruthless Georgian. And he had gravitated to where these talents could be put to excellent use: to the secretaryship of the party. At that time the Central Committee was still the policy-making body for a party in which the Congresses still counted. But under Stalin, the Secretariat began to lay a stealthy hold upon the party: for the Secretariat controlled admission to and expulsion from the party. The famous 'Lenin enrolment' of 1924, ostensibly a demonstration of affection for the departed leader, allowed Stalin to induct a large body of his pledged supporters into the party just as the struggle for succession opened.

For their different reasons, Kamenev and Zinoviev on the one hand and Stalin on the other were determined to prevent the accession of Trotsky. They contracted an alliance (the '*Troika*') and, against it, Trotsky and his supporters found themselves increasingly isolated in the party Congresses. By the time Zinoviev and Kamenev woke to the fact that Stalin represented a greater danger to them than Trotsky did, it was too late. The efforts of the two groups to unite against Stalin were dismissed by him as a 'mutual amnesty' and the Party Congress rejected them with scorn. In 1927 Trotsky was exiled for his persistent 'anti-party' activity. And, in the following year, Stalin came out with his own solution to the Russian economic problem and the future of her revolution. The world revolution had failed. Therefore all energies of the Soviet peoples must be harnessed to building up an industrial structure as fast as possible – for two reasons: first, to protect the U.S.S.R. against the powerful *bourgeois* nations of the West – the 'capitalist encirclement' – and secondly, to *create*, by sheer power, the industrial proletariat whose numbers and strength could alone save the revolution from the 'dark masses'. So was initiated the First Five-Year Plan: socialism was to be built in one country.

Henceforth all Stalin's energy was directed, to the very last year of his life, towards regimenting the Soviet peoples in a head-long, utterly ruthless drive to construct heavy industry. In 1930 the pressure was switched to the peasantry. Peasants who owned any worthwhile property were called kulaks ('fists') and stripped of their possessions, which were then handed over to their neighbours – on the condition, stringently enforced, that these merged their small-holdings into a collective farm. In this way, it was thought, mechanized farming could be introduced, the interdependency of town and countryside reinforced – and the peasantry subjected to state control.

In the party, where violent controversy ranged about the places where, and the ruthlessness with which these industrial and agricultural policies should be pressed, Zinoviev, Kamenev, Rykov and Bukharin moved into opposition to Stalin. It was in vain. From his vantage point in the Secretariat, Stalin now controlled the Congresses and he had no difficulty in first demoting his opponents and then, humiliatingly, re-admitting them to his conditional favour. From 1930 Stalin held the middle ground in the theoretical controversy; and the high ground in the struggle for the succession.

As the First Five-Year Plan was succeeded in 1932 by the Second, so the new socialist state moved towards totalitarianism. By this time, owing to his hold on the party machinery, Stalin was dominating the Central Committee and its Politbureau: decisions were taken by him and his adherents, and executed through the authority he enjoyed as the first secretary – the head and apex of the *apparat*, which he had enormously developed. Under the deep strains of industrialization and the necessity to deport the kulaks and quell the resistant countryside, the coercive organs of the state developed rapidly: the security police (G.P.U. or O.G.P.U.) began their rise to pre-eminence. For in 1934 Kirov, Stalin's personal protégé and heir apparent, was assassinated in Leningrad (in circumstances which have never been made clear). Thenceforward, by decree, the G.P.U. were empowered to arrest on the charge of counter-revolutionary crimes and try by secret court martial. In 1936, the year in which the 'liberal' Stalin Constitution was proclaimed, there began the great purges – of the armed forces, of the bureaucracy and of the party itself. In the next two years, half the officers in the armed forces were purged, and no less than one out of every four party members, charged with mostly fabricated counter-revolutionary crimes, were ejected from the party, exiled, imprisoned or executed. After 1936 Stalin was the personal despot of the Soviet Union, with Trotsky in exile in Mexico, and Zinoviev, Kamenev, Bukharin, Rykov, to name only a few of the great revolutionary generation, vilely executed for alleged conspiracy against the U.S.S.R. From that point on, the Soviet Union was wholly totalitarian. Not until Stalin's death in 1953 was the way open for a further struggle for the succession and, in the course of that struggle, a measure of liberalization.

But in the meantime the policy of industrialization had triumphed – how greatly can be seen from Table 19. Rapidly, a relatively backward and illiterate economy had been hammered into a modernizing, literate, urban society using advanced industrial techniques. Economically, the country advanced at a pace at least double that of the U.S.A., and a formidable heavy industry was created. Its Achilles' heel, then, as now, was agriculture. The attempt to create the large mechanized

TABLE 19. THE INDUSTRIALIZATION OF THE
U.S.S.R. 1913–60

Commodity	Unit	1913	1940	1950	1960
Pig iron	million metric tons	4·2	14·9	19·2	46·8
Steel	million metric tons	4·2	18·3	27·3	65·3
Coal	million metric tons	29·2	165·9	261·1	513·0
Petroleum	million metric tons	9·2	31·1	37·9	148·0
Electricity	billion kilowatt-hours	2·0	48·3	91·2	292·0
Machine tools	thousands	1·8	58·4	70·6	154·0

collective farms, between 1930 and 1934, failed in its purpose: food production lagged behind the production of iron and steel and cement. Moreover, while all emphasis was laid upon creating a heavy industry, consumer goods and their distribution were neglected. Much had been achieved: but at a terrible cost in life, in freedom and in happiness. These were the years of Russia's Iron Age.

(2) *The main political features*

Where the whole of society is politicized, as in the Soviet Union it is, the political system goes far beyond the constitutional and governmental institutions to which it is so largely confined in the liberal-democracies. It embraces the entire economic and social and cultural systems as well. Thus three matters have to be considered: the Stalin Constitution of 1936 which rationalized the governmental institutions of the U.S.S.R.; the economic ambit of the state which made the entire operation of industry, agriculture and commerce a part of the government's everyday duties; and the control and manipulation of all means of public self-expression in the interests and the image of the governing few.

(3) *The territorial arrangement of the U.S.S.R.:*
the federation

'The working man has no country', Karl Marx proclaimed. Logically, there was only one, unitary, international proletariat and logically there should be only one unitary, proletarian world state. Nevertheless, the national aspirations of the suppressed minorities of the Russian Empire could not be ignored. Therefore, from the very beginning there was a contradiction in the way the Bolsheviks approached the national problem in the great multinational state they had seized. The national minorities were entitled to a perfect independence. On the other hand, they ought to realize the identity of their interests as fellow proletarians. From 1917 to the Stalin Constitution of 1936, two organizing principles contended – and, effectively, both are realized in the Stalin Constitution. One solution was to grant a measure of cultural and administrative autonomy to the national minorities inside a single state: this was the policy realized in the 1918 Constitution of the R.S.F.S.R., which was the first Soviet Republic to be formally constituted and which served as a model to the later ones. The second solution was to establish and unite various national Republics, constituted on the R.S.F.S.R. model, into a federal union – in which the formal juridical equality of the constituent Republics and the voluntary nature of their union were recognized. This solution was realized in the Constitution of 1924, and perpetuated in the 1936 version. That the two solutions exist in the Soviet Union is a result of the historical circumstances in which it was formed, and to the deep perplexity and self-division on the matter inside the Bolshevik ranks.

The Russian Empire was a unitary and highly centralized state ruled by an autocrat, despite the fact that its inhabitants talked one hundred and one different languages. The Russians themselves formed the majority group: but only just. Of the remainder, constituting a little under half the total, some, like the Poles, were peoples of European and urban cultures; some were wanderers like the Eskimo of the North; others lived in quasi-feudal conditions as in Central Asia. All were subjected to a vigorous Russianizing policy which met with fierce nationalist resistance in Finland, in Poland, in the Baltic states, in the Ukraine, in Bessarabia, to mention only the more prominent areas of discontent. The Bolsheviks themselves called the Tsarist Empire a 'prison house of nationalities' and consequently one of their first decrees in 1917 was the 'Declaration of Rights of the Peoples of Russia'. This proclaimed the equality and sovereignty of the various peoples of Russia, and their right to 'free self-determination including secession and formation of independent states'.

What happened thereafter was due to no logic but to the ebb and flow of the civil war. In the western and south western fringes of the former Empire, in the lands of the Finns, the Baltic peoples, the Poles and the Romanians, the counter-revolution triumphed; hoist with their own petard, the Bolsheviks had no alternative but to recognize, with as much grace as they could muster, the independence of Finland, Estonia, Latvia, Lithuania and Poland. In the area of 'Great Russia', however, the Red Army triumphed, and the so-called R.S.F.S.R. was endowed with a constitution in 1918. This followed the unitary solution for the nationalities: those who lived in compact geographical regions were permitted to form 'autonomous' republics, regions or districts, where the degree of autonomy depended on their respective status – but all of which were only autonomous, not juridically co-equal with the central government.

In the other border territories, however – in White Russia, the Ukraine, the Caucasus and Central Asia, in all of which nationalist sentiment was strong – the course of battle swayed to and fro. In the last resort these areas were won for the Bolsheviks by the successes of the Red Army; but not before their formal 'independence' had been recognized. Hence in 1922, when these areas were all cleared of White Guards, the problem had to be faced of whether to merge them into the R.S.F.S.R., giving them 'autonomy', or whether to federate them, as juridical co-equals with the R.S.F.S.R., into a new *soyuz* or federal union. In the course of the wars, the R.S.F.S.R. had contracted treaties of military and economic alliance with these Republics. These pointed the way to a further union on federal lines and, after much debate and heart searching, this solution was adopted. Inside each of these

Republics, the lesser nationalities were granted 'autonomy' just as they had been inside the R.S.F.S.R.; but between the Republics themselves a federal union was formed. The Union was formally created with the ratification of the new Constitution in 1924, and at that date it consisted of only four Union Republics: the R.S.F.S.R., the Ukraine, White Russia, and the Transcaucasian Federation. In the course of time further Republics were created in Central Asia, and then, after the outbreak of the Second World War, in the border provinces which reverted to Bolshevik rule, namely, the Karelo-Finnish Republic, the three Baltic republics and the Moldavian Republic. By 1953 and the close of Stalin's era, the Union consisted of sixteen Union Republics (one of which, the Karelo-Finnish has subsequently been demoted to 'autonomous' status).

(a) The state organs of the U.S.S.R.

The Union thus comprises fifteen Union Republics. The federal government consists of the two-chamber Supreme Soviet, and the two bodies it elects: the Presidium, which acts on behalf of the Soviet when this is in recess, and the Council of Ministers (formerly the Council of People's Commissars). The federal principle is embodied in all these organs. The Supreme Soviet contains a lower chamber, the Soviet of the Union, elected by the people at large in the proportion of one deputy to each 300,000 voters; but the Upper Chamber, the Soviet of Nationalities, represents all the national units in the Union: each Republic elects twenty-five deputies, each autonomous republic eleven, each autonomous region five and each national area one. Likewise the Presidium, made up of thirty-two deputies including the chairman and secretary, contains fifteen vice-presidents, one from each of the fifteen Union Republics. And likewise the Council of Ministers, a very large body, includes the chairman of the council of ministers of each of the fifteen Union Republics.

The federal principle – the recognition of the 'sovereignty' of the constituent Republics – also affects the types of ministry. Three types exist: the all-Union, or entirely federal, ministries, operating their own offices throughout the Union; the Union-

Republic ministries, which operate through the offices of the corresponding ministry in each of the Union Republics and which are subject to the control both of the federal council of ministers and the Republic's own council of ministers (the so-called 'dual subordination' principle); and the Republic ministries, which fall exclusively under the control of the Republic's own council of ministers. By far the greater number of the ministries are of the first two types; their operation will be mentioned again later.

Unlike the Supreme Soviet of the U.S.S.R., the supreme soviets of the fifteen Union Republics have only one chamber, elected for a four-year term. Like the federal body, however, each of these elects its presidium and its council of ministers to which are subordinated the Union-Republic and the Republic ministries. And inside each of these fifteen Republics lie the various tiers of subordinate soviets. The highest ranking are those of the territories and the regions (*oblasts*). These contain lesser units, those of the areas and districts (*rayons*), which in turn contain borough and village soviets. All these are subordinate to the supreme soviet of the Republic in which they fall. But some of these territories, regions, areas or districts, namely, those inhabited wholly or largely by a distinct nationality, are given a special status. To begin with, some Union Republics contain within themselves 'autonomous republics'. At present nineteen of these exist. The guarantees of their autonomy are these: that the constitution is approved by the federal government, not the Union Republic, i.e., by the Supreme Soviet of the U.S.S.R. and not the Supreme Soviet of the Republic; that the boundaries specified in the constitution can only be changed by the Supreme Soviet of the U.S.S.R., not by that of the Union Republic in which the autonomous republic lies; and that the republic is directly represented in the Soviet of Nationalities of the Supreme Soviet of the U.S.S.R. An 'autonomous *region*' is granted considerably fewer substantive powers than the autonomous republic and the guarantees of its autonomy are reduced correspondingly. Like the latter, it is directly represented in the Soviet of Nationalities, and it is also permitted to communicate directly with the Presidium of the Supreme Soviet of the U.S.S.R., the Council of Ministers of the U.S.S.R. and the Supreme Court of the U.S.S.R. – in short with the main federal bodies. But, unlike the autonomous republic, its 'ordinance' is approved by the Supreme Soviet of the Union Republic in which it lies, and its boundaries may be altered by this body. Finally, the 'national areas' come within the full jurisdiction of the Union Republic, with only one apparent safeguard – that, like the other ethnic areas mentioned, they are directly represented in the Soviet of Nationalities of the U.S.S.R. (although, since this representation consists of only one deputy, the safeguard is clearly nominal).

Now one thing about Soviet federalism is quite clear: up to Union-Republic level, each organ – village and town soviet, district soviet, regional soviet – is entirely subordinate to the next highest one (subject only to what has already been said about the various ethnic units). Thus, at least up to the Union-Republic level, extreme centralization prevails. This is expressed, in a current legal textbook,[14] as the principle of *democratic centralism*. Already familiar to us as operational rule of the C.P.S.U., it now appears as applicable to the governmental units also.

> The principle [states the textbook] takes the following concrete forms . . .:
> 1. Electivity of all organs of state power. . . .
> 2. Responsibility and accountability of lower state organs to higher ones.
> 3. The obligatory nature of the directives of higher organs for the lower ones.
> 4. Control by the working people of the activity of state organs. . . .
> 5. Full conformity of the acts issued by lower state organs to those issued by higher ones.
> 6. Extensive development of local initiative by every state organ within the bounds of its own powers.
> 7. Application of the system of dual subordination especially in the work of executive and administrative organs. . . .

And at page 200, the authors further state: 'There is no need . . . for a higher state organ to interfere in the actions of a lower organ if these actions are lawful and expedient. The acts of higher state organs are, however, always binding upon lower state organs. . . .'

14. Denisov and Kirichenko, op. cit., p. 197.

Now elsewhere the authors say that the federal Union is a 'voluntary union of state formations differing in the national composition of their population', that they are 'organized along the lines of democratic centralism', *but* that the individual Union Republics are 'sovereign' except in respect to the federal matters specified in Article 14 of the Constitution. There is a muddle here; and all turns on whether the Union Republic is to be considered as a 'higher' organ or as a 'lower' organ. If the latter, then it is subject to the democratic-centralist principle, and subordinate in all matters which are either 'unlawful or inexpedient', to the directives of the federal government. In that case the Soviet Union is unitary, not federal. On the other hand, if the Union Republic is considered as one of the 'higher' organs, then it is subject to the control of the federal government only in so far as the Constitution specifies.

The puzzle cannot be settled by legal exegesis. Only inspection can divulge the truth of the matter. And here a sharp distinction ought to be drawn between the juridical position, as laid out in the Constitution, and the administrative practice 1924–57. (The post-1957 situation will be considered in the subsequent section.) Contrary to the view of many authorities on federalism, who regard the U.S.A. federal system as the paradigm state, it seems to me that in *strict juridical terms* the U.S.S.R. is a genuine federation, in that it guarantees the independent juridical status of the Union Republics *vis-à-vis* the federation.

The powers granted the federal government are admittedly much wider than those granted in the U.S.A. As laid down in Article 14, they concede to the Union full powers over all economic processes and resources, over the diplomatic-military-security functions and over social welfare. In addition the Union is granted the power to establish the 'basic principles' governing land tenure; mineral and agricultural resources; education, public health and labour legislation; marriage and family legislation; and the judicial system and the legal codes. Nevertheless the Republics also receive powers. Firstly, they may do anything not reserved to the federal government – though we may well wonder what such matters might be in view of the comprehensive powers granted to the Union. Next, they are empowered to establish their own constitutions, their legislatures and administrative organs. Thirdly, under Article 18 their territorial integrity is guaranteed. Fourthly and fifthly – and in these respects juridically far outrunning the U.S.A. system in the degree of States' rights – they have the right to establish diplomatic relations and to set up their own military formations.

The federal government receives great powers to enforce its views as against those of the Republics; and yet the Republics also receive great powers, far greater than those of the States of the American Union, to resist federal encroachment. The federal government's powers lie in the field of interpretation and amendment. Article 14 (d) gives it the power of 'control over the observance of the Constitution'; there is no independent judicial review of disputes. Article 20 states that, in cases of conflict, the federal law prevails as against the laws of the Republics. As to amendment, this is easier than in the U.S.A.: the Constitution is amendable by a two-thirds majority in each of the two chambers of the Supreme Soviet of the U.S.S.R. (Article 146). But, against this, it can be argued that the individual Republics have effective counter-powers. To take amendment first: the two-thirds requirement could be blocked in the Soviet of Nationalities by 226 votes, i.e., if eleven of the constituent Republics chose to vote together against the amendment. Furthermore, in the Presidium and in the Council of Ministers, where encroachments on states' rights are likely to be engendered or formulated, the Republics are directly represented. But, above all, the most effective of all their powers to resist federal encroachment of even a limited nature is to be found in Article 17: each Republic may, in law, secede from the Union! *If* the Constitution were taken as seriously in the U.S.S.R. as it is in the U.S.A., this single provision would effectively paralyse all federal activity that was not concurred in by each individual Republic, and all the powers and sanctions granted the Union by the Constitution could be thwarted by the mere threat of a Republic to secede! Juridically, therefore, only one conclusion is possible: not that the Soviet Union is a federation, but that the Stalin Constitution is a *federal document*. For, in fact, not only does the Union not act as federations are even minimally supposed to do: it is one of the most rigorously and extensively centralized states in the world. This is due to three spheres of practice: that of legislation, that of administration and that of party control.

The Republics are empowered to legislate on matters not reserved to the federation, namely, on matters 'of Republican importance'. This power might indeed turn out to be considerable. But an analysis of the laws passed by the Kazakh Republic between 1938 and 1957 shows that 'the republican legislation lives mostly according to Parkinson's Law and is concerned predominantly with the administration of the republican apparatus'. The list is as follows:

1. Laws on general matters (flag, alphabet, state structure) 9
2. Laws on administration (division of ministries, committees and town soviets) 56
3. Laws on administrative divisions 634
4. Electoral laws 16
5. Laws on commissions of the soviets 3
6. Laws on economic matters 6
7. Laws on foreign policy 1
8. Laws on titles 35
9. Laws on names and designations 6
10. Laws on structure of the courts, family law 50
11. Laws on labour relations 6
12. Laws on the use of water 2

It should be further remarked that the most important of these laws were passed at the end of the period, between 1956 and 1957, when, as will appear from the post-Stalin section of this chapter, important new powers were conceded to the Republics. Thus, four of the six laws on the economy were passed in this short period, as were all six of the labour laws and fifteen out of the fifty relating to the courts and family law.[15]

Nor do the Republics have much administrative discretion. The language used by Denisov and Kirichenko to describe their functions is instructive (the italics are mine and are intended to

15. These figures and comments are taken from Klaus von Beyme's paper to the sixth World Congress of the International Political Science Association, Geneva, 1964: *Federal Theory and Party Reality in the Soviet Union*.

illustrate how dependent the Republics are on the approval of the federal organs). According to the authors, the Republic government (1) '*approves*' the plan and state budget (which, as will be seen, is centrally formulated); (2) taxes '*in accordance with Federal legislation*'; (3) directs public health, social security and education '*according to Federal legislation*'; (4) supervises *Federal* enterprises; (5) '*co-operates*' in the work of the Union-Republic ministries. The only function, apparently independent of the federal authorities, is that of (6) 'directing the fulfilments of the budgets of the lower organs of government'.[16]

Thus the Republics' legislative and administrative discretions are, alike, trivial. On the other hand the federal authorities' administrative grip on these Republics is formidable. The State Procuracy – an office of legal-administrative challenge and control peculiar to the U.S.S.R. – was and remains a federal responsibility. In addition finance, budgeting and economic planning, all of them federal functions, subjected the Republics, until the partial relaxations of 1957, to a corset of controls. The Constitution vests the federal government with the contracting and granting of all loans; with the direction of currency and credit; and with the approval of the consolidated national budget, together with the determination of which taxes and revenues go to the Union, which to the Republics and which to their local budgets. Thus the Republics had absolutely no financial independence whatsoever – not even to decide how much to allocate to their own local authorities. Such powers were not granted them, as we shall shortly see, till the 1957 reform. And, finally, again till the 1957 reform, economic planning was a central matter, and most of it was administered either by all-Union ministries or by the Union-Republic ministries in which the official was responsible, partly to his own Republic government, but also to the Moscow headquarters.

But in the background loomed, and looms, a far more potent control than all of these: the control that renders the right to

16. Denisov and Kirichenko (op. cit.) mention a further two points – the Republics' supervision of the work of the economic councils and their establishment of legal codes. Both of these powers derived from the 1956–7 reforms and are dealt with below.

independent diplomatic representation, to independent military forces, to free secession from the Union alike nugatory: the party. The party, as had been seen, is a civic army, tightly centralized, responsive to direction from above. This organization, unitary and centralized, controls all the soviets in the fifteen Republics and provides their presidia and councils of ministers. These bodies are perpetually being reconstructed, not by local pressures and processes, but by the Politbureau and Secretariat; furthermore the key party secretaries in the Republics are by no means necessarily natives. On the contrary, they are arbitrarily appointed and recalled. From 1938 onwards there was a Russian at the head of the Ukrainian party; some officials served successfully as first secretaries in a succession of Republics – for instance, Brezhnev, who served as first secretary in the Moldavian and then in the Kazakh Republic, or the Ukranian Ponamerenko who was first secretary of the White Russian and then of the Kazakh Republic. And even in some of the Central Asiatic Republics, which have natives as first secretaries, evidence suggests that the second secretaryship – always held by a Russian – is the more important, controlling security as it does.

The Stalin Constitution, therefore, was a piece of window-dressing. That it is a federal *document* is not in doubt. Still less in doubt, however, was the reality that during the Stalin era (not to speak of the post-1957 period for the moment) the Soviet Union was governed and administered as a single, unitary and exceedingly centralized state.

But this was not the only sphere in which the document was window-dressing. The elective principle, the powers and duties allocated to the state organs, e.g., the Supreme Soviet, its Presidium and the Council of Ministers, were also fictions. They were simply gloves – the hands were the hands of the controlling organs of the Communist Party.

(b) The federal state machinery

Article 30 of the Constitution says that the 'highest organ of state power in the U.S.S.R. is the Supreme Soviet of the U.S.S.R.', and Article 32 that 'the legislative power of the U.S.S.R. is exercised exclusively by the Supreme Soviet of the U.S.S.R.'. The composition of its two chambers has already been noted. The Soviet's term is fixed at four years. At eighteen one has the right to vote. According to the Constitution, candidates may be nominated by any of the mass organizations, for example, trade unions or co-ops, and they may also be put up by the Communist Party – but not by any other political party at all. In practice, as already mentioned, ever since the first elections to the Supreme Soviet took place in 1937, the Communist Party and the leaders of other mass organizations, who in virtually every case are likely to be fellow-members of the Communist Party, meet together in order to decide upon the name of one single candidate to put before the electors. The electors are faced with merely one name, and thus have the alternatives of either voting for that name or of returning a spoiled paper or a negative against it.

Soviet electoral law ensures a much larger potential vote than does the electoral law in most liberal-democracies. In these it is usual to deny the vote to anybody who has not a residential qualification. In Britain, for instance, the register is made up once a year and, to qualify, the potential voter must be resident in one particular area for at least six months. Not so in the U.S.S.R. No matter where the citizen may be, the production of his passport for the appropriate authorities will entitle him to vote in that particular locality. Consequently the electoral list is always 'up to date'. In Britain it is reckoned that at least ten per cent of the people on the register have either moved residence or have died since the last registration took place, and that therefore only nine out of ten of the people registered in the United Kingdom are in fact able (or available) to vote at any particular election. In the Soviet Union the proportion will be one hundred per cent. Every effort is made by the Communist Party, the Komsomol and various other ancillaries to get people to the poll. Officials will even stalk the wards of hospitals in order to secure the votes of those who are sick. The results is a one hundred per cent turn-out. Officially voting is secret, and polling booths are erected to enable voters to cast their vote without the knowledge of the officials. Incidentally, all these are party members: and everybody knows it. In practice the secrecy of the vote is evaded by a very simple device: the election officers accept as valid an unmarked ballot slipped into the ballot box in their presence. It therefore follows that the only people who are likely to go into the polling booth are those who wish to mark their ballot in a way hostile to the single and official candidate. This, in itself, affords the presumption that those who vote in secrecy are hostile to the régime, and deters them very effectively. The result of these processes is a turn-out which seems incredible by any kind of liberal-democratic standard. In 1958, for instance, the voting in favour of the official candidates was declared to be 99·97 per cent of the total electorate, and in 1962, 99·95 per cent.

The work of the Supreme Soviet was and is a farce. It is supposed to meet twice a year. In Stalin's time (and until quite recently) it met once a year. Even if it meets more than once a year, however, it sits between four and seven days only in the course of the whole year. Moreover it is far too large to deliberate seriously, even if it wanted to. The Soviet of the Union currently consists of 791 deputies and that of Nationalities consists of 652 – a total of 1,443. It is the practice for these two chambers to deliberate jointly, not separately. In fact there is no deliberation – merely acclamation and approval. In the whole course of its history since 1937, never once in the Supreme Soviet has there been a single negative vote, or even a single abstention. In fact the true work of the Supreme Soviet is not in the field of legislation, deliberation and discussion at all, and certainly not in the field of controlling the government. It has two important functions. Its first is to ratify decrees which have been passed by higher organs during the periods when it is not in session. These decrees (or ukases) are far more numerous than laws. During the period from 1938 to 1956, less than twenty-five laws, as such, were passed in all, but many thousands of decrees. Its other task is to elect more operational organs. These are its presidium and the Council of Ministers.[17]

17. In parenthesis, this word 'presidium' which frequently crops up, demands a word of explanation. A presidium is simply, in Soviet parlance, a small and important executive committee. Thus, in the U.S.S.R. the Central Committee of the Communist Party used to have a smaller and more important executive and, as we shall see, the Council of Ministers itself has its own presidium.

The Presidium nowadays consists of thirty-three members: a president; fifteen vice-presidents, one representing each of the Union Republics; a secretary; and sixteen members at large, elected by the Supreme Soviet itself. In theory this Presidium merely acts on behalf of the Supreme Soviet during the intervals when the latter is not sitting. It is charged with a series of most important responsibilities. It issues decrees, it interprets the laws of the U.S.S.R., it convenes and dissolves the Supreme Soviet, it releases and appoints ministers, it awards decorations, orders, medals and titles of honour, it exercises the right of pardon, it appoints and removes the high command, and it can even, in the intervals between sessions of the Supreme Soviet, proclaim a state of war, or general or partial mobilization. It ratifies and denounces treaties, appoints ambassadors and receives them, and it can, in an emergency, proclaim martial law. In fact this Presidium is like the presidency of the U.S.A., but a presidency which is put into commission, a collective presidency rather than an individual one. Effectively, in working practice, the Presidium operates as a small working legislature, with a high degree of cross-membership of the top offices of the C.P.S.U. This is one of the workshops in which draft bills and draft decrees are made. The decrees will be put into effect and ratified by a subsequent session of the Supreme Soviet; the draft laws will either be introduced into the Supreme Soviet on the Presidium's own initiative or, if further discussion is felt necessary, they will be introduced into one of the standing committees on legislative proposals or on the budget which the Supreme Soviet establishes once it comes into being.

The other body which the Supreme Soviet elects is the Council of Ministers, and this is formally responsible to the Presidium. The Council of Ministers is the supreme administrative organ of the U.S.S.R. Its tasks are to co-ordinate and direct the work of all the ministries of the U.S.S.R., to plan the budget, to take measures for the maintenance of public order, to lay down principles of conduct for international relations, to direct the organization of the armed forces and to take all measures in respect of these. Since the sphere of government in the U.S.S.R. embraces the whole of the economic life of the country, the

Council of Ministers is particularly important. But it is an enormous body. Its full membership, which is laid down in Article 70 of the Constitution, is today no less than seventy-one members. This is because there are so many ministries in the U.S.S.R. and so many special boards besides. Consequently this body rarely meets in a plenary session, and when it does it is to hear reports rather than to discuss business. Therefore it too elects a presidium and it is this presidium which effectively carries out its work. It is the Presidium of the Council of Ministers which presides over groups of these ministries and co-ordinates them, supervises them and decides on general questions, which are then funnelled back to individual ministries, boards or groups of these for further amplification. The Council of Ministers can issue administrative decrees, some of which have the immediate force of law, while others, of more general importance, may have to go either through the Presidium or through the Supreme Soviet for ratification. The importance of the Council of Ministers is attested by the fact that its chairman is deemed, in the West, to be the premier of the Soviet Union, and by the fact that in the past the highest ranking Communist Party official has always held this post. Lenin held it, Stalin held it and Krushchev, after being first secretary of the party, also took the chairmanship of the Council of Ministers. And it is an index, perhaps, of instability in the leadership of the Soviet Union if the two top posts in the country, namely, the first secretaryship of the Communist Party, and the chairmanship of the Council of Ministers, are held by different people. (This has been the situation since 1964, with Brezhnev as the general secretary of the party and Kosygin as the chairman of the Council of Ministers.)

So much, then, for the central organs of state, as established under the Stalin Constitution. The decision-making bodies, therefore, are the Presidium of the Supreme Soviet on the one side, the Presidium of the Council of Ministers on the other. Both, by common membership, overlap with the highest echelon of the leadership in the Communist Party; and they exist in order to amplify, to translate into practical administrative or legislative proposals, or language, the directions which come to them through the Politbureau and the Secretariat. They are the glove of which the Communist Party is the hand. These relationships were established in 1936 by the Stalin Constitution. They have not materially changed since his death, and this is why, in the preceding paragraphs, we have dealt with them up to the present day.

(4) *Industry and labour*

Meanwhile the object of Stalin's personalist régime was that the Soviet Union should not so much be rich as be strong. It was in order to create the basis for defence against the so-called 'capitalist encirclement', that Stalin insisted on the crash programme for the construction of heavy industry. Thus was instituted the 'command economy'. The whole economy in the Soviet Union was (and is) in public ownership, and every single process was regulated from above. This apparatus consisted in the first place of a central planning body called Gosplan. It was this which drafted for the Politbureau's approval the general plan for development for the next five years. These general lines having been approved, the plan would then be funnelled down to the ministries for their comments, and from the ministries down to the individual administrative regions used by each ministry, and from those regions down to the trusts controlled by them, and from the trusts to the individual firms which were their components. Then the process would start in reverse as the views of the firms, the trusts, the regions were funnelled back to the ministries and back to Gosplan. In the end the proposals, brought once more before the Politbureau of the Communist Party, represented what was thought to be the workable translation of its views into administrative and economic practice. The ultimate decisions would be taken by the Communist Party leadership working through the Presidium and the Council of Ministers and assisted throughout by the opinions of the planners in Gosplan. Initially these plans were five-year plans which were broken up into annual and later quarterly reviews. Subsequently seven-year plans were adopted.

Now the first implication of planning on this scale is that raw material will be available. In fact the U.S.S.R. is singularly rich in raw materials; perhaps natural rubber is the only serious deficiency in this respect. The second is the availability of labour, and the third is the productivity of this labour with the available raw materials. And it is from consideration of these three components that it is possible for planners to draw up a sort of budget of manpower and materials and to work out what is possible, and in what directions, and in what time.

Engels said that, with the coming of communism, 'the political direction of man gives way to the administration of things and material processes'. This smoothly overlooks the fact that, in a plan so comprehensive and detailed, labour is just one commodity amongst others and that therefore the problem of managing the labour and of getting it to the right place at the right time and with the right skills becomes one of the key questions. It is primarily because it is impossible in the democratic conditions that have obtained in Britain, for example, that planning such as the Labour Party adumbrated from 1945 to 1951 could never be a success. Here labour was not treated as a commodity; it had to be induced to go into the right places at the right times, and the inducements offered were, on the whole, ineffectual. The first problem which Stalin faced in treating labour as a commodity came from the trade unions. It must be noted that trade unions in the U.S.S.R. were almost exclusively the creation of the state. There were indeed trade unions before 1917 and much is made of them and their heroism in communist literature. But industry was only feebly developed in the Russian Empire before 1917 and the trade unions themselves were extremely weak. After the Revolution, the party took it upon itself to see that workers organized themselves in trade unions, and, not unnaturally, their top leadership was Bolshevik. Once the decision to press on with industrial planning at a crash rate was taken in 1928, the leadership of the trade unions, Communist or not, was faced with a crux. Were the trade unions to act towards the state as they would towards a private employer, or were circumstances different? Tomsky, the leader of the trade union movement at that time, took the former view: that the job of the trade unions was to protect the workers and to improve, at all costs, their conditions of pay and employment. This was not the view taken by Stalin or his henchmen. In their view the job of the trade unions was to act as ancillaries to the state, increasing the general level of production; and it was elaborately argued that in this way the trade unions would benefit themselves because their increased output would return to themselves. This is demonstrably untrue, since it is possible for an individual union to secure advantages for itself over and above the general advantage which accrues to the rest of the community. Over this general issue Tomsky was dismissed in 1930; and from that point on, the trade unions became a mere administrative device, an adjunct to the planners in increasing labour discipline and labour productivity. Wage-fixing was laid down centrally by the Council of Ministers and the top leadership of the Trades Union Congress – which was the Communist Party under another hat. It was then broken down locally by the local management and the trade union shop stewards in each individual firm, and collective agreements were then drawn up. But the catch here was that, in so far as rule, piece-rates or bonuses were included in such collective agreements, they had to be approved centrally. In this way, therefore, the decision as to what demands concerning wages and conditions of employment should be satisfied was taken out of the hands of the local firm and fixed centrally. At the same time it was insisted that the trade union leadership in each factory had the positive task of assisting in maintaining discipline and increasing productivity.

Even this annexation of the trade unions did not solve the labour problem. During the First Five-Year Plan a serious labour shortage developed and workers wandered from factory to factory in order to obtain higher rewards. Internal passports were introduced to control them, but with the coming of the Second World War, in 1940, far more severe labour discipline was imposed. All movement was frozen and managers of factories were forbidden to hire any workman without first seeing his passport and noting where he had come from. Furthermore, all technical and skilled personnel were drafted into service. Thirdly, more and more use was made of forced labour from prison camps. The great purges of 1936–8 had turned the prison camps of the internal security force (now N.K.V.D.) into very large establishments. Certainly, it is very difficult to estimate how many people were included in them: captured documents suggest a minimum of one and a half million but higher estimates of some three and a half million seem to be more accurate. In addition to this, a labour levy was imposed on young persons leaving school; this would produce another two to two and a half million persons who could be moved to key points in the economy at the will of the state. In addition, about one million people of minor nationalities were moved out of the range of the invading Germans because their political reliability was suspect, and were put under N.K.V.D. surveillance. It is possible that after the Second World War as many as from seven to fourteen million people were at the disposal of the N.K.V.D., which thus became one of the largest single employers of labour in the whole of the U.S.S.R. And all of these people could be and were funnelled into jobs which needed doing according to the plan, but to which free labour had not gravitated.

Another difficulty in Stalin's five-year plans was the extremely low productivity of the Soviet workman. 'Socialist emulation', as represented in the Stakhanovite movement, was much featured by the Soviet state in an effort to overcome this, but this was increasingly supplemented by a system of rewards and punishments. During this period something like seventy-one per cent of industry was worked on piece-work and the differentials between the earnings of workmen were extremely high. There was no minimum wage and those who could not keep up with the agreed norms of productivity lived below a subsistence rate.

Punishments became increasingly severe, especially under the conditions of war. For lateness at work the punishment ranged from reprimand to dismissal. Dismissal could be extremely important because, under Soviet conditions, the workman at a factory is often entitled to living accommodation, and in this way a great national system of 'tied cottages' had grown up in the Soviet Union. Dismissal from work could therefore mean the loss of living quarters. For those who were persistently over twenty minutes late the punishment was even more severe; penalties could be imposed of either compulsory labour of up to six months at reduced wages, or from two to four months' imprisonment. Most of these measures could be justified by the war emergency, in which the Soviet Union was fighting for survival; but it is very important to notice that they followed a trend which had been in operation since 1930, and that they *remained fixed until the death of Stalin in 1953*.

The result of this great push forward was the creation of a substructure of heavy industry in the Soviet Union which made it a major industrial power within a short space of time. But at the same time the country had to feed itself. The Soviet Union originated as a largely agricultural state. That was not all. The Bolsheviks had come into power very largely by winning the allegiance of the peasantry, but they had not done so by putting forward their own peasant policy: on the contrary, they had won it by putting forward the policy of their allies, the Social Revolutionaries, and that policy was quite simply, 'the land to the peasants'. In fact this was the very opposite of what Bolsheviks thought appropriate or even safe. The one thing they feared was, indeed, the so-called masses of Russia, the peasantry. The peasantry were reactionary, the peasantry were religious, the peasantry on the whole tended to be loyal to old-established customs. The notion that these people should get hold of their own land and establish a 'peasantocracy' in the Soviet Union seemed to the Bolsheviks to be a threat to the establishment of the proletarian dictatorship to which they were dedicated. On the contrary, the important thing, from an economic aspect, was to throw together the peasants' minute plots of land and form them into large farms capable of being farmed by modern methods; this was also politically necessary, in order to control the peasantry and, in a sense, to urbanize it. Between 1924 and 1928, during the whole period of the struggle for succession between Trotsky and Stalin, discussion ranged upon what was the appropriate peasant policy. It was precisely because Trotsky was convinced that the peasantry was a massive conservative force, and that this could not be counter-balanced within the confines of the Soviet Union by the minute industrial basis of the state, that he looked towards the spreading of the revolution into the urbanized countries of the West, such as Germany. Stalin, having decided to cut loose from the notion of spreading the revolution into the urbanized and industrialized countries of the West, was stuck with the peasant problem. And, partly for political reasons and partly for the economic motives which we have described, in 1930 he laid down the policy of collectivization of the farms. Originally this was to be a voluntary movement. The peasants were to be encouraged to join together in collective, co-operative farms. The word soon went down to the party militants in the provinces that if the peasants did not wish to come in to these farms, and most of them did not, they were to be haled in, yea, even by the hair of their head. The way in which this was done and the kulaks were stripped of everything and sent in bullock carts to the labour camps of the frozen north, has been poignantly described in Mikhail Sholokhov's *Virgin Soil Upturned*. Thus millions of families, one in every twenty of the whole population, were in this way despoiled, reduced, dehumanized, in order to serve both the political and the economic objectives of the Communist Party.

But, for two reasons, this policy misfired. The first was that in certain areas, like the Ukraine and the Volga region, the peasants felt that if they were to lose their stock to the collective farms, then they might as well enjoy the satisfaction of eating these animals themselves. And so, during 1932 and 1933, flocks and herds of all kinds were destroyed throughout the southern regions of the U.S.S.R. From the enormous losses of those years the economy of the Soviet Union has still not recovered. The immediate result, however, was that in the bad harvests of 1933 thousands and thousands of peasants who had eaten up their own corn and stock faced famine. Stalin let them starve. It would teach them a lesson. The facts of this enormous famine in the south were first concealed, then glossed over and finally attenuated by Soviet propaganda; but that it existed on an enormous scale is no longer seriously contested by objective students.

The other difficulty of the policy, however, lay in the conditions of collectivization. The huge upsurge of the U.S.S.R. had been based entirely upon naked exploitation of the peasants. Officially, the state was governed by 'the proletariat in alliance with the peasants'. In practice, it was governed on behalf of the proletariat and at the expense of the peasantry. For the system on the collective farms as laid down by Stalin was as follows. The farmers' income was their crop. This they owned. But from it certain deductions had to be made. In the first place, the state fixed a quota of deliveries of farm products at prices which it laid down. It has since been publicly acknowledged in the Soviet Union that these prices were below the cost of production. They were, therefore, a form of theft. Secondly, the state established motor traction stations, which were brigades of tractors and their operators, the latter consisting, for the most part, of party members or people indoctrinated with the party line. The collective farms had to pay these motor traction brigades for the work they did in the harvest. Thirdly, they had to pay a household tax. Only after these three outgoings had been accounted for were they entitled to the residuum. This they were entitled to sell on the free market for whatever it would fetch. Two of the problems of this system were how to split up profits and at what stage the workers should be paid. Clearly, since crops are only gathered once a year, in principle the worker could only be paid out his share of the collective farm's net profit at the end of the year, unless some kind of credit arrangements were made. In most cases the credit arrangements were very bad or non-existent, so that the farmer would labour for several months at a time, perhaps, merely in expectation of what he would receive at the end of the year; and even this, of course, could not be guaranteed in advance.

All this added up to exploitation. The farmer was exploited by the taxes, by what he had to pay for the use of the tractors (a price which was arbitrarily set by the state) and above all because a proportion of the crop was taken from him at prices below the cost of production. This surplus was, of course, required by the state in order to feed the expanding towns with their growing population of factory workers. In revolt against the system, the peasants staged a go-slow. By way of a concession, they were therefore allowed to work, on their own private account, small plots, which in principle were to range between an acre and half an acre and on which they could keep cows, sheep, goats, hens and the like. What they produced in these gardens they were entitled to sell on the free market. Most peasants soon found that it was more profitable to work upon the private plots and sell their produce for what they could get, rather than put in work on the collective farm. (To this day about half of the meat and milk, nearly all of the eggs and much of the fruit and vegetables consumed by the Russian peoples still comes from these small private plots.) In reaction, the government decreed in 1939 that farmers must work a minimum number of work-days on their collective farms, but the policy failed for the war made it impossible to carry out. A vast amount of state land was incorporated piecemeal into these private plots which, in many parts of the Soviet Union, rose to more than their statutory figure. In 1946, with the close of the war, further attempts were made to divert the farmers from their private gardens to the collective farms, also unsuccessfully. In 1947, sharply progressive taxes were imposed on income from the sale of the farm surplus. But this, of course, merely increased the dissatisfaction of the farmers: it blatantly increased the exploitation to which they were subject.

The result, during the Stalin period and to some extent also today, was to stultify food production. Between 1928 and 1959 the population of the Soviet Union rose by roughly fifty per cent, yet the *per capita* amount of grain during that period only kept pace with this rise of population, and the number of cattle raised showed an actual *per capita* decline. There were sixty-seven million cattle in the Soviet Union in 1928, and only seventy-one million in 1959 (the number of cows in 1928 was identical with the number of cows in 1959); the number of sheep and goats had only minutely increased from 115 million in 1928 to 139 million in 1959; the number of horses had actually fallen (36 million in 1928 and only 12 million in 1959). Only in the number of hogs had there been an increase commensurate with the rise of population (28 million in 1928 to 49 million in 1959).

Thus the period was marked by the extension of the state's power over the whole of the economy. This led to the crash expansion of the industrial basis of the state. It also kept the Russian town worker and, more particularly, the village worker on very short commons indeed. It was truly Russia's Iron Age. All of this was paralleled by the increasing interference of the state with the private affairs of the citizens. This is registered by the developments in the field of civil liberties, and the similar developments in the secret police and in internal security organs.

(5) *Civil liberties and the Terror*

The Constitution of 1936 lays down the fundamental rights and duties of citizens. Citizens have the right to work, the right to rest and leisure, the right to maintenance in old age and in cases of sickness and disability, and so forth. These rights are unqualified. But when we come to Articles 125 and 126, which deal with the freedoms of speech, of the press, of assembly and demonstration, and the right to unite in public organizations, the observer will notice that the right *is* qualified. Unlike the preceding articles, Articles 125 and 126 which guarantee these basic freedoms are both preceded by the preliminary statement: 'in conformity with the interests of the working people, and in order to strengthen the Socialist system'. My interpretation, which may at first appear to be hypercritical, is not only borne out by the practice of the Soviet state, but also by the opinions of Soviet commentators. Vyshinsky's *Law of the Soviet State* still circulates as a university textbook: at page 617 the author comments: 'Freedom of speech, of the press, of assembly, of meetings, of street parades and of demonstrations are the property of all the citizens of the U.S.S.R., fully guaranteed by the state upon the single condition that they are utilized in accordance with the interests of the toilers and to the end of strengthening the socialist social order.'[18] And again, at the same page: 'In our state naturally there is, and can be, no place for freedom of speech, press and so on for the foes of socialism. Every sort of attempt on their part to utilize to the detriment of the state – that is to say, to the detriment of all the toilers – these freedoms granted to the toilers must be classified as a counter-revolutionary crime.' In fact, the state censors printing, meetings, and associations.

No private individual may own a printing establishment where labour is employed, simply because no individual may establish any business in which he employs labour. But no individual may

18. A. Y. Vyshinsky, *The Law of the Soviet State*, Macmillan, New York, 1948.

operate a handpress himself either; for the licensing instructions which permit of private enterprise without the use of employed labour specifically exept the operation of any printing apparatus. Thus nobody, either with others or by himself, may operate a printing press or mimeograph machine. As far as those print shops which are state-operated are concerned, they are censored under a law which requires that all matter prepared for reproduction goes to the *glavlit* (censor) prior to its publication. In short there is no freedom of the press in the Soviet Union.

Nor is there free assembly. It is required that all public meetings be licensed, whether held indoors or outdoors. Nor is there freedom of association. Every association has to be licensed, no matter what the purpose for which it is formed. Its constitution must be deposited at the offices of the Public Security of the area in which it is founded and the security officers may be present at any time during its meetings. Thus there is no opportunity for the Soviet citizen to print, to assemble, to form associations without the prior permission of the state. There is no opportunity, therefore, for any spontaneously formed associations in the Soviet Union; such an opportunity is, by contrast, the basic axiom upon which the liberal-democratic state is founded. Finally, as far as freedom of speech is concerned, this is governed by the courts, who may apply the criminal code if they think that freedom of speech is directed against the socialist order. (This we will deal with in more detail below.) Thus, during the Stalin régime, the Communist Party, led by Stalin, effectively suppressed all chance of private self-expression, of private assembly, of private associations. The state controlled the very existence of these and, if they did exist, their day-to-day operation. At the same time it was not just repressive. For it also controlled all the print shops and all the media of mass communication – the newspapers, the magazines, the cinemas, and subsequently the radio and the television. Thus a constant barrage of positive propaganda for the régime accompanied the five-year plans, with the complete suppression of all opposition views. And, finally, to back up what could not be achieved by mere censorship on the one side and positive propaganda on the other, there existed the secret police.

There had been a secret police force in Russia prior to the Revolution. This was the Tsarist *Okhrana*. In 1917, during the conditions of civil war, this was refounded as the revolutionary *Cheka*. In 1922, upon the founding of the Soviet Union, its name was changed to the G.P.U. – the State Political Administration. At that time its operations were mostly conducted against the N.E.P.-men, against the old intelligentsia, and against the kulaks, the million families who were despoiled and expelled from their homes. In 1934 the name of the G.P.U. was changed to the N.K.V.D. – the People's Commissariat for Internal Affairs. But from 1934, instead of largely confining itself to the counter-revolutionaries, the remnants of the *bourgeoisie* and the rich peasants, the N.K.V.D. was used by Stalin himself to weed out all potential opposition inside the party which he controlled. The true horrors of that régime, expressed in such books as that by Beck and Godin, *The Russian Purge and the Abstraction of Confessions*, have subsequently become known from Soviet sources themselves. Fabricated evidence; forced confessions; delation of opponents; the use of torture; the wholesale pro-scription not of opponents but of persons accused by others who had been forced to this by N.K.V.D. pressure: these were the order of the day. The climax came in between 1936 and 1938 when arrests amounted to millions. Zinoviev, Kamenev, Smirnov, Piatnikov, Radek, Sokolnikov, and then finally the highest ranking officers of the armies, such as Tukhachevsky and Yakov, together with those former collaborators of Lenin and Stalin, Bukharin and Rykov – all of these were brought to trial during these years, and nearly all of them were shot. The charges brought against them included collaboration with Trotsky (then in exile in Mexico) and collaboration with the Nazi High Com-mand. It was said that in the event of a Russo-German war they planned to open the front to the Nazi armies, that they sought not only to overturn Stalin and his government, but to reintro-duce capitalism into Russia. Since that date the untruth of these charges, indeed their absurdity, has been openly acknowledged even in the Soviet Union. It was first acknowledged in Krush-chev's 'secret speech' of 1956, which gave accounts of how the false confessions had been extracted, and subsequently most of the victims, though not all, (notably, not Trotsky) have been rehabilitated by name.

In this way, by 1939 Stalin and a few upper officials of the party, together with the secret police apparatus, had established a virtual reign of terror throughout the U.S.S.R. Henceforth all voices were stilled. The whole of this vast-ranging state apparatus was brought entirely under the hand of one man and his groups of personal collaborators – Stalin and his circle. In these circumstances, everybody, even in the party itself, shut their mouths. Not merely had the party lost nearly a third of its members between 1936 and 1939, but henceforth the elective principle was set aside in favour of a covert, appointive principle. The Congresses were not duly convened; the Central Committee did not meet; and on the eve of Stalin's death the members of the Politbureau, the highest ranking body of the C.P.S.U., went in daily fear of their own lives.

In this way Russia conformed in every major respect to the model of a totalitarian state. All opinion was politicized, all politics was reduced to one single standpoint. This single standpoint was reduced, in turn, to the standpoint of one individual and his knot of personal collaborators. And this policy was radiated throughout the whole of society in the Soviet Union by means of the party members, who had been reduced to a state of abject terror and blind obedience through the purge that had overtaken their comrades. It was received by the common people partly through the absence of any opportunities for complaint, partly as a result of the vast barrage of propaganda which accompanied it and, finally, through the fact that in the last resort there was an omnipresent secret police. This régime continued with no mitigation after the war. Indeed in 1952–3, with the so-called 'doctors' plot', it looked as if a further purge was on the way. Only with the death of Stalin in 1953 did a new chapter open in the life of this totalitarian state.

IV. KRUSHCHEV'S RUSSIA AND BEYOND: 1953–69

Sixteen years have now elapsed since Stalin's death. In these years the harshness of his system has been relaxed: the security organs have been brought under the control of the Politbureau, consumer goods are more readily available, the labour laws are much eased, the farmers are less exploited, the party rules are more overtly observed, the criminal code is less punitive and criminal procedures are far less arbitrary. But in all its essentials his system still remains. Measures taken to revitalize the elective principle in the party, particularly Rule 25, which, it will be remembered, was intended to secure a rapid turnover of party officials and committee-men, have been repealed. Others, to give more power to the Union Republics and to decentralize economic decision-taking, were first eroded and some of them were later repealed. The weight of the *apparatus* – the party bureaucracy and also the state bureaucracy – seems to have been too heavy to be altered easily. And for the rest, the essential features of Soviet totalitarianism – the monopolistic, monolithic and utterly pervasive dominance of the party over the whole of society, the political police, the politicized army – have remained unchanged and, if the Programme of the C.P.S.U. of 1961 is a true guide, are destined to remain so for ever.

(1) *Chronology* 1953–69

Stalin's personalist system endured in all its rigour for eight years after the close of the Second World War. That conflict had inflicted enormous losses on the U.S.S.R. She had lost one-tenth of her population, two thousand towns and seventy thousand villages, and factories that had employed four million workers. Of her railway network, never too good, two-fifths had been destroyed. Steel was produced at little more than one-half of its pre-war level, oil was much the same, pig iron was about twenty-five per cent down and, in 1945, farm production, never high, was only sixty per cent of the 1939 level. Exhausted by the horror years of the war, the population was ready to relax. It was not permitted to. Instead Stalin plunged it into yet another five-year-plan, to make good and even surpass the pre-war levels of heavy industry, and to this end all the forces of the totalitarian state were harnessed. And so the Iron Age continued. The harsh labour laws remained in force; the peasantry continued to be exploited;

the ubiquitous security forces, now called the M.V.D., headed by Lavrenti Beria, maintained and even extended their vast empire of slave camps, so vividly described by Solzhenitsyn in his *A Day in the Life of Ivan Denisovich*; and the atmosphere of frozen terror remained. In 1947 Zhdanov, head of the Leningrad apparatus, led the party into an attack on the writers and the intellectuals. In 1949 the 'Leningrad affair' sparked off a purge of the top leadership which involved the secret execution of such eminent members as Voznesensky, Kuznetzov and Rodionov. The party, now swollen to six million members by the wartime accession of two million new members, remained a pliant instrument. No Party Congress had been convened since the Eighteenth in 1939 and Stalin never bothered to convene even the Central Committee. Everywhere electivity had been very extensively replaced by nomination. The centralist principle had completely triumphed over the democratic one, and the party served merely as a transmission belt for the wishes of the Politbureau and Secretariat – which in the circumstances meant Stalin and his reigning favourites.

Not till 1952 was a Party Congress finally convened, thirteen years after the last, although the rules laid down that the Congress must meet every four years at least; and on its last day the first premonition of an approaching purge appeared. Summoning the newly 'elected' Central Committee of the party, Stalin denounced to it two of his oldest associates – Molotov and Mikoyan. Some two months later the new wave of terror appeared imminent: nine eminent doctors were publicly accused of systematically mistreating their high-ranking patients, including Zhdanov, and bringing about their deaths! This was the 'doctors' plot' and, if Krushchev's 'secret speech' of 1956 is at all credible, it struck panic into the hearts of Stalin's nearest associates who feared that they were to be associated with the guilt of the 'plotters' and summarily executed – others had been executed before them, with their acquiescence. But, within two months, Stalin was dead.

It would seem that for a space, throughout the Union, it was as if the sun stood still. Certainly the Politbureau feared widespread disorders. Hastily a temporary triumvirate was formed:

but from that point the struggle for succession was open.

Power was assumed by Molotov, an old Bolshevik who had survived the purges and had served as foreign secretary; by Malenkov, first secretary of the party; and by Lavrenti Beria, the head of the M.V.D. But the situation was unstable. First, by means so far unknown, Malenkov, who immediately assumed the post of chairman of the Council of Ministers as well as retaining his position of first secretary, was induced to yield up the latter to the former head of the Ukrainian apparatus, Nikita Krushchev. Then, some five months later, Beria was taken out and shot; he was accused of a crime as fanciful as those with which he had charged the victims of the pre-war purges – that ever since his earliest days of working with the Bolshevik organizations in the Caucasus he had in fact been a spy in the service of British intelligence! With him were shot a number of his close collaborators; the M.V.D. was reorganized and brought under the direct control of the Politbureau[19] and Secretariat, where it has since remained; and a widespread amnesty broke open the prison camps for all but the most hardened criminals and a few of the most redoubtable opponents of the régime.

From this point developed a covert struggle for supremacy between Georgi Malenkov and Nikita Krushchev, unresolved until 1957. It was certainly a struggle of personalities; but it was also a struggle over principles and issues. And these were far reaching. What was the future role of the party? Was it to remain the servile bureaucracy into which Stalin had converted it, or was it to be re-energized, and if so how? What was to be the role of the consumer? Was the Union to continue to pile up steel, cement, coal, oil, or at last to turn some of the products of her factories over to the public? What was to be the future of industrial planning, now centred on the vast bureaucratic ministries and their trusts in Moscow? How could the desperate food shortages be alleviated? In the sphere of cultural life and the realm of ideas, reduced by the party to arid Byzantinism, was control to continue or was there to be a 'thaw'? On all these issues, the different forces and the different personalities changed their views and their partners from time to time. In the end it

19. At that time and until 1966, this was known as the Presidium.

was Krushchev who won. But he enjoyed his supremacy only seven years, from 1957 to 1964; and when he was deposed much of his policy was undone.

In February 1955, publicly, Malenkov was forced to resign from his chairmanship of the Council of Ministers. In his place Bulganin, a political general, took the post. Thus began the Krushchev–Bulganin alliance. Then, just one year later in February 1956, at the Twentieth Party Congress, Krushchev made his celebrated 'secret speech'. He roundly indicted Stalin for his crimes in the purges of 1936–9 and later. He denounced him for failure to comprehend the Nazi menace, to take proper steps to defend the country and to conduct the Great Patriotic War. In place of Stalinism and its cult of personality, Krushchev promised a new course for the party, collective leadership and 'revolutionary legality'.

One year later, again in February, Krushchev raised a fresh issue. This was the future of industrial reorganization and at this, it appears, a group of the Politbureau rebelled. They were led by Molotov, who was joined by certain old Stalinists, such as Kaganovich, and in the last resort by one of the new men, Shepilov. They formed a majority. But Krushchev, who as first secretary had taken great pains to pack the Central Committee with his followers, was able to secure the convening of a meeting of the full Central Committee. There he was able to persuade the Central Committee that he was in the right and his opponents in the wrong! From that point on, his opponents were condemned and denounced as an 'anti-party *bloc* of splitters'. In this crucial matter the support of the army under General Zhukov seems to have turned the scale.

Within six months, in July 1957, the whole of this 'anti-party *bloc*' had been removed from the Politbureau, which Krushchev packed with his own supporters, mostly from the Secretariat, while Zhukov was given a place in the Politbureau – the first time a high-ranking general had ever held this place. Krushchev's position was now secure. Alarmed at Zhukov's attitude towards party control of the army, where the general sought to limit party activities, Krushchev felt strong enough, by the end of 1957, to force him out. Not only was he removed from the Politbureau, he was demoted and sent to some minor command in the middle of Asia. From that point on, the attacks on the so-called 'anti-party *bloc*' were continuous. They were renewed in December 1961 at the Twenty-second Congress of the Party, where it was clear, from the way in which Krushchev's remarks were received, that the whole of the party as represented in the Congress was now solidly behind him.

This position was only terminated in October 1964, when, in another surprise move, Krushchev himself was removed from his high offices, both as secretary of the Communist Party and as chairman of the Council of Ministers! Once again the circumstances surrounding this removal are obscure. At all events it was now his enemies who carried the day. The Central Committee confirmed his demotion and in his place once again a split leadership emerged with Brezhnev as general secretary, and Kosygin as chairman of the Council of Ministers.

(2) *The general lines of policy, 1953-69*

The policies elaborated during this period proceeded by zig-zags, because personalities intruded. But, briefly speaking, we can say that during this period a number of new directions were struck. Party initiative and risk-taking by individual members of the party was encouraged by re-establishing the Party Rules and by carrying them out. At the same time this newly re-invigorated party was thrust forward into open control not only of the state, but of the economy. This led, between 1957 and 1969, to a corresponding demotion of the technocracy, which proliferated in the ministries congregated in Moscow. Simultaneously with this, there had been a general softening of sanctions and an increase in rewards. At the Twenty-second Congress in 1961 all this was rationalized. It was claimed that socialism was at last accomplished and that the Soviet Union was now to move to the second stage, that is towards full communism. In Krushchev's view this would take twenty years.

With it he proclaimed the end of the 'dictatorship of the proletariat'. It was no longer a case of a section of the people having to repress other sections of the population in order to achieve the triumph of socialism: the other sections of the people, the farmers and the intelligentsia, were not hostile elements but allies of the proletariat. This was formulated as spelling the end of the dictatorship of the proletariat, and, in its lieu, the advent of 'the state of the whole people'. This formula, therefore, foreshadowed the long survival of a state apparatus, even under conditions of socialism. In this Krushchev seems to us to have turned his back on Lenin's formulation, which had stated that the state would come to an end as soon as one class had triumphed over its opponents, as soon, in fact, as the classless society had come about. Krushchev stressed what Western observers have always criticized in Lenin's theory of the state, that, given an elaborate and complicated industrial structure, machinery must exist to secure what is produced, where it is produced and how it is distributed, and that for these reasons alone it is necessary to retain a state apparatus. But, although maintaining that the state would have to continue for a very long time in order to exercise these basic economic functions, Krushchev foretold that being a 'state of the whole people' it would less and less need to use coercive sanctions in the future. And he correspondingly foretold that its functions would increasingly be turned over to elected bodies such as the local soviets and the Supreme Soviet, and to mass organizations such as the trade unions and the co-operatives. But, in order to secure that all these should operate harmoniously together, the Communist Party must not merely survive as 'a leading core and guide' of all these organizations: in every respect, as controller of the economy, as the formulator of policy, as the custodian of ideology and as the critic of art and culture, its role must be extended and strengthened.

(3) *The party, 1953–68*

We have already foreshadowed what took place in the matter of the party. An effort was made to reinvigorate it and to restore the confidence of party members after the experiences of the great purge. One way in which this was accomplished was strict conformity to the Rules. Not only have the Congresses been regularly held since that period,[20] but there has even been an extraordinary Congress. Not only have sessions of the Central Committee been held regularly, but sometimes there have even been full transcripts of the proceedings. Safeguards have been built into expulsions and purges from the party. These must be reported to the party's Control Commission before local parties are permitted to carry them out. At the same time, the membership of the party was increased. Between 1952 and 1961 one out of every two of the members was a newcomer. By 1961 one-quarter of the party was of less than three years' standing. Also Rule 25 was introduced, as described at page 378, only to be repealed at the post-Krushchev Congress in 1966.

The substantive changes in the party since Stalin's death do not appear to include any significant strengthening of the 'democratic' element in the 'democratic centralism' formula. They are to be found in the continued great numerical expansion of the membership – some two million new members were admitted between the Congress of 1961 and that of 1966, and the total is now double that of the immediate post-war years; in the greater youth and inexperience of the members; and in the increased emphasis on regular procedures. But these are marginal. Of central importance is the feature which is by no means a product of volition but of the force of circumstances: the greater coherence of the top leadership and the failure of any single personality to command for very long. Collective leadership does appear to have become established, not through lack of personal ambition, but through the multitude of such ambitions and the lesson which each senior party official learned from the Stalin era: never willingly to permit of a situation where their careers and lives were in thrall to any one of their colleagues however pre-eminent he might be.

(4) *Federalism and the federal government*

Elections are still organized as they were for the 1937 election, and the single-candidate system persists. Nor have the federal

20. Not quite, for the Twenty-second took place in December 1962 and the Twenty-third in April 1966 – three months overdue.

organs of government changed their role. They still function as previously described and, indeed, as long as the top leadership of the party takes the effective decisions, so long will they continue to remain otiose.

But in the relations between the federal government and the Union Republics, a degree of decentralization has occurred. Most of this – but not all – was due to the economic reforms of 1957–64 described below. As a result of these, a much larger slice of industrial activity was turned over to the supervision of the Republics, and by the same token they disposed of a far larger proportion of the state budget (namely, fifty per cent) than ever before; moreover, they were at last permitted to allocate their share of this budget between their own needs and those of their local authorities. (Previously, it will be recalled, this allocation had been decided by the federal authorities.) Next, each Republic was at long last permitted to draft its own legal code, while the supreme court of each Republic became, for the first time, the final court for crimes arising in that Republic's territory – provided always that in such cases federal and Republic law did not conflict.

It is vital to notice, however, the restrictions that still remain on Soviet federalism. In the first place, the economic reforms of 1957 were wholly repealed in 1964: once again all-Union and Union-Republic ministries assumed control of industry and the responsibilities of the Republics and the amount of the budget at their disposal were both curtailed. Next, although even in Stalin's day, in 1944, the Republics had been empowered by a constitutional amendment to raise their own armed forces and to conduct their own foreign policy, not one of them does so. The only effect of the amendment – and this is probably what was intended – was to permit the entry of the Ukraine and White Russia into the United Nations as sovereign states, i.e., as faggot-votes for the Soviet Union. Next, the office of Procurator-general, that peculiar amalgam in which an administrator is established to check upon the legality of all proceedings in the courts and in the administration and is thus entitled to challenge all their activities throughout the Union, remains a federal post. And, finally, the control of the party remains as all-pervasive as ever.

(5) *The economy*

For a time, however, it did seem as though a vital change, an enormous measure of decentralization, had been introduced into the administration of industry. One permanent characteristic of the post-Stalin era has been a relaxation of economic tempo and an increased effort to produce more consumer goods. The harsh labour laws have been repealed, the working day has been reduced, a minimum wage has been introduced considerably higher than that which millions of the most unskilled and inept workers were drawing. On the collective farms, as will be seen, incentives are replacing coercion, whose ineffectiveness had become ever more obvious. Attention has at last been riveted on housing, the vast majority of the population being squalidly overcrowded. A consumer goods industry – watches, champagne, television sets – has been set in train. Efforts are being made to improve distribution and eliminate the queuing for goods which takes hours of every working person's time. But as the economy reached and then greatly surpassed the pre-war levels, so its products became ever more variegated, and Stalin's 'command economy' became less and less capable of managing this now sophisticated and advanced industrial system. It was over his reforms in its administration that Krushchev made enemies of the 'anti-party *bloc*' in 1957; and it appears to have been the rashness of his reforms that led to his deposition by Brezhnev and Kosygin in 1964: the former was the chairman of the Presidium of the Supreme Soviet, the latter, significantly, the head of Gosplan, the central state planning agency, whose functions were severely restricted by the Krushchev reforms.

For one of the greatest problems of Soviet industrial administration turns on a perennial problem of public administration in general: namely, the clash between functionalism and regionalism. The 'command economy' was functionalist: most of industry fell under the control of highly centralized federal ministries whose offices and factories operated throughout the whole Union. Given the continuous shortages of manpower and materials in the Soviet Union, each ministry had long learned the necessity and the art of controlling everything needful for the continuous and efficient functioning of its plants, from the provision of labour and raw materials at one end of the process to the control of retail outlets at the other. Consequently, in any particular area there existed side by side enterprises which, because they fell under the respective control of different ministries at Moscow, would in fact give each other no co-operation. The result of this was an enormous increase of red tape, since requests from a local firm had to go all the way up to its Moscow headquarters, and be transmitted from there to the headquarters of another ministry in Moscow, and thence be transmitted back to the adjacent factory, before any local collaboration was possible between the two firms. By the same token there was also a fantastic duplication of demands upon freight services – and in these the Soviet Union is fairly backward.

To meet these problems, Krushchev envisaged the wholesale break-up of these great centralized ministries in Moscow and the transfer of their work to highly autonomous local councils. The Union was divided into over a hundred geographical areas, in each of which a committee, representing all the industries in the area, was to integrate the local economy. In so far as they fell within the jurisdiction of Union Republics, these committees were initially made accountable to the Union Republics.

The results of the change were, first, to increase party control, for, in so far as an area fell inside the area of a given Union Republic, it was automatically presided over by the local party chairman. This therefore gave the party very much stronger control over industrial activities than had been possible previously when control was held by powerful members of the federal Council of Ministers. A second result was more disappointing. Certainly the committees provided well co-ordinated services inside their respective areas, but these refused to collaborate with adjacent areas. They became autarkic! Consequently, in 1962, their number was sharply reduced and their area much enlarged, almost doubled, while, in 1963, a new central body was established – the Supreme Council of National Economy. This council reported straight to the Council of Ministers, and both Gosplan (responsible for long-range planning) and the Council of the National Economy (which dealt with current production) were subordinated to it. Thus the pendulum had already swung back towards some measure of centralization. But it was not deemed sufficient, and for this reason, if for no other, its architect had to go. With Krushchev deposed in 1964, his successors began to re-establish the old system of Union and Union-Republic ministries for some of the sectors of heavy industry, particularly those concerned with military procurement, and in 1966 the entire Krushchev system was scrapped. The system of Union and Union-Republic ministries has been reintroduced in its entirety. The only concession made to economic decentralization is a qualified experiment, confined to a few limited sections of the consumer industry, of 'Liebermanism': i.e., an effort to control the degree and quality of firms' production by the demand of the market, and to correlate firms' bonuses with the profit which they earn. That such an experiment should be undertaken is a tacit recognition that the problem of economic planning has changed, in that the 'command economy', suitable for producing a few standard raw materials and industrial products, has become inflexible and wasteful. That the Krushchev reforms have been repealed, as Party Rule 25 has been repealed, shows, however, that the industrial bureaucracy, no less than the party bureaucracy, exerts a *vis inertiae* that is not easily overcome.

Meanwhile reforms in agriculture have been carried out. This still remained the Achilles' heel of the Soviet economy. One method by which the ever-present grain crisis was to be overcome was the opening up of the 'virgin lands' in Central Asia, areas with a thin top soil but which nevertheless might well support arable crops. Unquestionably these virgin lands have added greatly needed supplies of grain to the Russian harvests. But their production is patchy and they are subject to drought and bad crop failures. At the same time, however, Krushchev recognized, belatedly, that the collective farms needed remanagement. He acknowledged, too, that Soviet industrialism had hitherto rested upon the exploitation of the collective farmers. From 1956–7 a set of far-reaching reforms was introduced, and these were capped in 1961. Briefly, these reforms amounted to a better deal in cash terms for the farmers. Better prices were offered for all dairy products, whether these were on the state quota or whether they were offered on the free market. An end was put to the so-called 'progressive' quota sanctions, for what had happened in the past was this: since a state quota had to be exacted from all farms and since some of the poorer farms simply could not manage it without eating up their seed corn, the quota collectors had gone back to the more well-to-do farms and taken more than they were entitled to. Steps were now taken to end this. Furthermore, in order to prevent the workers from deserting the collective farm for their own private plots, much higher pay was offered for *kolkhoz* work. On the other hand, this was balanced by a much higher household tax for their failure to fulfil their norm of work on the farm. Finally, the credit system of the farms was changed. Farmers were now to receive credit each month rather than having to wait longer periods – sometimes to the end of the year. Since 1946 much effort had gone into introducing P.P.U.s into the collective farms and this rendered the job of the motor traction station teams, mostly composed of Communists, otiose from a political aspect. Accordingly, these were now abolished and their machinery was sold to those collective farms which chose to bid for them. At the same time an effort was made to locate local responsibility for farm production in the hands of the local party secretary.

A further stage in encouraging the collective farmer to produce more by offering him more for his product came in 1961. Until this date, although state benefits for sickness, unemployment and retirement had been offered to all industrial workers, they had never been offered to the collective farmer. This was now redressed: at the end of 1961 the collective farmer was recognized as being on a par with his industrial colleague in the towns. Restrictions imposed by Krushchev on the ownership of private livestock, bitterly resented, were relaxed after his fall in 1964; prices paid to the farms were further increased in 1965; and, most important of all, from 1966 the collective farmer became entitled to a guaranteed minimum wage. Farm incomes have risen sharply.

(6) *Coercion*

So far the record of modification has been patchy: in the party, more procedural correctness, but little in the way of inner party democracy; in the administration of industry, a return to the *status quo*; in the fields of industrial relations, consumption goods, incentives and earnings, a significant relaxation; in the management of collectivized agriculture, an effort to buy good-will. In brief: the basic system has remained in force, but the carrot is waved more often than the stick. This is indeed the marked feature of the post-Stalin era – and nowhere more so than in the demotion of the secret police and the relaxation of the criminal codes; for, from the execution of Beria onwards, there has been a steady effort to tone down the coercive aspects of the régime and to subject the internal security organs to strict party control and to limit their arbitrary powers.

In 1953 a general amnesty was proclaimed. Some political prisoners were unquestionably not included in this, but the vast aggregates of labourers in the M.V.D.'s labour camps were for the most part broken up and returned to freedom. Many political prisoners also were released, as already mentioned, and after 1956 the rehabilitation of the victims of the purges began. In 1958 these foretokenings of a thaw in the coercive apparatus of the state were carried considerably further by the new Criminal Code of 1958. One of its most instructive aspects is the attention it draws to the policies which had hitherto applied. The 'Kirov Decrees' of 1934 were repealed. Also, it is made clear that in the past the law had been applied by analogy (i.e., if the law failed to specify a certain offence, it was open to the court to argue by analogy with the nearest crime on the statute book, and to punish for that). Again, the security organs had previously been permitted to punish without the sentence of a court. Courts had been wont to sentence when they deemed the accused to be a member of that category called 'an enemy of the working class'. It had also been permissible to find a prisoner guilty solely in the light of his past activity or associations with some criminal milieu, irrespective of the specific crime of which he had been accused. Again, in the past, treason was a crime even if it was unpremeditated. Now, under the new Criminal Code, all of these rules were abolished.

On the other hand, the code laid down positive crimes and the penalties for them. It is high treason to flee abroad or to refuse to return to the U.S.S.R., and the penalty ranges from fifteen years imprisonment to death. The crime of sabotage 'for the purpose of weakening the Soviet state' is again punishable by fifteen years or the death penalty. 'Anti-Soviet agitation and propaganda' is also a crime punishable by imprisonment for six months to seven years. This crime is defined as 'agitation or propaganda for the purpose of undermining or weakening Soviet rule and of committing especially dangerous crimes, the dissemination for this same purpose of slanderous fabrications defaming the Soviet state and social system, or the dissemination, production or keeping of literature of such content for the same purpose'.

Some of these crimes with their heavy penalties are exceptional by liberal-democratic standards; in no liberal-democracy is it high treason to flee abroad or to refuse to return to one's country; in none is the death penalty, or even a fifteen-year prison sentence, exacted for sabotage; and certainly in none can one be imprisoned for six months to seven years for agitation or propaganda to undermine the régime of the day. Thus despite the great liberalization, it is a liberalization only in contrast with what occurred during the Stalinist régime. It still gives the security organs and the courts ample power with which to repress anti-governmental activities. And, of course, the laws relating to censorship, and the laws restricting the freedoms of speech, of press, of association and the right to free election, still remain in their full force.

Nor is this all, for in certain respects the Criminal Code has invented new crimes and stiffened existing penalties. 'Social parasites', for instance, are defined as persons living with no evident means of income – loafers and black marketeers evidently – and under a law of 1961 they may be sentenced to banishment to remote areas for up to five years. And in 1961 also, it was enacted that certain forms of 'theft of socialist property', e.g., currency violation, were punishable by death.

(7) *Totalitarianism?*

When all the measures of liberalization are taken into account, the basic features of the Stalinist system still remain. To begin with, the state is ruled by a self-perpetuating bureaucracy which does not share its power in any significant respect with the remainder of the population. It is true that Nikita Krushchev foretold the day when more and more governmental responsibilities would be devolved upon the soviets and the 'public organizations'; but this has not yet occurred on any scale and, in any case, in that same speech at the Twenty-second Party Congress, he made it bluntly plain that the corollary of such devolution was that the party would control these organizations even more closely than heretofore. Again, it is true that both the worker and the farmer have received greater economic rewards; but the former is still denied any effective control over the level of his pay, not to speak of his continued incapacity to strike to enforce his demands; while the farmer still remains shackled to his collective farm.

Nor has totalitarian control over the arts and literature been relaxed. Certainly, a number of highly controversial books, critical of the régime, have from time to time appeared with official approval: for instance, Dudintsev's sombre indictment of the bureaucracy, *Not by Bread Alone*, and Solzhenitsyn's painful *A Day in the Life of Ivan Denisovich*. But both of these served Nikita Krushchev's turn (this is why he permitted them to appear), as alleged indictments of the Stalinist régime which he had denounced. Against this must be set more characteristic acts: the persecution of Pasternak after his *Dr Zhivago* had appeared in the West; and the trial and condemnation of Daniel and Sinyavsky in 1966, the suppression of Solzhenitsyn's writings, in 1969; the persecution of intellectuals in 1969–70. And Krushchev, in his speeches at the Twenty-second Congress, argued that such control over artistic, cultural and intellectual expression would have not only to continue but to be intensified. Nor are foreign ideas permitted free expression. The party still controls every conceivable medium of information; even foreign books may be admitted only by the permission of a special office, while travel abroad continues to be restricted to those favoured by the bureaucracy.

Finally, the national minorities continue to be denied full self-expression. On the ground of combating *bourgeois* nationalism, purges continue throughout some of the Republics. The deputy chairman of the Latvian council of ministers was dismissed in 1959 because he had allegedly complained that the massive immigration of Russians into his country was swamping its native population. Among those who suffered with him were the local chairman of the Trades Union Council, the first and second secretaries of the Komsomol and many others. Again, in 1962 the prime minister of the Kazakh Republic (where Russians are now the largest single ethnic group) was dismissed from his state and party posts on the charge that he had uttered nationalist sentiments in drinking parties with other Kazakhs, all of them party officials.

Altogether, the basic features of Stalinism remain. In what sense, then, can the U.S.S.R. be said to conform to or approach the totalitarian 'type' as described earlier in this book? There a totalitarian state was described as a state which directed the whole of society, no significant private areas existing, and where opinion was reduced to one single viewpoint and no others were tolerated. In both these respects the U.S.S.R. comes close to the model.

This can also be seen by contrasting the system with the liberal-democratic model. In the latter, the moral basis of government was said to derive from the free play of freely formed associations, either in consensus or otherwise. In a totalitarian state, it was argued, the moral basis was an artifact constructed by the government itself and radiated into mass associations which were likewise artifacts of the government. The U.S.S.R. certainly conforms to the model in this respect. Again, in the liberal-democratic state, the consensus or dissensus was said to be the end result of the free play of freely formed associations, whereas in the totalitarian model it was said to be artificially induced. Such is the case in the U.S.S.R. In the liberal-democratic state, the various groups and associations in society were said to be the sources and springs of activity from which the government itself emanated, whereas in the totalitarian model they were but the receptacles or agents of the government's activity. This is precisely what they are in the U.S.S.R. Finally, in the totalitarian model, it was argued that the channel of state activity was the tightly disciplined party of which the government was both head and guide, just as the party in its turn is the head and guide of all other associations. Again, this is fully true of the U.S.S.R. In each one of these major respects, therefore, the government of the U.S.S.R., for all the softening of the régime since 1953, exhibits the essential features of the totalitarian state.

Part Four

AUTOCRACY AND OLIGARCHY

Chapter 9

THE FAÇADE-DEMOCRACY

I. FAÇADE-DEMOCRACY AS A SYSTEM OF RULE

BY façade-democracy I mean a system where liberal-democratic institutions, processes and safeguards are established by law but are in practice so manipulated or violated by a historic oligarchy as to stay in office. The structure of the government is usually collegiate but for a time it may be superseded by an individual autocratic ruler using similar methods to perpetuate himself. Historically, this type of rule is associated with the social status and economic predominance of a traditional class and is the device by which they made the legal code of civil liberties and popular suffrage serve to perpetuate their own traditional power. The social correlates of *façade-democracy* were, and to some extent remain, what we might call 'the old oligarchy' or 'the old autocracy', as contrasted with the neo-oligarchy and neo-autocracy of the *quasi-democracy*.

In appearance the 'old oligarchy' or 'old autocracy' is a façade of liberal-democratic forms including a representative assembly; the reality is government by a loose confederation of 'bosses', or sometimes by a single super-boss – whereupon the régime temporarily becomes personalist. These bosses are those who by reason of their social and economic status can 'deliver the vote', and the elimination or falsification of the vote is the basis of the system. We have seen (Chapter 2) that the constitutive freedoms which are prerequisites of a liberal-democracy are the freedoms of speech and press, of association and of elections. If any of the first three are curtailed or abolished, the elections become *pro tanto* less than a true expression of public opinion. If, in addition, the elections themselves are falsified, then those in office perpetuate their hold on it or freely dispose of it on the strength of an entirely fictitious claim to the support of public opinion. In one way or another this is precisely how façade-democracy operates.

In his great work, *The Structure of Politics at the Accession of George III*, the late Professor Namier commented that the British parties of the eighteenth century bore a marked resemblance to those of Yugoslavia at the time he was writing (1930). And façade-democracies in their most sophisticated form resemble the British political system of the eighteenth century. In a small number of countries, façade-democracy has indeed been the parent of liberal-democracy. The existence of a socially dominant class, a narrowly restricted franchise and the lack of good communications are preconditions of façade-democracy. These existed in Britain in the eighteenth century, in continental Europe till well into the nineteenth century but in many countries of the Third World they still persist.

The French parliamentary experience until the advent of the Third Republic, Italian parliamentarism until the extension of the suffrage in 1911 and British parliamentarism until the Reform Act of 1832 and in some respects even till the Second Reform Act of 1867 – all had a great deal of the façade about them. The British experience is the most instructive because it started so much earlier than any other country. Until at least as late as 1832, the British political system though liberal, was not democratic. (A sharp contrast to the new Latin American republics of that era which were nominally democratic but never liberal.) Until 1830 no government had ever lost an election; on the contrary governments 'made' elections. Under the old potpourri of local franchises that constituted the 'unreformed' franchise up to 1832, election to the House of Commons rested in the hands of certain groups, namely: individual very wealthy noblemen, mostly of Whig family connexion; pettier but locally powerful notables, the so-called 'squires', predominantly the Tory or 'Court' party; certain town oligarchies – the close corporations; the government – in certain constituencies, e.g., dockyard constituencies; and for the rest, wealthy individuals who could buy a way into a disposable seat.

Contests there were in plenty, where a great landowner would contest debatable country with a rival – much as rival 'colonels' would contest with each other in the rural hinterlands of Brazil till very recently; and a few constituencies, with a popular suffrage, were genuincly 'open'. But until 1830, the Cabinet of the day, a coalition of the more powerful of the great landowners, could, assisted by their own wealth and the patronage which any government enjoyed in certain of the constituencies, reckon on securing the election of a favourable House of Commons. Once this had met, the Cabinet used military and civil commissions, ennoblement, and lucrative posts and contracts for M.P.s or their clients to help form a majority in the House and keep it together. The political upsets that occurred, occurred inside the House – through a Cabinet's failure to keep its supporters in line by these means and through the rivalry and subsequent self-division of the original group of notables and the consequent formation of differently constituted coalitions. That such governments were broadly in line with public opinion was not due to the electoral system at all, but to the liberal features in the Constitution: the absence of a standing army or a professional police; the jury system; and the extremely decentralized structure of government, in which the administration of public order, criminal justice and the social services was the responsibility of the local squires and the elective parish councils. When the franchise was reformed in 1832, it was tidied up indeed, but confined to the wealthier 750,000. The counties were still controlled by their local magnates, but the towns, with a greatly increased number of seats at their disposal, could be only marginally influenced by a Cabinet. Henceforth, despite the fact that ballot was by show of hands and that bribery and corruption were widespread, no outgoing government could guarantee its return to office. The system, operating through the alternation of two loose and locally based 'parties', still worked to the advantage of the old landlord oligarchy but gave the new industrial and commercial interests a decisive voice. It was not until the electorate was further enlarged in 1867 to take in large numbers of urban industrial workers and, shortly afterwards, the secrecy of the ballot and effective anti-corruption laws were introduced, that the transition to liberal-democracy was finally made. And the democratic element was then extended more and more, through successive acts widening the franchise, from 1884 down to 1969, when the voting age became eighteen years.

But until recently most of the Third World was as though stuck in the first, pre-Reform Bill stage of British parliamentarism – compounded, however, by a marked scarcity or total absence of indigenous liberal institutions; a disregard for civil liberties; a high degree of formal centralization; assiduous and ruthless police; and the pretensions of large standing armies. This not inaccurately describes the situation up to the turn of the century in all the Latin American republics, in the Balkan states and in the one or two other states, like Iran, which comprised the Third World of that era. A change only set in after the first decade of the twentieth century and has, piecemeal, run a course since then. But still, as we shall see, some seven states might still be regarded as façade-democracies.

These remarks should not be taken as meaning that states which have ceased to be façade-democracies have all followed the British pattern of evolution and become liberal-democracies. Some, such as Chile and Uruguay, have indeed evolved in this way, but the majority are currently military autocracies or quasi-democracies. Furthermore, change is not uni-directional. Because some façade-democracies have evolved into liberal-democracies, it does not follow that a liberal-democracy cannot regress into a façade-democracy. On the contrary, this is a perfectly possible pattern of change, and is precisely what happened in Nigeria between its independence in 1960 and the military revolutions of 1966. It might well be thought, from what has been said so far, that the façade-democracy is not a system in its own right but simply a pathological case of liberal-democracy. This is not so. Whether its supreme direction be collegiate or personalist, the structure of the façade-democracy is cellular, not hierarchical, and clientelist rather than centralized. This is because it is the political projection of the social oligarchy and its profile is therefore that of the social oligarchy – and this, by its very nature, is a geographically dispersed network of social equals, whose power and prestige rests upon their ability to command the vote of their social dependants. It is *cellular*, therefore, because the group of oligarchs in office depend upon the support of their fellows in the provinces, who in turn depend for their control of the vote upon the services of intermediaries. The governing clique grant favours to their provincial colleagues in return for the promise of their blocks of votes and these colleagues pass on a proportion of the favours to their middlemen, who return the service by 'delivering the vote' for the candidate of the governing clique. It is *clientelist* in that each of the actors in the game has a number of clients dependent on him, and they in their turn have more clients – until the level of the electorate is reached.

Perhaps an analogy from a liberal-democracy whose system has already been described may make this clearer: the U.S.A. Mention was made of the 'political machine' which exists in some towns, even today, as well as in rural areas. The old-fashioned machine as it grew up in the nineteenth century, such as Tammany Hall, was based on the control of the votes of new immigrants by various devices: by rendering services, for instance, or by outright bribery. When this resulted in the party winning control of office, the party workers were put on the public pay-roll; and so the party leaders were able to use the public treasury to reward them and to funnel out through them still further favours to the voters. These methods were often supported by others. For instance, the party used its control of office to alter the boundaries in which voting took place in such a way as to increase the number of seats it was likely to win – this was known as the 'gerrymandering' of electoral districts. In certain areas large numbers of opponents could be deprived of their franchise by the imposition of literacy tests or poll taxes. The latter methods have only recently been challenged in the Southern States where 'poor whites' (but, above all, Negroes who could be reckoned to be hostile to the racist policies of the dominant Democratic machines) were turned away from the voting booths in enormous numbers because they could not – officially – read or write or 'interpret the Constitution'. As a result of these and similar practices, then, there used to be, and to some extent still are, pockets of population whose votes can largely or wholly be guaranteed by their oganizer: in short, by the local 'boss'. And this boss, because he could deliver his block of votes in favour of a candidate for the State governorship, or to his party's State committee in favour of a particular presidential nominee, could, if 'his' candidate won, secure concessions for himself and 'his' voters in the shape of local housing projects, public works, or contracts for local firms, which perpetuated his hold on the electors.

But between the Third World and the U.S.A. at least two vast differences existed. In the first place, in the U.S.A., for all that the city machines played an important part in guaranteeing the success of Roosevelt in the presidential elections as late as the 1930s, they are ephermeal and in addition they are swamped by the very large numbers of independent voters up and down the rest of the country. In the façade-democracies of the Third World, however, their equivalents endured as long as the landed oligarchy itself, and the system was general, not localized, until (as we shall see) the rise of the great cities. Secondly, their 'bosses' were quite unlike the American boss in social and economic status. For the American boss is an entrepreneur – if one likes, he is a man who is making his business out of politics. He is a kind of broker, and may well be a very humble individual who has shown a flair for this sort of organizing and has risen to his position solely by virtue of his skill. His political position does not depend in the least upon his social origin and status. In the façade-democracy, on the other hand, the political equivalent of the American 'boss' was part of a traditional order of society, a member of the historic oligarchy who in one form or another had shaped the government of their country for decades or even centuries. In Latin America they were the great landlords, the *hacienderos* or *fazendeiros*, who owned vast estates and ran them like great manors of the European Middle Ages. In Arab countries great landlords and tribal sheikhs could guarantee the votes of their dependants or their tribesmen. In parts of Africa the chief would likewise deliver the vote of his tribe. In still other areas – in the Sudan, for instance – the oligarch might be able to do so as the leader of a religious sect. In the more urbanized societies these great potentates were supported by smaller fry: the village rich man, the money lender, the local philanthropist, each of whom had a following by virtue of being a big fish in a small and stagnant pond. In the small towns of Mexico, before the 1911 revolution, it could have been the local businessman, as described in Azuela's novel, *The Caciques*. (*Cacique* is the name given to such 'bosses' in Spanish and Spanish-American politics.)

I must stress that such phenomena are by no means absent from many Third-World states which enjoy highly competitive party politics inside a liberal-democratic framework and which I would classify as 'liberal-democracies'. It is the nature of society that sets the style. In largely agrarian societies, with poor physical communications (and hence considerable localism), where primary units such as the family, tribe, caste, clan or *ethnos* are still of major importance – in short in countries as disparate in other ways as India, the Philippines, the Lebanon and Somalia[1] – the bases of political allegiance, and the issues of politics, tend to be those of these local and primary units. Such bases are then built up, cell after cell, into larger agglomerations, into regional or national 'parties'. In such countries, at the local level at any rate, the structure of political party affiliation is *clientelist*; the votes are gathered in for huckstering, in return for local advantages, by a local 'boss', who may or may not be of high social status but is more and more frequently a 'new man' with a flair for political brokerage. To the extent that this is true, then, these 'agrarian democracies', as we might style them, resemble the façade-democracy in being cellular and clientelist.

Furthermore in some such countries the competition for the vote is itself imperfect: that is to say, it is intermixed with manipulation by the wealthy or by the socially powerful or esteemed.

For all that, these agrarian liberal-democracies differ signally from the façade-democracy. In the first place, the manipulation is not exclusively, and not usually even predominantly, in the hands of, or even the interests of, a historic oligarchy; indeed in some states like the Philippines, such oligarchies do not exist as a political factor. Secondly, even if manipulation is to some extent used, it is used by rivals, not by one sole grouping. Among the contenders for office there is genuine competition,

1. In its liberal-democratic phase up to the military take-over of October 1969.

and the local bosses, or 'vote brokers', can and often do shift their allegiance from one set of bidders to the other or others, from one election to another. In brief: it is not a question of a pre-arranged electoral result by a historic oligarchy but one of an open, vigorous and often fierce struggle between contenders who include, or are for the most part, *novi homines*. But the façade-democracy is, simply, the political projection of the social status and economic power of great personages, just as the political parties were in eighteenth-century Britain. They were a self-selected knot of potentates who reached down to the electorate, not for power – for they already held this – but for sacral anointing in popular and national sovereignty. Now there are certainly degrees in aristocracy: but above a certain level there remain only a number of peers. It is this fact that leads to the *collegiate* nature of the façade-democracy. This system by no means entails that the entire oligarchy act as one: on the contrary it entails fierce rivalries and jockeyings for position, but also an extreme unlikelihood of any one of these peers obtaining such pre-eminence that he can permanently destroy the social base on which the power of his rivals rested. Furthermore the system was *cellular* because the potentates themselves, in order to exploit their social and economic position, required the assistance of lesser men to influence or organize the votes on their behalf. And where, as in most instances, physical communication was difficult, the fact that these power bases were distant and regional was another reason why the assistance of lesser men was necessary.

Sometimes, however, the feuds of the potentates brought about such a damaging deadlock as to induce them to acquiesce in the temporary autocracy of one man. Sometimes the feuds erupted into actual fighting; in such cases the leader of the successful military coalition could impose his rule and sustain it by his command of the armed forces: and while some such, like Rosas of Argentina, might be oligarchs, there might be others like Porfirio Díaz of Mexico, a successful soldier of humble origin. And sometimes the going got too hard: the growth of physical communications, the rise of the cities and the spread of literacy, especially, all made it more and more difficult to apply the old manipulative methods successfully. In such cases the oligarchy had to rely increasingly on coercion. As·they did so their dependence on their armed forces increased, until the soldiers were effectively the policy-makers. And in these circumstances it was only a step for the military leaders to push their puppets aside and take over the government in their own name. Façade-democracies often moved into a twilight zone, sharing power with the military, then later being ruled by it.

II. THE METHODS OF FAÇADE-DEMOCRACY

The methods used to guarantee a pre-determined result affect some or all of the constitutive freedoms of the liberal-democratic political process. To begin with, the government may restrict the freedoms of speech and of the press. Sometimes this is managed under executive regulations, and amounts to harassment: the closing of the opposition presses, the denial of broadcasting opportunities; sometimes it is more general and is accompanied by the withdrawal of individual guarantees of the inviolability of the person and domicile. Such blanket suppressions of opposition are, in Latin America, achieved by the incumbent president's declaration of a 'state of siege'. This declaration is designed for use in the case of such calamities as invasion, armed insurrection or some natural disaster such as an earthquake. Its effect is to suspend all the constitutional guarantees of speech, press and assembly. But many Latin American republics have lived for years at a time in an almost continuous state of siege, which has been lifted for only a few days, perhaps for only one day, before elections.

All this is preliminary: the heart of the operation is the manipulation and delivery of the popular vote. First, the opponents of the government may be deprived of a man to vote for: for instance, in 1952 General Odría of Peru, who had seized power by a military coup in 1948, decided to hold elections and to stand as presidential candidate. The largest opposition party, the Alianza Popular Revolucionaria Americana (A.P.R.A.), was already proscribed. Nevertheless, a General Ernesto Montaigne decided to contest the election with Odría. But when he went to present his nomination papers to the electoral tribunal – appointed by General Odría's own government – this body found no difficulty in deciding they were invalid. The elections went off as scheduled and General Odría was triumphantly returned unopposed, on an eighty per cent poll. This device – the disqualification, imprisonment or intimidation of an electoral opponent – is in Latin America (which is rich in such terminology) described as the *candidato único* method – the single-candidate method.

Next, assuming that the opposition have been allowed to nominate candidates – thus conforming, in the sight of the outside world, more closely to liberal-democracy – comes the restriction of the right to vote, accompanied by blandishment and intimidation, by ballot-box stuffing and, in the last resort, by the government's falsification of the count.

In much of Latin America in the past, and in some of its republics to this day, a restricted franchise, together with fear of exposure, proved adequate. It stood to reason that where the electorate in a certain constituency was entirely or predominantly composed of the peasants working on a particular hacienda, the failure of the ranch-owner's candidate could be due only to the defection of his employees. The mere whisper that such defection would be punished by the dismissal of suspects was usually enough to ensure regularity of the vote. But, of course, a large number of the peasantry and villagers could be expected to vote for the ranch-owner's candidate of their own volition. He was a local benefactor and protector, not just somebody to be feared. Where the franchise was restricted, the control of the voters was made that much easier. In Latin America the literacy test is a favourite device for restriction. It means that in the rural countryside large numbers are debarred from voting. Brazil restricts its electorate in this way, as will be seen. So also does Guatemala. There, only the literate may vote in secret. This guarantees the perpetuation in office of the *Ladino* minority, amounting to about two fifths of the population. The remainder, the pure Indians, may indeed vote, but only publicly, in the presence of an official.

Next, intimidation or discrimination may be used at the polling stations. In many countries military cordons have been thrown around them to bar the booths to those not vouched for as 'regular' voters. In Mexico, under the 1857 Constitution, a curious situation obtained which lasted until the 1911 revolution. The rule was that the votes were to be counted by the first three voters to arrive at the polling station – the idea being, presumably, to guarantee impartial scrutiny by leaving the matter to a random group of voters. In practice, of course, a rush was made for the station. The contending factions would struggle among themselves to get there first, and whichever side managed to force its way in would claim to be the rightful tellers – whereupon they would either prevent their opponents from voting or, alternatively, falsify the count. As a consequence, rival parties got into the habit of making a dive for a particular building and, having occupied it, proclaiming it the official polling station. Thereupon they proceeded to count the votes as they came in – to their own advantage of course. Inevitably, all claimed to have won the election. But under the constitution it was the out-going Congress that validated the results in the case of disputed elections. So, such elections having been disputed, it fell to the party controlling Congress to decide and it invariably invalidated its opponents.

This brings us to the last stage in the manipulation and falsification of elections: the mode of validation. In some countries in Latin America this is left to the out-going Congress. In others, as in Nicaragua, it is left to a series of electoral tribunals: in that country each tribunal consists of five members, but the government always has a three to two majority on each of them. In other lands, the declaration of the results is left to the ministry of the interior. In all such cases, it is a simple task for the government to make the results conform to its own desires.

The limiting case of façade-democracy is, indeed, where the government of the day simply fabricates its own set of figures. Until the military revolution of 1958, Iraq provided a copy-book example. The political élite consisted of large landowners, tribal sheikhs, a sprinkling of professional men and wealthy traders, and the military forces. Parties were factions gathered around one or other of the outstanding men from among this narrow class.

The procedure for manipulating the elections was as follows. Having concluded that their political position would be strengthened by an accession of friends to the Assembly, the Cabinet in office – a clique of politicians of the types described – would decide to ask the king to dissolve the legislature, and then proceed to call an election. In all cases but one during the period 1934–58 it first drew up a private list of candidates, including not only the names of its supporters but those of selected opponents also. The latter operation was not mere window-dressing: it reflected the characteristics of the social oligarchy. It might well be that a powerful sheikh was a known enemy of the Cabinet, but prudence dictated that he be included as a deputy of the Assembly rather than left out, since his local power was such that it could otherwise raise his tribe in arms, with unpredictable consequences. And, *mutatis mutandis*, similar considerations of prudence dictated the names of other oppositionists to be included on the list. Then, the day before the election, this list was communicated to the polling officers throughout the country with instructions that these candidates were to be declared elected by the precise figures supplied by the government.[2]

The cellular-collegiate structure of rule appears even in régimes which at first glance appear to be highly personalist and autocratic, for example, the Mexico of Porfirio Díaz, 1876–1911. Mexico has a difficult geography and in those days the consequent localism was accentuated by lack of communications. The basis of power was therefore local. In each area, after bloody and cruel struggles, a *cacique* would establish himself and strive to dominate his neighbouring *caciques*. Broadly speaking, this was the situation throughout the first half of the nineteenth century. Porfirio Díaz was of mixed blood and so of low social status. But he was a professional soldier of great ability and a man of the utmost cunning and ruthlessness. He seized power in a typical military intervention in 1876 and set to work to impose order on the strife-ridden and divided state. He put down petty banditry in the countryside by creating forces of ruthless *rurales*

2. Since the 1958 military coup, there have been neither parliament nor elections – rigged or unrigged: a splendid example of the transition from old oligarchy to new.

(local police) often consisting of ex-bandits themselves. Conspirators got short shrift: they were shot 'while attempting to escape'. But the basis of power was still the local *jefe*. These *jefes* were all of a type. Each ran his own bit of territory in his own way, first building up a small clique of personal friends and supporters, with these dominating and cajoling the peasant mass, and then making accommodations with the locally powerful forces – the Church, the landowners, the local military. Unlike most of his predecessors, Díaz was too able and ruthless to be overrun by these local bosses; but he was not strong enough to eliminate them. He was strong enough, however, to 'beat them to a parley' and weld them into parts of his national 'machine'. The elections were held – to be rigged in the ways already described, so that the Congress was always packed with his supporters, and, with this compliant Congress, Díaz was able to name his own public officials.

Brazil is another vast country with poorly developed communications. Her history, though much more violent than is usually believed, was incomparably less disturbed and murderous than Mexico's. Here the façade-democracy operated with great subtlety, its heyday being the earlier period of the Republic, from 1889, until the rise of Getulio Vargas tore great rents in its fabric in 1930 (though the system still survives in the more rural states, as will shortly be seen). The way the system worked is splendidly described by Charles Morazé in his *Trois Ages du Brésil* from which the following lines are taken, and it rested, as we have already stressed and as Morazé in his earlier pages which are not quoted here makes categorically clear, on the fact that the local landowner could rely absolutely on the votes of his agricultural workers and other dependants.

We have seen that the persons we have been calling landlords and local squires had been local colonels during the heyday of the National Guard. After the fall of the Empire (1889) imperial titles lost their prestige, but not that of 'colonel'. This no longer signified that the title bearer was or had been an officer of the Guard: by it the people meant that he was an important personage who owned vast acres. The agricultural labourer and the peasant hardly dreamed of contesting the master's right to tell them how to vote. . . .

In the Republic every elector could choose between a number of candidates – but all belonged to the Republican Party. These candidates might draw up election manifestos – but all of them were the same and boiled down, in fact, to giving full support to the Federal Government. If the elector could not vote for a manifesto, was it not still possible for him to vote for a personality? But these candidates never carried out a campaign. What business did they have in the interior where the colonels ruled the land? To risk some slip of the tongue? To make an arduous journey and abandon the attractions of metropolitan society simply to get a more vivid impression of how heavy was the yoke of the colonel who did what he wanted – and who was in any case going to be loyal to his Deputy if the Deputy were loyal to him? Thus, the elector did not know his Deputies. Nor did he know the President of the Republic any better. To him, this was simply a name that emerged from party deliberations over there in the distant capital cities where the laws were made: from 1915 either a Republican from São Paulo or a Republican from Minas who was nominated and elected. At the end of four years the elector might have got used to the name of his President – but then a new name leapt from the blue to fall into the ballot box.

An old politician gave advice to a young one in more or less these words: 'If you try to run an election campaign all on your own your election will not be validated.' (Effectively, it was the retiring Chamber which decided on the validity of the elections replacing it, and it had not an instant's hesitation at the time of Pinheiro Machado or Washington Luis, in invalidating 80% of the opposition candidates.) 'Even worse your name will not appear on the ballot papers' (issued by the local authorities – that is to say, by the colonels). 'So what's the point since in no event will you be elected?' To have any chance of success it was necessary to be supported by a powerful colonel, who in any event willingly accepted the candidates suggested by their agents at Rio, i.e. the politicians they were already supporting. In that case all was clear and simple: the candidate was nominated, he obtained an ample majority and was validated at Rio. Provided he was docile, what a career to look forward to!

This mechanism worked smoothly for forty years and its essentials are still in place today. Certainly, there were quarrels between colonels. In that event it was prudent to stand clear. Such struggles could lead to bloodshed, bands of armed supporters faithfully defending one or the other of the adversaries and engaged in notorious ambushes; political murders occurred and went unpunished. Where this happened the public authorities tried to limit the form of the conflict but above all waited to see who would win and as soon as his victory seemed certain claimed him as a government supporter: a title from which, anyway, he had usually never derogated during the entire struggle any more than his opponent who had either surrendered or disappeared.

Brazil was a Federation of States. . . . A State President had a delicate task: to remain on good terms with the Federal President on one side and the powerful colonels of the interior on the other. One might even say that this was his unique preoccupation and as long as peace prevailed administration went on and rural and urban progress developed in an atmosphere of calm. But beware of battle! And yet – to speak true, if these became so serious as to warrant the despatch of federal troops the government won all along the line. The State President appealed to his friend the President of the Republic, a military force appeared, and the colonel who was on good terms with the Presidents won without any difficulty. In return for this service it goes without saying that the victorious colonel, as well as the State President who had been relieved of a great anxiety, would both remain in office and see that the people voted for the candidates nominated by the President of the Republic. However, federal intervention was not a matter to be abused – the army was no thing to scatter throughout all the cantons of Brazil. Hence arose that particular art of government which consisted of letting the local quarrels die out of their own accord without military expense or too much embarrassment over a costly preoccupation with justice and injustice, legality and illegality.

If a good President of the Republic had to hesitate before engaging federal troops in a local quarrel, a good colonel had to hesitate before he opposed the State, if the latter were on good terms with the federal government: the more so since if he acted as its electoral agent the colonel enjoyed a wide latitude often enabling him to try cases involving his own workers and neighbours. As to a State President, he had to reflect seriously before opposing the President of the Republic because, if a quarrel between colonels blew up, the federal government might well conclude an alliance with one of them in order to depose the recalcitrant State President. . . .[3]

III. THE PASSING OF FAÇADE-DEMOCRACY

The heyday of façade-democracy has passed, although survivals exist. In the Third World – in contrast with Britain, say – this system of oligarchical or even autocratic government, with its

3. C Morazé, *Les Trois Ages du Brésil*, Armand Colin, Paris, 1952, pp. 101–3.

façade of parliamentary forms, failed to adjust itself to the slow growth of towns and the rise of new classes; nor did it adjust itself to the appearance in many countries of military officers drunk with the heady amalgam of nationalism, popular sovereignty, economic independence and the like which, compounded, spell 'modernization'. For instance, as the pampas were transformed towards the end of the nineteenth century in Argentina, as the great beef export industry grew up, as immigrants poured in from Europe, so the towns began to grow, a professional and industrial sector arose, and with them, simultaneously, a middle class and a working class. But, until 1943, with a brief interregnum between 1916 and 1930, government was in the hands of the rural *estanciero* oligarchy or was so crushingly limited by them as to be valueless to the two new classes. This oligarchy fell from power in 1943 through the intervention of a military clique imbued with the ideals of modernization.

The system rarely adjusted itself because it was, as has been said, the political profile of a social and economic oligarchy. Moreover, it was ill-suited to the growth of towns. Simply by moving into urban areas, people had fled the traditional deferences of the countryside. And, as professional groups – artisans or industrial workers – they had nothing in common with the traditional oligarchy and its agrarian basis and outlook. Access to education, too, was easier in the towns and this whittled away the importance of a literacy qualification for the franchise, where this existed – as it did in Brazil. The electorates in the towns, therefore, more numerous than in the countryside, were less easily controlled in their voting. For all these reasons, a system based on the falsification of the vote became less and less effectual in the towns. In one or two countries, like Chile and Uruguay, the oligarchies adjusted themselves to a form of liberal-democracy. Elsewhere, the tension thus engendered produced – but often only after a number of intermediary forms had been thrown up – one of the following results: a popular insurrection broke out and was successful (as it was in Mexico and in Cuba; in the former, this led to military rule and then to quasi-democracy; in the latter it has led to a near-totalitarian form); a popular insurrection broke out but, being in general as distasteful to the military as it was to the landed oligarchy, it nearly always ended in violent suppression; where insurrection was not attempted but the 'constitution' was deadlocked, since its channels had been blocked or perverted by the oligarchy, the military turned against this and overthrew it.

In both the second and the third cases, therefore, a residual and derivative form of rule arose: the military régime. For in the former case, oligarchs, threatened by insurrection, were forced to rely on coercion to put it down. They thereby became dependent on the military. Armed forces which adhered to the principle of civil supremacy, like the Brazilian military between 1889 and 1930, and who therefore rallied to the support of the oligarchy, enabled the façade-democracy to continue. But others, sensing the new leverage which the unpopularity of the civil government gave to them, were not content to follow their orders so blindly. Instead they used this leverage to veto decisions which they did not like, or to impose policies which they did. Thus imperceptibly, a façade-democracy merged into a military régime of the indirect type. The line exists intellectually, though in practice it may prove hard to draw it: on the one side, obedient armed forces, buttressing the traditional oligarchy; on the other, autonomous armed forces imposing their policy on it. Alternatively, the military might tire of directing affairs at second hand, through the medium of civilian politicians whose tenure of power rested so heavily on their support. In that case, they would withdraw their support and take the government into their own hands, establishing a direct military régime.

Military intervention was also possible, however, even where the oligarchical electioneering machine continued to work smoothly. For it is in the nature of façade-democracy that it cannot be ended by constitutional means: these are corrupted at the source. Only an outside force can end it and if this is not popular revolution, as in Mexico, then it can only be the armed forces themselves. In a wide range of countries – Brazil in 1930, Argentina in 1943, Egypt in 1952, Iraq in 1958, Libya in 1969 – middle- and junior-ranking officers, seeking the modernization of their countries, came to despair of the oligarchy, conspired, and overthrew it by force.

But before these ultimate situations were reached many of the façade-democracies passed through profound constitutional crises. Brazil, whose façade-democracy has just been explained, provides a good example. Twice in the 1920s junior officers had attempted armed revolt against the system, but had failed. In 1930, after the full force of the system had been successfully thrown against the opposition presidential candidate, Getulio Vargas, they tried a third time. They marched on Rio, overthrew the constitutionally elected president and imposed Vargas in his stead. From 1930 to 1945 the rule of the colonels and the rural hinterland was suspended. But in 1945 the military, the force which had installed Vargas and buttressed his personalist rule, turned against him; and the old federal Constitution, with a number of modifications, was reintroduced. Brazil once more became a federation of States. And, as before, the arrangements followed those of the U.S.A. On the one side was the president, elected by popular vote; on the other was the Congress, with two houses – the Chamber of Deputies elected by the people at large and the Senate representing the various States. It was through these two branches of the government that the social conflict in Brazil, the confrontation of the old 'colonelism' with the urban masses, now took place.

For, since 1920, the towns have mushroomed: out of a population of some thirty millions in 1920, seven million lived in towns; out of a population of eighty million today, thirty-five million live in them. The majority are by no means industrial workers, as one would expect in Europe or the U.S.A. Though industry has greatly expanded in Brazil, little is situated in the towns and the largest part is sited on the great estates of the landlords themselves! While the towns were growing at six per cent per annum during this period, the factory population was growing at only three per cent. The towns have grown, partly as a result of general population growth, but also because they are the playgrounds of the very rich, so that they are the centres of service industries; they are also the centres of officialdom, so white-collar jobs are available there. Villagers flock in to pick up some service job or white-collar appointment, or simply to sample the attractions of the great city, and many remain unemployed. Thus the urban mass has no structure such as industrialization imposes on the European or North American masses. It is also both poor and credulous; it longs for the comforts it sees around it, pressing for greater social welfare benefits, full employment, better labour legislation and a high and secure standard of living.

In this way arises a confrontation between the presidency and the Congress. In the latter the Senate, representing the States, gives vastly disproportionate power to the agrarian interests of the interior, whose States outnumber the urban ones. In the Chamber, while it is true that each State's deputies are proportional to its population, it is equally true that each State's electorate is proportional to its *literate* population! So the votes of the illiterate States, the rural ones that are still controlled by the colonels, elect more seats than an equivalent number of votes in the literate States. The Congress, in fact, is dominated by the rural hinterland, i.e., by the colonels.

But not the presidency. For the president was[4] elected on a national vote and, as in the U.S.A., the vast town populations represent the margin between victory and defeat. So, every presidential candidate had to be a 'populist'. Though he knew that he could not fulfil his promises, he had to continue to make them, for otherwise he would have been beaten by others who had not hesitated to do so. Hence, after 1946, tension always existed between president and Congress. Even in defeat, after 1945, Vargas was a force. He set the style – the demagogic style – for all succeeding presidents. Dutra, President from 1946 to 1950, was Vargas's 'man'. In 1950 Vargas himself swept back into power as constitutionally elected president. His successors, Kubitschek, Quadros and Goulart, all followed his general political line and were supported by the party he had founded. But the Congress through all this period was in the hands of the conservative opposition.

Between the one and the other, the military have intervened, trying to preserve a balance, in their traditional role of the *poder moderador* – the arbitral power. In 1954, on the eve of new presidential elections, fearful that Vargas might illegally perpet-

4. Until 1965. Since then the Constitution has been changed at the hands of the military.

uate his power, they forced him to resign. But in the ensuing election Vargas's political heirs, Kubitschek and Goulart (the latter running for vice-president), were elected. The military accepted this despite the attempt of a group of right-wing officers to invalidate the election. After Kubitschek's term had expired, Quadros and Goulart won the elections, the latter as vice-presidential candidate once again. Now Goulart was considerably more radical than either of his running mates and when in 1961 President Quadros resigned, leaving him to accede to the presidency as the Constitution laid down, the right-wingers in the officer corps were seriously alarmed. Despite their efforts to prevent the accession, however, the rest of the military stood by the Constitution, so they tried for a compromise. Presidential prerogatives were transferred to the Cabinet, which, unlike the president, can be dismissed by the Congress. This compromise worked exceedingly badly and in 1964 the powers were transferred back to the presidency. At this stage the radical Goulart and the conservative Congress directly confronted one another. In 1964 Goulart sought to have the Constitution changed, not only to abolish many of the abuses of the latifundia and strengthen the peasant economy, but, far more radically, to extend the franchise to the illiterate! This would have ended for good and all the political role of the colonels. Up to this point the military course had tacked between Congress and president. Now (exacerbated further by Goulart's condonation of mutiny in the armed forces and his hint that the faults were on the officers' side) the armed forces struck. On 31 March 1964, they deposed Goulart, purged the Congress of his supporters, imposed the election of General Castelo Branco as president and gave him dictatorial powers.

So, façade-democracy was overtaken by changes in the social structure and the spread of a new political formula, both of them undermining the old traditional deference without which the system could not work without an excess of coercion. Where it did rely on coercion, it found itself subordinated to the military, its instrument of violence. Where it still had roots and worked smoothly, it antagonized modernizing elements among the officer corps, and they overthrew it.

Up to the 1920s, most of the Latin American countries, the

Balkan states, and Iraq, Egypt and Iran in the Middle East were façade-democracies but no more. Nowadays there are only seven. Very significantly, all are monarchies: Afghanistan, Cambodia, Ethiopia, Iran, Jordan, Morocco, Nepal. 'Significantly' because in every case it is the palace that rules from behind the manipulated liberal-democratic forms. (Of Liberia we have already spoken, as a state which falls between the façade-democracy and the quasi-democracy.)

Chapter 10

THE QUASI-DEMOCRACY

I. THE NATURE OF QUASI-DEMOCRACY

IN quasi-democracies, the right to form political parties is usually confined to only one, official body, and if, as in a few cases, like Mexico's, the right is extended, steps are taken to ensure that other parties are politically ineffectual. Furthermore, the freedom to form social and professional organizations such as trade unions and youth associations is also usually limited in that these are controlled by the dominant party. Finally, since restrictions such as these usually necessitate further restrictions, the freedoms of speech and the press, and guarantees of the inviolability of the person and of the domicile, are usually restricted also.

On the other hand, the quasi-democracy falls short of the totalitarian régime. Party discipline and cohesion are less firm. Loyalty is usually owed to a leader rather than to an impersonal doctrine. And, indeed, many of the parties which 'rule' in the quasi-democracies owe their cohesion, at the present moment at any rate, more to the common interests of their members as beneficiaries of government patronage than to any doctrinal commitment. Moreover, even if the ruling parties sought to control the whole of society, i.e., to become totalitarian in scope, the limited human and mechanical resources at their disposal make this impossible. Whatever their doctrine, the sheer ineffectiveness of such parties precludes the state becoming totalitarian.

Outside Africa, the sole example of a quasi-democracy is Mexico, which is at once the oldest and the most effective of the whole category. Until 1945, Turkey also was a quasi-democracy. In that year, however, the then ruling party permitted the formation of opposition parties of which the Democratic Party soon became the most important and it became a liberal-democratic régime for a time. But from 1956, when Tunisia became independent, one African state after another has moved over to this new form. At the moment of writing, the republics of Algeria, Burundi, Congo (B), Congo (K), Central African Republic, Libya, Mali, Nigeria, Somalia, Sudan, Togo, Upper Volta are military régimes and the United Arab Republic, for all its efforts to create a single official party (the Arab Socialist Union), ought also to be classed as such. Morocco and Ethiopia have been classed as façade-democracies and so, for different reasons, Liberia might be though this is a single-party state. In addition to these two states, Gambia, Zambia and Uganda have some claim to be considered as liberal-democracies but under severely repressive conditions.[1] The remainder of the African states, fourteen in number, are quasi-democracies.

In one sense quasi-democracy is simply a variant of the façade-democracy, in that it carries forward the electoral manipulation which is a characteristic of the façade-democracy to its logical conclusion, namely, the prohibition or neutralization of rival parties altogether; there are, however, important differences between the two types. Whereas the ruling group of the façade-democracy depends on its individual members who are important notables in their own right, the quasi-democracy is an oligarchy, but an oligarchy *of a new type*. Examples do indeed exist – the Northern Region of Nigeria or Mauritania – where the traditional ruling group still remain at the helm, having adapted their style of political campaigning and their objectives (towards economic modernization) to the new conditions of independence. But with these marginal exceptions (which pose a conceptual difficulty), the type of oligarchy that currently rules in most of the new African states is a self-styled and self-selected oligarchy of 'modernizers' – i.e., a minority of social upstarts whose popular appeal does not derive from their ascriptive but from their achieved status. To the extent that this is true in any particular state, then, each member of the ruling party is dependent upon the party itself for his power and influence; it is not, as in the façade-democracy, the other way round. So the party structure tends to be hierarchical rather than cellular; each party notable

1. This listing excludes three recent creations, namely Botswana, Barotse and Lesotho. (For Zambia and Uganda see p. 583.)

is a kind of functionary, and so on down the line. Furthermore, votes are garnered as a result of agitation and propaganda, not delivered out of immemorial custom and deference. Also, they do not come in clumps of common ethnic or religious background, but from individuals who are only reached through membership of or permeation by a territorial party branch. In short, the party in the quasi-democracy attempts to be the 'mass' party type, i.e., one that reaches past the traditional *cacique*, down to the people themselves. The extent to which the ruling parties of the African quasi-democracies do actually behave like this, however, varies considerably. The Ghanaian Convention People's Party (C.P.P.) certainly did so at first, only to lose its mass character after it took monopoly power to itself after 1960. In others, such as the Parti Démocratique de la Côte d'Ivoire (P.D.C.I.), which is the ruling party of the Ivory Coast, the party has simply transformed tribal sub-groupings into local party branches. In others, such as Chad, Gabon and Dahomey, the ruling parties never had deep local roots before independence and seem to have done little to create them afterwards.[2] In Algeria, notably, the Front de Libération Nationale (F.L.N.) was a party of guerrilla-militants and their sympathizers during the seven years' liberation struggle, and no local branch organization was established after independence in 1962. Even today no such organization exists.

For all this, the party in the quasi-democracy differs in both conception and style from that of the façade-democracy. For there the parties, where they exist (none are tolerated in Ethiopia for instance), tend to be weak in their organization, decentralized, personalist and only spasmodically active. The party comes alive only at election time; its organization goes no deeper than that of the local *cacique*; and the votes come to him out of deference with a touch or two of deceit and coercion thrown in for good measure. For all these reasons, the party has no need to propagandize and mobilize the masses to get their votes; these are there for the taking. By the same token, the party

2. cf. J. A. Ballard, *The Evolution of Single Party Systems in French Equatorial Africa*, seminar paper, Institute of African Studies, Ife, Ibadan, 1963 (mimeo).

has no ideology and often no specific programme; usually, it forms around some prominent personality and is held together by the hope of acquiring the spoils of office.

The party of the quasi-democracy, however, tends at least to be of the new 'mass' type, not what has been described as a party of 'cadres', i.e., of local and national notables; and, even when its local organization is weak, as in the states already mentioned, or it makes bargains with local traditional forces, such as chiefs or ulema, it still is *relatively* centralized, hierarchical, permanently active and popularly based by comparison with the façade-democracy type of party.

But the distinguishing mark of the quasi-democracy is not simply that its party is of this kind – for the parties of Somalia, where a two-party system existed were of this kind; the distinguishing mark is also that in the quasi-democracy the number of such parties is confined to one, or at least, only one is permitted to dominate.

Whether quasi-democracy in fact emerges as a form of government depends on two factors: what the leaders of such a mass party want to do and how far they are able to give effect to their wishes. These factors have varied from state to state. In Mexico, the now dominant party was deliberately created by a group of military leaders in order to perpetuate their own rule – and their successors were able to maintain and widely develop the cohesion of this party; likewise in Turkey, the Republican Party was the only party for many years until the strains within it became so great that in 1945 a group of its dissidents was permitted to hive off and to found opposition parties.

On the one hand, consider India, Pakistan and Burma, which were each overwhelmingly controlled by one party at the moment of independence in 1947; in none of these three states did the party leaders desire to proscribe the opposition – partly out of democratic commitment and partly because they were confident that they could retain their ruling position. But whereas the Indian Congress Party proved able to maintain its cohesion, the other two parties (the Moslem League in Pakistan, the Anti-Fascist People's Freedom League in Burma) broke up (ultimately inviting the intervention of the military).

In Africa, on the other hand, which as we have seen supplies all but one of the examples of the quasi-democratic type of government, either one mass party was overwhelmingly dominant at the moment of independence and subsequently took steps to legalize its monopoly of power, or, where several parties developed, they struggled for supremacy, until in the end one proscribed the rest. In the fragmented societies of sub-Saharan Africa, it was only to be expected that parties would spring up to represent particularist ethnic or religious loyalties or to re-evoke traditionalist ones. But such dangers had also existed in India, Pakistan and Burma. In the African context, however, the brutal expedient of maintaining power by multiplying the number of their own supporters and eliminating their rivals was the policy that commended itself in most cases. Thus, two things must be firmly distinguished: the fact that the establishment or at least the maintenance of the single or dominant party system was and is a deliberate act of will on the part of a group of rulers or would-be rulers; and the possibility that this choice of a form of government was a wise one – i.e., that the Pakistani or Burmese rulers might have done better for their country as well as for themselves if they had made a similar choice and suppressed their rivals. What is quite certain, however, is that, although in a few instances, such as Guinea, Tunisia, Tanzania and Malawi, the single party came about as a result of its overwhelming popularity at the time of independence, it is currently maintained by its deliberate act of will. (This point will be elaborated in Parts IV and V of this chapter where the particular ways and means by which the quasi-democracies were established in Africa, and the claims that are made in favour of them, are examined at greater length.)

The ruling parties of the quasi-democracies differ from one another in a wide number of respects. To begin with, while some tend to lay stress on official ideology and seek to encompass all significant associations within the society, others are more pragmatic and opportunist in their approach, and take a more limited view of their role in society. The parties of Mexico and Tunisia are excellent examples of the second type, with those of the Ivory Coast and Senegal not far behind. The parties in

Guinea, and the late C.P.P. of Ghana, are good examples of the first type. But the parties differ in many other respects also. They differ in origin, some, like the Mexican P.R.I., or the Algerian F.L.N. having a military origin, others – the vast majority – being evolved out of a civilian struggle. They differ in maturity. The Mexican P.R.I. and the Tunisian Néo-Destour are both over thirty years old; others have been formed only recently. They differ in the party's degree of monopoly. In Guinea and Tanzania, for instance, the ruling party is the only one permitted by law. Elsewhere, as in Mexico, other parties are permitted to operate. They differ greatly in the matter of local party organization. Some, like the Mexican P.R.I., the Tunisian Néo-Destour and the Parti Démocratique de Guinée (P.D.G.), have established branches in great number and everywhere. Others, like the Algerian F.L.N. and the parties in Gabon and Dahomey, have few functioning branches. They also differ signally in their degree of inner-party democracy. The Tanzanian African National Union (T.A.N.U.) permits members a very wide latitude in the nomination of candidates, and has operated this sytem justly and liberally, to judge by the election of 1965. The Mexican P.R.I. gives a degree of latitude to its various 'sectors'. But the Malawi Congress Party is the instrument of its leader Dr Hastings Banda, while the leaders of the so-called 'democratic centralist' parties of Mali and Guinea exert strict and one-way control over the local branches. Again, in some cases, as in Guinea, the party claims to substitute itself for the organs of government, while elsewhere, as in Tunisia and Mexico, the party is ancillary to the state machinery. The context of liberties within which the parties operate again differs widely: in Mexico, the public enjoys a wide liberty to criticize the ruling party and the government, in Tunisia it does not, but delation and violation of the person are infrequent or absent altogether, while in some other states, like Nkrumah's Ghana and Kéita's Mali,[3] all opposition was harshly punished. And finally, in some states (e.g., Nkrumah's Ghana, Mali, the Congo (Brazzaville)) the party made every effort to absorb other social organizations like the trade unions, the co-operatives and youth organizations,

3. Prior to its overthrow by the army, 1968.

while elsewhere[4] – as in Mexico – these are permitted to operate outside the party's limits.

II. MEXICO: THE PARTIDO REVOLUCIONARIO INSTITUCIONAL

Mexico's façade-democracy, pillared by the army, the Church and the landowners, and presided over and controlled by President Porfirio Díaz, was swept away by the Revolution of 1911. Díaz fled, and from then until 1922 all the separatist tendencies latent in Mexican political life burst into the open, compounded by murderous peasant and workers' grievances. For ten long years, the unhappy land was fought over, ravaged and destroyed by revolutionary armies. Over one million of her population were killed or starved to death, amid incredible barbarism, cruelty and destruction. The ancient landed aristocracy was swept from the stage. The decade is known as *el Tormento*.

Out of it was born the political importance of the peasant and the industrial worker; the triumph of the *mestizo* (person of mixed blood) over the old *criollo* aristocracy; the myth of 'the Revolution'; and the 1917 Constitution.

This is, at first sight, similar to the U.S. Constitution. Mexico is a federation of States, the Congress consists of a Chamber of Deputies and a Senate, the head of the executive is the president. But he is a more powerful figure than his North American counterpart. In Mexico, either a president is everything or he is nothing at all. Unlike the U.S. president, he can intervene in the States during emergencies, replacing their governors with his own choices. His secretary for home affairs (*Gobernación*) is responsible for administering elections and interpreting election law, and for validating contested elections so that the president can effectively 'make' his Congress. Thus, the likelihood of a conflict between it and him does not arise. The president is the government.

4. All were quasi-democracies; now (December 1969) Ghana has reverted to civilian rule, while the other two are military régimes.

The Constitution proved to be as much a façade as what it had replaced. When General Obregón established his supremacy in 1922, the political system was much the same as that of Díaz, except that the personnel had changed and so had the social basis.[5] Power was still localized in the hands of the military captains who had managed to establish themselves in a bit of territory and who made accommodations with the forces that now mattered – not the Church or the landowners, but the peasant leagues, or the trade unions, and what feeble political parties existed. Obregón, undisputed head of the military, established himself as *jefe máximo*, and combined these local *caciques* into a national machine by subjugating some and striking compacts with the rest.

It was Calles, the colleague of and successor to President Obregón, who transformed this arrangement into what later turned out to be the first move towards a quasi-democracy. In 1928, he persuaded Obregón to stand for re-election, getting a compliant Congress to alter the Constitution so as to make this possible. But after Obregón's triumphant re-election, he was assassinated. Calles, now the *éminence grise*, called together the various *caciques* in batches and persuaded them to support the candidature of Portes Gil, the boss of Tamaulipas State. But, in this last overt political gesture, Calles acted to perpetuate his influence, for he called together the most important *caciques*, both territorial and 'functional', and got them to ally themselves into a coalition, a single party, to be called the Partido Nacional Revolucionario (P.N.R.). It was not centralized. It was an amalgam of the local political machines, and various agricultural, labour and other interest groups. It included military *caudillos*, like Rodrigues of Sonora, Cárdenas of Michoacán, Cedillo of San Luis Potosí and Camacho of Pueblo, and civilian *caciques*,

5. Marxists, of course, would say this change of social basis is the all-important thing, the political arrangement being a mere form. But who gave *them* authority to decide what is form and what is substance? To them the substance is whether you are 'exploited' economically. Others might legitimately hold that the important thing was whether you were still being bullied or not; that *that* was the substance, while whether you were being bullied by a landowner or a party official was a question of mere form.

like Portes Gil of Tamaulipas and Tejeda of Vera Cruz. Each one
was to retain his separate organization, but to act under the
mandate of a national executive committee. The *caudillos* and
caciques were willing to do this, not because they wanted or
expected to surrender their independence but because this
stratagem afforded a temporary relief in a then clouded political
situation. Indeed, a number held off and refused to join. Later,
as the coalition proved its strength, these were to wither on the
vine. Of existing parties – both feebly organized – the Agraristas
were split, their leadership purged and their adhesion secured.
The Laboristas, representing the industrial workers, refused to
come in; but at that stage industrial labour was not important
enough to make this a source of weakness and their independence
was disregarded.

By means of this coalition, Calles – though not president – still
retained effective political control, for he was the *jefe máximo* of
the new 'party'. He used and manoeuvred this position in such a
way as to dominate the presidency: and many examples could be
cited in proof of this. For instance, alarmed at the pace of the
redistribution of land to the poorer peasantry, he was able to
terminate it by simply convening the governors of the States,
and telling them that it must stop – and it did. Meanwhile, the
'party' was strengthened by an administrative order, making
every state employee contribute seven days' pay per annum to its
funds. As a result, a party bureaucracy began to form, giving
direction to the coalition. At the same time, its officially favoured
status made it the vehicle through which government expenditures were funnelled down to the local political machines and the
associated organizations, to help them retain their grip on their
followers. In 1932, the success of this machine suggested further
improvements. Its confederal nature was abolished in favour of
the more orthodox hierarchical pattern of municipal, State, and
national conferences for decisions on policy and the nomination
of candidates.

Ten years of stable government, the expansion of the bureaucracy and the ever-increasing flow through this of the federal
patronage which kept the local *caciques* sweet and enabled them
to hold their followings together, generated a profound institu-

tional change. It exalted the office of the chief executive, the presidency, which controlled the bureaucracy and thus became the chief dispenser of the federal benefits – what in the U.S.A. is called the 'pork-barrel'. Calles had controlled the presidency from behind the scenes by virtue of his ties with the local *caciques* and his popularity with the army. For the presidential succession in 1934 he selected Lázaro Cárdenas, expecting to dominate him as he had dominated his predecessor, Portes Gil. But he had picked the wrong man. Cárdenas also was a revolutionary general: and equally popular with the armed forces. Furthermore, he was an adroit politician. He was an ex-president of the party; he had been governor of Michacán State; he had served as minister of defence; and he had also served as the secretary of the all-important office of *Gobernación*, which controlled elections. Furthermore, he was highly popular with the masses; he travelled widely, mixed freely. Cárdenas now re-activated the myth of 'the Revolution'. Land distribution had been halted. Cárdenas pushed it forward faster than ever before, and established peasant leagues throughout the States, finally bringing them together in a national federation, the National Farmers' Federation (Confederación Nacional Campesina, or C.N.C.). The trade unions had fallen into a decline. Cárdenas selected a rising trade union leader, Lombardo Toledano, and used his office to help him create a new trade union central – the Mexican Federation of Labourers (Confederación de Trabajadores de Mexico, or C.T.M.) in 1936. By 1936, he had woven his own web and created his own machine. When Calles challenged him, denouncing the leftward turn in social and political policy, a so-called 'Proletarian Defence Committee' immediately sprang to Cárdenas's defence, the bureaucracy fully supported him and the armed forces stayed neutral. Calles had no alternative but to flee and leave Cárdenas in sole command. The next year (1937) Cárdenas called for the dissolution of the P.N.R. and the formation of a new revolutionary party. The change took place in 1938, when its name was changed to the Partido de la Revolución Mexicana, (the P.R.M.), and its structure – and nature – completely altered.

The new structure was 'corporate' or 'functional', as well as being territorial. At each level – municipal, State and national – the party membership was grouped into four 'sectors': the agricultural sector, the industrial worker sector, the 'popular' sector and the military sector (the last being abolished in 1940). Peasant leagues and associations were grouped in the first, trade unions in the second. The third became a kind of residual sector for all other associations – white-collar workers, professional associations, civic associations and the like; but the interest it principally represented was that of the bureaucracy. To each sector a number of party candidatures was apportioned. Each met individually before a nominating convention of the whole party branch, in a sort of 'primary', to decide on the names to put forward. Then all four (after 1940, all three) sectors met together, and the list was finalized, after which it was understood it would be supported by the combined efforts of all. The presidential nomination – the most important of all – was also decided in this way. Until the abolition of the military sector in 1940, the rule was that three out of the four national sectors had to concur on a nomination for it to go forward; since that date, the concurrence of two out of the three sectors is required. With the qualifications to be noted below, this is the way the party works today.

Thenceforward, the entire style of politics began to change. Immemorially, and irrespective of its constitutional forms and appearances, it had rested on local bases. Now it began to rest on nation-wide functional foundations. The local *sectors*, in co-operation with the municipal and the State governments, jointly squeezed out the local *cacique*. They themselves relied increasingly upon the federal government – and on the party's Central Committee – for funds to help develop their local economies, and so the territorial basis of power was still further eroded. Furthermore, the party and its bureaucracy grew immensely stronger since, by virtue of aggregating trade unions, peasant leagues and the like, it now had ready sources for 'voluntary' collective contributions. And this powerful party buttressed the presidency, while the president himself became more and more influential because he was increasingly called on to arbitrate between the claims of the rival sectors.

The final stage in party reconstruction occurred in 1945, when a new nomination system was introduced – to be altered again in 1950 – and the party's name was changed to the Partido Revolucionario Institucional – the Party of Institutionalized Revolution. The current nominating system is as follows: any local group of over 200 members may submit a list of nominations to the local P.R.I. municipal committee: the latter comments on these and sends them to the State committee: this adds its comments: the National Committee then arbitrates and this process narrows the lists to two: these two are then re-submitted to the local P.R.I. nominating convention which continues, as before, to consist of three sectors each containing twenty delegates. It is for them to argue the matter between them to secure a satisfactory compromise.

The party claims a membership of three to four million – about forty per cent of the registered voters. The structure is pyramidal, headed by a National Assembly (triennial) which is officially the supreme organ, a Permanent Commission elected by this Assembly and a Central Committee elected by the Commission. It is this Central Committee which runs the party. It consists of seven members, the president of the party, his deputy, and five others; and of these, three are the national presidents of the three sectors respectively. Below these central organs, there operates a network of thirty-two regional executive committees which are elected by the municipal committees and on which, again, the three sectors are represented. And at the base, come the municipal committees themselves: each consisting of five members, who are *not* elected by the membership but are appointed by the Central Committee on the nomination of the appropriate regional committee. Here again, the three sectors are represented. There can be little doubt that the Central Committee, via the regional committees, keeps a firm check on nominations for municipal and State offices.

But the most important nominations are those for the federal government – for the House of Representatives and the Senate, and above all, for the presidency. These are in the hands of the Central Committee. But this has little latitude – if indeed it has any at all – in nominating the presidential candidate. For the

Mexican P.R.I. has solved the problem of peaceful succession where the C.P.S.U. has so signally failed. By a course of precedent and evolution the incoming president is selected by the one about to retire. As the leader of the party, as head of the national executive and as effective ruler of the entire state, the president is in the very strongest position to sense the balance of forces inside the party – the straining of the agricultural interest within it, or the restiveness of the industrial unions, and so forth; he is also best able to judge the orientation the country will require in the next six years. For the party is ridden with faction and conflicting interest; this arises from its very nature as a holding company for a host of functional associations whose interests by no means coincide. To select a candidate of an extreme complexion may – and often does – drive opposing factions into quitting the party and putting up their own candidate. The fact that such splinter groups have hitherto been electorally insignificant is as much a tribute to the skill in selecting presidential candidates as to the façade nature of the electoral process. A bad presidential nomination could well split the party open. It is significant, therefore, that the candidatures seem to have alternated between left-wing and right-wing tendencies: Calles was a man of the right, but Cárdenas turned out to be very much a man of the left. Alemán, who succeeded him, was, again, a man of the right.

The incumbent president, then, weighs up the balance of factions – and then, having selected the 'available' man, keeps his mouth shut for as long as possible. This is partly to prevent the rise of opposing factions until it is too late for them to rally an opposition, partly to protect his own pre-eminence until the last possible moment. So institutionalized is the practice of presidential selection that this is a matter not so much of criticism but of eager anticipation. The successor is known as *El Tapado*, 'the hidden one'. And the moment his name is made known, all the forces in the party – its assemblies and its sectors and its affiliated organizations – all hasten to endorse it. And naturally so; for there is no doubt that he will be elected and so it is wise to jump on his bandwagon. It is especially noteworthy that since 1940 all the presidents have been civilians, and that the last seven presidential candidates have made their mark by being the campaign supervisors and directors of the incumbent president.

Of the election of the P.R.I.'s candidate there is no doubt. For one thing, it is the office of *Gobernación* – under the control of the outgoing president – that administers electoral laws relating to whether a party may legally register, whether its nominations may appear on the ballot and how far it may participate in the election commissions. Furthermore, the Federal Election Commission, which is composed of seven members, of whom three are to be recognized representatives of competing parties, does in practice have a five-to-two majority of P.R.I. members. But quite apart from this, the choice of alternative is limited. The only opposition party to have a continuous existence since 1939 is the right-wing Partido Acción Nacionál (P.A.N.), itself badly divided. Despite its conservatism, it tries to attract dissident trade unions, and indeed it sometimes polls a considerable popular vote, especially for the congressional elections in a non-presidential year, when the P.R.I. vote tends to be much lower, since the presidency is not at stake. In 1955, for instance, P.A.N. secured thirty-six per cent of the votes for Congress – but, owing to the electoral system, received only five seats. Other opposition parties also spring into existence at election time, but tend to die away after their defeat, and new ones arise for the next election.

This system is, rightly, described by critical Mexicans as *imposición* – the imposition of candidates. The P.R.I. dominates Mexico. Its rivals have never won an election and would not be suffered to. Originally they were defeated by guile, force and fraud; this is no longer necessary since their support has withered away, while the P.R.I.'s command of all important patronage in the state is itself a factor that predisposes would-be dissidents to seek accommodations with it. And the electoral system also operates to its advantage: so much so that, in 1962, the Constitution was amended to ease the lot of the opposition parties. Parties which do not win any seats under the country's single-member constituency system (operating like the British or U.S. systems), but which, nevertheless, obtain 2·5 per cent of the total vote, are entitled to at least five seats and an additional seat for every additional 0·5 per cent up to a total of twenty seats. If a party wins some seats, but less than twenty, by majority vote in the single-member constituencies, it may bring its total representation up to twenty by adding 'party' deputies under the proportional arrangement outlined. The deputies thus elected are those of a party's candidates who came nearest to winning in their electoral contests.

But all this is far less than liberal-democracy, and the many critics of the system are opposing it for precisely this reason and by this standard. On the other hand, though not liberal-democratic, the Mexican system is broadly representative – even if it is not responsible; and it is far removed from totalitarianism.

First, it is representative of the broad currents of public opinion. Local grievances tend to be dealt with locally or by the sector from which the grievance comes, whether it be industrial or agrarian. If the local party or local government cannot handle it, they pass it to the higher echelons. The same thing happens at State level. By and large, through party meetings, grievances, complaints and demands filter up from the grass roots to the federal capital, and the programme of the party is based on a knowledge of them. Once they have reached federal level, they become a matter of hard bargaining between the three sectors. Unless they are accommodated there, the risk arises that affiliated associations will break away at election time; and while this is tolerable to some extent, it clearly could not be permitted on any large scale without threatening the supremacy of the party itself. This is the ultimate sanction behind any widespread and deeply-felt grievance.

Next, the party is by no means the only institution in Mexican society. It is neither the sole party, nor immune from outside criticism, nor all-embracing. For one thing, the constitution of the party has excluded two important interests – the capitalists and the Church. The latter, after a period of bitter persecution at the party's hands, has recovered its standing with the party – but it treats with it from the outside. The same is true for the employers – a class that has greatly multiplied and enriched itself in the shelter of the stability and corruption which the party system has brought to Mexico. The employers would, if they could, ensure the triumph of the P.A.N. or its right-wing offshoot, the *sinarquistas*. But they know they cannot – and so they, too, reach accommodations with the party through their associations. In short, both Church and private industry have important status in Mexican society, but they stand outside the party, and act on it as pressure groups.

Finally, the party operates inside a framework of civil liberties – the rights to speak, publish, assemble and associate with a considerable degree of freedom. The party has no official ideology, rigidly enforced upon its membership. Instead it has a myth, the myth of the Revolution – a very different matter and capable of meaning anything. The party imposes no discipline upon its members or affiliated bodies: they stay with it or leave it after a consideration of political principle and material self-advantage.

Since the Mexican quasi-democracy is the most liberal and well-established of this class of régime, it is as well to show how far short it falls of the well-established liberal-democracy as exemplified in Britain and the U.S.A. The sheer extensiveness, comprehensiveness and patronage of the P.R.I. ensure its dominance and self-perpetuation – and everybody knows it. The representative institutions envisaged in the Constitution have been stultified: for instance, the Congress has been degraded by the poor quality of the candidates and their lack of self-assertiveness. The primacy of the party and the extensive patronage that it confers on its lieutenants have vested enormous power in the State bosses. These are no longer the old traditional *caciques*, the pillars of the central government; they are new-style bosses whose careers are dependent on the central government. But for all that, as long as they remain in good standing, their area of discretion is prodigious: handling the flow of federal land distribution, controlling the *ejido*[6] programme, and involved in the placing of federal loans and investments, they have become rich and powerful, sometimes to the point of maintaining their private bands of *pistoleros* to reinforce their immunity to local criticism. Corruption (*la mordida*), an endemic trait in Latin

6. The programme (basic to the Mexican myth of the 1911 Revolution) of returning alienated common land to its village ownership.

American societies, still thrives in Mexico at federal and State levels, and the new party bosses are as often as not caught up with monopolies and black-marketing.

The Mexican citizen, as compared with the Englishman or the American, expects little fairness and scant consideration from the bureaucracy and the police. He feels much less free than they do to discuss politics. He believes elections to be corrupt. And yet, for all this, he believes in the value of elections and, even more surprisingly, believes to a quite high degree that he can, either alone or in combination with his fellows, 'do something' about an unfair law or local regulation. And although his pride in his national institutions is lower than that of the British or American citizen in theirs, it is far higher than that of the citizen of Western Germany or of Italy. The reason is that Mexicans have for over a generation been led by the P.R.I. to take pride in the Revolution; they have also been educated into a belief in the values of the Revolution – social justice and political participation. But at the same time, few of them believe that the P.R.I. has realized either of these. In fact, one-third of the party membership is alienated from the P.R.I., accusing it of selfishness, or seeing it as the betrayer of freedom and social welfare, and as misguided and reactionary. In Britain, only four per cent of Conservative Party members, and only four per cent of Labour Party members, saw their party in this light. In the U.S.A., the proportion of Republicans and Democrats alienated from their respective parties was much the same as in Britain – only four per cent and seven per cent respectively.[7]

Yet the last time a military revolt occurred was 1938, and since 1946 all presidents have been civilians. It can be confidently stated that never, in her entire history as an independent nation, has the government of Mexico been as broadly representative of public opinion as today, however much more so it might become under a competitive party system. And with even greater confidence it can be said that never in Mexican history, which numbers *one thousand pronunciamientos* (uprisings) between 1811 and 1940, has

7. These conclusions are derived from the tables in G. Almond and S. Verba, *The Civic Culture*, Princeton, 1963, which gives them quantitative expression.

the government been as stable as it is under the quasi-democratic system.

III. THE NÉO-DESTOUR PARTY OF TUNISIA

Roughly half the size of Britain and with a population of only about four million at the present time, Tunisia became a French protectorate in 1881. In 1954 it was granted extensive autonomy and in 1956 became independent. The Néo-Destour Party, claiming a membership of between one-third and one-fifth of the country's adult males, had held office, alone, from 1954.

The new state possessed certain advantages which those in sub-Saharan Africa lack. Tunisia had a continuous tradition of identity and of statehood (sometimes as a dependency, sometimes as an effectively independent unit) since earliest times. The society is ethnically and religiously homogeneous. The indigenous political structure, namely, the rule of the bey through his local *caids*, had been preserved. The principal class cleavage, namely, that between the large landowners and the masses (the peasants and farmers) was roughly equatable with the ethnic cleavage between European settlers and the native inhabitants, so that once independence was achieved there was no great social struggle for the Néo-Destour Party to resolve. And, finally, because French influence had been channelled through and mediated by the traditional political institutions, the nationalist and modernizing *élite* evolved gradually so that, when it succeeded to power after 1954, it was both experienced and mature.

It has been observed that anti-colonialist movements tend to evolve in three stages. After the first shock of colonial rule, a movement is launched by a small group of educated and highly-placed men, some from the professions but most drawn from the traditional high-status groups, to adapt their society to the new Western ways in order to reform and invigorate it. They do not envisage independence but think in terms of assimilation to the alien culture. This movement gives way to one in which the higher professional classes demand full political participation; they urge democratic reforms, demand internal autonomy for their country – but if they envisage independence at all it is for a distant future. This professional *élite* is then challenged by a radical group. It demands social as well as political reforms and it advocates full independence, immediately. The leaders are altogether humbler men, and they work through a mass movement appealing to and effectively organizing all sections of the population – a so-called 'populist' party.

The independence movements in India, Indonesia and Ghana, to cite only three instances, followed this threefold evolution; and certainly the Tunisian movement did. The first stage was that of the Young Tunisians, a movement which arose before the First World War and was effectively suppressed by the French in 1912. The second stage was led by a group of traditionalist-minded lawyers who founded the *Destour* (i.e., Constitution) Party in 1920 and rapidly gathered a quite unexpected mass support. The third stage began in 1934 when a radical group of Destourians, which included Habib Bourguiba, broke away and formed its own party, the *Néo*-Destour. They very soon won over the support of all significant sections of the population excepting the traditionalist classes. Their hard core lay in the middle class of the coastal towns but the party successfully appealed to the town artisans too, and soon attracted the significant and highly-influential support of the *soukhs* (bazaars) which were then suffering from the competition of cheap French imports. The students, always radical, readily joined it; and the leadership was quick to negotiate the adherence of the bedouin of the interior and the tribal groupings of southerners who, having migrated to the towns, formed therein a network of brotherhoods. The cliéntele of the Néo-Destour was virtually national in its scope. For four years it and its rival, the Destour, entered into deadly competition, but by 1938, it was all over, and the old Destour had become a mere ineffectual relic – and remains so today; so much so that the ruling Néo-Destour Party has not even bothered to order its formal suppression. From 1938, the Tunisian nation, the independence movement, and the Néo-Destour were one and the same.

In theory the party was organized exactly like the French Socialist Party (the S.F.I.O.). But it was illegalized (though sometimes tolerated *de facto*) from its foundation until the Accords of 1954. Also, between 1938 and 1943, and again between 1952 and 1954, its leaders were in gaol: thus, during that long period (1934–54), only two National Congresses ever met, and party policy was formulated by the National Council and Politbureau or – if the leaders were under arrest – by a shadow Politbureau and the leaders of the various local sectors (the 'federations'). Throughout that period, the various auxiliary bodies which the party had created also served to express and operate party policy. There were auxiliaries of this kind for the students, for the farmers and for the town artisans. In addition, Tunisia had a well-established trade-union organization, the Union Générale des Travailleurs Tunisiens (U.G.T.T.). Though it had emerged independently of the Néo-Destour, the leaderships overlapped. Because it was internationally recognized the French authorities did not dare suppress it so that it served in lieu of the party during the worst periods of repression.

The Néo-Destour's agitation was silenced by the Second World War, and the subsequent Vichy régime in North Africa; but the authorities continued to suppress the Néo-Destour even after the liberation, and Bourguiba had to flee to Cairo. Now began a protracted struggle between the French and the Néo-Destour. The grudging concessions offered by the French were persistently rejected by the party and in 1949, when Bourguiba returned from Cairo, he openly demanded autonomy. In 1950, the murder – allegedly by the *colons* – of the popular and able leader of the trade unions, Ferhat Hached, unleashed the beginnings of violence and the country fell prey to increasing terrorism. Arson, violence and murder became of daily occurrence. But in 1954, the remarkable Pierre Mendès-France became premier of France and in his spectacular '100 days' finally reached agreement with Bourguiba (who was still in exile). Tunisia was to be autonomous, though external affairs, defence and internal security would still remain in French hands.

To win support for the Accord, Bourguiba sent his emissaries to win over the Néo-Destour branches in Tunisia and he returned, in 1955, to a hero's welcome. But Ben Youssef, the party's general secretary, also returned from exile at the same time. He had been in Cairo, and came back full of the heady doctrines of pan-Arabism. (Nasser had won control of the Egyptian Free Officers'

Movement in the previous year.) Powerful in his home province of Djerba Island and attracting both the wealthy traditionalists and the rabble in Tunis, Youssef denounced the Accord and so threw down an open challenge to Bourguiba. The latter was well prepared, however. The Politbureau, which was loyal to him, expelled Ben Youssef and then, by shifty manoeuvres, isolated him at the party's National Conference and so secured his resounding defeat. He took to the interior, raising his own guerrilla bands until, defeated, he fled abroad once more. By this time, the French government was contemplating the cession of independence to Morocco, the other of her North African protectorates. Having decided to concede this in 1956, it appeared illogical to prolong the less-than-independent status of Tunisia; and so, in 1956, Tunisia became fully independent.

The Néo-Destour in power

'The system?' Bourguiba is said to have replied to a journalist's question; '*I* am the system.'

He fills this role by virtue of his dual capacity as undisputed head of the undisputed ruling party, and as the president of the state and so the chief of its executive agencies. The party and the state hierarchies run parallel, with much interchange of personnel between them, and much mutual interplay; but they are functionally distinct and Bourguiba, who takes advice from either or both as the feeling moves him, stands at the head of both.

The personal supremacy which this implies was not at all inevitable, despite Bourguiba's very considerable appeal and popularity and his high calibre as statesman as well as political tactician. He had to work for it. Ben Youssef; the Bey himself; powerful party figures like Ben Salah and Masmoudi – all were strong personalities, and in their different ways well placed to accede to the leadership. Ben Youssef was the most serious of these rivals. Though out-manoeuvred in 1955, he continued to attract considerable support in Tunisia from his places of exile. But in 1961, he was assassinated in a German hotel bedroom by persons unknown. As to the Bey: Moncef, who was the Bey until 1943, might well have played the same nationalist role that the monarchy was to play so successfully in Morocco. But the French authorities deposed Moncef in 1943, so that his successor, though he worked hard to make himself a nationalist pole of attraction, was from the start discredited in the eyes of all nationalists because of the vice of his 'French' origin. Next, the leader of the U.G.T.T. was always a potential threat to the party leader, since the organization claimed 150,000 members at the time of independence and disposed of much patronage. Its leader, Ben Salah, quarrelled openly with Bourguiba in 1957. A socialist, Ben Salah pressed for economic policies far to the left of what Bourguiba was prepared to consider, and insisted on the U.G.T.T.'s right to agitate for them. Bourguiba, for his part, insisted that such matters were political and that the U.G.T.T.'s proper role was confined to representing the material interests of its membership. Whereupon Bourguiba provoked a secession from the U.G.T.T. and then held out for Ben Salah's resignation as a precondition for re-uniting the labour movement. Ben Salah did resign and the U.G.T.T. was re-unified. Since then it has played the subordinate part which Bourguiba had decreed for it – while Ben Salah himself, after receiving his lesson, was subsequently made minister of planning. Finally, Masmoudi, an able and outspoken critic of Bourguiba, was likewise brought to heel. Masmoudi encouraged the official party organ (*L'Action*) to make critical attacks on Bourguiba's personal rule, and on the lack of democratic guarantees. He was expelled from the Politbureau, and, re-admitted some time later, committed the same offence as before. Once more he was expelled and, in addition, the party – i.e. Bourguiba – refused to re-nominate him as mayor of Malidia.

Just as Bourguiba effaced or outshone all his rivals, so the Néo-Destour Party effaced all rival parties. Independent elections were announced for a Constituent Assembly to decide on a constitution. Though the small Communist Party as well as the effete old Destour were permitted to contest these elections, the Néo-Destour leadership rejected proportional representation and decreed instead that all parties must nominate lists of candidates in the multi-member constituencies into which the country was divided, and that the party whose list obtained a majority of the votes cast would win all the seats in the constituency. This – as was intended – secured an absolute victory for the Néo-Destour. The small Communist Party was quite overwhelmed at the polls; the old Destour was represented in only one constituency by a 'League of Independents' – and this withdrew before the contest took place. As for the disaffected Néo-Destouriens, notably those who followed Ben Youssef, they had no other alternative but to abstain. And indeed many did. The forty-one per cent who abstained in Tunis, and the seventy-one per cent who did likewise in Djerba Island, bore silent witness for Ben Youssef and against Bourguiba. But all to no avail, for, of course, the Néo-Destour lists carried every constituency, so that the Constituent Assembly was one hundred per cent composed of Néo-Destouriens, hand-picked by Bourguiba and his colleagues on the Politbureau, in consultation with the leadership of the U.G.T.T. and the organizations representing the farmers and the artisans.

These organizations were brought still more firmly under party control once the elections were over and the political supremacy confirmed. The way in which the U.G.T.T. was reconstructed under more pliable leadership in 1957 has already been mentioned. The farmers' union (originally the Union Générale des Agriculteurs Tunisiens) had made the mistake of backing Ben Youssef in 1955. The party subverted it by promoting a secessionist movement, recognizing this as the official movement and then dissolving the old one. In 1962, the artisans' and traders' union was reconstructed and its elected regional councils were abolished in favour of appointed councils nominated by its general secretary, who is a member of the Néo-Destour's Politbureau. General freedom of association was limited by the law of 1959, which guaranteed the continued existence and status of the trade unions and professional associations on the condition that they confined themselves to non-political roles, but at the same time decreed that no other associations might be formed or continue to exist except with the permission of the minister of the interior.

Nor is the press much freer. Formally, no censorship exists but, in practice, newspapers and radio have to follow the wishes of the minister of information or face suspension or other forms of interference. *L'Action*, the official organ of the Néo-Destour (whose patron was that Masmoudi of whom we have had occasion to speak), was shut down for a week in 1957. Two years later, still under the protection of Masmoudi, it resumed its criticism of the régime. This time, the Politbureau withdrew support and it promptly collapsed. It reappeared in 1960 as *Afrique-Action*, but shortly afterwards began a series of articles on the personalist aspects of Bourguiba's rule. It was told that henceforth it might comment only on external affairs and, since then freedom of the press has, effectively, disappeared.

The party, then, is supreme – but who makes policy inside this party? The answer is, Bourguiba and those he chooses to consult – and these may include the various interest groups outside its ranks, the auxiliary party organizations that have been described, the ranks of the state bureaucracy, as well as such party members as he respects. The party organization still nominally follows that of the French Socialist Party with one major departure which was introduced in 1958 and ended in 1963. In 1958, the elected council at the 'federation' (regional) level was abolished in favour of a commissioner appointed by the Politbureau. In 1963, the commissioner was, in his turn, abolished in favour of an elected committee. In practice, however, policy continues to be formulated at the top and transmitted down the party hierarchy to the branches. These enjoy considerable latitude in expressing local grievances, provided they are not of such a nature as might be taken to impugn the régime; but policy is not discussed at branch level – it is explained and it is received. And a branch's nominations for its committee are screened by the 'federation' organization before they are allowed to go forward.

Nor do the higher organs of the party play much part in formulating its policies. Neither the National Conference nor the National Council have met very often. Since 1958, the former is supposed to convene every three years – and even this rule has not been observed. The latter never met at all between 1957 and 1962. In any event, even when they do meet, neither shows any independence. They meet to express solidarity and approval. Nor is the Politbureau as important as its name makes it sound. Not all its members are important figures and many important figures do not serve on it. It does not meet at regular intervals, but as Bourguiba convenes it. Its role is advisory. Its one important element of strength lies in that sometimes Bourguiba requires its corporate consent to a policy in order to legitimize it in the eyes of the party faithful. Perhaps it was the declining effectiveness of the Politbureau in its original form that led Bourguiba to the important policy reform of 1963: the Politbureau was then enlarged to a 150-member body and renamed the Central Committee while a new body of five appointed by Bourguiba himself, was established under the name of the Executive Committee. This change recognizes the facts of the situation.

Since the reorganization of 1958, the party organization parallels the administrative organization of the country. At the top, the Executive Committee parallels the ministries; at regional level, the 'federation' committee and its officers parallel the provincial governor; and at local level, the party branch parallels the municipal or village council. Bourguiba stands at the head of both hierarchies. From the beginning, he has insisted on the autonomy of the administrative machine. 'Some party leaders,' he said, 'especially those who claim a glorious past of struggle and of sacrifice, have paralysed the activities of the administration by their constant intervention.' He went on to insist that the governors, his representatives in the provinces, had to work in co-operation with the local party committees – and vice versa; and on the whole they do so. Where they do not, Bourguiba resolves the difficulty – usually by posting both the offenders to different parts of the country.

Quasi-democracy

Bourguiba's personal supremacy is reinforced by the status afforded him as president by the Constitution. Adopted in 1959, it provides a president elected by universal suffrage for a five-year term. He appoints his Cabinet which is responsible to himself and not to the Assembly. Nor can the latter even establish investigatory committees. In addition, the president can veto legislation and to override him a two-thirds majority of the Assembly is necessary. Why all these provisions should be necessary when the Assembly is composed exclusively of party members whose candidatures have been personally approved by the president in his capacity of party leader is beyond rational discussion. The intellectual qualifications of the deputies are without doubt high; but they meet in plenary session on only some fifteen occasions during the year and debate is almost non-existent. What work the Assembly does perform is carried out in secret in the legislative committees; the plenary session always gives their recommendations a unanimous approval.

Nor is village or municipal democracy any more vigorous. For one thing, local authorities are strictly controlled by the provincial governors on the French administrative model; for another, the elections, like the national ones, are a foregone conclusion. In the 1960 and 1963 elections, the government used pressure to force the withdrawal of the opposition lists, and the Néo-Destour lists were drawn up under central party direction. Local views tend to be expressed in the local party branches rather than in the councils and even there it is limited. The party branches serve as sounding boards by which the leaders of the party can keep in touch with public sentiment. For the rest, they serve as centres at which the *mots d'ordre*, the calls for support or the campaigns for collective tree-planting or road-building can be explained to the membership and passed on by them to the population at large. These functions of the branch – the representational and the informational – are assisted by devices such as the 'cadres' conferences, where local militants have informal meetings two or three times a year with the 'federation' level officers.

Yet the party still maintains its hold on public opinion. In the first place, it still enjoys an enormous fund of goodwill and prestige as the architect of independence. In the second place, it possesses in Bourguiba a leader of great popularity and prestige; he for his part has deliberately magnified this by indulging in a panoply of pomp and ceremonial as great as ever surrounded the Beys. And, finally, the party means jobs, land and state loans. The Néo-Destour is the one great avenue of social advancement. After independence, anybody who wanted a job or a bit of state land had to apply through the local branch and the application was handled by the party commissioner and the governor. In 1958, the scramble had become so great that President Bourguiba stepped in and, since then, the flow of patronage has slackened. Above all, its channels have been diverted. The supplicant may indeed approach the local branch – provided he feels that it is influential, as it might be; if not, he seeks aid from relatives in high places, or friends in the administration. Nevertheless, though it is no longer a sufficient condition that an applicant for an appointment should be a party member, it is still a necessary one.

In sum: what Tunisia has seen since 1954 is a wholly successful replacement of the authority and administration of the Bey by Bourguiba and his new men. And, indeed, this was the gravamen of the charge which Masmoudi brought against the régime in 1961 and which resulted in his disgrace. Here is what *Afrique-Action* had to say:

In the twentieth century one witnesses not so much the abolition of monarchy but its transformation into a power that differs from it only in two ways: it is not given by birth but is taken (and must therefore be kept); it is not handed down and therefore raises permanently the problem of succession. It is the *pouvoir personnel*. . . .

Today Bourguiba holds more power, in law and in fact, than did the Bey and the Resident General together. . . . All rival forces . . . are dislocated, subjugated, or eliminated: the judiciary, a deliberative assembly, trade unions or political parties, and the press continue to exist but their liberty of action does not exist any longer. . . . They constitute nothing more than supporting instruments of authority, which addresses itself to the people without any intermediary. Everything converges towards the holder of power who alone exists, decides, and in expressing himself expresses the country and incarnates it.

In the orbit of authority others can benefit from a certain consideration or play a role. Outside there is no possibility.

The police is not all powerful but it is everywhere. Imprisonment without trial exists but is used more as a means of intimidation. Anyone can be arrested but the prisons are not full. That is to say *pouvoir personnel* is not dictatorship. . . . It is a permanent compromise between democracy, difficult and unrealizable in some situations, and dictatorship. . . .[8]

8. Quoted in C. A. Micaud, *Tunisia*, Pall Mall Press, 1964, p. 113.

In all fairness, two qualifications ought to be made to Masmoudi's analysis, one deriving from the nature of the party, the other concerning the practice of consultation outside the party. As to the first: certainly, the party is directed from its highest levels, not driven from below; its internal processes are not democratic and there are no competing factions inside it, any more than there are opposition parties outside it. Yet there is no repression or delation inside it either; there is no official ideology, no attempt to 'open windows into men's souls'. And the party, though it embraces a large span of social life, does not embrace it all. Islam stands outside it, as does the family; and private industry, trade and agriculture persist.

Secondly, in a number of important matters, the party acts in a way not dissimilar from the P.R.I. of Mexico – as broker or arbitrator between competing pressure groups. The Social Security Law of 1960, for instance, was the product of no less than two years' consultation with the artisans' union (Union Tunisien des Artisans et Commerçants, or U.T.A.C.), the trade unions, the chambers of commerce, European business directors and the medical profession, and, in the course of it, the party was forced to mediate – successfully – between the antagonistic views of the trade unions and the artisans' organization, hammering out a compromise that was satisfactory to them both.

Mexican P.R.I and Tunisian Néo-Destour

Both Mexico and Tunisia possessed a long and continuous tradition of identity and statehood. In both, the ruling party is of long standing: the P.R.I. dates from 1928, the Néo-Destour from 1934, so that a whole generation has become accustomed to them. Again, both parties are prestigious: the first wrapped in the myth of the Revolution, the second, in the achievement of Independence. Neither party is dogmatic, both are opportunistic. In both, the functions of representation and patronage are more important than doctrine and discipline. In both states, the party, the bureaucracy and, for that matter, the army, form parallel hierarchies which undoubtedly interpenetrate and interact but are nevertheless distinct: the party neither supplants the other hierarchies nor directs them. And in neither state does the party seek to absorb or control all sectors of social life.

But the differences are revealing and important. In the first place, the P.R.I. is collegiate. Once elected, the president does indeed control it – but he must keep careful watch on its powerful sectors and the changing balance of power between and within them. Above all, he cannot succeed himself after his six years of office. The Néo-Destour, on the other hand, is a one-man-band and its history largely illustrates the skill with which Bourguiba has outmanoeuvred and reduced his opponents. In the second place, the Mexican party is clearly a far more complex animal than the Tunisian. Its most important difference is not merely that it contains many competing factions but that the existence and the struggle of these factions has been institutionalized. There is nothing of this kind in the Néo-Destour, whose membership is undifferentiated. As a result, the Mexican branches and sectors have much more influence upon party policies than their feeble equivalents in the Néo-Destour. And finally, the *de facto* freedoms of speech and association outside the party are much more pronounced in Mexico than they are in Tunisia. Compared with the examples we are about to consider, both P.R.I. and Néo-Destour are parties where the representative function runs ahead of the functions of indoctrination and integration; but the Mexican party expresses this in far higher degree than does the Néo-Destour.

IV. THE CONVENTION PEOPLE'S PARTY OF GHANA

Ghana did not become independent until 1957. There had once been an African state called Ghana – but it was mere memory with a highly debatable historic continuity, if any, with the new state called after it. Under British rule it consisted of the Gold Coast Colony, on the coast; Ashanti, the central forest region; the Northern Territories; and, later, a part of former German Togoland. These different areas had been annexed to the British Crown at different times. The Colony became a Crown Colony in 1874 – though it had been governed by the British since early in the nineteenth century. Ashanti, a powerful warrior kingdom, successfully fought off the British invaders until 1874, when Sir Garnett Wolsely succeeded, but only just, in capturing and sacking its capital, Kumasi; after a second defeat in 1895–6 – more of a British military demonstration than a war – and one final unsuccessful rising, it was annexed to the Crown in 1901. The Northern Territories – a detritus of ancient kingdoms – were brought under British protection at that same date. Thus, the state considered as a single territorial entity was a British creation, and hardly more than half a century old when its independence was proclaimed. Its regionalism was pronounced – the Fanti of the coast and the Ashanti of the interior were traditional foes, while the Brongs of the western part of the interior belt were anxious to throw off the yoke of the Ashanti who had conquered them in the heyday of the Ashanti Confederacy. In the east, in the Volta region, lived the Ewe people – ethnically identical with those living in the south of the neighbouring Togo Republic, and another illustration of the artificial nature of colonial frontiers. Not only were the people of these regions divided by their history, but they differed culturally as well. The people of the Coast had been in contact with the West for four hundred years, and their degree of literacy and modern political sophistication was considerably greater than that of the Ashanti, while the folk of the Northern Territories, also (like the Ashanti) organized in chieftaincies, were still more traditional in their ways than the Ashanti – as well as having a proportion of Moslems and animists among them in contradistinction to the primarily Christian peoples of the Coast.

Yet, for all these divisions and differences, Ghana was far more favoured than such states as Kenya or Uganda or Nigeria. Indeed, at the close of the Second World War, she was a relatively sophisticated society. By independence (1957) her national income, based largely on the export of cocoa, was high by world standards – about £50 per capita; the literacy rate in the coastal areas was, perhaps, one in three of the population; and in 1948, in the Colony and Ashanti, half the children in the infant–junior age group, and one-fifth of those in the senior–primary school group, were at school. Although chieftaincies were important, especially in the Brong–Ahafo, Ashanti and northern areas, they were an obstacle for an African succession government to negotiate rather than a wall to be blown down. The impediments to unity were, in fact, matters of degree rather than decisive and irreconcilable cleavages: the historic enmities of Coast and Ashanti, the communalism of Ga or Ewe and, above all, an intense localism.

A proto-nationalist movement had already sprung up before the Second World War. As soon as the war was over, it was taken up more actively, led by the United Gold Coast Convention whose leaders were the intelligentzia of the Coast – doctors, lawyers and the like. It demanded a gradual evolution towards autonomy and, ultimately, self-rule. The U.G.C.C. was founded in 1947, in which year its committee made a historic decision – to hire a young man, then in Britain, called Kwame Nkrumah to act as its organizing secretary. Volatile, energetic, a splendid organizer, a theatrical personality, the Marxian Nkrumah threw himself into the work of organizing the party on the British Labour Party model, forming branches in the villages and establishing or re-affiliating functional associations such as youth clubs, farmers' associations, trade unions. In the youth clubs, Nkrumah tapped an entirely new spring of political energy. In 1948, a series of riots suddenly broke out, to the amazement of the colonial authorities. The riots were ascribed by a committee of inquiry to a variety of pressing local grievances – food shortages, rising prices and the unpopular steps taken by the administration to check the growth of the cocoa disease. These sparked off a novel anti-colonial and nationalistic fervour. But with this went a new force – the revolt of the elementary-school leavers against not only the colonial régime but the chiefs as well. The marked characteristic of the Ghana school system was its large primary base and its relatively narrow secondary superstructure. The products of Grade VII of the elementary schools were very different, therefore, from the well-educated and established intelligentsia who conducted the U.G.C.C. They were primary-school teachers, clerks, local contractors and petty traders. These now spearheaded the nationalist movement. But their activities had long been familiar in the villages: even before the war the chiefs had found themselves confronted by the opposition of the 'youngmen' – i.e., the commoners, who increasingly challenged their handling of affairs; and youth associations began to spring up to voice their demands. When the 1948 riots broke out, the U.G.C.C. put itself at the head of these new forces. The authorities arrested the leaders and the chiefs struck back at their 'youngmen'.

At this point, a watershed opened; for the U.K. government accepted the chief recommendation of the Watson Commission of Inquiry – that a local committee should be set up to formulate proposals for a new constitution. The leadership of the U.G.C.C. agreed to serve, but Nkrumah demanded 'full self-government now', irrespective of the committee's findings. He pressed on with the formation of new youth associations which enthusiastically took the same uncompromising view. In 1949, the break came. Nkrumah was read out of the U.G.C.C., and responded by forming his own: the Convention People's Party (C.P.P.). When a new constitution was introduced as a result of the Coussey Committee's Report, he denounced it, calling for immediate self-government and proclaiming a campaign of 'positive action'. While he and many of his associates languished in prison, the government went on preparing for an election. The new C.P.P.'s slogans, 'Full Self-Government Now' and 'the Common Man', ran from one end of the colony to the other; the affiliated youth clubs formed a solid basis of support for the party; and the imprisonment of Nkrumah lent him an air of martyrdom. When the results of this 1951 election were declared, it was clear that in the 'popular' constituencies (as distinguished from the places reserved to chiefs, and other interests, under the new Coussey Constitution) Nkrumah's party had all but swept the board. The governor released him from prison and nominated him prime minister.

Once in office, the concern of the C.P.P. was to prepare the way for a new constitution, with a wider suffrage, and envisaging one single chamber elected from single-member constituencies, with all such provisions as reserved places for chiefs abolished; this, in its turn, was to be the precursor of full independent status.

In these years, the C.P.P. was formally pyramidal: its leader,

Nkrumah, was served by a Central Committee of nine, elected from a much larger National Executive Committee which was itself elected by the Annual National Conference. In fact it was far more inchoate than this. The Central Committee was not all-powerful as it later became, and indeed many important figures did not serve on it; and till 1953 the Conferences were still 'open' meetings where genuine debate took place over policy. In these years, the mass basis of the party was being greatly enlarged, rising to as many as 700,000 members – about one in three of the entire electorate. Money, which had hitherto been in short supply, began to flow in now that the party was in office, partly from wealthy contractors who wished to get into its good graces, partly from ancillary organizations such as the Cocoa Purchasing Committee, a loan agency which was directed by party personnel. A secretariat was established, a regional network created, and party auxiliaries were formed – the Ghana T.U.C., the Chamber of Commerce, the Farmers' Council, the important Women's Section, and so forth.

As the new Constitution was drafted and the time for the next election drew nigh, the defeated and embittered leaders of the old U.G.C.C. made common cause with the disgruntled chiefs of the interior and the north, and with other disaffected particularists such as the Ewe people of Togoland and with the Moslem minority. They were aided in this by the eruption of Ashanti nationalism which was offended (*inter alia*) by the delimitation of constituencies. In the new Parliament, Ashanti and Brong-Ahafo (then included as part of Ashanti) would receive only one-fifth of the total seats, though it was the mainstay of the national economy as well as being proud and jealous of its identity.

While the various oppositions made common cause, the C.P.P. ran into internal difficulties. Now that it was in office and very likely to be returned at the next election, a candidature became a considerable prize. It would bring wealth, influence and protection as well as esteem to the family and the associates of the victorious candidate. The local branches, therefore, insisted on nominating their own candidates irrespective of the wishes of C.P.P. headquarters. Hence, out of 323 candidates for the 1954 election, 160 were independents half of whom were C.P.P.

'rebels'. Many of these had bought their local nomination. Ashanti particularism was also affronted by the C.P.P. headquarters' attempts to 'impose' candidates on them.

This pointed up another difficulty facing the C.P.P. By now, Ashanti and even the Northern Protectorate were politically alert. Electoral success here required careful negotiations and cunning coalitions among the influential – the chiefs, the village headmen, the wealthier cattle-owners and traders and so forth. For this, the C.P.P. was, as yet, not equipped. It did not know the interior. The Northern People's Party, newly formed, was here on its home ground.

The colonial administration looked to the election results for a green light to prepare the way for full independence – as indeed did Nkrumah. Nor did the results disappoint them. Despite all its handicaps, the C.P.P. won handsomely. It received 55·4 per cent of the total vote, as against the combined opposition's 44·6 per cent, and seventy-two of the seats as against the opposition's thirty-two. Furthermore, some two-thirds of the opposition were independents. It was clear that only the C.P.P. could form a government, and that the opposition was in weak shape, though local movements were of some importance; the election also seemed to show that the next stage, independence, was in sight.

It was not. The grievances of Ashanti now flamed up and around them accreted a multitude of others. The C.P.P. was taken by surprise.

The Ashanti movement was set off by a Cocoa Duty and Development Funds Bill which named an official price to be paid to the farmers for cocoa: 72s. a load of 60 lb. To the Ashanti cocoa farmers this price seemed derisory. Cocoa was the mainstay of the Ashanti economy and the revolt of the farmers brought a large part of the tribal society into angry play, even dissociating from the C.P.P. the Ashanti Youth Organization that had been a spearhead of its successes in the 1949–51 period. The whole Ashanti nation was up in protest. The chiefs threw in their lot with it and so later did the Asantehene (chief of the Ashanti). Out of this protest movement was formed the National Liberation Movement demanding a federal constitution. Dr Busia of the old U.G.C.C. put himself at the head of it, as did other educated Ashanti like Joe Appiah; but, essentially, the N.L.M. was a particularist movement – this was its strength, but it was also a crying weakness in a general election. At first, Nkrumah seemed disposed to compromise with the demand for federalism, by offering some regional solution. Then, seeing that nothing short of a new election could overcome the difficulties, his party set to work with a will to familiarize itself again with the electoral geography of the interior. Its success was marked. No imperialist ever divided in order to conquer as effectively as did the C.P.P. in this operation. The party appealed to the common man – i.e., to the 'youngmen' dissidents in the chiefdoms. Again, all through Ashanti, there were pockets of non-Ashanti peoples: the C.P.P. appealed to their historic enmity to the Ashanti. Furthermore, almost every chiefdom had quarrels over the succession of the rights of the chiefs (stool disputes) and in these the C.P.P. intervened with great skill; where the chief was pro-N.L.M., it would approach his rivals – who became C.P.P. Nowhere was this tactic used with greater effect than among the Brongs, who were still smarting over their subjugation to Ashanti and desirous of breaking away.

But other tribal or regional groups were also prepared to fight the C.P.P. – the Ewe people of the Transvolta, as well as many of the peoples of the Northern Territories, and when the new election was called in 1956, the opposition parties felt confident they would win. They thought they would penetrate the Coast, and sweep the seats in the interior and the north. Meanwhile, the C.P.P. was regenerated by the new opposition: party solidarity was restored, the number of 'independent' candidatures fell away.

This was the last free election in Ghana and in it the C.P.P. scored a clear victory. It slightly improved its share of the vote – fifty-seven per cent as against the opposition parties' forty-three per cent; and it carried off seventy-one seats against the opposition's thirty-three. In the southern Colony area it had carried off every one of the forty-four seats; it had taken eight of the thirteen seats in the Transvolta region; and it had broken the northern front, taking eight of the twenty-one Ashanti seats and eleven of the twenty-six in the Northern Territories. The way to independence had been cleared. But, though it was obvious that the C.P.P. held a clear majority of votes and seats and that it was the only party with a national appeal, one other thing was also clear: it was still distrusted by over two-fifths of the population. There was opposition; and there was an Opposition.

Independence came in 1957 – among intimations of violence as the Ga tribe in Accra protested that their grievances were being overlooked and a minor Ewe revolt was put down by the army. These incidents provided the government with an excuse for strengthening its powers.

In the light of what came after, ending with the referendum of 1964, it seems clear that the moment independence was granted, Nkrumah was bent on sweeping away every vestige of organized opposition to his party and making himself the un-restrained ruler of the state. From July 1957 began those 'measures of a totalitarian kind', as he himself described them in his autobiography. The Avoidance of Discrimination Act, 1957, proscribed the formation of parties on a regional tribal or religious basis. The basis of N.L.M. strength in Ashanti was smashed by down-grading the N.L.M. chiefs or de-stooling them and at the same time up-grading the status of the C.P.P. chiefs. Every single N.L.M. chief, except the Asantehene himself, was removed, and the Brong allies were rewarded by the creation of a separate Brong–Ahafo region. Further measures to strike down the regional strength of the opposition parties were taken in the steps to dismantle the regional councils prescribed in the 1957 Constitution. First, their powers were restricted and then, in 1959, the councils were abolished altogether; instead, regional and district commissioners were appointed from the capital. Moreover, these were not civil servants but C.P.P. members.

These measures were accompanied by increasing violations of civil liberty: the Deportation Act of 1957, an Emergency Powers Act of the same year, and, in 1958, the Preventive Detention Act which permitted the government to imprison a citizen for up to five years without trial. In November, the government imprisoned thirty-eight of their political opponents; in December, they put two of their important leaders, Amponsah and Apaloo, into

gaol. The absorption of independent associations went on apace –
the co-operatives were brought into the party and the Builders
Brigades set up as a part of it – until few bodies outside the
university, the Church and the military were independent. The
C.P.P. guaranteed its finances by the Industrial Relations Act
of 1958, which made every member of the T.U.C. pay a compulsory levy of 2s. per month. And all this while, the cult of
Nkrumah's personality was expanding: his head appeared on
stamps and on coins, he was greeted as *Osagefyo*,[9] Liberator,
Messiah, the Christ of our Day; there were Nkrumah schools
and Nkrumah avenues or roads; statues were raised to him,
hymns sung in praise of him. As a result of the increasing
centralization and arbitrariness of his government, the opposition
in Parliament began to wither away. Of its thirty-two members,
Dr Busia was in exile, three were imprisoned, and twelve had
deserted and 'crossed the floor'.

In 1960, Nkrumah announced that he intended to hold a
referendum on a new and republican constitution for Ghana.
Dr Danquah, the former leader of the opposition, courageously
decided to contest it. He was allowed to publish and even hold
rallies though broadcasting facilities were denied him; and in
the towns, especially in Accra, the polling was honestly conducted.
However, the referendum was to be spread over three days, with
the Coast voting first. The Accra results of the first day were
profoundly disappointing to Nkrumah. For the turn-out was
very low – only forty-five per cent – and Dr Danquah received
no less than thirty-five per cent of the vote! From then on,
especially in the backlands, everything went right for the C.P.P.:
as Professor Austin says, 'not only . . . the right people voted,
but . . . the right number of papers were placed in the boxes'!
The result of this rigged election was a purported ninety per cent
vote for the Redeemer.

The new Constitution provided the foundation for a would-be
totalitarian state, and the punitive legislation that followed after
it as well as the blatant interference with the course of justice
proved a fitting superstructure. Under the 1960 Constitution, the
president (Nkrumah – elected by the same plebiscite) became the

9. Literally, 'war leader' (*osa* means 'war').

centre-piece of the state. Not only was he head of state and chief executive, but *de facto* prime minister as well. He selected his Cabinet colleagues. The president himself was to be elected in one of two possible ways: where a president died or resigned, his successor was picked by the M.P.s by secret ballot; while if his tenure ended as the automatic result of the dissolution of the Assembly, and an election, his successor was picked in accordance with preferences stated in advance by the parliamentary candidates. The president could dissolve the Assembly at any time, at least once every five years, although by so doing he ceased to be president. Among other powers granted him, was the right to remove the Chief Justice.

New repressive measures perfected the destruction of the opposition. The Sedition Act of 1960 punished with fifteen years' imprisonment those persons found guilty of intentionally exhorting the overthrow of the government by illegal means or inciting contempt of the government or the judiciary. By the Criminal Procedures Act of 1961, special courts were set up to try political crimes without a jury, and were empowered to pass sentences of death. The Emergency Powers Act of the same year enabled the president, with the approval of his Cabinet, to declare a state of emergency – and let it be remembered that, under the Constitution, the president both appointed and removed the members of his Cabinet.

From 1960, the period of economic fair weather, when the world price of cocoa was high, drew to an end while state expenditure soared. Also, political opposition, denied constitutional expression, turned to plots and efforts at assassination, which led to further repression and mass imprisonment. And, finally, the C.P.P. without the stimulus of electoral opposition, began to devour itself.

Nkrumah, intent on playing a world role, seemed to have lost his interest in organizing the party. His mind was on higher things. Now the electoral battles were over, the local branches of the party also began to lose their *raison d'être*, while the functional associations – the T.U.C., the Farmers' Council and the like – began to pull in different directions. To counteract this, Nkrumah laid stress on the need for an ideology to bind the party together, and for a vanguard detachment to spread it. So 'Nkrumaism' was developed. The book *Conscienscism* was ghost-written,[10] and the Winnebah Ideological Institute, purveying Marxian ideologies, was established:

As a consequence of the phenomenal growth of the party, the politically-conscious leadership is faced with the danger of being swamped by tribal, regional and other communal and ideological influences. Hence the party needs a vanguard of consciously dedicated activists and propagandists ideologically trained.

The tendency of this ideology – was it to be leftist or conservative? – became involved with intra-party quarrels of a personal nature. By this time, every party leader was telling tales on his colleagues. In his famous 'dawn broadcast' in 1961, Nkrumah declared that corruption had set in among the chief leaders. Botsio, the secretary of the Central Committee, was removed from his post which Nkrumah took over himself. Gbedemah, Botsio, Yeboah and Wiafe were all expelled from the party, and Edusei, Bensah, Inkumsah, Graft Dickson and others were forced to surrender their wealth over a certain limit. As they fell, so the radical ideologists on the left, Adamafio, Kofe Crabbe and Boateng, rose to favour, only to be ejected very soon. For now plots and murder attempts began to shake Nkrumah's trust and impede his political judgement. When, in 1962, an attempt was made on his life, the new favourites – Adamafio, Crabbe and Adjei – were arrested and thrown into prison to stand trial for suspected complicity, and their rivals – with the conspicuous exception of Gbedemah who had wisely fled abroad – came back to the leading posts.

But, when the Court delivered its verdict, it was to acquit Adamafio, Adjei and Crabbe. At this, the angry Nkrumah dismissed his Chief Justice, and his servile Assembly passed a retrospective Act permitting him to quash the decision of the Supreme Court. Nkrumah now took the final step towards totalitarianism. Two amendments to the 1960 Constitution were put to a referendum. By the first, all three of the High Court judges and not simply the Chief Justice were henceforth to be

10. K. Nkrumah, *Consciencism*, Heinemann, 1964.

liable to dismissal by the president. (This would ensure that there would always be a law court to sentence to death anybody whom the president thought was guilty.) The second was to declare the country a one-party state by permitting no party to exist other than the C.P.P., and declaring that elections should, henceforth, take place for one single national list of C.P.P. candidates.

Before the referendum could take place, a further attempt was made on Nkrumah's life in January 1964, after which the commissioner of police and eight of his officers were dismissed. The referendum was conducted with the most flagrant intimidation and falsification of election returns; also, Ghana was now a one-party state in law and not simply in fact. A second treason trial of Adjei, Adamafio and Kofe Crabbe now took place; given the first of the two amendments to the Constitution, the verdict was not surprising: guilty. The three were sentenced to death, although in response to world protests, the sentence was later commuted to twenty years' imprisonment. Then, in June 1965, a general election sealed the evolution of the Ghanaian political system. All the candidates were nominated by Nkrumah and his associates of the moment; all went uncontested; and all were returned as members. The parliamentary party, the nominees of the leader, then formally went through the ritual of unanimously re-electing Nkrumah as president.

'The C.P.P. is Ghana and Ghana is the C.P.P.', President Nkrumah had declared. The question in 1964–5 was whether this was the statement of a fact or a declaration of intent. To outward appearance, it was the former. The president controlled his party. He enjoyed wide powers of interference in the legislative, executive and judicial spheres. The party controlled the regions through its own regional commissioners. It had absorbed most of the key groups in society: the trade unions, the cocoa farmers, the co-operative movement, the women's and youth movements. It controlled the economy. It exercised a monopoly over the mass media. At the same time, through the machinery of the penal laws against civil liberties, it had suppressed the opposition, imprisoned several hundred of its opponents and driven others into exile. It was threatening both the Church and the university. To outward seeming, it was all-powerful and all-comprehending.

Ghana was not yet totalitarian, however – although in 1964 it formally adopted the title of 'People's Democracy', thus seeming to assert its identity with the Soviet-style totalitarian states of eastern Europe. The Church, though threatened, was still independent. Private property still existed. Distribution remained in private hands. The civil service, largely British-trained, and of considerable ability, maintained detachment. So did the armed forces, whose British commander-in-chief had been dismissed in 1961 and replaced by a Ghanaian. The Ghanaians themselves, outside the party ranks, seemed singularly unaffected by the high flights of party ideology. And private observers, including those most sympathetic to the régime, continued to assert that, in reality, the state was still high pluralist: that the party, unlike the parties of the Soviet-style states, was far from being a monolithic unity; that, on the contrary, it contained cliques and factions; and that the auxiliary associations themselves enjoyed considerable latitude.

Furthermore, as the economic climate worsened and murder plots succeeded one another, it was more and more frequently remarked how Nkrumah had grown aloof from the rank and file of his party, and how the party itself had grown aloof from the public. He shut himself up in Flagstaff House, which was surrounded by police lines and defended by a personal body-guard. The party in the legislature was not merely unrepresentative of the public, but, ever since the mock election of June 1965, was seen and known to be so. The party officials certainly carried out their tireless work of propaganda throughout their areas – but left their staffs and the civil service to administer. The party was unquestionably a powerful propagandizing force, but, apart from this, it survived largely as the representative of a nexus of interests – those of the members of the Assembly, of the regional commissioners and their staffs, of the party bureaucracy, of the officials of the ancillary organizations. It had shrunk, in fact, to a mere coalition of beneficiaries of the régime.

These were not necessarily the public at large – though the

two had been roughly identical in the 1950s. Rising prices, the collapse of the world cocoa price and the increased taxation necessitated by the drive to industrialization – all these had damped public enthusiasm. Indeed, the harsh budget of 1961 had caused the railway workers and dockers of Takoradi–Sekondi to go on strike, despite the fact that this was illegal under the 1958 Industrial Relations Act. Significantly, the strikers demanded political reforms, not just a redress of their economic grievances, and, although the strike was broken, their grievances persisted. By the end of 1965 the party leadership and its ideologists were regarded by the rank and file as an enigma, by the civil service as a squalid nuisance, by the non-party intellectuals as a joke and by the public as parasitic. All this qualified the outward appearance of a streamlined, monolithic party machine, run on the principles of democratic centralism, and incorporating and guiding the broad masses of the population. Where lay the truth? Was this the reality, or a façade?

An answer came on 24 February 1966, when, with Nkrumah absent on a mission to China, the army and police forces seized power, deposing Nkrumah, arresting his ministers, dissolving the Parliament and illegalizing the C.P.P., whose leaders were arrested. A self-appointed National Liberation Council of four army and four police officers took over. In the coup, the only groups whatsoever to offer resistance were the Russian- and Chinese-trained troops of the Palace Guard. For the rest, the population rejoiced, the various social and economic organizations expressed their support and – most significantly of all – in the ranks of 'the party' not a mouse stirred. Making all due allowance for the new government's show of bayonets and machine-guns, it is clear that, by this date, the rank and file of the party had lost whatever dedication they once had, and that its former mass support had quite disappeared.

It is hard to resist the conclusion that Nkrumah had, simultaneously, gone too far along the road to totalitarianism and yet not far enough. By harassing and subsequently illegalizing the opposition parties, the C.P.P. was, paradoxically, weakened and not strengthened. The elections of 1954 and 1956 had demonstrated that the more inevitable the party's electoral victory seemed to be, the more disunity and localism there was in its ranks. The rigging of the 1960 elections and, above all, the experience of the 1965 election, where the electorate were simply called on to endorse a list of C.P.P. candidates nominated by headquarters, bereft the party branches of all purpose. The electoral law was guaranteed to produce 'apoplexy at the centre and paralysis at the extremities'. It was, therefore, not a whit surprising that, at the centre, the leaders of the party intrigued against one another for Nkrumah's favour, like courtiers around the throne of Louis XV; nor that Nkrumah, in an effort to halt the disintegration and give the party back a sense of purpose, should have sought to endow it, through the Ideological Institute and the like, with an official philosophy. Unfortunately for him, as a result of its extreme cloudiness and highly personal character, this doctrine became a source of discord among the party's leaders and actually hastened the decay it was designed to prevent. As a result, factionalism in the party was neither eliminated nor institutionalized.

On the other hand, it could be – indeed, it is – argued that the party was not totalitarian enough; that, though the words and form were monist, society continued to be pluralist; in short, that the C.P.P. neither absorbed nor effectively controlled such elements as the civil service, the police and the armed forces. It is indeed true that trusted subordinates were placed at the head of these and that, in 1965, Nkrumah himself took over the control of the armed forces; but, imbued with the British traditions of professionalism and political neutrality, these organizations regarded themselves as functionally distinct from the party and held aloof from it. Senior civil servants in particular came to regard the party and the party ministers as inept or corrupt, or both, and resented their interference. In practice, therefore, the bureaucracy and the security forces operated as parallel hierarchies to the party. Nkrumah's efforts to build up a countervailing military force of Russian- and Chinese-trained soldiers, dedicated to his person, came too late to ward off the military intervention – and indeed there is some evidence that it might well have contributed to provoking it.

Ghana was a more vocal, politically more sophisticated and

more complex society than Tunisia; it was much more comparable to the Mexico of the twenties, in which the P.R.I. was founded, although Mexico had, at that date, a defined frontier and a sense of national identity which Ghana still lacked at independence. Ghanaian politics, like those of Mexico, were, therefore, bound to be factional. This factionalism might have been given self-expression through a multi-party system. If it be argued that the Ghanaian opposition parties were too parochial, too irresponsible and too violent to be tolerated (and there is substance in the charge) and that a single-party system was preferable or, indeed, necessary – then the factionalism could have been institutionalized inside this as it has been in the P.R.I. or, for that matter, in the Tanzanian single party, the T.A.N.U. Instead, Nkrumah imposed a more rigid and centralized framework on society than existed even in Tunisia – although, compared with Tunisia, Ghana was more heterogeneous, its sense of nationhood was less pronounced, and its political awareness was more alert, organized and vocal. Furthermore, the party that imposed this framework was only half as old as the Tunisian Néo-Destour. These differences might have suggested the need for greater flexibility and moderation on the C.P.P.'s part. Instead, it was committed to an official orthodoxy, while the Néo-Destour was almost free-wheeling; it pursued its enemies with a murderous harshness which the Tunisian counterpart found neither desirable nor necessary.

In short: compared with the Ghanaian party, the Tunisian ruling party had an inherently easier task in trying to encompass the diverse elements of society and went about this in a more relaxed way than did the C.P.P. The P.R.I., with a task of the same order of difficulty as the C.P.P.'s, handled it by making a virtue of pragmatism, and controlled the centrifugal elements within it by giving them institutional self-expression. In addition, both the P.R.I. and the Néo-Destour continued to enjoy their revolutionary prestige, to benefit from material success and, as a consequence, to show a degree of responsiveness to popular sentiment as the C.P.P., after 1960, did not. And yet, despite this, it still tried the methods of repression and conformism, while neglecting to ensure its control of the bureaucracy and the security forces: thus these were left in a position, of which they took advantage, to resist and then to overthrow it.

V. SUB-SAHARAN AFRICA

Practically every one of the new states of Africa commenced its independent life with more than one party. Today just under one-half of them are quasi-democracies. Opposition parties either 'crossed the floor' and merged with the government party out of conviction or self-interest; or else, deprived of government patronage, their followings fell away; or else they were harassed out of existence or brutally suppressed. Furthermore, in many instances, the monopoly position of the official party has been written into the constitution and the 'one-party state' proclaimed with fanfares of ideological justifications. The self-conscious rationalization of the system affords one marked contrast with the Mexican and Tunisian experiences; the artificial nature of many of these parties affords another; and the failure of many of them to strike roots among the common people affords a third.

For the sub-Saharan area, J. S. Coleman's recent symposium[11] offers an admirable conspectus of the reasons for the wide spread of this one-party tendency. Coleman lists four chief sets of reasons. To begin with, the situation at independence conduced to the quasi-democracy. The new *élites* did not inherit a liberal-democratic structure, but a modified autocracy. Their experience with a competitive party system was limited to the terminal years of colonialism. Also, some were threatened by the incoherence of the new state and the centrifugal tendencies of its component ethnic, linguistic, tribal and regional divisions. Furthermore, where these *élites* were modernizers, they were a minority to whom opposition smacked of the traditionalism they were sworn to supersede and of attachment to the colonial rule they had just thrown off. And lastly, as a modernizing minority they faced a task more exacting than that undertaken by their colonial

11. J. S. Coleman and C. C. Rosberg, eds., *Political Parties and National Integration in Tropical Africa*, California University Press, 1964.

predecessors – nothing less than to change the whole social and economic structure of their society.

Next, Coleman points out, sometimes the societies they controlled themselves facilitated the extension of the dominant party. While traditional elements usually opposed the modernizers, this was not always so. In such areas as Northern Nigeria and Brong–Ahafo in Ghana, the emirates of the former and the chieftaincies of the latter were both able and willing to lend their support and their 'clienteles' to the government party in return for favours; so that the party was able to secure footholds even in the traditional sectors. The degree to which it was able to do so depended in part upon the resilience and strength of those traditional elements and also on the extent to which they had been protected by the colonial power (as under indirect rule, by Britain) or eroded by it (as by the direct method of rule often practised by the French).

A third set of reasons lie, according to Coleman's analysis, in the impact of colonial rule itself. To begin with, the fact that it was autocratic is of prime importance. It was a system of bureaucratic centralism; Coleman says, 'one-party rule' and 'national party' government are simply post-colonial terms for this. . . . (In short – 'new presbyter is but old priest writ large'.) At the same time, the party under whom the state had achieved its independence basked in an aura of legitimacy – the state was its endowment. And this huge emotional advantage was often assisted by the electoral system bequeathed by the colonial government in its terminal period. The single-member constituency system, for instance, ensured the overwhelming triumph of the C.P.P. in Ghana in terms of parliamentary seats, although its rivals were only some ten per cent behind it in terms of votes. In the French-speaking states, the 'list' system of voting gave similar electoral advantages.

Finally, Coleman turns to what he calls the political culture of the modernizing *élite* – to its values and predilections. This he regards as probably the decisive factor – in which he is surely right. In that political culture, he isolates three factors. First, the elitism of the modernizing minority – a belief that they had a special claim to govern by virtue of their enlightenment. Next, their 'statism' – their belief that, given the self-appointed task of modernizing the society, the bureaucracy they inherited seemed the most obvious instrument to effectuate this. And finally, he claims, their nationalism led them to see any opposition as allied to traditionalism and as an attack on the integrity of the nation.

This analysis is admirable as far as it goes, but it is far too kind. One would never dream that ambition, cupidity or prejudice played a part in the process. They did. It would be difficult to underestimate the part that pure ambition and desire to dominate played in the careers of Nkrumah or Hastings Banda. Equally, it would be absurd to assume that their supporters – and, indeed, all the supporters of all the single- or dominant-party systems throughout the continent – do not realize that the single party offers them the very best of chances for keeping themselves in office. For they are a minority in their countries and are well aware of it. They cannot rely, as the traditional oligarchies did, on traditional deference. They cannot rely upon coercion, for their armies (save in Algeria, the U.A.R. and, latterly, the Congo (Kinshasa)) are weak and small. They must, therefore, cultivate the vote; and the easiest way of doing this is for them to multiply the number of their own supporters while, at the same time, harassing or suppressing their opponents. *The single party is the most obvious way to retain power in the post-colonial situation:* it really is as elementary as that!

Nor must one underrate sheer materialism. In a poor country, where it is hard to make a living out of business or the professions, politics is the best way to make a fortune; but where, in addition, property rights are insecure and liable to be invaded by government officials at any moment, as in these countries they are, the political career may indeed be the only way. The stakes are enormous, the more so since, for reasons discussed already, economic and cultural development in the new states are almost entirely in the hands of the government. To be in power is to be able to acquire wealth and to dispense it to one's friends; to be in opposition is to be poor at the very best, and in prison or dead at the worst. The party that controlled the government at the time of independence, therefore, enjoyed an enormous, indeed overwhelming, advantage over its opponents. But it could only be certain that it would retain this advantage by making the opposition ineffective or eliminating it altogether. Time and again, after an election in which several parties fought, the candidates elected for the minority party left their side of the house to join with the government; this 'floor crossing', as it is called, was not so much an implicit recognition that the interests of the opposition and the government were really one, as the single-party apologists claim, but a recognition that, once on the outside track, the race was lost forever.

Finally, there was the example of the Soviet Union. In French-speaking Africa, this made a notable impact because, in the terminal phases of colonial rule, the political parties in the French colonies were affiliated to their metropolitan counterparts: and, for the modernizing parties of national independence, this meant affiliation to the French Socialist Party and the French Communist Party. But, quite apart from such direct contact with Marxist circles, the Soviet Union appeared to many countries as an example of how a tiny but resolute minority, intolerant of the slightest opposition, could radically alter a society within a generation.

On the other hand, despite the Marxian jargon of leaders like Sékou Touré, Kéita, Nkrumah and Nyerere, it seems unlikely that Marxism has ever provided a practical basis for policy-making. Its role has rather been to rationalize action, and to provide a facile and plausible justification for the benefit of talkers and writers in the *Western* world. Except for the jargon talked, the structure and instruments of rule in some of the one-party states of Africa are hardly distinguishable from those of Mussolini's Italy. Nationalism – as in Italy; expansionism – with pan-Africanism substituted for Mussolini's *mare nostrum*; corporatism – through the forced affiliation of interest groups to the single party; 'corporative state' and state control over the private sector; autarchic tendencies in the economy; lavish public works programmes; one-party rule with the legislature reduced to a cipher; and, in some states like Ghana, a personality cult which, if anything, is more fulsome than that of Mussolini – these are the realities. Only the ideological justification differs.

But its role is that of Pareto's 'derivation' – to rationalize and justify. This phenomenon is common among populist parties in other areas of the Third World, not only Africa. As Torcuato di Tella has said, in his analysis 'Populism and Reform in Latin America':

> Reform parties in underdeveloped countries tend to adopt numerous elements from among the radical ideologies available in the world market. These ideologies (mostly varieties of socialism or Marxism) are based on the experience of the European working classes. But in the underdeveloped world, they are adopted by reform parties that comprise many social elements in addition to rural or urban workers. This does not create a great problem because the ideologies are used instrumentally, as a means of social control and mobilization of the masses, to an extent unparalleled in the older countries. The corpus of doctrine is reinterpreted and blended with national recognition. In India the Congress Party became socialist (or, rather, *socialistic*). Nasser also is converted to socialism. The Malagasi Republic has a government vowed to democratic socialism. *Aprismo* – derived from the initials of the Peruvian Alianza Popular Revolucionaria Americana party – claims to apply Marxism and dialectical materialism to Latin American conditions. The governing parties of Venezuela and Costa Rica are accepted as special members of the Socialist international. All this is meaningless. The word 'socialism' is now as malleable as the word 'Christian' and it is well on its way to becoming as useful for ruling the masses as it once was for arousing opposition against them.[12]

Remember, in the 1930s, when they said: 'If you want to drown your dog, first call him a Trotskyite.' Today, in many of these African quasi-democracies, particularly those approaching the totalitarian end of the spectrum, it could equally well be said: 'If you want to lock up the parliamentary opposition, first call them neo-colonialists.'

How have the ruling parties reached their present position? In the first place, they have done this by the conversion or the neutralization or even the suppression of the opposition. This is because the governments of these states dispose of such vast

12. Torcuato di Tella, 'Populism and Reform in Latin America', in C. Veliz (ed.), *Obstacles to Change in Latin America;* Oxford University Press, 1966, pp. 52–3.

powers. Supporters can be rewarded: by government appointments for themselves and their friends – and since the economies are 'socialist', there is an increasingly large number of boards, commissions and corporations of all sorts to which they can be appointed; by educational facilities – government scholarships for travel to Western universities or for undertaking special training; by allocations of funds to spend on public works in their constituencies; or by lucrative contracts for themselves or their clients. By the same token, opposition can be punished: by the withdrawal or refusal of favours such as the ones outlined above; by the harassment of opposition leaders; or, as happened in Cameroon, Chad, the Central African Republic, Dahomey, Ghana, Mauritania, Niger, Togo, the Upper Volta and Malawi, by the imprisonment or exile of the opposition. Secondly, a number of the governments have absorbed other associations and assimilated them to the ruling party. This has happened with varying emphases – in Guinea and, until the military coup, in Ghana and Mali, all or a large part of these associations were absorbed. (In the Ivory Coast, on the other hand, little assimilation of this kind has been attempted.) And finally, the ruling parties have manipulated the constitution or the electoral laws – sometimes by giving emergency powers to the government such as to make effective opposition impossible, sometimes by rigging the electoral system, as in Ghana, Mali and Guinea.

*

The merits and drawbacks of the quasi-democracy have generally been discussed with an eye to African régimes, south of the Sahara. On the whole it has been favourably regarded.

Its apologists have followed two main lines of argument, not incompatible. The first of these asserts that the single-party system confers positive advantages; the second argues that, however this may be, it is the only alternative to either anarchy or military rule.

It would seem that one or more of four advantages are alleged to accrue from the single-party system: (1) that it is a necessary prerequisite for rapid economic advance; (2) that it follows the 'natural' inclinations of the population; (3) that in some sense it is a necessary prerequisite for 'nation building'; and (4) that it guarantees political stability. As will be seen, however, not all these assertions are consistent with one another.

The economic argument

The argument seems to be that a strong coercive power, such as the single party is alleged to provide (but see below), is necessary if the state is to accumulate the large sums it requires for economic modernization, and to plan the growth of its economy.

If this be so, then as far as the first point – the accumulation of capital – is concerned, the single-party régimes are not coercive enough. The *investissement humain* programmes (how well the term sounds in French) have barely scratched the surface. Dumont, writing in 1962,[13] pointed out that China's programme realized some sixty days forced labour in the year, but that Guinea, over the period from 1959 to 1962, only planned for seven and failed even to reach this. Nor is this all. 'Human investment' is widely regarded by the peasants as simply *corvée* under another name and, not long ago, Togolese peasants clashed with party workers in resistance to it.[14] Taxation is another way of accumulating the necessary capital: yet many of the single-party régimes have been seriously weakened or even overthrown because of resentment at high taxation. It was this that sparked off the Takoradi–Sekondi strikes in Ghana in 1961, the repression of which permanently alienated a large body of workers from Nkrumah's régime. President Maga of Dahomey was overthrown in 1963 because his harsh budget had alienated the trade unions, and more budget cuts in 1965 again provoked them and paved the way for the second and third military coups at the end of the year. The same is true of the Upper Volta and the Central African Republic; in both cases austerity budgets, bearing heavily on the over-paid and over-privileged civil service, provoked unrest and led to the military

13. R. Dumont, *L'Afrique noire est mal partie*, Editions du Seuil, Paris, 1962.

14. And cf. *Africa Report*, Washington, D.C., November 1965, for the C.A.R.

coups in these countries. It is reckoned that, for adequate capital formation, the African states ought to raise some fifteen to twenty per cent of the national income in taxes. As matters stand, they most of them raise less than ten per cent.

Yet if the régimes are not coercive enough to raise the capital sums they require, some of them appear to have been too coercive in 'planning'. It is curious that those states which have had a reputation for possessing aggressive and centralized parties – notably Algeria, Ghana, Guinea and Mali – have also been the ones to embark on ambitious and comprehensive economic planning. The Algerian experiments had by 1968 landed that country with two million unemployed out of a population of ten million; the Nkrumah régime, as is well known, exhausted the country's foreign reserves, which had been substantial at independence, and ran it into a condition of imminent international bankruptcy; while the failure, accompanied by numerous unsavoury scandals, of the Guinean nationalized import agencies is notorious. By contrast, the easier, wheeling-dealing economy of the Ivory Coast advanced vigorously.

But quite apart from this, the single-party system, except in a tiny handful of states which includes Tanzania but few others, has caused substantial economic losses; for over most of the continent the single-party governments have indulged in a vast and profligate squandering of their scarce revenue and even scarcer foreign aid, partly on costly and uneconomic show-piece projects, but even more on swollen and highly privileged government apparatuses, grossly overpaid by European standards but fantastically so by reference to their own peasant compatriots. Dumont has observed[15] that the deputy's salary is usually in the order of £3,000 per annum; so that in six months he receives a sum which it takes a peasant thirty-six years of continuous toil to earn. Under the Ben Bella régime in Algeria, civil servants were earning in one month between four and twelve times what a fellah could earn in a whole year.[16] In Dahomey, just before the 1965/6 military coups, salaries made up two-thirds of the country's exiguous budget, and, although the country had an adverse trade balance, the imports of consumer goods outweighed

15. op. cit.   16. *Africa*, Number 13, London, 1965.

those of capital goods.[17] Furthermore, the trade unionist also is a privileged citizen; he tends to earn some twenty times more than his fellows on the land, and so he makes common cause with the civil servants in resisting any governmental effort to reduce salaries and wages. This coalition, together with that of the soldiery who take alarm lest similar cuts be imposed on them, has paved the way for the military takeovers in such states as Gabon, Dahomey, the Central African Republic and the Upper Volta.

It is hard to come by the comparative growth rates for all the various African states; in any case, since they differ markedly in human and natural resources, comparisons can only be made with great difficulty. From what is known it would appear that, if roughly comparable economies are considered, the single-party régimes do not do markedly better than those with competitive party systems – and, of course, vice versa. The point is that whether a régime has been single-party or not does not appear to have been decisive so far. And this disposes of the first apologia in its hard form, namely, that such a single-party system is a necessary prerequisite for rapid economic growth.

It could still be argued however that such a system is helpful when conjoined with other factors. But to establish this would require more economic data than exists at present and a sociologico-economic analysis more ambitious than anything yet attempted. We can, however, say fairly that the proposition that the single-party system in any sense guarantees rapid economic advance must be rejected.

The 'natural consensus' argument

Broadly, this argument asserts that the single-party system reflects a basic consensus of the population in the face of the tasks of national construction. In this sense, it is somehow 'natural'. But this argument takes two forms, and they are mutually inconsistent.

In its first form, the argument asserts national unity as a fact. It states that populations are unanimous. Certainly some ruling

17. *Africa*, Number 25, London, 1965.

parties first attained this position by virtue of a national unanimity. In Guinea, Tunisia, Tanzania, for instance, the party now ruling emerged immediately before or after independence as the clear favourite of the overwhelming mass of the population in fair and free elections. Given the role of these parties at the time as nationalist 'fronts' campaigning for the unique and sublime aim of independence, and given too the personality of leaders like Touré, Banda, Nyerere and Bourguiba, this is not at all surprising. Indeed what does surprise is that so many other countries should have thrown up, as they did, not one, but three or four rival parties in the period of the independence struggle.

Now in the latter countries, to the extent that they are 'single-party' states today, that single ruling party has emerged in one of two ways: either by the ruthless suppression of its rivals – as in Mauritania, the Central African Republic, Chad, Ghana, Niger and the Upper Volta – or by a hastily cobbled-up 'package' party, composed of the original competing factions, as in Congo (Brazzaville) (up to 1963), Dahomey (1961–3 and, again, 1963–6), Gabon and Togo. In the latter states the continued jostling of these factions made the so-called 'single party' more nominal than real and led to plots, civil disturbances and in every case the violent overturn of the first of the post-independence régimes. Therefore, as regards these states, the assertion that the populations are unanimous can be dismissed.

But what of those where the single party did indeed reach its ruling position by genuine popular acclaim? The question here is not whether it did so by the voluntary choice of the people at some point in the past, but whether it retains that position by such a voluntary choice today. In most cases there are ample proofs to the contrary. The P.D.G. of Guinea was the all but unanimous choice of the population after 1957. But it has discovered and suppressed no less than four 'plots' since 1960: a serious one in April 1960 when an attempt was made to found an opposition party (quite legal under the Constitution) which the government suppressed, claiming that it was a French plot; another and much bigger one in November 1961, when the Teachers' Union protested at a threatened change in teaching conditions, upon which the government declared a 'plot' inspired by trade unionists, students, communists, freemasons and General de Gaulle, and imprisoned fifty of the malcontents; a lesser plot in 1963 in which certain businessmen were charged with currency offences; and the November plot of 1965 when Mamadou Touré (significantly a native of the Fouta Djallon region, which has proved hostile to the régime) stood on the letter of the Constitution and deposited with the Minister of the interior the statutes of a proposed opposition party. The government claimed that this was the cover for a plot to overthrow or assassinate the Sékou Touré government, hatched up by the governments of the Ivory Coast, the Congo (Kinshasa), Niger and the Upper Volta, with the connivance of the French government. Over one hundred people were arrested and condemned, including two former ministers and a former ambassador to Moscow.[18] Again, in Tunisia, first the dissidents who followed Ben Youssef were repressed, and later even such party stalwarts as Masmoudi and Ben Salah were silenced. In Malawi a significant proportion of the ruling party has been in open rebellion since late 1964. Tanzania[19] is – with justice – regarded as the best supported and most liberal of the single-party régimes; yet even here the 1965 amnesty revealed that thirty-six persons were still imprisoned under the Preventive Detention Act, and, indeed, it was not until as late as September 1966 that all the mainland political prisoners were released – while many Zanzibaris are still in jail.

Political differences unquestionably exist both inside the ruling parties of these single-party states and outside them; and it is simply false that the only reason for the existence of a sole party in such states is that nobody there desires to have more than one.

At this point the argument shifts plane. It no longer asserts that the entire population is of one mind. It asserts that, even if

18. The official Guinean version of the plot will be found in *Africa Research Bulletin*, London, November 1965, quoting *Horoya*, 17 November 1965.

19. Here and elsewhere I intend by this only the Tanganyika portion of what is in effect a twin state, with twin single parties – the T.A.N.U. on the mainland and the Afro-Shirazi Party in Zanzibar.

it isn't, it ought to be. But this is a very different proposition.

It is supported by two different lines of reasoning. The first is this: that, given independence and the vast tasks entailed by modernization, differences among the population are bound to be limited and moreover confined to the choice of means rather than ends. This being so, such differences can be most constructively expressed, not through separate and rival organizations which tend to exaggerate and multiply differences, but within the bounds of one common fellowship – the single party. But where, one asks, save except in Tanzania and Kenya, does the party provide a constitutional machinery for expressing these 'minor' differences, and where, except there and in Tunisia, is a party member's life, let alone his career, safe if he dares to voice them? The only single-party states that appear (at the time of writing) to have been free of serious plots by former party members are: the Upper Volta, the Central African Republic, Mali, Kenya, the Malagasy Republic and Mauritania. And the overthrow of the governments of the first three by their military forces suggests a bottled-up latent discontent. As to Kenya, the breakaway faction of Oginga Odinga, though not so far imperilling the lives of the leaders, seems to have ruined their careers. So, leaving aside Mauritania and the Malagasy Republic[20] everywhere else plots and internal disturbances have marked the relationship between the leading faction of the party and its rivals. Some of these have already been mentioned in other connexions; and later many more will have to be mentioned when the issue of stability is confronted. At that stage I shall introduce a table of such plots and disturbances, so further illustrations need not be given at this point.

Thus, the first reason for asserting that the entire population

20. In Mauritania there has recently been serious trouble between 'Arab' and 'African' Mauritanians over a decree making Arabic compulsory in the secondary schools, but it is unclear how, if at all, this has involved the party leadership. The relative absence of plots in the Parti Social Démocratique (P.S.D.), the Malagasy ruling party, may well be due to the fact that officially the system is a competitive one, with the opposition holding three seats – so that if serious inner party opposition developed it could express itself in the form of a rival party.

ought to express itself through a single party breaks down, for the single party almost never provides machinery for the constitutional resolution of the differences that are bound to arise: on the contrary, it tends to suppress or punish those expressing such differences.

The second line of reasoning for the proposition is more metaphysical. It rests on the unproven axiom (if indeed it really is an axiom and not a covert recommendation) that political parties are the expression of class interests and only of class interests. Since – allegedly (and questionably) – there are no social classes in Africa, there is room for only one party or indeed for no party as such, only for a so-called 'national coalition'. The most widely quoted statement of this view is that of Sékou Touré of Guinea: 'The P.D.G. is not a political party in the European sense of the word [because] it is not the political instrument of a given social class. European parties express contradictions of interest between existing classes. . . . The P.D.G. cannot preach policies based on class, for the differentiation of social strata in Black Africa is not characterized by a fundamental difference or even an opposition of interests.'[21] The kernel of truth in this statement is that where social structure is homogeneous, dissent is less likely to occur and, when it does, is likely to be expressible within the confines of a single organization. This is the lesson of Tunisia's relatively stable single-party system, and of the systems of Tanzania and, possibly, the Malagasy Republic: in comparison with most of the single-party states elsewhere in Africa, their social structure is indeed homogeneous. But for the rest, Sékou Touré's much quoted and widely admired statement is bad Marxism, bad history and bad political science.

It is bad Marxism on two counts. In the first place, Marxism-Leninism has always asserted that in a *bourgeois* state the *bourgeoisie* may be and often is represented by a number of parties, not simply by one alone. In *The State and Revolution*, for instance, Lenin talks of 'the struggle for power of various bourgeois and petty bourgeois parties distributing and redistributing the spoils of official berths, the foundations of capitalist

21. Quoted in B. B. Burch, *Dictatorship and Totalitarianism*, Van Nostrand, New Jersey, 1964, p. 155.

society remaining all the while the same'.[22] Vyshinsky's *Law of the Soviet State* saw the political parties of the U.S.A. only as expressing the interests 'of separate cliques of big finance and industrial capital'. [23] Coming nearer home, we have it on Mr John Gollan's authority (1954) that the British Labour Party 'functioned . . . as the second party of capitalism in the so-called traditional British two-party system'.[24] Now if the *bourgeois* class can throw up two or more parties, why not the labouring masses?

Secondly, Sékou Touré and others like him appear to assume that where there is no industrial *bourgeoisie* and industrial proletariat, there is no class differentiation at all. But Marx never alleged that 'capitalist' and 'proletariat' exhausted the catalogue of classes, only that this would be the ultimate position as capitalism reached its term. In the pre-industrial period and in the nascent state of capitalism Marx and Engels recognized a whole multiplicity of social classes. For instance, in Germany in 1848 Engels counted no less than five – the nobility, the *bourgeoisie*, the small-trading and shopkeeper class, the artisan class and the peasantry.[25] Is none of these present in Africa? And may there not be still others, not mentioned by Marx and Engels?

But Sékou Touré's statement is also bad history and bad political science. It is bad history because it falsely assumes that the only causes of political disagreements are economic ones – as though religion, race, nationalism and the like are reducible to strictly economic terms. And it is bad political science because, although the industrial proletariat is a small class in most African states, substantial differences of outlook and economic interest exist between the townsman and the peasant, between the trader and the cocoa farmer and the subsistence farmer out in the bush, and between these last and the small but highly

22. V. I. Lenin, *The State and Revolution*, Foreign Languages Publishing House, Moscow, no date, Chapter II, Section 2, pp. 34–5.

23. A. Y. Vyshinsky, *The Law of the Soviet State*, Macmillan, New York, 1948, p. 241.

24. J. Gollan, *The British Political System*, Lawrence & Wishart, London, 1954, p. 10.

25. F. Engels, *Revolution and Counter-revolution in Germany*, London, Lawrence & Wishart, 1933, p. 13.

privileged class of 'proletarians' whose earnings are so enormously in excess of all the others.

Nor is this all. Let us take the argument *ad hominem*. Even if Guinea is not divided into conflicting economic classes, it is certainly divided regionally – the Fouta Djallon which is inhabited mainly by Fulani is notoriously disaffected – and equally certainly divided ethnically. The most important of its tribal groupings are the Mandé (including the Malinké) who number 600,000, the Fulani who number 850,000 and the Susu whose womenfolk some few years ago so charmed the strollers in Trafalgar Square, and who number 250,000. Is it purely coincidental that in the sixteen-strong Politbureau of the P.D.G. there are eleven Malinké (which is Sékou Touré's own tribe) as compared with only two Fulani (among whom opposition elements are strongest)? That the Malinké who make up twenty per cent of the population provide seventy-five per cent of the Politbureau, while the Fulani who make up thirty-three per cent of the population provide only twelve per cent of the membership? But it is otiose to labour the point that ethnic, religious or regional loyalties may and do provide the basis for political differences.

It is at this point that the argument changes again. I have just challenged and indeed refuted the ridiculous assertion that African society (unique in the world to hear the apologists speak!) never throws up differences substantial enough to warrant the formation of more than one party. The third major argument now makes its appearance. It tacitly admits that these religious and ethnic differences do exist but asserts that they are inimical; and because they are inimical, this argument continues, a single party is desirable because it alone can achieve two necessary things. It can rise above tribalism or communalism or regionalism by maintaining a balance of such elements within its ranks while simultaneously enthusing them all with a transcendent ideology, a vision of the nation. By doing this it will integrate the parallel and theretofore hermetic sectors which divide society. Such integration may be thought of as lateral, as though these sectors existed side by side. But at the same time this single party will provide a two-way flow of information between leaders and led, i.e., a vertical integration of leadership and population. This is the argument of 'nation building'.

The 'nation-building' argument

The nation-building argument is a popular and forceful one, and therefore it is not unfair to point out that it is totally inconsistent with the 'natural consensus' argument. One may be right or the other may be right. Both cannot be right and in fact both are wrong.

First of all, in practice few of the single-party states have managed to transcend regionalism or tribalism or communalism. Tanzania seems to have succeeded best and the reason may well be that all but a small proportion of its people are Bantu and speak a similar language so that, although they are divided into tribes, this has not the same significance as in neighbouring Kenya, and most of the West African states. The Malagasy Republic's success may also lie in the relative homogeneity of its people; the eighteen clans have indeed a history of rivalry, but the population is ethnically homogeneous and speaks the same tongue. The Ivory Coast seems also to have managed a balance though it has done this by going out to meet tribalism more than half way: the P.D.C.I. has made the ethnic groups the basis of its local branches – a practice that makes 'advanced' parties on the continent despise it for pandering to reactionary prejudices, but has the virtue of practicality. Senegal also strikes a good ethnic balance. But on the whole, the practice of the ruling parties diverges, some a little way, some a great distance, from the ideal. The C.P.P. of Ghana certainly had a national following – this was proved in the 1956 election; but its main strength unquestionably came from the southern Fanti peoples, the Brongs and particular northern chiefdoms which saw advantage in enlisting the power of the central government on behalf of their own local interests. In Chad the president and leader of the party (François Tombalbaye) depends on the support of the black African south (the majority), against the Arab moslem north, a situation which has led to civil war. In Mauritania, similarly divided, the situation is just the reverse; there the party is Arabist. The politics of Dahomey are simply incomprehensible if one does not take into consideration the mutual hatred of the people of the coast, of Abomey and of the north. And so one could go on.

And just as relatively few of the ruling parties have succeeded in transcending tribalism or religious differences,[26] so in virtually every case they have failed to establish that 'two-way flow of communication' which was to provide 'vertical integration'. The only two parties that can rightfully stake a claim to have done so are those in Tanzania and Tunisia in that order. Tanzania is, in the African context, a model. In Tunisia there is indeed a two-way flow by which complaints can be and often are funnelled upwards and come to the ears of the provincial governors or of the party leadership itself where they may be dealt with; but on policy matters the flow is in one direction only – policy is made at the top and explained and commended to those in the party meetings at the base. Something of the sort also appears in Senegal and the Ivory Coast.

Writing in 1961, Professor I. Wallerstein singled out Tunisia, Mali, Guinea and Tanganyika as 'models' of two-way communication, with Ghana, Togo and the Central African Republic 'running close behind'. Of the party in Guinea it is fair to say that it appears to have a most impressive network of local branches; but it is equally fair to add that they are mainly used to transmit policy downwards – and in an even more marked fashion than in Tunisia. The very party literature with its talk of 'democratic centralization' permits one to infer that this is the aim and not merely the practice. But the list of second-runners – Ghana, Togo and the Central African Republic – makes curious reading in 1969. In Ghana there was indeed a two-way flow in the C.P.P. up to about 1960 when Wallerstein was writing. But in that very year, as though deliberately to prove him wrong – and indeed the whole tenor of the argument we are at present discussing – a *de facto* single-party system was imposed: and this was the beginning of the end for the two-way flow. For, from that point, the local branches, which had thrived on fighting elections, lost their purpose and began to atrophy.

26. It is important to note that in one of the single-party states – Tunisia – this problem does not exist.

The 1964 constitutional amendment, which introduced voting by one single national list, finished the process. The party branches no longer had any say even in the nomination of candidates. By 1965 the two-way flow – indeed any significant flow at all – had fallen to a spasmodic trickle. As to the Central African Republic, notorious for the cleavage between its wretched peasantry and its upper crust of corrupt officials and wealthy coffee-planters, any dialogue between party headquarters and branches must have been a *dialogue des sourds*. Levine, writing in 1965, speaks of a gradual erosion of the militant solidarity of the party machine: 'Individual ministers and deputies have begun to carve out political fiefs of their own, and party militancy . . . [is] . . . less responsive to leadership's call for action.'[27] The bloodless overthrow of the president by his military cousin in 1966 confirms this impression that communication had broken down. Likewise for Mali, where the party was overthrown by the soldiers in 1968. Altogether, events seem to have outstripped Wallerstein's sanguine appreciation of nine years ago; and evidence from other states outside the list tends to confirm the view that, on the whole, two-way communication is poor and in many cases non-existent.[28] This is notoriously true of the far-famed F.L.N. of Algeria. This loosely-knit fighting organization was never reorganized after independence in 1962 and has no networks of party branches. Its policy is made by a few top leaders, in the name of a limited number of militants. Only in 1969 was serious attention given to creating a grass-roots organization; with little result to date. It is equally true of the Dahomean ruling party – whatever name this has borne (it has been continually remodelled since independence). What has remained constant is its largely nominal nature. Information from

27. Victor T. Levine, 'Insular Problems of an Inland State', *Africa Report*, November 1965.

28. It is odd that Togo is included in Wallerstein's list. There were four main parties in existence between 1960 and 1962, but by 1962 President Olympio had succeeded in banning or otherwise suppressing the rivals to his own party (the Comité pour l'Unité Togolèse), so that it is only from December 1962 that one could describe Togo as a *de facto* single-party state. Was it in the C.U.T. that the 'two-way flow' was so excellent, according to Wallerstein?

Chad is scanty; but, like the Central African Republic, it seems that 'the party' is, in practice, party functionaries and notables, assembled in conference to hear the words of the leader, rather than a network of functioning party branches – let alone a mechanism for transmitting the views of the rank and file to the leadership. In Kenya also, by 1965 the party 'network' had largely faded away if indeed it had ever existed: the 'party' was a loose confederation of local bosses over whom H.Q. imposed no effective control, and there had been no national conference since 1962.

This brings us to the fourth argument: that the single-party system is a prerequisite of political stability.

The 'stability' argument

This argument is connected with the third argument which we have just rejected; for one would expect, other things being equal, that a two-way flow of communication, by keeping leaders and population closely in touch, would prevent or at least fore-stall subversive movements. But just as the degree of two-way communication has been exaggerated, so has the degree of political stability. Indeed, of all the arguments advanced, this is the easiest to confute.

In the absence of better indicators, I will take as evidence for instability, (1) plots (real or alleged) against the government, and (2) the intervention (successful or not) of the armed forces. Algeria experienced the Ait Ahmed revolt (1963–5), the Oran troubles of 1963 and the Colonel Chaabani revolt of 1964, and has twice submitted to military intervention: in 1962, when the army of the exterior overthrew Ben Barka and installed Ben Bella in his place, and in 1965, when the army overthrew Ben Bella in his turn and installed its own commander-in-chief, Colonel Boumedienne. The Central African Republic appears not to have experienced plots but its government was overthrown by the military in January 1966. Chad experienced two major plots in 1963, and another, quite recently, in November 1965 and is currently in a condition of civil war. The Congo (Brazzaville) poses a problem of identification. It was not a one-party state

when the Youlou government was overthrown by rioting trade
unionists in 1963, but it became so in 1964; so that it could be
classed as being a one-party state when the recent military
attempt on the party headquarters was made in July 1966,
followed by the successful military takeover in 1968. Dahomey
is an even more difficult state to categorize because its party
system has been so fluid. Bascially, it has had three parties,
each regionally based, and each led by a powerful contender –
Apithy, Ahomedegbé and Maga; the manoeuvres of these
men make up most of the political history of that country.
In 1959 the three parties contended, in 1960 two of them
united against the third, and in 1961 this merged party, the
Parti Dahoméen de l'Unité, suppressed its rival, the Union
Démocratique Dahoméenne, and transformed Dahomey into a
de facto one-party state. It was in this condition when the first
military takeover occurred. Thereupon the P.D.U. was dissolved
and a new official ruling party, the Parti Démocratique Dahoméenne (P.D.D.), was formed in its place. It was in this situation
when the Parakou rising occurred in the north (contesting the
supremacy of this new party) and when the second and third
military takeovers subsequently occurred in 1965–6. As for
Ghana, this state became a *de facto* single-party state in 1960: it
is unnecessary to recount the several attempts upon Nkrumah's
life that followed, or the plots he claimed to have discovered.
They were numerous; and in February 1966 he was deposed by
the army. Guinea, as has been mentioned, experienced four
'plots', in 1960, 1961, 1963 and 1965 respectively. The Ivory
Coast uncovered two major plots in January and in August 1963,
though it has been quiet since. Kenya became a *de facto* one-
party state after 1964 when the Kenya African National Union
(K.A.N.U.) and Kenya African Democratic Union (K.A.D.U.)
merged, and so remained until recently when Oginga Odinga led
his breakaway faction out of the coalition, the country reverting
to one-party status, 1969. During that period there occurred the
military mutiny of January 1964. Liberia has not to the writer's
knowledge experienced any serious plots in the period from 1960
to the time of writing, nor has the Malagasy Republic. But in
Malawi, a section of the ruling party broke away into open

rebellion in 1964, and is still being pursued. Mali claimed to have uncovered a plot in 1962, allegedly led by the previous opposition party and the military overthrew the party, 1968. In Mauritania, light- and dark-skinned students fought one another over the 1966 language decree which made Arabic compulsory in secondary schools. In Niger, an assassination plot was discovered in 1965. In Senegal, there occurred in 1962, because of sedition by the prime minister, Mamadou Dia, a struggle between him and Léopold Senghor, the president. In this struggle the army took sides, and the stronger party (i.e., Senghor's, which had the paratroops) won. Tanzania has been free from internal plots of any consequence but experienced the military mutiny of 1964. Togo is another problem case in classification. It had four effective parties in 1960, but by 1962 the president, Olympio, had proscribed or otherwise repressed all but his own, so that it was effectively a one-party state at that point. During that period there were no less than three attempts to assassinate him. Ultimately, in 1963, a military revolt took place in which he was murdered. Thereafter the four parties were permitted to operate, but formed themselves into an electoral *bloc*, and this was the state of affairs when the second military coup, in January 1967, deposed Olympio's successor, President Grunitsky. Thus, during its single-party state, Togo experienced one military coup, that of 1963; it experienced the other during its multi-party stage. Tunisia has been relatively trouble-free, save for the Youssefist assassination plot against Bourguiba in 1963 in which some dissident military elements were involved. Finally comes the Upper Volta, free from serious plots until January 1966 when, among trade union riots, the military took over the government.[29]

29. I have not included the United Arab Republic among the one-party states. It was a multi-party state in 19ɔ2 when the military takeover occurred. Since then Nasser has made no less than three separate attempts to establish a single official party. It is clear to me, however, that, even if the present Arab Socialist Union is established, it is, for the moment at any rate, an arm of the régime, which is provided by the military caste. For this reason it does not seem proper to categorize the U.A.R. as a single-party state. In any case the U.A.R. has suffered much plotting – in 1966 no less than three separate treason trials were proceeding simultaneously, while 1967 saw the alleged treason of Hakim Amer.

The one-party régimes in Africa: reconsiderations

The state of play can best be illustrated by a table:

TABLE 20. INDICATORS OF POLITICAL INSTABILITY
IN SINGLE-PARTY STATES 1960–69

Total number of states	20
States suffering military intervention while in a single-party condition	11
States suffering plots or civil disturbances while in a single-party condition	13
States suffering both	6
States suffering neither (Malagasy Republic and Liberia)	2
Single-party states whose governments have been overturned by violence 1960–70:	8
of which, by the military	8

* The 1962 struggle in Senegal is not included as a military intervention.

Eight states out of twenty whose governments have been over-thrown by military violence within the short space of nine years, and only two from which we have no reports of either plots, civil disturbances or military intervention! These are not the statistics of stability but of nightmare.

Nor is this all. A variant upon the stability theme has been the argument that the single-party régime provides the only alternative to military intervention. Wallerstein was writing in 1962 that 'the choice has not been between one-party and multi-party states: it has been between one-party states and either anarchy or military régimes or various combinations of the two.'[30] Something of the same sort is hinted at in Janowitz's essay, *The Military in the Political Development of New Nations*,[31] where it is suggested that 'the takeover of power by the military in new nations has generally followed the collapse of efforts to create democratic-type institutions: the military has tended not to displace the single mass-party authoritarian régimes'. How in

30. I. Wallerstein, quoted in B. B. Burch, op. cit.
31. University of Chicago Press, 1964, p. 29.

fact do the single-party régimes in Africa compare with the multi-party ones?

Once again we are bedevilled by the problem of classification. There have been two main parties in Cameroon for the relevant time (1960–66) – but they were not competitive, nor does the opposition party play a great role in Zambia either. And so forth. Nevertheless, it is to such régimes that the apologists for single-party régimes refer when they discuss régimes which are not single-party. In Africa there are two such types: non-party régimes, like those of Ethiopia and Libya (the latter terminated in October 1969), and what we must therefore perforce call multi-party régimes. These comprise – or rather, at the time that any military coup occurred, they comprised – the following: Burundi; Cameroon; the Congo (Brazzaville) up to 1964; the Congo (Kinshasa); Gabon; Gambia; Morocco; Nigeria; Sierra Leone; Somalia; the Sudan; Togo, since 1963; the U.A.R. to 1952 when the military coup occurred; Uganda; and Zambia. In all, fifteen states which were multi-party *at the relevant time*. How did they fare compared with the single-party states, also at the relevant time? I am aware that the universes here are so small that one state can make all the difference to the percentages. The results are not statistically significant. For all that they are instructive (see Table 21).

TABLE 21. MILITARY INTERVENTIONS IN SINGLE-PARTY AND MULTI-PARTY STATES IN AFRICA, 1960–69

Number of multi-party states	15
Number of these experiencing military intervention	10* (66%)
Number of single-party states	20
Number of these experiencing military intervention	10 (55%)

* Namely Burundi, the Congo (Kinshasa), Gabon (in 1963), Nigeria, Sierra Leone, Somalia, Sudan, Togo, the U.A.R. (in 1952), Uganda.

In view of the tiny numbers involved, there is really little between them. So the claim that the single-party state provides greater stability than the multi-party state still has to be proven.

With this is concluded the first great line of argument in
defence of the single-party state: that it provides the society with
certain concrete benefits – economic advance, national representation, nation-building, stability. No one of these four claims
is true for every African state; all four are untrue for any one
African state; and most of them are untrue for most African
states. It is at this point that the second main argument enters.

The 'no alternative' argument

Irrespective of any intrinsic merits the single party may possess,
however, it is possible to argue that it is the only viable alternative
to either anarchy or military despotism. As can be seen from the
quotation already cited, this is Wallerstein's line. It has been
elaborated more recently by Mr Colin Legum, in a controversy
with Sir Arthur Lewis over the latter's brilliant and challenging
attack on the claims of the single-party system in his book
Politics in West Africa.[32] Legum had taken Lewis to argue that
the prime reason for the single-party system's spread in West
Africa was the baleful wilfulness of selfish politicians. In this
I believe he misinterpreted the book. However that may be, his
reply was concerned to point out the impersonal imperatives
that drove rulers of the new African states into erecting single-
party systems.

The new states, argued Legum, are states but not yet nations.
But their new rulers want to make them nations. The colonial
governing machinery that they inherit is unsuitable for this
purpose; indeed, this apparatus actually promotes internal dis-
harmonies. The new rulers, therefore, have to create a machinery.
They find themselves in a situation where they can rely either
on their popularity or on coercion. But with independence their
popularity wanes. They cannot fulfil the chiliastic expectations
that the campaign for independence has aroused, while their very
success in winning independence releases what Legum calls
'conflicting ethnic, regional and other particularist interest'. The
leaders can 'either abdicate, compromise or assert such powers

32. *Encounter*, London, December 1965, pp. 51–4.

as they can mobilize'. They choose the last two: hence the establishment of the single-party state.

And hence his conclusion: 'the one-party state is probably an inevitable transition between independence and the consolidation of the nation state.'

This conclusion does not follow: and it conceals a set of assumptions which seem, in various degrees, questionable. It assumes to begin with that the single party is a conscious response to conflicting ethnic, regional and other particularist interests. This is not a convincing account of the rise of the ruling parties of what are now Gabon, the Congo (Brazzaville) and Chad. As Ballard has shown, these resulted from a scramble for power between parties which served regional and even individual self-interest and possessed 'little ideology and no mass control nor committee control over the party leaders'; only after the acquisition of power did the victor establish the 'official' ruling party and the cult of the heroic leader.[33] Next, it assumes that these parties do really 'mobilize' the people. But I have already pointed out that some of the single parties are only nominally single, and also that many others are only nominally parties; that in states like Algeria, Chad, Mauritania, Niger and the Upper Volta these possess little in the way of local organization, and that in others, like Ghana, Kenya and the Central African Republic, such local organization as the party had created had atrophied. And it is increasingly doubtful how far the ruling parties 'mobilize' even their own members. More and more, it would seem, party members cohere as a set of beneficiaries or potential beneficiaries from what has become the source of all patronage, rather than as participants in a common cause. In short, in a high proportion of cases, the ruling party is more nominal than real; only this can account for the ease with which handfuls of armed men have overturned the party leaders in such states as Algeria, Ghana, the Central African Republic and the Upper Volta, without a shot fired by the party faithful. And finally the argument assumes that these single-party systems do in fact achieve

33. Ballard, op. cit. The P.S.D., the Malagasy ruling party, also evolved in this order.

'the consolidation of the nation state'. I have already given reasons for qualifying this assertion.

Even if these qualifications are shrugged aside, two objections remain. In the first place, let us suppose that the single-party state is, as suggested, the 'probably inevitable' consequence of the condition of African society: it does not also follow that it is therefore to be welcomed. On the contrary. Life confronts us with many things that are inevitable: they may well be deplorable. And if what I have said in the earlier part of this section is even partly true, then in many if not most of the new African states the single-party system has proved both unhappy and unconstructive. But, in the second place, does the single-party system follow so inevitably from the condition of African society? For on present form it seems that it offers no more secure bulwark against subversion or military intervention than other types of system.

If that is so, the only conclusion one can draw from Legum's analysis of African society is that the bulk of the African states are extremely unstable and likely to remain so for many years to come. In that event, the single-party system is no more an inevitable outcome than the multi-party system or the military régime; and the most likely event will be that for decades the majority of these new states will jolt precipitously and probably violently from one type of régime to another and back again, as each in turn wears out the patience of its supporters and the gratitude of its beneficiaries.

Chapter 11

THE MILITARY RÉGIME

MILITARY régimes come in all shapes and sizes; military intervention is pressed to different levels; and military coups have various antecedents. Sometimes (principally in Latin America and the Middle East) they have their antecedents in façade-democracies, and continue in alternation with these or with feebly functioning liberal-democracies. Sometimes (chiefly in Africa) their antecedents were self-styled one-party régimes. In eastern and south eastern Asia the antecedents have been either feeble liberal-democracies or façade-democracies.

Military intervention is not confined to the Third World. The military intervened in politics in pre-war Germany, Japan, Spain, and eastern Europe. Only eleven years ago they intervened in France; and at the moment of writing Greece has the 'régime of the colonels'. But for all that, the poorer, the newer and the extra-European states are the principal victims of military intervention in politics. The statistics are eloquent on this point. In the last eleven years, from January 1958 to November 1969, the military have made eighty-eight coups in fifty-two countries. By the end of this brief period twenty-two of the thirty-eight African states had been affected, fourteen of the twenty-six Asian states and eleven of the twenty-three Latin American and Caribbean ones. Again, of the states that were over 150 years old at the end of the period, only twenty-eight per cent were affected; of those between 149 and fifteen years old, thirty-seven per cent; but of the states created in the last fifteen years, no less than fifty-two per cent. And it is overwhelmingly the poorer that are affected. There were seventy-three states whose *per capita* income was less than $330 (1963 figures): of these forty-five suffered military coups, that is to say, sixty-two per cent of the total. Those in the $300–$899 range numbered twenty-five, and of them only five were affected – twenty per cent of the total. Of the wealthier states with a *per capita* income in excess of $900, numbering nineteen, only two – France and Czechoslovakia – were affected. Since the states that are poor, new and extra-European are, overwhelmingly, of the Third World, it is tempting to see military intervention as an exclusive Third World phenomenon. But it has occurred, and still does, in the industrialized Western and Northern countries also. Any explanation of this phenomenon must take account of these states also. What is required is not an explanation of 'the role of the military in under-developed countries', or 'the military in the political development of new nations' (to name two American titles) or similarly limited theses. What is required is a general theory of military intervention that can explain why this is rarer in the industrialized societies of the North and West than in the developing countries of the Third World: but why, nevertheless, it can happen and has happened there. We shall have to proceed, therefore, first to the general theory of military intervention: only thence to the military régimes: and finally, to the mutations these undergo and the problems of returning from them to some form of constitutionality.

I. THE GENERAL THEORY OF MILITARY
INTERVENTION

Military intervention (which is not at all the same as 'militarism', a term by which some have not scrupled to call it) may be defined formally, for our present purposes, thus: 'the constrained substitution of the military's personnel and/or policies for those of the civilian authorities'. It is the product of two complexes of forces: on the one side, the capacity and the propensity of the military to intervene in the sense given above; and on the other, certain societal factors.

Before proceeding to examine these, there are certain underlying factors which it is essential to bear in mind. I have already made mention of the continuing effects of the principles of the great French Revolution of 1789.[1] Two of these are particularly important for the role of the army in politics, namely the principle of nationality and the principle of popular sovereignty. As a

1. See above, Part I, Chapter 4.

consequence of the first, it is nowadays almost universal for *the nation* (rather than, say, the dynasty or the person of the ruler) to be regarded as the entity in whose name rulers can and do legitimately claim the allegiance of their subjects. Now this creates a possibility unknown to the dynastic state; the possibility, indeed the likelihood, of drawing a distinction between allegiance to the government of the day and allegiance to the perpetual corporation: the nation. As a consequence of the principle of *popular sovereignty* it is nowadays all but universally assumed that 'the people', rather than, say, the Divinity, is that entity whose voice legitimizes the exercise of power and gives it 'authority'. This means that any Tom, Dick or Harry may accede to rulership on the grounds that he 'represents the voice of the people'. The point is, however, that this might equally well be a General Tom, an Admiral Dick or an Air Marshal Harry.

A third factor in most contemporary states is the professionalization of the armed services. By means of military missions and the like this has spread from the great metropolitan countries of Europe and North America to even the most backward states like the Yemen. In the past the armed forces were feudal or aristocratic levies; in these circumstances those who led and directed field operations and those who ruled the state were one and the same, or at least were part of the same ruling oligarchy. But when forces are professionalized a cleavage opens between those who rule and those who fight; and there is no particular reason why the latter should regard the former as their clients. On the contrary, in the atmosphere of nationalism and popular sovereignty, the military leaders may well regard their client as being not the temporary incumbent of office but the enduring 'nation', or *Volk*, or 'people' which they make a profession of defending.

These three factors are to be found in the advanced industrial states as well as in the Third World. But there are two other underlying factors which are peculiar to the latter. First, as we have seen, most of the Third World states are new 'modernizing' states and self-divided societies. In consequence of this they are usually subject, as I have shown, to severe political stresses: and these, as will be seen, promote the likelihood of military intervention. Secondly, in a number of them (Algeria, Indonesia, Burma and most of the Latin American countries) the state owes its very existence to the armed forces. In states such as these the army has a tradition of being the custodian of a nation which it regards as its own creation, rather than a tradition of obedience to the rulers of the day.

(1) *The societal element*

Military intervention is obviously an exercise of volition, and be the prospects of society never so tempting, provoking or permissive, no intervention will take place if the military do not want to act. There are indeed a number of states where this is so. In Jordan, Iran, Morocco and Libya,[2] for instance, the rulers are exquisitely dependent on the support and goodwill of the armed services for retaining office, and the withdrawal of this support would end their rule. Nevertheless, in these countries the armed forces continue to support them, and so these régimes have sometimes been called '*military supportive*' ones. At the other extreme there are states where the conditions of society are such as to afford little prospect of a military coup making headway, but where, for all that, some military men do make the attempt: witness the Four Generals' Revolt in Algeria, in 1961. But in between there are the numerous cases where (1) the military are in certain circumstances prepared to act, and where (2) society is such as to create these circumstances.

What can be said is that the more abnormally dependent a government is upon the support of the military for retaining office, the greater the likelihood that a military disposition to intervene will be acted on. The less dependent the government is upon the military for its continuance in power, however, the less likely military intervention will be. The issue resolves itself into the existence or otherwise of what, in Part I, Chapter 4, I called '*organized public opinion*'. Where 'opinion' does not exist at all, or exists in only the narrowest public, the military with its

2. The Libyan army took over the government, October 1969. I leave the words as written 1968, because this military takeover illustrates so well the point made in the text.

advantages in organization, discipline, hierarchy, intercommunication and *esprit de corps* will be the strongest force in the society, and whether it intervenes or not will be at its own discretion. Even where 'opinion' does exist, but is feebly organized or not organized at all, these same advantages will still attach to the military. The same will also be true – but the government is likely to be far more out of tune with the population – in those numerous cases where opinion, feebly organized as it is, is in addition bitterly fragmented and self-divided. There are also cases where opinion *is* strongly organized, but at the same time bitterly polarized. This is why military intervention can take place, and has done so, in industrialized countries. In such circumstances no government can rely for its support on organized opinion alone because the opinion is not *public*; if it chooses to rely on one organized sector of opinion, it thereby alienates the others. This is what happened in France in 1958, in Greece in 1967 and in Germany through the years of the Weimar Republic. In these conditions the government of the day has to rely on military support as a makeweight against its organized enemies. It was (in theory) to avoid all these types of difficulty that African states took to the 'one-party' system: they hoped in this way to create an opinion which, if not public, would at least be so highly organized behind them as to guarantee their hold on office. It is because the Soviet Union and the east European people's democracies have both organized a supporting opinion and pulverized and silenced other potential sectors of opinion that the military in these countries, where it intervenes at all (as in the U.S.S.R. in 1957 or Czechoslovakia in 1967), intervenes to support one faction of the dominant party against another faction.

The greater the degree of consensus in society and the width and organization of this opinion, the less the likelihood of a military intervention and the less likely, in the event, its success. The questions to be asked are:

1. (a) To what extent does there exist a wide public approval of the procedures for transferring power and a corresponding belief that no exercise of power in breach of these procedures is legitimate? (b) To what extent does there likewise exist a wide public recognition of what or who constitutes the sovereign

authority and a corresponding belief that no other persons or centres of power are legitimate?

2. How wide is the political public and how well organized into secondary associations such as trade unions, churches, firms and enterprises, co-operatives, political parties?

It will be noticed that a positive answer to Question 1 does not entail a positive answer to Question 2, and vice versa. For, as in France (1958), or in the Weimar Republic, the political public may be strongly organized but strongly polarized. Something like the same situation – though in these cases the organization was not nearly as strong as in the two aforementioned cases – obtains in Argentina and in Turkey: in the former in the shape of the trade unions on the one side and the employers on the other, in the latter in the shape of the two main political parties. Where opinion is strongly organized but sharply polarized, the situation may be styled *overt political crisis*. On the other hand, as already seen, though consensus may exist (Question 1), it may be so feebly organized (Question 2) that the military is free to act. Or, alternatively, consensus may not exist (Question 1) and the expressions of public opinion may also be very feebly organized (Question 2), thus making 'opinion' doubly unreliable as a prop for the government. These last two situations may be styled *latent and chronic crisis*.

According to the answers to these questions, states can be arranged in a rank order; indeed, by selecting certain indicators it would be possible to give this ranking a statistical form. But as a crude approximation it is possible to put them into four groups, or levels, according to the answers given.

The first are states of *mature political culture*. By this is meant that their political consensus and its degree of organization are high: examples are Britain, the U.S.A., the Netherlands, Australia. In states like these the government's need for military support to maintain itself is at a minimum; and long habituation to this situation has brought not only the public but the armed services themselves to an almost unquestioning belief in the 'principle of civil supremacy', so that overt military intervention would be widely regarded as wholly unwarrantable. Not only would it fail to obtain public sanction: the well-organized secondary associations could be expected to react sharply against any such attempt. In so far as the military do harbour a disposition to intervene in policy-making in countries such as these, they are likely to do so through the constitutional channels open to them, although under cover of these they may on occasion sail perilously close to 'pressure' on the civilian authorities.

Next comes a category where the public is highly organized but where, from time to time, it becomes sharply polarized on either the legitimacy of its institutions and procedures – or on the incumbents who hold office as a consequence of these. These are the states of *developed political culture*. In these states, should opinion be inflamed in this way, the military may well attempt to intervene on their own account, by staging a coup. In that case they are likely to be resisted by well-organized sections of opinion – as indeed occurred in the Kapp putsch in Germany in 1920 and the Four Generals' Revolt in Algeria in 1961 – and as a consequence such putsches wither on the vine. The preferred methods of the military in such polarized situations tend to be pressure on the authorities; or even blackmail; that is to say, threats of non-co-operation with the government, or, alternatively, of co-operation with the rival sector of opinion. Such pressure or blackmail is usually intermittent; it is exercised at critical moments of political tension. This is how the military appear to have operated in the U.S.S.R., when they supported Malenkov and Molotov against Beria in 1953 and Khrushchev against the 'anti-party *bloc*' in 1957; or how the Czech military operated, when General Sejna was called in by President Novotny for support against his rivals in the party leadership. But such pressure and blackmail may be used fairly continuously, as by the Reichswehr in Weimar Germany or the Japanese army in the 1930s. If so, the result may be what I shall later call an *indirect-style military régime*.

In the third category come the states of *low political culture*; countries with narrow and weakly organized publics, often self-divided on the legitimacy of the régime or the incumbents in office. And with this group one enters fully into the Third World, with just a few countries like Spain or Greece outside. This category includes what by its own internal standards are developed societies, like those of Turkey or Argentina; but most of them are, like Syria, Iraq and South Vietnam, at the other end of the scale. All these governments are highly dependent upon the support of the armed forces. Therefore these can always effect a transfer of power from one group of civilians to another by simply announcing that they have transferred their support. Alternatively, they can take over the government themselves, since public opinion is too feeble or self-divided or both to offer any sustained resistance. In these states therefore the range of military options is much wider than in the first two groups. In the first place, the military may bring about the fall of one government by threatening to withhold support from it, so causing it to be replaced by another and more conventional one. A charming illustration comes from Ecuador, where a military quartet which had taken office in 1963 after a coup by the armed forces was removed from power in 1966 by those same armed forces and replaced by a civilian provisional president, Yerovi Indaburu. Or, alternatively, the armed forces may decline to protect the government from the violence of its enemies. This is what happened at one point in Indonesia. On 1 October 1966, an abortive coup occurred, initiated by the Communist Party. This failed, and the army took a terrible revenge, leaving it in a position of great strength against the president, Sukarno, who (it was widely suspected) was implicated in the Communist coup. In February 1967, after Sukarno had reasserted himself against the army by purging the Cabinet of his foes, violent student demonstrations took place which, though they mounted in intensity, were in no way countered by the military; Sukarno was forced to give in and conferred on General Suharto full powers to 'take measures required for the safeguarding and stability of government administration'. Thirdly, the armed forces may use open violence against the government and take it over themselves. This is what the armed forces of Argentina did, through the person of General Onganía, when they removed President Illía in June 1966.

There is a final group of states where to speak of a 'public opinion' is a misnomer: countries like the Central African Republic, or the Upper Volta, or Haiti, where for all practical purposes any government can rule provided it has military support. In these countries of *minimal political culture* there are no effective civilian counter-pressures against the military and whether these intervene or not, and whether they supplant the government or just control it, is a matter for the military leadership alone to decide.

It is in the third and fourth categories that military intervention occurs most frequently: and these are, for the most part, the countries of the Third World and subject to its burdens. What these are has already been described (Part I, Chapter 4). Such political 'opinion' as may exist is handicapped by the persistence of clan, localism, by the resistance of the sealed self-subsistent villages, by immemorial tradition, by the inadequacy of postal, road and rail communication systems, and by feeble mass media. Even if opinion does exist, it is feebly organized. Secondary groupings, trade unions, co-operatives, political parties and the like, are fluid: in contrast the primary groupings of family and clan and region, religious and linguistic community and so forth, are intensely durable; and these are divisive factors, unlike many secondary associations. Even where opinion is organized, it is at odds with itself; through class, or micronationalism, or communalism, or the like. Furthermore, as we have seen, most of these states are no longer ruled by traditional leaders who rely on the habitual defence of centuries, but by *novi homines* intent on modernizing: a process that increases the strains upon their tenure of office, since to modernize is to run counter to the traditional bases of allegiance, which were rooted in class and caste, in common faith, in common tribe, or clan, and to try to substitute for these some new ideology. Thus in these countries popular views about legitimacy, always supposing that there are any, are fragmented; and even where this is not so, the organized support they can give to the government and the régime is weak. Yet, at the same time, owing to their special economic and social programmes and problems, their governments need to be more than ordinarily powerful. It was precisely to try to acquire such strength factitiously that states like Ghana, Guinea and Mali introduced single-party rule.

In brief – most of these countries are in *latent chronic crisis*; the civilian counterpressure that can be exerted on the military is feeble and often self-divided and therefore all turns on the military's propensity to intervene. In some states, as has been said, this may not exist, but in many the propensity to intervene is unusually high. In some cases, this is because the state itself is, historically, the endowment of the national army, and even if the public would like to forget this, the military never do. Elsewhere, as in Turkey, Syria and Iraq, for example, the military enjoy a traditional esteem. Yet even in states where they do not do so initially, the situation can change rapidly as the mistakes or misfortunes of the civilian politicians tarnish their reputations for efficiency and honour. The decline of the politicians' prestige factitiously elevates that of the armed services. This is what has happened in Ghana, Nigeria and Pakistan.

An additional circumstance also leads the armed services – even those trained with a strict regard to this tradition, as in most of the African states and in Pakistan – to question the dogma of civilian supremacy. This circumstance is the impossibility of peaceful constitutional change. This is the condition of every façade-democracy and every one-party state. Neither contains within itself a process for changing the régime, nor for that matter even for changing the incumbents of office. When things begin to go badly in such régimes, the only outlets popular discontent can find are insurrection or a coup by the military – or, in some cases, both. But insurrection is difficult or even foredoomed against the armed services. Hence the population try to seduce it from its allegiance; and if they are not prepared to go this far, they let it be known to the military that a coup on their part would be popular. For their part, these officers are themselves likely to be affected by the condition of their country and the popular manifestations of discontent. They may undergo a crisis of conscience in deciding whether their duty lies in breaking the constitutional *impasse*. It is in this sense that Burke is to be understood when he wrote that a 'constitution without the means of change is a constitution without the means of self-preservation'. If the Pakistani, Ghanaian, Egyptian and Iraqui military had not effected their coups, it is certainly difficult to see how any change of régime could otherwise have come about.

(2) *The armed forces*

(a) The capacity to intervene

Military forces possess massive advantages over civilian organizations. For one thing, they are more strongly organized than the most powerful civilian association. They possess five characteristics not found in combination to anything like the same degree elsewhere: a highly centralized command, strict hierarchy, formidable discipline, extensive intercommunication and an *esprit de corps*. In addition, they have a symbolic character: they represent the guardian and custodian of the state against its external enemies; and with this goes an atavistic popular sentiment for the so-called military virtues of self-sacrifice, austerity, self-discipline, valour and the like. And finally, in all but a very few cases, they have a near monopoly of arms and a monopoly of heavy weaponry. At first sight, therefore, the military would seem to be irresistible. But at least two vitally important qualifications must be made.

In the first place, there is no correlation between the fire-power deployable by the military and the number of coups it attempts: the fact is that a piddling little infantry force may be sufficient to overthrow an entire régime. It only took 150 paratroopers to overthrow President M'Ba of Gabon and President Olympio of Togo in 1963; the coup that overthrew President Nkrumah of Ghana in February 1966 was carried out by only 600 men, whereas the total numbers in the army were around 9,000; and so one could go on.

The second qualification is much more important for what follows. It may even be put in the form of a query: can we really talk of '*the* military' as though this is a single solidary cohesive unit? For sometimes military *centralization* is defective. The larger the armed services the more they are split into different branches – like artillery, armour or signals – all of which sub-services and branches are parcelled into different commands and garrisons. A notable feature of the military coup is that it is often initiated by a mere fraction of the troops; the remainder either fall in with these activists out of *esprit de corps*, or (more rarely) remain loyal to the government. Again, military *hierarchy* is sometimes defective. For purposes of analysis it is convenient to assume that the 'military' is the same thing as the officer corps, and in most cases this is so. This was not true of the Cuban coup of 1933, however, when Sergeant Batista led a non-commissioned officers' revolt against both the officers and the government of the day. A similar non-commissioned-officer revolt took place in Sierra Leone in April 1968; the breakdown of the Congolese Force Publique in 1960 was occasioned by a non-commissioned-officers' revolt against the Belgian commissioned officers; and there is evidence, too, that the tension between Ibo and Hausa-Fulani officers in Nigeria, following the first coup of January 1966 – a tension which led to the tragic second counter-coup of July and sparked off the secession of Biafra and the subsequent civil war – was due to pressure by the rank and file on their officers.

These cases, however, if not exhaustive, must be nearly so up to the time of writing. On the whole the views and actions of the military are indeed those of the officer corps; but it must be noticed that in very many cases they are those of the junior officers, up to the rank of colonel, rather than those of the brigadiers and the generals. The conflict of generations between junior and senior officers adds another qualification to the concept of a unified 'military'. Other divisive factors may also make their appearance. The ethnic composition of the armed forces can fragment a force; it did so in Nigeria (1966) and in the Congo (Kinshasa) (1960 onwards). Similarly, a force may be split into hostile political factions. This is notoriously true of the Syrian army and largely accounts for the frequency of coups in that country (thirteen between 1948 and 1967). It has also been true of the Argentinian armed services; ever since elements of the Argentine military overthrew Perón in 1955 there have usually been three factions, one prepared to 'manage' the ex-Peronist vote, another anxious to suppress it, and a third which wanted to have no truck with parliamentarism at all, but to establish the military as a full-blooded ruling caste.

When describing military intervention it would therefore be far more accurate to talk of intervention by 'elements of the military' rather than by 'the military' as such; but for purposes of convenience it is so much easier to talk of 'the military', that this is the course I am going to follow. Sometimes 'the military' is indeed an accurate expression, signifying that all services and units are at one in promoting or supporting the intervention: this seems to have been the case in General Ongania's bloodless coup in Argentina in 1966. Where a case is analysed, therefore, the expression 'the military' will be used; but if the unity or the dis-unity of the armed services is of significance, then special mention will be made of that fact. Now it is tempting to assume that the more unitary the armed forces and the more centralized their command, the greater their armed might and *therefore* the greater the number of coups they will attempt. In fact, the exact reverse is the case. The more *inchoate* the armed forces, the greater will be the number of coups: the experience of the self-divided forces of Syria, Iraq, Argentina or Indonesia demonstrates this. By the same token, the weaker will be any régime which they establish: for the victorious elements find themselves threatened by other rebellious units. Often, as in the cases of the régimes of Perón in Argentina, Rojas in Colombia, Jiménez in Venezuela, to say nothing of the successive military régimes in Syria and Iraq, what was built up by reason of one military coup was cancelled by another.

(b) The motives for intervention

In some sense all armies are unique. Certainly it is unusual for two military interventions to show identical motivations. It should not be concluded from this, however, that each case is *sui generis*. This is nonsense. Inspection of over one hundred different cases elicits five basic motivations which operate singly or in combination. As this would mathematically permit of no less than *thirty-one* 'combinations' containing either five, four, three, two or only one of these motivations, it is not surprising that the number of cases which display identical military motivations in the military is limited.

These five basic motivations are: (1) concern for the national interest, either in the capacity of 'arbitrator' (the so-called *poder moderador*) or as the bearer of a substantive programme; (2) class interest; (3) regional, ethnic, communal – in short a particularistic interest; (4) corporate self-interest of the military *qua* military; and (5) the personal interest of coup leaders. How various the pattern of military motivations can be is illustrated in Table 22. This gives my personal estimation of the motivations which operated in each case. The Algeria case cited is that of Colonel Boumédienne's removal of Ben Bella in 1965. The

TABLE 22. MILITARY MOTIVATIONS, SELECTED COUPS, 1964-7

Interest:	Algeria	Ghana	Nigeria	Sierra Leone	Brazil	Argentina	Greece
National	x	x			x	x	x
Class					x		x
Particularist		possibly	x	x			
Corporate	x	x			x		x
Personal	x			x			

Ghana case is the February 1966 coup which removed President Nkrumah. The Nigerian case refers to two coups, the first in January 1965, and the second, the northern counter-coup, in July 1965. The Sierra Leone coup refers to the first, which took place in March 1967, where elements of the military first intervened to decide who had won the elections and then other elements decided to disregard these elections altogether and govern in their own name. The Brazil case is that of the military deposition of President Goulart at the hands of General Castelo Branco in 1964. The Argentine coup referred to is the bloodless removal of President Illía by General Onganía in 1966. And the Greek case is the first coup, of April 1967, which suppressed parliamentary government and established a military junta, led by Mr Papadopoulos and Colonel Pattakos, as the supreme governing authority.

It is common form for *all* leaders of military coups to claim an identification with the national interest, but this does not mean that one has to believe them. But it is wrong to conclude from this that military forces are never genuine in intervening in what they conceive is the national interest. Unless this plea is accepted certain important interventions of the military make no sense at all: for instance, that of the Burmese army in 1962, the Pakistani case (1958), the Ghana coup (1966).

This purported right or even duty to overthrow governments in the name of the nation reflects, as already pointed out, the professional status of the military in the modern state. The military claims to be outside party politics and in many cases this is true. It claims to be a neutral whose client is the state which it has been created specifically to defend. And the members of the military forces are indoctrinated throughout their training in the cult of the nation. It is not therefore surprising that so many military forces come to believe what ex-President Betancourt of Venezuela once described as 'the manifest destiny, the providential mission of the soldiers as saviours of their countries'.

However, the military's conception of the national interest is unlikely to be unaffected by the experiences and lives of the officers. To begin with it is likely to be coloured by their class interest. This has been amply demonstrated and documented as regards the German Reichswehr and the Japanese army in the years before the war, but it has clearly operated in many of the Latin American states, in Guatemala, Ecuador, Honduras and the Dominican Republic, to name but a sample. Furthermore, class interest also influences the policies adopted by a military government after a successful coup. It is impossible to account for the increasingly socialist emphasis of the Egyptian military caste if one ignores the fact that these soldiers derive from petty-middle-class backgrounds and were reared among fierce resentment of the effendis and landowners who controlled Egypt at the time. But the argument of Marxists that class interest provides the only or the overriding motive in military intervention is, in this form, quite untenable. To some extent at least the army plays an autonomous role. For instance: the Syrian army has launched no less than thirteen coups between 1948 and 1968. It is quite unreasonable to suppose that the class composition of the army relative to the governments of the day fluctuated thirteen times in this brief period. In addition it can be shown that military coups occur even where the army and the civilian government are drawn from the same class background; in the Ghana case of 1966, for instance, the backgrounds of the military-cum-police junta were in all major respects similar to those of the politicians they overthrew.

The corporate interest of the military is a very important factor. It is strongest where armies have long been accustomed to political and social deference, as they were in pre-war Germany or Japan and as they still are in Spain and most of Latin America. The military resist cuts in their budgets, limitations on their political influence and, above all, any form of rival 'popular' armed forces. In Brazil, in 1964, the incident that touched off the coup was the president's refusal to discipline naval mutineers and his subsequent dismissal of the minister who tried to do so. In Algeria, one of Colonel Boumédienne's motives in overthrowing President Ben Bella in 1965 was his resentment of the '*milices populaires*' which the president had established. In Ghana (so Colonel Afrifa, one of the authors of the coup, assures us) one of the motives of the military was resentment at the run-down state of their equipment and a corresponding jealousy and fear of the president's well-heeled Presidential Guard. It is often pointed out that in most of the sub-Saharan African states the armies are much less of a caste than in Latin America: but this has not prevented them also from acting in their own corporate interests. When Colonel Backasso overthrew Prime Minister Dacko in the Central African Republic in 1966, for instance, a principal reason was the army's discontent at the reduction of its budget. President Olympio of Togo was overthrown and killed in 1963 because he, too, had cut the military budget, thus evincing, in the words of a coup leader, 'his profound contempt for the military'.

Regional or ethnic divisions are usually carefully controlled, as in the Indian, Iraqi or Pakistani armies, for example: but how explosive they can be has been shown by the two bloody examples of Africa: the Congo (Kinshasa), whose army disintegrated after the 1960 mutiny into separate regional-cum-tribal bands of fighting men; and the Federation of Nigeria which erupted into a civil war between the Ibo people and their component of the armed forces, and the remainder of the army, drawn from the Hausa-Fulani in the North and the Yoruba in the West.

So, alone or in combination, motivations such as these, often coupled with the crude desire of officers for quick promotion or a well-paid administrative post, provide the disposition to intervene. What happens then depends upon the level of political culture, for this sets limits to the methods used, the level to which the intervention is pressed, and the resultant type of régime. This relation can be seen from Table 23.

II. THE MILITARY RÉGIMES

The most important way of classifying military régimes is structural: i.e., defining the relationship of the armed forces to the exercise and institutions of authority. Unless this is done we have no criteria for distinguishing a military régime from any other. That having been done, however, it is possible to classify the various cases both by reference to the political tendency of the régime (e.g., 'right' or 'left') and by reference to the role which the military adopts. A word or two is necessary on these last two approaches to classification before turning back to the cardinal one – the structural classification.

To classify the régimes by political tendency entails using expressions like 'right' and 'left', 'progressive' and 'reactionary', which are basically ideological expressions and refractory to any neutral and generally agreed definition. Classification according to role, however, is more rewarding. Broadly speaking, there are three roles the military can adopt, the first being the *programmatic* one. Herein the military take over power with the intention of carrying out a positive programme. This is the kind of role which the leaders of the Egyptian armed forces undertook after 1954, by which time the swithering between the various factions, personalized in the struggle between General Neguib and Colonel Nasser, had ended with the latter's victory: thenceforth the officers, as the armature of the new régime, were committed

TABLE 23

Level of politi-cal culture	Characteristics of public opinion	Typical methods of intervention	Levels to which intervention is pressed	Resultant régime
1. Mature	High organization, High consensus	(a) Constitutional methods, to (b) Collusion and/or competition with civilian elements	(a) Constitutional, to (b) Dubiously legitimate pressure on civilian authorities	Constitutional
2. Developed	High organization, High dissensus (= overt acute crisis)	(a) Collusion and/or competition with civilian elements, to (b) Blackmail*	(a) Constitutional, to (b) Dubiously legitimate pressure on civilian authorities, to (c) Blackmail	Constitutional, to Indirect military
3. Low	Feeble organization and possibly also High dissensus (= latent chronic crisis)	(a) Blackmail (b) Threats of violence (c) Violence	(a) Blackmail (b) Displacement of civilian cabinets (c) Self-substitution for civilians	Indirect or Direct military
4. Minimal	Insignificant organization, Insignificant political opinion (= power vacuum)	Any method	Any level	Indirect or Direct military

* Threats to withhold support, etc.

to an entire programme of government. Similarly, the Group of United Officers elaborated in Argentina a (rather vague) programme of reforms to be effected when they acceded to power, as they did in 1943. Likewise it appears that General Onganía, who deposed President Illia in Argentina in June 1966, did so with the intention of staying in power for ten years and carrying out a substantive programme in that period.

This programmatic role is, on the whole, a rare one. Much more common is the second role: the *transitional* one. This is essentially negative, and it takes two main forms. The first is fundamentally suppressive. The political and near political organizations of the country are stifled, either by restrictions or by outright abolition, and the military leadership rules on an empirical basis, not seeking to bring about a fundamental structural alteration to society. The suppressive régime of Pérez Jiménez of Venezuela (1948–58) would provide one example, the Mobutu régime in the Congo (Kinshasa) another. More common is the transactional role: the military hold power, or claim to do so, as a preparation for a new constitution or some new political alignment. The régimes in Ghana (1966–9), Nigeria, Brazil (1964–7), Pakistan (1969), are of this kind.

The third role is the purely *personal* one, where the military junta or leader takes power out of personal ambition. It is very hard to make this charge stick in any particular case, because the military leaders will never admit to it and throw up a smokescreen of patriotic motives for their action. But, to me at any rate, it seems impossible to attribute the seizure of power by Major Blake and his fellow conspirators in Sierra Leone (April 1967) to any other motive; likewise Colonel Backasso's deposition of President Dacko of the Central African Republic (1 January 1966), or Captain Micombero's deposition of King Charles of Burundi (in November 1966) seem to me to be ascribable to no other motives than those of personal conceit and love of power.

In many cases we find touches of two or even all three of these roles. Boumédienne's deposition of Ben Bella in Algeria in 1965 combined a programmatic role for the Algerian National Army and the Colonel's private ambitions. The Brazilian (Castelo Branco) takeover of 1964 was transitional but did have the broad outlines of a programme in mind also. Furthermore, a movement from one role to another often takes place once the military are installed. The Egyptian Free officers took power in 1952 with a transitional role in mind, but after Nasser's 1954 triumph their role became programmatic. The reverse has also taken place. For instance, the Group of United Officers who took over power in Argentina in 1942 had aspired to a programmatic role, but in the course of ruling they gradually abandoned this and assumed a transitional one only.

But, to return now to the cardinal method of classification – the structural one. What *is* a military régime? What forms can it take? And this is by no means as simple as it may seem to be. The stereotype of a military régime (by no means confined to popular opinion) is a state of affairs where a group of military leaders take over the functions of government in the name of the armed forces and then rule coercively through their support without a popular mandate. By this criterion, however, there are not very many military régimes in the world. The Onganía régime in Argentina would qualify because Onganía received his nomination as president of Argentina from the military junta which made the coup. On the other hand, the régime in Greece would not qualify, since the conspirators were 'invited' to become the government by King Constantine: a flimsy sort of legitimation, but a legitimation nevertheless. Nor is this all: the limitation to a 'group of military leaders who take over the functions of government' would also rule out many régimes which otherwise would be regarded as military ones. For instance, the Greek régime in its initial form consisted of a cabinet of nineteen members of whom only five were military figures. It was, and still is, headed by a civilian and the army chief of staff is only the vice-premier. The Togo régime of Lieutenant-Colonel Eyedama consists of a twelve-man cabinet of whom only four are soldiers. The Onganía Cabinet is almost entirely civilian. And so forth. And, finally, it has to be recognized that in some nominally civilian governments crucial decisions are taken from the instructions of the military. This was the position in Indonesia from the military counter-revolution of October 1965, till April 1967, when the People's Consultative Congress (incidentally largely nominated by the government) deposed President Sukarno and installed General Suharto in his place.

To decide whether a régime is military or even part military, the key question is: *whether the military leadership of the day is in practice the supreme, or at least the pre-eminent, source of decision-making*. True, it is often difficult to answer this question owing to the paucity of information; but it is answerable in principle.

On this criterion it is possible to recognize three principal types of military régime. The first – the stereotype – is *direct* military rule. By this I mean that the military leaders of the day themselves assume responsibility for the government though they may appoint a civilian cabinet to carry out their orders. This type breaks into two: the *direct* and the *direct:quasi-civilianized* form. In the latter the military leaders go through some fake or forced form of legitimization: by popular plebiscite, by the recognition of some captive assembly and so forth. At the other extremity there is *indirect military rule*. Nominally, a civilian government exercises authority, but in practice it is a façade for the military leaders who give it its instructions. This type also breaks into two. In the first the backstage influence of the military leaders ranges over the entire field of political activity. In the second, however, it is an intermittent activity, often limited to a simple veto rather than a positive programme.

In between there is a type best styled as '*dual*': here the military share power with organized civilian forces and the government of the day leans now on one support, now on the other. We thus arrive at the following five basic forms:

(1) *Direct*

Examples are the Military Council in Libya, the Ongania régime in Argentina or the 'colonels' régime' in Greece.

(2) *Direct: quasi-civilianized*

One example is Egypt, where Colonel Nasser, at the head of the military, is the ruling authority, but pretends to work through the

Arab Socialist Union and the National Assembly – which are in practice his creations.

(3) *Dual*

The most recent clear example of this type was that of Indonesia in the period between the failure of the outer islands' revolt in 1959 and the coup of October 1966 – the period called 'Nasakom'. This acronym denotes the union of the nationalist, religious and communist party forces in Indonesia. This civilian coalition was headed by Sukarno, while at the same time he rested also upon the support of the military. (In the end, as a result of the Communist-inspired coup of 30 September 1966, this equilibrium broke down and the army became ascendant, until in April 1967 Sukarno was forced out and General Suharto installed in his place). Another example of this type of régime was Perón's dictatorship in Argentina (1945–55). This rested on Perón's leadership of two distinct elements – the armed forces on the one side and the Peronist movement, particularly the trade unions and the Peronist party, on the other. Ayub Khan's presidential Régime (1962–9) provided another example.

(4) *Indirect: continuous*

Between the military coup of General Castelo Branco in Brazil in April 1964, and the 'election' of his successor (General Costa e Silva) in March 1967, the Republic was nominally ruled through its president (the General), its congress, and its provincial assemblies. In fact the civilian organizations did merely what they were told to do and if they demurred were rudely overridden. After an indirect/intermittent interlude (March 1967–December 1968) it reverted to this type. Similarly for Indonesia in the period between the failure of the Communist-inspired coup of 30 September 1966 and the formal designation of General Suharto as president in March 1967. In this interval the nominal supreme authority was President Sukarno. In practice the military called the tune.

(5) *Indirect: intermittent*

In such cases the military leaders stay aloof from the running of the country except for sudden incursions to block some proposed policy or, alternatively, to defend a sector in which they have claimed full authority, such as levels of military expenditure. If one extracts Chile, Mexico and Costa Rica from the Latin American state system, and then extracts the full-blooded direct régimes, most of the remainder are states of this type.

The routes by which the military leaders succeed in exercising power, whether direct, dual or indirect type, are very various. In fact only one basic dichotomy is to be noted: simply that, whereas a *direct* régime implies that the previous régime has been over-thrown and supplanted by the military leadership, all the other types of military régime can have come about *either* by a previous military takeover *or* by simple pressure and constraint on the civilian government. The various routes and the possibilities that branch out of them are shown diagrammatically in Table 24. And this table also takes into account the possibility that a military régime of whatever type may 're-civilianize' itself. This possibility can be realized either in a constitutional régime, or in an authoritarian one depending on the support of forces other than the military – usually the police.

III. THE TRANSIT OF RÉGIMES

The direct military régime in its unlegitimated form is a rarity, and even where it exists usually justifies itself on the ground that it is merely transitional, about to agree to its own demise. A régime of this sort is in fact a terminus and a starting point. The reasons for this are two. The junta that has taken control must assure itself of two things: the co-operation of key civilian sectors of society (that is to say, technological wherewithal) and the legitimacy of its rule. Without the latter it will rule by bayonets, whereas with legitimacy it will have 'converted right into might and obedience into duty'. Without the former it will prove

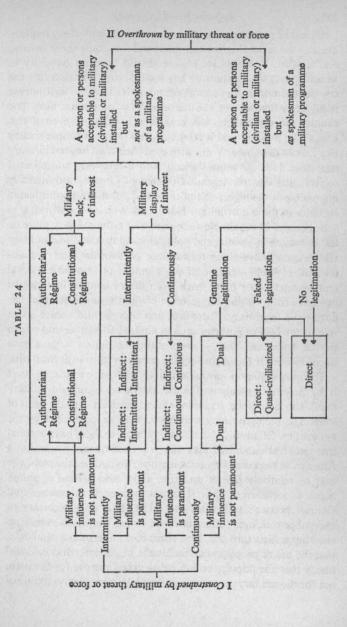

TABLE 24

inefficient at providing even essential services. Both these requirements – the technological and the moral – in some sense involve one another. A legitimate régime should have no difficulty in securing the co-operation of key sectors; and one that has the co-operation of the key sectors can smooth its way to legitimizing itself. They involve one another in another dimension also. The simpler the society, the less organized is opinion, even if this exists. The military find it relatively easy to run a simple society like that of the Upper Volta with even their own limited infantry resources. It is far more difficult with a relatively complicated society, like that of Argentina or that of Greece, and virtually impossible in the highly complicated and politically sophisticated societies in the industrialized North and West of the world.

So, except in the simplest societies where the military more or less dominate in a social and political vacuum, the direct military régime must move either forwards or backwards: either 'quasi-civilianize' itself – give itself the stigmata of popular approval and mandate – or move back from direct control in order to influence from behind the scenes a civilian government that has acquired a legitimacy. There is at first sight a third choice open: to quit the field of government and control altogether and return to the barracks. This – re-constitutionalization – is a rare phenomenon. It forms the limiting case of withdrawal from rule.

The most common way for a military régime to legitimate itself is by holding a plebiscite for the individual (usually a military man) who is, at once, its leader and spokesman, and the head of state. The plebiscite may well be coerced or controlled by the authorities. Often this is unnecessary because these have ensured that no rival candidate may run – a method known in Latin America as the *candidato único* method. Sometimes the plebiscite may be relatively free of pressure, and reflect a head of state's genuine popularity. Thus it is not necessary to assume that Colonel Nasser's plebiscites are faked. It is only necessary to remember that every effort is made to get people to vote, thus ensuring a high turn-out, that there is no alternative candidate, that the entire propaganda machine is at Nasser's disposal, and finally that the population are being asked to vote for the man, not for the military régime, since the plebiscites give no means of distinguishing between the two. That Nasser is popular with the masses is true though the degree of popularity is no doubt grossly overstated by the figures of affirmative votes: but that the military régime and the military themselves are extremely unpopular since their defeat in June 1967 is equally certain.

Another method of legitimation is by way of rigged elections. In Brazil, for example, the traditional mode of electing the president is by nation-wide popular vote. Despite limitations on opposition parties and the disqualification of former opponents from candidature, to name but two of the modes by which the military government of General Castelo Branco tried to strengthen its position, it became clear that a nation-wide vote might very well return a president obnoxious to the armed forces. Therefore the Constitution was changed by decree so that thenceforth it would be the Congress itself that would elect the president: for one thing Congress was more right-wing than the country generally, and for another it had been purged of outright opponents. It was accordingly from the hands of Congress that General Costa e Silva received the presidency in March 1967. In some countries, however, the elections may be reasonably free – free, that is, by reference to what one expects from a military régime. The Bolivian elections, which terminated the direct military régime in July 1966, seem to have been 'honest and democratic': but the antecedents must be noticed. First the military junta had established a party coalition with its own nominee as candidate (General Barrientos); next, the principal opposition party, the Partido Revolucionario de la Izquierda Nacional (P.R.I.N.) of Juan Lechin, did not dare contest the election and its leader was in exile; and, thirdly, the other opposition parties were not given much time to prepare their campaigns. It is impossible in these circumstances to say how much these factors contributed to the success of the military's nominee.

Other methods are more nominal still: 'authority' is conferred on the military junta by some suborned or controlled organ of government. For example, the Greek junta legitimized itself, as has been noticed, by purportedly receiving its nomination at the hand of the king; General Suharto was made president (and President Sukarno deposed) by the People's Consultative Congress, of which the majority were government nominees.

Even with the trappings of legitimization, however, the number of countries with régimes of the *direct* category is not unduly large; furthermore it changes very rapidly. At the moment of writing it comprises twenty-four states. Africa heads the list with twelve states: Algeria (though this is nominally ruled by a government formed from the largely non-existent F.L.N. party); Burundi; the Central African Republic; Congo (Brazzaville); Congo (Kinshasa); Egypt; Libya; Mali; Nigeria; Somalia; Sudan; Togo; and the Upper Volta. Only one of these régimes has lasted longer than ten years: the Egyptian, founded in 1952. Next comes Asia with seven direct military régimes. These are in: Burma; Indonesia; Iraq; Pakistan; Syria; Thailand; South Vietnam (despite the 'elected' status of the régime, since these elections were held in war-time conditions). Of these, Thailand has been ruled by one group of soldiers or another with only one short interruption since 1932, and Iraq by one or another group of soldiers since 1958. Latin America comes a very poor third with only Argentina, Bolivia and Peru classifiable in this direct category. In Europe there is only Greece.

Now all these are régimes where, as far as outward appearance goes, 'legitimation' is a sham and it is the military who not only rule but are known to rule. And this situation is not without its dangers. This is why the list of direct military régimes is so short and the régimes so transient.

To begin with, the military are not necessarily competent to govern even moderately complex societies. Their usual practice is to form teams with the civil bureaucracy; but to ensure success this civil bureaucracy must be competent, which is not always the case, and, if competent, it must be able to ensure that its advice is heeded and this it cannot guarantee, In some countries this military-civilian symbiosis has worked satisfactorily: in Ghana, for instance. But there have been instances of outstanding incompetence in military régimes – in Venezuela under Jiménez or in the Argentine under Perón or in Ecuador under the 1963 junta, for example; and it would be somewhat difficult to call the Iraqi and Syrian régimes competent except in the manufacture of revolutionary phraseology. The possibility must therefore be faced that the military régime may turn out to be as incompetent or corrupt, or both, as its predecessors.

However, unlike the pre-coup situation, the military are now not only in control but are seen to be: they have shed their previous neutrality and political innocence. Whereas the population under a faltering or corrupt civilian régime can turn to the military for relief, to whom can they turn when the military régime proves no better?

It is at this stage that the solidarity of the armed forces becomes of critical importance. Three things tend to happen. Policy differences open between members of the ruling element. Personality differences also come to the front. Add to both differences a divergence between the leading element and the remainder of the armed forces. As to the first, it is enough to recall that it is usually only an element, not the entire leadership, of the military that makes the coup and installs itself in power, and that it is very rare indeed for any such group to have a clear-cut policy programme laid out before it seizes power. I have already mentioned how cloudy were the notions of the Egyptian Free Officers when they took office and how a split soon developed between Neguib and his faction, who merely wanted to purge the political system and return to parliamentary rule, and those who followed Nasser and wanted to govern directly in order to bring about 'a revolution from above'. Take again the group that seized power in Turkey in 1960. This contained at least three political tendencies. The first group, the 'pashas', which was made up of older and senior officers including the coup leader, General Gursel, adhered to the Kemalist tradition of a neutral military and competitive and secular politics. Their intervention was made because they believed that the ruling (Democratic) party was falsifying the laws of the political game. The second group were younger and less senior, and also supported competitive politics on Kemalist lines, but were anxious to secure rapid economic development through a planned and controlled economy and for this purpose were less concerned about democratic niceties than the first. The third group were the followers of Alparslan Turkes; they numbered fourteen out of the thirty-eight-man junta and they were of the radical right; they wanted the military to remain in power, govern in its own name and launch a revolution from above. There are as many examples of these splits in the attitudes of the military junta as there are military takeovers and there is therefore no point at all in extending the list.

Next, there are personal differences. I once met a captain of the Iraqi Army who was in Europe on an administrative training course. Oddly, he was not at all well affected to the Iraqi president, General Arif, and the reason soon became clear. For he had served under the general when the latter was of much junior rank and had accounted himself a close friend. Indeed, just before Arif took over from his brother (who had died in a crash), he had received certain professional assurances from him. But two days later, just after Arif was installed as president, the captain found himself on half pay: compulsorily retired in mid-career! It must be understood that very often the person who succeeds to supreme power in the state is emphatically *not* the person adjudged 'most likely to succeed' in the cadet school or on active service.

Thirdly, it must be remembered that there are those beyond the charmed circle of the ruling junta. In many cases these are the junior officers, better trained technically, politically more radical than their seniors. If things go badly for the junta, these are likely to defect. Something of this kind brought about the fall of the military régime in the Sudan in 1964. It is true that the collapse of this régime was sparked off by the discontent of the intelligentsia, particularly the university and high school students, backed by the resentment of the two traditional major parties. But the régime would never have collapsed under their combined weight had it not been undermined from within by the cleavage of generations. To begin with, the feeling was growing among the junior officers that one could avoid a posting to the rebellious South Sudan if only one had enough pull with the generals who comprised the junta. Furthermore, these younger officers had received a quite different and much more advanced training than the generals of the junta, all of whom (except General Abboud) had been appointed and promoted during the Second World War. It was the disaffection of the bulk of the officer corps that made the junta throw in the towel when the students and then the civilians came on to the streets in protest.

One final point may be made. The more seriously the individual or junta who have seized power take the responsibilities of their new office, the greater the situation begins to resemble the previous one in the eyes of the active servicemen. For if these soldiers-turned-presidents begin to behave like presidents, to that extent they behave like civilians. They may even cut the military budget! In short, the new ex-military president may grow away from the military which hoisted him to power; but inside the military the same grievances and the same kind of plots will continue to ferment.

For all of these reasons, the continued direct exercise of power, whether with or without the baptism of popular mandate, is likely to be hazardous to the ruling group of officers. One consequence of this can be a succession of counter-coups, so that power is held by one group of officers after another. In Iraq, for instance, the 1958 coup was followed by an unsuccessful plot in 1959; a successful counter-coup in 1963, an unsuccessful one in 1966 and a third, successful one, in 1968. In the Sudan, the coup of 1958 was followed by a plot in 1959, a partially successful counter-coup in 1963, demise in 1964; another military takeover, 1969. In Syria the coup of 1962 was followed by another in 1962, a third in 1963 and a fourth in 1966 and a 'cold' coup in 1969. The other possible consequence is that the ruling junta may become aware of their isolation and difficulties and take steps to withdraw from their exposed position. This may mean that they decide to clear out of politics altogether, adopting a wholly neutral role as in Colombia; but this is not the most usual course. What they most frequently do is to move backward to some form or other of *indirect rule*. This is not to say that they do not perhaps want sincerely to disengage altogether. Often this is just what they wish to do. The trouble is that total disengagement is itself fraught with the most serious dangers.

To put the issue in its most concrete form: the Greek 'colonels' who made the April 1966 coup forthwith suppressed the parties of the left and the centre, rounded up their leaders and interned them, exiled them or tried them for treason. Just what fate would these same colonels meet if they withdrew from the political arena, leaving the field clear for these political opponents to stage a comeback to power? This is the prospect which haunts nearly all military juntas. Ever since 1955 the Argentine armed forces have dreaded the return of Perón (and, latterly, since Perón is now an old man, the Peronistas): for despite all their measures, the post-1955 governments of the country, whether military juntas or duly elected officials, have neither suppressed nor absorbed the Peronist voters. A similar prospect haunted the Turkish military leaders after the 1960 coup, directed as it was against the ruling Democratic Party and sealed by the execution of Menderes, its leader, and the trial and condemnation of over a hundred of his prominent supporters. A like anxiety gripped the National Liberation Council of Ghana as it faced up to the prospect of a return to free elections: what was to be done to safeguard against a return of Nkrumah and the Convention People's Party?

The difficulties are in fact threefold. The first is the possibility that in the future the military's political opponents will return to power thus threatening the very lives of the junta and its supporters. Next, since at least some of the military coups are made in the name of a principle (e.g., parliamentarism in Argentina, Kemalism in Turkey, competitive party politics in Ghana) there is the associated risk that, even if the lives of the military revolutionaries are spared, their principles will be sacrificed and their past intervention will have been made in vain. And finally, there is always the risk that, even if civilian opponents do not return to power, other elements in the armed services will make a coup on their own account. For those who make a coup breach legality; they set an example to everybody else to do the same. There is nothing sacrosanct about the authority of one particular element of the armed forces; since the path to that authority was paved by illegal violence, then it is open to rival military cliques to follow a parallel path, and this is what has happened in the faction-ridden armies of Syria and Iraq.

Such fears always attend the efforts of a military junta to disembarrass itself of the authority to govern. If their régime is proving unsuccessful or unrewarding for the reasons already outlined, they have an inducement to turn the country back to the civilians: but not to *any* civilians. At the least, they will wish to veto persons hostile and policies obnoxious to them; at the most, they will try to nominate their successors and dictate their policies. Out of a host of possible examples, those of Brazil and Ecuador are cited: the one because the military's precautions were so massive, the other because they were so ridiculous.

There were many reasons why the military-led government of General Castelo Branco should have wished to disengage from active politics after the 1964 coup. One was the wish to preserve the 'neutral' image of the military. The Brazilian military tradition has been to eschew active government; instead it tries to 'arbitrate' between the conflicting political forces, sometimes shifting left and sometimes right, vetoing here and supporting there, and attempting at all times to ensure a respect for legality. This was the famous tradition of the *poder moderador*, the arbitral power. Now, for the first time, the military were engaged openly in the business of government and they wanted to retreat from this, back to their *poder moderador*, as soon as it was safe to do so. But there were other and very pressing reasons for doing this. For one thing the opposition – which is to say the forces associated with the politics of ex-Presidents Kubitschek and Goulart – showed little disposition to acquiesce in the new situation and was disturbingly strong among the voters. Clearly, a nation-wide poll for a new president would risk the return of an opposition candidate: this is why Castelo Branco altered the mode of presidential election to an indirect election at the hands of the national Congress – a body that was more easily controllable than the population at large. But, in addition, the new régime faced military threats from the right (the 'hard liners' who wanted much more radical proscription of the opposition leadership and who seem to have been meditating another military coup in December 1965) and from the left where a group of former associates of Castelo Branco (including the veteran General Lott and two participants in the 1964 coup – Generals Filho and Kruel) accused the provisional president of having established a right-wing dictatorship. Castelo Branco also found himself opposed by a vocal section of the Catholic hierarchy; he had to face waves of student unrest from March to September,

1966; and the population was sullen because the deflationary measures of the government had brought about a recession without halting inflation (though it did check it somewhat).

For all these reasons Castelo Branco resolved to disengage the military from the direct exercise of political authority. But he had no intention whatsoever of seeing the principles of the 1964 coup abandoned, and equally no intention of allowing Goulart to return to power. By a number of 'Institutional Acts' and countless decrees and executive orders he created a situation where the army could at once relinquish direct authority and yet ensure the future. The political parties were reduced in number to two – a government-sponsored party, Aliança Renovadora Nacional (Arena) and an opposition one Movimento Democratico Brasiliero (M.D.B.) – under what was virtually a 'licensing procedure'. Large numbers of hostile or unreliable deputies, governors and prefects were deprived of their political rights. Certain deputies were deprived of their mandate, and when the Congress protested it was pushed out of the chamber. And the electoral laws were changed so that only the elections to the Congress and the State legislatures remained direct: the all-important State governors and the national president and vice-president were to be elected indirectly by the State legislatures and the national Congress respectively. It was not surprising, therefore, that the purged and intimidated national Congress should elect Costa e Silva as the president nor that the State legislatures should have elected the nominees of the government (Arena) party – the more so since the opposition (M.D.B.) deputies walked out and boycotted the latter elections in protest. And having thus secured the presidency and the governorships, Arena was able, by a not very large margin, to secure a majority in the Congress also – significantly, by the votes in the agricultural and backward areas, always susceptible to pressure. The tenure of the post-military régime was then further buttressed by three great Acts: a new Constitution which abolished the federal structure of Brazil and made it a unitary state, and provided for vastly increased executive powers for the president; a Press law which gave the executive sweeping control of the mass media; and, finally, a National Security Act which gave it extensive powers to act against the Communists and other elements deemed to be subversive. It is not too much to argue that, from the direct military régime of 1964, Brazil passed, in April 1967, into the stage of indirect military rule.

Ecuador presents an absurd caricature of this same process. Ecuador is highly unstable. Its governments hold or lose power at the will of the military. Between 1931 and 1937 there were six military coups, each of which led to a change in the head of state; in 1944 the head of state resigned in the face of military opposition – a coup was deemed unnecessary; there was another coup in 1947, and then a civilian–military coup again in that same year, leading to two further changes of the head of state. The next president, Velasco, resigned in 1961 in the face of civilian mass protests which the military showed no intention of repressing. His successor was Julio Arosemena Monroy and he was removed by another military coup in July 1963.

The government was taken over by a four man junta: one admiral, two generals and one colonel (the chief of staff of the air force). It promised to return to 'constitutional' government but did not. And it made a terrible hash of governing. It alienated the conservative mercantile community by raising tariffs, it alienated the landowners by sketching out land reforms, and the rest of the country was alienated because of soaring prices. During 1966 the junta faced strikes and riots and finally in March 1966 the high command of the three services itself told the junta it had to quit. In its stead they convened the major political parties (except the Communists) to choose a provisional president in anticipation of elections in six months' time. The choice fell on a non-political businessman and former minister of agriculture, Yerovi Indaburu. He appointed an all-party civilian Cabinet and elections were then held for a Constituent Assembly to draw up a new Constitution and also to appoint a president.

So far, so good; now for the farcical element. Provisional President Yerovi chose to submit to this Constituent Assembly a number of proposals designed to limit military intervention. Among other things, generals were henceforth to swear allegiance to the Constitution and the laws of the country, the military budget would be determined by Congress, military tribunals would no longer exercise jurisdiction over civil offences, the military would cease being responsible for internal security and the armed forces would be forbidden to take part in politics. This in a country where twelve heads of state had been overthrown in twenty-six years by the intervention of the military! The response was predictable: the chief of the general staff sent a letter to the Press on behalf of the services denouncing these proposals as 'unacceptable to the armed forces' as well as 'harmful to the country'. Yerovi was not elected president; instead a provisional president, Arosemena Gómez was installed, as non-obnoxious to the armed services.

Thus arises what I call the 'transit' of the military régimes. Save in a few cases, the pressures of office are such as to make a military government of the direct type wish to withdraw from this role; but, for the reasons outlined, it has to take steps to control the successor civilian régime. Thus military régimes of the *direct* type give way to those of the *indirect* type.

But this type of rule also has its disadvantages and dangers. For the course of internal politics is not easily predictable, as the resurgence of Peronist strength in the Argentine or Kubitschek–Goulart strength in Brazil or Justice Party strength in Turkey well illustrate. If the military withdraw too far or exercise their veto once too rarely they may find themselves with a *fait accompli*: the open manifestation of a public opinion controlled by their enemies, in circumstances where another coup would be difficult to justify and perhaps impossible to mount. On the other hand, if they govern with a tight rein, they are forced to superintend or rig elections, or pin their allegiance to one particular party (as the military had to pin their hopes on the Conservatives in Argentina in the 1930–43 period). This limits the military's freedom of action and the leadership may well find itself challenged by its own junior ranks, as the Argentine leadership was challenged by the majors and colonels in 1943. At the same time, too close an association with a particular political party destroys one of the most valuable of the military's assets, its claim to be national and to transcend party and faction. Thus an indefinitely protracted period of indirect military rule presents constant and nagging difficulties. These may lead the military to have to exercise so detailed a control over political developments as to wear out the patience of elements in the armed services. And it may also lead to the politicization of the military, which may develop an ambition to enjoy full discretion over public policies. A quarrel may then break out among the military leadership between those who want to continue indirect control and those who do not think this is worth the candle and want to take full control and responsibility for government. The Argentine military was split on this into the rival Blue and Red factions between 1958 and 1966, and in 1962 the opposing forces almost came to blows. The legalists (Blues) seemed to have won with the satisfactory popular election of the colourless Dr Illía in 1963; but the harbinger of change came when his chief of staff resigned in November 1965, for this was none other than General Onganía, the foremost of the former 'legalists'. On 28 June 1966, acting in the name of all three services, the general ejected Illía, assumed personal power, dissolved the Congress and the political parties and announced his intention to rule for the next ten years. Thus the wheel had come full circle: from direct rule (1955–8) after the ejection of Perón, to a period of chequered indirect rule (1958–66), to another spell of direct rule. But once the military assume direct responsibility they are back at the beginning of the cycle. The tensions and dangers I had described begin to mount and the move towards disengagement and indirect rule manifests itself once more. Lest this be thought fanciful, look at the pattern of military intervention in Argentina as a whole. In the modern period this began with the military coup of 1930. The continuance of direct rule was considered but discarded; instead, the military ensured the success of the Conservative Party and ruled from behind this party up to 1943. In that year the president was overthrown by a coup of the younger radical right-wing officers, the Group of United Officers, who were tired of indirect rule and plumped for direct rule. However, they found the going much harder than they had imagined. Their spell of direct rule did not last beyond 1945. In that year, realizing the weight of popular opinion against them, they put forward as their electoral candidate Juan Perón not because they liked him – for they distrusted and hated him – but because he seemed the best way out of a difficult situation. Perón won the elections easily and inaugurated a period of dual rule. He rested on the two rival pillars of the trade unions and the military (with the navy in opposition); he was overthrown by the military coup of 1955, with the navy playing the decisive role. A three-year spell of direct rule supervened (1955–8). Then came the self-division of the armed forces and the period of indirect rule (1958–66) mentioned above; until finally in 1966 another period of direct military rule was initiated.

It all sounds (suspiciously) like the Hindu wheel of existence, with souls being reborn in different shapes and racked for ever and ever in the cycle of birth and mortality – unless they can transcend *karma* and dissolve into the great cosmic mind. Is there a military equivalent of this transcendence? Is it not possible for the military to disengage fully and so break out of the vicious cycle? Yes. It *is* possible. But it is difficult and it is rare.

IV. MILITARY DISENGAGEMENT

There are two levels of military aloofness from active politics: what might be termed short-term and long-term, or contingent and necessary, or, better than these, disengaged and neutral. Let me put it this way. I have maintained that military intervention is the product of two sets of forces, the capacity and volition of the armed forces to intervene on the one hand and the condition of the society on the other. The cases I have been dealing with are those of the Third World where, as I have argued, the social conditions are favourable to military intervention and, on the whole, the will to intervene exists also. The states of mature political culture, on the other hand, are those where the will to intervene is lacking and also the conditions of society are unfavourable to intervention.

Now it is possible to conceive of states where the conditions are favourable to intervention: a latent chronic crisis of legitimacy exists, and all governments are abnormally dependent upon the support of the military – *but* the military lack volition. This is quite a different situation from one where, whether the military lack volition or not, a consensus exists, civilian counterforces are strongly organized and the conditions for the success of a military takeover are highly unfavourable.

In the first case cited, the military will be *disengaged* from active politics; in the second they will be *neutral*. In the first, the reason for the absence of military intervention is to be found in the mentality of the military leaders. In the second, irrespective of this mentality, it is to be found in the nature of the society itself. In the first, the situation may change with a change of military mentality. Not so in the second, where a profound cleavage of society would be necessary before any intervention could succeed. In the latter, the attitude of the military is a neutral one: to serve alternating sets of leaders with impartiality. In the first it is not neutral: it is temporarily uninterested.

In the Third World, military disengagement is not only possible, it is quite common. But military neutrality – that is another matter.

First, a number of states exist where the military have not hitherto intervened and where they show no current signs of wishing to do so. Such states include the Hashemite Kingdom of Jordan and the Kingdoms of Morocco, Arabia and of Nepal. But this is not to say that the armed forces of these countries are not liable to intervene in an immediate future. For, in the last resort, the rulers of all these and similar countries depend upon the support of their army. This has been put to the test several times in Jordan: in 1957, for instance, or in 1966 after the Samu raid. The reason the military have not intervened (apart from the abortive 1957 plot which was confined to a small element) is that on the whole it is well affected towards the person of the monarch and the kind of régime that he runs. If, on the other hand, King Hussein wished to make peace with Israel (for instance), it is more than conceivable that his army might depose him. In all these countries the military are the first reserve of the civil power, and it is in this sense that civil power exists by their complaisance: Libya is an example.

Additionally, there are a number of states where the military have intervened in the immediate past, but have since disengaged. They still form the first reserve of the civil power; they could, if they wished, overthrow this power as on past occasions; but they no longer have the disposition to do so. They permit the civilian authorities to govern, and they refrain from active interference. Portugal and Spain are European examples. Colombia, Paraguay, and South Korea provide further examples. Reasons why the military do not seek to intervene are various. In Colombia they are fairly clear: the military were used by the military president, Rojas Pinilla, in a particularly bloody and murderous campaign to put down the private warfare known as *la violencia*, and the Rojas régime was terminated by the army's withdrawal of its support, followed by a pact between the two rival parties (the Conservatives and Liberals) whose antagonism had – nominally – provided an excuse for *la violencia*. The military still find it in their interest to support this arrangement. In Spain the situation is not the same. The military support the régime, in the first place because they have confidence in the *Caudillo*, General Franco, and secondly because it is the sort of régime in which the traditionally privileged status of the military and its traditional hatreds (e.g., of Catalan separatism) have been fully recognized. Spain is not a military régime: the army does not as such play an important role in policy making. Nor is the army the main institution by which social discontent is subdued; this is done by the Civil Guard. But the military do constitute the great reserve of support to the régime. Much the same reasons – general contentment with their privileged position and confidence in the head of state – explain why the military support the régimes in Paraguay and South Korea, both of which issued from military coups.

All states of this kind – both those which have witnessed a military coup in the immediate past and those that have not done so – are what are sometimes described as *military supportive* states. In the Third World this is not only the commonest form of 'disengagement' from active intervention, but the only form possible. And the reason for this is that for an indefinite time to come the structure of society in the states of the Third World will continue to make their governments unduly dependent upon military support for their survival. As long as this condition obtains, so long the disengagement of the military will be of a temporary, contingent nature. This is likely to be as true of the recently-disengaged armies of Turkey, Ghana, Sierra Leone, Dahomey as it was of the Sudanese army, which, disengaged 1964-9, returned to active intervention in 1969.

But of long-term disengagement, disengagement of a 'necessary' character, there are few examples. Historically the best examples are those supplied by the régimes of Napoleon I and Napoleon III in France; of Kemal Ataturk in Turkey; of the P.R.I. party in Mexico; and of de Gaulle in France. And it may be that, in spite of what has been said about South Korea in the paragraph above, this country, too, may be on its way to a 'necessary' kind of disengagement.

In order to arrive at this disengagement, four conditions must obtain:

(1) Firstly, that the leader imposed by the military on the state (usually a military man but not necessarily so) shall positively *want* his troops to quit politics. This was true of both the Napoleons, of Ataturk, of the post-Cárdenas presidents of Mexico, and was true of de Gaulle and of Ayub Khan. It is, however, true of many other ex-military heads of state: for instance, of Jiménez of Venezuela, or Kassem of Iraq. It is in the interest of the head of state that the soldiers go back to their barracks; it gives him a free hand in running the country and at the same time seems to free him from military plots. But the second set of ex-military leaders cited did not meet the further conditions which include:

(2) That the ex-military leader, now the head of state, shall be able to establish a régime which is capable of functioning without further military support. This the Napoleons, Kemal Ataturk, the Mexicans and the former president de Gaulle have succeeded in doing; and it may be that General Park of Korea has really succeeded in this, too. But it is precisely on this point that nearly all other post-intervention régimes have failed. As has been pointed out, they still have to rely on military support as their reserve power, so that they are military supportive and not genuinely re-constitutionalized states;

(3) That this viable régime shall be favourable to the armed forces – as it was in all the cases cited;

(4) And finally, that these armed forces shall have sufficient

confidence in their leader, the head of state, to be prepared to return to the barracks when he tells them. This again was true in all the cases cited.

But these four conditions are to be found nowhere outside those cases. It may be that Nasser would like his soldiers to return to the barracks – but could the régime survive without them? Castelo Branco of Brazil sent his soldiers back to their barracks and they obeyed him; can the régime survive without them? Events subsequent to December 1968 suggest not. General Ongania does not want his officers to return to their barracks; nor does Colonel Pattakos of Greece – and so one could continue.

Each of these conditions, with the exception of the first, poses difficulties for a post-intervention régime in the Third World. For, as I have argued, these states are for the most part those of low or of minimal political culture – states of latent chronic crisis, where opinion is feeble and often self-divided. And because of this, all these states require a strong executive – a requirement the 'single party' was devised to meet, although it has failed to do so. To this extent all these states are ones whose governments are abnormally dependent on their armed forces. And indeed this is just why they *have* experienced military intervention: for in any such case of dependency the armed forces can simply blackmail a government out of existence by refusing to support it – let alone go to the trouble of overthrowing it.

The second of the four conditions will be just as hard to fulfil in the post-intervention phase as it was in the pre-intervention phase. These societies do not change overnight just because a general or a colonel or a captain has taken over the direction of the government.

Nor will the third and fourth conditions necessarily be complied with, though they are much more feasible than the one just cited which seems incapable of being met in any near future. For, as we have had occasion to see, it is not often that a post-intervention régime proves acceptable to the military: on the contrary, the military are wracked with anxiety lest their former opponents return. And finally, it is mistaken to suppose that the serving officers necessarily trust the military man who is now the head of state just because he has climbed there with their support. On the contrary, the annals of military intervention show more often than not that the ex-military head of state is, after a time, envied or even despised by his former supporters. Examples have already been cited from Brazil. To make the point one need only add that military leaders like Kassem (Iraq) or Rojas (Colombia) or Jiménez (Venezuela) soon become hated and feared by their former colleagues: and in the wake of defeat it is clear that Nasser also incurred the wrath and contempt of his former associates. And quite apart from these personal considerations, the cleavage of attitude between junior and senior officers, between the radicals and the reformers, will continue to create military unrest focused against the head of state.

The best the Third World states can look to, then, for the immediate present, is disengagement of a contingent and temporary nature. A genuine neutrality of the armed forces because they are satisfied with the régime, and because the régime for its part does not have to court their satisfaction, is only likely in the industrial societies of mature or at least developed political culture. The preconditions for neutrality are, in short, that the successor régime must be one that *neither needs the military nor is needed by it*. The latter precondition may be fulfilled, in the sense that the military may feel assured that its political future and the future of its leaders is secure. But the former is not likely to be realized. The most likely outcome of one military coup and one military régime in the Third World is a second coup and a second military régime, separated by bouts of indirect military rule, monopartism and feebly functioning competitive party politics – an alternation of these three types for a considerable age to come.

Chapter 12

COMPARATIVE GOVERNMENT

FOR two thousand years 'political science' was content to use a classification of régimes invented by Aristotle. In contrast, the last decade has seen the burgeoning of a wholesale variety of novel typologies, many of great power and originality. The one that I have advanced is both conservative and modest. I advance it simply as a first step to bring about some simplification and order in the innumerable factors and highly embrangled relationships which make up the data of comparative government. It does no more than provide a kind of map or chart on which régimes can be provisionally located, together with case examples by which the reader can question the map-reference for any particular régime, or indeed, the very validity of the map itself.

At least two more steps are required: the first by way of completing what has been done, the second by way of passing beyond it. The first stage requires additional criteria by which differences within any main type of government can be identified; for instance, the differences between the operation of the liberal-democratic procedures in, say, Britain and those in the Philippines or (to take a quite different social base from the Philippines') those in Chile; or, again, the differences between the operation of totalitarianism in the U.S.S.R. and the way it operates in, say, Yugoslavia or China.

But the second stage would be very different in kind and in object. This book has established criteria of differences between the main types of régime. The second stage presupposes these but is distinct from them. It is the stage of establishing similarities and contrasts *across* the main types. Whereas the text compares and contrasts different ganglia of structures, the second stage would be to compare and contrast different political *processes*. Emphasis has hitherto been laid on government; in the second stage it is laid on politics. In these concluding pages I propose first to lay out my chart of régimes, and point out some of the additional criteria necessary for refining it; and then to go on to indicate the kind of cross-category approach which might prove useful for the second stage, that of a comparative politics.

I. A SURVEY OF RÉGIMES[1]

(1) *Military régimes: direct, or direct/quasi-civilianized (25)*

Algeria, Argentina, Bolivia, Burma, Burundi, the Central African Republic, Congo (Brazzaville), Congo (Kinshasha), Greece, Indonesia, Iraq, Libya, Mali, Nigeria, Pakistan, Peru, Somalia, Sudan, Syria, South Vietnam, Thailand, Togo, the U.A.R., the Republic of the Upper Volta.

Haiti

First, a few notes on the status of one or two of these régimes. One is not strictly military at all since the coercive force that maintains the ruler is not the regular armed forces but a private army of cut-throats – the '*tonton macoutes*'. This country is Haiti. But in all other respects it conforms to the direct military régime model. Next, one of these states is in the terminal stage of the direct military régime: the rulers are currently preparing to re-civilianize; this state is Pakistan.

Next, these states can be further distinguished according to the criteria (the parameters) laid down in Chapter 1, and notably in respect of (a) the degree of reliance on coercion as opposed to other bases of power and (b) the degree of sub-group autonomy/ dependency.

(a) The coercive basis

A number of the named states rely upon a fair degree of manipulation as well as of coercion. This seems to me to be true of Indonesia, Thailand and South Vietnam.

(b) Sub-group autonomy

In trying to classify according to this criterion it is necessary to refine the criterion – which has not so far been done. Which

1. As at 1 December, 1969.

groups are to be taken as the indicators? For there are at least three main types (i) First, there are 'institutional' groupings (or 'apparats'): while a totalitarian régime by definition regiments all or most groupings in society, it may well be that these 'institutionalized' groupings compete fiercely with one another for a key role: e.g., the party against the civil bureaucracy or the army or the secret police[2] (ii) Next comes that class of specialized and differentiated groupings comprising political parties on the one hand and, on the other, bodies like trade unions, firms and civic associations which conform to the Western model of the 'interest' or the 'pressure' group. Such groups are less specific and less differentiated in the non-industrialized world, where their role is played – if at all – by primarily cultural groupings based on kinship, neighbourhood, lineage, language or religion. In so far as these play or have tended to play a continuous role in the political process, they constitute (iii) the socio-cultural groupings. For instance the marabouts of upper Senegal are still a potent political force and are courted by the ruling party to win support; likewise the Buddhists in Burma and in Vietnam.

In estimating sub-group autonomy/dependency it is necessary to specify which of these three classes of groupings is taken as the indicator. Here, I have confined myself to the second and the third; and notably to these: the press, the parties, the trade unions, industrial enterprises, student organizations, and also, where these have traditionally played a role, to the clerisy, the chiefs or sheikhs, and the like. Where all or most of these groupings have either been harnessed in the service of the government or simply silenced, sub-group dependency is high; where one or two still continue to play a critical role, then it is moderate; and where a number play such a role, then it is low.

With this set of criteria in mind, then, I estimate that the direct and quasi-civilianized military régimes in the relevant countries may be sub-classified thus:

(*a*) *High sub-group dependency:* Algeria, Burma, Burundi, the

2. See G. Ionescu, *The Politics of the East European Communist States,* Weidenfeld & Nicolson, London. 1967, to which I am indebted for this notion.

Central African Republic, Congo (B.) and Congo (K.), Greece, Haiti, Nigeria, Togo, the United Arab Republic, the Upper Volta.

(*b*) *Moderate sub-group dependency:* Argentina, Bolivia and Peru; where the Catholic priests, the trade unions and to some extent the unversity students, as well as employers' organizations continue to play significant roles despite efforts to contain or repress these forces; Syria and Iraq where the students' organizations have not been liquidated, where some political factions still survive, and where the clerisy forms a potentially hostile force; and three states which have only recently become appanages of a military clique, Libya, Somalia and the Sudan. The recency of the military takeover in these three states has led to the suppression of all party activity in them; but the military are not yet strong enough to dissolve the *de facto* power-groupings and the evidence suggests they are having to take account of these – for instance of the Senussi tribe in Libya, of the great clans in Somalia, and of the two major religious sects in the Sudan – (not to speak of the negroes of the southern half of this country).

(*c*) *Low sub-group dependency:* Notable here are Indonesia, Pakistan and Thailand. In Indonesia for instance most of the parties (the glaring exception being the Communist party) continue to function along with various civilian action-groups and functional associations. In Pakistan, the former Commander-in-Chief became Chief Martial Law Administrator, and then assumed the Presidency: he has permitted the political parties and other civilian action groups to function (though their freedom of assembly has been curtailed) and, likewise, has imposed no formal censorship on the press.

(2) *Military régimes: indirect/continous Brazil.* (1)

Between the election of General Costa e Silva in April 1967 and the events of December 1968, the régime is best styled as indirect/intermittent. Events since that date have changed the emphasis.

The radically revised Constitution and reorganized party system described above (p. 563) failed to give the army the freedom it desired. Matters came to a head when the army tried to pressure the Chamber of Deputies into raising the immunity of a Deputy who had publicly denounced the army as 'torturers'. In December 1968 the Chamber, including one hundred of the government's own party supporters, voted against the government on this issue. President Costa e Silva thereupon suspended the Congress indefinitely, imposed still further restriction on civil liberties, and followed this up by stricter press censorship and a wave of arrests. In 1969, however, the President was laid low by a stroke. The Army refused to permit the Vice-President to succeed him as by the Constitution he was authorized to do, and instead installed a three-man military junta to act *vice* the Presidency. Then, in October 1969 it declared the 'definitive' incapacity of President Costa e Silva, promulgated Institutional Act No. 16 declaring that the Presidency and Vice-Presidency were vacant, nominated its own candidates for these (a general and an admiral respectively), reconvened the Congress, and had it formally invest its candidates, 1 November 1969.

(3) *Military régimes: indirect/intermittent* (11)

Dahomey, the Dominican Republic, Ecuador, El Salvador, Guatemala, Honduras, Laos, Nicaragua, Panama, the South Yemen Republic, the Yemen Republic.

The parameters for classification were established at Chapter 11. It is a characteristic of these régimes as against the former type (with the possible exceptions of Indonesia and Thailand which begin to overlap with the present category) that, in all of them, manipulation is wedded to coercion, that 'representativeness' (as opposed to 'order') is present to some degree and that there is a moderate or high degree of sub-group autonomy.

(4) *Military régimes: dual* (5)

Paraguay, Portugal, South Korea, Spain, Taiwan.

All the parameters characteristic of the indirect/intermittent type of military régime are present in this sub-group, but better defined and to a higher degree. It is of the nature of these régimes that the government or head of state draws support from two sources, the military on the one hand and institutionalized civilian forces on the other. In South Korea, President (and ex-General) Park rests on the support of his parliamentary majority and the 1969 referendum, won in reasonably fair elections – but also upon his authority and prestige in the army with which he over-threw the parliamentary régime in 1961. It seems unlikely (to me) that the current revised system which Park resuscitated (in 1963) could survive without the active concurrence of the army which Park's person alone guarantees. Paraguay is a somewhat different spectacle; previously a direct régime, the president (Stroessner) now feels secure enough in the office he has occupied since 1954 to permit a certain limited opposition – provided, of course, that his own supporters win a majority in Congress. This is a more autocratic and less representative form than the Korean case. The Portuguese and Spanish cases are also pronouncedly auto-cratic, the legislators being empty of authority, the elections shamelessly managed. Here the heads of state repose on the support of social groupings (religious bodies, industrialists, land-owners and the like) and on 'official' political associations – while the military, at the moment, is 'disengaged'; it confines itself to passive support of the régime.

Taiwan is a puzzle. The legislature has not been elected; it is a rump parliament, established in 1947 and not renewed since that date. All its members are Kuomintang party members. The head of state, Chiang Kai-shek, stands at the head of the party hier-archy and the military forces which are very large. It is difficult to say whether either one or the other influences his decisions, or whether his own authority does not, at this stage in his career, enable him to make use of both. My assignment of this régime to the 'dual' is therefore highly provisional.

(5) *Dynastic régimes* (2)

Kuwait, Saudi Arabia.

(6) *Façade-democracies* (7)

Afghanistan, Cambodia, Ethiopia, Iran, Jordan, Morocco, Nepal.

The sub-distinctions lie in the parameters of order/representativeness and coercion/manipulation. Morocco and Jordan both comprise substantially more representative elements than Ethiopia and Nepal. Afghanistan, Cambodia and Ethiopia rely less on the coercive power of the military than Iran and Jordan, both of which have had to contend with restive opposition movements. The power and political influence of the Moroccan army, also, is currently on the increase, but this is a highly politically-pluralistic régime, with actively competing politica l parties.

(7) *Quasi-democracies* (15)

Cameroon, Chad, Gabon, Guinea, Ivory Coast, Kenya, Madagascar, Malawi, Mauritania, Mexico, Niger, Ruanda, Senegal, Tanzania, Tunisia. (Note that Zambia is, currently, moving into this group: while Yugoslavia, classed under (8) below, has strong claims to be in the present group.)

Three parameters can be applied to draw sub-distinctions here:

(a) Sub-group dependency–autonomy

The Press is unfree in all these states excepting Mexico and Kenya; and, with the same exceptions, the trade unions are unfree also, though in some states, like Tunisia and Senegal, they dispose of more influence in the counsels of the ruling party than they do in others and in some – Tanzania – are restive. In Chad, Niger, Senegal the clerisy is politically significant either as a support for the régime (Senegal) or as opposition (Chad, Niger). In many, despite official theory, chiefs are still politically important either as support or opposition – in contrast to Guinea, where they have been regimented by the rulers, or in the Ivory Coast where they form a part of the basic support of the ruling party.

(b) Present–future goals

Again, despite official theory, most of these states are oriented to the present; but Guinea and Tanzania stand out for their emphasis on future goals.

(c) Regimentation/manipulation/persuasion

In all these states the original basis for the seizure of power was regimentation: it was often coupled with coercion – but not always. In most cases, as the ruling parties have consolidated themselves, so they have shifted the basis of power from regimentation to manipulation: for example, in Cameroon, Gabon, the Ivory Coast, Madagascar, Malawi, Mauritania, Niger and Senegal regimentation is now blended with manipulation. On the other hand, the Mexican and to a lesser degree the Tanzanian régimes mix their regimentation with an appeal to cognition and rational persuasion. By contrast, the Chad government, faced with rebellion, has turned to coercion.

Scoring high on all three counts – regimentation, future goals and sub-group dependency is Guinea. Scoring low on all three are Mexico and Tunisia.

(8) *Totalitarian régimes* (14)

Albania, Bulgaria, China, Cuba, Czechoslovakia, German Democratic Republic, Hungary, Mongolia, North Korea, North Vietnam, Poland, Romania, U.S.S.R., Yugoslavia.

All these, of course, score high in the parameter of order/future goals, and all have a regimentary basis: the differentiation lies in the extent of sub-group dependency. Two sets of groups should be distinguished, the 'institutional' ones (i.e., what Ionescu calls the 'apparats') – the party, the civil bureaucracy, the military, the trade unions, the secret police and so forth – and the associations proper, notably nationality associations, writers' associations, the universities, the Churches. Régimes may be distinguished by the degree of competitiveness among the various 'apparats' – though more in theory than in practice, since information about the internal processes of these régimes is so scanty. In addition, they may be differentiated by the criterion of which 'apparat' is the 'key' one to which the others are subordinated. In principle this should always be the party; in practice – as in Stalin's U.S.S.R. – it might be the civil bureaucracy with the secret

582 Autocracy and Oligarchy

police. Likewise, it is conceivable that the military might emerge as a key 'apparat'. This criterion of difference is the one invented by Ionescu in his *Politics of the East European Communist States*.[3]

The other mode of distinguishing the régimes is by the dependence–autonomy of associations other than the institutional ones, and here again Ionescu's book is a valuable guide. It is clear first of all that the existence of tolerated minor parties side by side with the communist party does not of itself mean that a state has a higher degree of sub-group autonomy: these parties are licensed and subordinate. On the other hand, in some of these states, e.g., Hungary and Poland, the Church enjoys a partial autonomy and acts as a critic of the régime and a rival focus of loyalties. Similarly, in some, such as Czechoslovakia and Hungary, the 'writers' circles' have from time to time established a measure of autonomy and come out as critics of the régime. In Yugoslavia the nationalities with their individual assemblies and their own Communist League headquarters have emerged as partially autonomous entities which effectively check the central power, likewise the functional associations; while economic decentralization has likewise diluted the degree of sub-group dependence. Yugoslavia is, for these reasons, the least 'totalitarian' of the entire group, and indeed lies on the border of the 'quasi-democracy'.

(9) *Liberal-democratic régimes: functioning stably since 1948* (25)

> Australia, Austria, Belgium, Canada, Chile, Costa Rica, Denmark, Finland, German Federal Republic, Iceland, India, Irish Republic, Israel, Italy, Japan, Luxemburg, Netherlands, New Zealand, Norway, Philippine Republic, Sweden, Switzerland, U.K., Uruguay, U.S.A.

(10) *Liberal-democratic régimes: functioning with periods of instability since 1948* (8)

> Ceylon, Colombia, France, Lebanon, Malaya, Sudan, Turkey, Venezuela.

3. Ionescu, op. cit.

(11) *Liberal-democratic régimes: post-1948 states, functioning stably* (6)

Gambia, Jamaica, Malaya, Malta, Singapore, Somalia, Trinidad.

(12) *Liberal-democratic régimes: post-1948 states with tendency towards instability and/or one-party rule* (6)

Cyprus, Dahomey, Ghana, Guyana, Sierra Leone, Uganda, Zambia.

The liberal-democracies, besides forming the most numerous category also provide the most subtle variations on the original model. There are two principal – and pretty obvious – reasons for this.

In the first place, it is in the nature of this régime that it represents actual overt and freely expressed public opinions, a characteristic it shares with *none* of the other main types of régime. It therefore *presupposes* a fairly high degree of sub-group autonomy; and therefore, again, the substantive political issues reflect the tensions in the society while the style of political activity reflects the values held by these various social groupings. In no other main type of régime are these two characteristics present to anything like the same degree.

Hence arise enormous differences between the way a liberal-democratic régime operates in, say, the U.K. as compared with Somalia, or the Lebanon, or pre-military Nigeria. For all its bribery and violence Somalia did operate a competitive party system and its pre-military governments genuinely depended upon a parliamentary majority. Yet sixty per cent of its population are nomads and another fifteen per cent are semi-nomads. On inspection, it appears that below the ideological language with which the parties berated each other ('Greater Somalia', 'literacy', 'modernization', 'pro-Westernism', 'pro-Easternism', etc.) there lay the basic fact of Somali society: clan-alliance and clan-feud; and the parties chose or were compelled to rely upon this fact of social life for their organization, their support and their tactics. A great deal of the political infighting turned on the clash of the great Samaale clan with its rivals and then, in turn, on the rivalries of its sub-clans, the Hawiye and the Darood. When the two Somali ex-colonies united in 1960, new clans were brought into the competitive struggle; the picture became more complicated but also more polyarchic than ever. The main task of a Somali opposition was not to oppose the government's policy but to secure compensation for the leaders and the clans who supported it (the opposition); and the government maintained itself to the extent that it could distribute official favours and posts equitably among its principal clan supporters. All this is worlds away from a Britain where the parties are rooted in literate, urban, industrialized, mass society, and where the issues arise from the sectional or class interests of the population; yet the procedures and their main object – to conciliate the antagonisms of autonomous groupings and to allocate scarce favours among them – remained in essence the same in the two countries.

The second reason for the variations on the liberal-democratic model is that in no other form of government are formal procedures and formal authority so important. In military régimes, in façade-democracies or quasi-democracies and in the totalitarian régimes, formal and juridical norms of government are everywhere interpreted very elastically and sometimes totally ignored. To examine such régimes one has to look very hard for the practice, not for the formal requirements. But the liberal-democracies would cease to be such if, for instance, the constitutive freedoms of expression, assembly, association and elections did not exist, or if the balanced authority of the executive against the legislature and so forth could be overridden arbitrarily at the government's will. Yet these formal procedures and the authority-relationships between the organs of government differ in different liberal-democracies: so that one – e.g., France – may give more, and another – e.g., Israel – less, discretion to the executive; or the electoral laws may greatly distort the expression of opinion or may accurately reflect it; and so forth. Thus in liberal-democracies one set of variations turns on the differences in the *formal* provisions for civil liberties and in the balance between organs of government; another set of variations turns upon how far in *practice* these norms are observed – for instance, whether the courts are in fact independent and if so how far, or to what extent the government uses bribery or administrative pressure during elections. Clearly with a large number of these factors to bear in mind, and a wide range possible in each factor, there are bound to be many significant variations on the basic model.

II. THE NEXT STEPS IN COMPARATIVE ANALYSIS

So far, characteristic syndromes of structures and their inter-relation have been isolated and differentiated from one another: hence the main categories of régimes. This is not the end of the study of comparative government but the necessary first step. The next stage consists of pressing across these main categories to identify the procedures that make up the political process and to distinguish characteristic processes from one another.

As already stated (Chapter 1), I conceive the political process as being essentially a contest through which the various social groupings (and, in totalitarian states, the 'institutional' group-ings, i.e., the 'apparats') seek as far as possible to universalize their own interests or values by getting them sanctioned by the authority of the state: i.e., by giving them the status of *law*. The next step is to identify which of the procedures by which they do this are the most significant ones. These would include, notably, the following:

(1) The conditions in which individuals may use or form groups to further their objectives.

(2) The conditions in which these groups can give *political* expression to these objectives.

(3) The conditions in which groups which have done so can harness the authority of the state to secure these objectives.

In short, there are at least three significant sets of relationship, namely, the system of civil liberties, the system of representation and political expression,[4] and the system of inner-governmental relationships.

It is also possible to gradate the political relevance of the *sub-groups* in society by reference to their *access* to the policy

4. For example, a right 'freely to petition the government'.

makers and executors, i.e., the government or the ruler. There would be (a) a ring of social/cultural – i.e., ethnic, religious, regional and other (*crescive*) – groups. In the Third World these often play, in addition, the part which in the Western industrialized countries is played by the (b) specific interest groups. Next (c), comes an 'inner' group consisting of political parties and (d), the network of governmental agencies itself.

As a result of such analysis we find ourselves with: first, a set of processes present to a greater or lesser degree across all the main categories of governmental types; and secondly, a number of the most significant types of sub-groups. Each of the latter is at least potentially in competition with the others; hence, the behaviour of any one influences the behaviour of the others. And since these groups compete with each other via these processes, then both the groups and the processes influence one another also, as shown in Table 24.

In countries where all of these five sectors exist, each affects and is affected by all the rest. For instance, the structure, the values, the number of the social groupings in a given society will be affected by the framework of civil liberties, by the electoral or other representational procedures, by the form and structure and style of the political parties and by inner-governmental relationships and tensions. Equally, the inner-governmental relationships, the electoral and other representational procedures, the extent and degree of civil liberties, will all be affected by the number, type, character and organization of the groupings among the population.

Even in this preliminary and highly simplified form, a scheme of this kind holds certain evident advantages. For instance it becomes clear enough in the light of Table 25 how, in the U.S.S.R., the system of civil liberties both sustains the monopoly of the C.P.S.U. and also denatures and empties the public opinion groupings. So at one stroke are annulled both the formal constitutional guarantees of the electoral system and such checks and balances (e.g. the federal arrangements) as purportedly control the activities of the government. By the same token one could deduce the probable effect of substituting for this system of civil liberties one like that of Britain, for example. For, if adopted in the U.S.S.R., this would permit the free development of all manner of interest and value groupings and would also animate the electoral system; it would therefore weaken if not destroy altogether the constitutional and

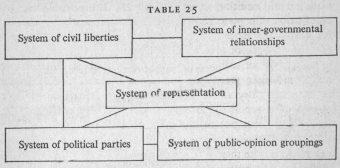

TABLE 25

System of civil liberties	System of inner-governmental relationships
System of representation	
System of political parties	System of public-opinion groupings

administrative provisions which forbid all parties except the C.P.S.U.; and it would end by endowing the agencies of government with the power to disagree among themselves. Of course the exact consequences of any such change in one part of the entire system could not be predicted with any certitude, except perhaps after intensive research on the details of the relationships which exist on the ground; more likely, what would emerge would be a number of probabilities – but a strictly limited number.

However, relatively few states contain or operate – in other than nominal form – all five sectors of this system. For instance the Ongania dictatorship in Argentina operates only two, thus:

System of inner-governmental relationships
↕
System of public-opinion groupings.

It is at this point that the five-element diagram has to be enlarged and new details added. For every one of the five components is in fact a little ganglion of interrelated units and procedures each of which also influences each of the others. For instance, inside the 'inner-governmental relationship system' one would normally expect to find the civil bureaucracy (itself divided into departments), the military (itself subdivided), the police, the secret police and counter-intelligence, the legislature, the cabinet or head of state – and so forth. The student of a particular state always examines these in their detail, especially with a view to ascertaining which, if any, are paramount over the others – or whether each influences each of the others. So the Argentine picture could be enlarged, as in Table 26, with possible lines of domination running as shown.

TABLE 26

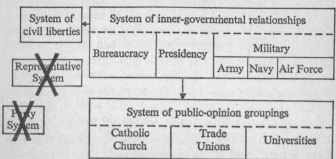

One final word is necessary: about the relationship of social structure to the form of government. Social structure, wealth and communications, and similar societal variables, *of course* affect the way in which a country is governed. A country with poor physical and telecommunications will not and cannot have, for instance, the same type of party structure as one where both types of communications are excellent, however hard its people try; a country of illiterate nomad clans will not form parties like the British Labour Party nor will they conduct party warfare with their rivals in the same way or over the same issues as the Labour Party and the Conservative Party do. It is *unthinkable* that anybody can understand the way in which a country is governed without first knowing something about the geography and about the people, their social structure and their history. But it does not in the least follow from this either that (a) politics is the same as sociology or is even 'a special branch' of sociology or that (b) there is a one-to-one correspondence between a given number of societal factors on the one side and a given form of government on the other. The first of these naïve beliefs, which has led to the current vogue for general systems analysis, is due to an initial failure to define politics and the political. For instance: because a state is clearly *some* kind of social system it does not follow that it is *any* kind of social system; and because a law is a kind of rule it does not follow that it is *any* kind of rule; and because trade unions have a government it does not follow that it is the same as what we style *the* government.

As to the second of these beliefs: much important work (on which, indeed, I greatly rely) has tried to identify and codify large numbers of societal variables such as areas, population, religious homogeneity and urbanization, and then to correlate these with one another and with various forms of government. Often one does indeed discover broad correlations: military coups, as I have pointed out, are more apt to occur in poor countries, not rich ones. The trouble is that some do happen in rich countries and some poor countries do escape! There are always 'deviant cases'. Lebanon practises competitive party politics: Mauritania does not. The U.S. and the U.S.S.R. are both urbanized and industrial; one is hyper-pluralistic, the other totalitarian and centralized.

Social structure generates the substantive issues of politics and colours the style in which these are disputed. It does not seem to me to *impose* any of the main forms of government I have catalogued and described. I concede no limitation on the form a government may take except the mutual forbearance of the population: if the people are individualistic, intolerant and arrogant then it is likely that their politics will be those of coercion or regimentation; if they are ignorant, quietist or deferential then their politics are likely to be those of manipulation. And always it must be admitted that harsh material conditions, low *per capita* income, glaring disparities in the distribution of wealth or status may set mortally low limits to mutual forbearance. But it is on this that, in the last resort, the form of the régime will depend. And forbearance is a human quality in very short supply. In the chronicles of time, some have indeed died for love, and many more have died for their faith; but incomparably the greatest number of those who have died violent deaths are those who have died for politics.

FURTHER READING

Note: This is a *select* bibliography. My intention is to suggest some ten to fifteen titles under each chapter heading. The bibliography consists only of English-language works. Furthermore, it excludes articles. Otherwise the list would have been very greatly extended.

Chapter 1

(GOVERNMENT: A PRELIMINARY SURVEY)

1. General

A. F. BENTLEY, *The Process of Government* (reprint), Harvard University Press, 1967.

B. CRICK, *In Defence of Politics*, Pelican, 1962.

A. P. D'ENTRÈVES, *The Notion of the State*, Clarendon Press, Oxford, 1967.

B. DE JOUVENEL, *Power*, Batchworth, 1948.

H. D. LASSWELL and A. KAPLAN, *Power and Society*, Routledge & Kegan Paul, 1952.

R. M. MACIVER, *The Web of Government*, Free Press, New York, 1964.

C. E. MERRIAM, *Political Power*, Free Press, New York, 1934.

G. MOSCA, *The Ruling Class*, McGraw Hill, New York, 1939.

V. PARETO (ed. S. E. FINER), *Sociological Writings*, Pall Mall Press, 1969.

G. PARRY, *Political Elites*, Allen & Unwin, 1969.

M. WEBER, *Theory of Economic and Social Organization*, W. Hodge, Edinburgh, 1947.

2. Systems of Classification

G. A. ALMOND and G. B. POWELL, *Comparative Politics*, Little, Brown, Boston, 1966.

D. APTER, *The Politics of Development*, Chicago University Press, 1965.

ARISTOTLE, *The Politics*, Penguin, 1962.

R. DAHL, *Modern Political Analysis*, Prentice Hall, New Jersey, 1963.

K. LOEWENSTEIN, *Political Power and the Government Process*, Chicago University Press, 1965.

Chapter 2

(THE LIBERAL-DEMOCRATIC STATE)

G. A. ALMOND and S. VERBA, *The Civic Culture*, Princeton University Press, 1963.

M. CRANSTON, *Freedom*, Longmans, 1953.

R. DAHL, *A Preface to Democratic Theory*, Chicago University Press, 1956.

J. LOCKE (ed. P. LASLETT), *Two Treatises of Government*, Mentor, New York, 1965.

A. L. LOWELL, *Public Opinion and Popular Government*, Longmans, 1926.

W. J. M. MACKENZIE, *Free Elections*, Allen & Unwin, 1958.

J. S. MILL, *Representative Government*, Blackwell, Oxford, 1946.

J. PLAMENATZ (ed.), *Readings from Liberal Writers*, Allen & Unwin, 1965.

G. DE RUGGIERO, *The History of European Liberalism*, Oxford University Press, 1927.

G. SARTORI, *Democratic Theory*, Praeger, New York, 1965.

J. A. SCHUMPETER, *Capitalism, Socialism and Democracy*, Allen & Unwin, 1947.

M. A. SELIGER, *The Liberal Politics of John Locke*, Allen & Unwin, 1969.

Chapter 3

(THE TOTALITARIAN STATE)

(*For specific references to the communist variety, see below under Chapter 8, p. 596.*)

Z. BARBU, *Democracy and Dictatorship*, Routledge, 1956.

E. BARKER, *Reflections on Government*, Oxford University Press, 1958.

N. H. BAYNES, *The Speeches of Adolf Hitler* (1922–1939), Oxford University Press, 1942.

H. FINER, *Mussolini's Italy*, Grosset & Dunlap, New York, 1965.

K. FRIEDRICH and Z. K. BRZEZINSKI, *Totalitarian Dictatorship and Autocracy*, Praeger, New York, 1961.

A. KOLNAI, *The War Against the West*, Gollancz, 1938.

W. KORNHAUSER, *The Politics of Mass Society*, Routledge, 1960.

F. M. MARX, *Government in the Third Reich*, McGraw Hill, 1937.

F. L. NEUMANN, *Behemoth*, Gollancz, 1942.

K. R. POPPER, *The Open Society and its Enemies*, Routledge, 1962.

H. RAUSCHNING, *Germany's Revolution of Destruction*, Heinemann, 1939.

J. L. TALMON, *The Origins of Totalitarian Democracy*, Heinemann, 1961.

S. J. WOOLF (ed.), *European Fascism*, Weidenfeld & Nicolson, 1968.

Chapter 4

(THE THIRD-WORLD STATES)

(And see below, under Chapters 9, 10, 11)

G. A. ALMOND and J. S. COLEMAN, *The Politics of the Developing Areas*, Princeton University Press, 1960.

D. APTER (Chapter 1 above, op cit.).

V. M. DEAN, *The Nature of the Non-Western World*, Mentor, New York, 1957.

G. IONESCU and E. GELLNER (ed.), *Populism*, Weidenfeld &Nicolson, 1969.

E. KEDOURIE, *Nationalism*, Hutchinson, 1960.

D. LERNER, *The Passing of Traditional Society*, Free Press, New York, 1958.

L. MAIR, *New Nations*, Weidenfeld & Nicolson, 1963.

F. R. VON DER MEHDEN, *Politics of the Developing Nations*, Prentice Hall, 1969.

M. F. MILLIKAN and D. L. BLACKMER, *The Emerging Nations*, Little, Brown, Boston, 1961.

M. PERHAM, *The Colonial Reckoning*, Collins, 1961.

L. W. PYE, *Aspects of Political Development*, Little, Brown, Boston, 1969.

E. SHILS, *Political Development in the New States*, Mouton, The Hague, 1962.

E. J. SIEYES (ed. S. E. FINER), *What Is the Third Estate?*, Pall Mall, 1963.

Chapter 5

(THE GOVERNMENT OF BRITAIN)

W. BAGEHOT (ed. R. H. S. CROSSMAN), *The English Constitution*, Fontana, 1963.

S. BEER, *British Politics in the Collectivist Age*, Knopf, New York, 1965.

R. BENEWICK and R. E. DOWSE, *Readings in British Politics and Government*, University of London Press, 1969.

A. H. BIRCH, *Representative and Responsible Government*, Allen & Unwin, 1964.

J. BLONDEL, *Voters, Parties and Leaders*, Pelican, 1963.

D. BUTLER and D. STOKES, *Political Change in Britain*, Macmillan, 1969.

R. BUTT, *The Power of Parliament*, Constable, 1969.

S. E. FINER, *Anonymous Empire: a Study of the Lobby in Britain* (2nd edn.), Pall Mall, 1966.

S. E. FINER, H. B. BERRINGTON and D. BARTHOLOMEW, *Backbench Opinion in the House of Commons*, Pergamon Press, 1961.

W. L. GUTTSMAN, *The British Political Elite*, McGibbon & Kee, 1963.

H.M.S.O., *Britain – an Official Survey*, 1970.

A. KING (ed.), *The British Prime Minister*, Macmillan, 1969.

A. KING (ed.), *British Politics: People, Parties and Parliament*, Heath, Boston, 1966.

J. P. MACKINTOSH, *The British Cabinet*, Stevens, 1962.

R. T. MCKENZIE, *British Political Parties*, Heinemann, 1964.

R. T. MCKENZIE and A. SILVER, *Angels in Marble: Working-class Conservatives in Urban England*, Heinemann, 1968.

P. G. PULZER, *Political Representation and Elections in Britain*, Allen & Unwin, 1967.

P. G. RICHARDS, *Honourable Members*, Faber, 1959.

R. ROSE, *Influencing Voters*, Faber, 1967.

M. RUSH, *The Selection of Parliamentary Candidates*, Nelson, 1969.

Chapter 6

(THE GOVERNMENT OF THE U.S.A.)

H. AGAR, *The U.S.A.: The Presidency, the Parties and the Constitution*, Eyre & Spottiswoode, 1950.

M. BELOFF, *The American Federal Government*, Oxford University Press, 1959.

M. BELOFF (ed.), *The Federalist*, Blackwell, Oxford, 1948.

J. M. BURNS, *The Deadlock of Democracy: Four-party Politics in the U.S.A.*, Calder, 1964.

M. CUNLIFFE, *American Presidents and the Presidency*, Eyre & Spottiswoode, 1969.

E. GRIFFITHS, *Congress: Its Contemporary Role*, New York University Press, 1961.

R. H. JACKSON, *The Supreme Court in the American System of Government*, Harvard University Press, 1951.

V. O. KEY, *Politics, Parties and Pressure Groups*, Crowell, New York, 1958.

V. O. KEY, *Public Opinion and American Democracy*, Knopf, New York, 1961.

J. LEES, *The Political System of the United States*, Faber, 1969.

C. W. MILLS, *The Power Elite*, Oxford University Press, 1959.

R. NEUSTADT, *Presidential Power*, Science Editions, New York, 1962.

D. T. STANLEY, D. S. MANN and J. S. DOIG, *Men who Govern*, The Brookings Institute, Washington, D.C., 1967.

P. WOHL, *American Government: Readings and Cases*, Little, Brown, Boston, 1965.

Chapter 7

(THE GOVERNMENT OF FRANCE)

J. S. AMBLER, *The French Army in Politics, 1949–58*, Ohio State University Press, 1966.

J. ARDAGH, *The New French Revolution*, Secker & Warburg, 1968.

R. ARON, *The Opium of the Intellectuals*, Secker & Warburg, 1957.

R. ARON, *France, Steadfast and Changing*, Harvard University Press, 1960.

P. AVRIL, *Politics in France*, Pelican, 1969.

J. BLONDEL and F. RIDLEY, *Public Administration in France*, Routledge & Kegan Paul, 1969.

C. BRINTON, *A Decade of Revolution 1789–1799*, Harper, New York, 1963.

D. W. BROGAN, *The Development of Modern France*, Hamish Hamilton, 1945.

P. CAMPBELL, *French Electoral Systems*, Faber, 1958.

B. CHAPMAN, *Introduction to French Local Government*, Allen & Unwin, 1953.

A. CRAWLEY, *de Gaulle*, Collins, 1969.

H. W. EHRMANN, *Organized Business in France*, Princeton University Press, 1958.

H. W. EHRMANN, *Politics in France*, Little, Brown, Boston, 1968.

H. S. HUGHES, *The Obstructed Path: French Thought, 1930–1960*, Harper, New York, 1966.

D. MACRAE, *Parliament, Parties and Society in France, 1946–58*, St Martin's Press, New York, 1967.

D. PICKLES, *The Fifth French Republic*, Methuen, 1965.

P. SEALE and M. MCCONVILLE, *French Revolution, 1968*, Penguin, 1968.

D. THOMSON, *Democracy in France*, Oxford University Press, 1967.

P. M. WILLIAMS, *Crisis and Compromise: Politics in the Fourth Republic*, Longmans, 1964.

P. M. WILLIAMS, *The French Parliament 1958–67*, Allen & Unwin, 1968.

Chapter 8

(THE GOVERNMENT OF THE U.S.S.R.)

1. The U.S.S.R.

F. BARGHOORN, *Politics in the U.S.S.R.*, Little, Brown, Boston, 1966

Z. K. BRZEZINSKI and S. HUNTINGTON, *Political Power, U.S.A./U.S.S.R.*, Chatto & Windus, 1963.

R. CONQUEST, *Power and Policy in the U.S.S.R.*, Macmillan, 1961.

R. CONQUEST, *Russia After Khrushchev*, Pall Mall, 1965.

A. DENISOV and M. KIRICHENKO, *Soviet State Law*, Foreign Languages Publishing House, Moscow, 1960.

I. DEUTSCHER, *Soviet Trade Unions*, Oxford University Press, 1950.

I. DEUTSCHER, *Stalin*, Pelican, 1966.

I. DEUTSCHER, *Trotsky*, Oxford University Press, 1954 and 1959.

M. FAINSOD, *How Russia is Ruled*, Oxford University Press, 1963.

G. FEIFER, *Justice in Moscow*, Bodley Head, 1964.

A. INKELES and K. GEIGER, *Soviet Society: a Book of Readings*, Houghton Mifflin, Boston, 1961.

P. S. ROMASHKIN (ed.), *Fundamentals of Soviet Law*, Foreign Languages Publishing House, Moscow.

L. SCHAPIRO, *The Origin of the Communist Autocracy*, Praeger, New York, 1965.

L. SCHAPIRO, *The Communist Party of the Soviet Union*, Methuen, 1963.

L. SCHAPIRO (ed.), *The U.S.S.R. and the Future*, Praeger, New York, 1963.

D. SCOTT, *Russian Political Institutions*, Allen & Unwin, 1969.

M. TATU, *Power in the Kremlin*, Collins, 1969.

ANON, *History of the Communist Party of the Soviet Union* (*Bolsheviks*) *Short Course*, Foreign Languages Publishing House, Moscow, 1938.

ANON, *History of the Communist Party of the Soviet Union*, Foreign Languages Publishing House, Moscow, 1960.

ANON, *The Road to Communism: Documents of the 22nd Congress of the C.P.S.U.* (*Oct. 1961*), Foreign Languages Publishing House, Moscow (n.d.).

2. Marxism/Leninism

V. I. LENIN, *What is to be Done?*, Foreign Languages Publishing House, Moscow (n.d.).

V. I. LENIN, *The State and Revolution*, Foreign Languages Publishing House, Moscow (n.d.).

V. I. LENIN, *Imperialism*, Foreign Languages Publishing House, Moscow (n.d.).

V. I. LENIN, *Against Revisionism*, Foreign Languages Publishing House, Moscow, 1959.

MARX, ENGELS, *Selected Works* (2 vols.), Foreign Languages Publishing House, Moscow, 1958.

3. Eastern Europe (General)

G. IONESCU, *The Politics of the East European Communist States*, Weidenfeld & Nicolson, 1967.

H. G. SKILLING, *The Governments of Communist East Europe*, Crowell, New York, 1966.

Chapter 9

(THE FAÇADE-DEMOCRACY)

Note: No theoretical work exists on this form of government, which is universally taken as either a precursor or a pathological degeneration of liberal-democracy, or some other and 'truer' form of democracy. The theoretical sketch of this type as found in my text, is derived from passages in Pareto's works, derogatory of the parliamentary democracy of his time. In his case, however, he reserved his strictures for what he styled *pluto-democracy* – whether of his own day or of the degeneracy of the Roman Republic. I have taken the hints further.

The few works cited below are meant to illustrate what has been said in the text.

L. BINDER, *Iran: Political Development in a Changing Society*, California University Press, 1967.

G. BRENAN, *The Spanish Labyrinth (Part I)*, California University Press, 1960.

R. CARR, *Spain, 1808–1939*, Oxford University Press, 1966.

M. KHADDURI, *Independent Iraq, 1932–1958*, Oxford University Press, 1960.

D. F. SARMIENTO, *Don Facundo: Life in the Argentine in the Days of the Tyrants*, Haffner, New York, 1960.

L. B. SIMPSON, *Many Mexicos*, California University Press, 1962.

Chapter 10

(THE QUASI-DEMOCRACY)

1. General

G. M. CARTER (ed.), *African One Party States*, Cornell University Press, 1962.

G. M. CARTER (ed.), *National Unity and Regionalism in Eight African States*, Cornell University Press, 1966.

J. S. COLEMAN and C. G. ROSBERG, *Political Parties and National Integration in Tropical Africa*, California University Press, 1966.

W. A. LEWIS, *Politics in West Africa*, Oxford University Press, 1965.

C. LEYS (ed.), *Politics and Change in Developing Countries*, California University Press, 1969.

K. POST, *The New States of West Africa*, Penguin, 1964.

A. R. ZOLBERG, *Creating Political Order: the Party States of West Africa*, Rand McNally, New York, 1966.

2. Ghana

D. E. APTER, *The Gold Coast in Transition*, Princeton University Press, 1955.

D. AUSTIN, *Politics in Ghana, 1946–1960*, Oxford University Press, 1964.

H. L. BRETTON, *The Rise and Fall of Kwame Nkruma*, Pall Mall, 1966.

3. Mexico

H. F. CLINE, *Mexico, Revolution to Evolution, 1940–1960*, Oxford University Press, 1962.

L. V. PADGETT, *The Mexican Political System*, Houghton Mifflin, New York, 1966.

R. E. SCOTT, *Mexican Government in Transition*, Illinois University Press, 1959.

W. P. TUCKER, *The Mexican Government Today*, Minnesota University Press, 1957.

4. Tunisia

D. E. ASHFORD, *National Development and Local Reform: Political Participation in Morocco, Tunisia and Pakistan*, Princeton University Press, 1967.

C. MICAUD, *Tunisia: The Politics of Modernization*, Pall Mall, 1964.

L. RUDEBECK, *Party and People: a Study of Political Change in Tunisia*, Almqvist & Wiksell, Stockholm, 1967.

Chapter 11

(THE MILITARY RÉGIME)

A. ABDEL MALIK, *Egypt – Military Society*, Random House, New York, 1968.

A. AFRIFA, *The Ghana Coup*, Cass, 1966.

E. BE'ERI, *Army Officers in Arab Politics and Society*, Praeger, New York, 1969.

H. BIENEN (ed.), *The Military Intervenes: Case Studies*, Russell Sage Foundation, New York, 1968.

J. VAN DOORN (ed.), *Armed Forces and Society*, Mouton, The Hague, 1968.

S. E. FINER, *The Man on Horseback: the Role of the Military in Politics*, Pall Mall, 1962.

W. F. GUTTERIDGE, *The Military in African Politics*, Methuen, 1969.

J. C. HUREWITZ, *Middle East Politics – the Military Dimension*, Praeger, New York, 1969.

J. F. JOHNSON (ed.), *The Role of the Military in Underdeveloped Countries*, Princeton University Press, 1962.

E. LIEUWEN, *Arms and Politics in Latin America*, Praeger, New York, 1960.

E. LIEUWEN, *Generals versus Presidents*, Pall Mall, 1964.

E. Luttwak, *Coup d'État*, Pelican, 1970.

P. J. Vatikiotis, *The Egyptian Army in Politics*, Indiana University Press, 1961.

P. J. Vatikiotis, *Politics and the Military in Jordan*, Cass, London, 1967.

W. F. Wecker, *The Turkish Revolution 1960–1961*, Brookings Institute, Washington, D.C., 1963.

Chapter 12

(COMPARATIVE GOVERNMENT)

1. Synoptic Surveys

J. C. Charlesworth (ed.), *Contemporary Political Analysis*, Free Press, New York, 1967.

W. J. M. Mackenzie, *Politics and Social Science*, Pelican, 1967.

V. van Dyke, *Political Science: a Philosophical Analysis*, Stanford University Press, 1967.

2. Cross-institutional

J. Blondel, *An Introduction to Comparative Government*, Weidenfeld & Nicolson, 1969.

H. Finer, *The Theory and Practice of Modern Government*, Methuen, 1949.

C. J. Friedrich, *Man and His Government*, McGraw Hill, New York, 1963.

3. Functionalism

G. A. Almond and G. B. Powell, *Comparative Politics*, Little, Brown, Boston, 1966.

4. Systems

D. Easton, *The Political System*, Knopf, New York, 1953.

D. Easton, *A Systems Analysis of Political Life*, John Wiley, New York, 1965.

5. Mathematical Approaches

H. R. Alker, *Mathematics and Politics*, Macmillan, New York, 1965.

J. M. Buchanan and G. Tullock, *The Calculus of Consent*, Michigan University Press, 1963.

W. H. Riker, *The Theory of Coalitions*, Yale University Press, 1962.

6. Communication

K. DEUTSCH, *The Nerves of Government*, Free Press, New York, 1966.
N. WIENER, *The Human Use of Human Beings*, Doubleday Anchor, New York, 1954.

7. Profiles

A. S. BANKS and R. B. TEXTOR, *A Cross-Polity Survey*, Massachusetts Institute of Technology Press, Cambridge, Mass., 1963.
S. M. LIPSET, *Political Man*, Heinemann, 1960.
B. M. RUSSETT *et al.*, *World Handbook of Political Indicators*, Yale University Press, 1964.

LIST OF ABBREVIATIONS

A.F.L.-C.I.O.	American Federation of Labor and Congress of Industrial Organizations
A.P.R.A.	Alianza Popular Revolucionaria Americana
Arena	Aliança Renovadora Nacional
C.A.R.	Central African Republic
C.F.T.C.	Confédération Française des Travailleurs Chrétiens
C.G.T.	Confédération Générale du Travail
C.N.I.	Centre National des Indépendants
C.N.I.P.	Comité National des Indépendants et des Paysans
C.P.P.	Convention People's Party
C.P.S.U.	Communist Party of the Soviet Union
F.G.D.S.	Fédération de la Gauche Démocratique et Socialiste
F.L.N.	Front de Libération Nationale
G.P.U.	see O.G.P.U.
K.A.D.U.	Kenya African Democratic Union
K.A.N.U.	Kenya African National Union
M.D.B.	Movimento Democratico Brasiliero
M.R.P.	Mouvement Républicain Populaire
M.V.D.	Ministerstvo Vnutrennykh Del (Ministry for Internal Affairs)
N.E.P.	Novaya Ekonomicheskaya Politika (New Economic Policy)
N.K.V.D.	Narodny Komisariat Vnutrennykh Del (People's Commissariat for Internal Affairs)
N.L.M.	National Liberation Movement
O.A.S.	Organisation de l'Armée Secrète
O.G.P.U.	Obedinennoe Gosudarstvennoe Politicheskoe Upravlenie (Joint State Political Administration)
P.A.N.	Partido Acción Nacional
P.C.F.	Parti Communiste Français
P.D.C.I.	Parti Démocratique de la Côte d'Ivoire
P.D.G.	Parti Démocratique de Guinée
P.N.R.	Partido Nacional Revolucionario
P.R.I.	Partido Revolucionario Institucional
P.R.I.N.	Partido Revolucionario de la Izquierda Nacional

P.R.L.	Parti Républicain de la Liberté
P.S.D.	Parti Social Democratique
P.S.U.	Parti Socialiste Unifié
R.P.F.	Rassemblement du Peuple Français
R.S.F.S.R.	Russian Soviet Federated Socialist Republic
S.F.I.O.	Section Française de l'Internationale Ouvrière
T.A.N.U.	Tanzanian African National Union
U.A.R.	United Arab Republic
U.D.S.R.	Union Démocratique et Socialiste de la Résistance
U.G.C.C.	United Gold Coast Convention
U.G.T.T.	Union Générale des Travailleurs Tunisiens
U.N.R.-U.D.T.	Union pour la Nouvelle République – Union Démocratique du Travail
U.D.R.	Union des Démocrates pour la République

INDEX

MORE ABOUT PENGUINS
AND PELICANS

Penguinews, which appears every month, contains details of all the new books issued by Penguins as they are published. From time to time it is supplemented by *Penguins in Print*, which is a complete list of all titles available. (There are some five thousand of these.)

A specimen copy of *Penguinews* will be sent to you free on request. For a year's issues (including the complete lists) please send 50p if you live in the British Isles, or 75p if you live elsewhere. Just write to Dept EP, Penguin Books Ltd, Harmondsworth, Middlesex, enclosing a cheque or postal order, and your name will be added to the mailing list.

In the U.S.A.: For a complete list of books available from Penguin in the United States write to Dept CS, Penguin Books Inc., 7110 Ambassador Road, Baltimore, Maryland 21207.

In Canada: For a complete list of books available from Penguin in Canada write to Penguin Books Canada Ltd, 41 Steelcase Road West, Markham, Ontario.

INTERNATIONAL POLITICS:
CONFLICT AND HARMONY

Joseph Frankel

Unlike the affairs of the citizen, international relations between states are not determined by social and legal pressures. The balance of peace is always precarious.

In *International Politics* Dr Frankel illustrates the patterns of conflict and harmony in the behaviour of states by a number of comparisons, contrasting, for example, the unity of the Roman Empire with the turbulent twentieth century. Today peace is harder than ever before to maintain, and the situation is aggravated by the growth of power blocs and ideologies, so that countries like Russia and China tend to become isolated. In the search for peace the author urges the West to accord equal weight to more exotic if less traditional modes of government, and not to regard failure as grounds for disillusion. He reminds us that to expect the worst is to invite the worst.

'It is possible to recommend his book as a judicious and comprehensive introduction to its subject for both students and teachers of international politics' – *The Times Literary Supplement*